Behavior and Existence
An Introduction to Empirical Humanistic Psychology

Behavior and Existence
An Introduction to Empirical Humanistic Psychology

Howard R. Pollio
The University of Tennessee

Brooks/Cole Publishing Company
Monterey, California

Brooks/Cole Publishing Company
A Division of Wadsworth, Inc.

Printed in the United States of America
10 9 8 7 6 5 4 3 2 1

Library of Congress Cataloging in Publication Data

Pollio, Howard R.
  Behavior and existence.

  Bibliography: p
  Includes index.
    1. Humanistic psychology. 2. Cognition. 3. Develop-
mental psychology. I. Title.
BF204.P64   150   81-1531
ISBN 0-8185-0425-0   AACR2

Cover.   *Spectre Riding a Headless Horse*, 1951-52, an
          original steel and bronze sculpture by David
          Smith. Hirshhorn Museum and Sculpture
          Garden, Smithsonian Institution.
Page 1.   *Voltri XV*, 1962, an original steel scuplture by
          David Smith. Hirshhorn Museum and Sculpture
          Garden, Smithsonian Institution.
Page 51. *The Hero*, 1952, an original steel scuplture by
          David Smith. Height 73 11/16 inches. Collection:
          The Brooklyn Museum, Dick S. Ramsey Fund.
Page 219. *Voltri VII*, by David Smith. National Gallery of Art,
          Washington, D.C. Ailsa Mellon Bruce Fund.

Subject Editor: *Ray Kingman*
Manuscript Editor: *Rephah Berg*
Production Editor: *Marlene Thom*
Production Assistant: *Louise Rixey*
Interior Design: *Jamie Sue Brooks*
Cover Design: *Katherine Minerva*
Photo Researcher: *Lyndsay Kefauver*
Typesetting: *Graphic Typesetting Service,
          Los Angeles, California*

Preface

This book is about people. Sometimes when I write, I like people; other times I don't. I've tried to write this when I like people. Maybe that's why it took six years to finish.

During those six years, I tried to answer a question that had bothered me since I was an undergraduate student: What can psychology say about human beings that is carefully and rigorously worked out and will have some significance to me as both a person and a psychologist?

This question occurred after my first course in psychology, in which all I read about was rats, electric shock, neurons, and salivating dogs. Whenever anything interesting came up in class, my textbook either tried to deny or ignore it or said that it would all be explained if and when we learned more about the nervous system, biochemistry, and the controlling effects on people of physical events known as stimuli. For a topic to be taken seriously, it had to pass the forefinger-and-thumb test—that is, if we couldn't hope to touch what it was we were talking about between our scientific thumbs and forefingers, we probably shouldn't be studying it.

Over the past decade or so, many psychologists have become less defensive about what they study and how they study it. One reason for this change in attitude was the development of cognitive psychology, in which the very human topics of speaking, planning, and thinking came to assume primary importance. A second was the great success that European ethologists (investigators of animal behavior) had in understanding the behavior of an animal from the animal's point of view. A third was the rise of humanistic psychology, in which meaningful human experience and action were given positions of crucial importance.

The present book owes a great deal to each of these developments. It represents my attempt to talk with the introductory student about significant human topics as they are experienced and lived by, and for, the human being(s) in question. For this reason, physiological psychology, in which the controlling role of biology is assumed from the start, is deemphasized. Similarly, our ability to step back from the world and reflect on it is given equal footing with our ability to be active in the world, whether we are concerned with shooting an arrow into a target (Chapter 7), feeding a baby (Chapter 11), having sexual intercourse (Chapters 1 and 10), testifying in court (Chapter 8), telling time (Chapter 9), or walking around on a crowded street in London or New York (Chapter 1). It is our experiences of, and actions in, the world of everyday human life that are important, and this seems a good starting place for psychology.

The overall direction of the book has been shaped with this idea in mind. The first part, containing Chapters 1 and 2, introduces some of the more pressing problems that must be dealt with in developing psychology as a "human science"; certain long-held ideas about human beings have to be examined once again. The most important of these is that the best way to describe human beings is to start by making a distinction between mind and body. Although such a distinction has been useful in the past, it does not seem helpful when the issue of first-person human experience is at stake. Rather, the study of human beings seems to require that we start with the world as directly experienced—that is, before we have done any special (scientific or philosophical) thinking about it.

When we approach psychology as the study of experience, we find that a whole new set of concepts is needed. These concepts include a theoretical distinction between my world, your world, and the scientist's world. They also include an explicit recognition of our rootedness in a particular society, in a particular historical era. Finally, they include an explicit attempt to recognize the world of everyday reality as the proper background for all our actions and theories.

In addition to placing psychology within the framework of social and historical concern, the first two chapters discuss what in other contexts would be called social psychology. Chapter 2, for example, deals with such topics as attitudes, social interactions, and the role of social influences in the personal self-world. In short, it deals with the significant role other people play in our own unique and individual self-worlds.

Part II, comprising Chapters 3 through 8, deals with the major processes historically studied by psychologists. Included among these are perceiving, thinking, speaking, remembering, and learning. The first three are activities that you or I do in the present; the last two concern past and projected actions. Because these topics are at the heart of contemporary psychology, it is important to emphasize that in writing about them I use many of the same facts as other authors; only my interpretation is a bit different so as to emphasize experience rather than movement. For example, although I do talk about learning as involving a progressive change in movement, I am equally interested in how experience changes as we get better at some task or activity.

Since mechanical movement is deemphasized relative to meaningful experience, an understanding of how I experience my body is an important topic. For this reason the whole of Part II is introduced by a discussion of the meaning and experience of my body as I go about dealing with my world.

Part III, consisting of Chapters 9 through 15, moves from a concern with psychological processes as these occur within an individual to a concern for the concrete realities of contemporary human life. This section describes the major developmental milestones and discusses three theoretical attempts to understand them.

Because not all of life progresses clearly and sensibly, some of us lose our way and for a time find our existence disordered and disturbing. Chapters 13 and 14 deal with the joint issues of how we deal with our lives when confused and how we and others try to help make it better. Finally, we all have to deal with the issue of aging and our own personal death. Although it may be hard for most of us to get excited about this issue at age 20, the issue does become progressively more important.

No picture of human life—or psychology, for that matter—can be complete without some consideration of time. For this reason, Part III begins with a discussion of what we know about psychological experiences in, and of, time. If this discussion is to be accurate, it also must consider our day-to-day relations to clock time. Although the exploration undertaken in Chapter 9 is a complicated one, it is necessary if we are to understand human reactions to one of the more important supports in human life—time.

Either of two points of view can be taken in describing human experience: that of a detached observer or that of a fully engaged person. I have chosen the latter alternative whenever possible. For this reason each of the major chapters in Part III was written from the "inside"—as if you or I were a 2-, 6-, 20-, 50-, or 80-year-old talking about his or her experiences of the world. Similarly, I have tried to write about personal madness as well as therapy from the inside. If I am successful at this, you ought to be able to experience a bit of what it's like to be mad and a bit of what it's like to be in therapy. In earlier chapters, you might also have experienced what it's like to be joyful, productive, competent, sexy.

This, then, is what the present book is about. It attempts to deal at an introductory level with a wide range of human issues and problems in ways that are both rigorous and meaningful. It tries to present an alternative to other ways of doing psychology, and I have written this book to show what such an alternative psychology might look like without throwing away the many significant techniques and insights achieved by scientific psychology. I have also tried to be interesting and not to hide who I am or what I believe. I am very much a part of this book.

Acknowledgments

Help in writing this book came mainly from two sources: students who were in my classes over the past three to four years and colleagues, at the University of Tennessee and elsewhere, who were buttonholed and interrogated whenever I got the chance and not released until they told me what they knew. Five colleagues at other universities also read the entire text in manuscript form and helped continue my education in existential phenomenology: Amedeo Giorgi and Constance Fischer of Duquesne University, Ernest Keen of Bucknell University, D. R. Lindberg of Green River Community College, and some modest, anonymous reviewer from an unknown university. In addition to serving as professional colleagues in the best sense of the term, they share my view that a text such as this is needed; I thank them for their professional and personal guidance and support.

My students, graduate and undergraduate, have been very patient with me as I worked through the ideas in this book. Not only were they a responsive and critical audience, they also suggested a number of useful changes. Two in particular, Michael Grande and Joy Cole, deserve special mention, and I am happy to acknowledge them.

A major portion of this book was written when I was a United States Senior Postdoctoral Fellow at Cambridge University in 1975–1976, for which I express gratitude and appreciation to the people of the United States. I thank my English host and friend, Brian Butterworth, for his hospitality and advice. I would also like to thank the following group of European scholars who were kind enough to discuss their work with me: Ference Marton of Goteberg, Sweden; Steiner Kvale and Boje Katznelson of Aarhus, Denmark; Ragnar Rommetveit and Jan Smedslund of Oslo, Norway; and J. H. Van Den Berg of Utrecht, Holland. As you can see, I got around a good deal in 1975 on what I have come to call my intellectual grand tour of Europe.

Other people helped in ways that are not easy to specify; even if I do not mention them by name, they will know how I feel about them. Three hardworking souls who deserve special mention are my former secretaries, Gail McKinney, Mary Roberson, and Carol O'Dell. All three typed, retyped, and retyped the present manuscript until, I'm sure, they now know it by heart. Ms. Roberson helped a great deal with references and permissions. Claire Verduin and Ray Kingman of Brooks/Cole were exactly what was called for in the way of editors: helpful, orderly, and pushy.

Finally, there is the continuing debt I owe my friend, colleague, and wife, Dr. Marilyn R. Pollio. In an earlier book on cognitive psychology (Pollio, 1974) I wrote the following dedication to her: "in Knoxville and elsewhere, her ability to put up with noisy kids, a crazy husband and a peripatetic existence has provided a thread of sanity and continuity to an otherwise freely-associated life style." The sentiment, emotion, and dedication remain the same; only the tempo has slowed to protect the author.

Howard R. Pollio

Contents

Behavior and Existence

An Introduction to Empirical Humanistic Psychology

Psychology as a
Human Science

1
Experience and Behavior

You and I, and all the You's and I's in this world, are in the midst of something we do not quite understand, and it is called living. Not that we don't try hard enough—every time there's a problem, there we are working at it—but no consistent or logical picture ever seems to come from all this mental work. All around us, in seeming disregard for what we would want, are wars and death, depression and gloom, separation and alienation. And surprisingly, at the same time all around us are laughter and creation, joy and satisfaction, and love and belonging. What at one moment is tragic can in the next be unimportant, and what at one moment is exciting can in the next be dull and ordinary. Are we never to understand?

I. EXPERIENCE

You might think that being a psychologist gives me some special insight into all this. Unfortunately, that is not true: like you, I have only my experience of the world, and this seems to be the point at which the two of us will have to start both as people and as psychologists. But what does it mean to say I "experience" the world? Sometimes it seems to mean that things happen to me and that I notice that they have happened. About the only thing I seem able to do actively is to think about things. For this reason, to experience can mean to be aware of the world intellectually.

There is, however, a different (and, I hope, more accurate) way to talk about human experience. For this way of looking at things each person goes out to meet his or her world at least as much as the world is there to be met. To experience is to be alive, to move around, and to do things in a world that was there before you and I were born and will be there after we die. Experiencing is more than intellectually understanding some "external" reality that determines what we do.

A. Experiencing the human body
1. Descartes' mind/body split. Even though my experience of the world is always larger than my understanding of it, I still do want to make some (intellectual) sense of the world and of my place in

it. For this reason, I often look around for a fairly straightforward way of ordering my experiences of the world. Here I fall back on what seems to be a very obvious fact: Some parts of my world can be kicked around or moved from place to place or broken into bits without seeming to mind what happens to them. Other parts of my world do seem to mind; indeed, they make elaborate plans to resist change or to shape other objects to their own ends. Those parts of my world that do not seem to care about their fate, I call objects or, more generally, *matter*. Those parts of my world that do seem to care, I call people or, more generally, *mind*.

The categories of mind and matter cover a lot of ground. After all, here am I, confused but thoughtful (mind), while over there, clear as can be, are rocks, trees, houses, boats, pencils, light bulbs—matter. Once we set up our understanding of the world in this way, all we have to do is show how the categories of mind and matter relate to each other. One way of doing this is to assume that they are the same thing, usually matter. In this case, mind reduces to brain and then conveniently disappears as a category in its own right. If we assume that all there is is mind, then each person's world is his or her own creation, and matter disappears as a separate category. Finally, we can acknowledge the duality (two-ness) of the world and say that mind and matter are forever different and that's that.

Psychologists have at different times accepted some or all of these possibilities. The one most often talked about, however, was that mind and matter are totally different aspects of the world. Under this assumption we were able to save something special for us as human beings (mind) and leave the rest of the world to matter. When pressed, however, we did admit that our bodies were made of matter—but "matter with a difference." This difference was, of course, conscious experience, or, more simply, mind. When I talked about me or you in terms of matter, I usually talked about my body or your body, so that as applied to human beings the categories of mind and matter were translated into the more restricted categories of mind and body.

Generally speaking, "mind" and "matter" have been good ways to think about things: they agree with some of our experiences and seem natural enough. The idea of a material world allows us to do many things—build boats, houses, rockets, planes, cars, locomotives, and so on. When we want to talk about people or even other animals, however, the idea that we are nothing but a bit of matter in the same sense that a car or a computer is a bit of matter seems somehow strained or even wrong.

Although we may think the view that a person is "only" a machine is too simple, it is quite strong even today. For example, when Christiaan Barnard did the first heart transplant some years ago, I happened to be in an auto-repair shop, and the mechanic I was talking to was working under my Triumph Spitfire. After the usual amount of clever garage banter, the mechanic came out from under my car holding a carburetor dripping with oil. The carburetor for a Spitfire is about the size of a man's hand, and it looked as if the mechanic had taken the heart (blood and all) out of the car and was coming to show it to me. Just to complete the image, as the mechanic approached me, he said "Hey, did you hear about that doctor in Africa or someplace who gave some guy a new heart?" Brr . . . .

The idea of a split between mind and body has a long history. It was not until the 17th century, however, that the great French philosopher and mathematician René Descartes (1596–1650) spelled out some of the implications to this kind of world view, which, accordingly, is called **Cartesian dualism.*** Descartes began his work because he was disappointed with philosophy and philosophers and decided to doubt everything he ever knew. When he did this, he came to the conclusion that the only thing he could not doubt was that he was doubting. As long as he doubted, he could not doubt that he existed; hence his famous phrase "Cogito ergo sum"—"I think, therefore I am."

Because Descartes was a religious man, and because he came to the idea that thinking defines what it means to be human, he concluded that God's truthfulness guaranteed that any idea he could think clearly must express something true. The task of a human being, according to Descartes,

was to determine which ideas are clear and which are not. For Descartes a clear idea had to meet only one criterion: did the reality it named take up space? For this reason, the only clear idea we could ever have of our body was that it took up space. Once we considered it in just this way, it seemed quite clear that my body must be an object no different from any other bit of matter.

Although simple, this point of view is loaded with consequences. For one, it gives the human being an essentially twofold, or dualistic, nature—the human being is both matter (body) and idea (mind). For another, it separates mind and body into two categories. Descartes, like our mechanic friend, could deal with the human body only as a machine that somehow or other had a second and more wonderful aspect to it known as consciousness, or mind.

Descartes and the mechanic are not alone in talking of a split between mind and body and in then concluding that the body can profitably be thought of as a machine. An eminent surgeon was quoted in the popular Sunday magazine *Parade* as saying that we should have the right to ask people to donate parts of their bodies to hospitals after they die. After all, he asked, since we already have cornea transplants, blood banks, and so on, why shouldn't we stockpile other body parts as well? We could maintain a kind of warehouse of parts for use in operations, transplants, and the like.

Actually, it may make good sense for physicians to look at the body in this mechanical way: If they didn't, it is doubtful they could perform surgery or autopsies. Looking at the body as a machine protects the physician from confronting the fact that the particular body he now sees before him has the same set of fears and emotions, needs and desires that he has; in short, this body is the repository for—or, more accurately, is—another human being. If physicians did not dehumanize the body to some degree, it is difficult to see how they could deal with terminal cancer patients, deformed children, and a hundred other impossibly painful aspects of their work.

This same kind of self-protecting approach sometimes applies to us in our everyday lives as well. If we consider our body a machine and believe that the important thing about us is something else, our mind or spirit, then we have nothing to fear about dying. After all, our spirit and the things we have

---

*Throughout the text, terms appearing in **boldface** are defined in the Glossary at the end of the chapter.

done live on; only our body decays and disappears. Here, the mind/body split has protective value in helping us handle the insoluble problems brought about by death and dying.

Jules Feiffer, in one of his extraordinarily insightful cartoons (Figure 1–1), illustrates a contemporary summary of the split between mind and body.

2. Physics, psychology, and human experience. Psychologists, biologists, and philosophers are not physicians, cartoonists, or theologians and, except occasionally, do not need the protection of a mind/body split. Why, then, should most of us be willing to accept the separation of mind from body as reasonable? Even Descartes long ago recognized the difficulty of this position, for what his famous split had done was to divide a unity—the person— into two separate parts, mind and body. From Descartes on, one aspect of the whole business of psychology (not to mention biology and philosophy) has been to try to restore the unity of mind and body on one or another basis: the mind is primary; the body is primary; they interact; or whatever. Even though our experience gives us the person as a unity, scientific psychology gives us only a fragmented entity.

The key word explaining how this state of affairs has come about is neither *mind* nor *body* but sci-

ence—more exactly, psychology's reading of one particular science, physics. If Descartes' philosophy did anything at all, it made a rational understanding of our world a very important and desirable goal for human beings (I *think*, therefore I am). Now the world, even the physicist's world, is a confusing place if we take it in an uncritical and naive way. For this reason physical scientists began to invent a theoretical world where everything would make sense if only they got it right. To construct a sensible world, the physicist began by taking observations and recording them. He or she then tried to develop a consistent theoretical picture of these observations and, through them, of the world. To this end, the physicist often invented such things as inches, minutes, or wavelengths to help order the worlds of space, time, and color.

At this point you may say: "But space, time, and color were always there; no one had to make them up. Everyone knows that space exists; it's there for all to see! As for color, there's red, there's blue— how can you say they don't exist? And as for time, just look here on my wrist or there on the wall, and you have time. How can you say that these things are made up, that they're invented, that they aren't real?"

All these questions have the same kind of answer: It isn't that we don't have watches to tell time or

Figure 1-1.   A modern mind/body split. *(Courtesy of Jules Feiffer)*

yardsticks to measure space or prisms to break up light into wavelengths; rather, all these measures already assume we know what it is that is being measured. Before the physicist can tell you that seeing red is caused by a band of light so and so many microscopic units wide, she must have already known what red was before she decided to think about it and measure it in terms of a unit such as wavelength. The same is true for space or time: before anyone, the scientist included, could talk about, let alone measure, space or time, he or she must already have had some experience with lived-in space and lived-through time. It seems fair to say that science is built up out of the world as directly experienced and that all science (physics included) represents an orderly second-level way of talking about a set of more disorderly initial experiences. As one philosopher put it, "Every scientific schema is an abstract and derivative sign-language, as is geography, in relation to the countryside in which we have learned beforehand what a forest, a prairie, or a river is" (Merleau-Ponty, 1962, p. ix).[1]

Does this mean that the physicist's constructions are useless? Hardly; the whole incredibly successful history of physical science is built on constructions such as these, on these "abstractions" of the countryside. The problems posed by forgetting that science is a derived language did not and do not seem critical for physics or chemistry but in fact are very critical if we return to our original starting point: my (your) life and my (your) experiences of my (your) life.

The idea of a constructed world is difficult to get hold of because we usually think of the physical world as real in some very final sense of the word *real*. It is only my experience of me that causes trouble. I just don't seem to be a *thing* that can be described fully in terms of centimeters, grams, and seconds. I do not feel like merely an organism, a living thing, a person, or even a "being"; rather, I seem to be "the absolute source of me."

> My existence does not stem from my antecedents, . . . instead it moves out towards them and sustains them, for I alone bring into being for myself the tradition which I elect to carry on. . . . Scientific points of view, according to which my existence is a moment of the

world's, are always both naive and at the same time dishonest, because they take for granted, without . . . mentioning it, the other point of view, namely that of consciousness, through which from the outset a world forms itself round me and begins to exist for me [Merleau-Ponty, 1962, p. ix].

Only if we realize that any physical description of me—as a machine, as a computer, or even as an organism—is not real in some fixed and final sense will we be able to pursue **psychology** in a way that is true to our experience and has any possibility of explaining what we do (how we behave) in the world in which we live.

Even if we recognize that the categories of physics are made up by human beings and do not represent the perfect (or final) description of our human world, we must not be misled to conclude that there would be no world if some intelligence or other did not "will it into existence." I have no doubt that there is a world; rather, what is open to change is how you or I choose to talk about that world. That it exists independently of us is not in question. I do not create a world; all I create is a particular picture (or geography) of the world.

3. Sex and the body. If the idea of the human body as a machine set over against the mind is not a realistic or even a useful one for psychology, how, then, should we go about talking about our bodies? One way to do this is to analyze the human being as he or she does something specific, and let that specific something be as interesting as possible and involve both mind and body in the ordinary sense of both words. The topic of human sexual behavior meets both criteria: sex is interesting, and it involves both "mental" and "physical" aspects. As *Ms.* magazine put it, sex is as much a matter of the head as it is of the genitals: "The mind is the ultimate erogenous zone."

Adult sexuality usually involves two persons, each having a body with its own particular characteristics. Probably the single most important philosophical notion to keep in mind in regard to sexual activity is that "erotic perception is not a *cogitatio* [thought] which aims at a *cogitatum* [object of thought]; through one body it aims at another body and [this] takes place in the world, not in a consciousness" (Merleau-Ponty, 1962, p. 157).

Since sexual events occur only when one "body" (person) makes contact with another, any analysis

[1]From *The Phenomenology of Perception*, by M. Merleau-Ponty. Copyright 1962 by Routledge and Kegan Paul, Ltd. and Humanities Press, Inc., New Jersey. This and all other quotations from this source are reprinted by permission.

of the body by way of sexuality must consider in detail what goes on in particular sexual situations. A careful reading of such encounters should allow us to see our bodies in a different light—a light that will not tolerate the person's mind up around the ceiling and his or her body down on the bed. Rather, mind and body will be together in the sexual situation.

Consider the following two situations.

Situation 1 involves a married couple in their middle to late twenties. They have one child, a boy just over 1 year old. The husband and wife are both college graduates and are very organized in planning their family. At present their plan is to have children (how many is undecided just now) on an average of one every two years. Their present problem concerns the rather sudden onset of impotence in the husband: for the past week or so, he has been increasingly angry and then depressed and has been unable to get an erection. At the end of this period, his sexual behavior suddenly returns.

In talking about his sudden recovery, the husband is reminded of one rather important fact—that the week-long period of impotence corresponded almost exactly with the wife's optimum time for pregnancy. This very planful pair had kept a careful chart for several months to get the very best estimate of when ovulation would occur. The husband was surely aware of this timetable, and his inability (or his unwillingness) to behave sexually was an implicit or explicit refusal to reproduce.

Some background: the husband always thought of himself as the least-liked child in his family, particularly after the birth of his younger sibling. Because of his love for his own infant son, he used his fairly exact knowledge of his wife's menstrual cycle to delay (or prevent altogether) having another child by the simple expedient of nonaction. Rather than being simply an inability to behave sexually, the husband's impotence represented one (admittedly unsatisfactory) solution to his problem.

In his sexual behavior (or, rather, in his lack of it), we can read the outlines of the husband's relationship to his own past. Although by interpretation it was possible to overcome the present difficulty, unraveling the meaning of his earlier conflict was not so easily done. All we need remember now, however, is that the specific properties of the husband's sexual behavior gave a clue by which to understand how he felt about his child and his own life.

Situation 2 concerns a married man and an unmarried woman who have been good, though not terribly intense, friends for five years. While on a business trip without his wife, the man meets the woman at a place where both have been before. On that earlier occasion, the woman was there with her boyfriend, and all three chatted amicably and pleasantly.

This time, after much discussion of the past and with not a little hesitancy, they jointly decide to go to her house to make love. All the while, they talk a good deal about the woman's life and where it is going, as well as about the man's life (including his wife and children) and where it is going. Since both parties are sexually experienced, the initial phases of lovemaking go smoothly. Up to the point of intercourse there is no problem. As soon as intercourse begins, however, the woman's body becomes tense so that the overall effect is one of closing up against the man's advances. Although he has entered, the woman has not made him feel at home or even welcome.

The ambivalence inherent in a relationship such as this is thus embodied by a subtle rejection occurring in the midst of a much more apparent acceptance. Even though the two parties did not lie about themselves or about their feelings for each other, complete acceptance is impossible in this situation. To make the issue completely clear, a fact both will laugh about, the woman some months later sends the man a commercial valentine: "You may have stolen my heart—but you're not going to get my belly button."

In both these situations a particular aspect of sexual behavior has meaning beyond the immediate sexual sphere. In the first situation, impotence was an attempt to avoid hurting a loved child; in the second, a moral, or at least an interpersonal, problem was stated in very obvious and dramatic bodily terms. In both cases, these bodies expressed an important pattern of existence for the people involved, and it is this pattern that makes both the bodily movements and their interpretations of interest.

One reason for talking about bodies as they do sexual things was to help us understand the mind/body question from a different point of view and thereby help us find words for talking about the human body different from the mechanical ones usually used. Both these situations point to one and the same conclusion: every human action, even one so seemingly tied to specific actions as sex, has a significance for the living human being, and such meanings are what is important about these movements, not the movements themselves.

Now, this is a difficult even if obvious point: what we do (behavior) is more than just a collection of movements; rather, what we do always expresses something about us as individuals. Hence, there can be no movement without meaning: whatever we do always carries meaning within itself, and there is no way to separate meaning from movement. Even if an action seems to be done "absent-mindedly" or by "habit," there is always meaning in that action.

Suppose, for example, you are listening to a particularly dull lecture, and you first begin to fidget and shuffle your feet and then finally lapse into silence with that special, empty, lackluster stare so characteristic of such situations. You may think there is no meaning or message in this habitual or absent-minded behavior. Yet we can all read the message. You may explain that you lapsed into silence because "You were tired," yet your "being tired" was not accidental; it expressed a lack of interest in the present situation. The important thing to remember is that there is no word, gesture, or action that does not express some meaning for, and about, the person doing it.

B. Unreflected and reflected experiencing

Once underway, sexual intercourse provides a particular and unique situation for the individuals involved. The initial stages of sexual activity often involve hesitancy and thinking, which disappear after a while so that such activity becomes more fluent and mutually regulated. If in the first stages there is a searching for particular bodily zones, in the middle stages such searching ceases and thinking evaporates as one body makes appropriate contact with the other and the other responds either by intensifying the contact or by making a different contact of its own. During this time, talking about my body as "where I am" or your body as "where you are" seems wrong and destructive of our experiences. I am not *in* my body; rather, I *am* my body, not as a process being looked at by someone else, but as one person in the midst of an upsurge against, and with, another person.

The look, the touch, the reach, and the general orientation of the partners' bodies next take on a new significance and come increasingly to regulate and complete each other in sexual contact. All this gets done without words, without thinking about what to do, and without any Cartesian dualism. One body responds to and is regulated by another body until both disappear for a time, only to return quietly and softly to each other and finally each to themselves. Talking, laughing, or other nonsexual actions begin to take over at this time until each individual is restored as a separate (thinking) consciousness to the appropriate body.

This description sets out a situation that requires something other than the usual categories of mind and body. Within the context of sexual behavior it does not seem fitting to talk about undirected movements. It also does not seem right to talk about thinking as consciousness of movement. It does, however, seem reasonable and correct to talk about a time during the sexual sequence when there seemed to be no thinking at all in the usual sense of the term—a time during which all actions and their outcomes seemed to occur simultaneously rather than in sequence. Does this mean that the behavior was without direction or that the persons involved didn't know exactly where they were or what they were doing? The answer is clearly no: the behavior of both parties was directed, did have a goal, and was mutually regulated even though there was no intervening activity that could be called thinking. As a matter of fact, had one of the individuals begun to "think," the total pattern might have been interfered with and the sequence disturbed.

A fine-grained description of sexual activity indicates that human beings are able to relate to one another and to a situation in a directed and regulated way in the absence of anything even vaguely resembling thinking. Human behavior that is not so dramatic as a sexual encounter also contains many examples of this unreflected or "un-thought-about" way of relating to the world. *Unreflected* does not mean stupid or without direction. It means that the behavior does not take place in the head and then in reality, so that the person first thinks about what he or she is doing and then does it. On the contrary, in all skilled acts—acts as varied as writing, walking, talking, and even thinking—the behavior is simply done, and that's all there is to it. To be sure, we may think about what we have done afterward (reflect on it), but at the moment of the doing there is no such reflection; all there is is the act itself.

Another example of unreflected moving is provided by an American tourist walking on a crowded English sidewalk. The usual tendency of an American is to go to the right if it looks as if he or she is going to bump into someone head on. In England the usual (unreflected) move is to the left. What this means is that two Americans will not bump into each other, two Britishers will not bump into each other, but if you are an American in London, be prepared for a collision. Americans or English people are never taught to go right (or left) when walking, nor do they reflect on doing this when they walk. It is just one of those regularities (rules) of social behavior that everyone follows and no one thinks about. We become aware of these regularities if (unreflectedly) we are operating on different sets of rules and these turn out to cause unexpected difficulties (bumping into someone).

Most of our difficulty in talking about our experiences—both reflected and unreflected—has to do with some of the rather peculiar ways we have come to talk about experience in general, ways that seem to separate us from our experience. For example, we usually say "I have a pain in the stomach" or "My stomach hurts." These expressions seem natural enough, but they are not necessarily true to our experience, only to our language. A pain in the stomach is not experienced by some mind that lets itself know "Oh-oh, pain—go find it—ah, there it is—pain in the stomach." Rather, pain is experienced much more directly and immediately—that is, "as the stomach painfully lived." Only when you or I try to describe this experience do we get caught by our language so that we speak as if pain, stomach, and person were separate from one another.

To take another commonplace example, we often say "Look at my hand; how sunburned it is!" Saying "my hand" makes it seem as if there were some Me that had a hand that was sunburned. The feeling I have about my hand when I hold hands with someone or when I write with it is quite different from my feeling about the hand that is sunburned. When holding hands or writing, my hand is doing something unreflectedly meaningful and is part of a total living movement. The sunburned hand is not part of my living situation; instead, I have reduced it to a possession of mine, a thing, and no longer consider it the living instrument by which I relate to, and work in, particular settings.

Is thinking so very different from other human activities? A good way to ask this question might be "Is thinking about thinking different from just plain thinking?" The answer is yes and no: If we are thinking₁ about thinking₂, then the first and the second *thinking*s are not the same. The first *thinking* is a process, it is something immediate and ongoing: it is what I am unreflectedly doing right now. The second *thinking*, however, is what I am thinking about and therefore is not a process, but the object or target of my ongoing thinking. The first *thinking* is what I am doing; the second is the topic of what I am doing.

Each of these cases—a pain, a sunburned hand, thinking about thinking, and sexual behavior—seems to involve two possible ways I, as a person, relate to my setting. If my relationship with my setting is immediate and ongoing, as in holding hands, thinking, living a stomach painfully, or mutually regulated sexual behavior, it is called an **unreflected experience**. If I think about any of these behaviors, then it is called a **reflected experience**.

Generally speaking, when we talk about consciousness, we usually think of reflected consciousness and tend to miss that the act of reflecting is itself an unreflected act. The tendency to consider only reflected consciousness as consciousness comes, of course, from Descartes. The *think* of his famous slogan "I think, therefore I am" refers to reflected, not unreflected, conscious experience. In one sense, Descartes tried to remove ongoing thinking from the world and to consider thought an achievement of the experience out of which it grew. Descartes' doubt does not signal the discovery of a mind or a self so much as it removes "mind" or "self" from the world in which it functioned well before Descartes talked about it. The conscious relationship "which says, 'I am' is not the consciousness which thinks . . . and Descartes' 'cogito' [mind] . . . is not Descartes doubting; it is Descartes reflecting on the doubting" (Barnes, 1956, p. 11).

C. Intentionality and consciousness[2]

Consciousness is a heavy word; it seems so loaded and final, so solid an achievement of intense thinking or hard work. Unfortunately, this is a very

---

[2]From here on we will have to make use of some new and fairly technical ideas. Although these ideas may seem a bit difficult to grasp on first reading, their meanings will unfold in the course of subsequent chapters. As is so often the case, you will have to see how I use these ideas in many contexts before you will be able to use or even define them in a consistent way. This is as it should be: formal definitions always assume we already know the territory of which they speak (see "Physics, Psychology, and Human Experience," above).

misleading way to look at consciousness. It would seem better to talk about consciousness as an open-ended project in a world of open projects.

The word *consciousness* misleads us into considering it a once-and-for-all achievement, not an ongoing process, because it is a noun and not a verb. In English, as in many other languages, nouns generally name relatively bounded and fixed things, such as chairs, trees, or boats. Now, psychology always has a tough time deciding what to do with nouns, particularly important ones like *love* or *life* or *behavior*. Consider, for example, the difference between the words *love* and *loving*. *Love*, the noun, is a once-and-for-all achievement—something we own or have—while *loving* implies that we have to work at it every day. This same distinction applies to *life* and *living*, *behavior* and *behaving*, *memory* and *remembering*, *perception* and *perceiving*, and all such process-versus-achievement pairs. If we are to understand human activity, we probably should replace all nouns with gerunds (nouns that are made from a verb plus the ending *-ing*). In this way psychology would concern itself with processing rather than with processes. Indeed, it seems reasonable to talk about psychology as the study of gerunds.

Unfortunately, *consciousness* seems forever determined to stay a noun; there is no easy gerund ("consciousing" sounds odd). Therefore, when we talk about consciousness, we must always remember two things—it refers to an active process on the part of some person (*my* consciousness), and it always deals with some target or topic. These points are important if we are to be true to our earlier use of conscious experiencing in sexual behavior, pain, and so on.

Consciousness is always consciousness *of* something, whether we are talking about grasping an idea or meeting a body unreflectedly in a sexual act. There is never just "consciousness" independent of some event, topic, or situation. Another way of saying this is that consciousness is always directed toward something or always intends something—that is, consciousness is **intentional.** Using the phrase *conscious of* rather than the blanket term *consciousness* will help remind us that there is always a target to our conscious experiencings. To understand is always to take in the total intention of an event—that unique mode of experience revealed by the ongoing relationship linking target and consciousness of target.

Since conscious experience can be reflected as well as unreflected, intentionality is a part of both. Intentionality in reflected consciousness is easy to understand. Usually what we mean when we talk about thinking, judging, or acting in any planful way captures what is meant here. That is, our thinking, judging, or acting always has a definite topic other than itself. In unreflected consciousness or activity, intentionality also makes sense. For example, in unreflected sexual activity, the target is the other person; in unreflected consciousness of pain, the target is the pain.

II. BEHAVIOR

Psychology, which used to be the study of the psyche, now describes itself as the study of **behavior.** Although most psychologists would probably agree with this definition, the term *behavior* can be confusing. It is a very general term and until we supply some specific adjective and speak of, say, problem-solving behavior, aggressive behavior, or sexual behavior, it seems to have very little meaning. Even then, the meaning is not very clear until we start talking about particular movements in particular situations. Only when we say something like "Problem-solving behavior means what 4-year-old Jonathan does when he finds himself in a room in which the cookies are on a shelf and he is on the floor, and the twain cannot meet" does the idea of problem-solving behavior begin to take shape, and only then can we see general implications even for this specific situation.

Let's follow out the Jonathan/cookie-jar situation and see if it won't tell us something about movements and behavior. First we have Jonathan—3 feet tall and hungry. Second, we have the unreachable cookie—delicious and 6 feet off the floor. What happens? Nothing until Jon notices the cookie and decides it's worth going after. Let's assume he does. He next walks over to the counter and tries to jump up in order to get to the shelf. Unfortunately, he can't jump 3 feet, and so his first effort fails.

What next? He borrows his brother's hockey stick and tries again to reach the cookie jar. But the stick is heavy and Jon is small, and the whole project collapses perilously close to his head. Jon steps back a bit, looks around, and finally sees a chair by the kitchen table. He grabs the chair, pushes it across the floor to the counter, and gets up on the chair—and voilà, the cookie is his.

A. The Dashiell-Melton diagram of adjustive behavior

What we have here is a quite ordinary example of problem-solving behavior, which is what we wanted. The episode described is so ordinary that it can be applied to many other situations. Except for certain small changes in goal (a banana for a chimp, sunflower seeds for a rat, raw fish for a cat) or in the movements involved (climbing a tree, running a maze, getting out of an enclosure called a puzzle box), our description of the Jon/cookie-jar situation applies equally well for other organisms. A number of psychologists (J. F. Dashiell and A. W. Melton, to name just two) have proposed a definition of problem-solving behavior based on an analysis of just this type of situation. The best way to approach their discussion is by using the Dashiell-Melton diagram of adjustive and/or problem-solving behavior (Figure 1–2).

Each of the five numbers in Figure 1–2 refers to some general aspect of adjustive behavior: "A motivated person (1), upon encountering an obstruction or difficulty (2), shows ... varied activity (3) until one of his variant ways of acting chances to take him around his difficulty (4) and a good or more nearly optimal situation is obtained (5)" (Dashiell, 1949, p. 405). In this way, Dashiell provides an abstract description of adjustive (problem-solving) behavior, certainly an important type of human and animal behavior.

Although all of living cannot be described in terms of the Dashiell-Melton diagram, it does help emphasize some important properties of behaving.

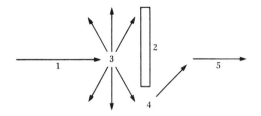

Figure 1-2.   Dashiell-Melton diagram of adjustive behavior leading to learning. *(From* Fundamentals of General Psychology, *Third Edition, by J. F. Dashiell. Copyright 1949 by Houghton Mifflin Company. Renewed 1976 by F. K. Dashiell. This and all other material from this source reprinted by permission.)*

The most notable aspect of the Dashiell-Melton diagram is that actions always have a direction and that this direction always involves the whole organism. Although this general description can be used for Jon as well as for a cat in a puzzle box, the specific properties of the situation determine what the actions in Phase 4 will look like—pushing a chair over to a counter to get a cookie or turning a knob to get a piece of fish. It may be possible to describe certain general aspects of behavior abstractly, but an accurate description of a particular behavior must take both the specifics of the situation and the organism into account.

B. Some characteristics of behavior

As long ago as 1932, another American psychologist, this time one particularly interested in rat behavior, E. C. Tolman, provided a list of the properties of behavior. Among others, he included the following three:

1. Behavior always seems to have the character of getting to or getting from a specific goal situation.
2. It always involves a mutual interchange between a behavior-act and its environmental setting.
3. Behavior is always an affair of the organism as a whole. As a type of commerce with the environment, it can take place only in a whole organism [paraphrased from Tolman, 1932].

Here, then, we have two lists that seem to describe what we mean when we use the word *behavior*. The lists are quite similar: both stress the directed aspect of behaving, both stress that it is necessary to take the particular situation into account in interpreting any given bit of behaving, and both stress that behaving always involves the total organism. What is interesting about these lists is that they are also similar to the list of properties that defined human experiencing when we started our definition from the point of view of experience rather than from the point of view of problem-solving behavior in young children or maze running in animals.

1. Intentionality.   Whether we start from conscious experience or from movements defined in laboratory tasks, it is impossible to talk only about movements; some interpretation regarding the purpose of these movements seems required before we can call moving "behaving." From the perspective of conscious experience, the meaning of a particular movement always concerns its (unreflected or reflected) **intentionality**—that is, its "directedness." From the perspective of laboratory psychology, the meaning of a particular piece of behavior usually concerns its goal—as Tolman put it, its "getting to or getting from a specific goal situation." To be of use for even animal or laboratory psychology, movements must have targets, and any movement is important to the degree that it expresses some intention for the behaving person or animal.

2. Constraint by situations. What a person does, will do, or can do is always limited by the situation in which he or she happens to be. For laboratory behavior as well as for "real world" behavior, different situations call for different behaviors, and any accurate description of behavior has to take this into account. This is true whether we describe behavior from the perspective of conscious experience or from the perspective of an analysis of movement.

All animals or human beings always find themselves in a **situation.** Such situations are defined by social conditions, historical period, personal talent, economic position, personal appearance, and so on. In philosophy, the fact that each person is always in a situation has sometimes been expressed by the phrase **Being-in-the-world,** which simply means that to understand behavior, the person's situation in a factual world must always be taken into account. To behave, human beings are always "somewhere," always acting in regard to "some-thing."

One of the most challenging responsibilities facing us as people is to deal with ourselves in our situation. The philosopher George Schrader (1967, p. 24) put it as follows:

If man is free to be himself, it is not just any self at all, but the particular self that he happens to be. Frequently he is unwilling to accept this restriction and wills not to be himself . . . but to be another self. Cinderella dreams of being a princess—and magically becomes one. The waitress dreams of becoming a movie star. Vicariously, millions of people enjoy lives of excitement and adventure through their identification with the heroes and heroines of the movies and television. . . . There [is nothing] deplorable about such dreaming [except] in so far as it represents a flight from oneself. One may forget oneself and temporarily identify with the

hero of one's dreams. But not for long can one escape from the realities of his existence.[3]

The idea of a situation also has something important to say to the continuing debate in psychology over the question of **free will** and human **freedom.** Many psychologists, most notably B. F. Skinner (1971), have argued that terms like *freedom* and *responsibility* have misled us into thinking we are free and responsible when, in fact, these terms are empty illusions and each of us is completely determined (made unfree) by his or her personal and social history. Although it is true that some philosophers, such as Sartre, have talked about radical freedom, it seems better to talk, with the philosopher Merleau-Ponty, about **action in situations.** In this view, free action (as is true of any and all activity) is always made in regard to a particular situation. The exercise of choice in a situation where limitations are present is a much more significant event than an action undertaken in a situation without limitations.

As a matter of fact, the idea of unconditional freedom—that is, action independent of situation—is a living impossibility, a lie told by past ages. Only if by *freedom* we mean a "**situationless freedom**" does Skinner's analysis have merit. Only if we accept the fact that we are always in the world and that no action ever frees us from our situation can we arrive at a better understanding of "free action." Freedom is not the possibility of escape from our situation; rather, it is the movement toward engagement in a new situation.

Perhaps the most human discussion of the relation between freedom and personal action was offered by the American psychologist/philosopher William James (1842–1910). To understand James' attitude, we need to know something about his life—most particularly, about a crisis that occurred in 1870 when he was 28 years old. It was during this period that young James experienced a profound depression in which he felt, as he put it, "a terrible fear for my own existence." This horrible fear took the form of an image of "a black-haired youth with greenish skin" who was subject to "fits of epilepsy" and who sat "all day on the back benches of an in-

[3]From *Existential Philosophers: Kierkegaard to Merleau-Ponty,* by G. A. Schrader, Jr. (Ed.). Copyright © 1967 by McGraw-Hill, Inc. Used with permission of McGraw-Hill Book Company.

sane asylum." This image, James was convinced, could in the extreme come to describe him, and there might be nothing he could do to defend himself against such a fate. Writing about his escape from this depression, James noted:

> I think yesterday I passed a crisis in my life. I had finished the first part of Renouvier's second *Essais* and see no reason why his definition of free-will—"the sustaining of a thought *because I choose to* when I might have other thoughts"—need be the definition of an illusion. At any rate, I will assume for the present—until next year—that it is no illusion. My first act of free-will shall be to believe in free-will [as quoted in Barrett, 1975, p. 59].

What James seems to be saying is that although it is always possible to argue about whether free will exists, there will never be a sure answer, and we are always free to set up our lives so as to take one or another attitude toward it.

James also suggests that a strong belief in free will has beneficial consequences for the believer. He gives an example of a mountain climber caught at the edge of an abyss, which he has to leap across in order to save himself. The gap is not so large that he can't make it, yet it is just large enough to give him reasonable cause for worry. What should the climber believe: that he can make it or that he cannot? If he believes that he can, James argues, the climber's energies will be increased by this belief, and therefore he will be much more likely to succeed in jumping across the gap safely. This success will also confirm the truth of his belief (Barrett, 1975).

So it is with free will. If we believe we are in control of at least some parts of our lives, we are more likely to undertake certain actions than if we do not. As James noted, if such a belief helps me, it seems reasonable to conclude that the belief is no illusion.

3. Involvement of the whole organism.   The final property of behaving that seems well agreed on is that it must involve the total animal or person. This idea seems to run contrary to the usual psychological experiment, in which a subject is taught to blink his eye in response to a quiet sound or to learn a set of nonsense syllables. Although laboratory psychologists often assume that who their subjects are as people in their lives outside the laboratory has little to do with the results of an experiment, more recent thinking has come to recognize that a complete human being works in the laboratory—not only an eye or a mouth or a hand. Although the experimental subject may lend the experimenter his or her eye, he or she never stops being a human being.

This understanding has been faced most directly and clearly by Martin T. Orne of the University of Pennsylvania in a series of studies dealing with what he has called the **demand properties** of an experiment. In one set of these experiments, for example, Orne was concerned with lie-detector tests such as are used by police. The galvanic skin response (GSR)—a measure of sweating—was used to detect lying by looking for large changes in sweating, presumably brought about by lying. In one early study (Ellson, Davis, Saltzman, & Burke, 1952) not done in Orne's laboratory, people were given two trials (testing periods). After the first trial, some of the people were told that their lies had been detected, and others were told that their lies had not. On Trial 2, those people who believed they had been found out became harder to detect; those who were told they had successfully faked the GSR on Trial 1 became easier to detect.

This is an extremely important result because in actual police work the suspect is told how hard it is to fool the lie detector; that is, he is told that he will be caught if he lies. If we believe the results obtained by Ellson et al., then telling a criminal how hard it is to fool the lie detector might have the same result as telling subjects that they have already been found out and that they are likely to be found out again on Trial 2. The very procedures used by the police to determine whether someone is lying should make lying harder to detect.

How can Ellson's results be understood—results that are so opposed to ordinary practice and common sense? The crucial issue here is what people taking lie-detector tests believe about themselves and about lie-detector tests. Orne (1969) reports, for example, that most college students believe that lie detectors using the GSR work only with normal people and that only habitual liars or psychopaths can fool the lie detector. If this is true, then it is important not to fool the lie detector if we are to be judged "normal." Since telling students that they had been found out meant "It's OK, you're normal," they then became harder to detect on Trial 2. And students who were told they had not been found out on Trial 1 (and hence were not "normal") became easier to detect on Trial 2 ("because they wanted to be normal").

To test this assumption experimentally, Gustafson and Orne (1965) told one group of 32 students:

"This is a detection of deception experiment. We are trying to see how well the lie detector works. As you know, it is not possible to detect lying in the case of psychopathic personalities or habitual liars. We want you to try your very best to fool the lie detector during this experiment. Good luck" [Orne, 1969, pp. 149–150].

These instructions were thought to be similar to the subjects' assumptions at work in the study by Ellson et al. As such, they ought to make for easier detection on Trial 2 if subjects were told they had not been detected on Trial 1. By the same token, if students were told they had been detected on Trial 1, they should become harder to detect on Trial 2.

The experiment went as follows: Students were given a series of numbers and told to keep one of them secret. (The experimenter actually knew the "secret" number.) After Trial 1, 16 subjects were told that GSR results indicated that "number so-and-so" was the one they were trying to keep secret. Of course, the experimenter was correct. For 16 other subjects the experimenter gave the wrong number.

In analyzing his results, Orne first looked at the data produced on Trial 1. If he had done the experiment without knowledge of the "correct" number, he should not have been able to detect the secret number on the basis of GSR results for any more people in the first group than in the second group, and this turned out to be the case.

On Trial 2, results were quite dramatic: Of the 16 students told that they had been detected, 12 could *not* be detected on Trial 2. Of the 16 students told they had *not* been detected, 14 could be detected on Trial 2. In short, the instructions given to the students changed the meaning of the lie-detector situation and thereby changed the ease with which lies could be detected. On this basis, the difference between the findings of Ellson et al. and the experience of police in using the lie-detector test could be resolved: Students show increased detectability only if *they* think such detectability is associated with being normal. Once assured of their normality, they become more difficult to detect.

This last study is extremely important, for it makes the experimental point that even within the confines of a "clean" scientific experiment, what people do depends on factors of intention, situation, and total-person involvement. This should not be too surprising, for whether we are analyzing sexual behavior, a child's attempt to get an unreachable cookie, or what subjects do in an experiment, we are always dealing with human beings who are forever destined to be human beings. There is no human response that is without meaning for the person doing it, and this is what we must understand if we are to make sense of what we do in this world.

Orne's experiment also has a very significant moral beyond the confines of the laboratory—that psychological analyses must consider every situation from the point of view of the person involved. Only in this way can we hope to gain some understanding of my particular understanding of the situation and of my particular reaction to it. Psychology needs to become a first-person science rather than one solely concerned with describing results from some third-person point of view, such as that of an experimenter. It is always *my* world that matters to me, never *his* or *her* third-person world. To get it right, we can never look only, or even primarily, at the third-person world of the abstract laboratory subject—rat, monkey, or, most especially, human being.

C. Experience, consciousness, and behavior

The three words *experience, consciousness,* and *behavior* all seem to deal with what it is any psychologist says he or she studies. Although at first glance they might appear to cover different territories, it also seems clear that they must be related in some obvious and straightforward way. Perhaps the simplest way to deal with these terms is to use the following (overly) simple set of descriptions, which make it clear that each of these three words emphasizes a different point of view: The concept of consciousness is a third-person reflection (often my own) on what I do (or did). The concept of behavior is a third-person reflection on what someone else does (or did). Experience is what I do, whether or not I reflect on it as I do it.

What this means is that of all three concepts, **experience** is *mine* in the most direct and immediate way possible. Both "behavior" and "consciousness" embody attempts at describing experience in an objective and third-person way. As such, they are terms used by disciplines such as philosophy or psychology and can never represent something as "real" to me as my own ongoing first-person experience. I experience; scholars deal with consciousness and/or behavior.

III. CAUTIONS IN USING PSYCHOLOGICAL WORDS

In one sense this book—or any book, for that matter—is nothing but a pile of dead words that come alive only by touching the personal experience of some reader. Because we are so thoroughly symbolic creatures, we tend to take words at face value and often overlook differences between the word and the experience it names. Sometimes we even treat all words of a certain class as if they related to experience in the same way. I have already talked about one part of this problem in connection with such words as *consciousness* and *behavior*, and I will have to discuss this issue over and over again many times.

Many people belonging to the philosophical movement known as "general semantics" (such as Korzybski, 1933, or Hayakawa, 1949) have been careful to point out how difficult it is to know what a word means and how easy it is to be trapped in misunderstandings. As a guide to the uninitiated, general semanticists have proposed a number of simple techniques, such as "dating," "etcetering," and "quotation marking," to help us avoid some of the difficulties brought about by careless speaking. Etcetering, the best known of these techniques, captures the idea that there is always more to an experience than the word that names it. If we add a silent "etc." to each word we speak or hear, we will never mistake a word, which is metaphorically a "**map**," for the "**territory**" it represents. So too for dating (giving each concept a definite time reference, as by specifying "the United States in 1920," "the United States in 1962," "the United States in 1980"), and so too for quoting (putting quotes around words that represent abstract ideas, such as *race* or *goodness*). In all these cases, we must never take the meaning of a word at face value; rather, to avoid semantic confusion, we must always be aware of the difficulties involved in the relation of word to world and world to word.

The philosopher Gilbert Ryle (1949) has described a different type of word/idea difficulty as what he calls a **category mistake**. The following anecdote gives one good example of this class of mistakes.

A foreigner visiting Oxford or Cambridge for the first time is shown a number of colleges, libraries, playing fields, museums, scientific departments and administrative offices. He then asks 'But where is the University? I have seen where the members of the Colleges live, where the Registrar works, where the scientists experiment and the rest. But I have not yet seen the University in which reside and work the members of your University.' It has then to be explained to him that the University is not another collateral institution, some ulterior counterpart to the colleges, laboratories and offices which he has seen. The University is just the way in which all that he has already seen is organized. When they are seen and when their co-ordination is understood, the University has been seen. His mistake lay in his innocent assumption that it was correct to speak of Christ Church, the Bodleian Library, the Ashmolean Museum *and* the University, to speak, that is, as if 'the University' stood for an extra member of the class of which these other units are members. He was mistakenly allocating the University to the same category as that to which the other institutions belong [Ryle, 1949, pp. 17–18].[4]

What this analysis means for psychology is that we should be very careful with our words and that often we may have to clear up ordinary ways of talking about things before we can get on with talking about them in a psychologically useful way. Considering some of the problems discussed in the present chapter, it seems worth noting that Ryle presented his ideas about category mistakes in a chapter called "Descartes' Myth." In his terms, mind/body dualism is simply a category mistake: minds and bodies are just not the same kind of thing. In Ryle's terms, it is wrong to contrast mind with body because such a contrast assumes that they are members of the same category. Making a contrast between the two is as improper as asking where Cambridge University is after seeing the various colleges, libraries, playing fields, and so on. From the logical point of view, Cambridge University is in a different category from St. John's College or from the playing field known as Parker's Piece.

By this analysis, Ryle does not mean to suggest that there are no "mental processes." What he

---

[4]From *The Concept of Mind*, by G. Ryle. Copyright 1949 by Penguin Books, Inc. Reprinted by permission of Harper & Row, Publishers, Inc.

means is that the phrase *mental processes* does not mean the same kind of thing as *physical processes*, even though the two topics can be labeled with the same word—*processes*. For this reason, Ryle concludes that the official Cartesian doctrine is empty and that it is reasonable to describe the Cartesian position on mind and body as "**the ghost in the machine.**" With this phrase, Ryle banishes the dichotomy from philosophy and psychology, and the means by which he does it is a careful analysis of words considered as concepts.

Ryle's analysis, however, should not be taken to mean that a poetic (mythic) use of words is always wrong—rather, that we always have to be careful in our myths and in the ways we express them. As a general rule, we ought to use our language as carefully and as objectively as possible. Wherever possible, we ought to try to make our language describe what we have seen and done when we present an observation or describe an experimental procedure. Although such language may never get exactly to the heart of the matter, it does allow strangers (psychologists, sociologists, philosophers, and so on) to talk to one another about experiments they have never done or about observations they have never taken.

Objective description, whether in the form of a photograph, a tape recording, or even highly descriptive third-person language, may be a valuable starting point for psychology. Any psychological investigation content to stay at this level, however, will surely be unable to deal with the complexities of behavior, human or animal. Of all possible descriptive systems, considered over the broadest range of situations, objective third-person description is likely to be the least wrong in the greatest number of cases but hardly ever the most revealing if an understanding of human behavior is what we seek. Objective description is always an appropriate place to start—never an appropriate place to stop.

IV. A FINAL WORD

In this chapter we seem to have come to the view that what we do as human beings is often a reflection of our mode of existing in the world at a particular time. No act is too small or inconsequential to tell something of our existence, even though all of our existence cannot always be read from even the most dramatic of human actions. The way in which

you and I live and come to make sense of our lives is through what we do, and this is something we must always keep in mind.

Now, you might think that the behavior of a small child getting a cookie or of a college student taking a lie-detector test or of a rat running down a maze is a slender thread on which to hang a theory of living and a comprehensive psychology, yet this is exactly what we must do. No behavioral situation is without meaning, and none fails to blend in with, and reveal the patterns of, our existence. What we do—how we behave—in the ordinary as well as in the dramatic situations of a life comes to define us; and if we try, our fate, yours and mine, more often than not can be read in both.

Psychologists tend to keep their private and scientific lives far apart. This is for good reason; no one likes to be considered just the human analogue of a white rat, a toad, or a computer. Rather, we like to think of ourselves as human and unique, but when we do, we run into a problem. Either we can be consistent and say "Even though I don't like it, what I expect to be true of my laboratory or clinical subjects is also true of me," or we can be inconsistent and say that our laboratory work, while interesting, is really irrelevant to us as people. This latter situation comes about when we assume that a physically based philosophy is an appropriate one for psychology.

Few psychologists have considered asking whether a philosophy useful to them in their very human daily lives could also be useful to them in their scientific work. The present chapter has tried to suggest that such an approach is possible and that the philosophical foundations underlying physics and chemistry may be wrong for psychology. The idea of psychology as a human science (Giorgi, 1970) requires a new basis on which to construct a discipline. This new basis can be described best as a philosophy of existence, where by *existence* we mean what we do in the world as human beings rather than as physical, chemical, or mechanical systems.

If we take this as our starting point, we have to recognize that we will always have to think of ourselves and our world as constantly changing. Consequently, there will never be a complete or final answer to any question. All we can hope for are provisional truths that will be useful for a while. This means that we must always be in constant discussion with ourselves and our world and never accept any solution to any problem as final. We must always look at who we are, where we are, and what we are trying to do.

Although this attempt at a final word is not designed to spell out a complete philosophy, it is meant to suggest certain things for you and me as people as well as, more narrowly, psychologists. To ask the question straight out: What does it mean to be a human being?

In terms of self-perception, it means that we must always consider ourselves an incomplete project—a task in need of completing. To be sure, there are lyrical moments when we seem to "have it all together," yet such integrations always seem to fall apart and, if we are lucky, to give rise to new projects. The project that we are is, and must remain, incomplete. Although human beings may actively seek solutions, completions, or resting places, such solutions can never be final, and the fine fragile syntheses we achieve occur only at separated points in a life.

In the moral domain, this approach suggests that we are what we do and that any moral evaluation of you or me in a situation must always begin with an honest critique of ourselves. We are never assured ahead of time, and independent of this honest evaluation in a particular situation, that we have (or have not) done the right thing.

From the perspective of me as person or of me as social scientist, there is no escaping from a continual evaluation of what I do. To come back to our starting point: You and I, and all the other You's and I's in this world, will just have to accept this as our situation and continue to evaluate and make new beginnings as we go along. Armed with this acceptance, we are now ready to step into that situation which calls itself contemporary psychology.

V. SUMMARY

In attempting to order our experiences, we usually divide the world into two major categories: that of objects, or matter, and that of people, or mind. There are two customary ways of dealing with mind and matter: assume they are the same thing (that is, interpret mind as matter or interpret matter as mind) or concede a permanent separation between the two. The latter alternative has been the position most often taken by psychology.

This dualism, first proposed by Descartes in the 17th century, has been very productive for physical science. In psychology, such an approach has tended to draw the focus away from an individual's experience of his or her life and has led us to forget that science itself is a human construction. Sexual activity is an example of a situation which has often been described in natural-science terms (that is, as involving only the body) yet which cannot be understood in terms of a dualistic separation of mind and body. Rather, it seems best understood through a careful analysis of human conscious experience.

Conscious experience—whether of sexual activity or of something else—can be either reflected or unreflected. An example of unreflected experiencing is that American pedestrians tend to go to the right to avoid sidewalk collisions, English pedestrians to the left. What is interesting here is that the Americans and the English are seldom taught which way to go, nor do they reflect on it as they walk.

Conscious experience is not an achievement, as the noun *experience* unfortunately suggests: when we speak of conscious experience, it must be remembered that such experience is always an integral part of some particular person, never an entity by itself independent of some particular situation. Conscious experience is an active process always directed at the world. Such directedness is called "intentionality."

Psychology has often been defined as "the study of behavior." It is important to keep three ideas in mind whenever the word *behavior* is used: (1) behavior is intentional, (2) it occurs in situations, and (3) it always involves a complete organism. For laboratory psychology, intentionality often means describing a behavior in terms of its goal or target. Situations have been seen to place limits on possible behaviors. These limits have often been interpreted by such psychologists as Skinner to mean that humans have no free choice. More existential philosophers, such as Merleau-Ponty or William James, emphasize the significant experience of free choice within the limits of a given situation. The third property of behavior, that it involves a complete organism, is not always taken into account in psychological experiments. As Orne's experiments on lie detection show, the person's perception of an experiment significantly influences how that person will respond. Even within the confines of a "clean" psychological experiment, what people do depends on who they are, what their goals are, how they perceive the situation, and, finally, what is important to them. This means that even an experiment must be looked at from the (first-person) point of view of the person involved.

Words are hollow symbols whose meanings become apparent only when in touch with the personal experiences of a listener or reader. It is difficult to know what a word means to someone else, and semanticists have suggested some techniques to avoid confusion, such as etcetering, dating, and quoting. These techniques provide reminders that words cannot always be taken at face value. A general rule in regard to words and concepts is that language should be used carefully and objectively. Although objective description is a good starting point for psychology, it is never an appropriate stopping place.

The category mistake is another word/idea difficulty. In Gilbert Ryle's (1949) anecdote, a foreign visitor is shown all the buildings that make up Cambridge University and then asks "But where is the university?" This visitor makes a category mistake in not understanding that "the university" is the organization and coordination of all he has seen—not simply another building. Ryle further explored category mistakes within his attack on Cartesian dualism. To contrast mind with body is as improper as asking where Cambridge University is after seeing the libraries, playing fields, and so on. On the basis of careful analysis of words, Ryle concluded that the official Cartesian doctrine was empty and banished the dichotomy from philosophy and psychology.

The separation of one's private and scientific life has been of concern to psychologists. One way psychologists have viewed themselves and their work is to adopt a physically based philosophy when doing laboratory psychology but to maintain that results achieved by such work are largely irrelevant to themselves as people. A different view is that even though they don't like it, what they expect to be true of their laboratory or clinical subjects must also be true of themselves. One way to deal with this problem is to wonder whether a philosophy that provides a foundation for physics and chemistry might not be wrong for psychology. The human sciences must find a new basis on which to build their discipline. This new approach can best be described as a philosophy of existence in which what we do in the world as human beings (rather than as physical or chemical systems) is what is important. In doing this, we consider ourselves as projects always in need of completion. This means that both as people and as psychologists, we must be in constant discussion with ourselves and our world and never accept as final any solution to any problem. Understanding, like human experience itself, is always open-ended.

VI. GLOSSARY OF IMPORTANT CONCEPTS

Action in situations. The idea that emphasizes that there is no absolute free will and that the limits of one's situation provide direction and horizons for one's activity.

Behavior. A description of one's mode of acting in the world at a particular time, as seen from a third-person viewpoint. It has three characteristics: (1) intentionality (behavior is directed toward something; there is no movement without meaning); (2) constraint by situation (human beings are always someplace acting with regard to something); (3) involvement of the whole organism.

Being-in-the-world. A term used by existentialist philosophy to mean that consciousness is always of, and directed toward, the world.

Cartesian dualism. The view, asserted by Descartes, that a person's being is composed of the physical body and a nonphysical aspect called mind.

Category mistake. A logical mistake inherent in Cartesianism pointed out by the philosopher Gilbert Ryle. This mistake is to assume that certain concepts are of the same logical category when in fact they are not.

Consciousness. An abstract description of the interchange between an organism and the world it lives in and through.

Demand properties. The features explicit or implicit in a particular situation (usually an experiment) that induce an unspoken belief in the subject. For example, people who are influenced to believe that a lie detector is effective are less likely to have their lies detected than those who believe that the detector is ineffective.

Experience. An active interchange between an individual and the world around her or him. It must be had by someone and be of something.

Freedom. Not an escape from our situation; rather, the possibility of "pointing at" and "going toward" a new situation by a particular individual; allied to "intentionality."

Free will. The assumption that people change the situations in which they act even if these situations presently limit their alternatives.

Ghost in the machine. A description of Cartesian dualism by the philosopher Gilbert Ryle, suggesting that such dualism is not useful.

Intentionality. In phenomenological philosophy, the directedness of consciousness toward some aspect of its situation.

Map and **territory.** A word is a map, a designator with no inherent meaning, which always designates some reality (a territory). Confusion of the two invariably breeds misunderstanding.

Psychology. The investigation of an organism's interrelationships with the world it lives in.

Reflected experience. Conscious experience directed toward an unreflected activity; directing oneself toward a consideration of one's ongoing behaving.

Situation. The environment of meanings, prospects, possibilities, and limitations within which conscious experience occurs.

Situationless freedom. The freedom of action that could occur only if consciousness were in a vacuum—in a situation in which there was no meaning to the ongoing activity.

Territory. See **map.**

Unreflected experience. Conscious experience in which the ongoing activity absorbs the person and is not itself thought about.

VII. SUGGESTED READINGS

The readings that follow are divided into two categories. The first, "Major Sources," is a collection of quite difficult books and articles that form the basis of much of the present chapter. They are intended for someone interested in serious further study.

The second category, "Secondary Sources," contains books that are much more easily understood. Many of them have been written for students and attempt to present the same ideas as works in the first category.

Major sources

Barrett, W. *Irrational man.* Garden City, N.Y.: Doubleday, 1958. Part 3, Appendix B.

Kvale, S., & Grenness, E. Skinner and Sartre. *Review of Existential Psychology and Psychiatry,* 1967, 7, 128–150.

Luijpen, W. A. *Existential phenomenology.* Pittsburgh: Duquesne University Press, 1969. Chapters 1–3.

Merleau-Ponty, M. *The phenomenology of perception.* London: Routledge and Kegan Paul, 1962. Preface; Part 1, Chapter 5; Part 3, Chapters 1, 3.

Ryle, G. *The concept of mind.* Harmondsworth, England: Penguin Books, 1949. Chapters 1, 2, 6, 8, 9.

Secondary (simpler) sources

Giorgi, A. *Psychology as a human science.* New York: Harper & Row, 1970.

Keen, E. *A primer in phenomenological psychology.* New York: Holt, Rinehart & Winston, 1975.

Lyons, J. *Experience: An introduction to a personal psychology.* New York: Harper & Row, 1973.

Schrader, G. A., Jr. (Ed.). *Existential philosophers: Kierkegaard to Merleau-Ponty.* New York: McGraw-Hill, 1967. Especially chapters on Merleau-Ponty, Marcel, Sartre, and Heidegger.

2

The Everyday World of Human Living

On the record album *In My Life* Judy Collins sings a song to the French Revolutionary hero Jean-Paul Marat, which in part goes as follows: "Marat, we're poor / And the poor stay poor. / Marat, don't make us / Wait any more. / We want our rights / And we don't care how / We want our revolution / Now."[1]

Although this song contains many important insights into how human society works, it is the line "And the poor stay poor" that gives the song its contemporary meaning. Why do the poor stay poor? Part of the answer must be that the poor stay poor because they have been brought up to be poor, because they have the habits of being poor, but mostly because they cannot see the world except from the perspective of being poor—other perspectives do not exist for them.

This answer sounds terribly abstract, and poor people live in the terribly concrete. What the song means on a day-to-day basis is that poor people have not been taught how to make use of systems and agencies set up for the benefit of all citizens, poor ones included. For example, it is almost beyond the possible for many poor people in North America to initiate a court action, to see their legislative representative, to question authority figures such as ministers or priests, to borrow money on appropriate credit terms, and a thousand other things that middle- and upper-class people do easily. It is not so much that these agencies don't or won't help; they simply are not a part of the first-person world of the poor. The habits of thinking and doing that are possible for most of us just do not exist for the poor. It is not so much a matter of being pushed away as a matter of not even knowing anything is there.

But how, then, do some of the children of the poor move to a different class—or, more dramatically, how do revolutions involving the poor ever come about? To help understand such events, think of your room at home and your usual way of dealing with it. In your room at home there are bookcases, lamps, desks, beds, and probably other furnishings. Without ever taking note of any of these things, you move about easily and comfortably within the room, never even noticing the constraints these objects put on your possible moves, seeming totally unimpressed by where and what things are. The situation changes, however, if you happen to look at your room through different eyes—say, when the lights are turned out or when a friend comments on how crowded your room is. Under these conditions the location of your furniture suddenly becomes very important, particularly if you have stubbed your toes or banged your knee on the bedpost.

In just this way, the poor stay poor: it never occurs to anyone that his or her space—his or her world—could be different until it is considered from a different point of view or until a social toe is stubbed against some of society's furniture known as institutions or their more formal counterparts, laws. Then and only then do the limitations of a particular situation become painfully obvious.

In our day, we have seen lots of toe stubbing, not only by the poor but by a number of other social groups that until recently had accepted a lot of amazingly useless social furniture forced on them by an unsympathetic society. Here, of course, we think of Native Americans, Blacks, students, and, most recently, women. Women present a particularly apt example: Did you know that until 1975 or 1976 in many states a divorced woman could not establish credit, while her divorced husband could? Did you know that women, on the average, earn about 20% less than men *doing the same job?* And how many men do you know who changed their last names when they got married? The list could go on for a good bit more.

The psychological significance of the women's movement lies in its ability to point out a large number of these seemingly "unchangeable" aspects of society and to show how—in the everyday situa-

[1]From *The Persecution and Assassination of Jean-Paul Marat as Performed by the Inmates of the Asylum of Charenton Under the Direction of the Marquis de Sade*, a play by Peter Weiss. Copyright © 1965 by John Calder, Ltd. Reprinted by permission of Atheneum Publishers and Marion Boyers Publishers, Ltd.

tion of a woman's life—these factors get bumped into. The world an old-fashioned person thinks a woman lives in has not changed; only some women's (and men's) perceptions of it have changed. What before was unthinkable now is possible. Only with a change in perspective such as this—that is, with a clear recognition of exactly how a society controls our day-to-day lives by the "furniture" it places in our way—do new ways of living become possible. This is true for women and no less for Blacks, poor people, students, and all of us in many subtle and as yet unperceived ways.

I. THE SOCIAL SITUATION

One reason for introducing the idea of a **social obstacle**—what we have been calling "furniture"—is to remind ourselves that people are always in a social situation and that any complete description of human experience must always take the person's perception of the situation into account. Although every situation must be talked about in individual ways for particular people, we do need general terms for dealing with the interrelatedness of people, situations, and society.

An easy way to do so is to use a diagram such as Figure 2-1, which emphasizes that a person is always unreflectedly in some particular situation in some larger social setting even if the person is not reflectedly aware of it. The ellipse around the situation is dashed to indicate that each situation may have different degrees of significance for the person

at any given time. To be perfectly consistent, all lines ought to be dashed, for an analysis might show that the boundaries of the person, P, also vary in importance, as do the unreflected limitations imposed by society. The purpose of this diagram is to provide a general way of looking at behavior; although it may be useful for talking about things in general, any more accurate description will always have to make a more specific use of this general scheme.

Figure 2-1 illustrates the perception of a single person in a rather unimportant situation. Most of our social behavior does not take place when we are alone, but when we are together with other people. Sometimes these people matter to us very much, as when we are with people we love; at other times they are strangers, as when we are but one of an anonymous audience at a play, a concert, or a ball game.

A. Being in an audience as a social situation

An audience situation seems unlikely to have much effect on how I respond to, and how much I say I enjoy, a particular performance. However, some observations by Murphy and Pollio (1975) suggest otherwise. In this experiment, two groups of students were asked to listen to comedy records, one performed by Bill Cosby and the other by Don Rickles. Cosby, of course, creates a world of the nice guy ruminating about the small misadventures of childhood and the perpetual battles a kid has with his archenemies, parents, and school. Rickles, in contrast, evokes a world of hostility, where failure, inferiority, and incompetence provide the guidelines. In this world there is always a target or scapegoat, usually some unfortunate soul in the audience whose verbal skills are nonexistent compared with those of the acid-tongued Rickles. The titles of their records clearly express these differences: Rickles' record is called *Hello, Dummy*; Cosby's is called *Wonderfulness*.

One audience group was made up entirely of strangers—people who had volunteered separately to serve in the experiment and who did not know one another. The second audience group was composed of friends who knew one another and who had come together to participate in the experiment. All students were told that they would listen to records by Cosby and Rickles. They were also told that

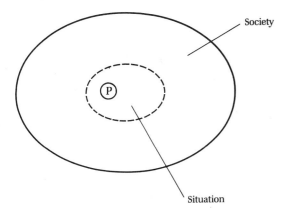

Figure 2-1. Schematic description of social relationships involving a single person, P.

(with their permission) their laughs, smiles, and other behaviors would be recorded on videotape.

Observations of these students were divided into three categories: (1) general movements, such as fidgeting, (2) group-interaction responses, including turning to look at and talk to someone else in the group, and (3) specific responses to humor, such as laughing and smiling. The observations revealed some striking differences between the two groups. For one, strangers moved around and looked at one another much less than friends, and this was true for people listening to both Cosby and Rickles. Although strangers talked to one another somewhat less when listening to Cosby than friends did, they were even more inhibited when listening to Rickles. The major differences, however, were found in laughing and smiling: friends laughed and smiled somewhat less than strangers when listening to Cosby but considerably more (by almost a 2 to 1 margin) when listening to Rickles. When students were asked which comedian they preferred, only 1 out of 50 students in the "strangers" audience said he preferred Rickles, whereas 17 out of 50 in the "friends" audience said they preferred Rickles.

Even in as uninvolving a situation as being a member of an audience, then, some striking effects can be seen by looking carefully at what goes on. Not only do people listening to Rickles respond differently when in an audience of friends rather than in an audience of strangers, they also say they like Rickles more. Contrary to common-sense notions, people do not like or dislike a performance on the basis of the presentation alone. The audience they share it with may strongly color not only their immediate reactions but later judgments as well.

B. The personal self-world

Although the results of the Cosby/Rickles experiment may run counter to common sense, they suggest quite plainly that we are affected by unreflected social influences we may not be aware of. Given this state of affairs, we need some way of talking about these quiet but significant background social conditions. Psychologists who study human behavior in the laboratory often try to rule out such conditions, but observers of animal behavior long ago stressed the peculiar properties of a particular animal's particular world—what they called the animal's "self-world," or *Umwelt*.

To understand what a self-world might be like, we could profit by having a guide such as the naturalist Jakob von Uexküll (1957, p. 5), to "help us stroll through the worlds of animals and men." To do this, von Uexküll suggests we first blow an imaginary "soap bubble around each creature to represent its own world, filled with the perceptions that it alone can know" (p. 5). Such a soap bubble represents the animal's self-world. For humans, the self-world is sometimes called the *Eigenwelt* (the world of the individual), as distinct from the more general term *Umwelt*, which refers to the surrounding world of a particular species (worm, rat, pigeon, human, and so on).

To illustrate the idea of *Umwelt*, von Uexküll enlisted the aid of an artist to draw how "the same reality"—in this case a tree—would appear in the self-worlds of six creatures. Figure 2-2a presents the thoroughly rational world of an old forester who must decide which trees are ready to be chopped down and how much wood will come from each. For this reason, he makes use of a measuring tape and is interested only in the dimensions of the tree; all other aspects, such as the gnarled branches, the texture of the trunk, or the leaves, do not appear in his self-world. Under a different purpose, the tree might have a different set of properties; however, in the present situation, the forester will see only its dimensions and how much wood it will produce.

In the magical self-world of a child, the tree takes on a frightening appearance (Figure 2-2b); the knobby bark looks like a face. The whole oak tree has now become a threatening demon, and the material world of the forester is nowhere in sight.

To a fox, von Uexküll continues (Figure 2-2c), the oak tree is significant only for its possible use as a lair, and the important parts—those represented in the *Umwelt*—are the roots. The "face," the height and width, and all other aspects are not represented. For the owl (Figure 2-2d), the tree also has a protective purpose, but the roots, which lie outside the owl's world, are not at all significant. This time it is the limbs that are important. In the ant's *Umwelt* (Figure 2-2e), the vast majority of the oak tree "vanishes," and all there is is the gnarled bark. Within this bark, the furrows are the ant's place. The bark-boring beetle lives under the bark (Figure 2-2f) and consequently inhabits a different *Umwelt*.

Does von Uexküll mean to suggest that the whole tree as we are likely to think of it in everyday lan-

Figure 2-2a. A tree as seen by an old forester.

Figure 2-2b. The tree as seen by a child.

Figure 2-2c. Fox's-eye view.

Figure 2-2d.   Owl's-eye view.

Figure 2-2e.   Ant's-eye view.

Figure 2-2f.   The tree as seen by a bark-boring beetle

(The preceding six drawings are from Instinctive Behavior, *by J. von Uexküll in C. H. Schiller (Ed.). Copyright © 1957 by International Universities Press, Inc. Reprinted by permission.)*

guage never appears to any of these creatures, the human included? The answer is yes. The "pure" oak tree as oak tree, with all its defining characteristics, exists only for the thinking human being, not for any of the six other creatures. Human beings, no less than other animals, never draw out all the abstract properties of their world except as they attempt to look at it as scientists or thinkers. What they do, rather, is live in a constantly shifting set of *Umwelten*. In these *Umwelten*, certain aspects that can be "seen" (understood) only from a totally abstract scientific or rational point of view never appear. They are invisible because they are irrelevant to the living being in its present situation. Behavior always occurs in a particular situation, and this situation is always structured by, and itself structures, the self-world of the living creature. This is no less true for me than for the ant. We all live in our own self-worlds.

C. The world of everyday reality

Even though there can be as many self-worlds as there are people and intentions, there is one "world" I as a person share with most other people in my society. I am alone in some of my worlds (as when I dream, read a book, or write a story), but I know that there is a world of everyday life and that this world is as "real" for other people as it is for me. Even more important, I experience this world as existing independently of me, as having been there before I came on the scene and likely to be there when I no longer am.

This means that everything I do, say, or think occurs within the context of a specific social world constructed by my particular society. While it may be difficult to realize that not every society constructs the same social reality as we do (see Chapter 9 for a different view concerning time), what is clear is that any understanding of me must take my social reality into account as the background against which what I do stands out.

What is this social reality like in a Western culture such as our own? Basically, it is organized around the "here" of my body and the "now" of my present as well as around the "here" and the "now" of your body and your present. Because all these "here's" and "now's" can and do change, I tend to experience things in terms of differing degrees of clearness both in space and in time. In general, the zone of everyday life closest to me

contains the world within my reach, the world in which I act so as to modify its reality, or the world in which I work. In this world of working . . . my attention is mainly determined by what I am doing, have done or plan to do in it. . . . It is *my* world par excellence. I know, of course, that the reality of everyday life contains zones that are not accessible to me in this manner. . . . Typically, my interest in the far zones is less intense and certainly less urgent. I am intensely interested in the cluster of objects involved in my daily occupation—say, the world of the garage, if I am a mechanic. I am interested, though less directly, in what goes on in the testing laboratories of the automobile industry in Detroit. . . . I may also be interested in what goes on at Cape Kennedy or in outer space, but this interest is a matter of private, "leisure-time" choice rather than an urgent necessity of my everyday life [Berger & Luckmann, 1966, pp. 22–23].[2]

I take this world of every day for granted: it is there and I know it is *real.* Even though, like Descartes, I may doubt everything I know or think I know, I must still come back to the ordinary world of every day once my doubting is done. The world of every day is as unproblematic and familiar to me as my room at home. It is only with great difficulty that I can see it as anything other than "there."

All of us, from time to time, do experience other "realities." The fact that each of us can become so absorbed in a book or movie has been interpreted by Berger and Luckmann (1966) to suggest that human beings regularly move in and out of many different "realities." We find it easy to enter and live in some of these realities because they are so clearly marked as "imaginary." The theater provides a good example: the change between "real" and "imaginary" is defined by the simple raising or lowering of a curtain. We have little or no problem stepping back and forth between the "created" world of the play and the "real" world of everyday life. Indeed, we carry on a perfectly ordinary life between the acts of the play.

What Berger and Luckmann are trying to do is to set personal experience (my experience) in the unspoken world of everyday reality. This is true whether my experience concerns something as ordinary as walking or something a bit more involving,

[2]Excerpts from *The Social Construction of Reality,* by Peter Berger and Thomas Luckmann. Copyright © 1966 by Peter L. Berger and Thomas Luckmann. Reprinted by permission of Doubleday & Company, Inc. and Penguin Books, Ltd.

such as reading a book or going to a play. In all cases, my activities always appear against the background of everyday reality. One important implication of this fact is that each person's self-world, regardless of what he or she is now doing, takes place within a socially constructed world. The specific (unreflected) nature of this everyday world (like the specific, unreflected nature of my room at home) provides a general set of possibilities for, and constraints on, what can go on in my specific self-world. The personal self-world is always a part of the "reality" possible in a given society, and this reality includes extraordinary as well as ordinary experiences in living. Whether we like it or not, our lives always occur in relation to some social reality provided for us by our ancestors.

D. Some ideas on social interaction

The self-world of the human being contains an enormous number of events and objects, of which by far the most interesting is another human being. There is just something different about being in the presence of another person—it is as if we immediately experience that he or she deals with the world in much the same way we do. When I enter a room, the objects and events in that room are given importance for me by me; I grant the same is true of you. When I am alone in a room, there is only one center to that room—me. When you walk in, the situation changes, for in that moment I know that you too form the room about yourself.

Although you and I both sense these possibilities, we each experience them from a different point of view: yours or mine. But we also are capable of knowing them from each other's point of view, so that it is quite proper to talk about "my perception of your perception." We can even talk about "your perception of my perception of your perception of my perception of . . ."—which follows from the fact that each of us is able to take not only our own point of view but the other's as well.

1. The Johari window.   But even in the simplest cases, how should we talk about the various points of view each of us can and does take? It depends on who the people are and what they are doing. A number of years back, two psychologists, Joseph Luft and Harry Ingram, developed a simple and general way of looking at how we take each other's point of view into account. The diagram

they developed for this purpose was playfully called the **Johari window** (named for Joe and Harry, its inventors) and was based on the idea that people do not know all there is to know about themselves or others.

The Johari window (Figure 2-3) contains four quadrants, each representing a class of information about myself which I am either aware of or unaware of and which you are either aware of or unaware of. For example, Quadrant 1, the "open quadrant," represents things that both you and I know about myself (behavior, motives, and so on). This information, along with the corresponding information that you and I have about you, constitutes our everyday world and forms the basis for our usual dealings with each other. Quadrant 3 represents information about myself that I hide from you. In interactions between you and me, the relative sizes of my first and third quadrants vary: If the relationship is close and intimate, Quadrant 1 predominates. If we are acquaintances rather than friends, Quadrant 3 will probably be larger.

Although you and I may try to deal openly with each other, this is sometimes impossible. Often I do not know why I do what I do. In Quadrant 2, the "blind quadrant," you know some things about me that I do not. You then have a decision to make—whether to tell me what you know or keep it to yourself. In some relationships, as between a patient and therapist, I may expect (but not always be ready for) you to tell me; at other times I may not want to know. There is a delicacy required in moving information from Quadrant 2 to Quadrant 1, and we are not always up to this task, either as a Me or as a You.

The fourth quadrant is not there just to fill up the remaining space in the diagram: it is meant to emphasize that some things about me are unknown to both of us. We may come to understand something about our relationship only after the fact—after something happened that neither of us expected. Luft (1969) feels that this quadrant "contains untapped resources" for the person and suggests that each person reaches his or her fullest scope only in dealing with others. Often what we can do together surprises both you and me.

Obviously, certain assumptions about what is valuable and important in human interactions are built into the Johari window. Using the words *open* and *blind* tells us that Luft and Ingram feel that the

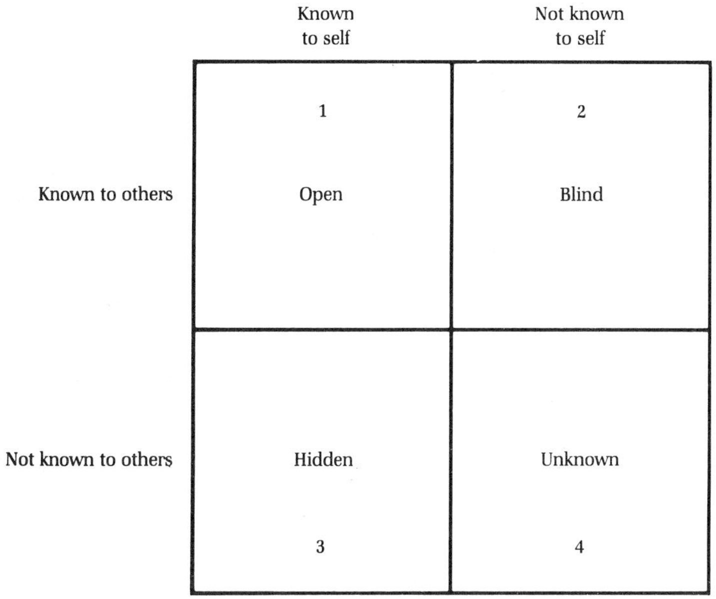

	Known to self	Not known to self
Known to others	1 Open	2 Blind
Not known to others	Hidden 3	Unknown 4

Figure 2-3. The Johari window. *(Figures 2-3 and 2-4 are adapted from* Group Processes: An Introduction to Group Dynamics, *by Joseph Luft. Reprinted by permission of Mayfield Publishing Company. Copyright © 1963, 1970 by Joseph Luft.)*

size of Quadrant 1 relative to Quadrant 2 gives a good indication of how well the person is getting on in his or her social world. As a matter of fact, Luft (1969, p. 22) makes this value quite explicit in describing the person whose interactions show a good deal of openness to the world:

> Much of his potential has been developed and realized . . . for this person . . . the area of the unknown may be even larger than it is for the average person. . . . Since he or she has a high degree of awareness of self, he or she is less preoccupied with defensiveness and distortion and has more access to inner resources. . . . Openness to the world implies a developed and ever-growing state, an experiencing, doing, enjoying, struggling, changing, creating, dreaming, agonizing, renewing, problem-solving, appreciating state of being with self and with others. Large tolerance for anxiety in self . . . and for the acceptance of differences in others are qualities in persons with a large first quadrant.[3]

However complex it may seem, the Johari window concerns only a single set of viewpoints. To

[3]From *Of Human Interaction*, by J. Luft. Copyright 1969 by National Press Books. Reprinted by permission of Mayfield Publishing Company.

talk of human interaction, we need to describe what goes on when two persons, each with his or her own open, hidden, blind, and unknown areas, deal with each other. Consider the case of two persons called Joe and Harry. Figure 2-4a presents all possible patterns, taking account of both Joe's and Harry's points of view. Figure 2-4b presents the situation from Joe's point of view, Figure 2-4c from Harry's. Each person is able to see the other's open and blind quadrants and his own hidden area but not his own blind area. Neither makes contact with his or the other's unknown area.

Every interaction begins with some knowledge common to the open areas of both parties. This does not mean that they agree—simply that they have something common in common. Furthermore, each knows both something more about himself (Quadrant 3) and something less about himself (Quadrant 2) than the other, and every interaction implicitly takes these unique inclusions and omissions into account. Thus, every social dealing Joe has with Harry involves all four quadrants, and what Joe sees or does not see in Harry tells us a good deal about Joe.

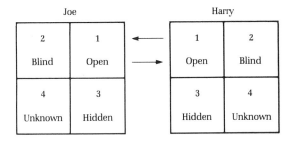

a. An abstract diagram of both Joe's and Harry's points of view

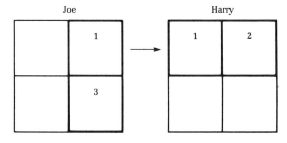

b. From Joe's point of view

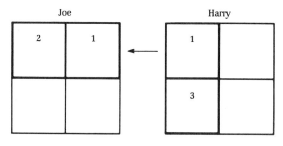

c. From Harry's point of view

Figure 2-4.   The matrix of interaction between two persons, Joe and Harry.

2. Reflections on social interactions: Attribution.   Because human interactions are so complex and ever-changing, we often try to get a more intellectual fix on what is going on by attributing more or less enduring meanings to things that we and other people do. We are not, as Rickles might put it, passive dummies in getting along with one another; rather, we try to evaluate what is going on and its significance for us. For example, I often want to know whether you're being nice to me because you like me, because you think it's the right thing to do, or because you want something from me.

Since the mid-1950s, social psychologists have come increasingly to study **attribution processes**— the ways people attribute meanings to the actions of themselves and others. Such processes would seem best described as the ways we categorize people and their actions so as to make the world a somewhat less chaotic and more predictable place in which to live.

As an example of such processes, consider a fairly obvious case: why do you always want to know whether the person you have just met comes from the same city as you do, whether he or she knows some of the same people you know, and so on? In trying to make sense of this behavior, you might attribute meanings to it as follows: If it turns out we have something in common, not only does it give us something to talk about, it also gives me some hints about what kind of person the stranger might be. It might also help me decide not only what to talk about but whether I want to go on talking with that person.

Although analyzing an attribution process can get fairly complicated, Shaver (1975) presents a fairly simple three-stage question-and-answer description of how it all works. For the situation diagramed in Figure 2-5, assume that you have come upon two men talking to each other animatedly. As you approach more closely, one of the men strikes the other, who falls to the ground. The first man then walks away. You will probably ask yourself "I wonder what happened." When you do this, you are in the midst of an attribution process whose outcome will be one of three decisions on why person A struck person B: (1) it was accidental, (2) it was provoked, or (3) person A is just a nasty guy. According to attribution theory, only alternatives (2) and (3) imply attribution—in one case, to the situation; in the other, to the person doing the act.

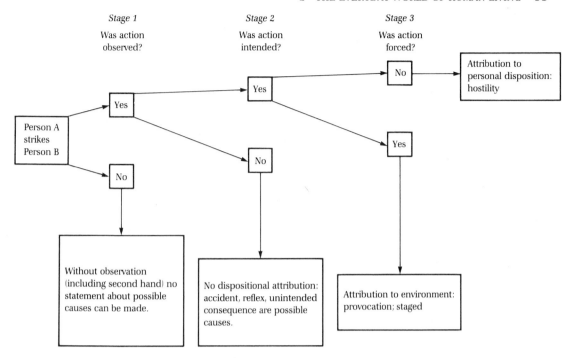

Figure 2-5.   Flow chart for attribution of an action. *(From* An Introduction to Attribution Process-*es, by K. G. Shaver. Copyright © 1975. Reprinted by permission of Winthrop Publishers, Inc., Cambridge, Massachusetts.)*

The sequence of questions and answers you produce in regard to these events consists of a series of choices that end up with you, the observer, deciding that A is to blame, B is to blame, or the event was "just an accident." The important thing to keep in mind about an attribution process is not whether the explanation is true or false but that it helps you (the perceiver) come to some understanding of a particular social situation or event. In addition, your future behavior will be altered. For example, if you decide person A is "hostile," you will be more likely to stay out of his way in the future than if you decide the whole thing was an accident.

3. Interaction rituals.   One of the major reasons attributions are hard to come by is that so many of our social interactions involve what the sociologist Erving Goffman has called "interaction rituals." Such rituals consist in an attempt by two persons to present themselves in accord with what they reflectedly or unreflectedly consider important to get across to each other. For example, my pre-

sentation of self may be as a scholar. The rules, words, postures, and gestures I bring to the situation are called my "line" and what my line is will be determined by the situation, my perceptions of it, and my intentions in it.

Because we all play with many different lines, Goffman has gone so far as to suggest that it might be helpful to look at all of human behavior as a set of constantly shifting performances. Goffman uses words like *performances* and *line* quite seriously, arguing that we are all actors who play out the parts provided for us by our society. Goffman argues that behind the armor of the parts we play, there may be an emptiness, a void. If there is anything there at all, it is "the simple desire to get on with people, . . . to be accepted and confirmed" (Hudson, 1975, p. 94). For Goffman, there is no inner core to human beings—only performances to be given and roles to be played.

Whether or not we accept the idea of person as "empty actor," we must always remember that social interaction is an ongoing event in which perceptions, presentations, corrections, postures, attributions, and heaven knows what else continually intermingle and modify one another. For this reason, it is easy to see why we are sometimes confused by our interactions and why we can never be sure that we have put someone in the right category. What we do know, however, is that we have made an assumption about another human being and that such assumptions help us order the flux of our social world.

E. Enduring reflections on social events: Attitudes

Attitude is a word that seems easy to understand: we all have attitudes toward this and attitudes toward that, and it should be no trouble to define *attitude* very simply and once and for all. Yet it is not so easy: psychologists have tossed out a number of definitions over the last 50 years, and none seems precisely right. Perhaps some of the difficulties involved can be seen if we look at an early study done by Richard LaPiere (1934).

LaPiere, using a common-sense definition of *attitude*, conducted his experiment in such a way that he not only asked people how they felt about something but also looked at whether they did what their "attitude" said they should. LaPiere toured the United States with a young Chinese student and his wife during a time when there seemed to be a great deal of anti-Oriental prejudice, at least if you asked Americans how they felt about people of Oriental descent. During their tour, LaPiere and his friends stayed at 66 hotels and motels and ate at 184 restaurants and cafés scattered throughout the United States. Only once in 67 times were they refused lodging at a hotel or motel, and they were never refused service at any of the restaurants.

Then LaPiere sent all the hotels, motels, and restaurants a questionnaire that asked "Will you accept members of the Chinese race as guests in your establishment?" Note that it did not ask "Do you like Chinese people?" or any other such question. Of 47 replies from hotels and motels, 43 unequivocally said no, 3 said "It depends," and only 1 said yes. These were the same 47 places at which these guests had in fact already secured lodging. Results for restaurants were roughly the same: of 81 restaurants that had served the touring couple, 75 said no, 6 said maybe, and none said yes.

These data seem to show that there is a big difference between a person's attitude and actions.

People don't always do what they tell attitude takers they will. A good example occurred in the presidential election of 1948. The pollsters—on the basis of good attitude questionnaires—predicted that Thomas E. Dewey would clearly win. When the voters went into the booths and marked their ballots, they selected Harry S Truman, not Thomas E. Dewey, as their president.

Such results have been repeated elsewhere. For example, Kutner, Wilkins, and Yarrow in 1952 found that many restaurant owners who failed to answer a request for reservations for a group including Blacks did serve a group of two White women and a Black woman when they showed up in person. Campbell (1963) reports that West Virginia coal miners showed little anti-Black prejudice on the issue of working in the mines but did show anti-Black behavior when integration in their town was the issue. In fact, 20% of the White miners in this town consistently refused to work with or live near Blacks, while 20% both worked with and lived near Blacks. The remaining 60% worked with, but did not live near, Blacks. This means that 60% of the White miners behaved differently in the mine (where they worked with Blacks) than in the town.

Despite these results, it is quite clear that there must be some consistency between the way someone answers an attitude questionnaire and what he or she subsequently does. The Truman result, after all, is an exception rather than the rule. One interpretation for such results has been offered by Campbell (1963), who notes that a restaurant manager is not being inconsistent by saying he won't serve a Chinese couple after he has already served them. Rather, it is the experimenter who is being careless in failing to understand the contrast. A face-to-face situation is of a different order from the situation of answering a questionnaire sent in the mail. Any attempt to predict what a restaurant manager would do without taking the specifics of the face-to-face situation into account could yield what might seem inconsistent results.

The difference between the questionnaire and face-to-face situations is important. With a questionnaire all the respondent has to go on is his or her own interpretation of the question—that is, how he or she would imagine the situation to be. For example, it is one thing to ask a person whether he would give his seat to someone in a crowded bus, not specifying whether the "someone" is a young girl, an old man, or just another tired shopper; it is another thing to observe the living situation in which it would be necessary for the person to get up or else stolidly avoid the eyes of the person in question. A reflected situation such as a questionnaire is not a lived situation, and the lived situation often contains elements different from those in the symbolic one.

One such "extra" element that can be quite important is the particular person who appears before you. As LaPiere was careful to point out, his Chinese friends were well dressed, spoke unaccented English, and, to use his words, "were very skillful smilers." When a clerk turns down a Chinese person sight unseen, all he can go on is his own (incomplete or negative) picture. When a specific person appears, no such anticipatory picture is necessary, and the ensuing behavior is appropriate to the lived situation as experienced by the clerk.

Here again, in the case of attitudes and attitude-related actions, the importance of knowing all about a given situation comes clearly to the fore. It is one thing to deal with a situation reflectedly and quite another to be in that situation. The more critical question about attitudes would seem to be "When will a verbal statement agree with what a person does, and when will it not?" As in so many areas, the basic question is under what conditions a person will behave in the same way in different situations and under what conditions the person will behave differently in different situations.

One way to make the correlation between attitudes and behavior a bit better is to ask more-specific questions. Two Israeli psychologists, Hans and Shulamith Kreitler (1976), have suggested that questions concerning four types of attitudes are necessary in order to do this: (1) attitudes about one's own behavior (for example, "I never lie"); (2) general attitudes ("People lie a lot"); (3) attitudes about social norms and rules ("People should not lie"); and (4) attitudes about goals ("I want to have fewer guilt feelings when I lie").

When Kreitler and Kreitler examined 117 attitude/behavior studies reported in the psychological research literature from 1940 to 1973, they found that only 34 studies had shown a positive relation between attitudes and behavior; 68 showed no relation, and 15 showed mixed (positive and negative) relations. Much more to the point, however, Kreitler and Kreitler found that 31 of the 34 "positive" studies had "attitude" questions concerning three or four of the issues described above, but only 5 of the

68 studies in which negative results were found asked about three or more of these issues. Looking at the other end of the scale, 45 of the 68 "negative" studies asked about only one of these issues, while none of the 34 "positive" studies asked about only one.

What all this means is that attitude questionnaires predict behavior to the degree that they ask not only about the person but about the person's perception of social norms, goals, and beliefs. Attitudes are useful in predicting behavior only if we remember that attitudes are always a particular person's attitudes (*my* attitudes) in a particular situation; they will not predict behavior if we consider them independent of person and setting. Attitudes are not "things" that exist independent of me, my place in my social world, or my perception of both.

For this reason, it may help to think of an attitude in accordance with one of the original meanings of the word—as a bodily posture preparatory to doing something—and ask what it is that allows a certain posture to lead to behavior. One answer is that postures give way to movements only if conditions are right. So too with attitudes: social postures (attitudes) turn into social actions only to the degree that the situation allows them to. Attitudes and behavior are interrelated in the same way that preparatory postures are related to moving: without appropriate conditions (social situations), an attitude will always remain a dead letter, never to be delivered into action.

One other thing that need be kept in mind is that a single question is not usually comprehensive enough to capture a person's attitude. Rather, we must ask our questions so as to get as complete a reflection as we can. Such a procedure must take account not only of my own personal beliefs but of my perceptions of the immediate situation within which the attitude is likely to become behavior. It isn't that attitudes don't relate to behavior—only that we must ask all the relevant questions.

II. SOCIAL INTERACTIONS BETWEEN TWO PERSONS

Of all the relationships possible among people, those involving two persons are surely among the most important. For this reason a special term, **dyad,** is used to mean a pair of persons in a relationship. Dyadic relationships are as diverse as those between lovers, parent and child, penitent and confessor, psychotherapist and patient, and an almost unlimited variety of more transient pairings.

A dyadic relationship can be represented as in Figure 2-6. The special relationship linking person 1 (P₁) and person 2 (P₂) is shown by the ellipse encircling both. The ellipse representing the immediate situation is dashed because the situation created by a dyadic relationship is usually more significant than that created by the immediate surroundings. As a matter of fact, strong two-person relationships, as between lovers, often create situations of their own so salient that they bypass certain social conventions. Although there is a mild general prohibition against people touching each other in public, lovers are exempt from this prohibition (within limits, of course). The gentle violation of this norm by people obviously in love makes both them and other members of the situation feel good.

A. Buber's ideas of I-Thou and I-It

Even if it were possible to describe every dyadic relationship in exhaustive detail, we would only end up with a catalogue of situations. It seems wiser to find a more general description of what is likely to happen that does not depend on knowing all the situations possible between two persons. The philosopher Martin Buber (1958) uses just such an approach in describing two classes of relations be-

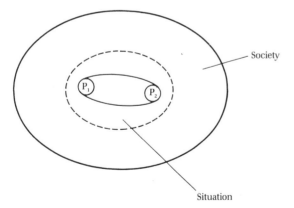

Figure 2-6. Schematic representation of a strong dyadic relationship. This type of diagram is derived from work initially presented by Kurt Lewin (1936). Although the diagram does not share all of Lewin's assumptions, it does agree with him in emphasizing the interrelatedness of people and their perceptions of social situations.

tween people and their world, called "I-**Thou**" and "I-**It**."

A person—an I—always takes some stand in relating to his or her world, and it is in that stand that the specific nature of the I (the person) appears. Because relating is of crucial importance here, the I of an I-Thou relationship is different from the I of an I-It relationship. In the case of I-It, the person relates to everything in his or her world as an object the I can use or manipulate. The world of an I-It relation is set in time and space: it involves order, categories, laws, and regulations. The world of It consists of things [other people included] entered in "the graph of place, in the framework of time and in the structure of isolated qualities" (Buber, 1958, p. 31). It is a world of things that can be sensed, understood, used.

The world Buber calls "Thou" is not set in the world of time and space as we usually understand them. It does not offer logic, use, or order as its prize. I-Thou is a domain of "pure relation" where all there is is relating—what Buber calls "meeting." In order to meet another human being as Thou, the I has to stop being a particular He or She or Person or Thing. If and when this happens, the other person ceases to be a "loose bundle of named qualities." When the other truly becomes a Thou, the I truly becomes an I, and both I and Thou live in the light of the pure relationship of I to Thou.

The idea of pure relation is difficult to get hold of, not because we cannot understand it intellectually but because such relations usually involve the complete person, not only his or her intellect. Buber suggests that one good way to think about an I-Thou relationship is in terms of a "true" **conversation** between people. He means a conversation in which the parties do not know how it will end up when it begins and in which they find themselves experiencing something they had no idea they were going to. The time spent in true conversation is outside time, just as the place where such conversation takes place is outside the network of It-space. Such conversations are always charged with "presentness"—that is, with a strong attachment to the "here-and-now." To understand what might be meant by presentness, try to experience the difference between the somewhat detached English phrase "far away" and the more "present" Zulu phrase: "There where a someone cries out 'Mother, I am lost.'"

It is impossible to do full justice to Buber's idea of I-Thou because he asks us to approach the world of people and objects in a completely new way. An I-It relationship to another person involves treating the person as a countable object in a world of countable objects, as a "being set in the coordinates of time and space" (Buber, 1958, p. 100). An I-Thou relationship can be thought of as pure here-and-now meeting in which neither person is trying to get the other to do anything and in which each maintains his or her unity while also being part of the larger unity involving both.

If I-Thou relationships are so important, why do we not try to remain in them all the time? Mostly because, as Buber says, it is "the exalted melancholy of our fate that every Thou must become an It." Even authentic loving cannot and does not endure in pure meeting:

> And love itself cannot persist in direct relation.... The human being who was even now [a Thou] ... has become again a *He* or a *She*.... Now I may take out from him the color of his hair or of his speech or of his goodness. But so long as I can do this he is no more my *Thou*....
>
> Every *Thou* in the world is by its nature fated to become a thing or continually to re-enter into the condition of things. In objective speech it would be said that every thing in the world, either before or after becoming a thing, is able to appear to an *I* as its *Thou*. But objective speech snatches only at a fringe of real life [Buber, 1958, p. 17].[4]

Is all this "only philosophy," or does Buber's approach have anything to say of general psychological import? Probably the most important implication of Buber's approach is that it suggests that human beings are always defined by the actions they take in regard to other people. Sometimes we fail to take into account the humanness of the Other. In that moment we treat him or her as an It—a thing no different from other things. Sometimes, if we are lucky, we enter into a complete relationship with another person that grants to the person a humanness equal to that we would hope for ourselves. In that moment we are changed, for the I that exists in humanness with another is itself made more human. Although we may want to experience such

meeting, it is not something that can be coaxed or taken from the world. Rather, only if we have "grace enough"—as Buber says—will such moments occur and thereby enrich the other parts of our life, which can be lived only in the world of It. Although the world of Thou is a difficult one in which to feel comfortable, it does provide a necessary moment in our history. Without Thou, we could never be fully human.

B. Reflected interactions within dyads: Games, gaming, and gamesmanship

When John F. Kennedy sat across from Nikita Khrushchev, or when Ulysses S. Grant sat across from Robert E. Lee, or Walter Reuther across from Henry Ford II, we had conditions appropriate for a dyad. These pairings, however, clearly were not ordinary dyads: each member of the pair was trying to get something from the other, each had carefully done his homework, and each had prepared some plan of attack. Strategic interactions such as these could be multiplied many times over—for example, when you see your instructor about changing a grade, when you bargain with a merchant, when you try to seduce someone. In each case your actions are not completely spontaneous; they flow from some preconceived pattern of what you want to happen. As such, they take account of the ongoing specifics only when absolutely necessary—and then only in order to get you what you want.

Social interchanges such as these indicate that people often have explicitly stated goals and strategies as they enter into social contact with another person. In a sense, the interaction is a game, and your strategy is the game plan. The advantage to such gaming is obvious—you can have things go your way if you're good at the game. The disadvantage is that if you play the game well, there is no possibility for immediacy or presentness in your dealings with another human being. You have to deal with the other person as an It, and under these conditions you are likely to miss the other person as a person.

The outcomes of a game can be described precisely: each person can either win or lose. Some mathematicians have described strategic interactions by means of a mathematical theory, game theory. **Game theory** describes the ways in which two persons, each having control over only his or her

---

[4]From *I and Thou*, by Martin Buber. Copyright 1958, 1970 by Charles Scribner's Sons and T & T Clark Ltd., Publishers. This and all other quotations from this source are reprinted by permission.

own behavior, seek to maximize their own payoffs in bargaining with each other.

C. Self-worlds revisited

An approach to interpersonal situations as rational or even partly rational games reminds us that a human being's (more or less rational) reflection on a situation can enter into what that person does. We must never be misled, however, into thinking that a rational analysis describes all there is to interpersonal behavior. There is always more, even in strategic interactions, and this "something more" is the self-world of the person as he or she deals with someone else.

An interesting historical example is given by Khrushchev in his memoirs as he reminisces about meeting with Kennedy. Khrushchev, the child of a peasant upbringing, reports that he was very impressed by Kennedy's bearing and manner—in short, with the Kennedy style. Even though Khrushchev knew what he wanted in this game, the interaction was necessarily colored by Khrushchev's perception of Kennedy the man. It seems reasonable to assume that Kennedy, for his part, also experienced some trouble with Khrushchev the man, as indeed many Americans did when Khrushchev banged his shoe on the table during a portion of a United Nations debate he did not particularly like.

History provides many cases in which the best (read "rationally best") decision was not made because other, unreflected aspects of the situation seemed more important. Think of the strange relationship between Adolf Hitler and Winston Churchill. There is no doubt in anyone's mind—at least not in any Briton's mind—that Churchill conned Hitler into believing that the United Kingdom was considerably stronger than it actually was in 1939–1940 or that had Hitler acted decisively during the early stages of World War II, he probably would have won it. To appreciate Churchill's ability, you need only listen to his wartime speeches. For example, at Christmas 1941, Churchill, then in charge of an army held together with glue and an air force running on rubber bands, made a speech to the Italian people in which he assured them that if they overthrew Mussolini right then, Britain would be happy to renew its long-lasting friendship with the present "descendants of the glorious Roman Empire." All this, mind you, while the main railway station in London was being defended by women and children having little more than pitchforks, water pistols, and English history on their side.

Any true picture of social interaction—strategic or not—must take into account both the reflected (rational or otherwise) and unreflected aspects of the situation for all the people involved. The diagrams presented earlier, no less than an analysis derived solely from game theory, are not so much false as incomplete. Every human act involves a person, and this means the person as he or she relates to a situation. Whether we examine presumably rational situations, such as games, or more lived situations, such as conversations, the conclusion must be the same: Human beings are more complicated than Descartes' *cogito* would suggest. There is no split—a complete person behaves, and a full description must always take this into account.

According to von Uexküll's analysis, every self-world contains all aspects of the world that presently guide what an organism will or will not do. For human beings this means that the self-world can never be static: rather, it must contain a series of constantly interacting and shifting perspectives and choices. The human self-world always includes what the person (rationally or otherwise) thinks he or she is doing as well as the meaning to himself or herself, in that situation, of what he or she is doing.

III. BEYOND THE DYAD: OTHER HUMAN GROUPINGS AND THEIR EFFECTS

Human beings seldom live only in dyads. Rather, we always move toward and live within **groups**. Some groups come together for a short time and then dissolve; other groups last longer, so that they come to lend a genuine sense of we-ness to their members.

The idea of we or **we-ness** is important, for a group that inspires we-ness is more than just a collection of You and You and You and Me; it is a social unit which has its own vigor and in which each You stops doing things alone and tries to coordinate his or her actions with every other You in the group. Because of this, there is a great difference between talking about a *We* that describes a genuine grouping, and a *We* that is just a shorthand way of saying You$_1$ + You$_2$ + You$_3$ + Me.

The idea that an authentic "we" involves something different from a simple addition of people is a good place to begin talking about human groupings larger than the dyad. One implication is that a person may behave differently in one group than in a different group or when alone. A group is not a simple congregating of people; it has properties of its own that often cannot be predicted from knowing something, even something important, about each of its members. Consequently, groups can produce unpredictable or at least unexpected results.

A. The risky-shift effect

One situation in which groups have been found to produce such unexpected results concerns the risky-shift effect. In almost all the many experiments on this topic, results have been the same: groups make riskier decisions than individuals, even the same individuals making decisions alone on the same issue. Being in a group seems to shift people to a more risky position.

The experimental situations in which risky shifts are found run somewhat as follows. Subjects (originally graduate students in industrial management) are brought into a room and asked to make decisions individually about a problem of the following type.

> Mr. A, an electrical engineer who is married and has one child, has been working for a large electronics corporation since graduating from college five years ago. He is assured of a life-time job with a modest, though adequate, salary, and liberal pension benefits upon retirement. On the other hand, it is very unlikely that his salary will increase much before he retires. While attending a convention, Mr. A is offered a job with a small, newly founded company with a highly uncertain future. The new job would pay more to start and would offer the possibility of a share in the ownership if the company survived the competition of the larger firms.
>
> Imagine that you are advising Mr. A. Listed below are several probabilities or odds of the new company's proving financially sound. Please check the *lowest* probability that you would consider acceptable to make it worthwhile for Mr. A to take the new job.
>
> (a) ☐ The chances are 1 in 10 that the company will prove financially sound.
> (b) ☐ The chances are 3 in 10 that the company will prove financially sound.
> (c) ☐ The chances are 5 in 10 that the company will prove financially sound.
> (d) ☐ The chances are 7 in 10 that the company will prove financially sound.
> (e) ☐ The chances are 9 in 10 that the company will prove financially sound.

> (f) ☐ Place a check here if you think Mr. A should *not* take the new job, no matter what the probabilities [Brown, 1965, p. 657].[5]

A conservative recommendation would be choice (e) or (f); a risky recommendation would be (a) or (b). In one experiment of this type (Stoner, 1961), subjects first recorded their decisions privately. Groups of six subjects were then formed and were asked to discuss the problem and come to some group decision. Most groups chose (b) although the average of the members' original choices was (c) or even (d).

To understand this phenomenon, imagine yourself in the group situation. First, you are in a group of graduate industrial-management students and are aware of what the group values in executive decision making. Second, you are a little bit relieved of the responsibility for the overall group response. That is, standing alone, you might have to defend your individual decision; no single group member will have to defend the group's decision. Responsibility seems to be diffused across the group. Finally, there is an excitement in the group that can easily overtake anyone arguing for a particular position, especially if that position is seen as socially valued and daring.

All these factors—value of risky decision, diffusion of responsibility, excited argument—have been mentioned as possible explanations for the risky-shift effect. One of the most complete explanations has been offered by Brown (1965), who sees the social value of risk taking as the most important single aspect of this situation. The concept of riskiness as a value, however, is hard to pin down, mostly because there is a subtle yet significant difference between being "bold" and being "foolhardy." If riskiness is a value, and if indeed the distinction between foolhardiness and daring is a fine one, then group discussion serves not to change your decision directly but to provide you with the group's definition of what is an "appropriate" level of risk. Discussion provides information because it tells you what other people think appropriate in the present situation.

An experiment by Levinger and Schneider (1969) supports at least a part of this analysis. Students were asked to respond to 12 executive-decision

[5]From *Social Psychology*, by R. Brown. Copyright © 1965 by The Free Press, a Division of the Macmillan Company. Reprinted by permission.

problems in three different ways: (1) by giving their own choice, (2) by giving what they believed their fellow students would choose, and (3) by saying which choice they would admire most. The results showed that students believed their own choices were riskier than most other students' choices, and they admired a choice even riskier than their own. In short, appropriate riskiness is a value, and most students before group discussion consider themselves bolder than most other members of the group.

If this is so, Brown argues, group discussion must serve an information-giving purpose: it tells you that you are not as bold as you thought you were. It also gives you a way of finding out what other people in your group think. The arguments pro and con are not important in themselves. Rather, it is the information about how other people answer that makes a person move toward greater risk after listening to discussion.

This analysis has one further implication, which ties the risky-shift effect to our more general experiences in group decision making. One reason the risky-shift phenomenon is of interest is that if people were asked to guess whether groups made more or less risky decisions than individuals, they would probably say that groups suppress risk taking and are likely to produce conservative decisions. Indeed, William F. Whyte in his influential book *The Organization Man* (1956) made just such an assertion: the team approach in industry, he argued, leads not only to the depersonalization of individuals but also to less innovative decisions. Experimental work by Nordhøy (1962, cited in Brown, 1965), in fact, has shown that not all risky-shift problems produce risky decisions. Nordhøy found that it was possible to get groups to behave more conservatively than individuals—to show what he called a "shift to caution."

How are we to explain both the usual shift to risk and the less usual shift to caution? Here as before, a value argument seems reasonable if we recognize that what is valued varies with the particular problem facing a particular group. Caution is a social virtue if the group defines a problem as foolhardy to attempt; risk is a virtue if the group defines a problem as solvable only by a bold solution. Once the value—risk or caution—is specified by group discussion, you know where everybody else is, and this takes some of the responsibility off your shoulders

for deciding between being "bold" and being "foolhardy." With the pressure off, your tendency in both cases is to overshoot the value a bit and advocate either more risk or more caution, depending on the situation. The risky-shift phenomenon thus depends on a more general consideration of what you see as valuable to you as a person and how your values relate to other people with whom you have established at least a transitory feeling of We.

B. How do groups work?

The risky-shift effect tells about what groups do when they have to make decisions. It even offers some suggestions on how they go about doing it. Yet it does seem a bit odd to talk about what groups do without looking at how a group works when it does its work. The obvious remedy is to observe groups of people as they go about doing things and see whether any general patterns emerge that will tell something about the ways things get done.

Although much of this work has been done in the laboratory, the categories developed out of this research do seem to be meaningful in naturally occurring groups. The major work on this topic has been done by Robert Bales and his associates at Harvard University, who after a great deal of preliminary work developed a 12-item set of categories for describing group work. Figure 2-7 presents the categories used in what has come to be called **Bales interaction analysis.** The 12 categories are broken down into four subgroups: A, B, C, and D. Categories A and D include what Bales has called socialemotional group reactions: A represents positive reactions, such as agreeing or telling nondisruptive jokes, and D represents negative reactions, such as disagreeing or deflating someone else in the group. Categories B and C are more task-oriented: C asks for questions and suggestions, while B provides the appropriate responses.

When groups and individuals in groups are looked at in this way, what kind of results emerge? One of the earliest results brought to light by the Bales procedure is presented in Figure 2-8, showing what kinds of things the members of 22 problem-solving groups said during group interaction; total group time was divided roughly into thirds. To relate these data to the Bales system, *Evaluation* refers to statements falling into categories 5 and 8; *Positive Reactions*, categories 1, 2, and 3; *Orientation*, categories 6 and 7; *Control*, categories 4 and 9; and *Neg-*

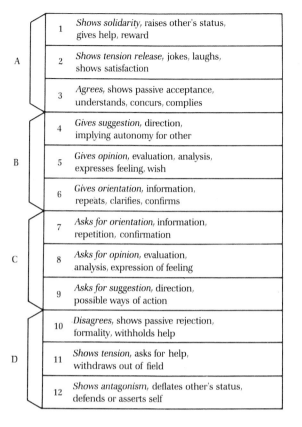

	1	*Shows solidarity*, raises other's status, gives help, reward
A	2	*Shows tension release*, jokes, laughs, shows satisfaction
	3	*Agrees*, shows passive acceptance, understands, concurs, complies
	4	*Gives suggestion*, direction, implying autonomy for other
B	5	*Gives opinion*, evaluation, analysis, expresses feeling, wish
	6	*Gives orientation*, information, repeats, clarifies, confirms
	7	*Asks for orientation*, information, repetition, confirmation
C	8	*Asks for opinion*, evaluation, analysis, expression of feeling
	9	*Asks for suggestion*, direction, possible ways of action
	10	*Disagrees*, shows passive rejection, formality, withholds help
D	11	*Shows tension*, asks for help, withdraws out of field
	12	*Shows antagonism*, deflates other's status, defends or asserts self

Figure 2-7. The Bales system used in recording group activity. (*From "Phases in Group Problem Solving," by R. F. Bales and F. L. Strodtbeck. In* Journal of Abnormal and Social Psychology, 46, *No. 4 (October 1951), 485–495. Copyright 1951 by the American Psychological Association.*)

ative Reactions, categories 10, 11, and 12. From this record, we can come to some conclusions concerning how groups go about solving problems.

Initially group process emphasizes problems of orientation (asking for or giving information, repeating the problem). This is followed by an interest in problems of evaluation (giving and getting opinions or analyses) and finally by an interest in problems of control (giving and getting suggestions and direction). To be sure, these strands crisscross and overlap, and the movement of the group may be deflected or even momentarily stopped; nonetheless, the flow does lead toward some sensible completion.

Concurrent with these problem-solving attempts

and sometimes giving direction or force to them are the emotional, or interpersonal, currents of group interaction. As discussion proceeds, both negative and positive emotional reactions increase, positive reactions increasing more sharply. If a group is to succeed, positive reactions must exceed negative ones, and there must be some final statement(s) of satisfaction by the time the group arrives at its decision.

The Bales interaction-analysis approach suggests ways to study many types of group process. Bales' observational techniques have been used to describe differences between satisfied and dissatisfied groups (in general, dissatisfied groups showed a much greater proportion of disagreements and a smaller proportion of agreements than satisfied groups; Bales, 1952) and to describe the properties of group leaders. A given person's behavior in a group can vary along three dimensions relevant to leadership: (1) how much the person talks, (2) how often the person makes appropriate problem-solving suggestions, and (3) how often other members respond positively to the person's contributions. Bales has found that during early sessions all three factors are interrelated: the person who makes the best suggestions is usually responded to favorably and gets to talk a lot. In later sessions, these three behaviors tend to disentangle (Bales, 1958), so that some individuals come to offer problem-solving suggestions, whereas others come to help support the group emotionally. Although there is a tendency for the same individual to perform both these roles, this does not always happen. The more general result is that, while there may be a "great man" in some extraordinary cases, the specifics of the situation often serve to select the leader.

Although the Bales observation system may seem a bit third-personish, it can provide a key by which to understand what goes on in a group without disturbing the process. What seems to be required is an ability to read behavior backward (that is, to read the intentions expressed by and through people's actions). To be sure, any such attempt is fraught with misunderstanding; just as sure, however, is that we can read the self-world of an individual (as well as that of an entire group) if we approach this task on the basis of sympathetic, rigorous, and continuing observation. Behavior is an appropriate topic for psychology only if we always keep this task well in mind.

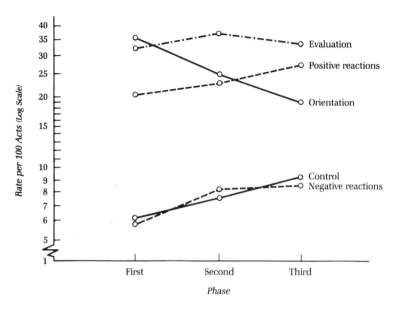

Figure 2-8. The course of group problem solving as described using the Bales system. *(From "Phases in Group Problem Solving," by R. F. Bales and F. L. Strodtbeck. In* Journal of Abnormal and Social Psychology, 46, *No. 4 (October 1951), 485–495. Copyright 1951 by the American Psychological Association.)*

C. Long-lasting social groupings: The family as example

The sense of we-ness that sometimes manages to surface in short-lived groups such as those studied by Bales is usually fragile and quickly passing. For a genuine sense of "we" to develop, continuing contact between people is necessary, and only here can an atmosphere of **off-stageness** develop—as described by the sociologist Erving Goffman (1967). Within this situation, people make no attempt to present a socially acceptable self; rather, we allow ourselves to be seen in ripped T-shirts, faded jeans, and unkempt attitudes.

One unit in our society that permits continuing interaction in a situation of off-stageness is the **family.** The family is not only experienced as an existing and functioning social grouping, it is also a significant social symbol as well. How else can we explain the long run of TV shows such as *Bonanza* or *The Waltons*—shows in which anything that happens to any of the leading characters, no matter how unexpected or trying, allows for a retreat into the wisdom and safety of an always helpful and defending family? Even less extraordinary families prove to have remarkable durability: think of the se-

ries of books about a pioneer family by Laura Ingalls Wilder, beginning with the book *The Little House in the Big Woods*. The protective qualities suggested by the title are enough to assure that little children and big adults will continue to be interested in this series for a long time to come.

But what about a "real" American family? What is it like and how does it work? In our society, families begin with a pair of individuals. Parents are drawn together for a variety of reasons, not the least of which is sexual. Parents join up voluntarily; children have no such option—they just get born. Once born, children give the family its usual organization, an organization based on generation (older and younger) and to a lesser extent on gender (males and females). Actually, a family is sometimes better considered to have two subgroups: children and parents. By unwritten rules, each group is allowed to do certain things and not allowed to do certain others. Some of the rules can be specified: older children generally take care of and teach younger children; parents are allowed sexual privileges with each other but not with their children; children are allowed no intrafamily sexual privileges; and in middle-class families, fathers take out the garbage.

In addition to these do's and don'ts, continuing family interaction takes place around, and for, significant events, such as eating, going to bed, and leisure-time activities. Within the family unit, each member has to coordinate his or her activities with other family members not only on projects the family does as a unit but on individual projects as well. This sometimes brings about conflict, so that families are almost always in states of "unstable stability." That is, there are always crises to be dealt with—children leaving home to go to work or school, illness of one or another family member, financial difficulties, and so on. A person's experience within the family is a constantly changing one in which family members are tied to one another by strong bonds. These bonds need continual readjusting, especially if all members are to develop as individuals. No less than other social units, families change, disintegrate, reintegrate, and provide support over time. In short, they are alive.

The function and structure of a family, as of other social units, also change over the course of the individual lives involved. Some families can be considered time-defined because they disintegrate when the youngest child leaves home and there is nothing more for the adult members to do. In this case, only a crisis situation for one or another child or parent can bring about the former sense of intimate we-ness enjoyed in the family unit. In other cultures such disintegration is less likely, particularly where the family unit includes grandparents, uncles and aunts, cousins, and so on. In our society, the best advice to give parents is to tell them to help their children grow away from, rather than toward, them. Such is the fate of the family unit in a fragmenting and fragmented society such as ours.

Figure 2-9 shows a typical time course for the American family. As can be seen, the American family can be described as going through eight phases, the first six taking about half of the years and the last two taking the other half. What this means is that a good deal of the time a couple are married, they are concerned more or less directly with raising children and related matters. The fact that some families disintegrate when there are no more children in the home suggests that such families see their job as to raise children, and when that job is finished, so is "the family."

Each phase, however, has its own set of possibilities and its own set of conflicts. These can be as obvious as having to deal with teenage children (Phase V in Figure 2-9) or as subtle as having to learn how to live with a romantic stranger (Phase I). In addition to these "internal" pressures, families exist as units within a larger society and are affected by the society's attitude toward the family unit. The society's changing evaluation of "the family" as a viable unit is quite important in setting up a ground against which individual family members think about their own particular family.

There can be no doubt about it: the American family is now under a good deal of pressure to change. The traditional ideal of being married and of raising children is fading, and an independent life as a single, even as a single parent, is emerging as a possible life-style. The idea of a monogamous sexual relationship at the core of family life is also declining, so that it now is possible to talk about open marriages (O'Neill & O'Neill, 1972) or marriages in which both partners engage in extramarital sexual liaisons, if not exactly with their spouses' blessings, then at least with their knowledge. And the divorce rate continues to increase, divorce becoming sufficiently socially acceptable that it no longer need be a political liability, particularly if a long-lasting second marriage follows. There is also the model of a fully employed husband/wife team who split the housework and who pursue independent careers and share in bringing up the children, if, in fact, children are wanted.

One reason for such drastic changes in the American family has to do with our changing attitudes toward intimate relationships, particularly sexual ones. Whereas the ideal of a few decades ago was a bride (and, to a lesser extent, a groom) dressed in white, the present model—if there is one—is to live together and if that works out, then possibly to settle on a more permanent arrangement so as to provide a secure base for children. The young, however, are not alone in being in the midst of a period of profound sexual change: their parents and even their grandparents are seeing on the stage and on the screen, as well as in their own lives, what was forbidden even to think a few years ago. These factors are giving the traditional American family a good deal of discomfort and stress.

Perhaps the best single exposition of this sexual theme was presented in the movie *Last Tango in Paris*. One recurring image tells it all: an elevated train moving on a metal bridge over the city. In the

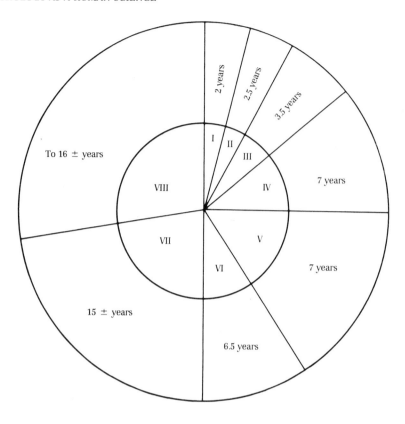

Family phase	Family description
I Beginning family	Married couple without children
II Childbearing family	Oldest child up to 30 months
III Families with preschool children	Oldest child 30 months to 6 years
IV Families with schoolchildren	Oldest child 6-13 years
V Families with teenagers	Oldest child 13-20 years
VI Families as launching centers	First child gone to last child leaving home
VII Families in the middle years	Empty nest to retirement
VIII Aging families	Retirement to death of both spouses

Figure 2-9.   The family life cycle. *(From* Marital and Family Therapy, *by I. D. Glick and D. R. Kessler. Copyright 1974 by Grune & Stratton, Inc. Reprinted by permission.)*

context of the film—whose plot is about a week-long affair between a 45-year-old man and a 20-year-old girl—the train has a double meaning: it is, of course, a symbol for maleness, and it is, of course, wholly mechanical. Mechanical sexuality hovers over our Western world and makes its influence felt in the 45-year-old—and 60-year-old—as well as in the 20-year-old. Such sexuality is sterile and leads in the end, as the movie suggests, only to

the annihilation of the older and the further mechanization of the younger. Although changing sexual values can free people from meaningless relationships, technical skill in such behavior is no guarantee of a better or more complete life.

Now completeness is what the family unit is all about—completeness in the sense of I-Thou relations in all possible pairings: between father and mother, mother and child, father and child, and child and child. The traditional roles of mothering and fathering need not be tied to gender; rather, both mothers and fathers can and do take care of and nourish the child, and both fathers and mothers can and do instruct and direct the child. Such activities provide us with ways of completing ourselves through mutual relatedness to one another. For this reason each society has provided a situation in which such behaviors occur, and despite wide variations within and between cultures in who "mothers" and who "fathers," the situation is always the same—the family.

Within a family the quality of relationships varies a great deal. One text on marital and family therapy (Glick & Kessler, 1974) has described such relationships under six styles:

A. *Mature*—Each person is differentiated for all others and seen for his or her own qualities. Everyone in the family relates to everyone else.

B. *Transference*—The personal self is differentiated from others in the family with "the other" seen as if he or she were someone else, usually a member of the person's family of origin. Everyone still relates to everyone else.

C. *Projection of good*—Each person is not differentiated from any other. In addition, the other is seen as if he or she were the embodiment of valued qualities. The person often feels he or she lacks enough of these qualities and would like more of them. Everyone still relates to everyone else.

D. *Projection of bad*—Each person is not differentiated from anyone else. The other is now seen as if he or she were the embodiment of the person's hated qualities, while the person usually does not acknowledge that he or she possesses these qualities. Some relatedness is still present.

E. *Fusion-merger*—The person and other family members are not differentiated from one another. All members still relate to one another.

F. *Self-relatedness*—No one relates to anyone else. Each person is alone; other family members are seen solely in terms of need-gratifying or frustrating properties.[6]

The quality of intrafamily relationships varies between those of zero relatedness (Level F) and those

[6]From *Marital and Family Therapy*, by I. D. Glick and D. R. Kessler. Copyright 1974 by Grune & Stratton, Inc. Reprinted by permission.

in which each person is an individual and grants the same right to everyone else (Level A). Although Level F may sound hopeless and Level A ideal, it is important to realize that all six modes of relating occur in most families. Families are not static, and there are times when mature relating is dominant and other times when selfishness predominates. What matters in talking about a particular family is which mode (or modes) occurs most often.

The family is clearly a special kind of group, not only in its off-stageness, duration, and stable instability but also, and most especially, in the strength of relationships linking individuals to one another. An enduring group such as the family must therefore be distinguished from more transient ones such as those studied by Bales and by Stoner. One way to do this is illustrated by Figure 2-10, where transient and family groups are described in the form of our now-familiar circle diagrams. The newly emergent group presented in Figure 2-10a is composed of a number of individuals who stay individuals but who still are able to perceive their immediate situation as that of a group—that is, as a situation having some degree of we-ness. Figure 2-10b, however, has an extra ellipse in it that encloses all possible pairs of individuals. This ellipse emphasizes that stable groupings, such as a family, come to form an enduring unit and that this unit is both a social and a personal reality. It also means that the family group, as group, can (and often does) create its own special social situation. As with a strong dyadic relationship, such situations allow individual family members to override certain social conventions (such as the general prohibition against touching).

IV. CROWDS AND MOBS

On Easter Sunday, March 25, 1894, a group of about 100 unemployed men set out on foot from north central Ohio for Washington, D.C. This "army" was led by Jacob Coxey, a successful Ohio farmer and businessman. Coxey had organized the march in order to deliver petitions to the U.S. Congress demanding that it take some responsibility for alleviating unemployment following the economic panic of 1893. The marchers gathered recruits along the way, so that by the time Coxey's Army reached Washington, it had some 600 people for the final march down Pennsylvania Avenue. Unfortunately, the group was not allowed to present its petitions

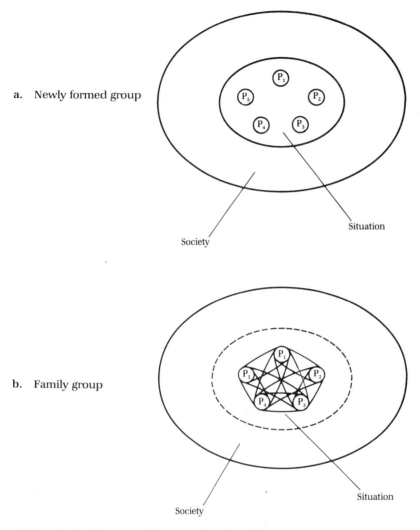

Figure 2-10.   Some possible groupings involving more than two people.

to Congress, and when the "army" reached the Capitol, police rushed the group, injuring more than 50 participants and spectators. Coxey and other leaders were ignominiously arrested, and the group disbanded shortly thereafter.

This is only one of a great many marches that have occurred in the recent and not so recent history of the United States. Only a few years ago, a similar march (again dealing with poverty) was led by Ralph Abernathy, and a short time before that, Martin Luther King gave a famous speech at the Washington Monument in which he spoke about

having "a dream in which Blacks and Whites would come to live together in equality and peace." Similarly, some of us recall the Armies of the Night marching on Washington against the war in Vietnam as well as the solemn memorial for the dead at Kent State.

All these historical events are valid social phenomena. As such, they must be considered in talking about the social world of everyday living. What we need to ask is what all these crowds have in common and how we can describe them in psychologically and personally meaningful terms. Essentially, each of the situations is an attempt to "stand up and be counted"—an attempt to add one's own body to a group of other bodies for the purpose of expressing a position or sentiment as strongly and emphatically as possible. As such, the situation is an attempt to describe a "WE" in capital letters, a "we" that is consonant with the opening phrase of the Constitution: "We the people . . ."—a *we* in which each individual as a unique entity disappears for a time so as to lend the crowd his or her body as a countable object.

For purposeful crowds such as these, each person, although not identifiable in his or her uniqueness, still assumes some degree of responsibility for both himself or herself and his or her peers. For this reason, such crowds usually disperse peacefully unless engaged by some outside force attempting to disrupt the sense of purpose and we-ness represented by the crowd. Under this latter condition WE often are arrested, as in the case of Coxey's Army, or murdered, as in the more recent case of Kent State.

But not all crowds are ordered and orderly or brought together within a setting in which each individual can and does take responsibility for his or her actions. Sometimes crowds congeal around highly charged social or personal issues, run amok, and perform antisocial acts such as vandalism or lynching; when this occurs, the group has changed from a condition of "Here I stand to be counted" to one of "Here I hide to be irresponsible." The crowd has then become a **mob,** and no individual is or wants to be responsible for what goes on. Some may even want mob activity and use the mob to hide in.

A. Mobs and history

Although sometimes mobs provide rallying points for further historical change—as in the storming of the Bastille or in the opening moments of the Russian Revolution—mobs are usually much more local in cause as well as in consequence. A historically significant mob is one that is able to transcend itself and become something other than a mob—a "something" that comes to embody and carry forward the ideas historians will later give to it. In the Russian Revolution, the mob served to embody the idea of an enslaved working class dominated by a privileged aristocratic class.

Does this mean that the workers and peasants who made up this mob were pushed by "historical forces" and surrendered themselves to the flow of history or to the demands of clever agitators? Merleau-Ponty (1962) feels that this cannot be the case and has analyzed this situation as follows:

> This does not mean that workers and peasants bring about revolution without being aware of it, and that we have here blind, "elementary forces" cleverly exploited by a few shrewd agitators. It is possibly in this light that the chief of police will view history. . . . Such ways of seeing things do not help [the chief of police] when faced with a genuine revolutionary situation, in which the slogans of the alleged agitators are immediately understood . . . and meet with concurrence on all sides, because they crystallize what is latent in the life of all productive workers. The revolutionary movement, like the work of the artist . . . creates its instruments and its means of expression. The revolutionary project is not the result of a deliberate judgment. . . . It [may be] these things in the case of the propagandist . . . or, in the case of the intellectual, because he regulates his life on the basis of his thoughts. But it does not . . . become a historical reality until it is worked out in the dealings men have with each other, and in the relations of the man to his job [pp. 445–446].

Revolutionary mob acts and the concrete details that come to "flesh out" a revolution usually end up being betrayed, no matter how committed the original leaders. In the end, it is Marat—the true revolutionary—who is murdered, and Stalin—the bureaucratic murderer—who assumes power. Although some progress is made, the cycle of tyranny begins again and should lead all of us to ask "whether there is not more future in a regime which does not claim to remake history but simply to change [it], and whether it is not this regime we should seek, instead of entering once again into the circle of revolution" (Merleau-Ponty, 1962, p. 420).

B. The individual in the mob

Mobs do not always lead to revolutions, and we are left with the problem of how the mob works. Almost everyone who has written about mobs attributes at least two significant properties to them: (1) the behavior of a mob is more than just the simple sum of the behavior of individuals; something like a "group mind" usually seems to emerge; (2) the mob often performs antisocial acts. When mob behavior is extraordinary, as in killing a referee at a soccer match or in a lynching, we feel that the individuals involved have done more than they would have done in a less extreme situation, and it is this "something more" that needs explaining.

The explanation seems to involve the relationship of each person to every other person in the mob. As in crowds expressing a social or political sentiment, each individual lends himself or herself to the total group so that the final number will be large and politically impressive. When a crowd becomes a mob, the individual as individual disappears and allows himself or herself to be caught up in the emerging flow of the crowd, thereby surrendering his or her individuality. Somehow the excitement of being in a mob as well as the tendency to give up one's individual identity brings about the characteristic behavior of a mob—destruction and terror.

Excitement is assured from the beginning, mostly because mobs generally direct themselves against a fundamental social norm. For urban mobs—in Watts or in Paris—it is the idea of private property; in lynchings, the sanctity of human life; in soccer matches, established authority; and so on. The violation of a strong social norm guarantees a certain excitement and power to the mob's surge.

But what about individual responsibility? Here the answer seems to be that under conditions of anonymity, people behave more uninhibitedly than under conditions of personal identity. This conclusion has been documented in the psychological laboratory, with one of the earliest studies done by Zimbardo (1969). In this experiment, groups of four girls were recruited, ostensibly to study how they responded to strangers. In one condition, each of the girls was greeted by name and wore a name tag throughout the experiment. Each girl, therefore, was highly individualized and identifiable. A second group of girls wore white lab coats, were never called by name, and even wore hoods over their faces. This, obviously, was the deindividualized group. If identifiability represents a situation of responsibility, girls in the second group, when given an opportunity, ought to behave more antisocially than girls in the first group. Indeed, being deindividualized produced a marked increase in antisocial aggression toward another human being: girls in the unidentifiable group gave girls not in the group *twice* as many electric shocks as members of the identifiable group did.

Figure 2-11 diagrams the person in a mob. In this figure, unlike all preceding ones, it is the boundary of the individual that is fuzzy and undefined. A

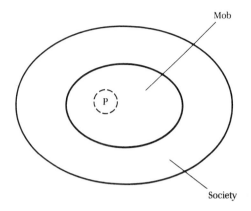

Figure 2-11. A person in a mob.

heavy line has been drawn around the group to emphasize that the situation, rather than the individual, is most salient and important. Although we might want to draw the person as considerably less porous in a crowd than in a mob in order to indicate his or her greater degree of personal participation, the fact remains that for describing mass social movements the person is important only as an element in a set rather than as a specific and unique human being. In this, the individual experiences himself or herself differently than in any of the situations described earlier in the present chapter.

V. SUMMARY

Judy Collins, in a song about Jean-Paul Marat, sings "The poor stay poor," and we wonder what this might mean. One reason the poor might stay poor is that they have learned to view the world around them from the perspective of being poor and are often unable to use social machinery set up to help them change their status. The recent experience of the women's movement suggests that aspects of our society once thought to be unchangeable are changeable when the person is helped to change his or her perception of these events.

When looking at what people do in their day-to-day lives, it is important to remember that each person is always in a particular situation in some larger social context. The person's behavior is always the focal point of a complex whole in which social events form the background. Murphy and Pollio's (1975) study of audience responses to comedy reveals that being in a situation with as little apparent involvement as an audience significantly influences one's enjoyment of that situation. This study suggests that we are open to many subtle and unreflected influences at all times.

"Self-world" (or *Umwelt*) is the concept used to describe the properties of a particular organism's particular world. Von Uexküll illustrates how a woodcutter, a child, an owl, a beetle, and other creatures all are sensitive only to certain aspects of a tree, demonstrating that each organism (or each person) lives in its own highly specific self-world. The oak tree that exists in the reflective experience of a human being as thinker is different from that experienced by each of von Uexküll's animals or by humans in unreflected experience. Behavior always occurs in a concrete situation, and this situation is always structured by, and itself structures, the self-world of the living being.

Perhaps the most important situation for ongoing human behavior is the lived world of everyday reality. This is the world I share with other people and the one in which I live on a day-to-day basis. Although I seldom reflect on this world, it defines the situation I would probably call "reality" if asked to explain what was meant by this term.

The "Johari window" illustrates the complexity of human relationships. This diagram divides information about a person into four categories: "open," "blind," "hidden," and "unknown." In each interpersonal encounter, what will happen to and between the persons involved depends greatly on how their knowledge, perceptions, and strategies are arranged within these four areas.

A different, more strictly cognitive approach to the study of human interactions involves what have come to be called "attribution processes"—the various ways in which people attribute meanings to their own or others' actions. Such attributions are valuable in helping each of us order the flux of our social worlds.

Attitudes represent another type of reflected social process. Although the predominant modern concept of an attitude sees it as something one "has" or "owns," the psychological problem is to determine how attitudes relate to what people do in regard to socially important issues. The general conclusion seems to be that although attitudes can influence subsequent behavior, they do not always relate directly to behavior in concrete situations. As contemporary research has shown, the more de-tailed and comprehensive the questions used to tap an attitude, the more likely it is that attitudes will correlate with the person's social behaviors.

Most human behavior takes place in combination with other people; one of the more important of these groupings is the two-person relationship known as a dyad. Martin Buber has described two general classes of relationship a person can have with his or her world as well as with other people: I-Thou and I-It. In an I-It relationship the person relates to everything in his or her world as an object the I can use and manipulate. I-It relationships occur in time and space and involve order, categories, laws, and regulations. An I-Thou relationship is not set in the world of time or space; rather, it exists in the domain of "pure relation" where all there is is relating. Unfortunately, as Buber writes, "It is the exalted melancholy of our fate that every Thou must become an It."

One major type of I-It social pattern is the game—a strategic dealing between two persons, in which each person can either win or lose. Mathematicians have used game theory to describe strategic interactions.

A different way to describe social behavior concerns the idea of a group. A group is more than just a collection of people, as shown most clearly by the fact that a person will behave differently in a group than when alone. Research on the "risky-shift" phenomenon shows that groups usually make riskier decisions (but sometimes less risky ones) than individuals, even the same individuals making decisions alone.

To study how groups work, Bales and others have proposed a 12-category scheme to capture the behavior of individuals in a group. From this work they have found that observational results do "make sense" in describing group experience in a great variety of settings.

It is through continuing contact in the context of "off-stage" dealings with one another that people come to develop a sense of we-ness. Goffman uses the term *off-stage* to describe a situation in which people make no attempt at a socially acceptable self-presentation. The chief unit in our society that permits continuing "off-stageness" is the family. Although we tend to think of the family as a relatively static unit, it is better described as always in a state of unstable stability. Families are special kinds of groups not only in their off-stageness and duration but also in the strength of relationships linking individuals to one another. In addition, they have a regular development over time that has come to be called "the life cycle of the family."

Crowds and mobs constitute less stable group situations because they exist more briefly and there is often a diffusion of individuality. A crowd can be defined as a large group in which individuals take responsibility for their own actions. Crowds become mobs when each individual chooses not to take personal responsibility for his or her actions. More specifically, mobs have been found to have the following characteristics: (1) the behavior of the mob is different from that of each person in the mob, so that a "group mind" seems to emerge; (2) mobs often perform antisocial acts. The excitement of breaking social norms plus the loss of personal identity and responsibility brings about mob action.

All these examples show that situations define our understanding of the social world and vice versa. Every human act involves a complete person in relation to a situation, and any careful picture of human action must take into account both the reflected and unreflected aspects of the situation as lived by, and for, all of the people involved.

VI. GLOSSARY OF IMPORTANT CONCEPTS

Attitude. A scientific fiction designed to summarize certain consistencies noted in a person's actions or statements in dealing with socially significant events.

Attribution processes. The processes by which people attribute meanings to the actions of other people; the ways we categorize people and their actions in order to make the world a more orderly and predictable place in which to live.

Bales interaction analysis. An analysis of group process that distinguishes 12 types of behavior in groups, reflecting social-emotional as well as task-oriented reactions.

Crowd. A group in which members submerge their own individuality in the pursuit of common values and goals yet in which each person retains responsibility for both self and other group members.

Dyad. A pair of persons in a relationship.

Family. A long-term social unit in which members are free to appear "off-stage." The family is unique in that members often coordinate their own projects as well as group activities with other members of the unit.

Game. An interaction in which one's actions flow from some preconceived pattern of the interaction and take account of the other person only when absolutely necessary in order to get what one wants.

Game theory. A theory that analyzes social interaction as a game wherein each "player" tries to outguess the other and thereby to maximize his or her benefit.

Group. A social unit that has its own vigor and is more than the sum of its members (has a sense of "we").

I-It. A two-person situation in which the person relates to the other person (and to everything in his or her world) as an object to use or manipulate (Martin Buber).

I-Thou. A two-person situation in which neither person is trying to get the other to do anything and in which each maintains his or her unity and at the same time is part of the larger unity; a "total relation" (Martin Buber).

Johari window. A diagram classifying information about myself into four categories: what both you and I know (my "open" area), what you know but I do not ("blind"), what I know but you do not ("hidden"), and what neither of us knows ("unknown").

Mob. A group in which members surrender their individuality and sense of responsibility to the group in such a way that the group's actions cease to be controlled by any individual members.

Off-stageness. An atmosphere in which people make no attempt at a socially acceptable self-presentation (Erving Goffman).

Presentation of self. The way one tries to appear to others, which varies with the situation and one's intentions (Erving Goffman).

Risky-shift effect. The difference between the riskiness of a set of individual decisions and the riskiness of a group decision made by the same people on the same issue. Generally, groups make riskier decisions than individuals, although not always.

Social obstacle. Limitations placed on a person's behavior by a particular social situation.

"True" conversation. A conversation in which the participants do not know where it will end when it begins and in which both parties find themselves somewhere they were not planning to go.

Umwelt. "Self-world"; one's "surrounding personal world," comprising those aspects of the world which are relevant to the individual and which are therefore "visible" to her or him (Jakob von Uexküll).

We or we-ness. A social unit which has its own vigor and in which, rather than doing things alone, each member tries to coordinate his or her actions with each other member's.

VII. SUGGESTED READINGS

Major sources

Berger, P. L., & Luckmann, T. *The social construction of reality.* Garden City, N.Y.: Doubleday, 1966.

Buber, M. *I and Thou.* New York: Scribner's, 1958. Parts 1 and 2.

Merleau-Ponty, M. *The phenomenology of perception.* London: Routledge and Kegan Paul, 1962. Part 3, Chapter 3.

von Uexküll, J. A stroll through the worlds of animals and men. In C. H. Schiller (Ed.), *Instinctive behavior.* New York: International Universities Press, 1957.

Secondary sources

Argyle, M. *Social interaction.* New York: Atherton, 1969.

Hollander, E. P. *Principles and methods of social psychology.* New York: Oxford University Press, 1971.

Luft, J. *Group processes: An introduction to group dynamics.* Palo Alto, Calif.: Mayfield, 1970. Chapters 1–4.

Psychological Processing

3

Prologue:
The Body Again

How do you and I know what we look like? This seems a simple, almost trivial question, yet tucked away in its answer are a number of very difficult problems. For one, the way the question is phrased suggests that we always look the same. Although a series of photographs would indeed show strong similarities over time, there are days when we don't like the way we look and other days when we feel like saying "Look out, world, here I come." Even within the same day there are times when I move with a loose and happy grace that tells how I feel and other times when I move with a wooden clod-dishness that also tells how I feel.

I. INTRODUCTION TO THE PSYCHOLOGICAL BODY

A. Double reactions

To answer the question "How do I know what I look like?" I need to do something that I can never do exactly right: I have to see myself in a third-person light—that is, as someone else might. To be sure, I can see my hands and feet, the front parts of my torso and legs, and the tips of my hair and nose in somewhat the same way as another person might, but I can never see all of me "from a distance." I can fill in some or all of the missing pieces—my face, my back, and so on—by touch, but this is not completely satisfactory, for in that moment when I touch myself, I can never be sure whether I am touching my nose with my hand or my hand with my nose; there is always a **double reaction,** as I am both doer and object at the same time.

Double reactions can be a very tricky business, as exemplified by active and passive touching. Hanna (1970) describes an experience/experiment of the following sort: Put your left hand palm down on the table and have your right hand look for the largest knuckle on your left hand. Now the right is the searching (active) hand, while the left is the searched hand. "But," Hanna asks, "does this mean your left hand isn't doing anything?" "No," he argues, "your left hand *is* perceiving passively. In terms of your sense of touch, to perceive [in this

way] means to *be felt, to surrender oneself to being felt.* . . . This does not mean that we are not perceiving, but rather that we are *not making any effort* to perceive anything . . . the left hand is just as busy perceiving as the right, only in a quite different manner" (pp. 203–204).

M. C. Escher, the Dutch artist, has caught some of the problem in his graphic work *Drawing Hands* (Figure 3-1). In this picture, the right hand is drawing the left hand, which is in the process of completing a drawing of the right hand, and so it goes. But which hand is drawing and which is being drawn? This process, of course, is similar to that in which my right hand touches my left hand as my left hand touches my right, producing an experience of double reactions.

The experience of double reactions applies not only to touch but to other senses. In fact, part of any answer to our original question "How do I know what I look like?" suggests that mirrors must play some role. Here again, in the case of mirroring, we seem to have the possibility of at least a double reaction and perhaps even more. For a long time mirrors have fascinated writers, painters, and poets, as well as other people interested in the question "What, if anything, do we mean by reality?" Part of this fascination has to do with the fact that mirrors seem to provide just that third-person point of view needed to see what we look like to someone else.

B. Some reflections on mirrors

To restrict mirrors and our experience with mirrors to this one function alone, however, is to lose sight of how much can be learned from a clear analysis of mirrors. To start with, the same word, *reflect,* describes what mirrors and minds do. To overlook this is to miss the powerful image that must have occurred when the word *reflect* was first used to describe either thinking or mirroring. The Latin root of *reflect* means "to bend back," and what better way to describe what it is we do with mirroring or thinking? Both provide a third-person view of me by allowing me for a moment to step outside my first-person world and "bend back" on myself as a separate object. The process of stepping

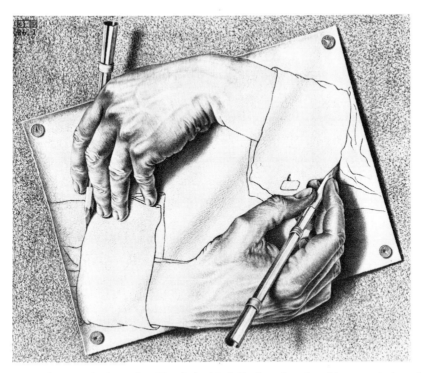

Figure 3-1. *Drawing Hands.* (Drawing Hands *by M. C. Escher. Reprinted by permission of the Escher Foundation, Haags Gemeentemuseum, The Hague.)*

outside myself is always incomplete, for I can never get back my glance when I look into my eyes in the mirror: all I get is a reflection of my eyeballs devoid of living glance. The mirror gives only an object, never a person, and in this sense there is only one person looking at his or her image, never another living eye looking into my living eye looking into it.

Mirrors can produce an infinite number of images if I look into a mirror in front of me in order to look into a mirror behind me so as to get a shot of my back. When I stand between two mirrors, I may lose sight of the fact that it is the front mirror that enables me to see my back side, and I am often left with the feeling that there is only a single rather than a double reflection. Sometimes, in a playful mood, I can repeat the process: front mirror, back mirror; front mirror, back mirror; me. In this way, I can get an image of my back side three times removed. When I carry this game through more doublings, my exact location may be in doubt for a moment.

The idea behind all this is that it is possible to "lose" my spatial location and that only by returning to my body can I make the infinity of mirrors and images disappear. These experiences also suggest that *my* body can never be just another object: rather, it must always be my unique and constantly changing region of the world. Mirrors and Descartes notwithstanding, my body is never anything other than that special place in the world which I can call mine and mine alone.

C. Infants and mirrors

Very young children do not immediately know how to deal with mirrors. A good deal of research has shown that infants placed before a mirror often try to talk with or touch the image. Slightly older children have been found to try to look behind the mirror when direct touching does not work, and only older children, age 2 or so, recognize the little person "in there" as none other than me. This development is not haphazard; rather, it progresses through a series of fairly regular stages.

Perhaps the most revealing of these confrontations between infant and mirror concerns some observations taken by Dixon in 1957. Dixon found that at about 1 year of age, infants were in a stage he called the "Who dat?—Who do dat when I do dat?" stage. During this time, the child tries out certain gestures, such as opening and closing his or her mouth, while observing his or her reflection in the mirror. Ajuriaguerra (1965), citing earlier work by Guillaume (1925), suggests that these gestures are broken up and undergo a process of reintegration in the mirror and in the child.

What this means is that the child has to correlate his or her first-person experiences of moving (such as are involved in opening and closing the mouth) with those that he or she sees occurring in the "child in the mirror." The infant has to learn that his or her first-person experiences of moving are connected with the more third-person movements occurring at the same time in the mirror. Only when this occurs can the child answer his or her own question "Who dat?," and the answer, of course, is "Dat me."

More generally, these observations suggest that before infants can respond in any reasonable way to their images in a mirror, they must already know a good deal about their bodies from a first-person point of view. The mirror only lets me recognize from a different point of view what I already know implicitly from my first-person point of view but have not yet explicitly claimed as mine. Such recognizing takes time and effort as the young child must learn that there is at least one perspective other than that of the first person—that is, other than mine.

D. Photographs and the body

A similar line of reasoning tells us how to deal with a photograph of my body. Photographs only let you (or me) recognize me; they never give much information about me as a living person. A photograph or any other representation from a third-person perspective (a painting, a video- or audiotape, a reflection in a pond) only lets you look at me, not know me. Indeed, we are often surprised at how we sound on tape or how we look in pictures, largely because these devices capture us from a different angle than the one we are used to. It is not so much that these perspectives are wrong; rather, they seem

strange to us because we have learned about our bodies from a first-person rather than an objective (third-person) point of view.

The human body is never just an object, and this is something we sometimes tend to forget as adults. Our adult point of view is often colored by how others have reacted to our body in the past (as powerful, as fat, as beautiful), so that the reflected adult image does not give a living body. It gives only our confused and confusing thoughts, attitudes, and reactions to a more unreflected experience of the human body, which surely preceded our present, somewhat intellectual attitude, in which the body is seen as an object given breath and intelligence by a magical process known as "mind." For this reason, in talking about the human body we must always go back to a time before the image of our body was formed, in order to recover the living body which precedes our adult body image and which presently sustains us in dealing with our world. The human body is that "place" at which I make a pact with the world and through which I form a system with it.

If this all seems even vaguely reasonable, what is the psychologist to do with it? Short of using only himself or herself as an object of study—which is basically not the method of psychology—the psychologist has been obliged to develop techniques to find out how human beings live, understand, and use their bodies. To this end, psychologists have observed human beings under one or more of the following four conditions: (1) as they engage in ordinary activities when healthy, (2) as they engage in similar activities when damaged by illness, (3) as they engage in highly skilled activities after years of practice, and (4) as they draw pictures of what they think human beings look like—that is, as they reflect on the human body. These four procedures have been designed to enable us to construct a detailed picture of the living human body as we go about the ordinary and extraordinary activities that make up our day-to-day lives.

II. DOING WHAT COMES NATURALLY— ORDINARY BODIES IN ORDINARY SITUATIONS

Standard wisdom would have us believe that the major way human beings communicate is by talking/listening and writing/reading. Yet any observer of human behavior knows that there is a lot more to communicating than simple "language use." To be sure, in the extreme (as in a book) we can and do communicate through the medium of language alone. Just as surely, however, in most situations we communicate in many other ways as well. Even within the seemingly pure medium of spoken language, human beings do an enormous number of things that are not strictly necessary for "the effective communication of ideas." So, for example, we pay attention to accents: what comic has not used a Brooklyn accent to emphasize an earthy urban approach to things, a mountain twang to emphasize an earthy rural approach, or an English-English accent to emphasize snobbery? We also pay attention to speech rate: in northeastern United States, the speech of intellectuals is rapid and clipped, whereas in the real Northeast (London, Cambridge, and so on), the proper thinker pauses and stammers a great deal to give evidence of difficult, ongoing thinking rather than speak in such a way as to suggest that he or she is a well-oiled and well-programmed thinking machine.

A. Paralinguistic communication

Pausing, however, is not the domain of the English lecturer alone; rather, as Goldman-Eisler (1968) and her students have shown, it is a common occurrence in all speaking. Whether we are reading (where pauses match grammatical structure), talking (where pauses reflect, among other things, uncertain word choice), or translating (where the translator uses the speaker's pauses to begin a translation), pauses are not without value. And they do more than help convey the content of the communication: Pauses that are filled (with sounds such as *uh, oh,* or *um*) or unfilled occur to tell not only that a grammatical boundary has been reached or an unlikely word uttered but that the speaker may be unsure of himself or herself or that the material being talked about is important or unimportant (Cook, 1969; Mahl & Schulze, 1964). MacClay and Osgood (1959) have gone so far as to suggest that many filled pauses have the purpose (and effect) of holding the floor. It is as if the speaker said "Wait a minute. I'm not through."

Pauses and other nonverbal aspects of speaking are usually lumped together under the heading of **paralinguistic** factors in communication. Communication has a great many other nonverbal aspects,

some as obvious as gesturing in combination with speaking, others as subtle as how close one person moves toward another in the course of a two-person interaction.

To take the simplest cases first: There is by now an enormous literature illustrating that not only do we communicate through words, but the whole person—hands, head, eyelids, and more—gets into the act. For example, Scheflen (1964) examined the coordination among a number of body parts, particularly in regard to the ends of statements and questions, and found downward (closing) movements of the head, eyelids, and hands at the end of a statement and upward (anticipating) movements when a question is asked or when the speaker will soon yield the floor (see Figure 3-2).

These and other results (for other examples, see Knapp, 1972) make the point that we communicate with our whole body. Looking down not only signals the end of a statement, it requests a pause that will make it difficult for anyone else to get the floor; looking up not only signals the end of a question, it requests a reply. Thus, a speaker's total intention is carried by the whole person, and making a statement or asking a question is an act of the total body (person), not of speech alone. (The words describing paralinguistic features agree with this picture—we "drop" our voice at the end of a sentence and "raise" it at a question.)

B. Touching

In the course of conversation we also often touch the person we are talking with. Much work has been done on this aspect of interpersonal conduct. Jourard (1966), who did one of the earliest studies on this topic, noted that the amount of touching observed between couples in cafés varied greatly by city. For example, in the course of an hour, he observed 180 contacts between couples in San Juan, 110 in Paris, 2 in Gainesville, Florida, and 0 in London. These results suggest that different cultures are differentially permissive in the degree to which they regard touching as appropriate.

People in our society touch not only in cafés but in other situations as well, and here again there are regularities. In the same study, Jourard asked students on which of 24 body regions they had been touched in the last 12 months by a friend of the same sex, a friend of the opposite sex, and a mother or father. Jourard's results are presented in Figure 3-3, which shows that females reported being

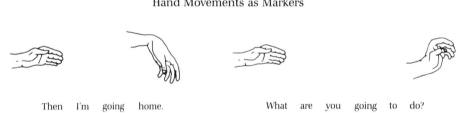

Figure 3-2.   Head and hand movements related to speaking. *(From "The Significance of Posture in Communication Systems," by A. E. Scheflen.* Psychiatry, 1964, 27, 316–331. *Copyright © 1964 by The William Alanson White Psychiatric Foundation, Inc. Reprinted by permission.)*

touched more frequently than males on more body sites and that many sons were seldom touched by their fathers on any body site other than the hands.

Although most of us pay little attention to these facts (strategic dating situations aside), such patterns do make meaningful social sense: Women are more likely than men to touch and be touched, and there are different degrees of touching in different cultures. In Western cultures, women are probably expected to be more expressive in using their below-the-neck bodies than men. Similarly, men primarily touch or are touched only at a distance

from their below-the-neck bodies—for instance, on the hands.

Considered more generally, these results suggest that most of what we do in our day-to-day lives is done unreflectedly. Even more important, they suggest the obvious but often-overlooked point that most of what we do "makes sense" in the context of what we are (unreflectedly) trying to do. To apply one of the concepts used in Chapter 1, this is but another example of the role of unreflected intentionality in human life—that is, that what we do expresses us and our way of dealing with the world in a meaningful and generally coherent way.

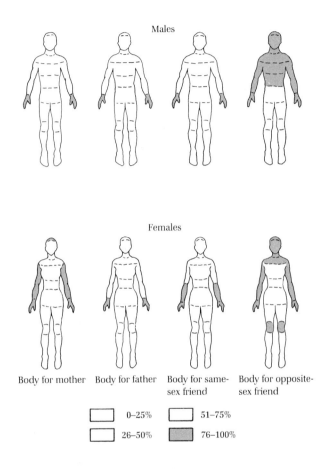

Figure 3-3.   Areas of the body involved in bodily contact for students during one year. *(From "An Exploratory Study of Body-Accessibility," by S. M. Jourard.* British Journal of Social and Clinical Psychology, *1966, 5, 221–231. Reprinted by permission of the British Psychological Society.)*

C. Proxemics and culture

Touch is one of the more intimate social behaviors. In order to touch, two persons have to be physically close to each other. The study of interpersonal closeness, **proxemics**, includes such things as how close people seat themselves for different tasks, how close they sit in order to talk, and the consistent preferences of individuals and cultures. As should be obvious from the touching results described earlier, North Americans and Northern Europeans stand farther apart in most situations than Latin Americans or members of other cultures, such as Middle Eastern ones. The usual distance in Western culture is about 5 feet, although Hall (1966) has noted that it is possible to describe four degrees of proximity: Intimate (less than 5 feet),

Casual Personal (4–6 feet), Social Consultative (6–10 feet), and Public (more than 10 feet). Five feet allows touching (should it be appropriate); larger distances, such as those involved in public interactions, rule out touching almost completely. To be sure, the numerical values are not absolute; they are not intended to apply to a New York subway train or a crowded party. Since all behavior occurs in a living context, absolute distances in different situations are not always completely meaningful: what we need to look at instead is distance within a given context.

D. Some general properties of nonverbal behavior

The psychological analysis of ordinary people doing ordinary things provides a certain satisfaction: from relatively simple data it has been possible to see what various everyday behaviors mean for the people doing them and how what they mean is altered by the situation in which they occur. In addition, the data reveal a surprising degree of congruence in many of the movements made—for example, lowering your voice, eyelids, and hands as you complete a sentence. For the psychologist to understand the meaning of a given piece of human behavior, it is always necessary to include an understanding of its meaning for the particular person doing it in his or her particular social context, and naturalistic observations such as those described above meet these criteria very well indeed.

In a different sense observations such as these seem atypical: The meanings seem to be too single-valued, too clearly expressed by a single set of behaviors. Surely human beings are harder to understand than that. And this, of course, is true. It is rare that everything a person does yields a single, consistent meaning, and it is even rarer that the person is able to express a single purpose in a single act. More usually, an act expresses more than one intention, and these intentions may even be in conflict. Sometimes the same bodily movement may even mean something different in a different situation.

Suppose, for example, that you see someone in a clinical psychologist's office, walking slowly back and forth over the same piece of floor, shoulders slumped forward, eyes downcast in a somewhat squinting expression. On the face of it, it seems reasonable to assume that he is "depressed" and feels "uncomfortable" in this situation. Suppose, however, you learn that he has just lost a contact lens. Far from expressing depression, the meaning of his present behavior is better understood as looking for a contact lens.

Thus, we must not always expect a close correspondence between a particular set of movements and the meaning of those movements for the person making them. A given bodily movement does not have a fixed, invariant meaning, so that the movement always means the same thing for the person making it. Behavior is not movement *plus* meaning; rather, behavior is the indissoluble union of movement and meaning. If we remember this, we are not likely to look for the meaning of an act independent of the total situation in which that act occurs.

Even unreflected movements whose meanings seem clear to a third-person observer when they occur alone have a way of combining with other movements so as to make the total pattern hard to understand. Analyzing nonverbal and verbal aspects of communication, Ekman (1965) has proposed six ways in which these classes of behaviors might relate in the first-person experience of the person producing them:

1. Nonverbal behavior can repeat what verbal behavior is about, as when I say "Turn right" and then point to the right.

2. Nonverbal behavior can emphasize verbal behavior, as when my son Jon takes hold of my face with his hands and says softly "I want you to listen to me."

3. Nonverbal behavior can complement verbal behavior, as when you stretch out and put your hands behind your head and say "Boy, do I feel good!"

4. Nonverbal behavior can substitute for verbal behavior, as when you look away from someone you don't want to talk to.

5. Nonverbal behavior can contradict verbal behavior, and vice versa, as when the well-practiced and poised-looking speaker says "Unaccustomed as I am to public speaking" or the novice speaker says "No, um, er, I can do it."

6. Nonverbal behavior can (unreflectedly) regulate the flow of verbal behavior without interfering with the ongoing flow. For a college lecturer, for example, the shuffling of feet by students often brings about a change of topic, while a room full of upturned, smiling faces tells the lecturer "Keep going."

In all these analyses we should be careful not to think of verbal and nonverbal communication as separate categories of human behavior. Both are aspects of a single human being, and neither can be understood (read, if you will) except in the light of the total person. Although it is possible to talk of verbal and nonverbal behavior as if they were separate, we must never take this *as if* as an *as is*—that is, we must never regard our categories and divisions as those experienced by the person doing the act. More likely, for the person involved, they are not even pieces. They are pieces only from the third-person point of view experienced by the observer.

With this precaution in mind, we can note that items 1 through 4 listed by Ekman all deal with cases in which the same intention is conveyed by verbal and nonverbal means. These four cases are the easy ones to understand, and, perhaps because they are so frequent, they have not been emphasized as much as they should. When we repeat, replace, emphasize, or complement verbal behavior by nonverbal means, we count on the total message getting across with a minimum of confusion. Indeed, this is what usually happens: we understand one another quite easily.

Similarly, we are all also sensitive to the regulating role played by nonverbal and paralinguistic behavior in human interacting. Scheflen's work on the use of head and eyelid movements and the work by Goldman-Eisler and by MacClay and Osgood on the use of such paralinguistic factors as pausing and "harrumphing" all give evidence of this regulating role. More extensive analyses by Dittman and Llewellyn (1968, 1969) have shown great regularities in the timing of head nodding—generally when the listener wants to speak or the talker wants some (small) response—as well as in the use of other body movements that indicate "I'm through (not through)—you can (cannot) have the floor." Perhaps the most interesting case, however, is provided by item 5 of Ekman's list, in which verbal and nonverbal behaviors express seemingly contradictory meanings. Indeed, it is this situation that has been most illuminating to clinical psychologists. It was not uncommon in Freud's early experience to find, for example, that a young woman who could not move her legs would say "Well, I'm really not too worried about that." This "beautiful indifference," typical of such cases of so-called hysterical paralysis, led Freud and other clinicians to try to understand the reason for this split between the distress that "should have been" caused by the disability and the patient's seeming indifference to it. Freud was usually able to show that although such behaviors appeared contradictory when taken at face value, there was some sense in which the contradictory combination was quite understandable. So, for example, Freud came to talk about the primary gain and secondary gain of a symptom—advantages of having the symptom. The primary gain might be not having to face the unpleasant situation that had brought about the symptom; secondary gains might include a decrease in anxiety and the receiving of attention from others (that is, the patient's seeming lack of concern encouraged others to take care of her "because she was such a good, brave person").

In short, in the ordinary and in the extraordinary aspects of human behavior, people tend to do things that, on the surface, appear contradictory. Further attempts at understanding, however, often show that the behavior makes sense if we look at its meaning from the point of view of the person involved. To be sure, there are contradictions, but just as surely contradiction is a basic aspect of human life, and the contradiction needs to be understood, not pushed aside. Although two "parts" of the person may not make sense for the outside observer, they often do make a sensible coherence for the person in question.

Hence, the best strategy to follow in regard to conflicting bodily responses is to realize that the conflict may be what is important and that conflict, as well as agreement, embodies human intentions and human meanings. The person is both a unity and separate pieces at the same time, and over and over again we shift from unity to fragment and back again. Various behaviors may emphasize, contradict, complement, and replace other behaviors—but it is the total person who does these various things. Separate acts have meaning only within this totality.

A description such as this suggests that contradictions apply not only to bodily actions but to the complete human being as well. After all, the conditions of our life are such that we can never know what it is we most dearly would like to know: "Does she love me or does she not?" "Am I a good person?" "When will I die?" and so on. Contradiction is a part of being human.

III. REFLECTING ON THE HUMAN BODY: FIGURE DRAWING

If you ask an adult to think about his or her body and then describe it to you, you are likely to get a long string of words. If you ask a child to think about his or her body and then tell you about it, you are just as likely to get a picture as a paragraph. As a matter of fact, if you simply ask a child to draw "anything you want," you are likely to get a picture of a human being. Drawing pictures of people is very natural for many children, if not for adults.

The fact that children will spontaneously draw the human body would seem to make drawing an ideal technique for dealing with the developing reflections a child has of his or her body. Such drawings do, indeed, turn out to be particularly useful in this regard if we look not only at pictures drawn by different children of the same age but at pictures drawn by different children at different ages. Figure 3-4 presents three drawings of a man produced by three different kindergarten children. The differences are striking: the picture on the left shows a great deal of detail in the face, torso, legs, and arms, while the picture on the right shows only a head without ears or hair. The middle picture is missing a few facial details but does seem to present a better grasp of what a human body might look like to someone else than the picture on the right.

. By contrast, consider the three drawings in Figure 3-5. W. C. Fields never looked so good as in the picture on the left; Disney would have to go to great lengths to improve on the bizarre figure presented on the right. These pictures were all drawn by 8-year-olds, and, as with the kindergarten children, there are striking differences among these three artists in representing the human body.

A comparison of Figures 3-4 and 3-5 shows some interesting things. For one, the bright 5-year-old's drawing is more complete than the dull 8-year-old's. More interesting are the systematic differences between the two ages. First, by age 8, all the bodies are in better proportion than at 5. Second, two of the three 8-year-olds' pictures present a profile view, while all three of the pictures by the 5-year-olds are full-face. Goodenough (1934) has suggested that children may come to draw figures in profile as they get older because a profile view makes it easier to show a figure in action, but no one knows for sure. Koppitz (1968) found that only 1 of 128 5-year-olds tested drew a figure in profile, whereas 3 of 131 6-year-olds did, 15 of 134 7-year-olds, 25 of 138 8-year-olds, and 30 of 52 12-year-olds. Similar trends were observed for drawing in details, such as a knee, nostrils, two legs, or four or more items of clothing.

Developmental data such as these suggest that human-figure drawings might yield some estimate of a child's intelligence. In fact, Goodenough (1926) suggested that it was possible to determine how

Figure 3-4. Drawings of a man by bright, average, and dull kindergarten children. *(Figures 3-4 and 3-5 are from* Measurement of Intelligence by Drawings, *by Florence L. Goodenough. Copyright 1926 by Harcourt Brace Jovanovich, Inc.; renewed 1954 by Florence L. Goodenough. Reproduced by permission of the publisher.)*

Figure 3-5. Drawings by bright, average, and dull 8-year-olds.

bright a child was by counting up the number of details he or she produced in a drawing of the human body. Although a satisfactory definition of intelligence is difficult to come by, for the moment let's say that "intelligence" is given by a child's score on a standardized IQ test, however fallible we know that test to be. When Goodenough and her collaborators (1926; Goodenough & Harris, 1950) as well as others (Koppitz, 1968) matched up estimates of intelligence derived from figure drawings and from more standard IQ tests, they found that for children up to age 10 (or thereabouts) such relationships were quite good.

Why should the number of details a child includes in a drawing of the human body have anything to do with how well he or she scores on an IQ test? The answer seems to be that a child's tendency to include details gives some indication of his or her reflective (thinking) ability. It is reasonable to expect that a child who is self-reflective—who notices and thinks about his or her body—is also likely to reflect about other parts of his or her world.

A. Figure drawing as an unreflected act

Drawing a human figure is an unreflected as well as a reflected act. It should therefore be possible to use human-figure drawings to tell us something about the good and the bad events in the artist's life as well as about how the child or adult experienced himself or herself during these events. All acts, figure drawings included, reveal more than the person producing them might realize, and it is often possible to read a further meaning in them.

Figure 3-6 is a drawing of one of the great moments in the life of a 5-year-old named Taneil, when she was permitted to sit with her family for the first time on Thanksgiving Day. First of all, note that Taneil is the biggest one at the table—it's her day. If that isn't perfectly clear, take a look at who got the turkey (as well as all the other food). To make the matter even clearer, the best part of this super day, as Taneil sees it, is that there is no plate in front of her archenemy, her little sister.

But drawings do not always express a happy situation for children, either in what is going on about them or in their feelings about themselves. Figure 3-7 is a drawing by a 7-year-old boy who stammered. The heavy shading Max drew around the mouth suggests that Max must have experienced great embarrassment over his inability to talk clearly.

Finally, family dynamics can be revealed in a drawing. Figure 3-8 is by Timothy, age 8.

Timothy was a youngster who had never known his father but longed for him with all his heart. Timothy was born out of wedlock to a girl of modest intellectual endowment and lived with his timid, dull mother, an indifferent uncle, his stern, domineering grandmother and the meek grandfather. The boy lived a sheltered and completely isolated life and filled the long and lonely hours with drawing and daydreaming. All of

Figure 3-6.   Taneil's drawing *(Figures 3-6, 3-7, and 3-8 are from* Psychological Evaluation of Children's Human Figure Drawings, *by E. M. Koppitz. Copyright 1968 by Grune & Stratton, Inc. Reprinted by permission.)*

Figure 3-7.   Max's drawing.

Timothy's drawings and fantasies centered around one topic only: his father. When he was asked to draw a picture of his family, he announced at once: "I have a Daddy too, but he lives far away on another planet." Then Timothy proceeded to draw his actual family according to their age and importance: ... the overpowering grandmother leads the procession; she is followed by the grandfather, then come the mother and the uncle, and finally there is Timothy himself. All the family members are lined up, one behind the other; they do not interact. Just when I thought that Timothy had finished his drawing, he introduced with bold strokes the object of his dreams, the absent and yet ever-present father. The father appears in this picture as Superman and informs the assembled family with a benign smile that he is going to return to them to stay. Timothy cannot talk about his father directly beyond saying that he has a father; but in his drawings, he can express most eloquently his dreams and wishes for the idealized father whom he has never known [Koppitz, 1968, p. 246].

In this drawing we can see Timothy's attempt to come to terms not only with his body but with his social situation. The picture and its story are not unique, nor is it unique to find that we tell a great deal about ourselves in our drawings. Not only do

Figure 3-8. Timothy's drawing.

we tell what we know of our bodies; we also give subtle and not so subtle hints about what is frightening to us and what is important to us. We do this not necessarily because we want to tell everybody about the things that bother us but rather because we have no alternative: everything a human being does reveals his or her mode of living, seeing, presenting, and/or understanding the world, and this is no less true in a drawing of the human body than in the attempt each of us makes to deal with the confusing business of living.

IV. DAMAGED BODIES, OR THE DIFFERENCE BETWEEN GRASPING AND POINTING

At the end of the First World War, a young German neurologist, Kurt Goldstein, set up a unique hospital whose purpose was to treat the living

waste left by war—young soldiers with brain damage who in previous years would have become objects of public charity. Goldstein and his coworkers, most notably a psychologist named Gelb, set up a neurological clinic in Frankfurt whose purpose was to observe the patients' everyday behavior and to study their lives and therapeutic progress in extensive and sympathetic detail. And study their behavior Goldstein and Gelb did—everything from how these young soldiers combed their hair and used mirrors to how they did special tasks involving the categorization of colors and shapes.

One of the more revealing observations concerned a difference between the everyday activities of grasping and pointing. In perhaps his most famous case study, Goldstein noted that a young soldier named Schneider could easily and accurately use his right hand to swat a fly that settled on his left forearm, but if Goldstein touched Schneider on the same spot with a ruler and asked him to point to it (or even to swat it), Schneider was totally unable to do so. There seemed to be some important difference between trying to grasp or swat the fly and pointing to a spot touched by a ruler when no immediate irritant was there.

After a great deal of analysis of this and other initially perplexing cases, Goldstein concluded that grasping is an immediate reaction made in response to a concrete event. Pointing is much less dependent on the concrete situation because the patient must point to an "as if" spot—that is, to point to a spot *as if* doing so were important to him and not simply an exercise designed to show that he could do it. Thus, swatting (or grasping) is a **concrete** movement made in response to an ongoing situation; pointing is an **abstract** movement made in response to nothing other than the question "Can you show me where I pointed to?" Pointing has no immediate, ongoing significance to the patient in his or her situation.

A. Abstract and concrete thinking in brain damage

In the distinction between grasping and pointing, Goldstein seemed to have found what it was the brain-damaged patient had lost: the ability to perform abstract movements. Schneider could move his hand to a certain spot in response to concrete events but never in response to imaginary ones. Schneider had not lost movements; rather, he had lost a mode of existence. To emphasize this further, Goldstein also found that Schneider was unable to point to the spot where he had just swatted a fly even though he had been able to swat the fly in the first place.

But how can we (and Goldstein) be so sure that what was lost is a way of dealing with the world rather than a specific skill? Here results gathered on a wide variety of other tasks and other patients become important. Consider the following examples:

1. A patient was asked to bring a comb from the table. She could not do this until she ran the comb through her hair to make sure, by using the object in her hand, that it was a comb.

2. A second patient was asked to say "The snow is black." The patient would not do so, because "it's not true," unless he mumbled immediately afterward: "No, snow is white." The same patient would also not say "The sun is shining" on a rainy day.

3. A different patient was unable to set the hands of a clock to an hour as requested but could tell time if shown a clock.

4. Another patient who used utensils while eating could not show how to use them when away from the table.

5. Still another patient never missed when throwing balls into three boxes located at different distances from him but was unable to say which of the boxes was nearest him.

6. A different patient could count only if started at number 1; if he was started at any other number, he was unable to continue unless he returned to 1 first.

7. Another patient could use a key to open a door but was unable to explain how to use a key in the absence of a door. Still another patient could drink out of a full glass but was unable to demonstrate how to use the glass when empty.

These observations could be multiplied many times over. And this list of observations, taken from a much longer list compiled by Goldstein and Scheerer (1941), contains clinical observations made by some of the foremost neurologists in the world: Sir Henry Head in England, Laura Bender in the United States, and J. Lhermitte in France, as well as Goldstein and Gelb and others in Germany. They all point to one inescapable conclusion: brain-damaged subjects have not only, nor even primarily, lost a specific bit of behavior; rather, what they have lost is an attitude, or orientation, to everything they do. The symptoms of brain damage are clear: patients function only in the immediate and concrete present, and then only if the movement required is to be put to some immediate use. Abstract movement is beyond them.

But what of the realm of thinking: does the brain-damaged patient also behave concretely if asked to do seemingly abstract tasks? Results here are no less clear. Consider the case of a patient asked to pick out all the red skeins of wool from a much larger multicolored collection. What some patients do is to place the colors in a row—from the lightest to the darkest red. Ordinarily this might be taken to mean that not only did the patient pick out all the reds, but he did so according to a very complex concept of brightness. On closer observation this assumption turns out not to be very plausible, for the following reasons: (1) if the patient is asked to order a set of reds by brightness, *he cannot do it in re-*

sponse to this specific request, and (2) if the examiner removes the last skein the patient placed down, the patient is unable to continue the series. These observations suggest that the patient was setting out his row on a skein-by-skein basis, not on the basis of an abstract concept of brightness. In the realm of ideas and thinking, the brain-damaged patient is no less concrete than in the realm of observable movements; in both cases it is possible to see the same kind of loss—a loss that is neither physical nor mental but is better described as a "total-person loss."

The evidence presented to this point all suggests that brain damage of the type studied by Goldstein brings about far-reaching changes in the living human being, changes that can best be described as the loss of an abstract attitude toward any and all activities. Anyone who has worked with brain-damaged individuals agrees that these changes come about in two stages. In the first phase, the patient appears to be in a state of general disorder: not only is he unable to perform tasks he was able to do before the accident, he is "restless, distracted, frightened, and very emotional. [The patient] is also unable to fulfill tasks in which he is apparently not organically damaged" (Goldstein, 1939, p. 218). This initial state is called the **catastrophic condition**, and patients often report afterward that during this time they felt "unfree, disordered, and shocked."

Following this initial stage, the patient tends to calm down, to show greater consistency in his or her behavior, and to behave across the board in what has been called a "concrete" way. This second stage is accordingly called the **concrete attitude**. Brain-damaged patients tend to be incredibly orderly and to avoid what Goldstein (1939) has called a "feeling of emptiness." This tendency is particularly striking because it sometimes produces somewhat bizarre behaviors. For example, brain-damaged patients showing language disturbance will often crowd their writing on the page so as to fill up the whole piece of paper. Such patients can be induced to separate their words and lines only with great difficulty, if at all.

Brain-damaged patients tend to be model patients because they quickly and effectively follow the routines set for them by hospital personnel. This tendency toward order is so marked that on one occasion when an examiner carelessly put a pencil across a piece of paper, the patient removed the pencil, set the paper in line with the edge of the table, and then set the pencil down parallel to the paper. When the examiner told the patient that "the pencil was to be left in a disorderly way," the patient acquiesced, "although with an expression of marked discomfort" (Goldstein, 1939, p. 43).

The existence of such discomfort suggests one way to understand these rigid, highly ordered behaviors. Brain-damaged patients have just been through an experience that shook them to the very foundations of their being, one that, Goldstein feels, produced a "subjective experience of being in danger of losing one's existence" (Goldstein, 1939, p. 9), and it is precisely this kind of experience they want to guard against. All their post-brain-damage behaviors give evidence of the power of this horrible state, and the development of ordered behaviors can be seen to represent an attempt to come to some kind of orderly and sensible relationship to the world. Since the world is not always orderly and sensible, the patient tries to shrink the world and do only those things that can be done without error most of the time. Thus, brain damage of any reasonably large extent brings about the concrete attitude as a protection against being overwhelmed by a new catastrophic condition, which would again bring about the overpowering experience of losing one's existence.

This danger to existence is experienced to some degree in all those conditions we usually call "sickness" and is not peculiar to brain damage. Goldstein has gone so far as to identify the catastrophic condition with the more general condition of anxiety that all of us experience to a greater or lesser degree at many times in our life. Goldstein makes no distinction between sicknesses that have to do with "physical" damage to the person and those that have to do with "psychological" damage—both affect the whole person, and both bring about a tendency to give up the abstract attitude, leading the person to try to exist in a much-reduced yet orderly world. Because what is given up is so precious, only in the extreme case of brain damage does the survivor continue to experience the world concretely. Although other life-threat survivors may show concrete behavior for a while, most do return to the more ordinary tensions brought about by living within both a concrete and an abstract attitude.

B. Actualization and personal "health"

Goldstein's position also has something to say about personal health. For Goldstein, health can be defined in terms of the unity, integration, and coherence of the person as well as in terms of the person's tendency to realize, or actualize, his or her individual nature and capacities in the world. Goldstein sees **self-actualization** as the major goal of all healthy human living—to be all that you can be. In the sick human being this tendency undergoes a dramatic change, as the patient is driven to use his or her now-diminished capacities in a way best suited to his or her present condition. This is done by reducing oneself to a state of being that tolerates very little disorder.

In a more general way, Goldstein (1939, p. 197) also has something to say to theorists such as Freud. He notes that the sick person

> is driven to maintain a certain state of living, and therefore sick life is very bare of productivity, development, and progress, and bare of the characteristic particularities of normal human life. Frequently, the law of maintaining the existent state is considered as the basic law of life. The tendency to maintain the existent state is characteristic for sick people and is a sign of decay of life. The tendency of normal life is toward activity and progress. For the sick, the only form of self-actualization which remains is the maintenance of the existent state. That, however, is not the tendency of the normal. It might be that sometimes the normal organism also tends primarily to avoid catastrophes, and to maintain a certain state which makes that possible; but this takes place under inadequate conditions and is not at all the usual behavior. Under adequate conditions the normal organism seeks further activity.

The work on brain damage has taken an unexpected, if speculative, turn: rather than center only on illness, it provides a new basis on which to understand human growth and health. It is only the fragmented organism, fearful of having to deal again with a catastrophic experience, who behaves in a rigid and nonspontaneous way; and it is only the intact, integrated person who has the courage to live and create in such a way as to allow maximum self-realization. Far from giving us a lecture on the separation of mind from body, Goldstein's analysis of brain damage leads to a new understanding of the unity of well-integrated human beings whose concerns are those of growing and changing rather

than those of stagnating and conserving. The human being is a unified being/event, open both to the world and to the changes he or she brings about in the world. It is only the world of the sick that needs to be continuously ordered so as to avoid both the threat and the anxiety of nonbeing.

C. Phantom limbs and anosognosia

If the world of the brain-damaged individual provides one ground out of which to understand integrated, healthy behavior, the occurrence of **phantom limbs** provides some interesting hints on how to describe the living, functioning human body. The experience of a phantom limb is about as eerie an experience as anyone could ever expect. It is extremely common for a patient who has lost a limb, either by accident or by surgery, to continue to experience the now-missing limb, usually beginning immediately after surgery. In a series of papers, Simmel (1961, 1962, 1967) has examined a number of cases and provides the following summary description:

> Immediately after the amputation, as he awakes from the anesthesia, the patient may not believe that the limb has been removed until he can convince himself by looking under the covers. But even once he knows beyond doubt that the extremity is gone, he typically continues to feel it as if it were still present. In the days—and years—to come the foot of the amputated leg may itch; as the patient reaches down to scratch it, he reaches for an empty space. He may feel the bedsheets on the arm or leg; he may feel a mild, perhaps pleasant, tingling; or much more rarely, he may feel pain. He may feel that he can wiggle his fingers or toes, flex or extend the wrist or ankle, and that he can perform these movements more or less at will. Despite his knowledge that the amputation has been performed, the patient may "forget" and reach out with the missing hand to grasp something, or to steady himself, or he may step on the phantom foot and fall. At least initially a good many amputees report that they are more aware of the phantom extremity than of the [opposite] intact limb [1967, p. 60][1]

In the beginning, the phantom is experienced as identical to the lost limb—the person fully expects

[1]From "The Body Percept in Physical Medicine and Rehabilitation," by M. L. Simmel. In *Journal of Health and Social Behavior*, 1967, 8, 60–64. Copyright 1967 by the American Sociological Association. Reprinted by permission.

it to be capable of any and all movements. In addition, limbs that were deformed before loss produce deformed phantoms. Two misconceptions that have been entertained about phantoms are that they are always painful (only rarely) and that the phantom assumes the position it had at the moment of injury (although some patients with painful limbs do report such experiences). Much more common is the experience of the disappearance of parts, in which an upper arm or thigh first fades while the lower arm and hand or lower leg and foot still remain. Ultimately such fading leaves the amputee with phantom fingers or toes and no phantom arm or leg. Correlated with the disappearance of parts (although not in all cases) is the telescoping of remaining parts to the stump. In the absence of a phantom arm, some patients report a "movement" of phantom fingers to the arm's stump.

Phantoms occur not only on the loss of an arm or leg but also after removal of other body parts—a nose, an eye, a breast, and so on. Although medical practice tends to think of amputation as the sole cause of phantom parts, Simmel (1962) reports that phantoms also occur after injuries that deprive the extremities of sensation. For example, a patient who has a complete transection of the spinal cord (and therefore has no sensation in the legs) will report phantom legs; if the spinal injury is high enough, the patient may experience phantoms in all four extremities.

An interesting observation has to do with the age at which amputation occurred. If the amputation occurred before 4 years of age, only 23% of the patients report phantoms. If the amputation occurred after 8 years of age, 100% of the patients report phantoms. Simmel also reports that if an amputation is performed on a limb that was not usable prior to amputation, there are no reports of phantoms; malformed arms and legs that did have some use do give rise to phantoms, especially if the patient was older than 8 at the time of amputation.

Finally, leprosy causes a gradual loss of use, sometimes taking 10 years or more, and patients who lose fingers and toes through absorption never experience phantoms. Patients suffering from leprosy who require surgical amputation almost uniformly do experience phantoms.

These data suggest two conclusions: (1) For a phantom limb to occur, removal must be dramatic and rapid. Slow loss of function, as in leprosy, does not produce phantoms, nor does amputation of previously nonfunctioning limbs. (2) The patient must have experienced this loss after about age 4.

Before it is possible to understand what these facts about phantoms might mean, we need to consider another phenomenon of damaged bodies, **anosognosia**. In this condition, the patient denies the existence of an injury even if, for example, it results in something as obvious as a totally paralyzed arm. One clinical neurology text (Elliott, 1971) notes that in damage to the right parietal lobe in the brain, the patient often tends to ignore the left side of his body.

> The patient may not use the left arm or leg, shaves only the right side of his face, and may attempt to dress only the right side of the body. He may even assert *that his left arm and leg belong to somebody else*, because he fails to recognize them as his own. Because the left side *has ceased* to exist for him, he fails to move the left arm and leg.... Furthermore, if the disease has [produced] paralysis, he may deny the paralysis.... A man with a right parietal lesion and left [paralysis] asserted that his only ailment was wax in the right ear, and he could not understand why he should have been brought into [the] hospital for so trivial an ailment (p. 419).[2]

Considered side by side, these two conditions challenge the usual (that is, physical) definitions of body and of body boundaries. In phantom limb the patient experiences a limb that is not there; in anosognosia the patient does not experience a limb that *is* there. Add the two "correct" cases, in which a patient has no limb and experiences none or has a limb and experiences it, and the picture is complete. Only the last two conditions seem right from our usual point of view: if it's there, it's there, and if it's not, it's not.

The problem we have in seeing the other two possibilities has to do with what we mean by "it's there." If by "it's there" we mean only that an outside observer can see it, then the phantom is clearly not there and the anosognosic limb clearly is. Since, however, we are looking at the world from a first-person point of view, it is necessary to argue that a

---

[2]From *Clinical Neurology, 2nd Edition*, by F. A. Elliott. Copyright 1971 by W. B. Saunders Company. Reprinted by permission.

useless arm, whether "there" or "not there," is useless and that an arm lost by amputation or one "really there" is still part of a body scheme that until recently was quite useful in possibility and/or in actuality.

From the patient's point of view, a useless limb is not part of the field of possibilities that defines his or her life and, for this reason, cannot be a part of the living body system. The amputated limb, which until recently was part of the field of possibilities, still represents an aspect of the body system and is lost slowly if at all. Here it is relevant to recall that the more mobile and useful parts of a limb (fingers and hand) remain as phantoms much longer than the less mobile and less useful parts (upper arm and forearm). It is also relevant that initially nonfunctional limbs or limbs lost slowly do not produce phantoms. Finally, age seems to be a factor, suggesting that there is probably no stable body system until at least age 3 or 4.

As with brain damage, a careful, first-person examination of certain very obvious damage done to the human body has taken a curious and revealing turn. These observations lead again to the conclusions that the human body cannot be an object like any other object and that the body *presents*—no, *is*—an I committed to certain possible actions in the world. The body is not a definite object having this or that shape, but rather, like conscious experience itself, is without fixed boundaries. Each I does not end (or, for that matter, begin) at the outside of the skin; each body is more than simply a physical form extending from the top of the head to the tips of the toes, fingers, and nose. Rather, each I (body) is a special and constantly changing region of the world defined by our projects, both real and possible. The person is a totality, and this totality is always alive and in the world as a living body.

This view of the human body has been well captured by Strand (1971) in his poem "Keeping Things Whole."[3]

Keeping Things Whole

In a field
I am the absence
of field.

This is
always the case.
Wherever I am
I am what is missing.

When I walk
I part the air
and always
the air moves in
to fill the spaces
where my body's been.

We all have reasons
for moving.
I move
to keep things whole.

V. SUPERIOR BODIES IN SPECIAL SITUATIONS

From the spectator's third-person point of view, feats performed by athletes and dancers are unbelievable. Take a football player—say, a pass-catching end or wide receiver. Generally, these players are relatively small—6'0", 190 pounds or so—with speed and agility their primary assets. Their task is to run down the field, make a sharp, veering movement, and finally meet their ultimate fate—collision with an angry and muscular 250-pound linebacker. If the wide receiver is lucky, he gets away untouched; if he is unlucky, the ball and the linebacker get to him at the same time.

Compounding this situation—which would seem enough to scare a mere mortal—is the fact that thousands of eyes, if not hundreds of thousands, are focused on the football player right there in the stadium, with millions more following his every move on television. Surely, the fear of physical collision and the possibility of being awkward or foolish before an enormous number of strangers who paid to see your skill ought to make professional football an entirely unreasonable and impossible activity.

Yet it is not impossible, and it seems reasonable to ask how it is done. The best explanation was provided by former wide receiver Paul Warfield a few years back when asked what he thought about when catching a football in the middle of a game. Warfield replied: "Nothing, because there isn't anything in the world but me and the ball." What this suggests is that if we take the athlete's first-person point of view rather than the spectator's third-

[3]From *Reasons for Moving*, by Mark Strand. Copyright © 1968 by Mark Strand. Reprinted by permission of Atheneum Publishers.

person point of view, catching a football is remarkably unaffected by the two events that would seem to make it difficult to accomplish—collision and public failure.

Coaches talk about this ability as concentration, but such a description implies that there is both someone to do the concentrating and something to concentrate on—or the more usual categories of mind and body, with mind serving to focus body. But Warfield didn't say "I first decide to blot everything out and pay attention only to the ball." What he said was that catching the ball became all of the world and that he automatically did what was necessary to achieve this end. In talking about "concentration," the coach speaks as a third-person spectator who sees only crowds and movements; the athlete speaks from his own point of view, in which body and will are one.

For the skilled athlete there is often no separation between intent and action, between will and performance, between mind and body. Both are given simultaneously by the athlete's movement in the here-and-now of his or her action. So overpowering is the immediacy of the athlete's behavior that some professional athletes talk about "getting into a different world," and it is this different world that is highly limited and highly regulated by rules and prior body training.

If an athlete's experience can be so immediate, how is his or her behavior regulated by the game situation? Here there are no sure answers—only a few hints from a rather remarkable article by the German coach/psychologist H. G. Hartgenbusch (1927), who tried to provide a first-person perspective on several sports, describing events that control the unreflected direction and flow of the athlete's behavior. In soccer, for example, Hartgenbusch notes that the goalkeeper standing before a rather large goal opening seems to be where the ball is more often than should be the case by chance alone. In explaining this, Hartgenbusch notes that a goalkeeper is the most dominant part of the goal mouth and for the ordinary soccer player undoubtedly serves as an aiming point—as a kind of target to be shot at. The expert player, however, has learned to disregard the goalkeeper as his or her target point and shoots instead at the open space surrounding the goalkeeper. A good kicker, then, is one who has "learned to reconstruct his field to change the phenomenal center of gravity from the

goalkeeper to another point in space [and] this [new point] comes to have the same attraction as the goalkeeper had before" (Hartgenbusch, 1927, p. 49).

There are a number of unusual words in this description, and a careful examination of what they mean will make Hartgenbusch's point of view a bit clearer. Words such as *attraction, center of gravity,* and *field* suggest that the first-person world of the athlete is not determined by first looking over the situation, next deciding what to do, and then doing it, but rather that it all occurs in a much more ongoing and unreflected way. For the well-trained athlete, appropriate action is an immediate result of the game situation in which the player is involved. "As soccer players move toward the goal, they see the playing ground as a field of changing lines whose direction leads toward the goal. . . . When I asked the player what he saw, [he said] I only saw a hole" (Hartgenbusch, 1927, p. 49).

Thus, the movement of an athlete, alone or in a team, is controlled by his or her unreflected perception of the situation. World-class athletes are those who are best able to deal with the existing structure, taking account of small variations and changes, and who consequently act with the most efficient movement to use these variations to their own advantage—that is, to move with perfect form. The player and the playing field, therefore, can be talked about as a constantly interrelated system, with many events emerging as significant from the overall structure at any given time. One such emergent event, which can be experienced directly only by the players yet can also be sensed by the crowd, is momentum. Sportscasters who know their sport from the inside can predict fairly accurately "where the momentum is" and how it will affect the accuracy of the team that has (or hasn't) got it.

The athlete deals in a "selfless" way with the ever-changing demands of his or her unreflected experience in a particular game situation. The world-class athlete responds to points of emphases, lines of force, and the like in an immediate way so as to use the most efficient movement system at his or her disposal. The world-class athlete also unreflectedly takes account not only of the immediately following movement but also of a string of movements whose final outcome is the desired goal—a series of passes in basketball, a series of shots in tennis.

It seems proper to talk of the athlete's experiences during a game in terms of his or her *Umwelt*, or self-world. This *Umwelt* always depends upon both the living being and the world, so that together they form a significant living situation having its own structure and its own effects. It is no more correct to say that the world stimulates the person than to say that the person selects the world—there is always an agreed-on sphere of possibilities.

The athletic self-world is defined by different events for different sports. In football (American style) the forces all converge on the goal line, and walls form to protect it or to penetrate it. In football (European style) the goal mouth and the goalkeeper form the focus, and all movement is for or against this focal point. Even within the same sport, different players have different focal points: for the runner in American football, it is the opening—the "daylight"—between linemen; for the wide receiver, side markings predominate. For the offensive lineman it is probably the defensive linemen he has been assigned to block, whereas for the defensive linebacker it is almost always the ball carrier, whoever and wherever he happens to be.

In some sports there are no clear "external" markings such as yard lines or goal post. Yet here too there are focal points. Hartgenbusch, in talking about weightlifting, describes a point of personal fixation that underlies the seemingly supersolid stance of the weightlifter. He tells of one contest in which all the athletes were performing considerably below their expected levels. One of the contestants soon found the reason. The competition was taking place in a brightly lighted hall, and there was no single place on the ceiling that the weightlifters could fixate. "The stability accompanying a fixed spatial orientation which is necessary for lifting heavy weights could not be achieved in this brightly lighted hall and the expected . . . performances did not appear" (Hartgenbusch, 1927, p. 49).

Because of what is known about skilled movements, it was somewhat surprising to find one of the participants able to diagnose his difficulty. Skilled performance is usually very much upset by self-conscious reflection of any sort, and the athlete who "has to think" either before or during an action usually does not perform as well as he or she might. The highly skilled athlete, dancer, or typist is very much in the here-and-now of his or her experience, and there is little or no time for reflection.

The orientation necessary for the correct movement is provided by the play of "perceived forces" in the athlete's self-world, and in that world the athlete or dancer exhibits the form necessary to get the job done.

Yet, in every field of movement there are also a few individuals who define the correct form for getting the job done: Ted Williams' swing in baseball, Sonny Jurgenson's release of the ball in football, Kareem Abdul-Jabbar's skyhook in basketball, Vaslav Nijinsky's leap in ballet. What such a person does becomes a definition of the exact and proper form for a game movement or set of movements: this form becomes the standard. *Form*, however, like *attraction* or *field of force*, is extremely difficult to define. **Good form** describes the smooth and unitary actions required for a given task, but it can never be extracted from the particular movements made by a particular individual. Form exists only insofar as it appears in movements: except as a fuzzy abstraction, it can never be independent of its realization in a particular moving body.

A. Developing skill

Even though reflection that occurs during an event tends to interfere with the ongoing performance, there is a place for such activity—the practice field. Here the athlete (either alone or in conjunction with a special observer known as a coach) takes apart, analyzes, and puts together the so-called elementary movements that must be mastered to achieve skilled performances. For highly skilled performers, practice is not so much a matter of learning new movements as one of reminding them of how it "looks" and "feels" to do the movement properly. For this reason, highly skilled athletes watch videotapes of their good performances and try to get back in touch with themselves as they were during those performances.

Less than highly skilled performers must learn new ways of doing things and note new parts of a situation. A classic paper by Bryan and Harter (1897) analyzing how telegraph operators learned to send and receive Morse code concluded that mastery of this skill proceeded through three phases. The first involved sending and receiving letters; the second, words; and the third, phrases and/or sentences. Skill in telegraphing seemed to involve enlarging the amount of material one could deal with at once.

Skilled performers, of course, do not only increase the amount of material they can deal with in any simple way; rather, what they do is continuously to develop a new form, a new unity, which makes a single, orderly movement out of what before was a series of separate movements. Just as it is wrong to say that the skilled swimmer makes more separate movements per unit time than the novice—in fact, he or she may not—so it is wrong to say that the skilled telegraph operator moves his or her fingers faster than the novice. Instead, it is better to say the skilled person has developed a new structure or form that is more efficient, and it is the ability to restructure and reorganize a series of fairly ordinary movements which we call skill. Every so often an individual performer comes along who expands the movement into a new structure, and from that time on the definition of good form and skill is forever changed.

The field of athletics and skilled movement generally gives a number of useful examples that help us understand the human body. For one, everyone at any level of skill clearly indicates the total absorption of the person in the event and the event in the person. Here, as elsewhere, the skin does not enclose the human being; rather, the person and his or her situation together form a living system. There is no separate mind and body—only a person in his or her situation as an indivisible unity. The special property of a skilled situation is given by the unity of intention and movement. In no other situation is the simultaneity of understanding and acting so totally a single event. The athlete does not "will" his or her body to a certain region of the field; he or she is there as the changing structures of the situation demand it.

But how do situations demand? The skilled performer who is totally within the situation has entered a special world where the structure of an event can be understood only in terms of patterns—patterns that describe the total field and that special region of the field known as the person. Person and field select each other in accordance with the rules of the event and the skills of the performer. The *Umwelt* of the athlete, no less than the *Umwelt* of the beetle, the mouse, or the woodsman, has specially noticeable aspects that appear to the performer, if not to the crowd. From the third-person perspective of the crowd, all markings on the field appear equally important—after all, they do define the permissible moves. From the first-

person perspective of the player, only the play matters.

The world of the athlete illustrates the unity of the person in his or her world perhaps better than any of the other situations considered in this chapter. This is as it should be—the skilled performer has worked long and hard to destroy the dualities that plague psychologists and psychological theory. And the way this destruction is brought about is through a careful and disciplined development of that place at which each of us and our world come together—namely, at the site of the human body, where by *body* we mean a region of possibilities rather than a biological machine governed by a disembodied spirit. I am always embodied, I am always situated in a place, and I am always my body immersed in my lived world.

VI. SUMMARY

There are basically two approaches we can take in trying to come to some understanding of the human body: that of some anonymous third person or that of first-person experience. Cameras, mirrors, photographs, and the act of reflecting all provide us with a third-person point of view by allowing us to step outside our first-person world and, thereby, to view ourselves as separate objects. This view is incomplete, for it gives us only an object, never a living body.

From the point of view of personal experience, a person never deals with his or her body as just another object. So, for example, the experience of double reactions illustrates the inseparable connection between doer and object that prevents us from considering ourselves in this light. Similarly, observations of infants responding to their images in the mirror indicate that first-person experience must be a more fundamental approach to body awareness than any third-person perspective could be.

Psychologists have studied the ways human beings understand and use their bodies through at least four procedures: observations of people as they engage in ordinary activities when healthy; figure drawings made by children and adults; observations of people engaging in ordinary activities when damaged by disease or surgery; and observations of (and reflections by) highly skilled people in special settings, such as athletics and dance.

Observing ordinary bodies in ordinary situations

reveals much about how we use our bodies in various interpersonal activities, particularly where communication is at issue. When we communicate with one another, our whole bodies get into the act, not just the muscles with which we speak. For this reason a very significant portion of all human communicating is paralinguistic (nonverbal). Personal closeness, or "proxemics," is also an integral part of communication. Any type of paralinguistic communication must be interpreted within the context of previous and subsequent movements in order to determine the significance of the act for the actor.

Any act can express more than a single meaning, and such meanings sometimes conflict. If we consider nonverbal and verbal behaviors as totally separate events, we can easily miss the meaning of the act for the person acting. Ekman has proposed six ways in which verbal and nonverbal behaviors relate to each other, five of which convey consistent intentions or meanings. When verbal and nonverbal behaviors appear to contradict each other, it is necessary to look at their meaning from a first-person point of view, as Freud and other clinical psychologists have done.

Any approach that looks only at what we do emphasizes a more general problem inherent in any third-person methodology: by categorizing separate acts and then combining them from a third-person point of view, we can lose sight of the unified experience of the person acting. Separate acts have meaning only within the totality of the person—a totality that is always changing as the person deals with the world.

Figure drawing is one way to learn about a person's perceptions of his or her body. As such, it provides an indication of the person's reflected and unreflected experiences of the body. For example, Koppitz's studies of children and their figure drawings not only detailed the extent of children's reflected thought about their bodies, which paralleled their intellectual development; they also indicated certain unreflected concerns children had about their bodies in the context of their interpersonal situations.

Observing people with certain types of brain damage engaged in ordinary activities, Goldstein and Gelb concluded that these people had lost the ability to perform abstract movements. One activity in which this loss was particularly noticeable concerned the distinction between grasping and point-ing. Although these two actions are superficially similar, grasping is an immediate response to a *concrete* situation, whereas pointing is an *abstract* movement made in response to an *as if* situation. "As if" movements cannot be performed by brain-damaged people who seem able to deal with their world only in terms of concrete realities.

Goldstein and Gelb interpreted these observations as examples of a total-person deficit in which a relatively major way of dealing with the world had been lost. By contrasting the rigid, orderly, and concrete movements of the brain-damaged person with the more spontaneous activities of the intact person, Gelb and Goldstein were able to gain a better appreciation for the integrated, healthy person, particularly insofar as such people deal with their world in a self-actualizing way.

Studying amputees yields new insights into body boundaries, contradicting the Cartesian idea that the body ends (or begins) at the skin. People who experience phantom limbs do not recognize the same bodily limits a third-person point of view considers obvious. Rather, these patients experience their body in accordance with past functions, so that the preamputation "boundaries" of the body are kept intact. For example, Simmel found that amputees did not experience phantom limbs if the amputated limb had not been usable prior to amputation. From the first-person point of view, a useless limb is "not there," whereas a once-useful but now-amputated limb is still part of the body scheme. The age at which amputation occurs has also been found to be critical. For amputations that occurred before age 4, most children do not report phantom limbs; for those occurring after age 8, most children do.

The skilled athlete's self-world provides the best example of simultaneity of will and movement. For the athlete, action and intent are a single, seamless event. Not only are "mind" and "body" unified, they also become part and parcel of the ongoing athletic situation.

The direction and orientation necessary for correct movement in skilled performance are provided by the pattern of forces in the athlete's self-world. All games impose constraints on the athlete's behavior, although within these constraints the athlete abandons himself or herself to the process, thereby forming a unified, living system of athlete and game situation. While training to master a skill, the athlete may experience some discomfort because at this time the movements are separate acts rather than a single unity. Through practice, the athlete integrates the dualities of "mind" and "body" as person and situation become a single, ongoing event.

The self-world of any human being is always agreed to by both the living being and the world, so that together they form a significant situation having its own structure and effects. The exceptionally skilled person develops a unique form for a movement, and it is the ability to restructure and reorganize a series of fairly ordinary movements that we call skill. For the highly skilled person, the duality of mind and body is abandoned and replaced by a unified, flowing system sensitive to the ongoing demands of the task or the game situation.

VII. GLOSSARY OF IMPORTANT CONCEPTS

Abstract action. See concrete action.

Anosognosia. Inability to recognize the existence of one's own bodily injury, as in the suppression of awareness of one side of the body after damage to the brain; this lack of awareness is itself not recognized.

Behavior. The union of movement and meaning.

Catastrophic condition. The early stage of brain damage, characterized by general disorder and a fear of losing one's existence. It includes restlessness, distraction, fear, and excess emotion.

Concrete (as distinguished from **abstract**) **action.** Acting in response to ongoing, "real" situations, as opposed to acting in response to "as if" (symbolic) situations—exemplified by grasping rather than pointing.

Concrete attitude. The stage of brain damage following the catastrophic condition and characterized by consistency or orderliness in behaving, with reliance on definite, specific points of reference in guiding one's behaving.

Double reaction. The simultaneous actions of perceiving and being perceived, where a single person is the actor and the object of the actions.

Good form. A quality of the smooth and unitary actions required for a skillful performance. Good form is inseparable from the particular movements made by a particular person in a particular situation.

Paralinguistic. Nonverbal aspects of speaking; emotional sounds and body "language" are basic aspects.

Phantom limb. A limb lost by amputation but still experienced as present.

Proxemics. The study of physical closeness and distance between people.

Reflect. To "bend back," to assume a third-person point of view on one's first-person experiences. A property of "mirrors and minds."

Self-actualization. Realization of one's individual capacities.

VIII. SUGGESTED READINGS

Major sources

Goldstein, K. *The organism.* New York: American Books, 1939.

Merleau-Ponty, M. *The phenomenology of perception.* London: Routledge and Kegan Paul, 1962. Part 1, Chapters 1–6.

Secondary sources

Hanna, T. *Bodies in revolt: A primer in somatic thinking.* New York: Holt, Rinehart & Winston, 1970.

Knapp, M. L. *Nonverbal communication in human interaction.* New York: Holt, Rinehart & Winston, 1972.

4

Perceiving

There are no impersonal eyes that see, tongues that taste, ears that hear, or hands that touch: all perceiving is done by the whole person, and people always have reasons for seeing, tasting, hearing, and touching. To look at a Van Gogh to determine how the paint was applied is quite different from looking to see his crows hovering over a cornfield. Tasting a wine to find out whether it is cold enough to drink is quite different from savoring its lightness or bouquet.

These differences in the reasons for seeing or tasting go along with other differences in what we do when we perceive. To find out whether a wine is lukewarm requires only a quick taste. To savor a wine, in contrast, is to look at it, to smell it, to sip it gently and slowly, and finally to let the liquid roll around on your tongue and only then to swallow it, with perhaps a certain sadness. Far from being unobservable, our reasons for perceiving do show up in how we go about the job. Such movements are often so well known that even a faker can go through the right motions.

I. MEASURING SENSATIONS AND THE HUMAN PERCEIVER

Nevertheless, psychologists interested in the general problem of perceiving have tried to ignore a person's reasons for perceiving. It is as if we asked human beings to lend us an eye, ear, tongue, or hand and then went on to ask them not to think about what they were doing. This approach grows out of the psychologist's attempt to learn about the workings of human perceptual systems in isolation. In order to do this, psychologists invented the methods of **psychophysics**—procedures designed to determine the relationships between psychological reactions and physical stimuli.

Using psychophysical methods, psychologists have given some fairly precise estimates of the minimal amount of energy the eye can see or the ear can hear. So, for example, we now know that human beings can see a candle flame at 30 miles on a clear, dark night or hear the tick of a watch under quiet conditions at 20 feet. We also know that the human observer can taste 1 teaspoon of sugar in 2 gallons of water or smell 1 drop of perfume diffused in the entire volume of a three-room apartment (Galanter, 1962).

Each of these values is called the **absolute threshold** for the appropriate sense and represents the outcome of one of the most carefully investigated areas of psychological research—psychophysics. As its name suggests, psychophysics is concerned with working out in a scientific way the exact relations between the physical and psychological worlds. Psychophysics assumes that matter and mind are separate realms and that the laboratory is a good place to work out their interrelations. Given this way of looking at things, it is reasonable to look for a threshold—to ask how much light has to stimulate my eye for me to say "I see it."

Psychologists' early attempts to answer questions of this type proceeded, for example, by bringing someone into a dark, quiet laboratory room, showing the person a series of lights from very dim to very bright, and asking the person to say when he or she sees the light. Even in the very earliest studies two disturbing facts came up: (1) the threshold value was lower if the light went from bright to dim than from dim to bright, and (2) perfectly responsible observers sometimes said "Yes, I see it" when in fact no light was presented.

Instead of treating such results as important in their own right, investigators considered them errors and concluded that a threshold could only be defined statistically—as, for example, "the physical value of a stimulus that evokes a positive response 50% of the time." Although from very early on psychophysicists described a threshold as being a statistical, rather than a "real," value, contemporary psychology (not psychophysics) sometimes plays fast and loose with the idea of threshold, often treating it as a "real" (rather than only a statistical) value. The idea of some fixed minimum energy seems too reasonable and too attractive a fiction to give up or to play carefully with all the time.

But psychophysicists are not the type of people to be satisfied with telling other people to be careful. Instead, a small group went back to the laboratory to demonstrate in a very rigorous way that thresholds were not fixed. This work on "signal detection," as it came to be called, initially had nothing to do with demonstrating a particular theoretical point; rather, it had to do with radar detection by somewhat unskilled observers. In the usual radar situation an observer is seated before a screen and is asked to decide whether one of the blips on the screen is or is not an approaching airplane.

Now this task would seem to involve a simple yes-or-no decision, but it turns out that most blips are not planes, and a false alarm—reporting there is a plane when there is none—can cause a great deal of confusion. If, however, the radar operator misses a real plane, a serious accident could result. Decisions, then, are not without their costs and payoffs.

In order to set the signal-detection problem in as clear a form as possible, psychophysicists decided on an experiment in which a signal was presented on some trials and not on others. In this kind of experiment the observer (a radar operator or an experimental subject) is always forced to say "Yes, I see it" or "No, I don't." It is then possible to describe the signal-detection situation in the form of Table 4-1. For the ideal observation situation, false alarms and misses should be 0, and hits and correct rejections should match the number of times the signal was and was not presented.

TABLE 4-1. Basic Outline for a Signal-Detection Experiment

Signal	OBSERVER'S RESPONSE	
	Yes	No
Present	hit	miss
Absent	false alarm	correct rejection

Suppose now that two experiments were done—one in which the signal was presented 90% of the time and a second in which the signal was presented only 10% of the time. If the signal were the only important factor, we should expect about the same percentage of hits in these two experiments—near 100%—and also about the same percentage of false alarms. The experimental truth of the matter, however, is that in many experiments for the 90% case the hit rate was .97 and the false-alarm rate was .62; in the 10% case the hit rate was .28 and the false-alarm rate, .04. That is, in the 90% case both hits and false alarms go up, whereas in the 10% case both hits and false alarms go down. In other

words, the value of a threshold can be moved around by how frequently the signal occurs.

Can other aspects of the threshold-detection situation also have an effect? One obvious factor would be the "cost" of a false alarm. During a war it is quite expensive to get your fighter pilots up and ready to attack a phantom plane: the cost is quite high. Still, if it is a matter of life and death, we would probably rather be safe than sorry.

Galanter (1962) has set up a hypothetical situation of this type in terms of what he calls a "payoff matrix." In the setup shown in Table 4-2, false alarms are not as heavily penalized as correct responses are rewarded. Under these conditions, an observer is more likely to say yes, since if he is wrong, he loses only 5¢, whereas if he is correct, he gets a dime. In this situation, when in doubt, it pays to guess.

TABLE 4-2. Payoff Matrix for Signal-Detection Situation

Signal	RESPONSE	
	Yes	No
Present	10¢	— 5¢
Absent	— 5¢	10¢

Adapted from *New Directions in Psychology I*, by Roger Brown, Eugene Galanter, Eckhard H. Hess, and George Mandler. Copyright © 1962 by Holt, Rinehart and Winston, Inc. Reprinted by permission of Holt, Rinehart and Winston.

The mathematical theory of signal detection gets more complicated than this, yet the essential point has been made: A person, not an eye, comes into the psychophysical situation, and it is the person who says yes or no. It is impossible for an observer simply to lend the experimenter an eye, even if he or she agrees to. The whole person responds even in this special situation, and the ideal objective observer who is sensitive only to the signal is a fiction. The classical psychophysical experiment is, for all its laboratory aura, a living situation, and people always behave as people, here as elsewhere.

Does this mean that the idea of a threshold is useless or that psychophysics has made no contribution to our understanding of human beings? In the language of "yes and no": Yes and no. The idea of a threshold seems so absolutely correct in a general sense that it is very difficult to give up entirely. But applying this idea always means determining some specific value in a laboratory—say, a candle flame at 20 feet—and here the experimental problem is almost impossible. In general, the *idea* of a threshold seems reasonable, but it is almost impossible to describe for any given sense modality (vision, hearing, and so on) a single value that will be correct under all conditions.

It is somewhat more difficult to come to a general conclusion about psychophysics. Perhaps it is best simply to say that this area has given us a great deal of information about the various senses, which has been put to good use in bringing about such technical advances as television, radar, and stereophonic sound. Whether psychophysics contributes to an understanding of human perceiving is somewhat moot. From an existential-phenomenological point of view, we have to be pleased with the ability of signal-detection theory to re-place thresholds within the realm of first-person events such as rewards and expectations. At the same time, we must realize that threshold data can be and have been used in isolation from the living person. This is particularly true in the psychophysicist's attempt to provide average values for the various senses, values that then are used to help the electronics engineer design your TV set or stereophonic recorder. When used in this way, psychophysics seems an approach far removed from human perceiving, although not from human technology.

II. UNITY (AND UNIQUENESS) OF THE VARIOUS SENSES

Signal-detection theory, then, restores the various senses to the perceiving person. But, even here there is a problem: if all perceiving is done by the "whole person," how is it proper to talk about any one sense—say, seeing—in isolation from the rest? Surely there must be some unity across the various senses. As the old country proverb says, you don't have to have your eyes open to know you're in a pigsty.

Cross-sense unity (and diversity) has been studied by examining experiences called **synesthesia**, in which stimulation of one sense is described in terms usually associated with another sense. A very common example of a synesthetic experience is color-music; the person reports that he or she "sees" colors (or shapes) when listening to music. Early work by Karwoski and Odbert (1938) found

that as many as 13% of college undergraduates regularly experienced such effects.

To examine this finding more carefully, Karwoski, Odbert, and Osgood (1942) asked a group of college students who usually had synesthetic experiences to draw what they "saw" while listening to music. The first thing Karwoski et al. noticed was that loudness was usually indicated by heaviness (that is, as a tone became louder, students drew heavier lines). They also found that each individual had a unique and personal way of translating sound into visual experience. In the second part of this study, a group of students who "never thought of seeing music" were asked to force themselves to draw something. Most of the students were able to. In addition, these students tended to use the same matchings (heavy line—loud sound) as those who usually and spontaneously "saw music."

If with a bit of coaxing students who do not normally "see" music can be made to do so, it seems reasonable to expect that artists might use cross-sensory experience in more subtle ways. Some work by the English linguist Stephen Ullmann (1959) is relevant. Ullmann was most interested in synesthesia in poetry. He looked at synesthetic language in 11 English and French poets of the 19th century, such as Keats and Shelley, to determine whether there were any regular ways in which the various senses were paired. For example, in Keats we find the line "*Taste* the *music* of that pale *vision*." Here there are two transfers: one from taste to hearing and one from hearing to vision.

To present his results systematically, Ullmann arranged the senses in order from what he called the least to the most differentiating. In this scheme, temperature and touch are at the bottom; hearing and vision are at the top. Using this procedure, Ullmann noted 2009 transfers. Of these transfers, 1665, or 83%, were from temperature or touch to hearing or sight, and only 344, or 17%, from hearing or sight to temperature or touch.

In discussing these results, Werner (1948) noted that transfer from a less differentiating to a more differentiating sense is not surprising, largely because children show an increasing use of more differentiating senses as they get older. In addition, synesthesia, which is uncommon for most adults, is much more frequent in children. For example, it is easy to find instances of synesthetic thinking in diaries about young children. Here Werner notes the case of a little boy "who opened his mouth when smelling" or of another 3-year-old who found that a lilac smelled "nice and yellow." Finally there is the exasperated child who told his resting mother: "Open your eyes or you won't hear what I'm saying." On the basis of these findings, Werner suggested that there is probably a primitive unity among the various senses, at least in young children.

Certain drugs also produce synesthetic experiences; there has been some recent work on mescaline, LSD, and so on. Early observers, such as Beringer (1927) and Klüver (1926), noted that the senses lose their separate identities and all tend to melt together during a drug state. One subject quoted by Werner (1948) noted: "I think that I hear noises and see faces, and yet everything is one and the same. I cannot tell whether I am seeing or hearing. I feel, taste, and smell the sound. It's all one. I, myself, am the tone" (p. 92).

There is an important general significance to these strange goings-on. The child, the sensitive adult, and the adult taking certain drugs all experience a unity among the senses that most of us ordinarily do not. It is as if in growing up we passed from a stage of intersense unity to an adult stage in which each of the senses is unique, stimulated only by its own special part of the world. Only the extraordinarily sensitive are still in contact with the original unity of the senses. The rest of us can recapture this unity, but only under special conditions that seem to destroy our ordinary abstract abilities or under special instructions that ask us to "see music" or to "touch light."

Sensory experience must have a primary unity that precedes its division into separate senses. This is quite reasonable once we recognize that each sense must provide us with access to the same world, even if in a different way. Synesthetic experiences suggest that each person constructs a single world from many different points of view and that this world, once achieved, always remains an open project requiring a never-ending integration of what the various senses tell us about it.

But how do we achieve such integration? Here we must go back to the notion of the living body (Chapter 3) and of its progressive development. Each sense initially is part of a unity that includes all others, and it is only the emergence of an abstract, adult point of view that gives us separate senses. Our bodies ordinarily do not need a translator to explain seeing to hearing or hearing to touch; rather, all are mutually understandable. Synesthetic experience clearly presents the case for the preabstract unity of our senses and thus helps us see why a nonmechanical view of the human body is so important for understanding all psychological processes, perceiving included.

III. STRUCTURING THE PERCEPTUAL WORLD: FIGURE AND GROUND

The most obvious first-person experience we have of the perceptual world is that of **figure** and **ground**. As the early Gestalt psychologists noted, some parts of the world catch our attention and become figural, while other parts recede from us as unimportant and become background. Figure/ground seems a very simple principle, but it is not always easy to recognize all that is involved. Take, for example, the pattern in Figure 4-1, originally presented by the Danish psychologist Edgar Rubin (1921). If we take the white area as figure, we see a vase against a black (back)ground. If we take the white area as ground and the black as figure, we see the profiles of twins facing each other. Thus, what is figure and what is ground can be changed, and it is obviously the perceiver who changes Figure 4-1

Figure 4-1.   Rubin's "twins and vase" figure.

from vase to twins and back again. The twins/vase pattern is an example of a **reversible figure.**

Rubin, who did the earliest work on figure/ground reversals, described figure and ground in the following terms:

1. The figure appears to have a definite form whereas the ground is much less definite.
2. The figure looks like a thing whereas the ground seems "thingless."
3. The figure appears nearer the observer than the ground.
4. The figure is more easily identified and described than the ground [Solley & Murphy, 1960, p. 263].

Using a modified version of the vase/twins picture, Osgood (1953) has shown how it is possible to change figure/ground relations. At the left in Figure 4-2, the "vase" and the "faces" are equally likely. The middle drawing is an attempt to make the vase dominant; the right-hand drawing, the faces. The additional lines in the middle drawing serve to make the vase more "thinglike" (hence, more like a figure); the lines in the right-hand drawing give the faces more "thingness." Reversibility can be diminished by deliberately emphasizing one part of the picture at the expense of the other.

Since one of the properties of reversible figure/ground patterns is that they are ambiguous and changing, it is possible to use this principle to hide or camouflage something. The original of the figure Rubin studied, for example, was supposed to represent two exiled Danish princes. As the story goes, a wicked government minister decided that no pic-

tures should be made of the princes, and it remained for a loyal follower to draw the original vase/twins figure. It was the perceiver who decided whether to see the vase or the princes; thus was the minister's decree thwarted.

More recent use of figure/ground principles can be seen in the use of camouflage in modern warfare. In an extremely interesting analysis of all kinds of illusions, Luckiesh (1965) has examined the role of figure/ground factors (among others) in camouflage. As he notes, one reason for painting battleships gray and tanks green is to make them fade into their usual grounds. This is similar to the natural camouflage of fish in which the top part is dark and the underpart light. Viewed from above, the dark color blends in with the ocean or river bottom; viewed from below, the light color disappears into the lighter color of the water surface and the sky.

Reversible figures remind us that the perceptual world is changeable and that perceiving always requires an active contribution from the perceiver. The perceiver, like the world, is never static, and the change of ground to figure or of figure to ground is not so extraordinary an event. As a matter of fact, much of what is involved in a "change of perspective" on some issue is nothing other than interchanging figure with ground. The perceptual world is always in flux and always involves relating one thing to another or to many others. The phenomena of figure/ground seem exactly suited to capture the mood of just these three aspects of perceiving: change, choice, and relationship.

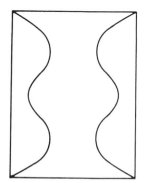 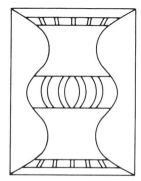 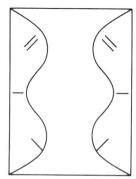

Figure 4-2. Manipulation of figure/ground relations. (*From* Method and Theory in Experimental Psychology, *by* C. E. Osgood. Copyright © 1953 by Oxford University Press, Inc. Reprinted by permission.)

A. What makes for a good figure?

In a reversible figure a single edge forms the boundary of two or more figures. The way the edge is perceived determines which is figure and which ground. For more ordinary objects—drawn or in the world—an edge is usually the boundary between a fairly definite object and "everything else." On this basis it seems reasonable to say, as Hochberg (1964) does: "The contour of a figure behaves like the ... edge of an object, which by its very nature has a shape on only one side, since past that edge, the object's surface ceases to exist" (p. 84).

Objects, unlike vases or simple profiles, are themselves usually composed of perceivable subparts. For example, an automobile has lights, windows, doors, a steering wheel, and other components, all of which can appear as figures in their own right or can be perceived as parts of a single, larger figure—the automobile itself. If the concept of pattern as an important aspect of the perceptual world is to be of any significance, it is not enough to deal with one part of the perceptual field as figure and all the rest as ground. Rather, we need to look at collections of "figures" and see how such a collection becomes (or does not become) a single, more inclusive figure. Although it seems reasonable to pursue this work in terms of objects or parts of objects, the earliest work on pattern organization involved simple line patterns usually containing more than a single item on a single field.

Since much of this work was done in German, the rules (or laws) of pattern organization took the German word *Gestalt* for their title. *Gestalt* translates reasonably well as *pattern, form,* or *configuration.* The laws of organization have come most often to be called the Gestalt laws of organization.

Consider the left-hand pattern in Figure 4-3. If we look at it for a while, we can see many organizations: first it appears as a single large square of boxes, then as a series of broken horizontal black lines, then as a series of vertical and horizontal white lines, then as a series of white crosses, and so on. No one perceptual experience dominates; in its own way this figure is as changeable as the vase/twins figure. Now look at the right-hand pattern. Here we experience much less variation and much more stability; rather, one organization, determined primarily by the cross of open circles, seems to predominate. The pattern provided by this set of elements structures the field to the exclusion of most others.

B. Reversible figures and Gestalt views on organization

Figures arrived at from the flux of experience need not produce a single Gestalt. Sometimes there is no doubt what is figure; at other times the nature of the figure can undergo continual change. The best-known example of this class of reversible figures is called the Necker cube. A simple example is shown at left in Figure 4-4. This figure seems to provide at least two organizations, which are emphasized in the next two drawings in Figure 4-4. It is also possible to see a third organization, which is not three-dimensional but appears as a collection of lines surrounding the small rectangle in the middle.

Although it is possible to see the Necker cube as two-dimensional, it is quite difficult. To make a figure of this type easy to see, Kopfermann (1930) presented the two figures shown in Figure 4-5. It is quite clear that the first one strongly produces a three-dimensional effect—it's our friend the Necker cube again—while the second is more easily seen as two-dimensional. This second figure, however, is only a cube drawn from a different point of view, and it is possible (even if difficult) to see it in three dimensions.

Hochberg and his associates (Hochberg, 1964; Hochberg & Brooks, 1960; Hochberg & McAlister, 1953) have suggested that one reason it is easier to see a cube in the first figure and a flat, six-sided figure in the second has to do with the simplicity of the figures. For Hochberg, simplicity is defined (and measured) by a number of properties of the drawing: how many lines there are, the number of angles within the pattern, the number of inside corners, and so on. When Hochberg and Brooks counted up these properties in Figure 4-5, it was clear that as the complexity of the two-dimensional figure increased from the first figure to the second, the less likely to be seen as three-dimensional the figure was. Not satisfied with simply measuring and explaining cubes, Hochberg and his associates went on to construct new figures having measurably simple and complex forms and were able to predict which of their new figures would be seen as flat and which as three-dimensional.

Results such as these can be interpreted as an attempt to quantify the Gestalt **law of Pragnanz**—"law of the good figure." The general idea of this law is quite simple: perceived figures tend to be "good"—that is, regular, simple and internally consistent. Whenever one figure is better (more regular and so

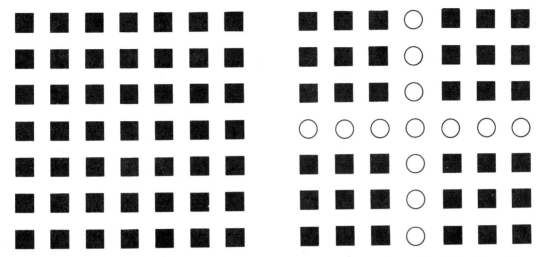

Figure 4-3.   Left: Arrangement of forms permitting alternate organizations while being observed. Right: Arrangement in which one dominant organization resists modification. (*From* Method and Theory in Experimental Psychology, *by C. E. Osgood. Copyright © 1953 by Oxford University Press, Inc. Reprinted by permission.*)

on) than another, it will be the one perceived. In a sense *Pragnanz*, or simplicity, presents a general statement of the Gestalt position: the figure experienced by the perceiver will be the best and simplest figure possible given the person, the pattern, and the situation.

Just to show that boxes are not the only patterns giving rise to more than a single figure, consider the famous case of the old woman and the young girl. As you look at Figure 4-6, which do you see? To help you see both figures, here's a hint: the old woman has a big nose and is in profile; the young girl has a black choker and is looking away from you.

The important point to all these demonstrations is that even within a single figure many organizations are possible and that the idea of a stable and unchanging world must be called into doubt. Even

in the seemingly sure world of what we see, it is not always sure what we will see. No less than the world of meanings and people, the world of lines and angles is also subject to fluctuation and change. You and I as well as our world are always in flux, and if we are true to our experience, we come to know the world and ourselves as much by what we choose to perceive as by simple reaction to solid fact.

C. Context effects

Grounds, not only figures, affect what we see. One of the best and most widely known demonstrations was first presented by the Gestalt psychologist Kurt Koffka in 1935. Figure 4-7 shows a uniform gray ring, which appears against both a black and a white background. If you put a pen, a card, a ruler, or any other straightedge over the edge where black

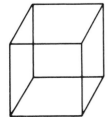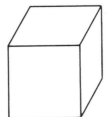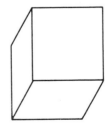

Figure 4-4.   Three views of the Necker cube. (*From* An Introduction to Perception, *by Irvin Rock. Copyright © 1975 by Irvin Rock. Reprinted with permission of Macmillan Publishing Co., Inc.*)

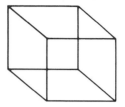

Figure 4-5. The role of figure simplicity in the perception of a three-dimensional figure. The two patterns are equally accurate drawings of a wire cube, yet the first is easy to see as a cube, while the second remains a flat pattern. (*From "Psychologische Untersuchungen über die Wirkung zweidimensionaler Darstellungen körperlicher Gebilde," by H. Kopfermann. In* Psychologische Forschung, *1930, 13, 293–364. Reprinted by permission of Springer-Verlag.*)

meets white, a double contrast will result; that is, the part of the ring surrounded by black will appear lighter than the part surrounded by white. This phenomenon is called a **contrast effect.**

This simple demonstration illustrates at least two Gestalt laws. The first is none other than *Pragnanz:* in the unaltered picture, a single ring is the simplest figure possible. The second, of course, is that of figure/ground contrast. Under Pragnanz we experience the ring as a single figure, and its brightness remains the same throughout. When we divide it into separate halves, we end up with two separate figures: a gray half-ring on a black ground and a gray half-ring on a white ground. Under these conditions, the half-ring on the white ground appears darker than the half-ring on the black ground. Dividing the figure breaks up the unity of the ring and gives us a new experience involving two separate half-circles. Because perception of the ring (the figure) is affected by its ground, this demonstration is an example of a **context effect.**

Context effects, however, are not confined to brightness. For an example concerning size, consider the two patterns in Figure 4-8. The two interior circles are exactly the same size; only the different grounds make them appear unequal. In addition, if you try to see a third dimension in Figure 4-8, the inner circle may appear closer than the outer circles on the right and farther away on the left. Again the conclusion is clear: figures always appear against some ground, and what this ground happens to be always plays some part in what is perceived.

D. Meaning and figure/ground

Some years ago a professional comedian invented a parlor game called Droodles. In this game, the players were presented with a seemingly nonsensical set of lines and asked to interpret it. For example, you might be presented with the Droodle in Figure 4-9a and asked to provide a caption that would make the lines into a meaningful picture. You might say it is a soldier and his dog passing an opening in a picket fence, and suddenly instead of meaningless scratchings on paper we have a meaningful picture. Figure 4-9b has at least two interpretations: a washerwoman cleaning the floor or a ghost watching TV. What is most impressive about these figures is that if you want to interpret them, you can and that, once interpreted, the lines always seem to form that figure, thereby making it difficult to see them as anything else. As a final example, what do you see in the possibly risqué Droodle in Figure 4-10?

In discussing figures such as these, Osgood (1953) notes that the meaning of an event is important not

Figure 4-6. The old woman and the young girl.

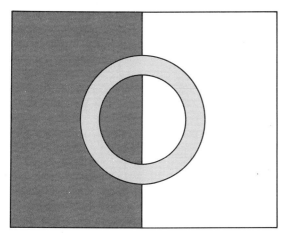

Figure 4-7. Demonstration of simultaneous contrast. (*From* Method and Theory in Experimental Psychology, *by C. E. Osgood. Copyright © 1953 by Oxford University Press, Inc. (Reprinted by permission.)*

only in visual line drawings but in perceiving language. For example, if you read English, the following set of letters is easily broken up into a meaningful Appalachian sentence:

E A T M O R E P O S S U M

If you do not know English—or, more precisely, Appalachian English—the letters may stay a collection of letters. If you know French, then you know that the phrase *Pas de lieu Rhone que nous* makes little or no sense. If you speak only English, you might hear it, when read aloud, as *Paddle your own canoe.* In these two cases it is clear that we break up language sounds in very predictable ways because we know something in addition to the sounds presented. This something extra, of course, is the meaning of the items.

In addition to simple figure/ground effects, FIGURE/ground effects, and figure/GROUND effects, knowing something about what you are perceiving can also serve to organize a collection of events into a figure. This is not surprising, for as perceivers we are more interested in what events mean to us than in how they are presented. It would be surprising if we had to wait to interpret everything we saw, tasted, or touched. As adults, we usually know immediately what object it is we are dealing with, regardless of how it is presented to us.

E. Perceptual constancy

For the human being, then, the world is normally experienced as relatively stable and populated by meaningful objects. Since meaningful objects have a certain permanence or constancy to them, it is surprising how little affected we are by vast changes in their physical properties. For example, I see a black

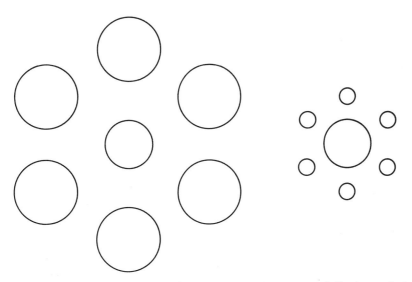

Figure 4-8. Equal circles appear unequal due to contrast. (*From* Visual Illusions: Their Causes, Characteristics, and Application, *by M. Luckiesh. Copyright 1965 by Dover Publications, Inc. Reprinted by permission.)*

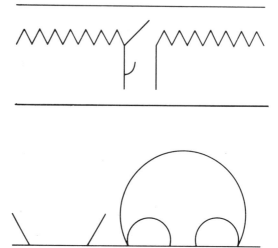

Figure 4-9. Two Droodles illustrating the influence of meaning on perceptual organization. (*From* Method and Theory in Experimental Psychology, *by C. E. Osgood. Copyright © 1953 by Oxford University Press, Inc. Reprinted by permission.*)

piece of paper in the sunlight and in the shade, and both times the paper is black to me. A friend walks away from me and then back toward me, and she seems neither to shrink nor to grow. Both cases are examples of perceptual stability, or, more technically, **perceptual constancy.**

For most perceptual situations, black paper in most living contexts stays black. It is possible, however, to set up a situation in which it does not, by removing black from its ordinary context. This can be done by hanging a piece of black paper

so that it is hit by a single beam of light and throws no shadow. The unsuspecting subject will report that the paper looks white, not black. This effect, first demonstrated by Gelb (1927), has come to be known as the Gelb effect.

The Gelb effect works only if there are no clues that a bright light is being projected onto a piece of black paper. If the light source is changed so that a bit of background is also hit by the same bright light, the perceiver immediately reports a piece of black paper in bright light. The human observer can work as a light meter if the situation is right—that is, only if there is no relevant context. One more aspect of this demonstration is also important: If the light is again projected onto the paper so that there is no overlap, the black paper will again be seen as white. Intellectual knowledge seems to have little effect.

An answer to the question why a black object stays black or a 5½-foot person stays 5½ feet tall is suggested by the Gelb effect: A human observer works like a light meter or a size detector only in the absence of context. In the presence of any kind of background or context, color and size will remain meaningfully constant. Should context be removed, we again see in accord with existing conditions of light reflectance or visual angle.

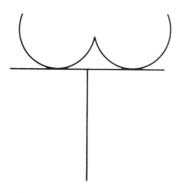

Figure 4-10. The Mystery Droodle.

Perceptual constancy is a very general phenomenon. Not only do brightness and size show constancy, so do shape, color, position, speed, and so on. Everywhere we turn, the perceptual world is experienced as a stable one, despite wide variations in the physical properties of the objects we perceive. The human observer seems to lose constancy—behave like a mechanical recording device—only in the laboratory where context is systematically manipulated or removed, so that all the observer can do is judge the amount of light or the visual angle of the object presented. Such a condition is made up, or devised, and, by definition, must always be a bit "unnatural." In the more usual situation of the natural world, perceiving is always done in context, always concerns meaningful objects, and always involves a perceiver who has a stake in what he or she perceives. Only in the constructed world of the laboratory is nonconstancy a serious possibility.

F. Space as ground

Perception's most important motto must be "figure and ground, figure and ground, figure and ground." As helpful as this notion is in most cases, there are times when what is ground in one context or for one particular person can become figure when seen against a larger ground or by a different person. For example, for any of the figures presented in this chapter—the old woman and the young girl, the vase and the twins, the Necker cube—the ground on which the figure appears includes not only the immediately surrounding white space on the page of this book but also the whole page on which the figure occurs. Then again, the book itself could be seen as a figure against the table, the table a figure against the floor, the floor a figure against the room, and so on.

Whenever the words *figure* and *ground* are used, we must expect the word *ground* to include both the immediate ground of the picture as it appears on a certain page and all the other grounds that stand behind that page. This is as it should be: everything is in relation to everything else. Even if we focus only on a particular figure in a particular ground (the old woman or the vase), all other grounds can be called on if we choose to do so. For there to be any particular figure (or ground) at all, there must be some larger, more permanent ground within which this all occurs. This larger ground is usually called "space." *Space*, however, does not

mean something abstract and intellectual; rather, it means something concrete and lived, or, as Gibson (1966) put it, something permanent in the world.

1. Perceiving space. An understanding of how we perceive space must be a basic problem for all perception. In a way, space can be considered the ultimate ground behind all our perceptions. If this is so, how should we understand what is meant by the term *space?* Surely we do not mean the contentless, bloodless, airless space described by geometry. Perhaps a better way to understand space is to look at the more unsophisticated meaning of the word *ground,* as in "Trees grow in the ground." To discover this way of describing space, we ought to stop looking at line drawings in books and go out and look at the natural world in as unprejudiced and open a way as we can.

What happens when we do go outside? First of all, we find a world that has a top and a bottom—what the little child draws as land and sky. The land looks solid, while the sky does not. As a matter of fact, the sky sometimes seems to drop behind the land, and clouds, as well as land, can stand out in front of the sky. There is also a special region of the outside, known as the horizon, where land and sky meet. If we now look at the land more closely, objects such as houses, trees, and people appear against the land as ground in much the same way as the land appeared against the sky.

A second thing we notice outside is that we move around. Ordinarily, it is very difficult to stay still or even to hold a single point of view for very long. If we try to, we find that our eyes wander even if our feet do not. To be in the world as a perceiver means to look at our world from continuously changing points of view. Only in the laboratory are both world and perceiver static. Outside, everything seems much more alive and changing.

2. Gibson's approach to space perception. One psychologist who has gone outside and looked at the world with a certain freshness is James Gibson. Although probably first forced out by pressing problems involved in wartime flying such as were common during World War II, Gibson has stayed outside in developing his approach to space perception. In this natural perceptual world, two things struck Gibson: (1) all spatial perception was done in regard to a textured ground (the earth); (2)

most perceivers were in motion, either because they were moving in some direction or other or because they moved their heads.

This second observation, though obvious, has some rather subtle implications. In an attempt to develop these implications, Gibson has described the pattern of flow that all of us experience as we walk along (see Figure 4-11). Although we do not usually notice this flow of events, it is there if we look. The perception of space as well as of objects in space is always a continuous process done by a moving perceiver in a highly textured visual world.

The abstract world that comes simply from thinking about (rather than from moving in or looking at) space always seems to give empty space—a space unfilled by objects or even by land, horizon, and sky. Reflections on space provide only an empty, "airy" world in which there are no textures, no directions, and no shapes. Gibson (1950) has gone so far as to suggest that an observer in a space of air

"might as well be in absolute darkness ... what [he or she] would perceive would not be space but the nearest thing to no perception at all.... Visual space, unlike abstract space, is perceived only by virtue of what fills it" (p. 5).

Does this mean that we should pay attention only to objects in the world and not worry about space? Gibson's answer is that the special character of the visual world is given not by an analysis of the objects in it but by a consideration of background against which objects become figure. Although the study of space involves objects, it must force itself to come to grips with the ground against which these objects appear. By a curious turn it is possible to describe the problem of space as a figure/ground reversal—that of getting the ground to become figure while still paying attention to the ground as ground. To see space we have to reverse our ordinary way of looking at things in the world; it is as if we had to be able to see both the vase and the

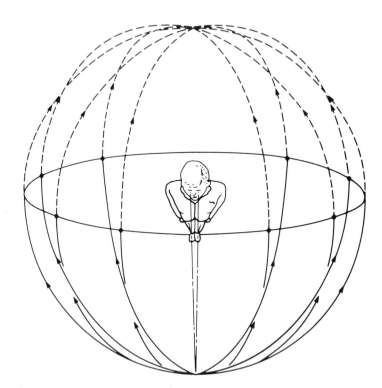

Figure 4-11.   The directions of deformations in the visual field during forward locomotion, as projected on a spherical surface around the head. (*From* The Perception of the Visual World, *by James J. Gibson. Copyright © 1950, renewed 1978. Used by permission of Houghton Mifflin Company.*)

twins simultaneously while still being able to see *either* the vase *or* the twins. To get to space, we have to perceive space. Unfortunately, there is no other ground big enough to serve as a ground for this perception, and so the task is extremely difficult.

3. Cues to perceiving distance. Probably because reversing our ordinary ways of looking at ground is so difficult, psychologists have tried to study space by studying the location and distance of objects in space. Historically, this effort has focused on the question of how a person knows how far away an object is. Here we have a lot of partial answers, mostly in the form of clues or cues to the distance of objects from the perceiver. Since we are primarily visual animals, most books talk about visual space even though it is clear that other senses must contribute to (and cue) our understanding of spatial relations. For vision, cues to the distance of objects are usually grouped according to whether they require one or two eyes. Cues requiring only one eye are called "monocular" or "pictorial" cues; cues requiring two eyes are called "binocular" cues.

Figure 4-12 shows four types of pictorial cues. Su-

perposition is the cue we use when one item is in front of another. Relative size works on the notion that, all other things equal, larger objects look closer. Height in a plane suggests that items lower in the plane are closer. Gradients of texture have been stressed by Gibson as providing a great deal of information not about the object but about the ground on which the object appears. In this case, the texture of the field becomes finer as it gets farther away.

In addition to these four cues, there are linear perspective, aerial perspective, and familiar size. Linear perspective is simply our ordinary perspective, in which parallel lines (such as railroad tracks) meet at the horizon. Aerial perspective takes advantage of the fact that distant objects usually appear more blurred than closer objects, although, as Rock (1975) points out, in the absence of any of the other cues, blurriness does not necessarily give distance. Familiar size is the cue of how big a known object looks; for example, a man who looks small will be seen as farther away than a man who looks much larger.

The major binocular cue is that of **binocular disparity.** It should not be surprising that there is basi-

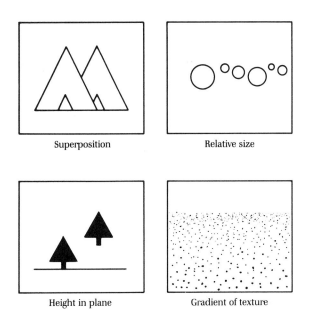

Superposition   Relative size

Height in plane   Gradient of texture

Figure 4-12. Four types of cues used in the perception of distance. (*From* Introduction to Psychology, Fourth Edition, *by Ernest R. Hilgard and Richard C. Atkinson. Copyright © 1967 by Harcourt Brace Jovanovich, Inc. Reproduced by permission of the publisher.*)

cally only one binocular cue, since people with one eye do have depth perception. Then, too, the printed page or the artist's canvas requires only a single eye to see the three-dimensional effects in pictures. Each of our two eyes gets a slightly different picture, and binocular disparity is the name of this difference. Two photographs taken from the positions of the eyes—about 60–70 mm apart—will produce a strong experience of depth if each photograph is shown to the appropriate eye, as in stereoscopic slides.

One class of distance cues is relevant not only to distance but to constancy as well. These cues occur when we are moving around. Movement cues to distance can be seen when riding in a car. As you look out the side window, the ground or bushes close to the car move in a direction opposite to the car's motion. As objects get farther away from the car, the backward motion is slower but is still backward. The distant mountains, however, seem to move with, not opposite, you. In fact, the whole world out of your window seems to be moving in a large circle around a reasonably distant, stationary central point. If you now look out the other window, a similar flow occurs on that side, so that you are at the edge of two flowing circles, one for each window.

Although it is hard to see what is happening above and below you, an airplane trip on a cloudy day produces the situation shown in Figure 4-13. A similar description applies to the road "eaten up" beneath your car or to the flow of trees over your head. With a naive attitude, each of us as we drive a car is at the very center of at least four flows—right, left, above, and below. Although the direction or the relative rate of the flow may tell us something about distance, under ordinary circumstances we feel and act as if we were riding along a stable, nonchanging highway. And indeed, except for the special attitude required to see this remarkable flow, we are.

In one sense our list of cues does have something to do with how we see space. In another sense, it

Figure 4-13. Motion perspective with an overcast or ceiling. (*From* The Perception of the Visual World, *by James J. Gibson. Copyright © 1950, renewed 1978. Used by permission of Houghton Mifflin Company.*)

misses the point entirely. In order for these cues to work in helping us determine the distance of a far-away object, we must already know something about space—something that the cues are cues to. Cues are useful only to the degree that they remind the perceiver of what he or she already knows. If we knew nothing about space, we would not find cues helpful, nor would we be able to develop abstract models of Space such as are given by geometry. The human being is born into space and always lives and moves in space. If this were not true, cues could not give us the appropriate experiences from which to develop a consistent feeling for space.

4. Reflected and unreflected space. To say that the human being lives in space or is a spatial being is not meant to be a fancy statement; it is a statement of fact. To say that the human being is a spatial being does not mean that the human infant, from birth on, has an innate ability to see distance or objects (although present work does tend to support this view). It also does not mean that young children can estimate or measure space very well or even that the infant's perception of space is in any sense identical to the adult's. The child's space is not the adult's space, and the adult's space is not the geometer's Space.

What it does mean is that living bodies move against a ground. Like all other aspects of human behavior, our skill in moving through space (or in thinking about space) must change dramatically as we gain experience in moving through (or thinking about) space. We move in what we will later call space long before we can understand or describe it abstractly, and the space we move in and respond to is ground to our perception of objects and movement. The abstract concept of Space occurs only much later and must surely grow out of our earlier lived experiences in grounded space.

The space we live in and perceive against is best thought of as unreflectedly perceived space, while the Space we theorize about must be a reflectedly created space. Human beings are always in the world, and the unreflected world (space) is the one we are usually in. No less than other aspects of our being in the world, perceiving is always dependent on what we are doing or trying to do. If perceiving is what we are trying to do, then we always have our reasons for perceiving. All perceiving is done by

the person and takes place against the complete context of our world.

IV. PERSONAL FACTORS IN PERCEIVING

What I see, taste, hear, or touch often depends as much (or more) on me as on the world. Of all the possible figures I might see, one stands out *for me.* Similarly, of all the possible grounds I might see this figure against, one presents itself to me as uniquely important. Any description of human perceiving must therefore not only look at the general ways in which figures and grounds appear to *most* people; it must consider some highly specific personal styles of perceiving as well. A few case studies in which the individual perceiver is at issue will help describe the unique contribution of the person in perceiving. Although these case studies all begin in the perceptual laboratory, their implications clearly reach out into the extra-laboratory world of events, objects, and people.

A. Of rods and frames: How to choose a ground
No object in our world stands alone. An object always occurs against some ground, and this combination gives us what we end up perceiving. The fact that our perceptions always occur within some context has suggested the more general notion that all of what we do also occurs in relation to some more global frame of reference. For example, in Chapter 2 I described Coxey's Army. To the men making up the "army," all of their complaints were seen as justified. To the U.S. attorney general opposing them, the marchers were seen to be nothing other than a ragtail group of men pressing for unjustified ends. Depending on one's frame of reference (marcher or attorney general), the event was seen as "just" or "absurd."

The word *see*, as used in the last paragraph, not only means to see some object; it can also mean to see the meaning of some event. Perceiving is such an important topic because its experiences, facts, and processes relate not only to hearing, seeing, and so on but to many other kinds of more general psychological processes. A frame of reference functions not only in seeing lines but in understanding social issues. Accordingly, laboratory demonstrations on perception often have importance far beyond the laboratory.

Consider one of the standard experiments concerning the role of a frame of reference in perceiving, the **rod-and-frame task.** This experiment uses a very simple piece of equipment—a movable rod within a picture frame. The experimental subject's task is to adjust the rod so that it appears vertical. To make this procedure interesting, the frame is often tilted to the right 30 or so degrees.

As Rock (1975) has noted, there are a number of ways a person can resolve the difficulties presented by this situation. Figure 4-14 shows three solutions. If the person orients the rod with regard to his or her body, the result on the left will occur. If the person aligns it with the frame, the middle arrangement will result. What usually happens is shown at the right: the person compromises and ends up with a slightly tilted rod in a very tilted frame.

The reason most subjects compromise is that somehow or other the left-hand configuration looks wrong. If it "looks wrong," the person then has the option of the middle configuration, but here again something is not quite right—the frame is not upright, and therefore it does not "feel" right to adjust the rod to the frame when neither matches the floor sensed through the body. What is surprising about the compromise shown at the right is the very powerful effect of a single empty picture frame: one such frame seems able successfully to oppose our usually upright position. Even though the perceiver never sees the frame as vertical, it is almost impossible to disregard it in setting the rod.

There are, however, situations in which our main frame of reference is tilted and we unhesitatingly perceive the top of the frame as up and the bottom as down. For example, when an airplane banks sharply on takeoff, almost everyone in the plane perceives the cabin ceiling as up, the floor as down, and the seat in front as vertical. In this situation, where the total context is organized in one way, the perceiver falls in step with the pattern, the earth notwithstanding.

Considering these results most broadly suggests that the context within which human beings make contact with the world is extremely powerful in determining what they end up perceiving. Perceiving always takes place within a frame of reference, and we must always keep this in (at least the back of our) mind. In the specific case of the rod and frame, it is possible to talk about "compromise" between body and field (nonbody) cues. Although most perceivers do compromise, different people handle the compromise differently. In 1954 Witkin and his collaborators found that they could group people into those who were very strongly affected by the frame and those who were hardly affected at all. Witkin called the first group of people "field-dependent" and the second "field-independent."

Once these two groups were identified, many interesting possibilities suggested themselves. Are people who depend on their bodies for frames of reference different from those who depend on the visual array? Are there differences according to age such that young children, with perhaps somewhat less well developed body systems, are more (or less) dependent on their bodies than adults?

The answers to both these questions turned out to be quite clear. Having tested a great many children, Witkin answered the second question: field dependence is high for young children of both sexes and declines to a stable level by age 13. At 15, however, early work by Witkin and his associates showed, field-dependence scores rise sharply for

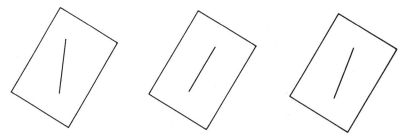

Figure 4-14. Three possible resolutions of the rod-and-frame task. (*From* An Introduction to Perception, *by Irvin Rock. Copyright © 1975 by Irvin Rock. Reprinted with permission of Macmillan Publishing Co., Inc.*)

women and only slightly for men. In answer to the first question, Witkin found that field-dependent young children draw more "primitive" human figures (according to established age norms) than field-independent children. Such findings, in combination with the fact that children are more field-dependent than adults, suggest that the less adequately developed a person's body image, the more likely the person will depend on a frame of reference other than his or her own body.

Thus, results of the rod-and-frame test have taken a very suggestive turn: how we perceive the vertical in dealing with a simple rod and an empty picture frame holds some rather important implications for far more significant matters, such as whether we base our perceptions on ourselves or on aspects of the world other than ourselves. Although other social implications could be drawn

from these results (for example, do field-dependent people respect their own opinions less than those suggested by others), it is enough, for our purposes, to note that who the perceiver is and how he or she selects a particular frame of reference make a big difference in what he or she ends up perceiving. The perceiver is always a part of the world, and what the world looks like to the person must take the particular perceiver into account. This is true whether we are concerned with rods and frames or with more significant matters of everyday living, such as opinions or attitudes.

B. Of windows, rooms, and trapezoids: How to choose a figure

One of the most famous modern illusions was created by Ames in the late 1940s. The **Ames illusion** is seen in Figure 4-15, which shows a man and

Figure 4-15. The Ames room. Is the woman really larger than the man? *(Photographed in the Ames Room, San Francisco Exploratorium. Adapted from* The Ames Demonstrations in Perception, *by W. H. Ittelson. Copyright © 1952 by Princeton University Press. Photo by Kay Y. James.)*

a woman in the photograph. The woman, whose head seems to touch the ceiling, looks much larger than the man. Is she really so huge and the man so small, or can the illusion be understood a bit more reasonably?

The missing piece of information is the shape of the room. Figure 4-16 supplies the missing details. As this diagram shows, the woman standing at the left is much farther from the perceiver. The illusion comes off largely because the back wall and windows are so constructed that they project a rectangular wall with rectangular windows. Since, in the laboratory, the subject looks at the room with one eye, he or she has no information that the room is not rectangular. Under these conditions the person assumes the room is rectangular, and the bizarre result is that women seem to shrink or grow as they cross the room.

Why should this illusion work? Consider a simpler situation: a line at different distances from the observer. Our everyday intuition is that the same-size object "gets smaller" as it moves away, or that it takes a bigger object to project the same-size image from farther away. The general geometric relations for two lines A and B can be drawn as in Figure 4-17. Lines A and B project images equal in size even though the lines themselves are unequal. From a geometric point of view, the "same image" can be produced by different lines.

Suppose we now complicate this diagram by adding lines C, D, E, and F (Figure 4-18). Now, not only do lines A and B produce the same-size geometric pattern, so do a whole family of lines (C through F). An infinite number of lines are also capable of producing the same-size image.

Does this mean that a given geometrical image can be produced by an infinite number of things? Yes; the principle of the line holds true for most of the things we see, "shrinking" and "growing" women included. In the case of the Incredible Growing Women, the family of equivalent events includes at least two objects: a rectangular wall with rectangular windows, viewed straight on, and a trapezoidal wall with trapezoidal windows, viewed obliquely. The perceiver has a choice of which of the two to see.

From this case we can see that perceiving, instead of being a predetermined event, suddenly comes to have a bit of choice to it. As is true of all choosing, however, there are limits to the choice, especially since the object chosen must be one of the family of equivalent configurations. But doesn't choice imply a mind to do the choosing or perhaps an "unconscious decision" about what is out there? The idea of choice would imply a mind only if all behavior were reflected. The whole mode of unreflected behavior, which is a more primary way of dealing with the world, seems very much in place

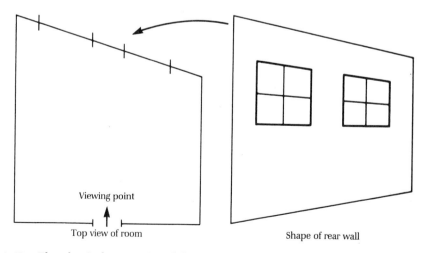

Viewing point

Top view of room

Shape of rear wall

Figure 4-16.   The physical properties of the Ames Room. (*From* An Introduction to Perception, *by Irvin Rock. Copyright © 1975 by Irvin Rock. Reprinted with permission of Macmillan Publishing Co., Inc.*)

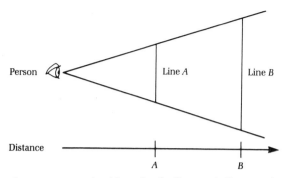

Figure 4-17. Relation between perceived length of a line and distance from perceiver.

in talking about choice in perceiving. The "choice" is given in the choosing: in perceiving, the person does not choose and then perceive; rather, what is perceived reveals what must have been chosen.

In talking about unreflected choosing in perception, it is possible to load the process too much on the side of choosing and thereby miss the constraints imposed by the world. Perceiving is built from two sides—the world's and mine. All perceiving requires the cooperation of me and some object; that is, both I (who I am, what I know, and so on) and the world (the object) co-constitute what it is I will see.

Ames and his coworkers (for example, Ittelson, 1951, 1960) have talked about perceiving in terms of "assumptions" about the world. Ames does not mean that a perceiver can tell in advance what he or she assumes in a given situation. Rather, what is seen reveals what was unreflectedly assumed. It requires a great deal of insight (not to mention an incredible amount of hard theoretical work) to state unreflected assumptions in clear form. This is

exactly what Ames and Ittelson have done: in constructing the trapezoidal room, they have uncovered (and put to work) some aspects of the unreflected world of the perceiver. In so doing they have developed a number of situations that reveal unreflected assumptions at work. Sometimes these assumptions help bring about unremarkable perceptions; at other times they bring about provocative perceptual illusions.

The case of the Ames room only confirms and extends what was suggested so many times previously: All perception takes place within a context, and the person, as well as his or her unreflected assumptions about the world, must be considered an aspect of that context. Every perceptual act also involves an element of choosing, for there would always seem to be a large family of objects capable of producing a given image. Choosing, in turn, implies a reason for one or another choice, and here the reason seems clear enough: to come to some useful and effective way of dealing with the world. The aim of all perception is not only to see

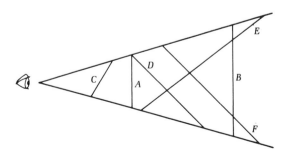

Figure 4-18. A family of lines producing the same-size image.

but to see what is important to me as a human being in my particular situation. We all have reasons for perceiving, the most general of these being to perceive usefully and clearly.

Robert White (1959, 1972) has raised this reason for perceiving to the status of a master motive in human life, the **competence motive,** describing it as an urge to obtain skill or competence in dealing with the world. According to White, this urge is most clearly seen in the playful activity of young children or in the relaxed conditions of adult life. Such playful and relaxed dealings with the world enable us to find out what we need to know about the world, how the world can be changed, and what happens when such changes occur. Such experiences provide us with a world of possibilities as well as with the wherewithal to develop, for whatever purpose, the unreflected world that lies behind our everyday perceptions and lives. Coming to some consistent but flexible orientation in the world is the sober purpose of competence even though that purpose is often first learned in playful or relaxed situations.

Not all of life, however, is playful or relaxed. There are times we are angry, times we are weak, and times we are detached, and each of these moods colors our world. The world of the scientist and the world of the poet differ not only from each other but also from the worlds of the scientist and the poet when they are satisfied, playful, or angry or when they just go about their everyday lives. Thus, the personal situations of perceiving must be considered in any description of perceiving, and it is to this task that we now turn.

C. Of Europe, dirty words, and paying attention: How you choose what you see

Writing around 1900, William James described four men returning from a trip to Europe. Since there were no airplanes or fast ships in those days, most Americans got their impressions of Europe from books or, occasionally, from firsthand observations by American travelers. Consequently, it was always a big event to talk to someone who had been to Europe. One of our four travelers was a gentleman of artistic temperament, one a gentleman of numbers, one a *bon vivant*, and the fourth a grouch. As James put it,

> One [of these men] will bring home only picturesque impressions—costumes and colors, parks and views and works of architecture, pictures and statues. To another all this will be non-existent; and distances and prices, populations and drainage-arrangements, door- and window-fastenings, and other useful statistics will take their place. A third will give a rich account of the theatres, restaurants, and public balls, and naught beside; whilst the fourth will perhaps have been so wrapped in his own subjective broodings as to tell little more than a few names of places through which he passed. Each has selected, out of the same mass of presented objects, those which suited his private interest and has made his experience thereby [1893, pp. 286–287].

These observations are not unusual. The sleeping mother awakens only to the cry of her baby; the home nurse, only to the appeal of his or her patient. Schoolchildren who have been paying almost no attention to their course work will suddenly perk up and be quiet when the teacher tells an anecdote. This is true not only of pleasant events but of unpleasant ones: Who has not turned away from the movie screen and looked elsewhere or shut his or her eyes so as to exclude a horrible movie image? In everyday living we also may shut our eyes or look away when there is something horrible or disfigured to be seen.

What these examples have in common is the tendency of people to select what they will or will not look at. The world presents an enormous array of interesting events, and it is characteristic of every perceiver to emphasize, ignore, unite, or fragment events in his or her world. Despite the seeming chaos, it is clear that human beings often agree on what to select, ignore, unite, fragment, or name. Although there are differences, there are also similarities, so that while each of us may emphasize or ignore some items in the world, we all end up with many of the same perceptions.

This is particularly true for the social world. Here, most of the members of a given society see the world in quite similar ways, particularly in regard to socially important events. Although, as we saw in Chapter 2, different societies may construct different social realities, all members of the same society are guided to "see" the same things. Members may not always admit that their world of everyday reality is partly constructed, but a visitor from some other society will often be able to point it out to them. Only under this new perspective does the world come to look somewhat different, and only in this way do we come to see our own unreflected assumptions at work. The everyday world we see always reflects the perceiver's choice and, like James' four travelers, contains points of difference as well as points of similarity across individual perceivers.

1. Experiments on perceptual defense and perceptual enhancement.

If the role of selecting and excluding is so obvious in everyday life, it is reasonable to ask whether it has been studied in the laboratory. Although much early work was done on attention, most of it had to do with fairly uninteresting events, such as buzzers or lights, and not until the mid-1940s did psychologists take their first new look at selectivity in perceiving. During the ensuing years, psychological work on selectivity in perceiving flowed into well over a thousand reports. Despite this enormous output, there were only two points at issue: **perceptual defense** (the tendency to delay the perception of an unpleasant event) and **perceptual enhancement** (the tendency to accept readily a familiar or personally important perception; under special conditions this is referred to as **perceptual vigilance**).

To start with the most notorious case: In 1949, McGinnies presented a list of 18 words to a group of eight male and eight female subjects. In the relatively tame days back then, 7 of the words were considered taboo, while 11 were seen as fairly neutral. Each word was presented visually for a very brief period—say, .005 second—and the duration of this presentation was gradually increased until the subject was able to report the word being presented. Figure 4-19 shows the results of this experiment for all 18 words for all 16 subjects. Except for the word *filth*, the taboo words took longer to recognize than the neutral words.

In an early experiment on perceptual enhancement, Postman, Bruner, and McGinnies (1948) first selected subjects on the basis of how they answered a questionnaire called the Allport-Vernon Scale of Values. This questionnaire is used to categorize individuals into one of six value groups—Theoretical, Esthetic, Economic, Social, Political, or Religious. Using the same type of procedure as McGinnies had used, Postman et al. found that subjects were able to recognize words in their "dominant value area" much faster than other words. For example, a person having Religion as a high value area would report the word *sacred* more rapidly than a person having Economics as a high value area. The Economic person, however, would report the word *income* faster, and so on for all value areas.

Perceptual enhancement turns into the more restricted case of **perceptual vigilance** when threatening events are presented. Here, the perceiver is thought to be specially attuned to such events and therefore recognizes them more quickly than nonthreatening ones.

2. Early criticisms of these experiments.

Experiments on perceptual enhancement, despite their plausibility, were soon attacked on several grounds. One of the first attacks was made in 1950 by Howes and Solomon, who had two criticisms of the McGinnies "dirty words" study. The first was that McGinnies' subjects were dealing with written

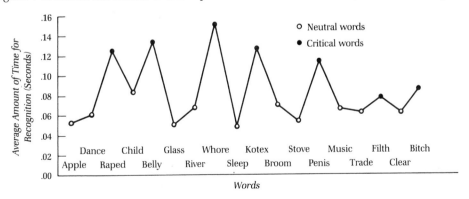

Figure 4-19. Results of the original McGinnies study, showing speed of recognition for 7 control and 11 neutral words.

words, and it was clear (in 1950, at any rate) that so-called taboo words occurred in print much less frequently than nontaboo words and should therefore take longer to recognize than "clean" words. To determine how frequently both clean and dirty words occurred in the language, Howes and Solomon used a book of word norms compiled by Thorndike and Lorge (1944).

The second criticism simply tried to look at things from the subject's point of view. Howes and Solomon argued that higher thresholds, rather than resulting from not *seeing* a taboo word, might be due to the students' reluctance to *say* such words until very confident of what they saw. It is quite one thing to be mistaken and say the word *clear* and quite another to be mistaken and say the word *penis.* Such "suppression" would make reporting take a good deal longer, even in the absence of any perceptual effect at all.

What seemed to be the final argument against perceptual defense was presented by Goldiamond in 1958, a short ten years after the original experiments. In a major experiment, Goldiamond and Hawkins (1958) had subjects see and pronounce a series of nonsense syllables for 1, 2, 5, 10, or 25 trials. Then all subjects were presented with a smudge and asked to report which of the nonsense syllables they thought they saw. To record how fast subjects "saw" these syllables, Goldiamond and Hawkins prepared answer sheets on which they had randomly ordered all the nonsense syllables. A smudge was counted as "correctly seen" when what the subject said matched the experimenter's answer sheet.

Even though in the final test trial no nonsense syllables were presented, only smudges, Goldiamond and Hawkins were able to show the usual finding of more ordinary studies—faster recognition for more frequently experienced items. They concluded that it was not even necessary to talk about perceptual defense; everything seemed to be accounted for on the basis of response bias—how likely subjects were to say a given word in a given context. No defense, no enhancement, no perception: only responses.

Even though Goldiamond's position was extreme, it fit in with many other less extreme ones, which have come to be called the **response bias** position (Dember, 1961). Such a position suggests that great care is needed to ensure that what is being measured in a perceptual-defense experiment has something to do with a person's response to events in the situation. For this reason it is absolutely necessary to rule out simple guessing strategies. One way to do so is to use a signal-detection methodology, which not only is sensitive to such things as response bias but uses such biases as a source of data (see the discussion of signal-detection theory earlier in this chapter).

3. Perceiving emotional items. Although there were other experiments on perceptual defense and perceptual enhancement in the years following Goldiamond's criticism, it remained for Erdelyi in 1974 to take a new look at these experiments. Drawing on a number of experiments, Erdelyi attacked the frequency, response-suppression, and response-guessing arguments head on. Against the frequency argument, for example, he noted that although research had shown a moderately strong relationship between a subject's ability to give the meaning of a neutral word and its frequency according to the Thorndike-Lorge list, no such relationship was found for taboo words. Hence, dirty words are probably more frequently used (and understood) than is suggested by published norms. Against the response-suppression argument—that is, that subjects suppress saying a taboo word until they are sure of it—Erdelyi cited other experiments in which subjects used a neutral word to indicate that they had seen a taboo one and a taboo word to indicate that they had seen a neutral one. Under these conditions taboo words still took longer to report.

The argument against the response-guessing hypothesis is both logical and experimental. Logically, the argument can be stated as follows: "Why should the subject emit the particular (target) word from several thousand likely words, if it isn't in some way related to the word presented?" The Goldiamond and Hawkins experiment, so the argument goes, tricked subjects by giving them false information. Under the conditions of this experiment, the subject did the only reasonable thing possible: guess in accordance with what he or she knew about the situation. Goldiamond's position seemed to suggest (as Erdelyi put it) not only that perceivers were biased but that they were blind as well!

Experimentally, Erdelyi and Appelbaum (1973) were able to show the disruptive effects of emotional stimuli on correct recognition, using a fairly so-phisticated signal-detection method. In their experiment, actively religious Jewish students were briefly shown a circle containing eight items surrounding a single center item. For one group, the center item was a Jewish symbol, the Star of David; for a second group it was a Nazi swastika; for a third group it was a drawing of a window containing the same number of lines as the swastika. When subjects were asked to recognize the array presented to them, the results indicated that they were more accurate in recognizing items having a neutral center element than in recognizing items having an emotional one, whether the emotional item was the star or the swastika.

Although this experiment does not prove perceptual enhancement or perceptual defense, it does present a strong case for the disturbing effects of an emotional event on perceiving. It seems clear that religious subjects paid more attention to an object relevant to them (the Star of David) than to one not relevant to them (the other eight items). Perceptual defense and enhancement aside, it is clear that there is a quite selective aspect to perceiving and that when such selectivity does not relate to the items being recognized, it will slow down the perceiver's ability to recognize them. When it does relate to the items, it will facilitate such recognition.

The laboratory road leading to a clear demonstration of selectivity in perceiving has not been easy to find or follow. And this is odd, especially since common-sense examples—such as the four travelers to Europe—are so very easy to come by. The reason perceptual selectivity has been difficult to demonstrate has nothing to do with whether it exists; it has to do with what many experimenters assumed about the nature of human perceiving. Most psychologists critical of the original perceptual-defense experiments seemed to think of perceiving as fitting the following simple scheme:

A.		B.		C.
Stimulus system	$\longrightarrow$	Perceptual system	$\longrightarrow$	Response system

Given this analysis, defense or enhancement could occur only at point A or B. Any selectivity occurring at point C could only be considered a response effect. Such an analysis of human perceiving is far too simple to do justice to the facts. First, it is always the total person who perceives—never a stimulus system, a perceptual system, or a response system. Second, there is no reason to consider that perceiving always (and exclusively) "flows in" from the outside. The human being is a living, choosing being, not a passive receiver of inputs. The real problem with this kind of single-level scheme is that it attempts to divide the living person into subparts and then to deny that the person is involved in any active way with either the world or his or her "subparts."

Finally, both the early proponents and opponents of perceptual defense seem to have taken the idea of a threshold out of context and at face value. If there is one thing we now know about thresholds, it is that they cannot be described as a type of gate that gets lowered or raised. "Higher thresholds for defense; lower thresholds for enhancement" suggests a far too mechanical and context-free analysis of how the human being sees words presented rapidly. Thresholds are always the outcome of what a particular person does in a particular situation in regard to a particular word; any analysis that removes thresholds from the person and the world is oversimplified. It is thinking of this type that brings about the single-level analysis described above.

4. Paying attention. The role of the person in perceiving is nowhere easier to see than in the phenomenon we usually call paying attention, a phenomenon that occurs in the world of every day as in the laboratory. A very obvious everyday example is the so-called **cocktail-party phenomenon**: in all the hubbub and noise of a cocktail party, the human being notes and understands what another person is saying even if a tape recording made in the same situation would give us only noise when replayed. Unlike the tape recorder, we selectively filter noise and hear sense.

It was observations of this type that gave a good push to recent attempts at understanding how human beings go about the seemingly magical process of **selective attention.** For reasons known only to history, the major investigators have been British, and here the early work of Colin Cherry (1953) and Donald Broadbent (1958) comes to mind. In Cherry's early studies, for example, subjects were asked to "shadow" stories presented to them via earphones—that is, to repeat back each word they heard as they heard it. Although this sounds like a fairly difficult task, it is quite easy. What Cherry was interested in, however, was not only how well the listener shadowed the material presented to one ear but what happened when different material was presented to the other ear and the listener was not asked to shadow it. Could the listener report this "unshadowed" material later?

Even though these experiments were done informally, results were clear: listeners were able to report voice changes (from male to female), tone changes, and even their names on the nonshadowing ear. What they were not able to report was also quite interesting. They did not notice changes in topic, changes from prose to poetry and back again, or even changes from English to French. It seems fair to say that subjects were able to report events from the nonshadowing ear that did not require them to interpret the meaning of those events.

Although this is a plausible description, the case of paying attention to one's name on the nonshadowing ear is particularly interesting. In the original study by Moray (1959)—also an Englishman—the usual shadowing procedure was used. The message presented to the nonshadowing ear was sometimes prefaced by the listener's name and sometimes not. When the message was preceded by the listener's name, the message was responded to even though presented to the nonshadowing ear.

Similar findings for the nonshadowing ear have been reported by Treisman. In one study, Treisman (1964) asked English/French bilingual listeners to ignore a French message played in one ear and to pay attention only to the English message played in the other ear. At first, the two messages were different. After a time the message presented in French was a translation of the English message. Under this condition many listeners reported that the messages were the same.

One thing these studies show is that certain types of meaningful material "force themselves" in on us and that in some sense we must be listening to nonshadowed messages some, if not all, of the time (Neisser, 1967). This seems consistent with the everyday observation that an automobile driver often does many things other than simply drive the car. Generally speaking, you or I can drive while talking to someone else, listening to the radio, looking at the person in the next car, having a fantasy, and so on. We very rarely hit another car. It seems that although there is a clear central sector to our experience, there is also a nonreflected "fringe" that

can become figural should the need arise. In driving, we may "switch off" our fantasies, radios, or conversations as we come to a dangerous intersection and then switch them back on when the intersection is past. The human being attends to events in the environment that demand attention as well as to those events he or she specifically selects to pay attention to.

Attending, then, is not a single-level event. At a minimum, any description must distinguish between reflected and unreflected attending. Almost all the shadowing studies make use of **reflected attention;** that is, the listener is told to make one message figure and the other fringe. Yet, as Moray's and Treisman's work suggests, the fringe ear does not turn off; rather, the person deals nonreflectedly (what Neisser has called "preattentively") with most of the message, bringing the fringe into focus only when the message might be something important for the person to know about or might be in agreement with the meaning of the figural message. These studies deal only with reflected attending, and only because it is impossible to detach the nonshadowing ear from the person do we find evidence for the less obvious process of nonreflected attending.

As a matter of fact, it seems reasonable to conclude that reflected attention, though much more obvious, is much less significant than **unreflected attention.** We do not bump into cars, chairs, or buildings although we hardly ever pay direct attention to them. Similarly, athletes do not "use" attention as a special faculty to guide their movements; rather, it seems better to say that the athlete attends to his or her task alone and that there is a loss of reflected attending during the course of the contest. Selecting and attending are not properties of rational thinking alone; they are characteristic of human functioning and, as such, are involved in all sorts of human behavior, perceptual and otherwise.

5. A conclusion or two. Case studies are interesting; general conclusions are better. What are we to conclude from the three sets of case studies presented? To start with the last one first: Perceiving is not a simple or unitary process; it includes a lot of selecting and disregarding. On what basis does such selecting occur? Here we must come back to a very general property of all human behavior: intentionality. To select (or reject) always implies a reason for selecting or not selecting a certain thing, and research suggests that we select, and are selected by, events that are important to us as people. Events can be personally important because they deal with me directly (they call my name), because they might be dangerous if not perceived (a stopped car in front of me), because they might be dangerous if seen (a horrible accident on the road), or because they are meaningful to me as a person (a Star of David for a Jewish person). In perceiving, as in all behaving, we must always take the person's intentions into account.

The theoretical need to take intentionality into account in perceiving is strongest in cases in which people select aspects of their world for further note or further action. This means that the total person is always involved in any perceptual act. Whether we are dealing (as in the present chapter) with synesthesia, figure/ground articulation, or a person's past experiences, it is the total person who is at issue. An understanding of perceiving is a primary concern for any attempt to understand the more general nature of the human being, for in perceiving we see the operation neither of a totally rational being nor of one passively submitting to the world. What we see is a human being committed to making sense of his or her world and to trying to deal with that world in a personally meaningful way.

Perceiving, however, does not deal only with the perceiver; it always occurs in some context, or setting. In certain situations, trapezoidal rooms appear rectangular, and we may have difficulty saying which side is up. What we see, hear, feel, taste is always perceived against some background, and in the absence of such background, perceiving is confused and confusing. Objects and events always carry with them one or another background, whether it be that of my body or some other aspect of the perceptual world, and their relation to that background is crucial to what I end up perceiving.

Everywhere we turn, perceiving involves a series of relationships: relationships among such things as who I am, what is important to me, what the world presents, what I choose or reject, what situation I find myself in, and so on. Perceiving deals with patterns, and any attempt to understand perception must always concern itself with the patterns of our unique and very individual perceptual worlds.

V. SUMMARY

Perceiving is an activity that can be considered only in the context of all that is involved—a unique balance among the perceiver, the world, and the situation. Psychologists do a disservice to the topic of perceiving by trying to dissect it into components in order to experiment with each one separately. Although thresholds may "exist" a certain percentage of the time (for example, a person can taste less than 1 teaspoon of sugar in 2 gallons of water), early concepts of psychophysics, which assume a separation between matter and mind, can be misleading. Evidence of this is presented by experiments described from the signal-detection point of view in which expectancies and payoffs have both been found to affect a person's ability to detect "a stimulus." Technological advances, such as stereophonic sound, may come about on the basis of studying sensory experiences in isolation. A more accurate understanding of perceiving, however, must encompass the act, the actor, and the particular environment all as a single event.

The need for considering the person in any description of perceiving can be understood more readily by studying cross-sense experiences called "synesthesia." For instance, music need not only be heard; it can also be seen, tasted, and even felt—that is, experienced from many different but integrated sensory points of view. The phrase *point of view* suggests that sensory experience (like all perceiving) occurs within a frame of reference. No perceptual experience ever takes place in isolation.

The concepts of figure and ground are important in understanding perceiving. My response to any figure/ground pattern may be highly individualistic, but similarities do exist among perceivers. Factors that organize separate items into figures include nearness, continuity, and closure. All these can be seen as but different aspects of the law of Pragnanz, which says that "good" figures tend to be regular, simple, and internally consistent. Figures with these attributes tend to be the ones most often seen.

The field, or ground, within (and upon) which a figure is perceived also affects perception of the figure, even in so simple a case as that of a gray ring. Contrast, color, distance, angle, size, shape, position, and meaning all play an important role in how one perceives things. Each of these factors can serve to highlight one or another aspect of any given event, thereby changing what the figure will be like for me in the present context.

The most important ground for all of our perceptions is the full, rich, textured world we encounter outside the experimental laboratory. Gibson has been most effective in describing the character of lived space (not the same as abstract Space) and the role of context gradients in our ability to see distance. Such gradients place objects in space in an unchanging way and thereby serve as reliable indicators of how far away an object is or might be.

One important property of human perceiving in all contexts is that we are selective. Although it is possible to deal with this fact in different ways, the most direct interpretation would seem to be that we select (and are selected by) events that are important for and to us. The quest after personal meaning may explain why it is possible for fellow travelers to bring back strikingly different accounts of the same trip. It also helps us understand phenomena as diverse as perceptual defense and enhancement as well as all the phenomena we usually describe under the topic of "attention."

Although it may be too strong to say that the perceiver is free to choose among alternative perceptions, it does not seem too strong to conclude that the world and the perceiver jointly co-constitute what is seen. The "choices" a perceiver makes are not arbitrary; they include unreflected elements of one's past experiences, present feelings, needs, desires, hopes, and attitudes. In this, they express the very general property of all human behaviors—intentionality. In perceiving, as in all behaving, we must always take the person's intentions (reflected and unreflected) into account. The total person is involved in any perceptual act, and to miss this point is perhaps to miss what human perceiving is all about.

VI. GLOSSARY OF IMPORTANT CONCEPTS

Absolute threshold. The smallest amount of stimulation that can be perceived, usually defined as that point at which a stimulus is perceived 50% of the time. The "absolute" threshold is never absolute; it depends greatly on such factors as the context, whether the intensity of the stimulation is varied from least to greatest or vice versa, the expected frequency of the stimulus, and the consequences of perceiving and misperceiving.

Ames illusion. The distortion in size produced by placing an object in a special room. The room is built so that, from a front view, the back wall is perceived as being perpendicular to the line of sight when, in fact, one back corner of the room is much farther away than the other.

Binocular disparity. The slight difference between the retinal images of the two eyes caused by their separation; thought to be involved in the perception of depth.

Cocktail-party phenomenon. Ability to make sense of a conversation in a mixture of noise.

Competence motive. The urge to obtain skill in dealing with the world, elevated to a master motive by Robert White. It has been described as one of the major aims of perception.

Context effect. Changes in the perception of a figure brought about by the ground, or context, against which it is perceived.

Contrast effect. A phenomenon in which a quality of a figure is made to seem more extreme by a contrasting ground. For example, a gray figure is made darker by a white background or lighter by a black background.

Figure. That part of a perceptual array which is salient. What gets looked at.

Gestalt. A form, structure, or pattern; that which emerges out of the relation between figure and ground; a perceptual whole. Factors that organize elements into a Gestalt are nearness, continuity, closure, and similarity.

Ground. The context in which a perceptual object (or figure) occurs and against which it is perceived. In contrast with the figure, the ground seems more indistinct in form, less like a thing (more indefinite), farther away, and less easily identified.

Law of Pragnanz. The idea that perceived figures tend to demonstrate certain properties, such as regularity, simplicity, and consistency.

Perceptual constancy. The stability of an object's color, size, shape, and so on, even when it undergoes a spatial or temporal transition in relation to the perceiver.

Perceptual defense. The tendency not to perceive (that is, to defend against) stimuli that are threatening to the perceiver.

Perceptual enhancement. The tendency to recognize a personally significant figure more readily than a personally unimportant one.

Perceptual vigilance. The tendency to recognize unpleasant or personally threatening events more readily than neutral ones; a variety of perceptual enhancement.

Psychophysics. A method for studying the limits of sensory-perceptual systems. The method originally implied an attempt to discover the relationship between physical and psychological dimensions.

Reflected attention. Attention, in the conventional meaning of the phrase "to pay attention." Deliberate action with respect to one thing in particular and not another or the choice of one arrangement over another. The obvious thing people do when told "Look at (listen to, taste, smell) this."

Response bias. The tendency of a perceiver to respond in ways predictable from previous experience in similar situations.

Reversible figure. A figure that seems to undergo change because its components alternate as figure and as ground, such as the Rubin twins/vase figure.

Rod-and-frame task. A laboratory procedure designed to explore the influence of a frame of reference on perception of the upright. The apparatus consists of a rod and frame, both movable. When asked to place the rod vertical, some subjects are influenced by the tilt of the frame.

Selective attention. Attending to the relevant portion of experience as defined by the person. For example, a person can understand what is being said at a loud cocktail party even though an audiotape would record only noise.

Synesthesia. A phenomenon in which stimulation of one sense leads to an experience usually associated with another sense—for example, on hearing music a person "sees" colors and shapes.

Unreflected attention. The fringe of our attention (outside the focal center of attention). Most of the time that we move in a familiar environment, our attention is of this sort. When the message on the fringe of attention becomes personally important, we center reflected attention on it.

VII. SUGGESTED READINGS

Major sources

Gibson, J. J. *The perception of the visual world.* Boston: Houghton Mifflin, 1950.

Köhler, W. *Gestalt psychology.* New York: New American Library, 1947.

Merleau-Ponty, M. *The phenomenology of perception.* London: Routledge and Kegan Paul, 1962. Part 2, Chapters 1–3.

Neisser, U. *Cognitive psychology.* New York: Appleton-Century-Crofts, 1967.

Secondary sources

Haber, R. N., & Hershenson, M. *The psychology of visual perception.* New York: Holt, Rinehart & Winston, 1973.

Rock, I. *An introduction to perception.* New York: Macmillan, 1975.

5

Thinking and Creating

Genuine human thinking has much the same grace and power as the flight of an eagle. When the eagle soars, dives, or rides an air current, we sense its skill, its beauty, and its seeming aloofness. Should our own thinking fly as the eagle flies, we surely would soon lose contact with much of our familiar intellectual landscape—and yet only during moments of flight is it possible for us to experience a new point of view.

If thinking can be like this, why do we often talk about it as dry and unemotional? The answer concerns the fact that human beings are able to separate thinking from other types of doing. Advice such as "Think before you act" means there are important advantages in planning how to do something before you get down to the business of doing it. It is surely much wiser and easier to figure out how your clock or car works before you take it apart than to take it apart first and try to figure out how it works later.

Although "Think before you act" is a good motto, it can have far-reaching side effects. If you *always* think before you act, you may find that you are not doing very much and that when you do do something, it is not very exciting, especially if you have figured out in advance what will happen. Too much planning (thinking in advance of doing) produces an unemotional and flat existence. It is just this kind of superplanned life that gives the feeling that thinking must be dull and is only a preparation for future doings.

I. THINKING AS A HUMAN ACT

If, however, we recognize thinking as a unique way of relating to and of being related to our world, then thinking stops being a preface to action and becomes an activity in its own right. A life spent in authentic thinking—thinking which involves the person completely and which seeks to go beyond itself—can be as exciting as a life spent in hurrying about. If we approach thinking with the same gusto as jumping, dancing, or playing tennis, we open up one more possible way of relating to the world as a total human being. Complex books on logic notwithstanding, thinking need not be dry.

History provides many examples of just how ex-

citing thinking can be. Take Archimedes and his famous cry "Eureka!"—"I've got it!" The year is something or other B.C.; the place, Syracuse, Sicily. Archimedes is royal physicist to the court of Hiero. As the story opens, Hiero has presented Archimedes with a problem: "Here is a crown," Hiero says, "supposedly of pure gold. Yet, I suspect it has some silver mixed in. How should we find out whether it is made of pure gold or mixed with silver?"

Archimedes accepts the task (not that he has any real choice—Hiero is king). He knows from the work of many people that different metals have different weights per unit volume, so that if he could melt the crown into a brick and compare its weight with that of a same-size brick of pure gold, he could easily solve the king's problem. To do that, however, would be to destroy the crown; hence the problem remains, and remains and remains.

For long days Archimedes is obsessed with the problem; it gives him no rest and he gives it no rest. One day, tired from his labors, he goes to the baths. There, surrounded by slave girls, perfumes, and steamy air, Archimedes, giving himself over to bathing, steps into the tub and sits down. A very ordinary thing happens: the level of his bathwater rises above the level it had before he stepped in. He absent-mindedly notes this fact and returns to the heat and luxury of the bath.

Suddenly, without benefit of towel, he jumps up and shouts: "Eureka—I've got it!" And what exactly has he got? The solution to Hiero's problem. If an object—his body—placed in water displaces a regular amount of water, then the amount by which the water level rises could be used as a simple measure of volume. If this is true for his body, it should also be true for other irregularly shaped objects—particularly crowns made of gold. In just this way did Archimedes decide how to measure the volume of Hiero's crown, and in just this way did he come to a general theory of the displacement of bodies in water. No wonder he jumped from the tub shouting "Eureka!"—not only had he solved the specific problem at hand, he had made a general discovery that ultimately would lead to the physical law known as Archimedes' principle.

Genuinely inventive thinking of the type done by

Archimedes is neither dull nor unemotional. If we take this story as our text, we are struck by the fact that it is a complete person who thinks and gets excited by thinking—not only, nor even mainly, some special part called "mind." It is the person Archimedes who is concerned with the king's problem; it is the person Archimedes who bodily jumps from the tub; and it is the person Archimedes who shouts "Eureka!" The idea of thinking as going on in some unique or special part of the person is belied by this case history of human thinking.

A. William James and the stream of consciousness

All this still leaves us with the problem of describing what we mean when we say a human being *thinks*. Although no one has ever given a perfectly satisfactory definition, William James (1890/1950) did give us a list of characteristics that he felt captured the nature of human thinking.

Although we will use James' list to help us describe thinking, James himself wavered between using this list as a description of all of adult experience and more narrowly as a description of human thinking. Since thinking is a part of the more general **stream of consciousness,** nothing will be lost in considering the list more narrowly in regard to thinking. In this we follow the master.

James' list, updated and compressed, boils down to five major points:

1. Every thought is always part of some person.
2. Within each person, thinking is always changing.
3. Within each person, thinking is always sensibly continuous.
4. Thinking always *seems* to deal with objects, events, or experiences independent of itself.
5. Thinking always selects among its objects and events.

James' first point simply tells us that no thought ever exists independent of a thinker. It is always "I think," never just "thoughts exist." For this reason, any description of thinking must take the thinker—the I—into account: who I am, what language I speak, how much I know, and so on. Thinking is always done by some person, whether the person does it with an uppercase I or not.

The idea of thinking as flight is captured in James' second and third points. Indeed, it was James who first compared human thinking to the life of a bird, consisting, as he put it "of an alternation of flights and perchings." Although James had a somewhat smaller bird in mind than our eagle, his analogy was meant to emphasize that thinking seems to have two parts: one that deals with content, such as images, ideas, or thoughts, and a second that deals with transitions between such points of content.

If we think casually about our own thinking, we sometimes feel that it consists only of "**stopping points**"—ideas, images, and so on. This suggests that thinking is not the flight of some great (or small) bird, but rather is better described as a train of ideas tied together because they have followed one another in the past and continue to do so in the present. Instead of describing thinking as a train or even a bird's flight, James suggests that we think of it as a stream. By this word picture, James means to suggest that a person's mental life is continuous and should not be described as a series of separate railroad cars only loosely connected to one another. The stream of conscious experience is unbroken.

Perhaps the major reason it is tempting to describe thinking (or, more generally, conscious experience) as a train or a chain is that our ideas and images are much more compelling than the transitions between them. Transitions are often difficult, if not impossible, to capture directly. If transitions are but flights to a conclusion, to stop the flight before it comes to its conclusion is to destroy it. If, however, we wait for the next conclusion, this new junction is ever so much more vivid than the transition to it, and again we miss the transition for the stopping point.

To catch a glimpse of transitions in the stream of our mental life, we need to approach them from the side, unawares. Here James suggests we think of our experience of such words as "Wait!," "Look!," or "Watch out!" Aside from unreflected differences in the bodily reactions produced, each word also brings about a distinctive and unique anticipation. Although we never know in advance what it is we are waiting, looking, or watching out for, we all do experience a distinct feeling of waiting, looking, or watching.

The purpose of this discussion is to restore transitions and similar events, such as anticipations, to their proper place in the stream we call "thinking." Thinking is not composed of content alone, such as images and ideas that stand like solid parts in the stream; rather, what we call thinking is the stream itself. Perhaps there are no preexisting islands within the stream until we develop them. Ideas and thoughts cannot exist independent of the thinking of them. Thinking brings them into existence rather than discovering them as always having been there. To be sure, a new idea (once thought) will be available for us again. For this reason, thinking is not only the discovery of preexisting ideas but also their actual creation and re-creation. Perhaps we often feel that ideas have a preexisting life because we glance at them over our shoulder rather than in front of us. It is only in retrospect that an idea is solid and clear; in prospect nothing may have been there but a sense of imbalance, or what many thinkers have called a "gap"—an unreflected opening in the ongoing stream.

The conclusion suggested by James' analysis must be that thinking has two parts, one clear and the other vague. The first part consists of ideas, images, thoughts, and so on—those parts of consciousness that can be easily recognized and held onto. Round about these "solid" places is a halo, an overtone, or a fuzzy fringe. Thus, thinking has both a main line and a fringe, and when we speak of a train of thought or a chain of logic, we really are talking only about the main line, hardly ever about its more smudgy transitional flow.

B. Objects of thought: Focus and fringe

Adult human thinking, to come to James' fourth point, always appears to deal with objects independent of itself. We always seem able to step back from our stream and reflect it so as to make the process of thinking appear as an object of thinking. Philosophers have concluded that reflected consciousness is necessary for there to be any thinking at all; that is, not until a human being is able to take a third-person point of view of some activity is it proper to talk of thinking. The ability of human beings to take an objective point of view is usually what is meant by such terms as *ego* or, more philosophically, *cogito*—in short, by all the terms psychologists and philosophers use to specify that reflected thought occurs.

Although thinking can and often does differentiate between itself and its content, it need not always do so. Consider the situation of watching a movie or listening to a record. We say that the movie *involves* you just to the degree that you become so engrossed in what is going on in the film that you have no experience whatever of you as separate from it. If the film catches you, it catches all of you. Even if occasionally you do come back to you as-sitting-in-this-dark-place, in-this-comfortable-chair, next-to-this-or-that-person, this occurs only when you are "bored" by the picture. An engrossing event has its own presentness, which does away with the experience of "me watching me watch a movie." To be sure, it is *me* who watches the movie or listens to the record, but there are no secure boundaries to personal experience during that moment. I am "there" with the events of the movie, rather than "here" in my chair watching the movie. It is only an objective, or third-person, point of view that gives Me *and* the Movie, rather than Me/Movie/Me/Movie....

Thinking, then, only *appears* to be separate from its object, and then only at some times. At other times, my consciousness includes and is included by its "object." For this reason, it seems appropriate to say that the movie (or any "object of thinking") is never independent of the person attending to it. Since thinking consists of not only a **focus** but a **fringe** as well, it seems reasonable to describe an object of thinking not as a single, clearly defined object but rather as the total first-person experience of the event—fringe, thinker, and all.

With this extended (and perhaps vague) notion of a mental object, we all know that certain objects more completely capture a person than others. That is James' fifth point: not all objects move from fringe to focus with equal ease. Although this property of thinking was also seen in selective perceiving (see Chapter 4), it is equally obvious in reasoning. The successful thinker—the man of genius, as James called him—is one "who will always stick in his bill at the right point and take out the right element—'reason' if the emergency be theoretical, 'means' if it be practical.... [This view] suffices to show that Reasoning is but another form of ... selective activity" (1890/1950, p. 287).

The gospel according to James concludes that human conscious experience always involves a number of simultaneous possibilities. Acts of thinking use the threefold ability to select, throw away, and ignore. Fortunately, what I choose to select often agrees with what you choose to select. Since we usually name what we select, it is fair to conclude that most of the people in a given society agree on what they will name and notice, or notice and name.

Despite our usual agreement, there is one extraordinary case in which no two persons (even in the same society) ever select exactly alike. There is, as James said, one "great splitting of the universe made by each of us." In this split there is almost always one part in which I am more interested. If, along with James, we call these parts Me and Not-Me, it is clear which part is the more important. No matter how hard I try, I can never be as interested in the Not-Me as in the Me, in the Yours as in the Mine. My *Me* always stands out against the ground of my Not-Me, which, whether you like it or not, includes You. Fortunately for You, however, you feel the same way about your Me and Not-Me, and consequently you and I split the world at different places.

What seems important in James' model of conscious experience is that I am the unique center of my world, that my conscious experiences are sensibly continuous (even if changing), and that although I may have some inkling of a special part of the world known as "mind," I often think with sufficient force and excitement to overrun the more narrowly defined banks of the stream of my mental life. Human consciousness is always much larger than rational thinking.

C. The daydreamer and the fisherman

Almost all writers concerned with human thinking make a distinction between thinking that is relatively free-flowing and thinking undertaken to solve a problem. Pollio (1974) has termed the corresponding styles of thinkers the **Daydreamer** (in honor of Marcel Proust's narrator in the book *Swann's Way*) and the **Fisherman** (in honor of Hemingway's hero in the book *The Old Man and the Sea*). Proust's narrator is a dreamy fellow, given to going along with his stream of ideas in a haphazard and undirected way. Hemingway's fisherman is an extraordinarily planful man who approaches his task, catching the fish, with care and order.

For the Daydreamer, the flow of ideas moves from one to another in an informal and somewhat chaotic way. For the Fisherman, thinking is directed, has a clear purpose, and frequently bends back on itself to see how well it is doing. For planful thinking, the total sequence of thoughts and ideas can be described as under the overall control of a single idea, such as "Solve the problem." In more

leisurely (or at least less planful) thinking, one idea seems to connect fairly directly with the next. The type of thinking done by the Daydreamer is technically called **associative thinking**, while that done by the Fisherman is called **directed thinking**.

II. ASSOCIATIVE THINKING

The idea of an associative flow, such as A→B→C→D→E ..., suggests that Idea A usually makes us think of Idea B, that Idea B makes us think of C, C of D, and so on. Although Idea A may also have connections with Ideas C, D, E, and so on, it is the pairing of adjacent items (A-B, B-C, C-D, etc.) that directs the overall sequence as experienced.

A. Word association

If associative thinking involves pairs of items, it should be possible, in part, to see how associative processes work by looking at what human beings do when asked to give one response to one word. In word-association tasks a person is given a single word, such as *book*, and is asked to give the first other word that comes to mind. The first thing to note about this procedure is how simple and easy it is to do; no one ever has any problem in producing a response.

From so simple a procedure it is possible to get a great many different responses, and it is reasonable to wonder whether all words have the same or roughly similar patterns of response. The answer is no. For example, the word *boy* most often produces the word *girl* as a response (for 77 to 100 respondents). *Long* often produces *short* (76/100); *man*, *woman* (.77); *woman*, *man* (.65). Not all words have such high-probability responses: *cheese* produces *crackers* 11% of the time; *baby* produces *boy* 16% of the time. The pattern of responses to a given word, ranked in order of frequency, is called the **associative response hierarchy** for the word. Words such as *boy* and *long*, which produce a small number of different words as responses, are said to have steep associative response hierarchies; words such as *cheese* and *baby*, which produce many responses, are said to have flat ones.

Given the existence of unequal probabilities, it is reasonable to wonder whether they relate to other differences in verbal activity. One positive answer to this question is that the higher the probability of a response, the faster it is given. This fact of word association, discovered about a century ago by a German psychologist named Karl Marbe, is called Marbe's law.

1. Word association and creativity. Building on this type of research work, Mednick (1962) and his collaborators (Mednick & Andrews, 1967; Mednick, Mednick, & Jung, 1964) suggested that different people have different tendencies in producing responses. Some people produce a great many different responses to almost any word; others produce only one or a few. Probably the most important consequence to draw from these differences is that people having no single dominant response ought to be more creative than people who always tend to have a single dominant response. This idea, in fact, has been the major assumption behind much of Mednick's work on creativity.

To understand this assumption, we must begin with Mednick's analysis of the creative process. This analysis assumes that creative thinking involves making new and useful combinations from old elements. As an example, Mednick reports that a well-known physicist trains for creative thinking by randomly picking items out of the index in an introductory physics text and trying to relate them to a single (new) idea. Obviously, if he gets *force* and *mass*, he draws again; for only if the items drawn are not already related will the exercise have any effect. Mednick notes that what the physicist is trying to do is to establish new connections between unrelated or remotely related elements. His exercise should therefore facilitate the essential aspect of any creative act: producing novel connections among initially remote elements.

To measure how well people can produce such connections, Mednick developed a test he calls the **Remote Associates Test** (RAT). As examples of items on this test, look at the following four sets of words and try to supply the one word that "makes sense" in connection with the three given. As you do this task, occasionally "bend back" on your own thinking and see how you would describe what it is you are doing. Answers are given in a footnote at the end of this chapter.

Set 1   railroad   girl   class

_____

Set 2   surprise   line   birthday

_____

Set 3   wheel   electric   high

_____

Set 4   out   dog   cat

_____

If the answer is immediately obvious (as it is for me in Set 3), the task seems little more than an exercise in word association: all three words are followed by the same word, which makes sense for all three. Set 1 requires a bit more ingenuity, for although both *girl* and *class* follow a certain word, it takes more thinking to recall that an admittedly familiar folk song links that word with *railroad*.

The actual items used on the RAT are somewhat more difficult than these. Even such simple examples, however, tell us something about how one word gets together with another: they both suggest or are suggested by the same word. In the RAT, the word we are to find is called the "mediating word" because it mediates between the words given.

2. Continuous word association. Typical studies of word association use only a single pair of words. If the psychological laboratory is to approach the idea of a stream of associations experimentally, the person ought to be asked for more than a single response. Studies of **continuous word association** do exactly this: each subject is given a single word, such as *house* or *flower*, and is asked to give as many other words as he or she can that are suggested by the original word.

One of the earliest studies of this type was done by Bousfield and Sedgewick in 1944. The first result they found was that subjects tended to run out of associations: after producing 5, 10, or 20 responses, the person said "That's it; I can't give any more." Bousfield and Sedgewick then took a careful look at the sequence of responses produced by their subjects and found that no subject ever produced all 5, 10, or 20 responses at an even rate. Instead, subjects tended to cluster their responses in time, then pause, then produce another cluster, then pause, and so on. The words contained in any one burst seemed to go together. For example, if subjects were asked to name all the pieces of *furniture* they could think of, the record might look like this: *table, chair, sideboard, sink, dishwasher, breadbox,* (pause) *bed, chair, dresser, mirror, lamp,* (pause) *sofa, TV set, table, bookcase,* and so on. It is easy to see the pattern here: first the person named items found in the kitchen, then in the bedroom, then in the living room. Thus, ideas were produced in related bunches that made sense together. As in James' stream of consciousness, continuous-word-association records give evidence both for solid islands (word clusters) and for periods of transition. In this, the word-association task makes contact with more general properties of human thinking.

B. Daydreaming

The associative stream studied in the psychology laboratory comes nowhere near the complexity of the associative stream each of us experiences in our private lives. For this reason, it is necessary to step outside the laboratory and look directly at the phenomenon we started with: **daydreaming**. After Proust's daydreamer Marcel, perhaps the most famous bit of literary daydreaming was done by Molly Bloom in James Joyce's *Ulysses* (1934). In her daydream, Molly begins by being impatient and then angry at having to wait for her husband. Having nothing to do, and unable to fall asleep, she looks around her apartment. In looking around, she notices the clock, the wallpaper, and other objects immediately at hand. Each of these objects serves as a starting point for a chain of thoughts. Ultimately, her images all melt together until finally Molly gets back to the days of her courtship with Leopold, most particularly to the first time she said yes to him, and on this note she drifts off to sleep.

In commenting on Molly's daydream, Singer (1966) notes that she comes progressively to give herself over to it particularly when her wake-a-day situation is experienced as monotonous. For us, as for Molly, daydreaming usually takes place during quiet or boring times: just before sleep, on a train, while waiting for someone, or as an escape from an unpleasant situation. Singer is quite emphatic in pointing out that most daydreaming is not done as a fantasy escape from unpleasant events or as wish-fulfilling; rather, it occurs in situations in which the person is not held by present interest. The reason for daydreaming would seem to be providing the person with an opportunity to do something more exciting than what is going on at present.

What little evidence there is on the amount of daydreaming shows it to be remarkably widespread. Singer found that 96% of the people who responded to a questionnaire reported that they engaged in some sort of daydreaming every day. Most people did not report that they engaged in wish-fulfilling or escape daydreams; rather, the most frequently reported daydreams concerned future plans and events. Although many of Singer's respondents did have frequent daydreams concerning sexual activities or personal achievement, it seems best to look on daydreaming not as wish-fulfilling but as "attempts at exploring the future. . . . The predominant content . . . seems to reflect a fairly practical concern with life situations" (Singer, 1966, p. 58).

In addition to giving us clues to content, the case of Molly Bloom suggests that daydreaming occurs most often between wakefulness and sleep: either when going to bed or when waking up. Although hard and fast estimates are extremely scarce, McKellar (1957) found that 63% of the people he interviewed experienced one or another kind of daydream before going to sleep and that about 21% reported such daydreams in the drowsy state before being fully awake in the morning.

As Singer notes, most daydreams—his own particularly—do not necessarily withdraw the daydreamer from the world or substitute fantasy for achievement. Rather, daydreams often serve to make an unstimulating situation more exciting and to help in future planning. As one advocate of autonomous imagery, Robert McKim (1972), put it, "Daydreaming possesses the paradoxical characteristic of purposeful-purposelessness" (p. 95). He means that daydreaming can be used productively in helping us gain access to a significant source of possibly innovative imagery.

To find out at what ages people daydream most often, Singer asked respondents to report how often they remembered daydreaming at various ages. Generally speaking, daydreaming reached its greatest peak between 18 and 27 years, with decreases reported up to age 50. Because no elderly people were included in this study, it is unknown whether such decreases would continue. It seems more likely that they would not, for it is reasonable to assume that older people might show a reemergence of daytime reverie, especially of a reminiscing sort.

The fact that daydreaming hits one peak during late adolescence suggests that such activity can have both an escape-from-reality and a problem-solving aspect. In its defensive (or escape-from-reality) role, daydreaming provides an antidote to present frustrations—the girl or boy I didn't get to go out with, the prize I didn't win. In this form daydreaming never solves problems. In its problem-solving role, however, daydreaming allows the person to try out different modes of approach to a problem situation. Even if the daydream does not solve the problem, it can at least help me see which solutions might work and which would not. In either case, daydreaming can serve to brighten up my life when it is at its most confusing (as in adolescence) or at its most boring (during any part of my life).

C. Free association in psychotherapy

No discussion of associative processes could be complete without some mention of the clinical technique of **free association,** invented by Freud. The patient is asked to sit comfortably and tell the therapist "whatever comes to mind," censoring nothing, no matter how odd or unrelated it may appear. Although people differ in their ability to follow these quite simple-sounding instructions, the first thing almost everybody reports is how difficult they are to follow. It is very hard to say *everything* that comes to mind. Along with this difficulty is the fact of long silences or, in more active patients, extended and beside-the-point joking or conversation.

When these initial resistances are overcome and the patient comes increasingly to trust the therapist, a stream of free association such as the following is often reported:

"You've asked me about my father ... He wasn't a particularly large man, as I think about him as an adult ... He was more distant than anything else ... Oh I must tell you about an incident that I'm now thinking of that occurred a few years ago.

"While driving downtown I met a policeman ... I became tense and trembled with fear even before he spoke to me ... He merely asked me for a ride down the street ... The officer turned out to be one of our company guards who had recognized me ...

"On a few occasions when I happened to be present in the same restaurant as a uniformed officer, I preferred to leave rather than stay and struggle with my acutely painful and nervous feelings ...

"It is important to remember that ever since childhood I had been uncomfortable in the presence of policemen. I had no real reason to fear the police, yet a simple warning from a traffic officer was enough to set my heart pounding ...

"Let's see, where were we before I started talking about policemen? Oh yes ..., we were talking about my father ..." [Adapted from Knight, 1950].

Probably the most significant part of this fragment is the way it sticks to the topic and does not stick to the topic. The original question must have asked the patient for some information about his father. Although the patient begins by providing a relatively straightforward description, after some hesitancy he jumps to an unrelated topic, policemen. Without any warning, he next produces two memories: an incident in which he mistook a person he knows (the guard) for a more remote policeman and another incident in which he experienced tremendous anxiety in dealing with a policeman over a minor infraction. Then he recognizes that he has gone off topic and comes back to the original question about his father.

This excerpt is a rather ordinary fragment of a clinically produced associative stream. It is representative of free associations that occur early in therapy and illustrates some of the more important phenomena. As in other continuous mental tasks, the behavior is episodic—the patient talks, stops, talks, stops, and so on. And as in other associative tasks, the parts surrounded by pauses usually make some kind of internal sense—at least they all deal with the same topic. The one problem in this record is the way in which the patient gets from Father to Guard to Policeman to Father and it is precisely at this point that Freud comes in.

In one sense the Father, the Guard, and the Policeman are all part of the same topic—"authority figures." Freud assumed that when sequential topics did not make immediate sense, it was the therapist's job to understand why a jump had come about, often by stopping the patient and asking him or her to free-associate to one or the other topic in hopes of finding a meaningful link between them. In the course of associating to Policeman and then to Father, the missing link would become apparent to patient and therapist. Sometimes the link would be apparent only to the therapist. Here the patient would be asked to associate further, or the therapist might provide an interpretation connecting the two initially separate ideas.

The fact that patients are often unable to see the connection at first glance, coupled with similar phenomena from everyday life, such as forgetting something well-known, making slips of the tongue, but most especially having strange dreams, led Freud to the revolutionary idea of an "unconscious" mental life. By this he meant a mental life not known to the patient, one that operated on the basis of rules different from those describing activities, such as planning a vacation or adding a column of numbers. The stream of conscious experience described by James—fringe and all—is incredibly orderly and understandable compared with what goes on in dreams and free associations. Because Freud felt that dream symbolism represented an earlier (more infantile) and more primary level of human thinking, he called the process by which it was produced **primary process** to distinguish it from thinking that developed only as the child grew older, which Freud called **secondary process** thinking.

Primary-process thinking, if we accept Freud's word, is quite chaotic and undisciplined. It follows none of the usual constraints imposed by our logical understanding of time and space. Things long gone can coexist with things now present. Orderly, three-dimensional space is everywhere violated, and beautiful and disfigured images easily run with one another. As for transformations, primary process is positively mad with them: first a tree, now a rocket, then a pencil (all three wearing skullcaps) tumble into a river, which obligingly gives way to an oyster shell opening to reveal the Botticelli Venus wearing a No-Care bra by Playtex. As Freud noted, the closest we ever come to experiencing primary-process thinking is during our dreams—in that situation where everything is possible and where the wish is as good as the deed.

If we compare Freud's two modes of thinking with James' stream of consciousness, it is possible to describe secondary process as quite like rational thinking, with a bit of the Jamesian fringe thrown in. Primary-process thinking may have something in common with James' fringe consciousness, but it is quite clear that such thinking is well beyond the fringe in its ability to bring together things that are not now nor have ever been together. The absolutely unbridled flow of images and transformations in primary process seems to carry us into deeper (or at least into different) waters than those described by James.

The major difference between James' fringe and Freud's primary process seems to be that for Freud the central factor directing the flow of all our transformations is a sexual or aggressive wish or desire that cannot be expressed directly. Although James did recognize the role of such wishes in directing the flow of a person's thought, it remained for Freud to emphasize that what we dream (or think about) is often tied to concerns not usually talked about in polite society. Freud's hypothesis is not so much in contrast to James' as much as it is in addition to it. No doubt, James would agree that trees, rockets, or pencils that tumble into a river and are then transformed into a beautiful offspring might represent a rather graphic, even if somewhat hidden, description of a sexual act. It also seems reasonable to suppose that James might feel that Freudian symbolism has been carried rather too far by assuming certain direct equivalences—for example, that a tree always equals a penis. Just as surely he would agree that such symbolism does occur and is meaningful both to the thinker and to the person with whom the thinker shares his or her thought.

D. Imaging

The words *image* and *imagery* have popped up in a number of places, and the time has come to deal with them in some detail. Usually, when we think of imaging, we talk about "getting an image," and the whole process *seems* very much like "seeing" an internal picture. Even if we do not actually see the image (or hear it, for that matter), this view underlies much of the work on this topic.

The idea that imaging is the same kind of process as seeing was first put to experimental test by Perky in 1910. In this experiment, the observer was brought into a very well lighted room and asked to look at a special point on a screen and then to imagine an object, such as a banana or a leaf. Unknown to the subject, a faint picture of a banana or leaf was projected onto the screen at a low level of illumination (that is, below a previously determined brightness threshold). As the observer looked at the screen, the illumination was raised little by little until the subject reported that he or she "had an image." Under those conditions, Perky reported two effects: all her subjects mistook the picture for their image (even though some did comment on its strange location or size), and the brightness used for the image was considerably brighter than that which would have been seen under earlier, more ordinary threshold-detection conditions. This second finding was taken to suggest that we are less sensitive to brightness (and perhaps to all stimulation) when we are imaging than when we are not.

To examine the so-called **Perky effect** (confusion of the projected image with an imagined one), Segal and her collaborators (Segal & Nathan, 1964; Segal & Fusella, 1969, 1970) performed a series of studies, which repeated the results but not the interpretation put on them by Perky. Although early in an experiment of this type most subjects do not distinguish between their own image and the one projected on the screen by the experimenters, it soon becomes clear to some subjects that there is a picture projected there. Once this is realized, subjects try to ignore it or to incorporate it into their own image. Results gathered by Segal showed some tendency for subjects who were good imagers—that is, who reported they normally used imagery in thinking—to report the projected image sooner than people who were habitually poor imagers. Some subjects, when questioned, did say they knew their image was different from the one projected but thought the experimenter might want to see how well they could produce images anyway (see the discussion of demand characteristics in Chapter 1).

Imagery, in its vivid or washed-out form, is clearly a phenomenon of our mental life. Only in recent years, however, has there been a return to this topic, and then only because it has been possible to demonstrate that imagery clearly affects more verbal sorts of learning. Perhaps the leading experimenter in this area is Allen Paivio of the University of Western Ontario, whose laboratory research has shown the powerful effects of imagery on the ease with which human subjects learn paired items (Paivio, 1969, 1971). For example, Paivio has shown that human subjects learn high-imagery word pairs, such as *house-tree*, much faster than word pairs not producing high imagery, such as *beauty-truth*. Nouns, by and large, evoke images more easily than adjectives, and early work showed that the first word in a given pair predicts how fast the pair will be learned. For example, Lambert and Paivio (1956) found that the pair *house-large* was more easily learned than *large-house*, even though *house large* is not a grammatical English phrase and *large house* is.

If we accept the fact that **imagery** occurs, we still need some way to talk about it. From earliest times on, the usual way has been to describe imagery as a type of "inner perceiving"—a "seeing in the mind's eye" or a "hearing of things in the head." The philosopher Gilbert Ryle (1949) has suggested that although it may be all right for ordinary purposes to talk about an "inner eye" or "inner ear," it clearly will not do for psychology to be quite that sloppy. Ryle's argument is simply that imagery occurs but that images are not seen or heard in any of the usual senses of these terms.

Why is Ryle so strong in insisting that "images do not generally exist in the head" and that "the familiar faith that people are constantly seeing things in their mind's eye . . . is no proof that there exist things which they see and hear, or that people are seeing or hearing" (p. 243)? Probably the major reason has to do with his distrust of Descartes' distinction between mind and body (see Chapter 1). Ryle believes that although this distinction might once have been a useful way of looking at the human being, it no longer is. If the idea of mind and body is simply a category mistake, as Ryle maintains, there can be no *inner* or *outer*. To talk of imagery as "seeing things in the mind's inner picture gallery" must be misleading.

Imagery is better considered as a special way of doing things that need make no appeal to "faint copies" or "inner seeing." To image, or, more generally, to imagine, is to do something that human beings do. It is perfectly all right to say "imaging is like seeing" as long as we remember the two little words *is like*. Imaging is not seeing; it is its own unique way of dealing with one or another task, and as long as we remember that imaging (an action) does not in any ordinary sense of the term involve seeing pictures in our mind, we will be all right.

III. DIRECTED THINKING

How do you divide 4372 by 84? If you're like me, very slowly, and if you're like me, you also do it by using a very mechanical procedure that goes something as follows:

Step 1: Does 84 divide into 43? Answer: No.

Step 2: Does 84 divide into 437? Answer: Yes.

Step 3: How many times? Answer: 5 times ($5 \times 84 = 420$).

Step 4: Is there anything left over? Answer: Yes, 17.

Step 5: Are there any numbers left in 4372? Answer: Yes, 2.

And so on until the answer 52 and 4/84 is reached.

In working out this problem, you are following a set procedure that guarantees a solution to any problem in long division. Technically, such a procedure is called an **algorithm**—a procedure that guarantees a correct answer for a particular class of problems.

If algorithms always enable you to solve a problem, why hasn't someone invented an algorithm for such games as chess or, perhaps more easily, checkers? The answer has to do with the enormous number of possible moves in a game as "simple" as checkers. Generally speaking, algorithms are constructed by considering the total number of moves possible in a game. In checkers, the complete exploration of every possible move requires something like 10^{40} choices of moves, which, as one author notes, "at 3 choices per thousandth of a second would still take 10 centuries to consider" (Samuel, 1961, p. 211). In chess, the total number of possible patterns has been estimated to be 10^{120}, give or take a few powers.

For all practical purposes it is impossible to construct an algorithm for checkers, let alone chess. Yet we have all read about checker-playing computers; how do such computers do it? The answer is that they use a **heuristic**—a procedure that drastically limits the thinker to a highly selective search of possible move patterns. Generally speaking, a heuristic considers only a small number of future moves; for chess the search can be extended only for the most significant pieces.

Algorithms and heuristics are obviously related, although an algorithm will always produce a victory (or solution), while a heuristic need not. A heuristic, however, requires a much less exhaustive analysis of the logical structure of a game (or problem) and often provides the only possible procedure for an enormously complicated game or problem. Since most problems do not admit of a simple enumeration of all possible alternatives in the near and far future, there are only a few useful algorithms. Far and away the great bulk of our game-playing or problem-solving activity must be based on heuristic procedures.

A. Computers as thinkers, thinkers as computers

All this talk about heuristics and algorithms derives from the invention and widespread use of the electronic computer. Although the whirring wheels of tape, the blinking lights, and the perforated cards are now part of our everyday life, the important part of computer technology for psychology is not its physical or electronic parts, but rather its logical structure—its "software," as the computer people call it.

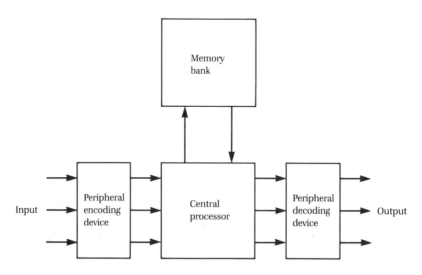

Figure 5-1. Computer "behavior": A graphic representation of the sequence of component operations between the input of a problem and the output of a solution. (*From* Experimental Psychology and Information Processing, *by D. W. Massaro. Copyright © 1975 by Rand McNally College Publishing Company. Reprinted by permission.*)

Logically speaking, computers can be described by Figure 5-1, which begins with the input of information at the left and the output of an answer at the right. In between, information of any and all kinds is first encoded (put into a form suitable for the computer to work on), and after the computer has done its work, the information is decoded (put into a form suitable for us to read). Neither encoding nor decoding affects how the computer works; they are simply conveniences—first for the computer and second for us. We could learn the computer's "language," or it could learn ours, but it turns out to be more convenient to let the computer work as it will and us as we will.

The most important part of this whole process for psychology is contained in the relations of the central processor to the memory bank. It is in this interaction that most computational work ("thinking") goes on. The interaction between memory and processing is contained in the program—the set of operations that the computer performs on information held in immediate or more long-term storage. It is here that algorithms, heuristics, strategies, or, more generally, rules for doing come into the picture.

The rules for doing in a computer are usually described in a set of statements called a program, which is often presented in the form of a flow diagram. A somewhat facetious example (computer people are like that) of how a flow chart might look in describing the sequence of things a man might do in going to work in the morning is presented in Figure 5-2. The figure labeled "Oversimplification" (Figure 5-2a) divides the sequence into three parts: getting up, getting ready, and going. The larger figure provides a more complete description, although it is not nearly as complete or detailed as it might be. In this second figure, the simple sequence presented in Figure 5-2a seems suddenly to have a lot of twists and repetitions. So, for example, if the question "Is it dark?" is answered yes, there is still a further something to be done: turn on the light. In addition, there are loops, or repetitions, as in the sequence Groan—Shake wife; Groan—Shake wife. The same is true for the question "Keys?," where a "No" answer forces a loop.

B. Computers and cognitive psychology

This brief example of flow charts, though oversimplified, does present a good many of the important concepts and procedures that have found their way into psychological theory—particularly in that branch known as cognitive psychology (see Neisser, 1967, or Massaro, 1975). One of the facts that guides cognitive psychology is that behavior can be described at many levels, as in the "Oversimplification" diagram and the more complete flow chart, which expands it by filling in more details. Every act can be broken down into as many subcompartments as necessary. What needs special emphasis is that "we are not talking about directly observable behavior, but about theoretical descriptions of this behavior. Descriptions of different levels . . . are all different descriptions of the same behaviors, each made for its own purpose" (Pollio, 1974, p. 44)

The loops contained in any flow chart point to another important idea in cognitive psychology: that of feedback. Put in most general terms, feedback involves two phases: a *test* phase and a *do* or *operate* phase. In the getting-up-in-the-morning flow chart, the input to the test phase for (Keys) would be to ask "Where are my keys?" If the answer is "Here they are," the test has been met, and the person can exit the loop.

Does this computational theory describe anything besides the operation of a computer—say, a person solving a problem? As an answer, the mathematician George Polya (1945) suggests that he has found three computerlike heuristics to be of use in his own work and in teaching. One of **Polya's heuristics** is called "working backward." This approach involves starting out with what we want to prove and working back, step by step, to the information originally given. A second heuristic is the "make-a-plan" approach, in which we think of a similar problem we have solved in the past and use that approach—appropriately modified—in the present case. Polya's third heuristic, "means-end analysis," is the most important for psychological work. Means-end analyses work by asking the would-be problem solver to compare his or her current state of affairs with what he or she would like to happen and then to look for some procedure that will reduce the difference between the two. If this procedure does not work, the thinker is supposed to go through a new means-end analysis until the difference no longer remains.

Heuristics such as these can be used in programming a computer to solve problems. One of the most successful and well-developed attempts has been undertaken at the Carnegie-Mellon Institute of

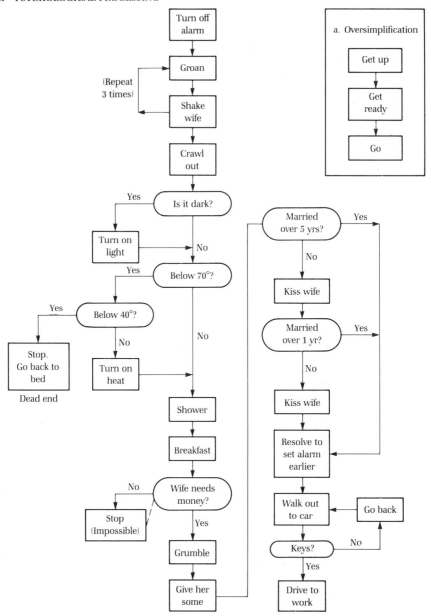

Figure 5-2.   Flow chart: How to get to work in the morning. (*From* The Psychology of Symbolic Activity, *by H. R. Pollio. Copyright © 1974 by Addison-Wesley, Reading, Massachusetts. Reprinted with permission.*)

Technology by Simon, Newell, Shaw, and their associates (Newell, Simon, & Shaw, 1960; Simon & Newell, 1971). In their attempt to develop a General Problem-Solver (GPS) program for the computer to follow, they have made use of Polya's means-end heuristic. The GPS program works by trying to reduce the difference between where the problem solver—human or machine—is now and where he, she, or it would like to be. To give some idea of how GPS works, Newell, Simon, and Shaw (1960) provide the following more or less common-sense example:

I want to take my son to nursery school. What's the difference between what I have and what I want? One of distance. What changes distance? My automobile. My automobile won't work. What's needed to make it work? A new battery. What has new batteries? An auto repair shop. I want the repair shop to put in a new battery; but the shop doesn't know I need one. What is the difficulty? One of communication. What allows communication? A telephone ... And so on [p. 258].[1]

Thus, GPS works by classifying things in terms of what they do and then trying to develop some means of bringing about what is needed. For example, "What changes distance? My automobile." Although it is possible to eliminate differences between states in any order you want, in practice GPS does it by eliminating differences in order of difficulty. In addition, the GPS program includes a planning heuristic whose job is to change the originally complex problem into a series of simpler ones and then order which subproblems will be done first and which ones later. Finally, GPS has a variable component, called its "task environment," which deals with the particular task at hand. Such task environments contain different information if GPS is trying to solve a problem in logic, in chess, or in taking a son to nursery school.

The end state desired for GPS is not only that it work but that it simulate—that is, work like—a flesh-and-blood human being trying to solve the same problem. To do this, GPS is set up to print out a running commentary of what it is doing during each step it performs. To have an appropriate point of comparison, a human subject is asked to talk aloud as she or he goes about solving the same problem. To compare human protocols with computer printouts, Simon and Newell (1971) suggest the use of a problem–behavior graph, which shows what the subject knows at any given point in problem solving as well as what he or she does to get to the next state. Such protocols end, for both the computer and the human subject, when the problem is solved (or is found to be insoluble by that method). They allow the investigator to find the total number of states produced as well as the exact steps used in solving the problem.

Although the problem–behavior graph is not a foolproof way of describing the sequence of prob-

lem-solving steps—for example, sometimes the human subject gets so involved in working on the problem that he or she forgets to talk aloud—it does provide one way of comparing computers with people. When such comparisons are carried out, at least on the range of problems studied at the Carnegie-Mellon Institute, agreements between them and us are sometimes quite good. Human subjects often report quite spontaneously that they use means-end heuristics, and the operation of such heuristics is obvious in the things they have said and done. This is not surprising; after all, the idea of a means-end heuristic came from a careful (reflected) analysis of human thinking by a very good human thinker named George Polya.

C. Thinking in open and closed systems

So far, most analyses of human problem solving have concerned well-defined problems: games such as checkers or chess, how to get your son from one side of town to the other, how to do long division. Because many significant problems are just not that orderly, Sir Frederic Bartlett has suggested that psychologists ought to deal with at least two types of thinking in talking about human problem solving: **closed-system** and **open-system thinking**. In closed-system thinking there are a limited number of units, which do not change as thinking progresses. All the problem solver has to do is to use the elements provided in such a way as to reach the solution required. In open-system (or adventurous) thinking, the problem solver has to go beyond the information given. The task may require changing the original elements or even developing new ones.

Although it is important to distinguish between these two types of thinking, it is also important to remember that in nonresearch situations the distinction is not as clear as it might appear in the laboratory. And although the problem a person is confronted with may be described as an "open task," he or she may choose to deal with it in a closed way. For example, if we have to make a decision about changing jobs and we do this by making a list of "pluses" and "minuses" and then deciding "yes" or "no" by counting them up, we have closed a task that could have been done in a more open way.

All of Bartlett's work on problem solving (Bartlett, 1958) was designed to help us understand how we accomplish what in everyday language would be

---

[1] "Report on a General Problem-solving Program," by A. Newell, H. Simon and J. C. Shaw. In *Proceedings of the International Conference on Information Processing*, Paris, UNESCO, 1960, 256–264. © UNESCO 1969. Reproduced by permission of UNESCO.

called "real hard thinking." Real hard thinking, in the laboratory or out, is usually undertaken when the evidence or information given is incomplete. One purpose of thinking is to fill in the gaps—in a closed system, by using the information available; in an open system, by getting or developing new information. Real hard thinking always has a direction, and this direction is given by a vague feeling that "something is missing," that "something is out of balance." Although what is missing or what is out of balance often cannot be described very clearly, we do experience such gaps quite frequently.

Consider the tip-of-the-tongue phenomenon: you are sure you know someone's name or address, only you can't recall it just now. What you feel, however dimly, is what is meant by a gap in thinking. And it isn't enough that you experience the gap; you feel compelled to return to it over and over again until you fill it or, with a strong act of will, disregard it. Brown and McNeill (1966) have described the tip-of-the-tongue state as being like getting ready to sneeze but not having any sneeze occur. This experience of a gap in speaking is close to what is meant by a gap in thinking: a feeling of discomfort which obstructs the continuing flow of thinking and in which we cannot say in advance what is required to fill it but will recognize the correct "filler" the minute we think of it.

The hallmark of real hard thinking is that it is not so much a matter of rearranging already-known information as it is one of developing new and different ways of going about things. In any innovative work, whether it be in science, art, or technology, our usual feeling is that the thinker must go beyond the limits imposed by a particular problem. The catch to this kind of problem solving was described by Socrates some 2000 years ago: How can we set out to look for something whose nature we do not know? Which among all the things we do not know is the one that we are looking for, and if by chance we should stumble on it, how will we recognize it as right, since we do not know exactly what we are looking for? And yet we do recognize it.

In order to answer such questions, Gestalt psychologists, such as Max Wertheimer, Kurt Koffka, and Wolfgang Köhler, have attempted to analyze a number of situations in which—to use their term—productive thinking occurs. Strangely enough, not all or even many of these activities are ones that would be thought of immediately as having some-

thing to do with thinking: for Wertheimer an interesting case was provided by two boys playing badminton; for Koffka it involved an analysis of jokes; for Köhler it concerned monkeys trying to reach bananas suspended above their heads.

1. A game of badminton.   Two boys are playing badminton, and the older is much better than the younger. His service is so clean and accurate that the second child hardly ever returns it. After several sets, the younger child—child A—throws down his racquet and refuses to play. The older boy, child B, sits down beside him and tries to get him to play by telling him that he isn't being a good sport.

Child B, however, doesn't feel very nice about being quite so mean to child A and soon says "I'm sorry—I really am." After a little while, child B turns to A again and says "This game is silly, the way we're playing it. I'm hitting the bird in such a way that you can't return it, and then there's really no game. Is there any way we can get it to work better?" Suddenly B's face lights up, and he says to A: "Look, I have an idea. Why don't we play a new game: let's see how many times we can get the bird to go back and forth over the net. Let's start with easy serves, and if we reach 10 or 15, then let's begin with a harder serve and see if we can do it again." Child A responds enthusiastically to this suggestion, and a new game begins.

A story such as this deserves not only a happy ending but a moral or two. As Wertheimer (1959) notes, he saw the two boys playing again a few days later, and child A's playing had greatly improved. It also turned out to be a good experience for child B: he had discovered something by his own productive thinking, and that something went well beyond the solving of a simple problem in playing badminton.

This story also has a moral for the psychology of problem solving; it concerns the changing way child B saw the game. At the beginning he saw it only from his own point of view. From this perspective, child A was not another person—simply an opponent in B's game. The first change in perspective was brought about by A's refusal to continue the game. This event forced B to **recenter** his view of the situation and look at it from A's point of view. In this new situation, B came to experience that the world didn't look so nice from A's point of view. Finally, B saw the game not from his own or from A's point of view; rather, he came to a different point of view, in which the game, not the players, was at issue.

Since the nature of the game itself had caused the interruption in the first place, it remained for B to take one further and quite decisive step. In his initial understanding of the game there were two points: having a good time with another person and beating him. The original situation of the game was one of competing, in which there is an I who wants to beat a You. The meaning of the situation changed when the I and the You became a We and competing changed to cooperating. From this point of view, the original game was seen as unfair, since beating a younger opponent was not very satisfying.

The overall course of this very human bit of problem solving involved several steps. The first was the change from a one-sided to a two-sided view of the situation. From this new perspective, things looked different; A was no longer an enemy to be beaten, only a younger boy quite unhappy at what was happening. This new point of view then led to a second change in perspective, in which A and B were no longer seen as opponents, but rather as a We trying to have a good time. With this new change, B was able "to face the issue honestly . . . [and to go] straight to fundamentals" (Wertheimer, 1959, p. 179).

In regard to this last point, Wertheimer notes that, although a word like *honestly* may seem out of place in a discussion of problem solving, it is "only an artificial and narrow view which conceives of thinking as an intellectual operation and separates it entirely from questions of human attitude, feeling and emotion" (1959, p. 179). Not only when the problem has emotional overtones is this important: even seemingly abstract and intellectual tasks always reveal a human attitude. As Wertheimer put it, the productive thinker must always reveal a "willingness to face issues and to deal with them firmly, honestly and surely" (p. 179). Unless the productive thinker is able to do this, he or she is likely to stay centered on a single mode of attack and thereby proceed in a single, highly mechanical way.

2. A joke.   What can a joke and a problem possibly have in common? They seem so unlike: problems are so serious and important, jokes so frivolous and insignificant. The similarities may be more obvious if we keep in mind that the word *wit* refers to humor as well as to problem solving and that the saying "Keep your wits about you" is not advice to a king about his court jesters. Pushing on, we may also note that in order to understand a joke, a person must know something about the elements of the joke and then be able to see how they fit together in a funny way. Finally, the idea of a *puzzle* applies both to jokes and to problems, again suggesting that jokes and problems are related in some quite significant way.

In *The Act of Creation* (1964) the novelist Arthur Koestler describes parallels between making jokes and solving problems. Consider the following joke reported by Koestler:

> In the good old days, a dashing but penniless young Austrian officer tried to obtain the favors of a fashionable contessa. To shake off this unwanted suitor she explained to him that her heart was, alas, no longer free. He replied politely: Mademoiselle, I never aimed as high as that [p. 36].[2]

Koestler points out that in order to understand this joke, it is necessary to understand the word *heart* in at least two ways—one relating to affections, the other to location. The joke comes about because we are able to see both meanings of *heart* and because they are somewhat ambiguous in this context at first glance. After the punch line has been delivered, however, we see how effective the officer was at pressing his own advantage.

Tying together two separate ideas in a single word or phrase is for Koestler the essence of humor as well as other creative acts. Only if we know something about the two ideas joined is it possible to get the point of a joke or of a new idea. A person who has laughed at a joke will necessarily see component parts from a different point of view after the joke has been understood. Like creative problem solving, "getting" a joke involves a complex reorganization of our usual ways of looking at things. Only if this occurs can we say that the joke worked.

One further relationship between jokes and problem solving concerns the idea of a riddle or puzzle. When children are at about 8 or 9 years of age, riddlemania takes over many households, and parents

---

[2]From *The Act of Creation*, by A. Koestler. Copyright 1964 by Macmillan Publishing Company, Inc. Reprinted by permission of Macmillan Publishing Company, Inc., and A. D. Peters & Co., Ltd.

and brothers and sisters of the afflicted child are often puzzled by puzzlers such as these:

Q. What's a crick?

A. The noise made by a Japanese camera.

Q. What's the best way to drive a baby buggy?

A. Tickle its feet.

Although the first riddle comes close to being a groaner, it does not depend for its effect on sound alone—the listener must also know that Japanese speakers have difficulty pronouncing the English letter *l*. The second riddle is a bit more interesting: the phrase "to drive a baby buggy" has two meanings, and the answer—tickle its feet—makes the peripheral meaning dominant. After the joke has been understood in the sense of molesting an infant, the answer is not funny a second time, for it has now become difficult to see *buggy* as a type of carriage rather than as a mental condition.

Although most adults do not go in for riddles, it is clear that word play is not without importance for children or adults. Perhaps for this reason, the major attempt to relate jokes to problems, in addition to that by Koestler, was made by the rather austere Gestalt psychologist Kurt Koffka (1935). For Koffka there are two parts to understanding a joke (and to solving a problem). The first is to make contact with first one and then other meanings of the various parts of a joke. For example, in a pun used by Phyllis Diller in her nightclub act, "I'm descended from a very old line my mother fell for," the listener must know both meanings of "old line"—as in ancestry and in seducing. These two meanings set up a direction to the flow of thought in accordance with the context given by "I'm descended." At first, the direction suggests ancestry. With this direction set up, the joke works, as the listener is fooled, but only for a moment, by the unexpected ending indicating it was seducing, not ancestry, that was meant. With this new direction, both meanings can still be seen at once, as the fittingness and the fooling come together in my own feeling of cleverness at being able to break an original direction and come to see not only the second meaning but both meanings at the same time.

Joking and reasoning do have a good deal in common; yet there are also differences. As one early Gestalt psychologist put it, one of these must be that in humor the person steps outside his or her ordinary way of looking at the world (Maier, 1932), whereas in problem solving this need not necessarily occur. Only within this altered frame of mind can we laugh at an old lady slipping on a banana peel or at a distinguished professor getting hit in the face with a pie. Only in the special world set up by a joke could such events seem funny. But even in this world, more ordinary rules of directional thinking still apply, so that in order for some act or situation to be funny, it must have a sensibly nonsensical progression of ideas that can be followed from start to (moderately unexpected) finish.

3. Some insightful apes. Any discussion of problem solving that did not deal with the idea of insight would be a strange one; yet to discuss it using apes as examples would seem to be stranger still. There is a connection, however, since the role of insight in problem solving was first brought to the attention of psychologists through work done by Wolfgang Köhler (1925) with the help of a group of chimpanzees. To make the story even more unlikely, Köhler studied insight in chimpanzees not because he was particularly interested in chimpanzees (or even in insight, for that matter) but because as a German citizen he happened to get himself caught on the British island of Tenerife during World War I, where there was no equipment for studying perception but there was a colony of chimpanzees.

Probably because Köhler had not been trained in animal psychology, he started his work with careful and detailed observations of chimps and what they did. From this work he became absolutely sure that the American psychologist Edward Thorndike had vastly underrated the ability of animals to behave intelligently. Köhler came to feel that Thorndike denied that animals could behave intelligently because he had observed them in very restricted environments in which it was impossible for them to see all of a given problem situation at once. For example, Thorndike confined cats to boxes, where they had to perform the very uncatlike behavior of pressing a latch to be released.

Köhler believed that if he could present problems to animals in such a way that unnatural movements would not be required of them and all pieces of the problem were readily in view, he could examine problem solving in a more naturalistically meaningful way. In one of his best-known studies, a chimp subject was seated behind bars, and a banana was placed on the floor on the other side of the bars.

Also in the area were a number of hollow bamboo sticks and other objects—a piece of wire, a blanket, an old straw hat, and so on. What does a chimp or ape do in this situation? First most chimps tried to reach the banana by putting a hand through the bars. One particularly clever ape, Sultan by name, next tried to reach the banana with one of the sticks. Although the stick was too short, Sultan kept working at it for an hour or more. Then he stopped, walked away from the bars, sat down, and began to play with the sticks. In the course of playing with the hollow bamboo sticks, Sultan found himself holding one rod in each hand in such a way that they formed a straight line. He then jammed the smaller one into the larger one, ran to the bars, and got the banana with the now-double-size stick.

Not all chimps were tested with these sticks. Even those who were often used other "tools" in place of the sticks. One chimp, for example, used a blanket: she flapped at the fruit and succeeded in beating it toward her and into the cage. In another case, when the banana rolled onto the blanket, the chimp changed immediately from vigorous beating movements to drawing in the blanket slowly and gently so as not to dislodge the banana. In all these cases, the two sticks (or the blanket) were used only after the animal had looked over the situation, tried to use the most direct route possible, and found it unusable. It does not seem unreasonable to call the two sticks or the blanket a "tool," nor does it seem wrong to say that these animals showed "insight" in solving their problem.

But what does it mean to say "the animals showed insight"? To define *insight* in terms of what they did, it seems proper to say that an insightful solution was reached if (1) it occurred suddenly, (2) it was novel to the animal observed, (3) the solution sequence was done smoothly, and (4) it served to end the problem situation (Osgood, 1953). These criteria simply identify what an animal has to do before we, as third-person observers, are likely to say that "insight occurred."

Another way to describe insight is from a first-person point of view. Here the description is quite difficult to specify in detail except to say that there is a sudden reorganization of how everything looks: confusion gives way to a clear, precise plan, which is then put into action in overcoming the problem. The way we come to this plan, according to Köhler, involves a change in the way the situation looks to us. From our first-person point of view the blanket is no longer seen as something to cover ourselves with; rather, it becomes—"is seen as"—an extension of our bodies. Its function has changed within the demands of this situation. Similarly, a stick is no longer only for poking; it is now an implement for extending our reach. The essential process involved in an insightful solution requires us to release a needed object from its usual function and then use it in a new way. The crucial step is to unfix the function of a needed object.

4. Functional fixity and the idea of stupid thinking.   Sometimes it is impossible to see a blanket as anything other than something to cover yourself with: the blanket stays fixed in its function. Probably because **functional fixity** so often hinders problem solving, psychologists have been very interested in studying how functional fixity arises and how it is overcome. The basic procedure used to study this effect was first reported by Karl Duncker in 1945. In these experiments, several ordinary objects were left on a table in a very disorderly way. In one of Duncker's problems the crucial item was a pair of pliers, and the subject's job was to construct a small table from the following objects: the pliers, a board, a wooden bar, and two iron joints (the two joints are irrelevant to the solution). Figure 5-3 shows these materials and one of the correct solutions.

For one group of subjects—the experimental group—the wooden bar was nailed to the center of the board and had to be freed from the board by using the pliers. For the second, or control, group, the bar was simply tied to the board and had to be untied before it could be used. The results of this and similar procedures showed that subjects in the experimental group had much more trouble setting up the table than subjects in the control group. For example, 50 of 51 subjects in the control group solved the problem, while only 37 of 49 subjects solved it in the experimental group.

If objects get "fixed," Adamson and Taylor (1954) were interested in finding out how long such effects might last. In their experiment, subjects were given a relay and a switch and were asked to perform two tasks. During the first phase, some subjects were asked to wire the switch, other subjects the relay. Before subjects did the second task, in which they were asked to use one of the objects as a weight,

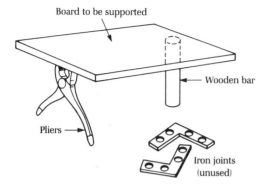

Solution of the "flower stand" problem

Figure 5-3. When the subject is presented with the objects shown, the problem is to construct a flower stand using any of the items given, not necessarily all of them. The best result is obtained by using the pliers in an unusual way, as shown. (*From* The Psychology of Symbolic Activity, *by H. R. Pollio. Copyright © 1974 by Addison-Wesley, Reading, Massachusetts. Reprinted with permission.*)

they waited varying amounts of time. One group waited 1 minute; a second group, 30 minutes; a third group, 60 minutes; a fourth group, 1 day; and a fifth group, 1 week. The results showed that the tendency to use the object *not* used in the pretest did not decrease to 50-50 until after a week had passed. After all other intervals, the object not used in the first task was always used more frequently in the second task.

The results of these experiments have been subject to many interpretations, yet the one originally offered by Duncker seems best: objects are functionally fixed to the degree that we can see them for only a single use—pliers for prying, switches for regulating electrical current, blankets for covering. To emphasize these ordinary functions, subjects are asked to use an object in its usual way. Such experience fixes the conventional meaning of the object for a subject so that it becomes unavailable for a different use.

Directed thinking at its most productive demands that we destroy our ordinary ways of looking at and thinking about problems. With this phase of the process underway, we are then ready to try out a new organization for the situation at hand. Both as-

pects of this process must involve the whole person, suggesting that disembodied intellects do not solve problems: people do. After a problem has been solved, we may be able to describe the steps we went through in solving it, but while we were working on the problem, our experience was one of dissatisfaction or incompleteness. This is as it should be: if we were not dissatisfied, there would be no reason to change, no reason to see the world afresh, and hence no reason to solve the problem.

Thus, problem solving involves a continuing process of destroying and building, destroying and building, destroying and building. In open-system thinking we are sure to be disappointed if we expect this cycle to end and final solutions to be reached once and for all. What we achieve, instead, are fragile syntheses—resting places—that will be undone when a new thinker comes along and sees the solution from a new and unique perspective. Thinking always outruns itself and always presents an incomplete synthesis; it is an operation that fulfills more than it promises, and one is never able to describe the process in a totally logical way. Thinking occurs, and I follow on until I understand what I have done. Only then can I tell others what I now know.

IV. CREATIVE THINKING AND THE STREAM OF CONSCIOUS EXPERIENCE

Productive thinking is available to all of us, yet sometimes a particular one of us comes to some idea, invention, or conclusion that changes the nature of the world all of us will live and work in from then on. Sometimes it is a highly speculative idea, such as Descartes' split of mind from body or Einstein's theory of relativity; sometimes it is a new invention, such as a steam engine or a light bulb; sometimes it is a new medicine, such as penicillin, or a new technique, such as anesthesia; and sometimes it is a new artistic style, such as impressionism or jazz.

The person who brings off such a piece of far-reaching thinking is usually called a genius or, at minimum, a person of great creativity. To label someone a genius does not tell us how this or that special bit of thinking was achieved—it simply suggests that we couldn't have done it ourselves. With the idea of a creative act we are on more familiar ground, for all of us from time to time do have the experience that we have done something new and original—in short, that we have been creative.

A. How do creative acts come about?

In order to describe the process by which creative acts and solutions are accomplished, it is necessary to look at the way in which great discoverers brought about their great discoveries. Only in this way will it be possible to distinguish the significant act of a significant thinker from the lesser act of a lesser thinker.

Consider the case of Frederick von Kekulé, who proposed the far-reaching notion that certain organic compounds are not linear structures but can better be considered as closed rings. Just before he devised his theory of the benzene ring, von Kekulé reported he experienced the following dreamlike incident:

I turned my chair to the fire and dozed, he relates. Again the atoms were gambolling before my eyes. This time the smaller groups kept modestly in the background. My mental eye, rendered more acute by repeated visions of this kind, could now distinguish larger structures, of manifold conformation; long rows, sometimes more closely fitted together; all twining and twisting in snakelike motion. But look! What was that? One of the snakes had seized hold of its own tail, and the form whirled mockingly before my eyes. As if by a flash of lightning I awoke.... Let us learn to dream, gentlemen [cited in Koestler, 1964, p. 118].[3]

If this were an isolated case, perhaps we could disregard it as a simple curiosity. But it is not: a book by the mathematician Jacques Hadamard (1945) documents the tremendous importance of dreams and dreamlike states in creative mathematical thinking. Among other examples, there is the famous case of Poincaré, who reported that during one sleepless night he found that his ideas "rose in crowds; I felt them collide until pairs interlocked, so to speak, making a stable combination"—thereby leading to a general solution (cited in Koestler, 1964, p. 116).

Koestler mentions other, similar examples:

1. Coleridge, in writing the poem *Kubla Khan*, explains that he dozed off after taking some medicine (probably opium) and that on waking he recollected 200–300 lines he had written *while* asleep. "On waking I constantly and eagerly wrote down the lines [of the poem]."

2. After deciding that nerve cells were stimulated chemically, Otto Loewi could not figure out how to test the theory experimentally. For the next 17 years or so he worked on the problem from time to time. In 1920, on the night before Easter Sunday, he reports:

I awoke, turned on the light, and jotted down a few notes on a tiny slip of thin paper. Then I fell asleep again. It occurred to me at six o'clock in the morning that during the night I had written down something most important, but I was unable to decipher the scrawl. The next night, at three o'clock, the idea returned. It was the design of an experiment to determine whether or not the hypothesis of chemical transmission that I had uttered seventeen years ago was correct. I got up immediately, went to the laboratory, and performed a simple experiment on a frog heart according to the nocturnal design [cited in Koestler, 1964, p. 206].[4]

Thus, Loewi had to solve his problem in dreams not once but twice.

3. Finally, there is the case of Michael Faraday, who knew little or no mathematics and yet made many of the most significant inventions of the past 300 years. Faraday often reported seeing "lines of force" surrounding magnets. Without mathematics, now considered absolutely necessary for physical invention, he invented the dynamo and electric motor—all, as he put it, by the use of his peculiar visual imagery.

These surely are strange histories for seemingly rational thinkers such as von Kekulé, Poincaré, Coleridge, Loewi, and Faraday (not to mention Archimedes and his bath). These cases, drawn from so many different fields, all seem to support the notion that not all high-level, creative thinking goes on in the clear light of day; rather, there seem to be hidden, almost underground games constantly at work behind the rational scene. Hadamard (1945) was so impressed by these underground games as to suggest that there must be some "unconscious" process at work in almost all creative acts. By "unconscious" Hadamard does not mean a simple

---

[3]From *A Hundred Years of Chemistry, Second Edition*, by A. Findlay. Copyright 1948 by Duckworth Ltd. Reprinted by permission.

[4]From "Autobiographical Sketch," by Otto Loewi. In *Perspectives in Biology and Medicine*, Vol. IV, No. 1. Copyright 1960 by the University of Chicago Press. Reprinted by permission.

process, but rather a much more complex one that ranges all the way from James' "fringe" to Freud's "primary process."

In trying to describe his understanding of "unconscious processes" Hadamard quotes two descriptions, the first by Galton and the second by Taine:

> When I am engaged in trying to think anything out, the process of doing so appears to me to be this: The ideas that lie at any moment within my full consciousness seem to attract of their own accord the most appropriate out of a number of other ideas that are lying close at hand, but imperfectly within the range of my consciousness. There seems to be a presence-chamber in my mind where full consciousness holds court and an ante-chamber full of more or less allied ideas situated just beyond the full ken of consciousness. Out of this ante-chamber the ideas most nearly allied to those in the presence-chamber appear to be summoned in a mechanically logical way, and to have their turn of audience [p. 25].

> You may compare the mind of a man to the stage of a theatre, very narrow at the footlights but constantly broadening as it goes back. At the footlights, there is hardly room for more than one actor. . . . As one goes further and further away from the footlights, there are other figures less and less distinct as they are more distant from the lights. And beyond these groups, in the wings and altogether in the background, are innumerable obscure shapes that a sudden call may bring forward and even within direct range of the footlights. Undefined evolutions constantly take place throughout this seething mass of actors of all kinds, to furnish the chorus leaders who in turn, as in a magic lantern picture, pass before our eyes [p. 27].

Putting both these views together gives a much more complex picture of the stream of human conscious experience than that first described by James. Not only does thinking depend on fringe consciousness; it even depends on processes still further removed from center stage. In addition, the composite stream of consciousness must have easy and quick commerce between certain parts (as between focus, fringe, and antechamber) as well as more difficult commerce between other parts (as between focus and primary process).

Largely because it is so difficult to get from back to center stage—from primary to secondary process—such commerce seems to require a special set of circumstances. One of these is clearly suggested by Kekulé's advice to his students:

"Gentlemen, let us learn to dream." The testimony of a great many individuals who have been recognized as creative suggests that dreamlike or reverie states facilitate the opening of channels between primary and secondary process. On the basis of such evidence it seems reasonable to conclude, as Hadamard did, that unconscious thinking helps bring about creative combinations that otherwise would have been impossible.

To state the matter just this way and let it go at that is to overlook much that is involved in creative thinking. The click of insight that produces the excitement of "Eureka!" is only one step in a much more continuous and ongoing process. As a matter of fact, a number of writers (among them Hadamard) suggest the Eureka step as only the third in a series of four. In these analyses (Hadamard, 1945; Wallas, 1926) the first and second stages preceding Eureka are called "preparation" and "incubation," and the one after it is called "verification." Thus, most creative acts begin with a period during which the thinker prepares himself or herself by studying what is known about a given topic. Although creative thinkers differ on this point, most suggest that during the preparation stage the would-be problem solver must get to know important questions, even if not their answers.

During the second stage, the thinker lets the problem rest. It may be for a few minutes, a few hours, or a few days: in some extraordinary cases, it may require up to 17 years (see the story of Loewi). At this point, the person must "think to the side" and allow "back-stage games" to progress. If an original intuition was correct, and if preparation was adequate, the fortunate thinker will someday experience the excitement that goes with the flash of illumination. Sometimes, depending on the thinker's character, it explodes as incredible excitement (Archimedes); in other cases it is described as a small excitement followed by a quieter feeling of satisfaction (Poincaré). In either case, the person is totally there when it occurs.

Following Eureka come the less exciting jobs of verifying a conclusion and of communicating the discovery to someone else. This latter, more directly reflective work consists of at least three tasks, which Hadamard has called "verifying," "precising," and "continuing." In mathematics, to *verify* means to work out a detailed and communicable proof; in science, it means to do the experiment; in art, it means to decide whether the artifact is as good as the intuition. To *precise* means to make the most economical and precise statement possible of the solution, as when the mathematician takes out unneeded steps in a proof or the writer removes extra words. Finally, to *continue* means to see further applications of a discovery, applications often not seen in the other stages.

Analyzing the significant creative act into four major (and three minor) steps seems a bit too neat. Thinking is a much more ongoing process, and these steps often overlap and intermingle. To make the matter even more complex, the steps of different problems may intertwine, as when I am incubating one problem and precising a second. Thinking is an ongoing, living process, and as James noted, nothing ever occurs in the neat sequence we describe in our textbooks. All parts of a creative act overlap, and the divisions we talk about are only the "precising" work of third-person reflection, not the work of first-person experience.

B. Hadamard and Einstein on the stream of consciousness

As part of his investigation into creative thinking in mathematics, Hadamard wrote out a description of his own methods of work and submitted it for comment to other mathematicians and physicists. In his description, Hadamard noted that during the process of mathematical invention he tended to function in terms of what he called "full consciousness": totally centered thinking that dealt only with the problems at hand. In our metaphor of the stage, "full consciousness" is thinking that is center stage, down front, and in full, close spotlight.

Hadamard reports that when he is thinking in full consciousness, there are few if any movements going on in his body. In addition, the center of his stream of consciousness is occupied not with words or symbols but with images and fanciful figures. The bits of "logical argument wait, so to speak, in the antechamber to be introduced later, when the stream widens" (Hadamard, 1945, p. 80).

In discussing this aspect of Hadamard's description, Einstein noted that full consciousness rarely if ever occurred for him. Rather, he considered it a limiting case that was never fully accomplished. In agreement with Hadamard's description, Einstein reported that he used conventional symbols, such as words or mathematical solutions, only after productive thinking had been completed, and then only quite laboriously. "Combinatory play seems to be the essential feature in productive thought—before there is any connection with logical construction in words (or in other kinds of signs)" (Einstein, 1949, p. 142).

If we can generalize from these descriptions, recognized productive thinkers do not primarily use conventional symbols. Rather, they create their own representations, sometimes visual, sometimes auditory, sometimes motor, and sometimes of no identifiable nature at all. On the basis of these reports, innovative human thinking cannot be described as the rational, wordy sequence that seems to be our major way of talking about it. It is much more chaotic and individualistic than most third-person descriptions suggest. It is probably better described as a restless, moving stream composed of narrow and wide parts, which can be deep or shallow. The concentrated, totally compressed, and fully focused line of thinking seems only a theoretical limit, never an actual fact of experience.

In the course of the present chapter, the flight of a bird has metamorphosed into the flow of a somewhat erratic and powerful river. This is perhaps as it should be, for a bird's flight seems too fragile an image to describe human thinking except for some extraordinarily delicate soul. A stream, with its more hardy and robust nature, seems better suited to capture how human thinking is experienced by the thinker. Like thinking, the stream can be narrow at places and wide at others; like thinking, it can be shallow at places and deep at others; and, as in thinking, we never know when we are the stream, where the stream comes from, or where it will get to. What we do know is that the stream moves as thinking moves and that moving is a condition of human experience.

The idea of thinking as a living stream reminds us again of the adventure of existence—thinking or otherwise. Thinking, more than almost any other activity, illustrates the open-ended and ongoing nature of human experience. Thinking produces its resting places and procedures in advance of being sure of a final outcome. This is as it should be, for future developments will always occur to take us beyond where we now rest. Thinking, like the world, is never fully realized in the form of some final system. "It is this capacity of going beyond created structures to create others . . . which constitutes the very nature of human existence. We must speak of personal knowledge in the sense that there is no system or set of formulae which will enable us to comprehend the world completely in a detached manner; we come to know by acts of personal involvement whose presuppositions can never be fully known and whose fulfillments are always uncertain" (Bolton, 1972, p. 235).[5]

V. SUMMARY

Thinking and doing are often considered distinctly different ways of relating to the world. In this point of view, thinking is always seen to be a preface or a postscript to action, never an activity in its own right. Such an approach assumes a separation of mind (thinking) and body (doing) and overlooks the fact that thinking is not a substitute for doing, but is its own special type of doing. The story of Archimedes and his cry of "Eureka!" illustrates the excitement possible in authentic thinking. The whole person thinks and is excited by it—not some special part called "mind."

To describe his understanding of what goes on when a person thinks, William James offered a list of five characteristics important in defining human thought: (1) every thought is always part of some person; (2) within each person, thinking is always changing; (3) within each person, thinking is always sensibly continuous; (4) thinking always *seems* to deal with objects, events, or experiences independent of itself; (5) thinking always selects among its objects and events.

James also introduced the metaphor of a stream as a good way of talking about human thinking. By this he meant to suggest that one's subjective life was continuous, not a series of loosely connected "railroad cars." Because our ideas and images are usually more compelling than the transitions between them, thinking has often been described as a train or a chain. James, however, was correct in noting that thinking must be composed of two parts: (1) a focus, consisting of ideas, images, thoughts, and so on that can be easily recognized, and (2) a fringe, consisting of transitions between the items contained in the focus.

Any theorist (James included) who has ever tried to describe human thinking has found it necessary to distinguish at least two types: associative thinking (the Daydreamer) and directed thinking (the Fisherman). Associative thinking involves a relatively sustained and seemingly disjointed flow of ideas, whereas directed thinking seems a more orderly process designed to produce a specific action in regard to some goal.

Associative thinking has often been studied using the word-association task. Given a sample of people responding to a particular stimulus word, it is possible to plot an associative response hierarchy, which shows the number of popular and unpopular responses to that word. Such hierarchies may be steep or flat, depending on the diversity of responses produced.

Using the fact of different response hierarchies as his starting point, Mednick suggested that people who have many responses to a stimulus word may be more creative than those who have few, since they are able to produce and utilize more diverse elements in thinking. On this basis, Mednick developed the Remote Associates Test to measure differences in the ability of different people to make novel associations between originally unrelated stimuli.

Bousfield and Sedgewick, using continuous word association as their starting point, found that there were a consistent number of responses given to individual stimulus words and that responses tended to be produced in bursts, or clusters. Such bursts would seem to support James' view that a focal idea cluster is followed by a fringelike transition, which, in turn, is followed by another idea cluster, and so on.

Daydreaming represents still another type of associative thinking. Singer contends that daydreaming occurs as a reaction to an uncompelling present situation. As such, it is not simply an escape from that situation, but an attractive alternative to it. Singer found that 96% of respondents to a questionnaire reported daydreaming as a daily routine, with most daydreaming occurring immediately before or after sleep. Two types of daydreams were described: one in which the person entered into a familiar and well-worked scene and a second in which the person used the daydream as an ongoing comment to an ongoing activity.

Associative thinking in the form of free associa-

[5]From *The Psychology of Thinking*, by N. Bolton. Copyright 1972 by Methuen & Co. Ltd. Reprinted by permission of Associated Book Publishers Ltd.

tion can also be studied in the context of psycho-therapy. The patient is asked to say everything that comes to mind (a difficult task). Behavior in this situation is again episodic, and patients are often unable to describe how they got from one idea to the next. Using this observation and similar phenomena from everyday life (slips of the tongue, strange dreams, and so on), Freud postulated the idea of an unconscious mental life. Within this domain, according to Freud, we tend to think in somewhat primitive ways, which he described as primary-process thinking. Such thinking must be distinguished from more mature thinking, called second-ary process, the type we usually use in our ordinary, wake-a-day lives.

Imaging is often thought of as "seeing things in the mind's picture gallery." The idea that imaging follows much the same rules as ordinary seeing or hearing has been studied by several investigators, beginning with Perky in 1910. Imaging is not exclusively visual; it can include hearing, tasting, smelling, and so on. The ability to produce an image seems possible for most people, although some report clearer images than others. Paivio reports that the ease with which an image is produced in response to a word is related to ease in remembering a word pair beginning with that word. Finally, Ryle suggests that imaging *is like* seeing but must not be confused with seeing: "is like" does not mean "is."

Directed thinking, the second major type of human thinking, can be seen quite clearly in the use of algorithms, such as the one used to solve problems in long division. Although algorithms are possible for some tasks, even computers are unable to use such procedures in playing checkers or chess because of the incredible number of potential moves in the game. Instead, computers are often programmed with heuristic procedures—more flexible and less extensive plans that allow a selective search of possible actions in a given situation. Many heuristics are based on the strategies of "working backward," "making a plan," or "means-end analysis" described by Polya. All these procedures have been used in developing a computer program called the "General Problem Solver" (GPS), which was designed to simulate human problem-solving activity. The problem-solving behavior of GPS often agrees quite closely with protocols produced by human subjects solving the same or similar problems.

Computer programs such as GPS often deal with problem solving in closed-system situations, such as occur in a game of checkers or in a mathematical proof. Most task situations, however, are not so clearly structured and are better described as requiring open-system thinking. Perhaps the best descriptions of how such thinking progresses have been provided by Gestalt psychologists, such as Wertheimer, Köhler, and Koffka. Wertheimer, for example, described a game of badminton in which a younger child became frustrated in playing against an older child. The older child resolved the problem inherent in this situation by restructuring the game under new, more cooperative rules. Koffka described the similarity between understanding a joke and solving a problem. In both cases a person has to complete a conceptual gap in an unusual or unexpected way. Finally, Köhler studied insight in chimpanzees. For insight to occur, the would-be problem solver, human or animal, has to make use of objects in a novel way—that is, reconstrue the meaning or function of the object or situation. Other Gestalt psychologists, such as Duncker, have investigated directed thinking along similar lines. Their experiments almost always require the person to overcome functional fixity and thereby come to a new use for a well-known object.

Productive thinking is available to all; sometimes, however, a particular someone develops an idea, invention, or conclusion that changes the nature of the world all of us will live in from then on. The person who brings off such a bit of far-reaching thinking is usually called a genius or a person of great creativity. Several important discoveries, inventions, and works of art have come to the person while he or she was dreaming. Thinking, then, depends not only on focus and fringe consciousness (James) but also on processes such as primary process (Freud) that are further removed from center stage. Creative thinking, thus, often requires the person to move from back to center stage (and back and forth again)—a difficult and challenging feat.

A number of analyses have described four steps in creative human thinking: (1) preparation, (2) incubation, (3) "Eureka!" or insight, and (4) verification. These steps are not a neat, progressive series ultimately leading to a creative solution; they overlap and intermingle and only infrequently lead to a genuinely creative outcome.

In human creative activity, unconscious or at least nonrational processes are sometimes better able to solve difficult problems than more reflected, conscious ones. However, to split creative thinking into two is to miss the fact that both processes go on in the same person as he or she thinks. Thinking, more than most other activities, shows the open-ended and ongoing nature of human living. Thinking produces its resting places in advance of being sure of a final outcome, and such exhilarating uncertainty is as much a part of "good hard thinking" as is the solution attained. In this we can all join Archimedes in the adventure of innovative thinking.

VI. GLOSSARY OF IMPORTANT CONCEPTS

Algorithm. A procedure or formula that always solves problems of a given class.

Associative response hierarchy. A ranking of responses to a stimulus word in a word-association task, established by testing many subjects. A steep hierarchy has few total responses; a flat hierarchy has many responses.

Associative thinking. A type of thinking in which the flow of ideas occurs in an episodic sequence. The first idea in a sequence has a direct connection to the second, the second links directly to the third, and so on. Although the first idea may also have some connection with the third, fourth, or fifth (or any other idea in the chain), it is the connection of adjacent ideas that gives direction to the overall sequence.

Closed-system thinking. As identified by Frederic Bartlett, a type of thinking that uses a limited number of elements, which do not change as thinking progresses.

Continuous word association. A procedure in which the person gives as many responses as possible to a single cue word. Responses are usually produced in bursts.

"Daydreamer." A poetic term for one whose thinking is relatively free-floating and unconstrained. It is a literary allusion to Proust's narrator in *Swann's Way.* (See **associative thinking**.)

Daydreaming. Private, personal manifestations of an associative stream of consciousness. It can occur in two forms. In one, the thinker escapes into familiar and well-worked scenes; in the other, the thinker's daydream seems to occur as an ongoing comment on an activity in progress. This second type usually is rooted in some fairly definite object, idea, or problem and gradually assumes proportionately more of the focus of thinking.

Directed thinking. Thinking that is clearly purposive and planful.

"Fisherman." A poetic term for one who thinks directly in order to solve a reasonably concrete (or practical) problem. It is a literary allusion to Hemingway's hero in *The Old Man and the Sea.* (See **directed thinking**.)

Focus and fringe. Aspects of the stream of conscious experience. Focus is the object occupying "center stage"; fringe, occupying "back stage" and "wings," is composed of connotations, related objects, anticipations, and the like.

Free association. The therapeutic technique of talking about whatever comes to mind even if it seems unrelated to what was said before; introduced by Freud.

Functional fixity. The tendency to see objects as having only one use; the degree to which we put them to only one use.

Heuristic. A limited procedure for an orderly search of some possible "moves" in a problem-solving situation. It does not exhaust all possibilities, nor does it guarantee a correct result.

Imagery. A special way of doing things that has been described as "seeing things in the mind's picture gallery." To image (imagine) is better described as a unique method of working on various tasks, not necessarily related to literal seeing.

Open-system thinking. As identified by Frederic Bartlett, thinking requiring one to go beyond the given information to come to a conclusion; it may involve changing old elements or developing new ones.

Perky effect. Confusion of a faint projected image with one imaged.

Polya's heuristics. (1) "Working backward"—start from what is to be solved and work back to the original problem. (2) "Make-a-plan"—solve present problem on the basis of similar past problems. (3) "Means-end analysis"—compare situation with a desired situation; then get procedure(s) to reduce differences.

Primary process. In Freud's theory, the process by which dreams and dream symbolism are produced. Primary-process thinking (in Freud's opinion) is extremely chaotic, undisciplined, and desire-oriented.

Recentering. A process in which a thinker changes from the ordinary first-person view of a task so as to see it from a new perspective.

Remote Associates Test. Mednick's test for verbal creativity, in which the subject gives a word that relates three seemingly unrelated words.

Secondary process. In Freud's theory, rational, mature thinking that mediates between desire and external necessity.

"Stopping points." The objects, ideas, and so on of which the stream of thinking seems to be formed; often emphasized to the detriment of *transitions* between stopping points.

Stream of consciousness. William James' interpretation of consciousness, stressing the continuous nature of thinking, rather than its apparent segmented content. James described it as having five properties: (1) Every thought is always a part of some person. (2) Within each person, thinking is always changing. (3) Within each person, thinking is always sensibly continuous. (4) Thinking always *seems* to deal with objects, events, and experiences independent of itself. (5) Thinking always selects among its objects and events.

VII. SUGGESTED READINGS

Major sources

James, W. *The principles of psychology.* (2 vols.). New York: Dover, 1950. (Originally published, 1890.) Chapters 8, 9, 11–13, 18, 19, 22.

Koestler, A. *The act of creation.* New York: Macmillan, 1964. Book 1.

Wertheimer, M. *Productive thinking.* New York: Harper & Row, 1959.

Secondary sources

Lindsay, P. H., & Norman, D. A. *Human information processing.* New York: Academic Press, 1972.

McKellar, P. *Experience and behavior.* Harmondsworth, England: Penguin Books, 1968. Chapters 1–4.

Pollio, H. R. *The psychology of symbolic activity.* Reading, Mass.: Addison-Wesley, 1974. Chapters 1–4, 6, 8–10.

Answers to test items, page 109: Correct responses for Sets 1–4, respectively, are: *working, party, chair,* and *house.*

6

Speaking and Language

Saying "I love you" and meaning I love you is different from saying "I love you" and meaning I want something from you. In the first case, the words are spoken by the whole person, and they change the world for both of us in a very special and unique way. From then on, everything, myself included, exists in the light of the world newly created by my words.

Often the simple act of saying "I love you" surprises the person saying it. This happens when the lover did not realize his or her love until saying it spontaneously for the first time. In a one-sided love affair, in contrast, the person in love longs to hear "I love you," confident that a genuine saying will make it so. Unfortunately, forcing someone to say it may have a reverse effect: when the person says "I love you," it may become all too clear that he or she does not, and what before was possible is now impossible.

Sometimes when people have been lovers for a long time, the spontaneous saying of "I love you" around the breakfast table or during a quiet time at evening again reveals the world anew. Every time a statement honestly expresses some previously unsaid feeling, I am changed by the very act of expressing it. **Authentic speaking** brings a world into existence, and the surprise and pleasure of this discovery in so ordinary a place as the breakfast room comes pleasantly upon both speaker and hearer.

How different is what happens when we say "Very truly yours" or "Do come over sometime"! Here our world is not changed; nothing important happens. "Very truly yours" means only that I have finished writing you a letter; "Come over sometime" means that you and I have just finished a conversation and I now have to go. Rather than opening up a new way of looking at the world or suggesting future actions, well-worked phrases close things down and leave no open future.

A strategic "I love you" is said to get something. The speaker is not surprised by his or her speaking of this phrase. "I love you" is used in a planned and manipulative way: the speaker keeps something in reserve, some element of control for himself or herself. If the listener is not deceived, a strategic "I love you" is pleasant or annoying, depending on mood.

In general, however, it serves to close up the listener by suggesting that he or she also hold something in reserve from the speaker.

I. SPEAKING

Speaking and listening are complex and interrelated events. Authentic speaking has the power to change my way of looking at the world. Strategic or clichéd speech can only close things down or bring about distance between people. Like the other things human beings do, speaking often tells us something about what they would like to happen in the future. **Speaking,** no less than any other act, requires us to understand it from the point of view of the people involved: who they are, how they feel about one another, what is important to them, and so on.

A. The role of context in speaking

Facts such as these are often considered irrelevant to understanding human language. We assume that words and sentences have meaning independent of the situations in which they are used or the people using them. After all, there are dictionaries and thesauruses to give us our words and meanings; there are style books to give us our grammar. But does knowing the words and the grammar of a language tell all there is to know about speaking? If it did, if we could disregard the speaking situation—the here-and-now when I speak to you or you to me—then "I love you" would be the same as I love you. Even if these two sentences were said differently, they would look alike in a love letter, in which the reader has no clues to detect differences in tone, speed, or accent.

Speaking and language are very much related, and differences between the two are good starting points for thinking about language and speaking. There are only a few times when we pick our words first and speak later; from the point of view of personal experience, we seem to speak all at once. Our speaking is done in accord not only with what is permissible in a given language but also with hidden aspects of the situation. Unlike language, speaking always occurs in a situation, and how we understand and deal with this fact quite strongly affects what we say and understand.

Suppose, for example, we are talking to a schizophrenic patient in a mental hospital, and he says "I too was invited, I went to the ball . . . and it rolled and rolled away" (Rommetveit, 1974). Our initial reaction is likely to be confusion. Although we understand the two parts, *I went to the ball* and *it [the ball] rolled and rolled away*, the total act makes no sense to us. It is as if we have been deceived or rejected—no real communication takes place, and the notion that speaker and listener share a world is not borne out. In discussing this case Rommetveit makes the point that far from making no sense, this communication tells us that the speaker does indeed not share the "same world" or even the same set of rules for talking as we do. The speech act, no less than other acts, reveals the interperson break between the schizophrenic and us. His words have nothing to do with a fancy ball but deal instead with his rejection of our world. The message has meaning even if the words do not. We may have thought that we shared an interpersonal pact with the patient; his speech tells us how wrong we were.

Suppose, however, that we are listening to a poet, and she tells us:

> I too was invited,
> I went to the ball . . .
> It rolled
> And rolled away . . .

Even though we may not understand immediately, we are not nearly as bewildered as in our dealings with the patient. The listener may say "I think I understand, but I can't quite put it into words" or "I think the poet has captured some of those conditions of human life where we are surprised that things are never what we expect them to be" (Rommetveit, 1974, p. 57). In both interpretations we have given the writer "poetic license" to play with language in unexpected ways. Although the dictionary meanings of the words used are the same when spoken by the schizophrenic and the poet, what is understood by the listener is not. Situation makes all the difference in the world.

The philosopher Ludwig Wittgenstein (1896–1959) in his later philosophical works, compared the use of language to a game—more exactly, to a set of games (1963). To play a game we must know the pieces and the rules that tell us how to use the pieces. But we must also know when a particular set of rules applies and when it does not. Although volleyball and soccer use roughly the same-size ball, touching the ball with your hands is a forbidden move in one game (except for the goalkeeper) and absolutely necessary in the other. Neither the hands that touch nor the object touched is changed: only the rules of the game have changed. In the case of the schizophrenic and the poet, neither the words nor their dictionary meanings are changed—only the living context within which they occur.

To talk about speaking and the human use of language, it is always necessary to know something about the **living context** of speaking—the situation in which the person is speaking, the preceding sentence or sentences, who the speaker and listener are and what they know, and the relationship between them. If we do not take all this into account, we cannot be describing the human experience of speaking and listening. Instead we can only be talking about some abstract system of use and meaning called **language**. We have taken speaking out of its living situation—out of its here-and-now—and have made it into an abstract possibility that has neither a particular time nor a particular place.

Yet dictionaries and grammar books do exist, and these facts need to be dealt with. One part of the problem concerns Merleau-Ponty's distinction between **originating** and *repeated* speech. When I say "I love you" and it is true, or when Descartes says "I think, therefore I am," my world or Descartes' world is forever changed. When I say "In response to your letter" or "Come and see me sometime," my world and your world are left unchanged. The dictionary, the thesaurus, and the grammar book refer to the past; they record, from a third-person point of view, the ways words have been used and the ways most people now use them. The dictionary and thesaurus can only give us hints to what words might mean at some future time. Before you fall in love, the word *love* for you is quite different from what it will be from then on.

When we speak, we often go back and forth between originating and repeated speech. This is true even if we should say the "same" words again and again. Consider an actor playing a role in a theater for the second, third, or umpteenth time. Each time the actor says his lines and performs his gestures for a new audience, the speaking situation is alive with possibilities—especially if he is responsive to his audience. To speak the same lines is not the same if he enters fully into the present situation.

One speaking situation in which repeating the same words can be meaningful is in prayer. Reciting a well-known prayer can be an act of intense affirmation or nothing but a mechanical act having little or nothing to do with me and my relationship to God. Saying the same prayer over and over again is not important; what is important is my intention in offering the act.

B. Dictionaries and word change

Dictionaries are quite useful in reminding us that words have a history and that even seemingly fixed meanings have changed over time. Perhaps more than anyone else, the linguist Gustave Stern (1931/1954) has attempted to trace historical changes in words. Take a seemingly simple word like *horn*. Originally *horn* referred to a part of an animal. When people discovered that horns made noise, *horn* referred to an instrument used as a warning device. Then the word came to mean any of many types of brass instruments, and even today it is used as a slang expression for a trumpet or cornet. While this musical development was taking place, *horn* was also undergoing a different sort of change, a change that led to such uses as *to horn in*, *shoehorn*, or *horny*. Exactly how this latter change came about is left as an exercise in creative language use for the reader.

Deese (1967) has shown how a very simple word, *compact*, has changed drastically from 1920 until now. Originally *compact* meant "small." With the widespread use of cosmetics in the 1920s, women needed a compact case to carry their powder, and this came to be called a *compact*. In 1955, the United States got smart and began to look into the use of small automobiles. From 1955 onward, the word *compact* has come to mean a small car. With the advent of the VW bug, *compact* seems to be returning to its original use as an adjective, as in the phrase "compact economy car."

Language, however, is defined not only in terms of words and their meanings; it can also be defined in terms of sounds and letters. Here too we can trace historical changes. About 200 years ago the letter *s* was written as a kind of *f* for its first occurrence in a word, so that *original sin* was written *original fin*. Although we cannot be as sure about pronunciation, we do know from looking at early rhymes (as in Shakespeare) that *clean* was originally pronounced *clane* and rhymed with *lane*. Like the meaning of words, the very sounds and scribbles used to bring words to life have undergone continuing change over the past 1000 years or so. Despite the existence of dictionaries of all sorts, the history of language is one of change rather than one of standing still.

If change seems to describe everything there is to say about speaking and language, how is it that we ever understand one another? To approach this problem, let us begin with a quotation from the great Russian novelist Leo Tolstoy. In this episode of the novel *Anna Karenina*, we read of a declaration of love between two characters, Kitty and Levin. The dialogue opens with Levin speaking first:

> "I have long wished to ask you something."
> "Please do."
> "This," he said, and wrote the initial letters: W y a: i c n b d y m t o n. These letters meant: "When you answered: it can not be, did you mean then or never?" It seemed impossible that she would be able to understand the complicated sentence.
> "I understand," she said, blushing.
> "What word is that?" he asked, pointing to the n which stood for "never."
> "The word is 'never,'" she said, "But that is not true." He quickly erased what he had written, handed her the chalk, and rose. She wrote: I c n a o t.
> His face brightened suddenly: he had understood. It meant: "I could not answer otherwise then."
> She wrote the initial letters: s t y m f a f w h. This meant: "So that you might forget and forgive what happened."
> He seized the chalk with tense, trembling fingers, broke it, and wrote the initial letters of the following: "I have nothing to forget and forgive. I never ceased loving you."
> "I understand," she whispered. He sat down and wrote a long sentence. She understood it all and, without asking him whether she was right, took the chalk and answered at once. For a long time he could not make out what she had written, and he kept looking up into her eyes. His mind was dazed with happiness. He was quite unable to fill in the words she had meant; but in her lovely, radiantly happy eyes he read all that he needed to know. And he wrote down three letters. Before he had finished writing she was already reading under his hand, and she finished the sentence herself and wrote the answer, "yes." Everything had been said in their conversation: that she loved him, and would tell her father and mother that he would call in the morning [Tolstoy, 1944, pp. 403–404].

This example is extraordinary not only because the communication works between Levin and Kitty but also because it works even though "he was quite unable to fill in the words she had meant." In all sorts of intimate relationships the partners build a shared world that allows and even encourages them to talk in what Vygotsky (1962) has called **abbreviated speech**. To speak in a shared world is to speak differently than in a world of strangers.

Unfortunately, most scholars concerned with speaking and language are strangers to one another. They spend much of their time in solitary thought or observation, not in interperson contact. Thus, their writing and speaking tend to be dry and artificial, bereft of genuine emphasis. And because scholars generally are strangers to one another, they tend to base their analysis of all language on an analysis of distant, rather than intimate, speech. Speaking always involves a communication to, or a pact with, your listener, and only in those cases in which we are most unsure of the listener or of our ideas do we talk in the most precise and well-defined way that we can.

As Vygotsky noted, people do not do that for all kinds of speaking, particularly between intimates. We can see that in order to understand human speaking, it is always necessary to know the degree of relationship between speaker and listener. This necessity, combined with the fact that speaking and listening always take place in a specific here-and-now situation, suggests that we must always take the *here*, the *now*, and the *who* into account in talking about speaking.

C. The situation of speaking

Rommetveit (1974), for one, has tried to take all these factors into account and suggests that a diagram such as Figure 6-1 might be useful. The *before-after* line simply stresses the obvious fact that time is important—that is, when in your personal history a particular bit of speaking takes place. The *here-there* line indicates that situation is important; the *I-You* line indicates that both speaker and listener must be considered. Every speech act involves a listener, even if the "listener" is only implied, as when I write a book for an audience of readers I do not know (although I may have some general ideas about them).

The three lines of the figure give only the very simplest listing of what must be considered in describing speaking and language. Each line suggests a whole range of problems. For example, to consid-

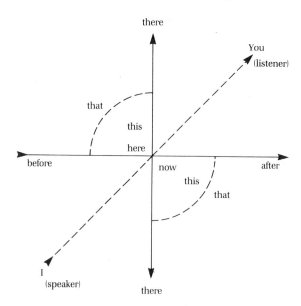

Figure 6-1. The situation of interperson speaking. (*From* On Message Structure: A Conceptual Framework for the Study of Language and Communication, *by R. Rommetveit. Copyright 1974 by John Wiley & Sons, Inc. Reprinted by permission.*)

er the *I-You* line, any would-be describer must take into account the nature of the relationship between You and Me and all that it might imply. Similarly, it is always necessary to take the speaker's (and listener's) intentions into account: "I love you" does not always mean I love you.

Some words in the diagram are at varying distances from the point where the three lines cross. Closest in to this point are the words *here* and *now;* a bit farther out in both directions from the center we find the word *this,* and even farther on we find the word *that.* It is often difficult to know, here and now, what *this* and what *that* we mean. In order for you or for me to know exactly what I mean by the word *this* or *that,* we must share some common information. *This* and *here* generally refer to something you and I are paying attention to at present and in our location; *that* and *there* refer to something we paid attention to at another time or something farther from us than *this.*

Words such as *this, that, here,* and *there* occur in almost all languages to point out or to indicate things. Such words are called **deictic elements in speaking,** after the Greek *deixis,* meaning to indicate or point out. What deictic elements point out more clearly than most other words is the need to take factors other than language into account in thinking about how we understand even the simplest of words. These nonlinguistic factors also change over time, so that in order to talk about *deixis*—as well as many other aspects of speaking—we must keep in mind that speakers and listeners share a *changing* verbal world fabricated out of their implicit agreement to talk sensibly to one another.

Such words as *it, he, she, you, I, us,* and *they* also depend in part on shared verbal worlds. The personal pronoun *she,* which occurs in many languages, always seems to single out an already-talked-about female who is not engaged as a You or an I in the present speech act.

Deictic elements and pronouns bring us back to the idea that to understand, it is necessary to look at the situation from the continuously changing first-person perspectives of the people involved. Communication takes place in a constantly changing world, and the here-and-now that constitutes human dialogue is neither completely public nor purely private, but must be thought of as an inter-person agreement established at one time, which is likely to change over the course of further conversa-tions. Such further conversations clarify what each of us knows about the world and each other, and on this basis we come to take the other person's point of view more easily and more knowledgeably.

Cases of understanding as well as of misunderstanding grow out of the more or less temporarily shared worlds that stand behind speaking. Merleau-Ponty (1962) has called this shared ground of assumptions or experiences a certain kind of silence. A conversation emerges as a figure out of this ground of silence in precisely the same way that a visual figure emerges out of a particular perceptual ground. Just as a set of geometrical lines leads to a different percept if the background or the perceiver is changed, so what is meant and understood depends on the silence out of which it emerges.

But understanding is possible only if we speak in accordance with the rules of a particular language system. Speaking, then, has both an ongoing creative aspect and an ordered preexisting one. We have the latter in mind when we talk about a child's *having* language. But it would be wrong to talk about "having language" if we meant *having* in the same sense that we talk about having a pen or a bottle. Rather, to "have language" is to have the possibility for a different kind of world—a world that is always in the process of changing and becoming.

D. Social aspects of speaking

Speaking tells us more about what is going on with the speaker than what he or she is talking about. A great many unreflected things go on when one human being talks to another, and many of these have little to do with content. Such a state of affairs should not surprise us, for like all the things people do, speaking is done by some person for one or another reason in some context.

The English linguist Roger Fowler (1974, pp. 241–242) presents the following rather ordinary exchange between himself and the bartender at a local pub. The bartender opens the conversation:

1. *Bartender:* Morning, sir.
2. *R. F.:* Morning. Not a bad morning, either. It's quite hot.
3. *Bartender:* Yes, the forecast said it would be warm. What can I get you?
4. *R. F.:* Pint of bitter, please.
5. *Bartender:* (pouring) You like [Brand X], don't you (?)
6. *R. F.:* How are they getting on with decorating the other bar?

7. *Bartender:* Oh, shouldn't be long now. They've finished the ceiling and are on the windows now. End of the week, they say. I'll be glad to see the back of them, makes such a ruddy mess—dust all over the glasses and that.
8. *R. F.:* Still, it'll be nice when it's done. It was very scruffy before.
9. *Bartender:* Oh, yes, but it's an upheaval. Sixteen pence, please.
10. *R. F.:* Thank you.
11. *Bartender:* (giving change) Thank you. Do you want to order anything?
12. *R. F.:* No, I'll wait a bit.[1]

This conversation, though not one of the great dialogues of all time, does have some interesting features. For one, it is very brief (the conversation has to be completed in the time it takes to pour a glass of beer); for another, much of it has little to do with the dictionary meanings of words used. For example, in Exchange 1, the word *morning* is used as a greeting, not as a statement about the time of day. Exchanges 2 and 3 continue the opening greeting, and (since it's England) both participants begin a discussion of the weather. Although how hot it is could help R. F. decide whether to sit outside, the talk about weather has to do with greeting the bartender (B. T.). The end of Exchange 3 gets to the real business at hand—a drink; Exchange 4 tells what it is that is wanted. Exchange 5 seems to deal with the problem at hand, yet a closer look tells us that B. T. never really waited for an answer. Exchanges 6–9 do seem to "talk about things," although it seems unlikely that R. F. is all that interested in the other bar. Exchanges 6–9 seem better described as "small talk," or that kind of talk designed to keep a conversation going where silence may indicate that I do not like or respect you. The bartender plays the same game and keeps the ball rolling until the total exchange ends with R. F. having his glass of bitter and B. T. having his 16 pence.

If you asked B. T. what went on between him and R. F., he would probably tell you he had a friendly chat. It is doubtful he would call part of their dialogue "small talk" (even if he knew it to be such), and he might even seem a bit insulted to hear that most of what went on was designed to fill the time between asking for a drink and paying for it. We all like to think we are talking about important ideas and events, even if we know we are not.

This conversation shows that some of the ways we use language do not depend for their importance on the dictionary meanings of words. R. F. gets a drink, B. T. gets his money; R. F. and B. T. talk for so-and-so many seconds, and both feel better for it. Speaking was not done mainly to transmit information or ideas; it was used to greet, to request, and to cover a possibly embarrassing silence. During this latter period the language used was "politely familiar," and each speaker understood the social distance between a college professor and a bartender. Finally, some of the words could not be understood except in this context; for example, *anything* in Exchange 11 really means *sandwiches* and is not a random comment.

1. Pronunciation and social class.   Although it is not always obvious to everyday observation, sociolinguists have shown that certain aspects of speaking tell the careful listener a great deal about the speaker. For example, Labov (1966) has shown that the occurrence (or nonoccurrence) of a particular sound in the speech of people living in New York City tells about their so-called social class. In some New York dialects the letter *r* is not pronounced at certain positions in words. *Fourth floor* is often pronounced *fawth flaw*. On the basis of his own intuitions, Labov assumed that upper-class speakers would be more likely to have an *r* in their speech than lower-class speakers. As one test of this hunch, Labov went to three department stores that could be described as of high, medium, and low status. To get a "natural" pronunciation, Labov tape-recorded answers to such questions as "Where are men's shoes?," knowing in advance that the answer would be "fourth floor." On the basis of 240 speakers he found that 30% of the salespeople in the high-status store did not pronounce the *r*, 49% did not pronounce it in the middle-status store, and 83% did not pronounce it in the low-status store.

One reason Labov asked his question in a naturally occurring situation is that people often speak differently when asked to pronounce something in a linguist's office than if asked a question on the street. In addition, most New York City speakers are at least vaguely aware that television and radio announcers do have an *r* in their speech and that not

[1]From *Understanding Language*, by R. Fowler. Copyright © by Routledge & Kegan Paul, Ltd. This and all other quotations from this source are reprinted by permission.

pronouncing the *r* is a bit of a giveaway as to the speaker's social class: no *r*, lower status.

To determine what effect different tasks would have on the pronunciation or nonpronunciation of the *r*, Labov listened to speakers during four tasks: reading a list of words, reading a passage of prose, speaking formally, and speaking casually. Figure 6-2 shows the results of this experiment for lower-class, lower-working-class, upper-working-class, lower-middle-class, and upper-middle-class speakers. With the exception of one point (the last one for lower-middle-class speakers), the results produce a remarkably systematic pattern: more *r*s are pronounced not only as social class increases but also as the formality of the speech situation increases. The one exception to this general trend (for lower-middle-class speakers reading a word list) is perhaps the most revealing of all. These speakers seem to be overcorrecting for the clearly nonprestigious pronunciation of dropping the *r*. As the *second*-highest class, they "try harder" to achieve the most prestigious pronunciation and overshoot, by about 20%, the 40–45% value produced by upper-middle-class speakers.

2. Familiar and polite pronouns. Pronunciation is not the only aspect of speaking that differs in different situations. Word choice also varies across contexts, and here we need only think of the difference between *tu* and *vous* in French or *du* and *Sie* in German—in short, the difference between the "familiar" and "polite" ways of saying "you." This distinction is also made in Italian, Spanish, Dutch, Swedish, Norwegian, Greek, Russian, and some other languages.

As you remember from high school French, German, or Spanish, familiar usage is used for speaking to people we are on casual terms with; polite usage is reserved for speaking to someone we do not know very well or to a person in authority. You would say *tu* to your girl- or boyfriend and *vous* to your teacher or boss. To the beginning speaker of any of these languages, such differences are hard to get the hang of—not only must you learn the grammatical forms of the verbs that go with the two kinds of pronouns; you would seem, at least the first few times, to have to make a judgment about how friendly or distant you are with a particular *tu* or *vous* to whom you are speaking.

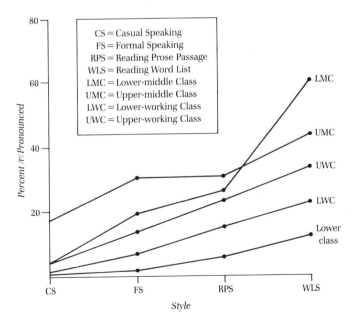

Figure 6-2. Social-class and style differentiation of postvocalic /r/ in New York City (after Labov, 1966). *(From* Sociolinguistics: An Introduction, *by P. Trudgill. Copyright © 1974 by Penguin Books, Ltd. Reprinted by permission.)*

The more important psychological point, however, is that speaking deals with much more than the simple communication of information; calling another person *tu* is quite different from calling him or her *vous*. It is not so much that the words are different; the very uttering of *tu* (or *vous*) gives the listener a clue to how he or she is being seen and reacted to. A very striking case in point involves the use of *du* and *Sie* in German. Brown and Gilman (1960) note that in Germany in 1940 a prostitute and her client said *du* (informal) when they met; *du* in bed; but *Sie* (polite) once their business was complete. Was *du* ever appropriate?

3. Male/female differences. Some societies have different speaking conventions for men and women. The classic case, reported in the 17th century, was the Carib Indians. One amateur anthropologist went so far as to claim that men and women "spoke different languages." As it turns out, there are some differences in certain aspects of male and female speech, but nowhere near what would be required to support the idea of a totally different language.

One example of these differences is provided by the ways male and female speakers of the Native American language Koasati say certain words and phrases. Although it is difficult to describe the differences and similarities exactly, Trudgill (1974) has noted that two facts seem of some importance: (1) female forms are used mainly by older (women) speakers, with younger women basically using male forms, and (2) adult speakers seem equally familiar with both male and female forms, so that, for example, if a man told a story involving a woman, he would use the appropriate female form when a female character spoke. Similarly, mothers would correct the speech of their younger male children from an (incorrect) female form to a more correct male form.

The second of these observations indicates that there is probably no taboo about using the female or male form: both men and women may use either, depending on context. The first observation, however, suggests that "female forms" may be historically older than male forms and that the group as a whole seems to be moving toward the use of the male form. When asked, most Koasati speakers indicated that the female form was the "better" or

"more appropriate" form than the male but that there was little anyone—male or female—could do about the fact that more and more people were now using the male form.

4. Silence. Speaking always strikes the listener as being surrounded by silence. Yet not all silences are the same—compare a "restful silence" with a "frightened silence"—silence can sometimes be the message, more than what was actually said. People who "aren't talking to each other" suggest that silence says as much as talking: it is not true that the person who is silent says nothing.

The American anthropologist K. H. Basso (1972) has described the profound significance of silence in the Western Apache culture. In this work, Basso found six situations in which, as his informants put it, "it is right to give up on words": (1) on meeting strangers, (2) during the initial stages of courtship, (3) between parents and children when the children have just come home from "Anglo" schools, (4) in the process of getting "cussed out" by another person, whether you (the listener) deserve it or not, (5) during a time of mourning, and (6) while attending certain ceremonies designed to pray for the sick. These six situations seem a rather random collection. Basso suggests, however, that they all represent a response to unpredictability or uncertainty in social relations. These are situations in which people do not know what is expected of them or what they can expect from others. In courting, for example, being silent with a male is taken as not knowing what to do with men, while easy talking during courting can be taken as knowing what to do with men and, therefore, as a sign of having had much experience (in all ways) with men.

One other point is worth noting in regard to silence among the members of many Native American tribes. The usual picture of the Native American as taciturn or aloof seems to have arisen because not talking is a widespread Native American practice in situations of social uncertainty. Thus, the Native American is quiet in dealing with outsiders not because of "instinctive dignity" or an "impoverished language," but because silence is the socially appropriate response to such situations. The meaning of silence has to be understood not from my quasi-European point of view, but rather from the Native American's very particular first-person point of view.

5. Speaking as an act in the world. The conclusion to be drawn from all this research is that there is hardly any social factor that does not figure into the "speaking-world" created by two persons talking to each other. The nature of this world grows out of differences and similarities in social class, power, intimacy, sex, and almost any other social factor involved in human activities. A wagging tongue is only one part of the complex living act known as speaking. Human speaking, as much as or perhaps more than any other human activity, not only exhibits the speaker and his or her social realities; it also depends on such realities for its proper interpretation. The understanding of speaking must always include some mention of the situation within which it occurs.

The idea that speaking is an act much like any other seems contrary to the idea that people speak so as to tell someone else what is on their mind. Although sociolinguists have talked about the social and interpersonal importance of speaking, it remained for two philosophers (Austin, 1962; Searle, 1969) to point out that we do things with words other than simply talk about things.

Consider the case of the 3-year-old who says "Could you get me a drink?" after being put to bed. If we look only at the dictionary meanings of the six words making up this sentence, we have to conclude that the child wants a drink. The proper reading of such a sentence would surely have to make some mention that the child does not want to go to bed just now, and although she may (or may not) "really" want a drink, one sure purpose of asking for a drink is to stay awake.

Pollio (1974) reports the anecdotal case of his daughter, then 2½ years old. At that time, Pollio was interested in having Michele learn to speak and, for this reason, commented favorably on almost anything she said. In the particular situation at hand, Michele had just got her father angry, and he began to approach her "somewhat menacingly." And what did Michele do at this point? She started walking slowly away from him and began to name objects in the room: "See table, Daddy . . . lamp . . . chair" and so on. And what could the poor father do except say "Good, Michele, that's a table . . . that's a lamp . . . that's a chair"? Score another point for Michele.

In this instance, as in "Could you get me a drink?," the meaning or importance of what was said was not given by the words used; rather, it had to do with what the words did. In one case they provided a bedtime reprieve; in the other, they seemed to ward off an angry father. Although the philosopher J. L. Austin would agree that such cases do reveal speaking to be a kind of doing, he preferred to talk more simply about how people "do things with words." For this reason, he began his discussion of speaking by considering such words as *promise, warn, command,* and *apologize*—that is, words that count as an action when said. For example, if you say "I'm sorry," you've done the act of apologizing; there is nothing more to do. Similarly, if you say "I do" at a marriage ceremony, you've gone and done it—you've got married. Legally, there is nothing else you need do.

Although such statements look just like any other statement, they do have one unique logical property: they cannot be declared false. For example, if I say "I'm sure it rained yesterday," and you say "That's not true," you don't mean that it is not true that "I'm sure"; only that it's not true that it rained yesterday. The reason for distinguishing between utterances that can be false and utterances that cannot is that philosophers and linguists often talk about the truth or falsity of a sentence and that this approach will not do if we start describing sentences as "speech-acts" rather than as "logical propositions." Austin's approach, in fact, suggests that we must stop asking questions such as "What does this sentence mean?" or "Is this sentence true or false?" and start asking questions such as "What does this sentence do?"

This type of shift asks us to think about talking as what happens when one particular human being talks to another particular human being in a particular situation for a particular reason. No less than any human act, speaking is one way of dealing with many of the things that need dealing with in the human world. As Fowler (1974) put it:

> We speak to make statements, ask questions, command, persuade, threaten, cajole, entertain; to proclaim our feelings and individual identities; to work out problems and to increase and stabilize our command over the world of things and ideas; to amuse ourselves (literature is, among other things, a sophisticated form of verbal play); to record and preserve experience; to perform rituals (marriage, legal sentence, cursing, etc.); to assist

and co-ordinate physical work (sea chanteys, children's skipping rhymes); to explore and to translate experiences; and so on [p. 243].

Speaking is always an act, never an imprecise attempt at presenting a logical proposition.

II. SPEAKING POETICALLY

Sociolinguistic research on speaking stresses the general properties that speaking shares with other human actions. Unlike other actions, however, speaking always deals with individual expression and interperson communication, which come about through the use of language. This last point is important, for it means that every speaker must re-create from the materials given by his or her culture what it is that now needs communicating. Even though each person may "use language" in a different way, and even though each person can be recognized by his or her pronunciation or word choice, there are limits on any individual's specific use of language. There is, after all, something in common between you, me, and Shakespeare, and that something is the system we call the English language.

I have a great deal of freedom within the limits language sets, however, particularly if I happen to be a skilled language user, such as a poet. If I am not a poet, I can still experience some of this freedom if I choose to speak poetically. Although poetic speaking might seem rare, Pollio, Barlow, Fine, and Pollio (1977) found that even the most ordinary of speakers uses between three and five figures of speech in every 100 or so words he or she speaks. On this basis, if we assume a speaking life of 2 hours a day for 60 years, each of us will use something on the order of 15 million instances of poetic speech.

We need not turn to arithmetic, however, to see how frequently we speak poetically. We cannot control ourselves when it comes to figures of speech: we borrow or invent them, good and bad, by the hundreds, by the millions. In terms of parts of the body, we say things like the *head* (foot) of a bed, the *mouth* of a river, the *finger* of fate, being *nosy*, having *eyes* for someone or something, *male* plugs and *female* sockets, *hairy* problems, and a list as long as your arm. Perceiving also gives us an earful: mood *indigo*, true-*blue*, a *cool* manner, a *red*-letter day,

frigid, *purple* passion or prose, *green* with envy, and *bright*-eyed, as well as many other colorful examples. Treating people as animals is still another good source: *goose*, *hawks* and *doves*, to *wolf* food, a *whale* of a time, a *snake* in the grass, and a flock of others. A list such as this is enough to make the stout-hearted blanch—or at least turn slightly green.

A. Figurative speaking in psychotherapy

The general conclusion is that speaking poetically or figuratively is not the special privilege of a few specially gifted speakers. Rather, we all use and understand poetic speech. Consider the following bit of dialogue taken from a psychotherapy interview.

Therapist: Right. [Pause.] Yeah, I think I felt a little of your sadness, then . . . and what came to mind to me was this idea of somehow deep inside of not wanting to change . . . like it's better to keep on wearing the white hat . . . that sort of confirms the suspicion you had about yourself all along . . . it's hard to take it off [the white hat].

Patient: It seems like it's sort of turned gray [faint laugh].

T: Your white hat, you mean?

P: Yeah. [Both chuckle.] A little dirty.

T: Getting a little dirty, huh?

P: I find myself on . . . like, uh . . . when, you know, like selling my car. It's sort of like . . . I'm not the nice little . . . uh . . . I don't find myself wearing a white hat . . . [Pause.] I don't know.

T: Are you afraid if you take your white hat off, you are gonna end up being the angry monster?

P: Yeah, I think I might.

T: Yeah, let's look at it this way . . . maybe the angry monster—

P: Is a little mouse about that big [holds index finger and thumb close together, laughs nervously]—the mouse that roared.

T: That would be scary, wouldn't it? Maybe the angry monster is just as much an illusion as the white hat. The mouse that roared.

In this particular case the patient was an undergraduate college student and the therapist a graduate student not particularly interested in the role of figurative language in psychotherapy. Both patient and therapist nevertheless knew a good thing when they heard one, and both made good use of poetic figures—*the white hat* and *the mouse that roared*—in trying to deal with the patient's problem.

From even a very superficial analysis of this situation, it seems clear that speaking poetically helped the patient come to some understanding of who he was, what had been happening to him, and what he might do about it. Speaking poetically turned out to be very helpful: it allowed the patient to talk about a problem he had not been able to talk about before and in such a way that he did not have to be frightened of it. As one therapist put it, poetic usage "has a half-playful, half-serious quality which permits a therapist to talk about intimate characteristics without appearing to intrude on the patient" (Lenrow, 1966, p. 145).

To study this use of poetic speaking, Pollio and Barlow (1975) looked at 1 hour of psychotherapy in which the therapist very self-consciously asked the patient to speak poetically. In order to look experimentally at the role of such speech during this hour, three independent raters first selected every example of poetic usage they could find in a written transcript of the interview. Early in the rating procedure, it was clear that patient and therapist spoke poetically in two ways. In one, the figure seemed newly created for the present situation; in the other, the patient simply repeated a standard, or clichéd, piece of poetic usage. For example, to call a stubborn person "hard" or to call a thief "crooked" is to use words that, though not exactly literal, occur very frequently in everyday speech. Such clichéd examples are called **frozen figures of speech** to contrast them with more innovative or novel uses, such as *the white hat* or *the mouse that roared*. The term *poetic usage* or *poetic figures* seems better reserved for the latter kind of phrase.

Pollio and Barlow found that the patient produced frozen figures of speech at a fairly regular rate—one almost every time the patient spoke for any length of time. Novel figures, in contrast, were produced in widely separated bursts. As an example of how Audrey, this particular patient, spoke during one of these bursts, consider the following bit of dialogue.

Audrey: Uh-huh, oh, I'm talking to the anger. [Pause.] So I won't have to hide it anymore, now, do I? I'm not asking you . . . 'cause it's there. I don't hide it. It's a failure to try and hide it 'cause it can't be hidden, even from myself. So now what am I going to do with it? 'Cause I am going to get angry. This isn't going to solve the problem of anger. I am going to get angry.

Well, I think I'll just go in and punch the pillow. That's the best I can do right now, though the kids will think I'm kind of silly . . . but they won't really.

Therapist: All right, so who's going to be thinking you're silly? What part of you is going to be calling you silly when you do this?

A: The adult side.

T: Okay, will you be the adult side of you and pretend you're sitting next to the chair and tell yourself how silly you are for doing something like that? Be your—

A: Oh, yes. I'm the moral, I'm the moral, I'm the moral Audrey [last name eliminated]. There, she's angry, she's punching the pillow . . . Oh, Audrey, you're just silly, you're just acting like a child. And . . . that's how I feel, only much more cold. There's warmth in that, and that moral Audrey just hasn't any warmth at all, not any.

T: And what does the human Audrey say back to that?

As can be seen from this excerpt, Audrey began by talking about (and, in this case, talking to) her anger—a topic that made her feel uncomfortable and silly. Responding to this, the therapist asked "Who's going to be thinking you're silly?," which then led both of them to the idea of an "adult side" and later to a moral side called "moral" Audrey. With the division of Audrey into a moral and a human Audrey, the therapist proposed a conversation between the two, hoping to provide some way for Audrey to explore her feelings toward herself as both an angry and an overly demanding person.

This analysis only demonstrates what most therapists and counselors already know: speaking poetically plays an important role in helping people come to important decisions in their lives. For Audrey, the therapist first encouraged a general discussion of her problem, then focused—with the help of poetic language—on setting up the problem in a novel way. Finally, he enabled Audrey to move out of her figure of speech into a more realistic view of herself and her problem.

But how, exactly, does speaking figuratively help problem setting and problem solving, in psychotherapy or in other situations? Problem solving requires a person to cast a familiar problem in an unfamiliar light or to cast an unfamiliar problem in a familiar light or some combination of both. Figurative speaking made the familiar—Audrey's inability to deal realistically with her feelings of anger—unfamiliar by building her supermoralist attitudes into the poetic flesh of "moral Audrey." The therapist's task was mainly to allow Audrey to see her familiar problem in this unfamiliar light and then to help her move from this way of looking at things back to her ordinary world.

B. Poetic speaking in complex problem solving

A more general description of how poetic language works in human problem solving has been made not by a therapist but by an artist/entrepreneur turned psychologist, William J. J. Gordon, in his book *Synectics* (1961). The word *synectics,* manufactured by Gordon from two Greek words, means the fitting together of diverse elements. Synectics theory is concerned with creativity and invention, particularly in industrial settings, and has been used to train members of a "problem-stating, problem-solving" group. Gordon describes his approach as a theory designed to help make us aware of the psychological mechanisms of human creative activity. The synectics approach involves trying to help the would-be problem solver to make the strange familiar (that is, to understand the problem as given, with all its various implications) and to make the familiar strange (that is, to distort, invert, or transpose the problem so that it can be viewed from a new angle). Gordon suggests the following procedures to make the familiar strange. Each involves speaking (and thinking) poetically.

1. *Personal analogy.* The person becomes the object or situation involved in a particular problem and tries to feel, think, and act as that situation or object would.

2. *Direct analogy.* The person is asked to compare the present problem with information or facts available in other (seemingly similar) problems. In actual industrial practice, the Synectics Group has found analogies from the biological sciences to be most useful.

3. *Symbolic analogy.* The person is asked to describe the elements of a problem in whatever terms seem appropriate, no matter how bizarre they might seem. Gordon sees this description as a poetic response that sums up what has been said in earlier stages. More often than not it takes the form of a poetic figure.

Although this approach may sound a bit like magic, research undertaken by this group has shown that it works. The synectics approach has been used in industry (where the standard of evaluation is a new or improved product or invention) and in science education (where grades and student comfort have been used as standards). In both cases results have been impressive: better products and better teaching.

In one attempt to look at the synectics process in a somewhat different way, Mawardi (1959) examined the patterns of communication in a highly successful industrial consulting group using synectics methods. Her analysis revealed that speaking poetically often played a significant role in defining and then in solving problems set for this group. She came to this conclusion by categorizing everything that was said during problem-solving sessions. After long and careful analysis Mawardi found that every statement could be placed into one of four categories: orientational (O), instrumental (I), abstract (A), and metaphorical (M). An orientational response was defined as any statement designed to praise, scold, redirect, or instruct the group. An instrumental statement dealt with the group's attempt to produce a possible solution; an abstract communication concerned any "intangible notion" proposed by a group member; a metaphorical response was defined as any poetic use of words. From pattern analysis Mawardi concluded that the sequence A-M-I-O was the most successful in producing a reasonable solution to the problem at hand.

C. Other aspects of poetic speaking

What all of this work on figurative language suggests is that speaking poetically is unavoidable in presenting a new idea, whether this idea be in psychology or physics. The philosopher James M. Edie (1963) has argued that this occurs because "man is not pure consciousness; he becomes conscious, little by little" (p. 545), and it is by speaking that more and more of the world becomes available. Poetic language is useful because it helps put difficult abstract concepts back in contact with the living world and thus helps us make contact with concepts. For example, Edie talks of Plato's dramatic use of sexual words in his discussion of thinking: to *conceive* an idea, to have *intercourse* with the world, *knowing* something inside and out, and so on. It is hard to describe thinking as dull when figures of speech such as these are used.

The very optimistic view of speaking poetically that has been presented to this point has not been agreed to by everyone. In a series of papers going as far back as 1900, some writers have described such speaking in much less friendly terms. Their basic idea has been that speaking poetically (like all symbolic expression, such as occurs in dreams, slips of the tongue, and so on) represents a mask for unacceptable sexual or aggressive urges. Like other symbols, ordinary vocabulary items clothe such urges in respectability and let the speaker hide the "real" meaning or intent of his or her words. For example, by speaking poetically a patient may keep the therapist from significant problem areas, and only by asking the patient why he or she is using such "funny" language can the therapist unmask what is being hidden.

We need not take a therapeutically based point of view to realize that poetic speaking can be used to hide behind. A politician put on the spot often resorts to speaking in platitudes (frozen figures) to smother an embarrassing question. In fact, public speakers are often taught explicitly (see Osborn & Ehninger, 1962) to speak in clichéd (frozen poetic) ways so as to provoke an expected response in the political listener. Calling a Communist a "Red" or a person on relief a "freeloader" presents examples of this kind of talk. In political speech, new ideas are often pushed aside in favor of those that can be counted on to arouse the audience in predictable ways.

One final aspect of poetic expression is that poets often seem to violate the ordinary rules of speaking or writing—as in e. e. cummings' use of lower-case letters where ordinary rules demanded capital ones. Poets prefer to think that they extend, rather than violate or destroy, language. The French poet Paul Valéry has noted that the poet is a person who has decided to change "the walking of prose to the dancing of poetry." Prose always has a definite aim, and it can approach a universal idea only when a speaker decides to dance—momentarily, as in poetic expression, or more enduringly, as in a great poem.

In poetry, and to a lesser extent in all human speaking, it is possible to see that speaking is both for us the speakers and for the people to whom we speak. Were speaking only for us, we could speak in completely personal and subjective ways. As it is, each of us is also responsible for saying something that can be understood by someone else. The tension between personal and interperson speaking is nowhere more easily seen than in poets practicing their craft or in more ordinary people speaking poetically. Poetic speech is the narrow borderland between first-person talk and interperson communication.

III. LANGUAGE

If no one spoke, could there be such a thing as language? Our first reaction must surely be "Why, yes, of course, what a silly question!" Yet if we think about it for a moment, our answer will be much less sure. The example of dead languages—that is, those no longer spoken, such as classic Greek or ancient Sumerian—would seem to say "Yes, there can be languages even if no one speaks them." If we think a bit more, however, it is clear that people must have spoken the dead language once upon a time, and it seems much more reasonable to conclude that speaking precedes language. If no one *ever* spoke, there could be no such thing as language.

This is as it should be, for even though we can say someone *uses* this or that language, what we mean more exactly is that he or she *does* something with a special set of sounds, words, phrases, and sentences, whether that something is writing, speaking, or reading. Language is not something we use in the same way we use a razor or a hammer; we only know someone "uses" English, French, or Chinese because that person speaks (or writes or reads) in a special way.

Language, then, is always an inference from what speakers do; we never "see" language directly. Although we may feel that we all know what language is, all we ever know is speaking people. Language with a capital L is an abstract system made up out of our desire to describe the orderly events that happen when a person speaks. As first-person speakers, we are hardly ever aware of the systematic nature of our speech. To recognize and describe this order, we must step back into a third-person point of view and seek order in the speaking of other people.

The French linguist Ferdinand de Saussure was the first to make a distinction between language and speech. For de Saussure (1916/1959) *language* refers to an abstract system, whereas *speech* refers to ongoing behavior. Language appears only after analysis; speech is what speakers do. Although this distinction may not sound important, an example may make its importance clearer. Every time a Russian speaks, he or she is adding to the sum of speech that goes on in his or her community. Each Russian speaker is in no way adding to the Russian language. The abstraction known as the Russian language is subject to different sorts of factors from those affecting a Russian speaking. The conclusion is that speaking is living, ongoing *behavior* and that language is a useful abstraction derived from the ongoing flow of speech.

Fortunately, there is a great deal of order to speaking, and the science of language, **linguistics,** has been quite successful in describing this order in useful and general ways. Originally, at the turn of the century, linguistics was part of anthropology, and the major job of linguists was to provide an alphabet for so-called primitive languages that did not yet have a way of converting speech to writing. Consider the scope of language problems facing a linguist at the turn of the century: He or she arrives at a distant land, and a strange flood of sounds strikes the ear. The sounds are jumbled; there seem to be no breaks between what will later be called words and phrases, and only occasionally does a speaker pause in the middle of speaking. It goes without saying that very little is understood. Although the linguist and the speaker can and do point to things as needed (and this pointing will later serve to teach linguists and speakers some of the words in each other's language), that is not enough help at the beginning.

If this sounds hard to imagine, think back (or ahead) to your first trip to a non-English-speaking country. When you step off your plane at the Istanbul airport, everything everyone is saying sounds like an undistinguishable blur of strange noises. Although the bellboy may be smiling, it does little to calm your fear that you don't know what's going on. Announcements over the P.A. system in two languages you don't understand are of little help, and you wonder what you are doing here. Until you hear that first word of English (or even French), you feel totally adrift, with no signposts to tell you which way to go.

Fortunately, your "cool" doesn't desert you entirely, and you begin to look for a friendly face, meaning one who looks as if he or she might speak English, or at least one who will be patient while you go through the motions of conveying that you

would sure like to know where the bars, restaurants, and toilets are. Depending on what your priorities are at that moment, you'll find it easy or difficult to pantomime your wish.

Although a fairly direct and graphic "gesture language" will help you get along for a while, you soon need some words. In order to get them, you extend your gesture language to include something like "How do you say X?"—while pointing to your shoe, belt, or whatever. Although you may not be able to make out the word the first time, a few repetitions will yield not only the missing word but some of the sounds of the language as well.

The early linguist regularly faced problems of this sort. There is a difference, however, between our problems and the linguist's. We want to learn how to talk so as to satisfy our needs. The linguist must not only learn how to talk, he or she must also get the native speakers to talk about talking. We intend to use our newly learned skills to speak of everyday matters; the linguist wants to develop a third-person description of someone's first-person experience within the presently unknown language. Just talking is not enough; the linguist has to invent special procedures to record as clearly and as consistently as possible the language he or she hears.

There are three special classes of information the linguist must find out and systematize for a language: its sounds, its grammar, and its meanings. In the special terminology of linguistics, the linguist studies **phonology** (sounds), **syntax** (grammar), and **semantics** (meanings), and these three areas are the major working divisions of linguistic science.

A. Phonology

Consider the sounds of a language such as English. You might think that all the linguist has to find is the 26 letters of our alphabet, and the job of writing down the sounds of English is done. But see how many different spoken sounds are produced by the same letters in the following poem. (This poem, by the way, was written for a young girl learning English. For best effect, read the poem aloud.)

Lines on the Pronunciation of English

Dearest creature in Creation,
Studying English pronunciation,
I will teach you in my verse
Sounds like corpse, corps, horse and worse.

Just compare heart, beard and heard,
Dies and diet, lord and word,
Sword and sward, retain and Britain,
(Mind the latter, how it's written!)

But be careful how you speak,
Say break, steak, but bleak and streak;
Previous, precious, fuchsia, via;
Pipe, swipe; recipe and choir.

From "desire," desirable—admirable from "admire";
Lumber, plumber, bier, but brier;

And your pronunciation is O.K.
When you say correctly croquet;
Rounded, wounded; grieve, and sieve;
Friend and fiend; heave and heaven;
Rachel, ache, moustache, eleven. . . .

And so on, for 80 more lines, until the last four:

Finally, which rimes with "enough,"
Though, through, plough, cough, hough or tough?
Hiccough has the sound of "cup" . . .
My advice is—Give it up.

If consonants weren't trouble enough, there are still the vowels: the letter *a* can be pronounced in about eight ways according to a good English dictionary. It is easy to see that it is impossible to use only the 26 letters of our alphabet to represent all the sounds that occur even in English. (Most linguists record from 31 to 35 sounds in the speech of English-speaking people.)

Linguists therefore invented a set of symbols to record as many sounds as they could hear in a number of languages. The total list is called the International Phonetic Alphabet—"phonetic" because it deals with sound and "international" because it is meant to be used with all languages. In this alphabet, for example, *the* is written [ðə], where ð is read as "th" and the upside-down *e* is read as "uh." The word *ball* is written [bɔl]. Because a consonant does not take many forms, ordinary English letters are often used. Most of the new symbols invented for use in the International Phonetic Alphabet stand for vowel sounds, which are more varied in most languages.

Although the International Phonetic Alphabet has well over 80 symbols, not all languages use all of them. So, for example, the sound [ts], which occurs in Hebrew, does not occur in English, and the prob-

lem becomes one of finding the smallest number of sounds in a language that "make a difference." In English it turns out to be about 33 symbols—slightly more (35) or fewer (31), depending on where you live—and these are called the **phonemes** of English.

To see what a phonemic transcription looks like for English, consider the following exercise, taken from a workbook in linguistics (Gleason, 1961):

> ðə stiyd bit ɨz mæster,
> haw keym ðɨs tə pæнs?
> hiy hərd ðə gud pæstər
> kray, ɔнl fleš ɨz græнs.

The translation is as follows:

The steed bit his master
How came this to pass?
He heard the good pastor
Cry, all flesh is grass.[2]

Phonemics is tricky business to the uninitiated. To help just a bit more, consider the following anecdotal case history of a young child who had only a single pheneme for /k/ and /t/; that is, she did not distinguish between them. Four words caused terrible problems: *cake, take, Kate,* and *Tate.* Each word was responded to as if it were any of the other three. For example, this child would just as often say "take," "Kate," or "Tate" when she was pointing to a piece of cake. The sentence "Take Kate Tate cake" sounded to this child like the same word said four times. From little Kate Tate's first-person point of view, these words were all acceptable variations on one another.

Linguists are proud of their work in developing the phoneme. Such pride does seem justified, for not only does the discovery of a phoneme meet the most rigorous of third-person objective standards, it also takes into account the first-person point of view of the mature speaker. To define a phoneme properly, the linguist must first collect a set of sounds peculiar to a given language. Without many presuppositions, he or she looks for regularities and overlap in the sounds collected. Only when the linguist feels almost sure that a unique sound grouping has been uncovered will this grouping be presented to a native speaker for verification. To define

---

[2] From *Workbook in Descriptive Linguistics*, by Henry Allan Gleason, Jr. Copyright 1955 by Holt, Rinehart and Winston, Inc. Reprinted by permission of Holt, Rinehart and Winston.

a phoneme as a unit of sound that makes a difference to a native speaker of the language is to include both first- and third-person points of view.

Like the idea of language itself, the phoneme is an abstraction—a concept—and exists only when we deal reflectedly with language. Phonemes never appear to the speaking person unless he or she is specially asked to notice how something that is said sounds. Such situations do not usually occur in speaking; they are more likely to occur if we are asked to spell something, especially if we have never spelled it before. To some degree, we all can do what the linguist does; if not, no one would be able to spell. In speaking, however, there are no phonemes for the speaker, only speaking. From a first-person point of view, we speak and the sounds take care of themselves.

B. Syntax

The fact that language in its spoken form seems to go from beginning to end and in written form (in English) from left to right suggests that we ought to be able to describe sentences as going in a straight line from beginning to end. Such a suggestion seems quite plausible if we follow a procedure suggested by Philip Broughton of the United States Public Health Service. As we all know, government forms are filled with their own particular brands of jargon, and the Public Health Service is no exception. To help in getting a memo through the system, Broughton offers the three columns of "popular words" in Table 6-1, designed to make it appear

that the speaker or writer knows what he or she is talking about.

The procedure is simple: think of a three-digit number—for example, 937. Looking now at Broughton's table, 937 turns out to be the phrase *balanced reciprocal projection,* and who in his or her right mind would admit to not knowing what a balanced reciprocal projection was? If we try any set of three numbers, such as 000 *(integrated management options),* the phrases do sound as if we knew what we were talking about.

What is most important about this technique from a linguistic point of view is that it shows how easy it is to produce perfectly good English phrases by picking words in a preset order. In Table 6-1, at least, going from left to right produces a perfectly good grammatical phrase. Unfortunately, word order is not the most important part of producing meaningful phrases in some other languages, such as German. If this were the only problem with Broughton's approach, we might well shrug our shoulders and say "Well, it works for English, anyway."

Unfortunately, this is not the case even for English. One very obvious problem can be seen if we look at the following sentences, proposed by the American linguist Noam Chomsky: (1) "Visiting relatives can be boring." (2) "They are cooking apples." Consider Sentence 1. Nothing very important seems to be involved. Yet looks are deceiving, for it is soon clear that we cannot tell what can be boring—to visit relatives or relatives who visit. The same sentence can have different meanings, and that does

TABLE 6-1. How to Win at Wordsmanship

Column 1	Column 2	Column 3
0. integrated	0. management	0. options
1. total	1. organizational	1. flexibility
2. systematized	2. monitored	2. capability
3. parallel	3. reciprocal	3. mobility
4. functional	4. digital	4. programming
5. responsive	5. logistical	5. concept
6. optimal	6. transitional	6. time-phase
7. synchronized	7. incremental	7. projection
8. compatible	8. third-generation	8. hardware
9. balanced	9. policy	9. contingency

Source: From "How to Win at Wordsmanship: New Peak for Newspeak," by P. Broughton. Copyright 1968 by Newsweek, Inc. All Rights Reserved. Reprinted by permission.

not seem such a good thing for any logical analysis of the system known as the English language.

The problem is not as serious as it seems, for, after all, I was able to describe both possible meanings, and you were able to understand both grammatical structures. A *grammatical* pun, such as "Visiting relatives can be boring," is possible only because human beings make tacit (unreflected) use of this structure in speaking. Human speakers not only respond to the grammatical nature of a particular sentence; it is an absolute necessity that we know a good deal more about grammatical structure if we are to speak or understand sentences at all. Although words may come out in a left-to-right sequence, we understand the sentence as a whole, never a piece at a time.

To explain how we understand sentences, linguists have suggested that language must be seen not only as a system but as a rule-governed system in which rules go from very general to very specific. But how exactly should we understand what linguists mean when they use the term *rule?* One psychologist, Ulrich Neisser (1967), pointed out that the word *rule* can have two meanings: as a restriction and as a recipe. A "Keep off the Grass" sign is an example of rule-as-restriction. The idea of rule-as-recipe is given by statements found in a cookbook: "Take the white of two eggs, beat in a dash of cinnamon, fold gently. . . ." When linguists talk of a rule of grammar, they mean a recipelike procedure that, when applied, will generate good, clear grammatical sentences.

But what does it mean to say "Rules generate sentences"? When linguists talk about a rule generating a sentence, they do not mean that a speaker produces sentences on the basis of one or another grammatical rule. Rather, rules allow us to describe the structure of any and all sentences that could be produced in a language. A **generative grammar** is a system of rules that allows us to say whether any given sentence could or could not be produced in a particular language. Generative rules do not help speakers make sentences; rather, they allow the linguist to generate or produce an abstract pattern that, in turn, enables us to decide whether a given set of words is a possible sentence in that language.

The idea of a generative grammar reminds us that linguists deal with grammar as they deal with words—as part of an abstract system known as language, not with a speaking person. The logical form of what is said is important to the linguist, not how it was produced by a flesh-and-blood speaker. It is only because linguistic descriptions *are* abstract (not specific to speakers) that they can be used to describe what is possible in a given language.

C. Semantics

If we are looking for a "speaker-free" way of talking about meaning in language, we have two examples to choose from—the dictionary and the thesaurus. A dictionary contains all the words considered by some group of people to be important for a particular language. These words are gathered together, put in alphabetical order, and given precise-sounding definitions. From our point of view as would-be users, we can find the meaning of a word only if we already know the word. It is very difficult, if not impossible, to begin with a meaning and find a word.

But how, exactly, does a dictionary tell us what a word means? Usually by providing other words that the word in question is related to. Sometimes we find a picture, and often we find the word used in a sentence or phrase. In addition, there are markings identifying the word's grammatical class (noun, verb, and so on), and if the dictionary is an expensive one, there may even be a brief history of the word and its ancestors.

Considered as a model for how human beings use words meaningfully, the dictionary has a great many limitations. Most important are that it is ordered by the not-very-useful but orderly principle of the alphabet, that it requires you to know a word before you can look it up, and that it sometimes gives a definition that may not be understood. Although a dictionary may be perfectly useful in reading or in looking up how to spell a word, it does seem a bit awkward for use in speaking—that is, for telling us what word it is whose meaning we want to express. In speaking (or writing), the usual experience seems to be knowing what you want to say first and then finding the word or words later.

For this reason a thesaurus seems a better model for word meaning. First, the thesaurus was set up to help us when we know what we want to say but do not have the right word to say it with. Second, words are not only arranged alphabetically, they are also ordered on the basis of some 1000 or so categories, which fall into about six or seven major ones. The 200,000 or so words (give or take 50,000) entered in *Roget's Thesaurus* are divided into categories such as Abstract Relations, Space, and Matter. Each of these major categories is then subdivided into lower-level categories, which in turn are divided into still more precise categories, until individual words appear in the narrowest category. Behind the use of any given word is a clearly organized set of categories. The overall organization of these categories is nothing less than an impressionistic representation of what it is human beings know, talk, and write about.

One other very important aspect of the thesaurus is that it contains two indexes. In one index, words are organized on a category-by-category basis; in the other, they are organized alphabetically. In this second index, the categories too appear alphabetically. Thus, it is possible to get from a word to other words as well as from ideas to words. Although a thesaurus does not define a word in the same way a dictionary does (it does, however, tell parts of speech), it is capable of putting you in the right ball park, so that an initially unfamiliar word can be made less strange by looking it up in the thesaurus.

For these reasons it seems better to talk about meaning in terms of a thesaurus rather than a dictionary. Although the thesaurus does not give a perfectly specifiable sentence or phrase defining a word, it does provide enough clues to give us an approximate meaning. Similarly, in listening to speech we often come to the meaning of a word on the basis of a rough understanding rather than a highly polished definition. In fact, it is well known that we can use new words in meaningful and reasonable ways long before we can go through the rather strange business of providing a fully developed and precise dictionary definition.

The thesaurus seems to be what we seek. Before it is possible to say amen, it is necessary to handle one further bit of business, and this concerns finding (or inventing) the categories a speaker might have in mind when he or she uses a particular word. As some help in showing how a linguist might go about discovering these categories, consider the following eight words: *father, aunt, uncle, daughter, mother, son, niece, nephew.* Suppose a linguist asked you, as a native speaker of English, to divide them into two groups of four each. It seems reasonable that you might break them up as follows:

A_1 father, mother, son, daughter
A_2 uncle, aunt, niece, nephew

Suppose you were then asked to break them up into two new groups of four each, and you did it as follows:

B_1 father, mother, uncle, aunt
B_2 son, daughter, nephew, niece

And finally suppose you did it once more and produced the following groupings:

C_1 father, son, uncle, nephew
C_2 mother, daughter, aunt, niece

Each of the three divisions is made on the basis of one or another concept. The four words in one group share that concept, and the other four words do not. A_1 contains members of the immediate family; A_2 contains more "distant" relatives. B_1 is older than B_2. C_1 is male and C_2 is female. The groups produced suggest that we can say three concepts serve to organize this set of words: concept A is degree of relationship; concept B is age; concept C is sex.

Given these three concepts, it is possible to diagram this particular set of eight words as in Table 6-2. Within this approach each word can be described in terms of its set of pluses and zeros. For example, *father* can be represented as $[+,0;+,0;+,0]$. *Niece* can be represented as $[0,+;0,+;0,+]$. It is usual to simplify this system by representing a "plus, zero" condition under a given concept as a plus and representing a "zero, plus" condition as a minus. Thus, *father* can be represented as $[+,+,+]$; *niece* becomes $[-,-,-]$. Representing the meaning of a word in this way has a number of very nice consequences. For one, it is possible to describe the degree of similarity between any two words in the set in terms of how many concepts (pluses and minuses) they have in common. So, for example, *father* and *niece* have no concepts in common, whereas *father* $[+,+,+]$ and *son* $[+,-,+]$ share two of three.

Perhaps the major gain from looking at things in this way is that it becomes easy to organize lots of words with only a few semantic concepts. In a perfectly organizable system of words—that is, where it is possible to describe each word as "having" $(+)$ or

TABLE 6-2. Classification of Eight Relationship Terms under Three Concepts

	A Relationship		B Age		C Sex	
Word	Near	Far	Old	Young	Male	Female
Father	+	0	+	0	+	0
Mother	+	0	+	0	0	+
Son	+	0	0	+	+	0
Daughter	+	0	0	+	0	+
Uncle	0	+	+	0	+	0
Aunt	0	+	+	0	0	+
Nephew	0	+	0	+	+	0
Niece	0	+	0	+	0	+

"not having" ($-$) a concept—the total number of words that can be organized is equal to 2^C, where C is the number of concepts. The number is 2^C because each concept can have one of two values ($+$ or $-$). Therefore, three concepts can cover exactly 2^3, or 8, perfectly organizable words: *father, mother, son, daughter,* and so on. A little arithmetic will show that five concepts will be able to handle 32 words, ten concepts will be able to handle 1024 words, and only 20 concepts will be able to handle a perfectly ordered set of over 1 million words.

Now this is a very exciting possibility: imagine being able to describe over 1 million different words with only 20 categories. There is a logical elegance in talking about word meanings in this way, and it is therefore not surprising to find that linguists and psychologists were very enthusiastic about such models of word meaning when they first appeared in linguistics. Unfortunately, the economy achieved by this way of talking about meaning is more theoretical than real, mostly because words do not have fixed meaning-concepts. Rather, words can always be used in a new way, and this new way prevents us from ever exhausting all that we or some speaker may mean by a word.

Consider the word *blue.* If we take it to mean a color, then phrases such as *a blue dress* or *sky-blue* can be easily understood. If, however, we still take it to mean a color but use it poetically (as in *blue baby* or *blue Monday*), the meaning of *blue* is quite different; no longer is it a moderately pleasant or even a neutral word. In the context of these two phrases, *blue* has crossed the boundary from a "pleasing" to a "sad" word. Without much imagination we can talk about a *blue* film; now *blue* has changed from pleasant to unpleasant to downright sexy. A *blue* ribbon, however, would seem to get *blue* almost

back where it started. In the course of going from *blue* to *blue* to *blue* back to *blue,* we seem to need the following meaning-concepts: color ($+,-$), pleasant ($+,-$), happy ($+,-$), sexy ($+,-$).

What is at issue here is that the idea of a meaning-concept, which appears so reasonable at first glance, is not very clear. If meaning-concepts are to be useful, they need to describe something that is relevant for all or most of the words we use and understand. Unfortunately, there are no threads that go across all the words in our vocabulary. Instead, we find concepts that are relevant only to a small subset of vocabulary items, such as family (*mother, father,* and so on), animal names, or types of games. Although *Roget's Thesaurus* suggests that it should be possible to find general concepts, the truth is that it is not. Even the thesaurus was forced to invent a rather hodgepodge category, Disjunctive-Conjunctive-Quantity, under its more general category of Abstract Relations.

Dictionaries and thesauruses, then, do not help in describing a universally meaningful organization of words. These books are not so much collections of *speaking* words as of *spoken* words. The dictionary, like the thesaurus (and the grammar book), tells us how a timeless, situationless, and ideal speaker *has* used this or that word in this or that sentence. It can never predict how the word may be used by some living person, having some living reason, in some living speech context.

This limitation of dictionaries is not surprising if we remember what the linguist is trying to do. For the linguist, the meaning of a word need not have much to do with its relation to the world or to a speaker; rather, meaning is described in terms of relations among different words in the language system. In this, the linguist's work is an intellectual exercise more akin to logic and mathematics than to poetry or fiction.

D. A postscript on speaking and language

Even though no one seems to know how to deal with language in a satisfactory way, it is clear that the idea of language does mean something. Even though the dictionary or the thesaurus may not be a good model for how the human being deals with words, it is certainly true that dictionaries and thesauruses exist for many languages. Similarly, books of grammar exist for many languages, and to say that all there is to language is speaking is to overlook the very obvious fact that Russian is not Chinese and both are not English.

What, then, *is* the relation between speaking and language? To speak is to draw on the past of a particular community so as to say something in the present. Although not one of us would describe language as the linguist does, we all do use a very special set of highly patterned noises when we talk. To talk is always to talk in some special situation, and this situation is defined not only by speaker, listener, and context, but by the language as well. To speak, therefore, is to use already-established possibilities for present purposes. Language is a cultural inheritance passed on from one generation to the next. Like all such gifts, it must be used to be owned. The ready-made sounds, words, and sentences of a language become our sounds, our words, and our sentences only to the degree that we use them to invoke the contours of our experiences in ourselves and in someone else. This is what we do to claim our inheritance: to talk genuinely from ourselves and thereby bring new worlds out of old words. We will find nothing new in language if we fail to put something new into it—and what we put into it, of course, is ourselves.

IV. SPEAKING, LANGUAGE AND THINKING; SPEAKING, LANGUAGE AND SEEING

Do we take our own language too seriously? Does it really matter whether you or I speak English, Swahili, or Arabic—aren't they "really" all the same? Although on a day-to-day basis most of us are not terribly concerned with what language we speak, there are enough examples in history to tell us that political leaders do not share our casual attitude.

The number of legal prohibitions against one or another language is astounding, and the following is only a partial list.

1. In Franco's Spain, beginning in about 1940, the Catalonian language (which has some 7 million speakers in Valencia and on the Balearic Islands) was banned from the public schools. Departments of Catalonian language and literature were abolished at the University of Barcelona and elsewhere. Textbooks, legal and political documents, and newspapers could be printed only in Spanish, and the use of Catalonian was everywhere forbidden in an attempt to outlaw the separatist tendencies of Catalonian-speaking citizens.

2. Following the 1917 revolution in Russia, official policy was to encourage each of the 200 or so ethnic groups to make use of its own language. Unhappily, under Stalin, there was a tendency to demand a single central language, although some ethnic languages, such as Georgian (Stalin's native language), were granted privileged status. As part of Stalin's centralization scheme, Russian was to be written in the Cyrillic rather than in the Latin alphabet, and certain minority languages, such as Yiddish, were to be discouraged. Although Russian is still officially the "second native language" of the Soviet Union, long articles appear in *Pravda* and elsewhere praising it as an "unfailing source of enrichment" for minority languages. In addition, all new technical words are coined in Russian, never in any other Russian language.

3. Finally, there is the paradoxical case of South Africa, where minority languages have been encouraged rather than suppressed. Thus, such languages as Zulu or Xhosa were encouraged for the various tribal groups, while English and Afrikaans were never taught to them. The Bantu Education Department, which was set up to educate all Africans in their mother tongue, can be seen as an attempt to isolate each tribe from every other, as well as from the ruling elite, international literature, and so on. (In the past decade or so, this policy has been reversed, with English and Afrikaans now being taught in tribal schools.)

This third case is an interesting one. Here, political policy dictated strengthening rather than weakening different ethnic languages. Thus, similar political ends—consolidating the power of a ruling central government—were served by two completely different means. But why should the use of one or another language be important politically? The usual answer is that separate languages promote separate identities, and separate identities can be dangerous (as in Franco's Spain or Stalinist Russia) or desirable (as in South Africa). Yet the question remains why one or another language should (or should not) make you feel a greater kinship to your own or a different ethnic group.

A. The Whorf hypothesis

There is more here than meets the eye. For openers, there is the implicit assumption that all languages talk of the same world even if the words and grammatical constructions are different: a rose by any other name would, after all, still smell as sweet. For this point of view language simply lets us talk about "the world"; in no way does it affect how we see or understand that world. All languages are different ways to talk about the same thing.

But is it the "same" if we talk about this or that part of the world in Zulu, Russian, or English? Does how you talk about something make a difference to how you will think about, or perhaps even perceive, what that "something" is like? Consider again the case of *tu* and *vous*. From a very personal first-person point of view, it seems that it will sometimes matter a good deal if my language has a polite and a more intimate mode of address. It certainly would matter to a wife or lover if she was called *tu* or *vous*. If I speak only English, I might not so easily recognize (or signal) different degrees of intimacy as would be true if I spoke French.

Surely the other person is not a different person if I call her *vous* than if I call her *tu*. It is likely, however, that if I call you *tu*, I also behave differently toward you than if I call you *vous*. As a consequence, you probably also behave differently toward me. The world is changed—our perspectives, actions, and understanding have been shifted by the use of one or another word—and this shift seems more likely in a language that has a *tu* and a *vous* form than in one that does not.

But surely a word does not make such a big difference in how I see, understand, and act toward other parts of the world that are not people? Here we need only think of the psychologically important words and phrases that have occurred in earlier chapters: *mind/body* (Chapter 1); imagining as

seeing pictures in the mind's picture gallery (Chapter 5); *love* rather than *loving* (Chapter 1); *the mouse that roared* (Chapter 6); and so on. These examples show what a difference a word or phrase can make. In each of these cases, the way we came to understand a particular psychological process or a particular philosophical idea was strongly colored by the particular words we used to talk about that process or idea.

Events such as these occur not only in the ivory tower but in industrial settings as well. Benjamin Lee Whorf, the American linguist/anthropologist who most strongly pushed the idea that "language shapes rather than mirrors reality" (1956), an idea now called the **Whorf hypothesis,** first came to be interested in this problem as part of his work as a claims adjuster for an insurance company. In this job he found that many industrial fires were caused not only by people throwing lighted matches where they should not but by an inappropriate understanding of certain words. For example, when a gasoline or kerosene drum has been emptied of its gasoline or kerosene, highly inflammable vapors remain for a fairly long time. We will then ordinarily say "The gasoline drum is empty," and this is taken to mean that there is nothing in it. Given that the drum now "has nothing in it," it is all right to smoke in the area, and given that it is all right to smoke in the area—Kaboom! Here comes Whorf the Adjuster.

All these examples—*tu* and *vous, empty, seeing pictures in the mind's picture gallery*, and the rest—involve difficulties within a single language, be it French, German, English, or whatever. Whorf's analysis really picks up steam, however, not by comparing words and concepts in the same language but by looking at differences across different language communities. Because Whorf knew most about Native American and Eskimo languages, many of his examples involve a comparison between these languages and a collection of Indo-European languages made up of English, French, German, and Italian, which he lumped together and called "Standard Average European" (SAE).

In one of his best-known contrasts, Whorf noted that SAE had only one word, *snow*, to describe a large class of things that included falling snow, icy snow, good-packing snow, and so on. The Eskimo has many words for the various kinds of snow and finds the idea of a single word impossibly limiting. To the Aztec, the situation is quite different: not only is there only one word for all the great varieties of snow; the same Aztec word also means "ice" and "cold" as well as "snow."

Even more important than these specific word differences are differences in grammar between different languages. For example, consider something as simple as the difference between nouns and verbs. If we think about this difference in a very general way, somehow or other we have the feeling that nouns name relatively long-lasting events, such as houses and tables, whereas verbs, such as *turn* or *run*, name events that are over and done with quickly. If so, Whorf asked, why are *fist*, *lightning*, and *spasm* classified as nouns and *keep*, *possess*, and *persist* classified as verbs? If we object that *keep* and *possess* are verbs because they deal with stable relations rather than with stable perceptions (whatever those might be), we will still be unable to handle such nouns as *current* or *equilibrium*.

Because of phenomena such as these, it seems that to classify a word as a noun or a verb means to classify it according to the grammar of a language. A noun *is* a noun because it fills a certain grammatical role in our language, not because there is some category in the world demanding to be called by nouns. Although it may be possible to define nouns and verbs in some abstract way ("a noun names a thing, place, person . . ."), there are enough exceptions to suggest that we do not define nouns or verbs "from nature" but from grammatical constraints in our language.

If this is true, we should find that different languages put different words into each of these categories. And so they do. In Hopi, for example, *wave*, *flame*, and *meteor* are classified as "verbs"—that is, they are in the grammatical class that Hopi language reserves for events that are over and done quickly. Words such as *cloud* and *storm* are at the lower limit for "nouns," because Hopi classifies words along a fairly strict time dimension. Hopi gives us two classes that resemble our English nouns and verbs, although the "rules" that sort a word into one of the two classes differ somewhat between the two languages. In the Nootka language (which is spoken on the Vancouver and nearby islands in Canada), there is only a single class, so that it is equally proper, in Nootka, to say "a house occurs" and "it houses." For Nootka, nature is not divided into categories of "things that *are*" (nouns) and "things that *do*" (verbs); rather, nature is always talked about as in process. Even the most "noun-like" of events, such as houses or boats, have "verb-like" qualities.

Speaking is thus not the handmaiden of thinking. The categories of a language constrain and shape what is "thinkable" by the people speaking that language. Poets such as W. H. Auden have gone so far as to say that "words will tell you things you never thought or felt before." Words are not incidental to communicating; rather, they serve to shape what we think and say. Since words always occur within a language, the grammar of the language is as important as its words in shaping what is thinkable in a particular language community. For Whorf, to speak a language is to make the world it expresses one's own, and each language brings into existence its own unique world.

But what about a person who speaks two or more languages—does he or she live in two worlds? The answer is that one of the two languages usually presents the everyday world in which the person lives. Consider the remarkable testimony of an Englishman, Lawrence of Arabia, who not only spoke two languages but actually lived for many years as an Arab among Arabs:

> In my case, the effort for these years to live in the dress of Arabs, and to imitate their mental foundation, quitted me of my English self, and let me look at the West and its conventions with new eyes. . . . At the same time I could not sincerely take on the Arab skin. . . . Easily was a man made an infidel, but hardly might he be converted to another faith. I had dropped one form and not taken on the other. Such detachment came at times to a man exhausted mechanically, while his reasonable mind left him, and from without looked down critically on him. Sometimes these selves would converse in the void; and then madness was very near, as I believe it would be near the man who could see things through the veils at once of two customs, two educations, two environments [cited in Merleau-Ponty, 1962, pp. 187–188].[3]

For just these reasons it seems impossible to think that one and the same person could live in the very specific linguistic worlds presented by two

[3]Excerpted from *The Seven Pillars of Wisdom* by T. E. Lawrence. Copyright 1926, 1935 by Doubleday & Company, Inc. Reprinted by permission of Doubleday & Company, Inc. and Jonathan Cape, Ltd.

languages, especially if they could not be directly coordinated with each other—for example, Arabic and English. Even people who speak two languages seem to live in the light of only one culture at a time. If they tried to live simultaneously in both, madness, in Lawrence's words, would surely be near.

Speaking within a given language brings about a special way of relating to the world. Even within the same language, the use of a special word or phrase set in a new or different context can bring about a new way of dealing with a problem. Speaking poetically reveals a situation in a new and transformed way: the word or phrase used not only expresses an idea but may bring it uniquely into existence for the first time. Our ideas live only in the light of the words and phrases used to express them, and each language provides its own pattern of light and shadow.

B. Whorf's hypothesis and the world of color

If any of these assumptions has value, we ought to be able to demonstrate differences in thinking or perceiving between people speaking vastly different languages. To do this systematically, it is necessary to find some aspect of the world that is described differently by a number of languages. It would also be quite helpful if this same "something" could be described in terms of some third-person language system. One obvious candidate is color: different languages have different numbers of color words and it is possible to describe color in the perfectly objective third-person language of physics.

Figure 6-3 shows a portion of the color spectrum as labeled in four languages (physical description being one of these languages). The top line represents the physicist's approach to color. In this system, there are no separate names, just a continuous series so-and-so many nanometers long. The second line represents the Jalé language of central New Guinea, which has only two color words: *sing* (roughly equivalent to *black*) and *holo* (roughly equivalent to *white*). For the speaker of Jalé, blood is called *sing;* a lemon is labeled *holo.* The third line represents the Ibibio language of Nigeria. In this language there are four color words: *afia* (white), *ah-babit* (black), *ndaidat* (red), and *awawa* (blue-green). The English labels are not exact, and *awawa* actually covers some colors that would be called yellow-green as well as some that would be called blue in English. The final line represents a portion of American English color usage, where the total collection contains 11 basic color names: *white, black, red, green, yellow, blue, brown, pink, purple, orange,* and *gray.*

These, then, are the color-worlds presented by four languages. For the physicist, there are no discrete categories, whereas for the English speaker there are 11 major and a great many minor ones (some estimates, including combined words like *blue-green,* suggest over 1000 different words). For the Ibibio speaker there are four major and a small number of minor names. For the Jalé speaker there

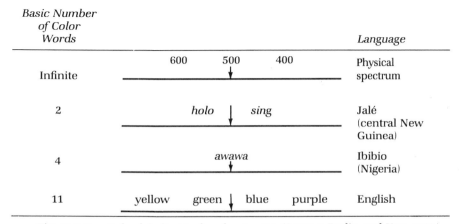

Figure 6-3. Color labeling in four languages. (Source: Berlin and Kay, 1969.)

are two major and some very highly specific ones. For example, in Jalé the word *piano* is the name of a plant whose leaves are used to dye objects a sort of "green" color. *Piano*, however, is never used as a name for a "green" object, such as a leaf. Leaves are called either *sing* or *holo*, depending on whether they are dark or light green (Berlin & Kay, 1969).

Now look at the arrow in Figure 6-3, which appears in the same place on all four lines. In Jalé, there is no word; in Ibibio, it falls in the middle of the *awawa* range; in English it falls at the "boundary" between *blue* and *green*; for the physicist it falls at 500 nanometers. The physicist and the Ibibio speaker will have little trouble labeling the color represented by the arrow. The Jalé speaker will have to invent a word or call it *sing* or *holo*, depending on how bright it is; the English speaker will have to use a composite name, such as *blue-green*. The "same" color is thus not labeled with the same ease in these four languages; that is, the "codability" of this color varies among the languages. The question to be asked by Whorf's hypothesis must be "Do differences in color labeling affect other kinds of behavior?" If the answer turns out to be yes, it would provide some support for Whorf's more general views.

The first experiment in recent years to study this question was done by Brown and Lenneberg in 1954. College students were first asked to name a set of 24 color chips. Some colors were given the same name by all the students, and others were not. The degree to which the students agreed with one another was called the "codability" of a particular color chip. With the problem of defining codability taken care of, it was then possible to find out whether codability affected how people did other tasks. One task chosen by Brown and Lenneberg concerned the effects of codability on the ease with which subjects recognized and remembered color chips. Subjects were first shown a set of four different chips. After waiting a few seconds, they were asked to pick out the four chips they had just seen from a large array of chips. Chips that were more codable in words were also better recognized in the later test. This finding lends some support to Whorf's hypothesis: where there is a label, there is better recognition.

Brown and Lenneberg's experiment deals only with differences within English; what about cross-language effects? To do this experiment, it is necessary to find a language that cuts the color spectrum at different places than English does. The language of the Zuñi tribe meets this requirement quite well: in Zuñi there seems to be only one term for yellow and orange. If Whorf's hypothesis is correct, Zuñi speakers should have poorer recognition for yellow and orange chips than English speakers. A study testing this hypothesis did show that Zuñi speakers had greater trouble recognizing yellow and orange chips than English-speaking subjects. Since Zuñi does have words for brown and green, results also showed that Zuñi subjects—like English-speaking ones—had little or no trouble recognizing green and brown chips.

Both experiments suggest that where a language provides a clear label, native speakers are able to deal quite easily with objects falling under that label. If the language does not provide a unique label, speakers have somewhat more trouble dealing with the objects presented. These experiments do not prove the Whorf hypothesis. What they suggest, instead, is that for some tasks having a verbal label helps in doing the job. In no way do they show that people could not recognize colors if there were no specific words in their language. Widely different languages seem able to express color in their own terms, even if some languages do have a much more extensive and precise collection of color words to begin with. In this regard, Berlin and Kay (1969) note that even if a language such as Ibibio has only one color for a portion of the spectrum where English has two, the rest of the spectrum is labeled in much the same way as in English. Thus, the remaining three color words in Ibibio label colors similar to what *red*, *black*, and *white* label in English.

The most important fact for the Whorf hypothesis is that almost all languages agree on which areas of the spectrum are to be named. Even though Ibibio does not have different words for blue and green, it does have a red, and if Ibibio speakers are asked to select color chips representing their color words, *red* in Ibibio turns out to be similar to *red* in English.

C. Whorf's hypothesis and translating from one language to another

The issue of color-naming practices across different languages, though interesting in its own right, is part of the much larger problem of translating from one language to another. In regard to the Whorf hypothesis, it is quite clear that Whorf was able to make English speakers understand examples from Native American languages they did not speak. Obviously, some of his key words were translatable, however crudely, from one set of languages to another. Here, then, is one real nub to Whorf's problem: how well can we translate the words and concepts of one language into the words and concepts of a vastly different second language?

As a start on this problem, we all know that certain words and phrases do not translate very well, and for this reason we often import foreign words into English. One reason for doing this is that English does not already have a word to express the meaning we want. Just as surely, however, we import words and phrases because we, the English speakers, mean to suggest the culture standing behind the word.

Calling someone a *schlemiel* (a Yiddish word) is not only meant to call someone a fool, but to call him a fool within the very special historical and social context of Yiddish culture. The *schlemiel* is only one of many kinds of foolish persons distinguished in Yiddish, and calling someone a fool within a language and culture capable of labeling a wide range of fools is quite different from calling someone a fool in English. A word is sometimes used not because a substitute cannot be found, but because the meaning of that word in one culture does not translate (except crudely) into another culture. To know the meaning of a word is to know and live in the culture (history and all) from which that word comes. Lawrence of Arabia surely knew this when he feared going crazy should he continue to live simultaneously within both Arab and English cultures.

Many words are translatable, however, and here we come again upon the meaning of the Whorf hypothesis and, through it, to Whorf's warning: although we may be able to translate words from one language to another, we can often understand them only from our own particular (cultural/linguistic) point of view. To understand a word means to know a great deal not only about the language from which it comes but also about a particular view of the world. For this reason, poetry—in which the widest possible meaning for each and every word is at issue—is almost totally untranslatable. We may have the "right" words, considered one at a time;

what we do not have is the right ground out of which they grow in speaking and already-spoken contexts. Translation, at best, does no better than approximate.

The Whorf hypothesis, then, has both a weak and a strong form. In its strong version, any and all translation is impossible; in its weak version, translation is only approximate. If we accept the weak version, what Whorf has done is to call attention to the fact that speaking is not simply a mirror of thinking but often controls what is or is not thinkable by the person speaking that language. The language that lets me go beyond myself if I use it poetically is the same language that may imprison me in its categories without my ever knowing it. Words and speaking create a world at least as much as they are created by that world, and it does not seem too strong to conclude that in the beginning there were both the word and the world.

V. SUMMARY

Speaking, no less than any other human activity, must be understood from the point of view of the participants. Too often we assume that sentences have meaning independent of the situation in which they are used. Unlike language, speaking always occurs in a situation, and how we understand and speak is very much affected by this fact. Saying reveals what we ourselves may not have known until then; authentic speaking changes my way of looking at the world. Strategic or well-worked speech closes things down or brings about distance between people. Originating speaking changes the world; trite speaking leaves the world unchanged.

The act of speaking is best described as an ongoing process of creation performed within the preexisting and agreed-upon rules of some particular language. For this reason, any interpretation of speech must take into account the where, the when, and the who of those communicating. The rules of communication, no less than other aspects of speaking, change over time, and change seems to describe almost everything there is to say about speaking and language.

Speaking is not only a means of "transmitting" ideas. For instance, it is very often used to initiate and maintain social contact. As such, it can yield a great deal of information about the speaker independent of the content of his or her speech. For example, formality, word choice, and pronunciation are clear functions of social class. Anthropologists have shown that females tend to be more grammatically "correct" because more "correct" social behavior is expected of women. Silence too can speak, as exemplified by the list of instances in Apache culture where words are deemed unnecessary for communication. In addition, silence always acts as a ground from which speaking emerges.

Speaking poetically (or figuratively) is done by all of us. Therapists use poetic speech to talk about intimate characteristics without appearing to intrude on the patient. Speaking figuratively aids in problem setting and problem solving: a familiar problem is cast into an unfamiliar light, or an unfamiliar problem is cast into a familiar light.

Making the strange familiar (or the familiar strange) is put to use in the synectics approach to problem solving and the promotion of creative human activity. Figurative speech, however, can also serve to disguise and may be used to avoid concentrating on the issue at hand or to mislead attempts at understanding. Figurative speech can be equally effective as a disguise or as a bridge to new ideas. Considered more generally, poetic speaking is the narrow border between personal expression and interperson communicating.

Speaking is behavior; language is an abstraction from speech and appears only after analysis. Linguistics, the science of speech, studies language in terms of phonology (sound), syntax (grammar), and semantics (meaning). Most important for contemporary linguistic theory is the study of syntax. Grammatical convention is necessary for common understanding, and the rules of grammar provide a "recipe" for the generation of clear sentences to ease this process. Sentences must be looked at as a whole for proper understanding. As argued by Chomsky, the central aspect of language is neither sound nor meaning; rather, it is the logical form of the language as embodied in its grammar.

The study of semantics is more difficult than that of either phonology or syntax. In studying words, which are understood only in the context of some situation and which are always moving and changing, semantics can only tell us how a word has been used, not how it may be used in the future. Semantics can only study relations within language itself, whereas meanings are never independent of situation.

Speaking and language are not independent of thinking. Using a language promotes identification with the community of people who use that language, and control of language can mean control of identification. The Whorf hypothesis states that perceptions and understandings are dictated and constrained by language. For example, where language provides a clear label for an object, that object may be unambiguously dealt with in the world. Where a label does not exist, the object may not be dealt with as easily. According to Whorf, language shapes rather than mirrors "reality." Language tends to encompass a whole world, as exemplified by Lawrence of Arabia, who found that to live in two cultures meant to live in two worlds that did not mix culturally or linguistically.

Speaking and thinking thus interact with each other, sensitive to the particulars of the task or situation at hand. It is not surprising that speaking says so much about an individual and that language controls to such a large extent what we say, think, and perceive. If speaking creates a situation, language may be said to express a culture.

VI. GLOSSARY OF IMPORTANT CONCEPTS

Abbreviated speech. Language shared by people in intimate interpersonal relationships.

A certain kind of silence. As described by Merleau-Ponty, a shared fringe of background assumptions or experiences; the ground out of which conversation emerges.

Authentic speaking. Speaking that expresses what one is genuinely experiencing at the moment; as such, it is usually spontaneous, rather than forced or planned. Such speaking usually opens up ways of looking at the world or suggests unsuspected future actions.

Deictic elements in speaking. Words such as *this*, *that*, *here*, and *there* that serve to point out or indicate things.

Frozen figures of speech. Clichéd examples of poetic usage (such as "crooked thief ") produced at regular intervals in conversation.

Generative grammar. As proposed by Noam Chomsky, a system of grammatical rules that allows the linguist to decide whether a given set of words is a possible sentence in one or another language.

International Phonetic Alphabet. A set of symbols used to record all the sounds that can be distinguished in a large number of languages.

Language. An abstract system of symbols and rules for their use, independent of the social situation in which it is used. It describes the orderly behavior that occurs in speech, inferred from what speakers do.

Linguistics. The study of language, usually divided into three parts: *phonology*, the study of the sounds of a language; *syntax* (grammar), the study of the rules by which words combine to produce sentences; *semantics*, the study of meanings and how they relate to one another.

Living context. All the variables that give meaning to speaking. These include the situation in which the person is speaking, the preceding sentences, who the speaker and listener are and what they know, and the relationship between speaker and listener.

Originating speech. Speech that results in change in the world (see **authentic speaking**).

Phoneme. The smallest unit of speech that distinguishes one sound from another in a given language community.

Phonology. The study and systematic classification of sounds made in speaking.

Poetic usage or **poetic figures.** Genuinely novel use of language, usually produced in periodic bursts.

Semantics. The study of meaning in language.

Speaking. An act of verbal communication (generally involving two or more people) that occurs in a particular situation and relates who the participants are, how they feel about one another, and what is important to them.

Synectics. The process of fitting together two diverse elements. Synectic theory concerns itself with creativity, invention, problem solving, and poetic language.

Syntax. The way words are put together to form phrases, clauses, and sentences; the grammar of a language.

Whorf hypothesis. The view that language shapes other activities, such as perceiving and thinking.

VII. SUGGESTED READINGS

Major sources

Gusdorf, G. *Speaking* (P. T. Brockelman, trans.). Evanston, Ill.: Northwestern University Press, 1965.

Pollio, H. R., Barlow, J., Fine, H., and Pollio, M. R. *The poetics of growth: Figurative language in psychology, psychotherapy, and education.* Hillsdale, N. J.: Erlbaum, 1977.

Rommetveit, R. *On message structure: A conceptual framework for the study of language and communication.* London: Wiley, 1974. Part 1.

Whorf, B. L. *Language, thought, and reality: Selected papers.* Cambridge, Mass.: MIT Press, 1956.

Secondary sources

Fowler, R. *Understanding language.* Boston: Routledge and Kegan Paul, 1974.

Trudgill, P. *Sociolinguistics: An introduction.* Baltimore: Penguin Books, 1974.

7

Learning

Between the first and second world wars a German professor by the name of Eugen Herrigel went to teach philosophy in Japan. This act, by itself, wouldn't be all that noteworthy if Herrigel did not also go to Japan specifically to learn, as he called it, the art of archery. In the Western world, if we think about archery at all, we think of it as a sport involving me, an arrow, a bow, and a bull's-eye that needs hitting. For us, the idea that archery is an *art* seems out of place in describing what it is we do when we shoot arrows at targets. At first glance, it seems a bit degrading to associate archery with art.

In Japan the situation is different: archery, like many other ancient arts, such as swordsmanship, karate, dance, and even flower arranging or tea service, is not meant to be useful or even pretty; rather, it is meant to serve as a vehicle by which a profound change is brought about in the person mastering the art. The Master Archer, like the master swordsman, is not trained to hit bull's-eyes or to kill. He is trained to experience what Zen theory—the major religious creed in much of Japan—calls the "Great Doctrine." For the Great Doctrine of Zen, to know how to do something well, really well, means to lose all of oneself in the activity so that actor and activity are no longer separate. When this occurs the **Zen Master** is at one with the world.

To learn how to shoot a bow with skill is no small achievement, for he who masters the art not only has learned archery but is at union with the rest of the world. Given the magnitude of this outcome, it is not surprising to find that Herrigel took six years to learn how to do it. Even then, like all true masters of any art, he came to consider himself only a beginner. Although the reason Herrigel undertook the difficult task of learning archery had to do with his attempt to understand Zen theory "from the inside," the record of his training presents psychology with an extraordinarily rich diary of a person in the process of learning a complicated skill. A careful reading of this document, called *Zen in the Art of Archery* (1964), ought surely to give some insight into the learning process.

I. ZEN IN THE ART OF ARCHERY

Where to begin? As a Zen Master might say: at the end, of course. Herrigel provides us with a rather remarkable first-person account of how he, as Master Archer, now approaches his difficult art. As Master he begins each session of archery by doing a special ceremony consisting of a series of quite specific steps and postures, which ends in a state of "deep concentration." All that occupies the Master Archer during this period is the regular breathing that must precede each shot if it is to be a true shot. And what is the state of the Master Archer like during this time? Herrigel tells us about it in one of his final conversations with his Master:

> "Do you now understand," the Master asked me one day after a particularly good shot, "what I mean by 'It shoots,' 'It hits'?"
> "I'm afraid I don't understand anything more at all," I answered, "even the simplest things have got in a muddle. Is it 'I' who draws the bow, or is it the bow that draws me into the state of highest tension? Do 'I' hit the goal, or does the goal hit me? Is 'It' spiritual when seen by the eyes of the body; and corporeal when seen by the eyes of the spirit . . . ? Bow, arrow, goal and ego, all melt into one another, so that I can no longer separate them. And even the need to separate has gone. For as soon as I take the bow and shoot, everything becomes so clear and straightforward and so ridiculously simple . . ."
> "Now at last," the Master broke in, "the bowstring has cut right through you" [Herrigel, 1964, p. 88].[1]

In our earlier descriptions of the body and skill (Chapter 3), we recall, many skilled performers have talked about a selfless state. Paul Warfield talked about it while catching a football; other anonymous master performers described it in weightlifting, running, playing soccer, broad-jumping, and so on. To be skillful in a task is to experience the world quite differently than the person who is not skillful or the skilled performer when he or she is not doing his or her skilled activity. The first-person world of a master is always different from that of the pupil or novice.

But how did that world become different? Because Herrigel began his training as an adult, many, if not all, of the movements required to shoot a bow were already known to him before he began. All he had to do was learn how to organize them into an

[1]From *Zen in the Art of Archery*, by E. Herrigel. Copyright 1964 by Pantheon Books, a Division of Random House, Inc. Reprinted by permission.

appropriate sequence. To take one simple example: the Master Zen archer releases his arrow only in a state of complete body relaxation. Although Herrigel could imitate the moves of the Master, for well over a year he could not learn how to relax first one and then another body part. He would tense his forearm or his shoulder. Or if he seemed to have his upper body completely relaxed, he found that he was tensing his calf muscle. The tension seemed to move around on its own.

Only when Herrigel threw down his bow and refused to continue did the Master offer him a way out by teaching him how to breathe in such a way that all tension disappeared. There followed a long period of practice during which the good professor made excellent progress except that he was still unable to let go of the arrow in exactly the right way— as the Master put it, "by having the bowstring cut right through his hand." He was able to do this only after about three more years of practicing. During each practice session he was carefully watched over by the Master, who initially praised him every time he almost did it right. Later the Master praised him only as he ever more closely approximated the correct movements. Finally, the entire process led to a new first-person organization in which bow, arrow, target, and person formed a seamless unit. To enter this enviable state of affairs, Herrigel went through an elaborate ritual that called up the desired state prior to shooting the arrow.

Herrigel's diary not only provides a good example of how an adult goes about learning a new skill; it also gives hints about how to look at diverse learning phenomena. Although the good professor's diary describes mainly the first-person world of a pupil, it also describes how a master must deal with his or her student. In every learning situation there are two points of view: that of the learner and that of the Master. The world of the pupil gives the changing nature of a learner's first-person experience of what he or she is doing (or not doing) in practicing a task. Sometimes a particularly sensitive master (teacher) "knows" from his or her own previous learning what the learner is now experiencing; in this way, master and pupil share the pupil's point of view. Similarly, a particularly apt pupil sometimes catches a glimpse of the Master's world while practicing. Unfortunately, in many situations, teacher and student do not share or even try to share a common point of view, much to the detriment of both.

II. FIRST-PERSON AND THIRD-PERSON POINTS OF VIEW ON LEARNING

The psychologist interested in learning can talk about it from the point of view of the learner or that of some other person observing the learner, be this "other person" a teacher, a parent, or a psychologist. Generally speaking, the psychologist has most often taken the "other" point of view and has been content to describe not what he or she thinks or knows about the learner's experience but simply what he or she sees and can record in numbers. The world of the learner seldom appears, and we are content to count the changing number of correct responses made by the learner.

Because psychologists have been little concerned with the learner's first-person point of view, they have been perfectly content to study animals. Under these conditions, they never did feel a need to interpret the animal's learning-world and for this reason felt quite safe from the possibility of misunderstanding the learner's experience. Using animals seemed a good idea not only because they were more convenient but because they discouraged the psychologist from looking at the world from the learner's point of view. Laws of learning discovered from working with animals could only produce an accurate third-person collection of if-then statements, such as "If a rat has been given 20 trials in learning to go to the right for food, then it is likely to run faster than another rat given only 2 trials." *Learning* could then be defined without reference to experience. It came to be defined as an inference from performance—what the animal or human subject did—which was reflected by a progressive change in performance measured in terms of fewer errors, more correct responses, faster moving, or whatever was convenient to measure. In this way, learning turned into a scientific fiction assumed to have taken place when an animal changed the way it did something.

The only problem with this way of looking at things is that it gives only half the story—the experimenter's half. Fortunately, very few experimenters were able to stick to their side alone. In one way or another, most of them managed to sneak in the learner's point of view. For example, B. F. Skinner (1907–   ), one of the leading American authorities on animal and human learning, notes quite openly: "I have found it useful to regard myself exactly as I regard the pigeons, rats and other people [I study]" (Skinner, 1964, p. 99).

Another psychologist who tried to imagine what might be going on in the learner's first-person world was Edward Tolman (1888–1962). For example, in his work on the way rats learned the correct turn in a T maze, Tolman observed that animals often turned to the right and then to the left before they ran left or right. Tolman observed that this behavior seemed to give his rats an opportunity to get information on the correct direction, and he assumed that they were "casing the joint" before they started running. Such goings-on in rats were called "vicarious trial-and-error behavior."

Tolman was not content, however, to intuit vicarious trial-and-error behavior. He also assumed that his rats developed a quite general plan of their situation, which he called a "cognitive map." Such maps were thought to systematize the rat's knowledge of its task and therefore to change in detail as learning progressed. Vicarious trial-and-error behavior was tied to learning when Tolman found that animals that looked more often than other animals also learned more rapidly. Tolman came to describe the rat's strategy in learning a maze as consisting of a series of "hypotheses" the animal tried to confirm by looking carefully at the maze. Obviously Tolman, like Skinner, had very little hesitation about sneaking in the learner's world—hypotheses, cognitive maps, and all.

This is as it should be: experimenters, like other mortals, often fall back on their own experience in trying to understand the behavior of other organisms, be they people or rats. Skinner, Tolman, and many other learning psychologists often drew on their own experiences in describing how learning occurred. Tolman explicitly acknowledged this strategy and then tried to define exactly when a "hypothesis" or a piece of "vicarious trial-and-error behavior" occurred. Although Skinner does much the same thing in thinking about his experiments, he is much more careful in creating events for the animal's world. Putting yourself in the learner's place is allowed by Skinner only in coming to an *informal* description. For a formal one, Skinner would prefer not to use his intuitions. Instead he prefers simply to say what he did and what he saw and let it go at that.

For two of the most important learning psychologists, then, the learner's world became a silent partner to much of what they (and we) have learned about learning. One of the first and most important of the world's learning psychologists, Ivan Pavlov

(1849–1936), resolutely refused to give the learner's experience a role in his theory. For Pavlov, when an animal learns something, a connection has been established between a stimulus event and a response event, nothing more. Stimulus events, in turn, are defined quite precisely in terms of physical units (volts for electricity, cycles per second for sound, and so on); response events are defined in terms of the size of a movement or in terms of how quickly it occurred. In this, Pavlov was always true to his original role as an objective observer.

Perhaps because of Pavlov's eminence in the field of learning, few theoretical or experimental descriptions of learning—human or otherwise—have explicitly taken the learner's experiences into account. Although we as experimenters are willing to guess about what a learner might be experiencing, we, like Skinner, save it for our private conversations and hardly ever investigate it in its own right. The learner's first-person world remains largely a mystery, only a very few daring souls ever venturing to try their hand at describing it in a systematic and rigorous way.

III. PHENOMENOLOGICAL ATTEMPTS TO DESCRIBE THE LEARNER'S WORLD

How do you go about mapping the learner's world—what a learner experiences during a learning task? In perhaps the most ambitious attempt, Colaizzi (1969, 1973) asked 50 subjects to perform one of ten tasks. (Each task was performed by five subjects.) Some of these ten tasks were procedures that are often used in the psychological laboratory, such as learning a list of ten nonsense syllables or tracing a line between the boundaries of a six-pointed star as seen in a mirror. Others involved activities that occur in more or less natural settings; these included learning how to walk with crutches and what turned out to be the most revealing task—disassembling and then reassembling a Colt .45 automatic pistol.

After a subject had completed one of the tasks to some criterion or other—reciting all ten nonsense syllables correctly or putting the revolver together in less than 2 minutes—he or she was asked to fill out a questionnaire. In order not to prejudice the subjects' responses, the word *learning* was never used. Instead, all questions were asked in terms of "changes that occurred" during the course of doing an activity. The most important questions asked of the subjects were (1) to describe in detail the changes that occurred, (2) to distinguish (if they could) between changes in the activity and in themselves, and (3) to describe fully what they believed to be the purpose of the investigation (including the investigator's reasons for having them complete that question).

As an example of what the subjects wrote, consider the following answers written by Subject 5 after he had learned to assemble the revolver.

> These changes occurred: the gun became more familiar to me; more specifically, the gun's parts became more familiar to me. One thing led to the next. If I came cold to the whole thing and if the parts did not become familiar, I would have been bogged down. The gun's parts changed from chaos to meaningful interrelations. That is to say, they made sense with each other. This was not true in the beginning, even though I tried to keep on to it.
>
> As learning progressed: I became more "involved"— lost sense of "ego"—task captured me—began to like it.... Involvement is a personal thing. Activity concerns the aspects of the situation involved specifically with the objective characteristics of the material with which one is working. I became more involved with it. It "grabbed" me. The activity changes from noninvolvement and perception of disarray to involvement and feelings.
>
> Changes came about through practice; through ... my commitment to the task. I think that it was my decision to involve myself in the whole thing....
>
> I was grabbed by the desire to resolve the puzzlement of the task and of the material I was working with in the task....
>
> I'm sure I changed. I felt these changes; and the results from the changes justified my feelings that changes were occurring as I continued in the practice of the task [Colaizzi, 1973, pp. 163–164].[2]

Colaizzi summarized each subject's statements, using the subject's own words as often as possible, so that for Subject 5 a reduced description came out as follows:

> Progress in the task occurs as the parts of the material became more familiar, less chaotic, meaningfully interrelated, and making sense. With commitment to task, become involved in it, losing sense of ego. The certainty

of these changes is "self-sufficient" in that it is the self who is involved [Colaizzi, pp. 173–174].

After all protocols had been examined, Colaizzi then devised a very much reduced form to provide what he called the fundamental structure of learning from the learner's first-person point of view. Although the description finally achieved contained fairly technical terms, it can be paraphrased as follows: "**Learning** is the prereflective organizing of a to-be-learned content whereby the person comes progressively to adopt a changing style of functioning in the learning situation. This style amounts to a new point of view, which the learner comes to feel represents a useful way of behaving in that situation."

Almost all subjects also reported progressive changes in experiencing their bodies, not only in their reactions to the task. It was not uncommon for subjects to report that they felt awkward and clumsy and that they ached and perspired early in learning. Many subjects also reported a feeling of order and smoothness when they finished the task. For many subjects, the body was initially experienced as an aching or uncomfortable burden that had to be carefully observed and thought about as it related to performance. With practice it was gradually eliminated altogether until it became the agent of performance. It returned to the foreground of awareness only when relapses of bodily performance occurred (paraphrased from Colaizzi, 1973, p. 77).

In overall reactions to the task, subjects experienced a change from an initially strange and unknown situation to one in which the learner knew what to do and did it. "Initially the context appeared alien and consisted of confused, disorganized and strange parts ... [at the conclusion] it was related to other information and procedures used by the person.... [Finally] the task was seen as made up of parts that are now sharply differentiated and which are arranged ... and inter-related ... in a reasonable and sensible unit" (p. 77).

For all these descriptions, the purpose has been to explore the first-person world of the learner and to see what implications such a description might have for understanding the nature of learning. Although Colaizzi's work used a large number of tasks, they were all tasks that were set *for* the learner rather than *by* the learner. In this experiment the learner was responding to someone else's request,

---

[2]From *Reflection and Research in Psychology: A Phenomenological Study of Learning*, by P. F. Colaizzi. Copyright 1973 by Kendall/Hunt Publishing Company, Dubuque, Iowa. This and all other quotations from this source are reprinted by permission.

not to his or her own attempt to do something new.

Perhaps it was for this reason that Giorgi (1975) tried to map the learner's world for a more natural task. Consider the following bit of a protocol reported in his study (1975, pp. 84–85). The subject speaking is E.W., a 24-year-old female, a homemaker and educational researcher.

Researcher: Could you describe in as much detail as possible a situation in which learning occurred for you?

Subject: The first thing that comes to mind is what I learned about interior decorating from Myrtis. She was telling me about the way you see things.... She told me that when you come into a room you don't usually notice how many vertical and horizontal lines there are, at least consciously, you don't notice. And yet, if you were to take someone who knows what's going on in the field of interior decorating, they would intuitively feel if there were the right number of vertical and horizontal lines. So, I went home, and I started looking at the lines in our living room, and I counted the number of horizontal and vertical lines, many of which I had never realized were lines before. A beam ... I had never really thought of that as [horizontal] before, just as a protrusion from the wall. [Laughs.] I found out what was wrong with our living room design: many, too many, horizontal lines and not enough vertical. So I started trying to move things around and change the way it looked. I did this by moving several pieces of furniture and taking out several knick-knacks, deemphasizing certain lines, and ... it really looked differently to me.... My husband came home several hours later and I said, "Look at the living room; it's all different." Not knowing this,..., he didn't look at it in the same way I did. He saw things ... were moved, but he wasn't able to verbalize that there was a deemphasis on the horizontal lines and more of an emphasis on the vertical. So I felt I had learned something!

R. What part of that experience would you consider learning?

S. The knowledge part that a room is made up of horizontal and vertical lines. The application of that to another room; applying it to something that had been bothering me for quite a long time and I could never put my finger on it. I think the actual learning was what was horizontal and vertical about a room. The learning that was left with me was a way of looking at rooms.

R. Are you saying then that the learning was what you learned from Myrtis, what you learned when you tried to apply ... ?

S. Since I did apply it, I feel that I learned when I did apply it. I would have *thought* that I learned it only by having that knowledge, *but* having gone through the act of application, I really don't feel I would have learned it. I could honestly say, I had learned it at that time.[3]

Once Giorgi had this transcript in hand, his next job was to define the central themes of each statement and then try to reduce them to a general description of learning. For subject E.W., the first theme was taken to be "the role of vertical and horizontal lines in interior decorating." After many further reductions the learning that had occurred in this situation was captured as follows: Learning "happened" for E.W. when she was directly told something quite specific by an important other person about a problem situation that had been bothering her for a long time. The learning took place when she could apply that information to a new situation after having seen a few prior examples.

Even though E.W. is only one person, a careful reading of her approach to learning yields some interesting results. For one, the interperson nature of human learning comes through loud and clear: Not only does E.W. learn about vertical and horizontal lines from her friend Myrtis, she finds confirmation of her new way of looking at things by comparing it with her husband's less precise statement that "the room looks different." A second important point is that learning is sensed by the learner as "a new way of looking at things" that leads to new, previously impossible changes. Learning, from a first-person point of view, always seems to include a person's experiential history, for "a new way of looking at things" implies that there was an "old way." In addition, learning outside the laboratory always seems to involve an interpersonal context. For learning to have occurred, the learner must perceive or behave in a new way with respect to his or her own personal history, a way that was not previously possible.

IV. BEHAVIORAL ATTEMPTS TO DESCRIBE THE LEARNER'S WORLD

For Giorgi, as for Colaizzi and Herrigel before him, the learner's world is best described in terms of the

[3]From "An Application of Phenomenological Method in Psychology," by A. Giorgi. In A. Giorgi, C. T. Fischer, E. L. Murray (Eds.), *Duquesne Studies in Phenomenological Psychology: Volume II.* Copyright 1975 by Duquesne University Press. Reprinted by permission.

learner's first-person statements about a particular situation. For Herrigel, such a description involved a personal diary; for Giorgi and Colaizzi, it involved reducing subjects' descriptions by a careful and patient experimenter. Psychologists, however, are often wary of how people describe situations, not only because we are a suspicious lot but because many of the more important things that the person needs to attend to cannot be directly reported. Indeed, it is possible to describe what Giorgi and Colaizzi did as making explicit the implicit, or making reflected what was unreflected for the learner.

A. Learning how to learn

There is, however, another way to go at the job of reflecting the unreflected: careful and sympathetic third-person observation of a learning situation that extends for a reasonably long period. In modern psychological research, perhaps the best example of such work is a 30-year series of studies on **learning**

how to learn undertaken by Harry Harlow of the University of Wisconsin in the early 1940s. Because Harlow is director of a primate laboratory, most of his studies were done on monkeys; it is a tribute to his careful experimentation, intuition, and long-term knowledge of monkeys that much of what he described as true of the animal learner's *Umwelt* also turned out to be true of the human learner's self-world.

Harlow's general procedure is simple and uses the apparatus shown in Figure 7-1. In case there is any doubt, the experimenter is on the right and the subject is on the left. For the particular problem being tested, two objects are on the tray, a barrel-shaped object to the monkey's left and a cube-shaped object to the right. Under the barrel-shaped object is a raisin, and if the monkey picks it up, he gets to eat it. The positions of the objects shift between right and left for any given series of six trials. At the end of Trial 6 a different pair of objects is

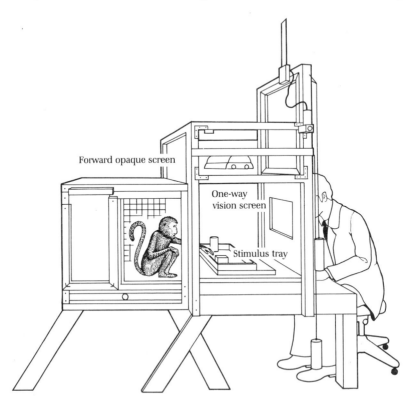

Forward opaque screen

One-way vision screen

Stimulus tray

Figure 7-1.   Wisconsin General Test Apparatus. *(From "Learning Set and Error Factor Theory," by H. F. Harlow. In S. Koch (Ed.),* Psychology: A Study of a Science, Volume 2. *Copyright 1959 by Mc-Graw-Hill, Inc. Reprinted by permission of McGraw-Hill Book Company.)*

presented, and the animal has to learn which new object hides the raisin.

The results of an enormous number of studies are quite consistent, and Harlow's most famous **learning curve** is shown in Figure 7-2. In the study represented by this curve, each animal was presented with 312 problems, and each problem was presented for six trials. Since the animal has no way of knowing for any new problem which object hides the raisin, Trial 1 responses are always about 50% correct: half the time the monkey gets the raisin and half the time he does not. For this reason it is better to look at Trial 2 responses. If the monkey got the idea on Trial 1 and he "understands" the task, he will get the raisin on Trial 2; if he does not "understand," he may or may not. Figure 7-2 shows that monkeys get progressively better on Trial 2 as they do more and more problems. On Problems 1–8, monkeys get raisins 54% of the time on Trial 2, compared with 93% of the time on Problems 201–312.

Harlow's work has a great many implications. The most important for our purpose concerns Harlow's analysis of what happens as monkeys solve more

and more problems. To put the matter most simply, they learn not to do certain things if they want the raisin. For example, a given monkey may have a preference for barrel-shaped objects. If the raisin is under that object, well and good; if the raisin is not under that object and the monkey picks it anyway, no raisin. Some animals prefer picking objects to their right; if the raisin is there, well and good; if not, the preference must be overcome to solve the problem.

In this situation learning consists in finding out what is not correct to do and then not doing it. For monkeys, as for people, the world is an interesting place, and learning often means figuring out what is important to notice and to do in a particular task. In this situation, the reason for learning is the raisin, and each of the objects used represents an impediment to getting this raisin. Only if the monkey suppresses his interest in parts of the world that are not related to getting the raisin will he be able to circumvent the attraction of those other objects and keep his eye on the reward.

Thus, various parts of the monkey learner's world can be described as changing as the animal has fur-

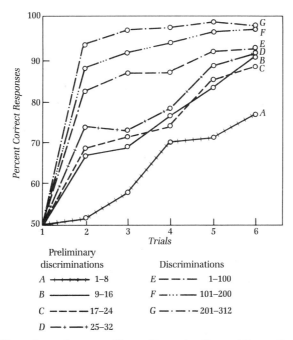

Figure 7-2. Family of learning-set curves. *(From "Learning Set and Error Factor Theory," by H. F. Harlow. In S. Koch (Ed.), Psychology: A Study of a Science, Volume 2. Copyright 1959 by McGraw-Hill, Inc. Reprinted by permission of McGraw-Hill Book Company.)*

ther experience in that situation. In the Harlow/raisin/monkey case it is not so much a matter of learning how to do a certain thing; rather, it is a matter of not doing certain things, thereby letting other behaviors occur. Just as in the description reached on the basis of self-reports provided by human subjects, what is the "correct thing" to do in a task can be defined only against the background of what it is the learner usually does. New behavior is new only against the animal's very own personal history, and only when that history is followed carefully do we come to the conclusion that learning may involve discriminating the relevant from the irrelevant rather than learning how to do something new.

B. Simple human concept learning

Although there is much to recommend Harlow's careful observations of monkeys learning how to learn, human beings would seem better subjects because they can tell us about their experiences as they learn how to do a task. As an example, consider the following classroom experiment. A set of words was presented to a group of students who were told that some of the words represented a "hidden" concept while others did not. The students were given the following instructions: "For each word that you get correct I [the experimenter] will give you a quarter" (actually, the original experiment was done so long ago that pennies worked).

The first word on the list is *boys*. Let us assume that you say "Yes"—it is an example of the correct category. Let us also assume that I say "Correct; you've just earned a quarter." Here is the rest of the list, with correct answers.

Word	Correct?
1. Boys	Yes
2. Girls	Yes
3. Men	Yes
4. Desk	No
5. Elephant	No
6. Man	No
7. Ruler	No
8. Pencil	No
9. Trails	Yes
10. Toys	Yes
11. Story	No
12. Desks	Yes

Probably up to Word 5 you categorized all the words correctly. You probably did not get Word 6 correct and at that point felt somewhat confused about why that word was not an example of the category. By around number 7 you probably recovered, so that after Word 11 you knew what the correct category was.[4]

If we had tested a group of ten students, the learning curve for this task might look like Figure 7-3. Up to Word 5 the curve rises almost regularly. At Word 6, however, catastrophe strikes, and most students do not categorize the sixth word correctly. Then everybody gets Words 7 and 8 as not being part of the concept, but the curve drops again at Word 9, only to rise slowly again through to Word 12, by which time almost everybody has figured out the concept.

For a moment, let us suppress the fact that our ten subjects can talk, and look only at what they

[4]Plural words.

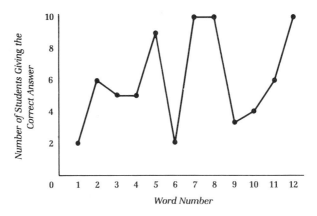

Figure 7-3.   Learning curve for concept-learning task.

did. We must keep in mind that by chance alone we would expect five students to be correct on every trial; if values are below five, we need to ask what might be going on with our subjects. The same is true for values above five. Now, three of the twelve trials fell exactly at five (Words 3, 4, and 11), while two of the trials fell either at four (Word 2) or at six (Word 10). If we assume the subjects were "just guessing" at all these points (that is, they had no clear notion of the concept), we note that "just guessing" occurs in two runs—one including Words 2, 3, and 4 and the other, Words 10 and 11.

This conclusion seems strange, mostly because very good (that is, correct) responding occurred at Word 5 (just after the first run of "just guessing") and at Words 7 and 8 (just before the second run). In addition, there is Word 6, which nobody got right and which falls between the three highest points in the first part of the experiment. As a matter of fact, if we omit the value for Word 6, it looks as if nothing happened between Word 5 and Words 7 and 8, with results produced at Word 6 "just an accident." Unfortunately for this explanation, there is another precipitous drop at Word 9, and responses recover only by Word 12.

Is it possible to "read" this curve so as to determine what our subjects were experiencing? As a start, note that the curve seems to have two quite distinct and comparable sections: one running from Word 1 through Word 8 (with the exception of Word 6) and the other running from Word 9 through Word 12. Since Word 6 is so out of line, it seems a good place to begin our inquiry.

Why should Word 6 have been difficult? The word itself is not rare; certainly subjects understood what it meant. If we look at Word 6 in the context of the five words preceding it, we notice a clear pattern: all the "yes-words," *boys*, *girls*, *men*, denote people; both "no-words," *desk* and *elephant*, do not. Word 6, *man*, is also a "people-word," and it seems reasonable to assume that for Words 1–5 our subjects must have come up with a concept such as "Yes-words are people; no-words are not." Unfortunately, this is not the correct solution, but it yields the correct answer for Words 1–5 as well as for Words 7 and 8. For this reason, subjects probably continue to use the "yes-words are people" concept up through Word 9. Words 1 through 8 (except 6) therefore compose the first run, for which a usable rule is "Yes for people; no for everything else."

Unfortunately, Words 9 and 10, *trails* and *toys*, do not follow this rule, and subjects get them wrong. By Word 11, our subjects probably no longer believe their own rule and start looking around for another one. Here the order of words presented comes to their aid because a non-person word (*desk*) that was incorrect earlier (in its singular form) is now correct in its plural form. All ten subjects note this, and ten of ten are correct on Word 12. We can be pretty sure that ten of ten would be correct from Word 12 onward because we feel confident that our learners now know the correct concept.

The important point in all this detective work is that we were able to reach our (correct) conclusions without asking our subjects anything at all. From the very objective numerical data provided by the experiment, a skillful experimenter is often able to reconstruct the subjects' experience. Unfortunately, many experimenters suppress intuitions about their subjects when they write up an experiment to present to their colleagues. The "dirty truth" of the matter is that most experiments begin and end with the experimenter's intuitions.

But human subjects can talk, and it would seem a shame not to ask them about their experiences. We need only look both at what subjects say they are doing and at what they do. Usually subjects' reports only confirm what the experimenter concluded from a careful and sensitive reading of the data. Sometimes, however, subjects' reports do not agree with the experimenter's analysis, and the experimenter must decide whether the subjects' reflected reports capture their experience better or whether the experimenter's descriptive analysis is the more revealing. Because there is no easy way to decide, many experimental psychologists have decided to do away with a verbal report entirely, preferring to let the numbers speak.

C. Verplanck's experiments on saying versus doing

A different approach to this problem was taken by W. S. Verplanck of the University of Tennessee. Verplanck (1962) wondered how what subjects said they were going to do was related to what they did. In his experiment, subjects were given a set of 110 children's playing cards like those that come in bubble-gum packages. The subject's job was to put the cards, one at a time, either to the left or to the right. After each card was placed, the student was told "right" or "wrong" according to the experimenter's decision about what constituted a correct response.

Unknown to the subjects, they were treated according to one of three procedures. Before testing each subject, the experimenter decided on a "concept"—for example, all cards with one object on them go to the left, all cards with more than one object go to the right. Subjects in what Verplanck called the P group were told "right" or "wrong" on each trial according to whether the card was *placed* correctly. Subjects in the Ph group were treated the same way except that they were asked to tell the experimenter what rule (or *hypothesis*) they followed in placing the card. Such statements of hypotheses had to be made before the subject placed the card to the right or left. Subjects in the pH group were treated exactly like subjects in the Ph group except that they were told "right" or "wrong" for their statement of the hypothesis rather than for their placement of the card.

The experiment was run in two phases. In Part 1 all subjects were told "right" for each correct response and "wrong" for each incorrect response. Subjects during Part 1 were run until they made ten correct placements. In Part 2 subjects were still told "wrong" when they were in fact wrong, but they were told "right" for only six out of every ten correct responses. For the remaining four trials they were told "wrong." As in Part 1, all statements of "right" and "wrong" during Part 2 were given for the response chosen for that group: for groups P and Ph, placing the card; for group pH, stating the hypothesis.

There was no difference in how long it took the three groups to get ten correct during Part 1. The more important data concern what subjects did in the second part of the experiment. During Part 2 subjects in all three groups produced about 73% correct placements. Table 7-1, however, presents the more interesting data for the subjects' descriptions of what rule (hypothesis) they said they were following. As may be seen from the table, subjects in the Ph group were able to state the correct hypothesis only 48% of the time. Subjects in the pH group, however, stated the rule correctly 94% of the time. If we take these data in combination with the fact that correct placement was about 73% for both groups, it is clear that on about 25% of the cases (73 − 48), subjects in the Ph group placed

TABLE 7-1. Percent Correct and Incorrect Hypotheses Produced during Part 2 of Verplanck's Experiment

Hypothesis	Group	
	pH	Ph
Correct	94	48
Incorrect	6	52

their cards correctly but did not state the correct rule. Subjects in the pH group, however, were able to state the correct rule 21% of the time (94 − 73) more than they were able to place their cards correctly.

These are most interesting results. They seem to show that subjects are able to separate statements of what they said they would do from what they in fact do. We really must wonder whether a verbal report is ever a valid index of a subject's intentions or, more generally, whether a verbal report is a useful experimental indicator of the subject's unreflected experiences in a given experiment. Results of this work led Verplanck to conclude somewhat dramatically: "As an experimental strategy, then, let us remain unaware of awareness, but let us diligently ask the subject what he is or 'thinks' he is doing, and let us . . . determine how such verbal statements behave, and . . . are related to . . . other ongoing activities" (1962, p. 157).

The upshot of this experiment seems to be that unreflected experiencing and verbal report cannot be considered interchangeable in all contexts. In many cases they may be, but not always. Although under some circumstances it may be profitable to remain unaware of awareness as Verplanck suggests, his own strategy seems more sensible: Look carefully at the conditions under which verbal and nonverbal behaviors are related and accept neither the placement nor the verbal statement as the more valid description of a subject's experience. Experimentally, both placements and hypothesis are done by a single subject, and their relation (or lack of it) ought to tell us something about how to get the best description of a subject's first-person experience in a particular experiment.

D. Dulany and O'Connell's experiments
Although Verplanck's cautions against the uncritical use of verbal reports as indicating what the subject experienced seem well taken, it remained for

Dulany and O'Connell (1963) to clear up what was going on in the original study. Dulany and O'Connell argued that some of the cards Verplanck used were not completely clear. For example, if a correct rule (hypothesis) was that "pictures with one item go to the right and pictures with more than one item go to the left," a picture of a vase with a bunch of flowers in it could be an unclear example. Does such a picture contain one object (a vase with flowers) or many objects (a vase and many flowers)? If a subject were to consider the vase and flowers as more than a single item and state the (correct) rule, "Pictures with one item go to the right," and then place the item to the left, he or she would show a correct hypothesis and an incorrect placement (since by Verplanck's criteria the vase with flowers was considered a single item).

Dulany and O'Connell were able to show that 15% of all the cards used were unclear in just this way. In their study, subjects in the group reinforced for correct hypotheses produced 92% correct hypotheses but only about 75% correct placements, and this difference could be accounted for just about perfectly by the 15% difference; that is, 92% − 15% = 77%, which is close to the 75% observed.

Dulany and O'Connell then turned their attention to the group rewarded for correct placements. For this group, results showed about 73% correct placements but only 50% correct hypotheses. Here Dulany and O'Connell argued that in the cases in which subjects misstated a rule, they could still get half of the placements correct by chance alone. Therefore 50% (for correct hypotheses) + ½ × 50% (for incorrect hypotheses) = 50% + 25% = 75%, which is only 2% different from the value of 73% actually observed in both experiments.

The most important conclusion that can be drawn from these studies concerns what we mean by the word *awareness*. Both studies showed that subjects who were told "right" for hypothesis stating (group pH) were extremely careful about their hypotheses. And subjects who were rewarded for correct placements almost never misplaced an unclear card, whereas subjects who were not rewarded for correct placements misplaced such cards about 17% of the time. In short, all subjects paid attention to (were aware of?) those behaviors that led to reward, whether such behaviors were placements or hypotheses. To be sure, people usually do what they say they intend to do, but the correlation is perfect only if the task is clear or if being told they

are correct depends on both doing and describing things correctly. If the situation is unclear, it is possible to get the subject to be more careful about one or the other behavior.

Given this possible outcome, it seems wise not to assume that there is any one royal road toward a perfect description of the learner's first-person experience. As these experiments show, many different procedures must be used in describing such experiences. The experiments also suggest that it is probably not helpful to talk simply about awareness; rather, we must be much more specific about what it is awareness is aware of. Again we are reminded that awareness, like all consciousness, is always intentional. That is, consciousness is always consciousness *of* something, be this "something" a placement, a statement, a person, or a reward.

V. REINFORCEMENT AND LEARNING

Why should rewards work in directing the behavior of people doing a task? The answer is at once simple and important: a reward works only to the degree that it relates to something that is important to the learner. For Verplanck's and Dulany and O'Connell's subjects, "being correct" was important, and it was being told that one was correct that directed what the learner paid attention to and did. To say that something is important to a person tells us something even more important about rewards: what a person works for reveals what the person is like and how he or she sees the world from his or her own unique first-person point of view. Thus, if we know what kinds of events—praise, money, sex, or whatever—direct a person, we know a good deal about his or her style of being in the world.

Reward, or **reinforcement**, to use the more technical term, is always specific to a particular person in a particular situation doing a particular task. Nothing is capable of being a reinforcer for a particular person all the time. Even food will not be reinforcing unless the person is hungry—a person who has just eaten a big meal is not likely to work for food. Water is reinforcing only after deprivation—never after drinking. Thus, it is the learner who defines what is rewarding—never the Master, teacher, or learning psychologist. The Master provides reinforcement, but an event will be reinforcing only if it agrees with the learner's wishes, whether or not the learner reflectedly "knows" what his or her wishes are in a particular situation.

Because reinforcement reveals not only what is important to the person but something about his or her style of life as well, it is not surprising to find that much of contemporary learning theory deals with the role and nature of reinforcement in learning. The psychology of learning is sometimes not much more than an attempt to work out the very complicated relationship of reinforcement to changes in behavior, whether the behavior be that of a human being learning a social skill or of a white rat or pigeon learning how to behave in the laboratory. Precisely how psychology came to this point of view forms a very interesting story, and we can do no better than to let the Master of Reinforcement, B. F. Skinner, tell us how it all came to pass.

A. Skinner's approach to the learner's world

If we are to take Skinner's word for how he came to see reinforcement as the single most important aspect of learning, we have to believe that it came about quite by accident. It all began about 40 years ago when Skinner was a graduate student. As part of his research, he was interested in finding out how long it took rats to get back to a starting box once they had got some food for running down an alley. The original test apparatus was an oblong box with food in one corner and a starting area in the other. Although the young Skinner was quite optimistic about discovering the laws of behavior from this piece of apparatus, there was a problem:

> There was one annoying detail.... The rat would often wait an inordinately long time at the food ramp before starting down the back alley on the next run. There seemed to be no explanation for this. When I timed these delays with a stop watch, however, and plotted them, they seemed to show orderly changes. This was, of course, the kind of thing I was looking for. But there was no reason why the runway had to be 8 ft. long ... I saw no reason why the rat could not deliver its own reinforcement.

A new apparatus was built. In Figure [7-4] we see the rat eating a piece of food just after completing a run. It produced the food by its own action. As it ran down the back alley A to the far end of the rectangular runway, its weight caused the whole runway to tilt slightly on the axis C; and this movement turned the wooden disc D, permitting a piece of food in one of the holes around its perimeter to drop through a funnel into a food dish. The food was pearl barley—the only kind I could find in the grocery stores in reasonably uniform pieces. The rat had only to complete its journey by coming down the home stretch B to enjoy its reward.

The experimenter was able to enjoy his reward at the same time, for he had only to load the magazine, put in a rat, and relax. Each tilt was recorded on a slowly moving kymograph....

Eventually, of course, the runway was seen to be unnecessary. The rat could simply reach into a covered tray for pieces of food, and each movement of the cover could ... move a pen one step in a cumulative curve. The first major change in rate observed in this way was due to ingestion. Curves showing how the rate of eating declined with the time of eating comprised the other part of my thesis. But a refinement was needed. The behavior of the rat in pushing open the door was not a normal part of the ingestive behavior of *Rattus rattus*. The act was obviously learned, but its status as part of the final performance was not clear. It seemed wise to add an initial conditioned response connected with ingestion in a quite arbitrary way. I chose the first device which came to hand—a horizontal bar or lever placed where it could be conveniently depressed by the rat to close a switch which operated a magnetic magazine. Ingestion curves obtained with this initial response in the chain were found to have the same properties as those without it [Skinner, 1959, pp. 365–367].[5]

This, then, was the first Skinner box. Over the 40 years since, the exact nature of the box has changed, although its basic idea remained the same: let the animal do something first and then give it a reinforcement if it did something you wanted it to do. Within this situation all the experimenter has to do is keep a continuous record of an animal's behavior, most especially of a criterion

[5] From "A Case History in Scientific Method," by B. F. Skinner. In S. Koch (Ed.), *Psychology: A Study of a Science* (Vol. 2). Copyright 1959 by McGraw-Hill, Inc. and the American Psychological Association, 1956. Reprinted by permission of the author and the publisher.

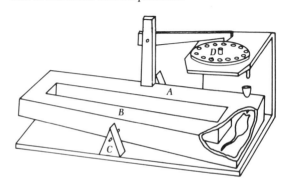

Figure 7-4.   An early form of the Skinner box. *(Skinner, 1959. Reprinted by permission.)*

response, such as pressing a bar or (for a pigeon) pecking a key.

The problem of how to keep such a record is an important one, and Skinner solved it in a quite simple and elegant way. Consider the data in Figure 7-5, produced, let us say, by a rat pushing a bar in a Skinner box (each blip on the curve indicates a response). Once the data are presented in this way, a few things stand out. The times between Responses 1, 2, and 3 are about equal and relatively long; the times between Responses 3, 4, and 5 are about equal and relatively short. In fact, the total record suggests that the animal might have been "warming up" slowly and then got into a "burst" of behavior.

Presenting the data for an ongoing performance in this way is a bit inconvenient. For this reason, Skinner developed what he called the **cumulative response curve.** For the five responses shown in Figure 7-5, the curve would look as in Figure 7-6. This curve shows that this particular animal produced five total responses and that there were two distinct rates. The slower rate is given by the slope of line A, the faster by the slope of line B. In cumulative curves it is always possible to read the relative rate at which an animal is doing something from the slope of the line: steeper slope, faster rate.

B. The issue of behavioral control

One further implication of viewing behavior through the glasses of a Master Reinforcer concerns the experiences of the Reinforcer. One word sums it

Figure 7-5.   A simple way of recording performance in a Skinner box.

up: *power.* Any honest person who has ever reinforced another person or even a lowly rat will tell you of the rather strong feelings of power that go along with controlling someone else's behavior. Even though this may be a bit scary, it should be explicitly recognized whenever we talk about reinforcing behavior.

Although it is possible to deal with this state of affairs in a lighthearted way (see Figure 7-7), there are some quite serious issues for both psychologists and their subjects. These deal with the idea of one human being's having control over another. Skinner did not invent reinforcement; what he did was to call attention to its unsystematic use as a controller in everyday life.

One reason we as human beings react (or overreact) to the idea of behavioral control is that we have seen a lot of political controlling in history, and the possibility that it could be done more efficiently must cause us a bit of concern. Control changes a Master/Pupil relationship into a Master/Slave one. The Pupil who becomes a slave ceases to be a person and becomes an object, an It to be manipulat-

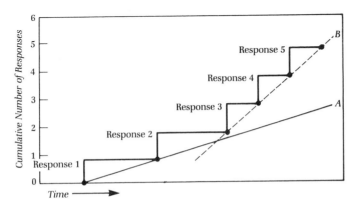

Figure 7-6.   A typical cumulative response graph showing a record of the first five responses. A and B denote slope—hence, rate—of responses. (*From* Learning, Second Edition, *by S. A. Mednick, H. R. Pollio, and E. F. Loftus, p. 43.* © 1973 by Prentice-Hall, Inc., Englewood Cliffs, New Jersey. Reprinted by permission.)

ed. A pupil is always another human being even if he or she submits to a master; a slave is never a full person. This situation also matters for the Master: the Master of a pupil is very much a human being; the master of a slave, however, is as much caught up in the depersonalizing aspects of the situation as the slave. Although Figure 7-7 says it nicely, it does present a truism: he who would control is as controlled by his controlling as the person controlled. In a Master/Slave situation, there are no masters—only slaves.

Reinforcement, by itself, is neither good nor bad. It is simply a fact of human existence. What is socially and politically important about reinforcement is the intention of the Reinforcer—be it a psychologist, a parent, a teacher, a politician, or a dictator. If reinforcement is used in such a way as to reduce the person (or animal) to a thing or object, then both Master and Pupil are in a dehumanizing situation. If reinforcement is used in such a way that it recognizes the essential humanness of the human being (or the essential animalness of the animal), we need not worry about reinforcement "robbing" us of our freedom. In the end it is the intentionality of the person who reinforces that matters, not the fact that reinforcement works.

C. Some experimental findings on reinforcement

Reinforcement psychology, or operant conditioning, as it is often called, was born in the laboratory, and most of the early work relating reinforcement to learning was also done there. Once the original Skinner box was set up and the first cumulative response curve plotted, it became a simple matter to try out all kinds of experimental manipulations. One of the first of these was to determine how the number of reinforcements a rat or person was given affected the subject's behavior. This question was answered in terms of how long it took an animal to stop making a response after the response had been reinforced so-and-so many times and reinforcement was then withdrawn.

Although there are complications, the most general finding is that as the number of reinforcements increases, it takes longer for an animal to stop responding. A special term, *extinction*, was invented to describe this condition of "stop responding." In terms of the cumulative curve first described in Figure 7-6, extinction is said to have occurred when

"Boy, have I got this guy conditioned. Every time I press the bar, he drops a piece of food."

Figure 7-7. (From Learning, Second Edition, by S. A. Mednick, H. R. Pollio, and E. F. Loftus, p. 42. © 1973 by Prentice-Hall, Inc., Englewood Cliffs, New Jersey. Reprinted by permission.)

the curve has no slope—that is, when it is parallel to the X-axis. In Figure 7-8, the point marked by an arrow tells when the animal no longer responded. In the jargon of the learning psychologist, we say that the animal has extinguished this or that response.

1. Effects of continuous and partial schedules on extinction. If it is a fairly simple matter to see what effect the number of reinforcements has on response rate (remember that the slope of a curve gives the animal's rate of response), it seems reasonable to ask what would happen to an animal's rate if reinforcement were not given after

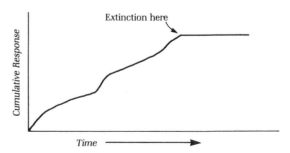

Figure 7-8. Cumulative response graph indicating point of extinction. (*Adapted from Skinner, 1938, p. 75.*)

every response. We can give the animal one reinforcement every so-and-so many minutes—that is, reward it on an **interval schedule**. Or we can give the animal a reward every so-and-so many responses—that is, reward it on a **ratio schedule**. Because what happens to the animal's behavior is so predictable, it is possible to draw typical curves, as in Figure 7-9. The curve marked **fixed interval** shows what happens if we divide the time into regular intervals and give the subject an appropriate reinforcer at the end of each interval during which it made a response at least once (in the figure, the interval is 10 minutes). The curve marked **fixed ratio** shows what happens if we give a reinforcer after every nth response (here n is about 200). (For the moment let us disregard the curves labeled "variable ratio" and "variable interval.")

The first thing to note about these curves is that the slope of the fixed-ratio curve is much steeper than that of the fixed-interval curve: the rate of responding is higher. This makes very good sense if we look at the world from the subject's point of view. If, on a fixed-ratio schedule, I get paid (reinforced) for every 200 responses, then I rush to do all 200 responses. If I get paid for the first response I make every 10 minutes regardless of what I do dur-

ing the remaining 9.99 minutes, then I am likely to rush only every 10 minutes or so. Hence, a fixed-interval schedule produces a slower overall rate than a fixed-ratio schedule.

If I am a pigeon or a rat, and I have no watch, then I cannot be sure when 10 minutes have passed. In order to be sure I get reinforced as soon as possible, I start responding a few minutes or seconds before the 10 minutes are up and stop responding after I get my reward. My behavior in this situation can be described as follows: "Don't do anything just after you've got a reinforcement, and begin, first slowly and then more rapidly, to do what you need to do as you come close to the appropriate interval." Although no animal ever said it just this way, it didn't have to: the cumulative graph for behavior performed under a fixed-interval schedule clearly tells it all.

What is important about all this work is how simple and sensible it is: although it is not always easy to understand how a particular learner is looking at or understanding the world, a careful reading of what an animal does can sometimes tell us what the first-person world was like for the animal while it was doing the task. If reinforcement reveals intentionality, it is also true that the "hows" and "whats"

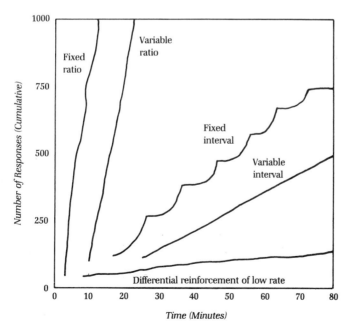

Figure 7-9. Typical curves for different reinforcement schedules.

of behavior can tell us about the unreflected first-person world of the behaver. In the case of reinforcement, we can check whether we have correctly understood the subject's intentionality by reinforcing different responses and seeing whether the subject's behavior changes. In the case of behavior, we can tell whether we have correctly understood the first-person world of the learner by changing schedules and then seeing whether we have changed the animal's behavior in ways that make sense given our original understanding.

Now look at the two curves in Figure 7-9 labeled **variable ratio** and **variable interval**. These curves tell us what happens when an experimenter gives the subject a reinforcer *on the average* of every 200 responses or *on the average* of every 10 minutes. In the variable-interval curve, two things are immediately clear: the response rate is slower than on the fixed-interval schedule, and the stop/start pattern of the fixed-interval schedule has disappeared. This also makes sense: if the interval is not fixed, neither is the behavior it controls.

Although the difference is not nearly so dramatic between variable-ratio and fixed-ratio schedules, there is still a slowdown in rate under the variable schedule. What is important about these comparisons is not only the specific patterns of behavior that the schedules produce but the extraordinary control that reinforcing a learner has on his or her behavior.

Since schedules of reinforcement seem to have such a profound effect on what the learner does, it is reasonable to ask whether such schedules also affect how long an animal will continue to do the thing it has just learned once reinforcement stops. The experimental problem is to determine how schedules of reinforcement during learning affect "resistance to extinction."

The most dramatic finding concerns the difference in resistance to extinction brought about by continuous and partial schedules. A **continuous schedule** is one in which the animal is given a reinforcement for every correct response. A **partial schedule** gives the animal a reinforcement for only some of its correct responses. Two partial schedules have already been described—the interval and the ratio schedule (and most work has used these schedules). The overall conclusion on this topic is presented in some classic work reported by Jenkins, McFann, and Clayton in 1950 (see Figure 7-10). Continuously reinforced animals extinguished after about 600 responses; partially reinforced animals produced 2500 responses in 6 hours and probably were not finished even then. Responding continued that long even though animals in both groups received 200 reinforcements before reinforcement was discontinued.

2. Beyond reinforcement.   Reinforcement is an extremely important and general phenomenon

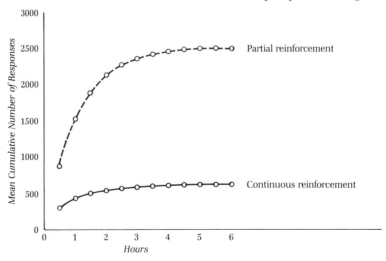

Figure 7-10.   Cumulative extinction curves following intermittent and continuous reinforcement. *(From Jenkins, McFann, & Clayton, 1950.)*

of learning and doing, whether the learner is a rat pressing a bar in a Skinner box or a human being giving his or her answers to a concept task. In all cases the rule seems quite clear: if you reinforce, I *do*. Yet all this is so mechanical, so "third-person-ish," that it leads one to wonder whether I, as learner, always have to be a passive object waiting for someone else to reinforce me for doing something. Isn't it also possible for me to do things that require no "outside" reinforcement, things I do just because they are meaningful to me? Just doing something or learning how to do something may be its own reward, and it is not necessary to have you tell me what you want me to do. Sometimes I decide for myself. An example is my going swimming, which is really not reinforced now (or ever) by anyone or anything outside my just wanting to do it. There seems to be a whole class of things people do (which we call pleasurable or simply "just fun") that are not directly or indirectly controlled by reinforcements administered by someone else.

Once before, in the chapter on perceiving, we came up against these peculiar carryings-on—carryings-on that Robert White (1972) described as related to our becoming complete, competent people. For this class of behavior the closest thing to "reinforcement" is to become competent human beings in whatever we do. For perceiving, it is to perceive clearly; for moving, it is to move with ease and good form. Certain activities are done because you find the doing of them good for you. Some tasks come to be "self-rewarding" even though they started as ways to earn an external reward. It is wrong to say that such tasks are resistant to extinction; it is better to say "Who would ever think of not doing them?"

When we start paying somewhat closer attention to first-person experience, another part of the reinforcement story also appears. It concerns differences between the Zen Master and the Master Reinforcer and their respective pupils. Professor Herrigel, our Zen archer, did not take up archery because someone told him to or because he particularly wanted to learn archery. He took it up because it was the only way for *him* to experience Zen theory directly. Herrigel's reason for learning (his intentionality, if you will) was self-produced, and it seems unlikely that he would have completed the six-year course had he not been totally committed to learning about Zen. Indeed, the Master "tested"

the strength of the professor's desire by not immediately taking him on as a student: only once the Master was sure Herrigel would finish did they begin.

How different this is from the case of a rat being reinforced for pressing a bar in a Skinner box or, more comparably, for a human being reinforced for increasing the rate at which he or she gives correct statements of a concept. In neither case is it the learner (the subject) who decides to do what gets done; it is the experimenter who (so to speak), without the consent of the subject, not only delivers the reinforcement but sets up the task as well. To reinforce is of course to take the learner into account, but it is quite one thing when the learner is a willing pupil and quite another when the learner is neutral to what the Reinforcer is trying to get him or her to do.

3. Shaping.   In almost all the work on reinforcing people and animals to do things, the thing to be done—the response—is already possible for the subject. But where do new responses, things a learner is now unable to do, come from? To ask the question in just this simple way does not mean that psychologists can train any person or animal to do anything they want—humans cannot make honey from nectar, nor can bees swim underwater. What the question does mean is how we learn to do something that others have come to learn to do.

Consider the very practical problem of teaching an active child to speak more quietly. Here, Pollio (1974) presents the case of Michele. The first thing to do is to get a baseline value for loudness. This is accomplished by observing how loudly Michele speaks on a number of occasions—say, on 100 occasions. We will then have a list 100 occasions long telling us the level of loudness Michele used on each occasion. If we take an average of these 100 occasions, we will know the usual loudness with which Michele speaks. Once we set up our analysis in this way, one way to describe what we want Michele to do is to say that we want her "average loudness" to move from where it is now to some lower level. But how do we go about doing this?

Already, Michele often speaks much more loudly and much more softly than her average value, and she is above and below this value about an equal number of times. What is crucial is that she sometimes speaks more softly. All we have to do is get her to speak softly more often—that is, to lower her average. Because we cannot expect her to get there all at once, we, as experimenters (or parents), begin by taking some intermediate point as our criterion and begin reinforcing everything Michele says that falls at or below this level. During training we never reinforce anything above that level. What we are doing is trying to get Michele to the desired level by having her learn intermediate steps well within her present range. After we have reinforced Michele's speech by this criterion a number of times, we will want to take a new set of, say, 100 observations. If we did the job of reinforcing correctly, we would have succeeded in moving the whole set of responses away from the original (baseline) average toward a new, softer value.

Since we are not really interested in stopping at this new level—it's still too loud—we go through another set of steps, using a lower loudness level as our new criterion. If we do this properly and take another set of 100 observations, we will end up with the new level as the average. When this happens, we have achieved our original goal: Michele now speaks softly most of the time.

The procedure described above is called **shaping**. The name seems a good one, for what we seem to be doing is "shaping" the behavior we want. To shape some person or animal to do something, we must decide on the desired outcome at the very beginning. With this done we must discover whether the desired final behavior (or something similar to it) is already possible for the learner; if it is, all we need do is progressively reinforce the learner's approximations to that behavior until in the end we get this new piece of behavior to occur more frequently.

The use of reinforcement in shaping demonstrates the guiding ethic of learning through reinforcement: the teacher must always know the desired final behavior in advance of the learner. In addition, this "final place" must be described in sufficient and precise detail so that both teacher and learner know when it has been reached. A teacher need never be cruel, only patient, for sooner or later the living, behaving person will undoubtedly do something that comes close enough to (approximates) the desired final outcome.

Unfortunately, some psychologists have taken this emphasis on "doing something" to mean that we need concern ourselves only with movements. If

we take this position seriously, it would be almost impossible for anyone to reinforce anyone to do anything. The whole idea of reinforcement (not to mention our ability to reinforce) depends on taking the learner's unreflected self-world, complete with its intentions and perceptions, into account. Reinforcement is not a static or unitary process: it changes with the person, the situation, and the task. Despite statements to the contrary, the reinforcement psychologist does a bit of (secret) phenomenology every time he or she does an experiment.

After all, a careful description of behavior that is more than a simple listing of movements must always take the organism—human or animal—and his or her first-person world into account. Who could ever describe in purely physical terms the movements that make up "pressing the bar" in a Skinner box or "walking to the door in my house"? As noted in Chapter 1, a complete description of a person's behavior in a given situation almost always turns out to be similar to a complete description of that person's experience in that situation. If considered properly, experience and behavior are but two different openings into the world of first-person existence.

4. Discriminative stimuli: Stop on red, go on green. Stopping your car when the light is red or starting it when the light is green is one of a large class of behaviors that seem to be under the control of one or another specific part of the environment. The lights in a theater go off at the beginning of a play, and we sit down and are quiet; the house lights go on between acts, and we get up, move around, and talk. A father and a son are arguing, and as the father begins to get angry, the son comes on a bit less strong; the good-looking person smiles at you on the street corner, and you run your hands through your hair, walk over, and go through the rest of your act.

In each of these cases the behavior you do (or do not do) depends very much on the presence or absence of a very specific event. This event does not force you to respond; rather, it sets the occasion for your making one response rather than another. Such an event is called a **discriminative stimulus**, usually abbreviated S^D, because it has been discriminated out of all the possible confusion that surrounds us to serve as a signal that one or another behavior is appropriate: go on green; stop on red. In terms of reinforcement, the S^D signals that something good will happen (that is, a reinforcement will occur) if the correct behavior is performed. For the reinforcement psychologist, the S^D brings responding under the control of a specific part of the experimenter's (and the learner's) world. By controlling reinforcement, the psychologist comes to control the rate and persistence of responses; by controlling S^Ds, the psychologist comes to control when the response will or will not be made.

It is quite simple to bring behavior under stimulus control. Consider a pigeon pecking a clear plastic key that can change color from red to green to yellow and so on. Suppose that we deliver reinforcement only when the key is red. We can expect to find that the pigeon will peck the key only when it is red (red = S^D), not when it is any other color.

For a more rigorous demonstration, Reynolds (1968) suggests the following four-part experiment involving a key that can become one of three colors: red, orange, or yellow. During Part 1 of this experiment, we reinforce responding to all three colors. During Part 2 we reinforce the pigeon only while the key is red, never while it is orange or yellow. During Part 3 we do not reinforce any color, red in-

cluded. During Part 4 we again reinforce only the red key. What happens can be seen in Figure 7-11. During Part 1 the pigeon responds to all three colors at about the same rate (about 50 responses per minute). During Part 2 responding to orange and yellow both drop off to 0 responses per minute (for yellow) or 5–7 responses per minute (for orange). During Part 3 all responding drops to zero. During Part 4 responding to the red key goes back to its Part 2 level of about 60 per minute, while responding to orange and yellow first increases (to about 20 per minute) and then drops off again (to about 5 per minute). In the end, red wins.

One further consistent aspect of these results concerns how fast the pigeon responds to orange and yellow during Parts 2 and 4. Orange always seems to come out on top. Red and orange and red and yellow are not equally different, as shown both by what we know about hue from the physicist and by what we have just observed from the pigeon. Red and yellow seem to "go together" less well than red and orange. Another way of saying this, from the pigeon's point of view, is that there is a greater degree of generalization from red to orange than from yellow to red.

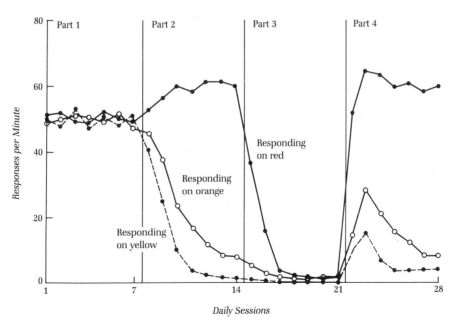

Figure 7-11. Some effects of generalization on the formation of a discrimination. *(From* A Primer of Operant Conditioning, *by G. S. Reynolds. Copyright © 1968 by Scott, Foresman and Company. Reprinted by permission.)*

The occurrence of generalization has been considered a very basic learning phenomenon by most psychologists. Unfortunately, generalization has been thought to tell us a great deal about the relation of (human and animal) behavior to physical stimuli. It has only infrequently been thought to tell us something about the living organism itself. When an organism gives us a generalization effect, it is "telling us" which items "go together"—that is, are similar for it. If it turns out that the subject of a generalization experiment categorizes aspects of the world, such as color, in the same way that the physicist does, well and good. If the living being does not, should we say that it has made a mistake, that it hasn't read its physics textbook? The answer is no; human beings and animals behave, and if such behavior agrees with a physical description of the world, it does not necessarily mean that physical description is the only appropriate one for the living organism. If physics and living do not agree—if generalization does not fit the physicist's description of the world—then as psychologists we must always go with a behavioral rather than a physical description of the situation. Behavior reveals the self-world a living being inhabits; physical description only gives us a world appropriate to the purposes of physics.

VI. REINFORCEMENT AND PSYCHOLOGICAL TECHNOLOGY

There can be no doubt about it, Skinner is a clever and inventive fellow, not only in laboratory psychology but in more practical things as well. Although his solutions at first may sound rather far-fetched, they do work. Take the case of Skinner's patriotic pigeon and the guided missile. The time is World War II, and the problem is to direct a missile unerringly to its target. At this time electronic guidance systems were not only expensive, they were not yet totally accurate. Enter Skinner and the idea of directing a missile using the pigeon as a kamikaze pilot.

The idea is quite simple. A pigeon is taught to peck a round screen on which the picture of a ship is projected. The pigeon is reinforced only to the degree that it pecks the center of the ship on its screen. A metal tip is attached to the pigeon's beak, and a sensory device locates the pigeon's pecks on the screen, thereby guiding the missile toward the

target. The missile gets on course as the pigeon pecks the middle of the screen. In this way the pigeon guides the missile to the target. In presenting this bit of pigeon technology, Skinner chose to display it in the form of Figure 7-12, which tries to present the world from the pigeon's first-bird point of view.

A. Behavioral medicine

Most reinforcement technology is not as esoteric as this. Probably the two major areas to which such technology has been applied concern therapy for inappropriate behaviors and the attempt to make education more orderly and appealing to the learner. In the area of psychologically inappropriate behaviors, the usual procedure has been to extinguish maladaptive responses while reinforcing personally helpful ones. Because these techniques are quite complicated in their specific application, we will discuss them in greater detail later (Chapter 14). For the moment let us turn to a different class of maladaptive response that has been shown to be affected by reinforcement techniques: bodily processes such as heart rate, intestinal contraction and relaxation, and blood pressure.

Figure 7-12. The kamikaze pigeon's first-bird point of view. (Adapted *from "Pigeons in a Pelican," by B. F. Skinner. In* American Psychologist, *1960, 15, 28–37. Copyright 1960 by the American Psychological Association. Reprinted by permission.)*

Each of these bodily response systems can be damaged if it functions improperly, as in high blood pressure, ulcers, or irregular heartbeat. In the early 1960s Jasper Brener, now of Hull University and then of the University of London, asked whether it would be possible to modify bodily reactions such as heart rate using reinforcement procedures. Such procedures would have the advantage of allowing the patient to control heart rate, blood pressure, and so on without depending on medications, which are not always successful and which may have undesirable side effects.

In Brener's original study (1966) he first determined the person's usual heart rate. With these baseline data in hand, Brener shaped some of his subjects to increase the interval between beats, thereby slowing heart rate, by reinforcing progressively longer intervals. The remaining subjects were gradually shaped to decrease their interbeat interval, thereby speeding up heart rate. The outcome of Brener's experiment was quite clear in showing that heart rate could be significantly increased or decreased by reinforcement procedures.

It was still not proved that the heart had been retrained directly. It is always possible to argue that some other, more easily controllable system, such as the muscles that control breathing, had been conditioned and that heart rate changed only as a secondary effect. To answer this question, Neil Miller and his associates at Rockefeller University in New York first injected rats with curare, a drug that paralyzes skeletal muscles but does not interfere with internal organs, such as the heart. Because breathing is controlled by skeletal muscles, it was necessary to put the rat into a respirator, where it was run through the shaping procedure. Using this technique, Miller and DiCara (1967) and Miller and Banuazizi (1968) were able to produce changes not only in heart rate but in visceral contractions as well. These studies indicated that it was possible to condition organ systems directly, even if the subject was unable to move.

Although Miller was originally quite optimistic about the exciting medical possibilities opened up by reinforcement procedures, more recent work suggests that so-called psychosomatic diseases will not easily let themselves be reinforced out of existence. Although some patients do maintain control over heart rate or blood pressure when they return home, many others do not. It is possible to get or-

gan systems to change in the laboratory, but it is quite difficult to prevent the extinction of such changes once the patient leaves the laboratory. Constant follow-up is needed.

This work on organ learning has one further implication for a first-person approach to the psychology of learning: Even though I might want to lower my blood pressure or change my heart rate voluntarily, I am unable to do it just by wanting it to be so. If there is one thing these experiments demonstrate, it is that sometimes another person is needed to teach me how to do something I want to do. Unreflected activities are not changeable on the basis of my reflected first-person desire to change. It seems that maladaptive responses are beyond a reflected act of will and that once a particular mode of unreflected responding has been set up, the pattern can be broken only by having the person learn another unreflected act. In almost none of these experiments could the person "will" his or her heart to beat more slowly or his or her blood pressure to decrease.

B. Programmed instruction

Perhaps the most widely known technological change brought about by reinforcement psychology concerns the development of teaching machines. Although the word *machine* must strike terror into the heart of every well-intentioned educator, what is important about teaching machines is not the machine but the **program** that lies behind it. By and large, this procedure is a straightforward extension of shaping procedures, in a form known as **programmed instruction.**

To illustrate how programmed instruction works, consider the following three questions for an introductory physics text (Skinner, 1958, pp. 969–977).[6]

1. The important parts of a flashlight are the battery and the bulb. When we "turn on" a flashlight, we close a switch which connects the battery with the

   _____ .

   Response: bulb

2. When we turn on a flashlight, an electric current flows through the fine wire in the _____ and causes it to grow hot.

   Response: bulb

[6]Question examples are from "Teaching Machines," by B. F. Skinner. In *Science*, Vol. 128, pp. 969–977, Table 2, 24 October 1958. Copyright 1958 by the American Association for the Advancement of Science. Reprinted by permission.

3. When the hot wire glows brightly, we say that it gives off or sends out heat and _____ .

Response: light

The answer to the first question is quite obvious, and we would expect a learner to produce it without trouble and to be immediately reinforced by learning that he or she had got the correct answer. Question 2 has *bulb* as its answer, and since the learner has already said *bulb* in response to the first question, it is quite likely to be produced (and reinforced) again. Question 3 takes up the cue given by Questions 1 and 2 and asks a slightly different but still quite clearly related question. Again the correct response is given and reinforcement follows.

So far everything seems so simple that we must wonder how far a learner can get with such a program. Consider now Questions 29 and 31 (Skinner, 1958, pp. 969–977).

29. A nearly "dead" battery may make a flashlight bulb warm to the touch, but the filament may still not be hot enough to emit light, in other words the filament will not be _____ at that temperature.

Response: incandescent

31. When raised to any temperature above 800 degrees Celsius, an object such as an iron bar will emit light. Although the bar may melt or vaporize, its particles will be _____ no matter how hot they get.

Response: incandescent

Without knowing the intervening steps, it is quite clear that the learner has got quite far indeed: it is a long way from *fine wire* to *filament* and from *hot wire* to *incandescent*.

It requires no great stretch of the imagination to see how such educational machinery comes from shaping procedures developed in the laboratory. The basic idea is clear enough: make sure the learner has the required response in his or her repertoire, and never make the learner do anything he or she will have to unlearn. Under this set of conditions each successive step is an approximation to the final desired bit of learning. In this way the technique of programmed instruction makes direct contact with the laboratory procedure of shaping.

A great many advantages are claimed for programmed instruction: For one, the student need never be frustrated by not having the attention of his or her teacher—a teaching machine always works for each student alone. Two, reinforcement is always immediate—no need to wait for the teacher to notice. Three, the teacher is free to deal with children about personal issues, since much of the routine teaching that goes on in an elementary or high school classroom is done by the program. In addition, each student is allowed to progress at his or her own rate and need never be "bored" if the rest of the class goes too slowly or be "left behind" if it goes too fast. Finally, programmed instruction seems to take the learner's first-person skills and knowledge clearly into account at every step of the way.

With all these seeming advantages, we ought to go right out and organize a campaign to bring programmed instruction to each and every school in the Western world. Yet educators have not been enthusiastic about the reinforcement revolution in education, and there seem to be perfectly valid arguments against the indiscriminate use of programmed instruction in the classroom. Perhaps the major argument has already been made in regard to the difference between the Zen Master and the Master Reinforcer: for the Master Reinforcer, education is designed to teach facts independent of the person doing the teaching. Although it may seem theoretically reasonable to separate the teacher from the teaching of unpleasant or just plain boring material, it is clear that we, as learners, learn most about our teacher's (and society's) attitude toward learning in just these "boring" or "uninspiring" cases. If we let the human teacher deal with his or her pupils only for the "fun stuff," then the discipline of learning is made an evil to be avoided, not a necessary part of learning. To learn requires a learner to do some routine tasks, such as memorizing multiplication tables, and if we do not allow teachers to show children their dedication and humanness in teaching all kinds of material— multiplication tables included—we do not present a clear picture of what learning is about. It's not that it's good to suffer; rather, if you, the learner, know why something is important, you are not likely to suffer very much.

Perhaps the most important objection that can be raised against programmed instruction concerns the idea of a clearly specified "correct answer," or a clearly defined behavioral objective. The process of education is not so much a piling up of correct answers as it is the developing of an attitude toward the open-ended nature of human knowing and understanding. If we teach a child, by our clear objectives and our clear analyses, that there always is *an answer*, the child is likely to overlook the fact that knowledge is always incomplete and that many of our most important questions have no final answer. Learning, like living itself, is best thought of as open-ended, and any attempt to close it in with a mess of "correct answers" benefits neither education nor living. Reinforcement and clear objectives are important concepts in the psychology of learning but, by themselves, are not as important as they have been made to appear.

VII. CLASSICAL CONDITIONING AND THE LEARNER'S WORLD

One of the best-known phenomena of learning is salivary conditioning, a phenomenon that was discovered almost by accident around 1900. The place was Russia, and the discoverer was the distinguished physiologist I. P. Pavlov (1849–1936). As early as 1880, in the course of his studies on digestive processes, Pavlov had found that if a dog with an opening in its throat was given a piece of food, the stomach produced gastric secretions even though the food never got to the stomach. To Pavlov this suggested that simply presenting a piece of food to an animal could serve as a cue for an anticipatory (or, as he called it, a "psychic") secretion.

Despite this early observation, Pavlov continued his studies on gastric secretions (work for which he won the Nobel Prize in 1902) and did not begin a systematic study of "psychic secretions" until just about that time. Because the original surgical procedure of making an opening in the dog's throat was so difficult, Pavlov (1928) decided to use the much simpler operation of exposing a salivary gland in the dog's cheek. Although he began his work by seeing how much saliva was produced when an animal saw (but did not eat) a piece of bread, he soon came to use another event as a cue for "psychic salivation." For example, in many of the early studies a bell was first rung and then some food powder or weak acid was put on the animal's tongue, causing it to salivate. After a number of pairings of bell with food, the bell alone came to produce an increase in the flow of saliva even if no food was given.

In the intervening half-century and more, a great variety of events—lights, noises, touches, smells, buzzers—have been used in place of the original bell. Any of these events, which originally did not cause the animal to salivate, is called the "conditioned stimulus" because it is an event to which salivation is conditioned. The response of salivating (together with a whole host of other behaviors) is called the "conditioned response." Two other concepts complete the Pavlovian picture: the "unconditioned stimulus" (such as food), which evokes a response without being conditioned to do so, and the "unconditioned response" (such as salivation), which occurs without prior learning when the unconditioned stimulus is presented.

Well, there you have it: four terms and a few relationships among them, and that's **classical conditioning.** The procedure for bringing such learning about is quite simple: take some neutral and easily manipulable event, such as a bell (the conditioned stimulus), and pair it with a second event, such as food (the unconditioned stimulus), that regularly evokes a specific and measurable response, such as salivating (the unconditioned response). If you pair the two often enough, the first stimulus will come to evoke the unconditioned response, thereby making it a conditioned response to that stimulus.

These results are so simple that it is hard to understand why they should be considered such an important experimental finding. Surely we all have had the experience of thinking about a steak (or even of the word *saliva*) and sensing the flow of saliva on our tongues. What, then, is so important about these findings that the word *conditioned* has come into our vocabulary as almost synonymous with *learned* and that American psychology has come to embrace such events as crucial for human and animal learning? Probably the major reasons American psychology was so strongly impressed had to do with two aspects of the conditioning experiment: (1) all parts were out in the open so that any unbiased observer could see them, and (2) the experiment seemed directly relatable to a popular philosophical analysis of learning called "associationism."

The first of these two factors meant that anybody could do a conditioning experiment: it could be replicated easily. This feature, of course, is in the best tradition of experimental science. Not only could such experiments be replicated, they could also be systematically varied, one variable at a time. It was therefore possible to ask (and answer) such questions as these:

1. What happens if I change the original conditioned stimulus in one or another way? (Answer: generalization.)

2. What happens if I stop pairing the unconditioned stimulus (UCS) with the conditioned stimulus (CS)? (Answer: extinction.)

3. What happens if I pair the CS and UCS only some of the time? (Answer: great resistance to extinction—the partial reinforcement effect.)

4. What is the absolutely best time interval between CS and UCS for conditioning to occur? (Answer: about .5 sec, with CS preceding USC.)

5. Can I condition animals other than dogs? (Answer: yes; almost every animal in the world is conditionable.)

6. Do I always have to use "pleasant" events, such as food, for UCSs, or can other events also be used? (Answer: "unpleasant" events, such as shock, not only work, they usually work better, producing faster conditioning and slower extinction.)

This list of questions (and their answers) ought to show that Pavlov's experiment easily led investigators to an almost endless series of clearly answerable research questions. These experiments were easy to do and seemed to clarify many of the basic phenomena of learning. (Almost all the phenomena discovered for the first time in the classical conditioning laboratory were later replicated through use of reinforcement techniques, and each of the facts listed above applies both to Pavlovian and to Skinnerian situations.) The phenomena of learning seem hardy and relatively unaffected by certain rather dramatic changes in task.

The second major reason psychologists liked the conditioning technique had to do with theory, or with an attempt to explain how learning came about. The major theory of how learning occurred was first developed in the 17th and 18th centuries by the philosophers Hobbes, Hume, and Locke. These philosophers argued that the "human mind" was greatly increased in power by learning. In fact, the infant was seen as an essentially unfit organism devoid of all but the most elementary responses.

Locke went so far as to call the newborn infant a "blank slate" that only became a human being as it learned new ideas and rearranged old ones. And how was all this learning and rearranging to happen? Quite simply: an idea was learned if we came into contact with it, and one idea became connected to another idea because they occurred in close contact with each other.

The major principle of learning, then, was the so-called **Law of Contiguity**, which stated that two ideas were learned as going together to the degree that they occurred together. Although the Law of Contiguity was originally proposed in terms of "ideas," the argument could be generalized to any two events in the experience of a human being or animal. From psychology's point of view, the most important of these events were stimuli and responses, and here one version of the Law of Contiguity went as follows: an initially neutral stimulus will come to evoke a given response to the degree that the two events have occurred together in the past.

Pavlov's very scientific procedure seemed a good way to study the "invisible" ideas proposed by philosophers. If contiguity was the major principle by which people and animals learned, then the conditioning procedure ought to serve "to bring the mind into being" in a clear and experimentally useful way.

A. Conditioning in advertising

Since one outcome of the classical conditioning procedure is "to make the mind visible," it will come as no surprise that conditioning principles have been used quite extensively in describing human thinking. One example concerns advertising, in which the pairing of two items is commonplace. Although it may seem quite unimportant that Farrah Fawcett bathes in Adolph's meat tenderizer, advertising logic seems to demand that we hear all about it. The assumption is that the product will become associated with some of the star's attributes and that if you like the star, you will become conditioned also to like the product.

Sometimes advertisers attempt a more complicated pairing. Consider the hypervirile specimen known as the "Marlboro man." Although it hardly seems possible now, there was a time when smoking filter-tipped cigarettes was considered unmanly (did you ever see Humphrey Bogart smoking a filter tip?). How do you get rid of the "sissy" idea evoked by a filter tip? Easy: pair it over and over again with a virile-looking sea captain or cowboy, and over the course of five years of advertising the sissy stigma of the filter tip disappears.

But what about women smokers? It would be a rather empty victory if the advertiser alienated half the market. Here there are two answers: (1) filter-tip advertisements also stress "lowered tar and nicotine," and that appeals equally to women and to men, and (2) for a woman, the idea of virility (suggested by the male smoker in the ad) is sexiness, and there is nothing bad about smoking a sexy cigarette. Male smokers are told to do it all the time, as in the ad for Muriel cigars in which an actress resembling Mae West croons "Why don'tcha pick me up and smoke me sometime?"

All this could be only a lot of smoky speculation if we had no experimental evidence to back it up. The first supporting evidence comes from Pavlov, who demonstrated the phenomenon called **higher-order conditioning**. Pavlov first established a conditioned response—say, salivating in response to a light as a conditioned stimulus. Once the light quite regularly evoked the conditioned response of salivating, it was paired with a tone. If Pavlov then presented the tone by itself, the animal salivated, even though the tone and the original unconditioned stimulus (food) were never directly paired. What seems to have happened is that the first conditioned stimulus—the light—was sufficiently well conditioned to evoke the salivary response in the dog so that it could now be used as an unconditioned stimulus for the tone—hence, transfer of the conditioned response from light to tone.

The implication for advertising (and higher-order reaction transfers generally) is that any stimulus capable of regularly evoking one or another response should be able to transfer that response to some other stimulus—as, for example, feelings of sexiness are transferred to filter-tip cigarettes by way of cowboys. This type of higher-order transfer is also theoretically neat because it requires only the pairing of stimuli: light and tone or cowboy and filter-tip cigarette. Such results suggest that the law of contiguity works in higher-order conditioning as in simpler situations.

All this is plausible, but the question remains: can we demonstrate experimentally the "transfer" of a "reaction" from one word to another? The an-

swer is yes. The most relevant studies were done by Staats and Staats (1957, 1959a). To begin, they needed a series of words to serve as unconditioned stimulus items—that is, words known to evoke a particular reaction before the experiment began. To get such words, they asked college students to rate a large number of words as pleasant, unpleasant, or somewhere in between. From this collection they selected two sets of words, one all pleasant and one all unpleasant. They argued that if an experimenter paired a nonsense syllable, such as GEJ (which initially is rated as neither pleasant nor unpleasant), with pleasant words, such as *love, sweet,* and *pretty,* the nonsense syllable ought to come to be rated as more pleasant than if paired with negative words, such as *putrid, sour,* and *nasty.* Many experiments confirmed this prediction. When a nonsense word had been paired with pleasant words, it was rated as more pleasant than when it had been paired with unpleasant words. In addition, Staats and Staats reported that many of their subjects were unable to describe why they rated the nonsense syllable as they did except to note that somehow it "felt" more pleasant (or unpleasant).

Perhaps the set of studies most relevant to the advertising case concerned the "conditioning of meaning" to names of nationalities, such as *Japanese, Turkish,* and *Russian.* Staats and Staats found that they could affect the good/bad ratings given a national group by pairing its name with good or bad adjectives. Here again, some subjects were unable to say exactly why they rated the groups as they did.

The classical conditioning procedure, which is described with words like *evoke* and *response,* seems a good one for both advertising and propaganda—at least from the perspective of the advertiser or propagandist, not of the consumer or the citizen. After all, what is wanted is an immediate (conditioned) reaction to a particular product or a social group. If it is possible to produce a mechanically obedient subject in regard to some event or other, isn't this just the aim of advertising or propaganda? To be a good advertiser (or a good propagandist) is to restrict my choices so that I become robotlike in regard to your product (or ideology): show me the stimulus and I want it.

Although advertising (and propaganda) aims for this type of reaction, consumers are scarcely ever conditioned quite that strongly. For one thing, there are too many competing advertisers. More important, the conditions of initial pairing are often too weak to bring about purely reflexive buying. Although second-order conditioning does occur, it is easily subject to extinction. Unless the original CS—the light—is soon paired again with the original UCS—food—the animal soon stops salivating. The light is then no longer able to serve as a UCS for the tone, and second-order conditioning becomes impossible.

B. Electric shock and the mechanization of behavior

In contrast to food, certain other events, such as electric shock, produce much more long-lasting effects, not only for second-order conditioning but for other phenomena as well. Classical conditioning based on "negative" (noxious) stimulus events seems more long-lasting and much more likely to cause highly mechanical and robotlike behavior than more benign events, such as food on the tongue or sexy cowboys on the billboard. Although many examples can be found in the laboratory, a strong phobia in a human being shows the same rigidly mechanized and totally maladaptive responding found in laboratory animals trained with shock. Although most of us have experienced the exasperating loss of freedom that goes along with even a mild fear of flying, heights, particular foods (brains, testes, snails), animals, small places, and so on, the total mechanization of behavior brought about by aversive stimuli can be seen best in the clinic or in laboratory learning based on shock.

Pavlov never used electric shock with his animals. A contemporary of Pavlov, Vladimir Bechterev, was the first to use such stimuli in the conditioning experiment. Bechterev believed that psychology ought to concern itself with movements of an intact animal rather than with surgically prepared animals such as Pavlov had used. Bechterev's experiment was quite simple: he would touch the animal (usually a dog) on the left hind paw (conditioned stimulus) and then give the animal a moderate-level shock to the right front paw. An unconditioned response would occur when the dog lifted his right front paw. Conditioning was shown when the dog would lift his right paw simply in response to a touch on the left hind paw. In this experiment it is important to note that lifting the right paw does not prevent the shock; learning is shown by an anticipa-

tory lifting of this paw in response to the conditioned stimulus alone.

Although this procedure is almost identical to the Pavlovian one using food, it is a bit more awkward from the animal's point of view: there is nothing the dog can do to avoid getting shocked. What happens in this situation, as Bechterev in Russia and Liddell (1926) in America noted, was that the dog gets very still in response to the conditioned stimulus and makes the minimal move possible as the shock comes on. Probably a more important event, however, does not concern the paw, but concerns changes in the animal's breathing and in other bodily responses, such as sweating, urinating, and defecating. Here Liddell's results were quite clear in showing that even though the animal (in his case, a sheep) became quite still and even pricked up his ears in response to the conditioned stimulus, there were strong and quite clearly measurable changes in how much the animal sweated and how rapidly he breathed, and these events occurred well before the shock came on. Results such as these suggested that not only does the conditioned stimulus come to control a specific movement, such as flexing the paw, but it also controls other bodily reactions even though not all of them can easily be seen.

1. Avoidance learning. The lot of animals subject to this type of procedure is a sad and unfair one: there is little they can do to help themselves. But what happens if animal subjects are able to avoid the shock? Do they behave in such a way as to avoid the shock, or do they show some of the same helpless characteristics as the trapped animals? An early series of studies by Solomon and his associates (Solomon & Wynne, 1953; Solomon, Kamin, & Wynne, 1953) is relevant. In these experiments, a dog was put into a two-compartment box. A buzzer was used as a conditioned stimulus to warn the dog that a very strong shock was to follow in 10 sec. To avoid the shock, the dog had to jump to the opposite compartment. When the buzzer came on again, the dog could avoid the shock once more if it responded within 10 sec. The phenomenon these experiments illustrate is called **avoidance learning** because the subject must learn to perform a response in order to avoid some noxious event.

Figure 7-13 shows results for a typical dog in this experiment. The line drawn across the graph repre-

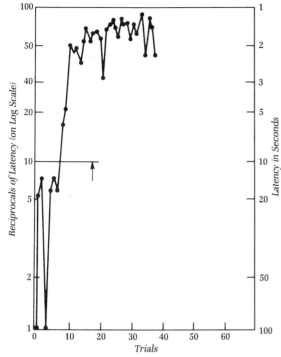

Figure 7-13. Performance of a single typical dog in avoidance conditioning with strong shock as unconditioned stimulus. The horizontal line is drawn at 10 sec. Responses below this line were escape trials; responses above it were avoidance trials. Shock was turned off permanently at Trial 17. *(From "Traumatic Avoidance Learning: Acquisition in Normal Dogs," by R. L. Solomon and L. C. Wynne. In* Psychological Monographs, *1953, 67, No. 4 (Whole No. 354). Copyright 1953 by the American Psychological Association. Reprinted by permission.)*

What was good, adaptive behavior at the beginning of the experiment turned out to be rather unnecessary and mechanical behavior at the end. The animal, once conditioned, never tried to determine (by staying around for a bit more than 10 sec) whether the situation had changed. Even when an animal, for one reason or another, did not jump within the 10-sec limit on a particular trial (and should have noticed that his situation had changed), the dog continued to respond well within the 10-sec limit on the next trial. The animal's behavior, therefore, was no longer sensitive to changes in his situation; rather, the dog seemed controlled (like a robot) so that he had to repeat behavior that had worked previously. It is as if in this situation, the conditioned stimulus came to dominate all of the animal's experience, leaving no room for any new experiences to alter what he might do.

Under these conditions, the feared event or object (the buzzer) seemed to be what the animal was escaping from; the original situation of pain brought about by the shock now seemed much less relevant. And this, unfortunately, is as it has to be: the buzzer is in the present, the shock long gone. To be sure, the buzzer came to capture the subject by being paired with the shock, but just as surely it is escape from the buzzer that is now of importance, not avoidance of the shock. The sequence, then, is quite straightforward, quite understandable, and quite mechanical.

In human beings, we often label strong, unpleasant bodily reactions brought about by earlier aversive conditioning as "fear." When we have such reactions, as in so-called fear-objects or even phobias, we probably are escaping more from ourselves than from a situation that at present could hurt us. It is our fear that we fear, and the mechanical and controlling nature of such conditioning is so powerful as to close down our options in a particular situation. When the feared object appears, we respond in mechanical and repetitive ways that restrict our intelligence and flexibility. Fear narrows the world, making us rigid and unfree.

2. Persistence of avoidance responses. How long do such effects last? According to the clinical literature on phobias, the answer can be a lifetime. The answer given by more experimental situations is still a very long time. Consider a set of observations made by Edwards and Acker (1962) on 20 ex-

sents 10 sec, so that any response that is over the line means the animal avoided the shock. This dog was able to avoid the shock from Trial 7 on, and he got progressively faster at it throughout the entire experiment. The most important part of the experiment, however, is shown by the arrow at Trial 17. At this point Solomon and Wynne turned off the shock, so that, strictly speaking, the animal would not have to do anything to avoid shock. But the dog continued to respond before 10 sec were up and, for this reason, never found out that the situation was no longer dangerous.

servicemen in a Veterans Administration hospital. All the men tested were some 15 years past their service experience in World War II, so that any of the reactions to be described had to be at least that old. Some of the men had served in the Army, others in the Navy. Only the ex-sailors had experience with a special series of gongs used to call seamen to battle during wartime. In the experiment, all the subjects were exposed to a series of sounds, including the gongs used to indicate a naval battle. As the gongs were sounded, Edwards and Acker recorded physiological indexes of emotional response—sweating, changes in breathing rate, and so on. Results were quite conclusive in showing considerably larger reactions for seamen than for soldiers even though they had not been in a combat situation for over 15 years. It seems quite clear that fear conditioning lasts for a very long time.

Although not quite as impressive, laboratory results provided by Solomon, Kamin, and Wynne (1953) are still dramatic in their own context. In this series of experiments, dogs were trained to avoid a very powerful shock by responding within 10 sec to a warning buzzer. If the crucial event making an avoidance response so difficult to extinguish is that the animal never tests whether there is still shock in the situation, it should be possible to speed up extinction by keeping the animal in the feared situation so that he can come to know that the shock has been turned off. Because animals will not stay in the situation on their own, Solomon and his collaborators kept them from jumping. In one procedure, dogs were forcibly restrained in the shock compartment by a glass barrier; in another, they were shocked for jumping into the second compartment. Although it seems as if both these procedures should work, only 2 of 9 dogs showed any extinction under the glass-barrier procedure, and only 3 of 13 showed any extinction when shocked for jumping.

Thus, only 5 of 22 dogs showed extinction when prevented from escaping from the buzzer. Although it is difficult to say exactly why avoidance conditioning is so hard to extinguish, Solomon and Wynne proposed that two factors seemed to be involved. First, dogs generally escaped from the fear box in about 1.5 sec, far too quickly for the "emotional" responses to decrease when the buzzer was present. Thus, quick jumping "saves" these re-

sponses from extinguishing. More important, Solomon and Wynne argue that behavior learned on the basis of very strong shock is partly irreversible, so that, once learned, such responses are capable of affecting behavior for a very long time unless directly competed against by other responses.

3. Conditioning in phobias.   A classic study on "fear conditioning" shows what kinds of principles might be involved in breaking the very strong and rigid sequence of conditioned stimulus/fear/escape from fear . . . found in phobic reactions. The year is about 1920; the experimenters are John B. Watson and Rosalie Rayner; the subject is a 9-month-old infant named Albert. The experiment begins with Watson and Rayner showing Albert a tame white rat. At first, the rat only aroused Albert's curiosity, and since it was clear Albert was not afraid of the rat, it was removed from Albert's sight. A little later the rat was again presented. This time, however, the experimenters made a very loud and startling noise behind Albert. This noise frightened Albert, causing him to cry. After pairing the rat with the harsh noise for about five trials, the experimenters presented the rat alone. This time the sight of the rat was enough to make Albert cry.

If we substitute the Pavlovian terminology of conditioned stimulus for rat, unconditioned stimulus for harsh noise, and unconditioned response (and later conditioned response) for Albert's crying, we have a model of how an infant might learn to fear something through conditioning. This observation also confirms the idea that if an animal or person is unable to avoid a noxious stimulus, he or she is likely to learn a series of bodily reactions as a response to the originally neutral conditioned stimulus.

The troubles of little Albert did not come to an end when the white rat was removed, for now not only did the sight of a white rat frighten him, so did anything similar to the rat, such as a ball of cotton, a rabbit, and a white mask. Watson and Rayner (1920) found that Albert was not frightened by any object that did not resemble the white rat (say, a block of wood). Here we have an example of the generalization of fear, based in this case on something being white and fuzzy.

This experiment would have been of only passing interest—a hint about how fear is learned—if not for a follow-up study done by Mary Cover Jones. In this experiment a 3-year-old boy by the name of Peter was brought to Jones' laboratory because he was afraid of white rats, as well as rabbits, fur coats, cotton balls, and so on—in short, a natural replication of the case of little Albert. Jones tried a number of approaches to helping Peter get rid of his fear. The one that worked best was to pair the feared object—the rat—with a pleasant event: eating Peter's favorite dessert. First the caged rat was brought into the same room as Peter but was kept far away from him. While Peter kept track of the rat, he was fed ice cream. The next day the rat moved a little closer while Peter again ate. Notice that Peter was eating in the presence of the rat and that eating involves movements that are incompatible with crying. After a number of such sessions, Peter and the rat were happily reunited. One caution in using this technique: the situation must be handled with finesse, for rather than teaching Peter to be happy with the rat, Jones might have caused Peter to fear his dessert.

The principle involved is clear: Find some response pattern that is incompatible with the bodily reactions aroused by the conditioned stimulus. Next pair the stimulus producing this pattern with the feared object, making sure that the incompatible response is evoked more strongly than fear (for example, in the beginning keep the rat far away from the child). Once fear is extinguished at this distance, reintroduce the incompatible response with a slightly stronger version of the conditioned stimulus, again making sure the incompatible response is the stronger of the two. Over a number of presentations, fear will be "unlearned."

Although this is a highly reasonable and highly successful procedure, it was almost 35 years before anyone systematically tried to use it to desensitize people to feared objects. An early attempt was made by a psychiatrist named Joseph Wolpe (1958). Wolpe's basic hypothesis is that most cases of phobia depend on the evocation of fear or anxiety in the presence of certain objects or situations. To overcome a phobia, it is necessary only to relax the patient and then ask him or her to think of these anxiety-evoking situations. According to the logic of this procedure, relaxation training must be sufficiently strong to overcome such responses as fast heart rate or sweaty palms, which are associated with fear. The specific procedures developed by Wolpe are a good deal more elaborate than this and will be described in Chapter 14. For the moment, it is enough to know that procedures have been developed to deal with phobic reactions in human beings and that these involve teaching the patient to perform a series of responses ("relaxation") incompatible with being afraid.

4. Learned helplessness. The original observations by Bechterev and Liddell pointed out that animals behaved in the no-escape/no-avoid situation with helplessness and passivity. More recent work by Seligman and his associates (Seligman, 1974; Seligman, Maier, & Geer, 1968) has been directed at understanding the phenomenon they have come to call **learned helplessness.** The experimental facts are simple and straightforward: if an animal is classically conditioned to an unavoidable shock, it is subsequently less likely, and perhaps totally unable, to learn to escape from shock in a new situation. For example, if dogs were first kept in a situation in which shock was unavoidable and then put into a two-compartment box, they were unable to escape to the safe side. Even if one of these dogs occasionally did get over the barrier and escape the shock, on the next trial he returned to his old, helpless ways. In addition to these direct behavioral effects, such dogs showed a decrease in appetite and a subsequent loss of weight.

Once learned, such behavior was extremely resistant to extinction. Some dogs took over 200 trials of being actually dragged over the barrier before they finally were able to break out of the learned-helplessness symptom. Why should this behavior be so resistant to extinction? Again we may talk about the all-involving nature of a strong negative stimulus event. That does not seem quite enough, however, because if animals were first trained with an equally negative shock in a situation in which they could escape by doing something, they had no later problem in jumping from one compartment to the other. The critical ingredient seems to be that helplessness is learned in response to a powerful, negative situation that allows no exit regardless of what the animal does. Helplessness results only when an animal or person has not experienced mastery in regard to dealing with negative events in his or her world. Give the living organism a situation in which it can have some effect, and the probability of learned helplessness is greatly reduced.

C. Classical conditioning and human learning: A concluding comment

Of all the procedures used to study learning, human and otherwise, classical conditioning is least concerned with the learner's experience. Although it seems unfair to consider classical conditioning simply a bit of laboratory technology, it does not seem wrong to say the idea of conditioning is appropriate only to a limited number of situations—situations in which the learner is reduced to a simple stimulus-response machine. In this type of situation, the learner's experience consists mainly of insistent bodily reactions, reactions often labeled by the word *fear*. Classical conditioning seems to describe how learning occurs for certain types of aversive events that demand their due in terms of a total response by the learner.

Thus, behavior learned in connection with certain types of stimuli binds the learner to a simple set of reactions. And these reactions seem to occur automatically when a painful or traumatic stimulus is presented. An aversive event, such as shock, restricts a person's or an animal's world to such a degree that the learned signal for that situation reduces the organism's possibilities to one: get away from it. Under this condition, the signal makes a direct appeal to the subject's first-person world, an appeal so strong and so compelling that it can be broken only with great difficulty and patience.

The very compellingness of the reaction we call "fear" seems to remove the person from experiencing any other aspect of the world except the phobic event. There is good reason to pay exclusive attention to events that signal harmful or dangerous situations, but the reason seems less good if we never check to see whether the danger is still present. When we come to this state of affairs, we respond mechanically to escape fear. The cycle is as entrapping as it is vicious, and there is little we can do about it. Powerful traumatic events reduce us to a bit of mechanical push-pull, and it is here we become a "Clockwork Orange."

Fortunately, such situations are rare in our lives (unfortunately, not rare enough), and it is usually improper to describe us in terms of stimuli evoking responses. Rather, our experience of the world is a good deal more open. The Pavlovian world is really one in which the learner's experience is denied or at least suppressed. For Pavlov, that was all right, as he was interested mainly in describing the living being as a bit of biology. For a *psychology* of learning to talk about human behavior in this way is inappropriate and unreasonable. Each of us experiences more than a stimulus-response world, and to base psychology on the idea that we are robots following the dictates of the world's stimuli is accurate only in very reduced behavior, such as occurs in phobias or when a person has been surgically altered.

In short, the self-world provided by classical conditioning is too empty to serve as a general model for the learner's world. The Skinnerian world—in both description and fact—is a bit fuller, but it too is far too timid in its explicit recognition of the learner's experience. Although I have tried to show (as did the Scandinavian psychologists Kvale & Grenness, 1967) that Skinner and Merleau-Ponty are not at opposite ends of the world, the idea of Skinner the phenomenologist (or Merleau-Ponty the behaviorist) is not easily accepted. The learner's world described by phenomenological psychologists such as Giorgi and Colaizzi is rich enough; unfortunately, it depends too much on the learner's verbal report for its specific mappings. Reflected consciousness is not all there is, and here Harlow's and Skinner's more directly behavioral methods also seem appropriate. But we have to be careful not only to observe and measure responses; rather, what we have to observe, measure, and describe is the world of the learner as experienced by the learner.

One conclusion to be stressed is that the human learner always experiences something both during the course of learning how to do something and in his or her reports about it afterward. To try to describe learning without taking the learner and his or her world into account is to miss the mark, whether the learning is the kind that produces phobic behavior or the kind achieved by a Zen Master. The human world is always a world of first-person experience, whether we talk about it from the point of view of reflected experience or that of observed behavior.

VIII. SUMMARY

Mastery of a complex skill such as archery may produce the experience of a "selfless self." This rich first-person experience is rarely (if ever) taken into account by the learning psychologist, who prefers instead to describe what he or she can see and record in numbers. The world of the learner seldom appears in such calculations, and psychology has been content to describe learning in terms of the changing number of correct responses made by a learner. This approach ultimately produces a definition of learning as only an inference to be drawn from changes in observable performance.

Few experimental psychologists have tried to use a learner's first-person experience in their theoretical analyses of learning. Edward Tolman, working with rats in T mazes, intuited "vicarious trial-and-error learning" on the basis of having noted that many of his (rodent) subjects looked both ways before running down the alley of their choice. Tolman later related such behavior to learning when he found that rats that looked more often also learned more readily.

B. F. Skinner has always been willing to look at the first-person world of the learner, although he does not use his intuitions in a formal way. Ivan Pavlov, the father of conditioning, resolutely refused to give the learner's experience any role in theory. Perhaps because of this stand, learning is most often described from a third-person point of view, and the "learner's world" remains relatively uncharted.

A few experimenters, however, have tried to describe the learner's first-person world in a systematic and rigorous way. Colaizzi had subjects learn different tasks and then describe their experiences in terms of changes in their reactions to the tasks presented. As a result of this work, Colaizzi concluded that learning often involved a new way of looking at (and dealing with) tasks and situations. Sometimes this meant that the learner had to learn how to discriminate the relevant from the irrelevant in a situation rather than how to do something entirely new.

In an earlier attempt to describe the learner's world using only third-person observation, Harlow found support for the view that learning can be defined in terms of learning not to do something rather than in terms of learning to do something new. In the hands of a skillful observer such as Harlow, objective data can be used to reconstruct the first-person world of the learner, particularly as he or she becomes progressively more skillful in dealing with a given class of problems—that is, as the learner learns how to learn in a given problem situation.

Since human subjects can talk, it seems a shame not to ask them about their experiences during learning. Verplanck has argued that it is necessary to look carefully at the conditions under which verbal and nonverbal behaviors are related, stressing that neither movements nor verbal statements should be taken as a more valid description of experience. He concludes that it is not helpful to talk simply about awareness; rather, we must always talk about the directed (intentional) aspects of awareness (what Verplanck has called "awareness of").

If we know what kinds of events—praise, money, sex, and so on—direct a person, we should be able to get him or her to do things for these events. When we change a person's behavior on this basis, we are said to be reinforcing the person. For reinforcement to work, however, we must always consider the particular person involved: who he or she is, what he or she values, how he or she experiences the present situation, and so on. In the end it is the learner who defines what is reinforcing. Thus, reinforcement reveals intentionality; that is, it tells us what is important to the person in the present situation.

To study the effects of reinforcement on learning, Skinner invented a special apparatus that has come to be called (by others) the Skinner box. The idea behind a reinforcement approach to learning is to let an animal do something first and then reinforce it if it did what the experimenter wanted. Because it is the experimenter who selects which response is correct and will be reinforced, the experience of reinforcing someone else often gives the experimenter a feeling of power. For this reason, the rights of the learner sometimes get overlooked, particularly if the experimenter is careless or insensitive.

Despite this danger, reinforcement techniques have been used for therapeutic purposes. The therapist works to extinguish inappropriate and maladaptive behaviors while reinforcing personally helpful ones. Reinforcement techniques have also been used profitably in teaching patients to control their heart rate or blood pressure. Subjects have been found to be unable to control heart rate or blood pressure on their own. Rather, they seem to require the intervention of an outside observer/teacher to help them come to respond (unreflectedly) in a more adaptive and personally helpful way.

Reinforcement procedures have also been used

in education. In programmed instruction the student is taken from his or her present state of knowledge to a more desirable state. Programmed instruction works on the basis of shaping procedures, in which successive approximations to some preset final level are reinforced until the learner reaches criterion performance. When this happens, the student is said to have learned or mastered the material or task.

In spite of its obvious advantages, programmed learning has the decided disadvantage of leading a learner to expect correct answers to any and all questions. Learning, like living itself, is better described as open-ended, and any attempt to close it in with the idea of an unfailing correct answer to every problem benefits neither the educational system nor the learner. It is important to teach the student that certain important questions do not have a uniquely correct answer. In these cases understanding the question is as important as knowing its answer.

In a final look at learning we must consider Pavlovian conditioning. This approach to learning has clearly left its mark on American psychology, not to mention our advertising and propaganda. Experiments in classical conditioning have shown that it is possible to train an animal to respond in mechanical, stereotyped ways to mechanical, stereotyped situations. In experiments such as those done by Pavlov's colleague Bechterev, conditioning shrank the learner's world so that it came to contain only the conditioned stimulus. For an animal in a no-escape/no-avoid condition, the only possible response to conditioning is an emotional one—and this the animal or human subject always learns.

Animals exposed to situations in which they cannot avoid shock, as in Solomon and Seligman's more recent experiments, become passive and helpless. A comparable process occurs in human phobic reactions: the person continues to respond in stereotyped and repetitive ways even though the present situation is no longer dangerous.

We must always remember that each person experiences more than a stimulus-response world. To base psychology on the idea that we are but mechanical robots pushed around by stimuli seems accurate only for people whose behavior is reduced, as occurs in phobic reactions. The human world is always one of varied and changing first-person experience. This is true whether we talk about it from the point of view of reflected experience or from that of careful third-person observation. The human learner always experiences something during the course of his or her learning, and the job of the psychologist is to capture that world of experience, whether it is the world of a phobic patient or that of a master archer. Both worlds are real for the person experiencing them, and both should be described effectively and rigorously by any psychology of learning.

IX. GLOSSARY OF IMPORTANT CONCEPTS

Avoidance learning. A form of learning that occurs in response to noxious stimuli. This type of learning is difficult to extinguish because it is based on an escape from fear, not on an avoidance of punishment.

Baseline. The rate of behavior at the outset of a learning experiment, before any conditioning occurs.

Classical conditioning. A learning procedure developed by Pavlov, that works by pairing some neutral event (the *conditioned stimulus*) with a second event (the *unconditioned stimulus*) that regularly evokes a specific and measurable response (the *unconditioned response*). After repeated pairings, the conditioned stimulus will evoke the unconditioned response, thereby making it a *conditioned response* to that stimulus.

Continuous schedule. A learning schedule in which reinforcement is given for every correct response.

Cumulative response curve. A method for presenting the data for an ongoing performance of some behavior in which slope tells response rate (steep slope means fast rate).

Discriminative stimulus (S^D). A stimulus that sets the occasion for making one rather than another response.

Extinction. The cessation of a particular learned response, often due to the withdrawal of reinforcement.

Fixed-interval schedule. A learning schedule in which reinforcement is given at regular time intervals.

Fixed-ratio schedule. A learning schedule in which reinforcement is given every time a certain number of responses have occurred.

Higher-order conditioning. A conditioning procedure in which a conditioned stimulus is used as an unconditioned stimulus to a new conditioned stimulus.

Interval schedule. A learning schedule in which reinforcement is given at a rate based on a time interval.

Law of contiguity. The "law" that two ideas are learned as going together to the degree that they occur together. As applied to learning theory, the idea that an initially neutral stimulus will come to evoke a given response to the degree that the two events have occurred together in the past.

Learned helplessness. The tendency of animals not to avoid or escape from an aversive situation as a result of previous experience in an aversive situation where escape or avoidance was impossible.

Learner's world. The first-person experience of the learner.

Learning. As described by Colaizzi, the prereflective organization of a to-be-learned content whereby the person comes progressively to adopt a changing style of functioning.

Learning curve. A graph plotting the course of learning, in which the vertical axis shows a measure of proficiency (for example, amount per unit time, time per unit amount, or errors) and the horizontal axis shows some measure of practice (for example, trials or time).

Learning how to learn. A type of learning in which an animal's rate of learning gradually improves over a series of problems of the same general type.

Operant conditioning. A technique of inducing behavioral change brought about by reinforcing responses selected by the investigator. Emphasized, and named initially, by B. F. Skinner.

Partial schedule. A learning schedule in which reinforcement is given after only some responses.

Program. When used in connection with teaching, a set of materials arranged in sequences of units, called frames, so that learning can proceed with a minimum of error. The program can be presented in book form as well as in a form suitable for use with a teaching machine.

Programmed instruction. An educational technique, based on shaping procedures, that enables the learner to work at his or her own pace and receive immediate feedback at each step in the learning process.

Ratio schedule. A learning schedule in which reinforcement is given at a rate based on number of responses.

Reinforcement. Any event that serves to direct the behavior of people (or animals) doing a particular task. A reinforcer is not defined absolutely, but is relative to what the learner considers (reflectedly or unreflectedly) important or valuable in a particular situation.

Shaping. Progressive reinforcement of the learner's approximations of a desired behavior, used to guide the learner to some particular desired behavior, such as talking more quietly or having a slower heart rate.

Variable-interval schedule. A learning schedule in which reinforcement is given at irregular time intervals.

Variable-ratio schedule. A learning schedule in which reinforcement is given after every so many responses, where the number of responses between rewards is varied.

Zen Master. A person attaining the highest level of skill in performing some activity. According to the "Great Doctrine" of Zen theory, the Master performs his or her art so well that actor and activity are not experienced as separate.

X. SUGGESTED READINGS

Major sources

Colaizzi, P. F. *Reflection and research in psychology: A phenomenological study of learning.* Dubuque, Iowa: Kendall/Hunt, 1973.

Herrigel, E. *Zen in the art of archery.* New York: Pantheon, 1964.

Kvale, S., & Grenness, C. Skinner and Sartre. *Review of Existential Psychology and Psychiatry*, 1967, 7, 128–150.

Merleau-Ponty, M. *The structure of behavior.* Boston: Beacon Press, 1963. Introduction, pp. 93–124; Part 3, Part 4.

Skinner, B. F. A case history in scientific method. In S. Koch (Ed.), *Psychology: A study of a science* (Vol. 2). New York: McGraw-Hill, 1959.

Secondary sources

Bower, G. H., & Hilgard, E. R. *Theories of learning* (5th ed.). Englewood Cliffs, N.J.: Prentice-Hall, 1980.

Mednick, S. A., Pollio, H. R., & Loftus, E. F. *Learning.* Englewood Cliffs, N.J.: Prentice-Hall, 1973.

8

Remembering

It is quite one thing to remember something for a judge, a psychotherapist, a priest, or a loved one and quite another to remember something for a psychologist studying you in the laboratory. Each of these situations creates its own unique set of demands, each determining not only how but also what you finally do remember. Remembering, like every other human act, is always of the present. As such, it can be described only in terms of a particular person trying to remember a particular something for a particular reason in a particular setting. Even though remembering surely deals with things past, it always deals with them in the *now* of our experience.

I. RECAPTURING THE PAST

Many times we are made aware of past events not because we are asked to recall them but because a bit of the past breaks in on us quite unexpectedly. J. H. Van Den Berg describes the following bit of **personal recall** in *The Changing Nature of Man* (1961)[1].

> Turning over the leaves of [a book] to verify a quotation, I became aware of the smell so peculiar to old books. Suddenly the memory of my own youth came back to me, still vague and not exactly determined in time, but alive, real, and pregnant, more real than it would have been if I had tried to recall it without opening the book. But it was more fleeting, more transient as well; only a minute later the impression had gone again, the past was submerged, from then on to emit unconnected facts until once more a smell, a sound, a word, an incident, or an object recalls the past as it was; as it can speak to me as "my past" [pp. 32–33].

Van Den Berg goes on to note that the memory intruding itself on him was not necessarily true in many or even in any details. What was true and is even more important was that the past was recaptured for him not by his looking for it but by its finding him. The past we invite by remembering is quite different from the past that "shows itself" to

[1]From *The Changing Nature of Man*, by J. H. Van Den Berg. Copyright 1961 by Dell Publishing Company. This and all other quotations from this source are reprinted by permission of W. W. Norton & Company, Inc.

us without being asked. The significance of a given piece of remembering is to be found not in the correctness of the event reported, but rather in what the event means to us now. For the individual, a memory is always important in relation to a whole life, never in regard to a single moment of an obscure past.

People in psychotherapy often become concerned about knowing exactly how something happened in the past. They want "factual" truth, not their chaotic and individual relationships to it. The past as remembered, however, is the only true past a person can now have, and past events speak differently to us as we change. A rejected lover may "remember" that his girlfriend stole a ring when, in fact, it was only misplaced. Until the lover is able to accept what happened, the ring will stay "stolen."

The observation that some memories seem able to break in on us suggests that certain very significant past events are ever alive for us, waiting only for an appropriate present event to let them again show themselves. It is no accident that it is not *any* past that breaks in on us, only a past that is still important: old books for Van Den Berg, the idea of the ring wrongly taken for the rejected lover.

Van Den Berg's description, though helpful in pointing out that bits of the past do seem to break in on us, tells little about how such things happen. To find some hints, it is better to consider a much fuller description of "uninvited memory." An example is provided by the French novelist Marcel Proust in his series of books called *Remembrance of Things Past* (1934). The narrator is daydreaming about his earlier life in the city of Combray.

> Many years had elapsed during which nothing of Combray . . . had any existence for me, when one day in winter, as I came home, my mother offered me some tea . . . I declined at first, and then, for no particular reason, changed my mind. She sent out for one of those short, plump little cakes called "petites madeleines," which look as though they had been moulded in the fluted scallop of a pilgrim's shell. And soon, mechanically, weary after a dull day with the prospect of a depressing morrow, I raised to my lips a spoonful of the tea in which I had soaked a morsel of the cake. No sooner had the warm liquid, and the crumbs with it, touched my palate than a shudder ran through my

whole body, and I stopped, intent upon the extraordinary changes that were taking place. An exquisite pleasure had invaded my senses ... with no suggestion of its origin. And at once the vicissitudes of life had become indifferent to me—this new sensation having had on me the effect which love has of filling me with a precious essence; ... I had ceased now to feel mediocre, accidental, mortal. Whence could it have come to me, this all-powerful joy? I was conscious that it was connected with the taste of tea and cake, but that it infinitely transcended those savours, could not, indeed, be of the same nature as theirs. Whence did it come? What did it signify? How could I seize upon and define it? ...

And suddenly the memory returns. The taste was that of the little crumb of madeleine which on Sunday mornings at Combray (because on those mornings I did not go out before church-time), when I went to say good day to her in her bedroom my aunt Leonie used to give me, dipping it first in her own cup of tea. The sight of the little madeleine had recalled nothing to my mind before I tasted it; perhaps because I had so often seen such things in the interval, without tasting them, on the trays in pastry-cooks' windows, that their image had dissociated itself from those Combray days to take its place among others more recent; perhaps because of those memories, so long abandoned and put out of mind, nothing now survived, everything was scattered. ...

And once I had recognized the taste of the crumb of madeleine soaked in her decoction of lime-flowers which my aunt used to give me, ... immediately the old grey house upon the street, where her room was, rose up like the scenery of a theatre to attach itself to the little pavilion, opening on to the garden, which had been built out behind it for my parents, and with the house the town, from morning to night and in all weathers, the Square where I was sent before luncheon, the streets along which I used to run errands, the country roads we took when it was fine. And just as the Japanese amuse themselves by filling a porcelain bowl with water and steeping in it little crumbs of paper which until then are without character or form, but, the moment they become wet, stretch themselves and bend, take on color and distinctive shape, become flowers or houses or people, permanent and recognisable, so in that moment all the flowers in our garden and in Swann's park, and the water-lilies on the Vivonne and the good folk of the village and their little dwellings and the parish church and the whole of Combray and of its surroundings, taking their proper shapes and growing solid, sprang into being, town and gardens alike, from my cup of tea [pp. 61–63].

Now that's remembering—and all of it from the taste of a little cookie soaked in tea. Here, then, is a more complete record of an uninvited memory that gives enough detail to work on. First, there is the emotion: the memory is not neutral or bland; it is full, rich, and exciting. Not only is it exciting, it is experienced—lived through—in the present: "a shudder ran through my body ... I had ceased to feel mediocre, accidental, mortal."

A second point is that the memory seems to sneak in from Marcel's sense of taste in much the same way that Van Den Berg's memory sneaked in from his sense of smell. Both these senses are not the ones we use most often, nor are they the ones that give us most of our information about the world. Despite (or perhaps because of) this, memories evoked by taste and smell seem quite vivid and compelling. Such memories not only remind us intellectually of some event past, they seem to recapture us for it. That Van Den Berg and Proust both have the past recapture them through smell and taste suggests that the "lower" senses are more compelling than the "higher" senses in producing experiences. We recall (Chapter 4) that poets more often talk about sight and hearing in terms of smell and taste than the other way around; it seems they too know this fact.

There is another difference between vision and taste in their ability to reevoke the past, and here Proust gives us a hint: "The sight of the little madeleine had recalled nothing to my mind ... perhaps because I had so often seen such things in the interval ... that their image had dissociated itself from those Combray days ..." This passage suggests that the sight of the madeleine cake had become "detached" from Marcel's earlier experience. Although he could remember that he used to have such cakes in his aunt's house, this memory was more difficult to come by and much less compelling. *Seeing* the madeleine in a great many contexts seemed to interfere with the Combray memory, so that the *sight* of the cookie only produced a rather diffuse set of memories.

The final part of Marcel's report that is important for any understanding of how we remember involves the very complex, yet highly structured, nature of the recall produced. The images of Marcel's past are not chaotic; they are ordered in a very special and obvious way. They progress from Marcel's aunt's room to her house, to the little pavilion, to the garden, then to the town ("from morning to night and in all weathers"), to the Square, then to the streets, and finally to the country roads. The orderliness of this recall is, of course, the orderliness of a walk—a walk from Marcel's aunt's room to the outskirts by way of town.

This order, however, is too orderly, too constructed. It is as if some person other than Marcel were describing Marcel's route from a third-person point of view. And indeed this is the case: the third person is none other than Marcel as an adult, who tells about his town after having just experienced it in a much more vivid and chaotic first-person way. The Marcel who remembers and seeks the past is different from the Marcel who was recaptured by that past.

For Marcel, as for all of us, there are two types of experience that can be described as **remembering**. One of these is unexpected and chaotic and absorbs all of the present so that, for the moment, past is present and there is a break in time. Such remembering is rare. A second, and more usual, experience occurs when we take a stand firmly anchored in the present to look back at some past event. This type of remembering invokes an almost logical, third-person look at our previous first-person experiences. Because we cannot, from this third-person point of view, enter the center of an earlier self-world, our experience is much less chaotic and much less compelling.

Remembering, then, is different from memory: it is an act of the present designed for one or another purpose to recapture our past. We try to remember for many reasons, and each of these reasons imposes its own set of constraints on what we come up with as a consequence of the process of remembering. Marcel's attempt to remember was guided by the very obvious desire to define the origin of an "exquisite pleasure"; for Van Den Berg, there was no attempt to reconstruct (to remember)—simply a desire to be present to his own past. Perhaps that is why Van Den Berg could only point out that he experienced such-and-such a memory and only Proust could describe the act of remembering with such delicacy and precision.

Proust, however, also knows that the past can never be recaptured by remembering. As he put it, "It is a labor in vain to attempt to recapture [our past]: all the efforts of our intellect must prove futile. The past is hidden somewhere outside the realm, beyond the reach of intellect, in some material object which we do not suspect. And as for that object, it depends on chance whether we come upon it or not before we ourselves must die" (p. 61).

II. THE WITNESS REMEMBERS

The idea that remembering is an act of the present undertaken for one or another personal purpose seems best exemplified in that special recall situation known as the courtroom. No one would doubt that there are strong personal reasons for saying whatever it is one says in court, whether one is the defendant or just a witness. Although telling the truth, the whole truth, and nothing but the truth would seem a fairly simple job, the bulk of evidence—both legal and psychological—indicates that it is not.

A. The courtroom as a recall situation
Even when no one would gain from confusing the issue, eyewitnesses often disagree. This is not an isolated fact and seems to represent a very stable aspect of witness behavior: different witnesses, even with the best of motives, usually differ in their reports of an event. One reason is our tendency to pay attention only to events that concern us— hence, different events for different folks. More important, but much less obvious, is our inability to say "I don't know." In one early analysis, Stern (1939) found that of 59 answers brought out under cross-examination of laboratory subjects, only 7 (or 11%) were of the "I don't know" kind. The surprising part of this report was that subjects were questioned in a fairly relaxed situation and the events to be remembered were pictures, not events to be described as at a trial.

What does it mean to say "I don't know" in a court (or, for that matter, in a classroom)? One interpretation is that the person is being lazy or, worse, not cooperating. Within the context of a courtroom, being questioned demands a reply, and if you, as witness, do not give one, you are either uncooperative or lying. As Stern noted, however, saying "I don't know" may also be the reply of an independent-minded person who will not respond unless reasonably sure of what he or she experienced. It is difficult to say "I don't know" against the insistence of an inquirer who repeats the question, hammering away at the person in forceful phrases.

Another aspect of the legal question-and-answer

game is the so-called **leading question.** Stern reports that when he showed children and young adults relatively simple pictures they had never seen before, fully 25% of the answers given to leading questions were "Yes, I do remember." In one case Stern was able to get a 12-year-old witness to remember a nonexistent item in such detail that she reported it had "two doors," was "brown," and had a "flowerpot" standing on top of it.

How is it that perfectly honest citizens with nothing to gain come to produce such obviously led remembrances? The answer would seem to be that witnesses, like other people, want to be of help. When testifying, this means they want to produce the best and most logically complete description they possibly can. For example, Stern reports a laboratory experiment involving a picture in which a group of movers were helping an artist carry out crates of his work. A woman was also in the picture, seated on a sofa. Many witnesses reported as a "true fact" (that is, a fact they were certain of and would swear to) that the woman was sitting on a packing box. Remembering the packing-box-as-seat seems to be the result of a process Stern has called **logification:** the witness remembered movers, boxes, and a seated woman—what could be more logical than seating the woman on the packing boxes?

B. The nature of courtroom testimony

Another source of witness error has to do with the process of testimony itself. Stern finds that many witnesses remember their first description of an event more clearly than the event itself. If, on some future occasion, witnesses are asked "What happened?," they are likely to tell the same story again—even, as Stern found, in the same words. Another problem is that what a word or phrase means can change on different occasions. For example, one subject described the moving-artist picture as having something to do with letting the painter "approach the *gateway* of a new life." A few weeks later, on requestioning, the subject noted: "A moving van was passing through a narrow *gateway*." The memory of the subject's own words changed between Testimony 1 and Testimony 2.

Language and speaking affect remembering in still another way, most especially in testimony given at a trial. Generally, when a witness answers a question in court, it is not the first time he or she has told the story. In the beginning there was a report

to the investigating officer, later to one or another of the attorneys, then a rehearsal to oneself, and finally, at the end of this long process, the testimony in the courtroom. Even if the witness may seem to produce an entirely spontaneous account in court, good coaching tells.

In this connection, Stern (1939) reports the case of a female witness, age 14½, who gave the court a very detailed account of the activities of a male teacher accused of sexual offenses with female pupils, including herself. Ordinarily, detailed testimony is considered quite conclusive; if the witness can describe in a fairly spontaneous way exactly what happened, judges and juries are impressed. In this particular case, the origin of the girl's testimony was determined only after careful questioning of the investigating detective. When asked "How did you question the girl?," the detective replied that the "girl was reluctant at first to give positive items. In order to help her I asked 'Did he (the defendant) do this . . . or this?' In each case I supplied a specific description of what the defendant might have done" (p. 15). When the girl's testimony was reexamined, it was found that she used many of the same phrases that had been suggested to her by the detective.

Another significant part of a courtroom situation concerns the nature of that rather curious legal procedure called "cross-examination." As is well known from television, there are always at least two lawyers in an American courtroom: one for the defense and one for the prosecution. The assumption is that somehow or other the "truth" can be found through the action of two opposing forces, each cutting away distortions introduced by a skillful and partisan retelling of a particular event. Although there are strong arguments in the legal profession (who ever heard of weak arguments in the legal profession?) over the significance of cross-examination, it is part of our legal system even if not that of other countries. (In some European countries it is the judge who summons the witnesses and conducts cross-examination.)

For psychology, as for American legal practice, the idea of cross-examination has to do with helping (or hindering) a witness in his or her attempt to present a balanced description of a past event. The use of cross-examination assumes that different witnesses will have different versions of an event and that only by careful probing will it be possible to come to some understanding of "what really happened" independent of the particular person providing the testimony. A "balanced" description in a court of law is like "objective truth" in the laboratory: it satisfies no one completely but annoys everyone less than any other possible description.

Thus, the courtroom is not your ordinary, run-of-the-mill question-and-answer situation. Yet it is here that witnesses talk about past events. For this reason the psychology of testimony and its tamer laboratory counterpart, the psychology of remembering, both become interested in the effects of questions on what gets reported as being remembered.

One of the earliest "naturalistic" experiments attempting to tie the laboratory to the courtroom was done by the German criminologist F. von Liszt. In his experiment, which has been repeated countless times in countless classrooms, two students began a (prearranged) academic discussion, which grew progressively more bitter until, at last, one of the two students drew a revolver and fired a (blank) shot at the other. At this point, Professor von Liszt stopped the dramatization and asked for an oral and written description of what had happened.

Although almost all his "witnesses" were law students (who should have been very careful in giving testimony), results showed from 4 to 12 errors. Students also tended to produce increasingly more incorrect statements when describing the second half of the event, when things got progressively more dangerous.

To determine whether only dangerous situations bring about inaccurate testimony, Stern (1939) designed an experiment in which students were asked to describe a very ordinary event of a week earlier. Stern made use of a graduate-student seminar group that usually met in his library. He had a rule that no one was allowed to borrow books from his library. During one class period, however, a stranger entered the library, asked Professor Stern's permission to look at a book in the library, read it for a short while as the class went on, and finally left, taking the book with him—that is, he stole the book. A week later the students were asked, among other questions, "What happened to the book the man was reading?" To this straightforward question, the majority answered "He put it back in the bookcase."

For an ordinary event as well as a dangerous one,

many witnesses seem unable to recall what happened in a reliable way. Thus, "being there" does not guarantee that a witness "saw anything" or that he or she will be able to recall anything of importance later on. Yet these are exactly the conditions under which most witnesses testify: they are asked to describe an event that may have frightened them or an event that was of only marginal interest to them. As Stern (1939, p. 12) put it, "Very often bodily presence may go along with complete lack of attention [and/or] . . . observation . . . [and then] the inquirer's insistence—'The event happened before your eyes; you must have observed it'—is psychologically unsound and often nothing but a misleading suggestion."

C. Testimony as a theory of remembering

Before it is possible to analyze the relation of testimony to a theory of memory, it is necessary to look at some of the more recent experimental techniques used in studying testimony. One of the major modern techniques, developed by Elizabeth Loftus of the University of Washington, involves showing a group of students (sometimes as many as 100 at a time) a film of an automobile accident. In this film, a car makes a turn into the stream of traffic and causes a five-car, bumper-to-bumper collision. After viewing the film, witnesses are asked a series of questions. For one of her experimental groups, Loftus worded the initial question as follows: "Did you see *a* broken headlight?" For a second group, the question was worded slightly differently: "Did you see *the* broken headlight?" Although this may seem a minor difference, the *"a* question" seems tentative, while the *"the* question" seems much surer. In fact, 15% of *"the* question" witnesses answered yes, whereas only 7% of *"a* question" witnesses said yes. The frequency of "I don't know" answers was 38% for *"a* questions" and only 13% for *"the* questions."Thus, the use of *a* or *the* in a question makes a big difference in leading the witness to report a nonexistent aspect of an accident (Loftus, 1975).

In a different experiment using the same film (Loftus & Palmer, 1974), witnesses were asked to estimate the speed as one car *hit/smashed/bumped/ collided with/or contacted* another car. *Smashed* cars were estimated to be going at 41 mph, *collided with* cars 39 mph, *bumped* cars 38 mph, *hit* cars 34 mph, and *contacted* cars 32 mph. A change of words produced a range of average differences of 9 mph. Other experiments (Loftus & Zanni, 1975) have also shown that how a question is worded affects what is recalled. For example, using the same accident film, 53% of people asked "How fast was Car A going when it ran the stop sign?" reported they saw a stop sign. Only 35% asked "How fast was Car A going when it turned right?" reported seeing one.

Some of the basic results, then, suggest that asking a person one type of question rather than another may change his or her report of a previously experienced event. Even for the most scrupulously honest subject, information given (or, perhaps more important, asked for) after an event has been experienced will affect what is remembered about that event. These experiments make the important points that questioning can help a person recall a nonexistent or an "actual" event and that recalls produced after initial questioning may alter what is later remembered.

Such results provide the real meaning of the testimony experiment for a psychology of remembering: every bit of what we recall is always recalled in some context or other, after one or another intervening experience, and the recall situation and the intervening event(s) strongly determine what we will produce as our recall right now. Every memory partakes as much of the present as of the past, and to recall always represents an attempt to speak with the past, with me as the living link between then and now.

For this reason, it is not surprising to find that my past sometimes speaks to me in ways I cannot understand or even recover. If I am unable to remember something I "ought to be able to," such a lapse must have some personal significance for me. Forgetting and remembering, like all the activities of a life, reveal us to ourselves and to others. This idea, although now obvious, was first pointed out only about 70 years ago by Sigmund Freud, and it is to his consulting room that we now go.

III. THE PATIENT REMEMBERS

The year is 1901; the place, Vienna. A young Austrian doctor named Sigmund Freud has just published a book, *The Psychopathology of Everyday Life*, with a curious hypothesis: that many of the little annoying things that just seem to happen to us during the course of an ordinary day do not "just happen to us," but that, in fact, we are doing them to ourselves. For example, if we make a slip of the tongue, misplace a book, lose a pair of glasses, misremember the name of a place, forget the name of a friend, miswrite a sentence, or have a peculiar or impossible dream, these odd goings-on tell something about what is or is not important to us.

To understand events such as these, Freud believed, a third-person point of view was required. Such events gave Freud some of the very earliest clues to a style of dealing with the world that he came to call "the unconscious." To tie very ordinary lapses of speaking and memory to his theory of the unconscious, Freud began with an analysis of slips of the tongue. Because his discussion was so persuasive, we now call such slips **Freudian slips** in honor of his argument.

Although some of Freud's examples appear a bit dated, they do reveal his method of analysis clearly. Consider the following three events:

1. A professor, at the end of a lecture in which he is sure no one has understood the ideas presented, says: "I can hardly believe you all understood this . . . Persons who understand this, even in a country of millions, can be counted on *one finger*—I mean on the fingers of one hand."
2. A politician, in talking about a rival politician, introduces him as "a *bottle*-scarred veteran."
3. One woman, on seeing another woman in a new dress, notes: "How lovely, I'm sure you must have just *thrown* it together yourself—I mean *sewn* it together yourself."

It is easy to see that each "speaking error" expressed what the speaker wanted to say but did not: the professor "knew" there was only one person who really understood (namely, himself); the politician "knew" what he was talking about in describing his rival; and the woman "knew" that the dress was not skillfully made, just "thrown together." Such slips are not necessarily errors; rather, they reveal what it is the speaker would like to say but feels is inappropriate to say in the present context.

This, of course, is not a surprising conclusion: Everything we do tells something about us. It surely is no more improper to look at the meaning of error than to look at the meaning of a correct or expected act. Freud made new assumptions, however, that the meaning of the slip was unconscious. By this he meant to suggest that it was held away from conscious experience by a strong counterforce called "repression."

A. Conscious and unconscious processes

Freud saw the need to assume two major parts to the human psyche: the conscious and the unconscious. The conscious is that part of our mental life which we experience directly and which we can talk about—what we usually call thinking, planning, and so on. For Freud—and here remember the year is 1905—the greater part of our mental life is unconscious and therefore unknown to us. Not only do we not reflectedly know the content of our unconscious life, we are quite unaware of its existence. (For a more extended discussion of these differences, see Chapter 5.)

Even though we do not experience the unconscious directly, it "tells" about itself in many of the ordinary actions of our everyday lives. Since much of the unconscious is concerned with antisocial and aggressive matters, Freud saw it as having to do with the psychopathological (that is, unhealthy) aspects of the person. Perhaps it was for this reason that he called his book *The Psychopathology of Everyday Life* rather than simply *Errors of Everyday Life.* This book was designed to provide the reader with concrete experiences of unconscious events in his or her everyday life. "The unconscious" was not meant to be some remote, artificial theoretical construct concocted by a serious and scholarly Viennese doctor; quite the contrary, Freud meant to show that with the proper attitude, we could all experience unconscious processes in the rather ordinary day-to-day events of our lives.

B. Repression of memories

Freud defined consciousness as approximately equivalent to what is now called "reflected experience." Unconsciousness, in contrast, was something biological, something primitive, something to be pushed away from higher human conscious activity by human civilization. Although unconscious processes may determine what human beings do, such processes are unavailable to conscious experience.

If events are not known to us, how can they bring about slips of the tongue or lapses of memory? According to Freud, by "forcing their way" into consciousness; by slipping (or fighting) past a "censor" who guards us from having to deal with primitive and messy impulses. The name of this sentry is **repression**, and it is his job, as Freud put it, "to turn back events from the unconscious [so that] they are 'incapable of becoming conscious.' . . . Being repressed . . . means being unable to pass out of the unconscious system because of the doorkeeper's refusal of admittance" (Freud, 1935, p. 260).

The major argument against this way of describing unconscious processes is that unconscious events become known only if and when they slip past the doorkeeper (that is, repression); in some sense, however, we must know what it is we are avoiding if we are to avoid it successfully. To avoid a memory, I must first know where not to look. For this reason, repressed events must be just as well known as nonrepressed ones.

A seemingly similar case was described in Chapter 2 when noting that you are able to avoid bumping into the furniture in your room. Without consciously attending to the pieces of furniture, you unreflectedly take account of their location. There is, however, a great difference between an unreflected and a repressed event: under rather ordinary conditions I can come to have reflected awareness of the objects in my room; only under the far more special and demanding conditions of psychotherapy can I come to have reflected awareness of repressed events. The whole idea of repression indicates not only that I have lost something from the past which I can no longer recover without help but that I have learned to act in such a way in the present as to guarantee that I will not now come in contact with these events. I have become a skillful broken-field runner in regard to certain difficult past experiences. I skip by them with such agility that I never see them now. Repression is an act of the present done by a particular person in regard to some aspect of his or her life, which cannot be reflected upon as long as the repression continues. The ability to "recover" repressed events, unlike unreflected experiences, is not easy to come by until I understand the personal reasons for my having learned to avoid them in the first place.

C. Repression as a theory of remembering

Perhaps a few examples will clarify the role of repression in remembering (and nonremembering). An early case given by Freud concerns a young man and a misplaced book. The young man tells his story:

A few years ago there were misunderstandings between me and my wife.... One day, on coming in from a walk, she brought me a book which she had bought me because she thought it would interest me. I thanked her for her little attention, promised to read the book, put it among my things and never could find it again. Months passed by and occasionally I thought of this derelict book and tried in vain to find it. About six months later my dear mother, who lived some distance away, fell ill. My wife left our house to go and nurse her mother-in-law, who became seriously ill, giving my wife an opportunity of showing her best qualities. One evening I came home full of enthusiasm and gratitude towards my wife. I walked up to my writing desk and opened a certain drawer in it, without a definite intention but with a kind of somnambulistic sureness, and there before me lay the lost book which I had so often looked for.[2]

A second case concerns the familiar experience of being unable to recall someone's name. A certain Mr. X fell in love with Miss Z, who unfortunately (for X) married Mr. R. Although Mr. X had already known Mr. R for a number of years and even had business dealings with him, he constantly forgot his name, so that even now when he wants to talk to Mr. R, he always has to ask his secretary for R's name.

Examples such as these could be multiplied many times over. They all make the same point: forgetting does not "just happen"; rather, it expresses an intention not to remember. Remembering is neither a simple nor a mechanical act that I do in regard to some event past. Instead, like all acts, it works or does not work because it does or does not make sense to me now. The husband who forgot where he put the book from his wife "had not really lost the book, but neither did he know where it was. Everything connected with his wife had ceased to exist for him, he had shut it out of his life" (Merleau-Ponty, 1962, p. 162).

This conclusion seems a strong one to base on a simple case of forgetting—harmless or not. To demonstrate more forcefully the role of personal intentions in remembering and forgetting, it is necessary to consider more extreme cases in which a person's whole life is affected by being unable to recall some event. Consider the case reported by the American therapist Morton Prince early in this century. The

basic outline of this case—which has come to be called the "belltower case"—is as follows:

A woman had a phobia for towers and church steeples, especially those in which bells might ring, and she was totally unable to explain it. While she was in a condition of hypnosis she remembered an incident from her childhood. Under hypnosis she wrote: "G——M—— church and my father, took my mother to Bi——where she died, and we went to Br——and they cut my mother. I prayed and cried all the time that she would live, and the church bells were always ringing and I hated them." As she wrote this she wept. After being awakened she was able to tell a good part of the story, under guiding questions from the therapist. Her mother had undergone a major surgical operation which killed her. The overly conscientious daughter who feared she had not given her every care during the nursing period was in a very great agony of mixed grief and remorse—"and the church bells were always ringing."

This later recall of the full story did not at first shake the phobia. It persisted until the patient was convinced that her (childhood) attentions to her mother had actually been most devoted and that the fatal outcome was due to a sequence of events not at all of her doing [Prince, 1929, pp. 34–35].

The first thing to note about this case is that it is serious: it does not deal with the seemingly trivial phenomena of slips of the tongue or forgetting a name or forgetting the location of a book. The patient is afraid of steeples, belltowers, and bells, and she is in extreme distress over this inexplicable state of affairs.

A second significant aspect of this case is that all the events repressed seem to belong to the patient's childhood. Many events that turn out to be important in helping patients understand a significant detail of their lives are from childhood. Freud was so impressed with this recurring clinical fact that he came to the idea that many of the most important things that happen to people occur during their childhood years and that there is a general tendency to forget most, if not all, of these crucial early events, a tendency termed *childhood amnesia*.

There is also the curious clinical fact that many of Freud's patients were able to produce vivid remembrances of certain early experiences and events. What was most surprising was that many of these early memories did not seem to be meaningful in any ordinary sense of the term: they concerned trivial, almost meaningless events. Freud and most psychologists and novelists along with him have been committed to the view that we remember events that are important to us and forget (or repress) those that are painful; it seems reasonable to expect that young children ought to remember according to these same rules. For this reason Freud felt sure that the "trivial childhood memories" we all recall so easily must turn out to represent a very significant complex of events.

In one of his summary statements of how psychoanalysis works, Freud wrote that psychoanalytic therapy is successful to the "degree that all gaps in a patient's memory are filled in, that his amnesia is removed." Such "amnesia" is removed by getting the patient to talk about his or her memories, however slight they may at first appear, and then by helping the patient reconstruct the significance of these memories.

It is at this point that the patient and the witness make contact: The witness faces a friendly (or hostile) lawyer or judge who asks the person to reconstruct the past in one or another way. The patient faces a friendly (or hostile) therapist who helps the person try to reconstruct his or her past. In both cases the technique is similar: ask the person to fill in details that do not seem entirely clear or consistent to the questioner.

Does this mean that there may be "mistakes" in a patient's recall of things past as well as personal aspects to a witness' story? Surely, the answer is yes: no less than the witness, the patient is directed and guided by the questioner's questions. But what of the "true" facts in the case: what if the patient fills in "unremembered" facts in just the same way the witness fills in "unremembered" facts in his or her testimony? It does not matter very much in the patient's case, for two reasons: First, the whole story— the patient's life—has to make sense to him and his therapist. Second, there is no good reason for determining what "really happened" if the reconstruction makes sense now. The purpose of therapeutic recall is not to fill in the facts so much as to fill in their meaning for the person. A patient does not suffer from knowing or not knowing X, but from not knowing why knowing or not knowing X is important to his or her present life. It is the patient's relationship to the meaning of his or her past that needs to be recaptured, not the past itself.

Thus, there are reasons for remembering and forgetting, just as there are reasons for perceiving, talking, moving, thinking, and so on. In recall, as in all other acts of a human life, the human being is destined to look for sense and significance rather than for objective truth. To be sure, there are times we do try to remember exactly, and most times, when that is what is required, we do. But just as surely we also try to develop a continuously renewing relationship to our past, and who and what we are now must surely affect not only how we do the job but what we end up recalling.

IV. THE PROFESSIONAL REMEMBERS

Despite results provided by Stern and Freud, we often do recall certain events quite accurately, even when the material to be recalled is without much present significance. To overlook the results of testimony or therapy is to miss one part of the story of human rememberings; to overlook the fact that we do recall accurately is to miss a different part of the story. To understand this whole story, it is necessary to look at the work of people who regularly recall words, people, and events without error: orators and **mnemonists** ("professional rememberers")—in short, just those people who must remember a great many things that are not always personally important to them.

The great day of the orator is past. We now have typewriters and teleprompters, and no one considers it wrong for a speaker (we no longer dare call them orators) to read his or her speech. In ancient Greece or even in more contemporary England, an orator not only wrote his own material, he was expected to deliver it with style and flair, and the words mattered: the ancient orator was an actor who needed to know lines.

A. Simonides and the method of locations
For this reason it is not surprising to find that orators were also often professional rememberers as well as poets; many anecdotes were told about the phenomenal ability of certain poets to remember everything. For example, Cicero (in *De Oratore*) reports the story of the Greek poet Simonides, who had been hired to read his poetry to a group of guests invited by a wealthy nobleman named Scopus. Unfortunately, Simonides discovered that being a nobleman did not mean a man acted nobly: at the end of his recital he sadly discovered that Scopus offered to pay him only half the fee they originally agreed on.

Here the story becomes a bit murky: it is not clear whether the gods Castor and Pollux sent a messenger to Simonides or whether someone else did. What is sure is that Simonides was called from the banquet hall and went outside to talk with the messenger. Moments later, the roof of Scopus' hall caved in, and all the guests were crushed beyond recognition. Because it was very important for ceremonial reasons to bury each guest under his or her correct name, the relatives of those buried in the rubble asked Simonides whether he could remember the names of the people who had attended his poetry reading. Simonides found that if he imagined the hall as it had been, he could identify where each person had been sitting. The location each person had occupied in the hall helped him recall his or her name.

Simonides, the poet/orator, was quite impressed with the fact that it was possible to remember so many names without ever really trying. It all seemed so easy if you could just reimagine where everyone sat. On the basis of this experience, Cicero reports, Simonides came to the idea that he, as an orator, might be able to recall ideas (and objects) by assigning them a fixed and unique location in some real or imaginary space. For obvious reasons, Simonides' technique has come to be called the **method of locations**, or the **method of loci**.

B. Tricks for remembering

The method of loci worked for Simonides and Cicero; will it also work for nonprofessionals? In an experiment, Groninger (1971) first taught one group of subjects (the location group) the method of locations and asked them to think of a situation having 25 quite specific locations. He then gave them a set of 25 words to learn in order, using their newly formed plan for remembering. A second (control) group of subjects was simply given the 25 words and asked to learn them in order. Both groups were then tested, and it was found that all subjects in both groups had learned the list.

The major difference between the location and control groups did not appear until 1 to 5 weeks later. After 1 week, subjects in the location group were able to recall 92% of the words, subjects in the control group only 64%. After 5 weeks, the location group still got 80% of the words correct, while the control group was down to 36%. There can be no doubt about it: the method of locations helped

these subjects recall more items—and it had taken subjects only about 10 minutes to develop the location map they would later use so successfully.

This is quite an important point, for if people are interested in learning a trick to help them learn how to do something, it is reasonable to worry about how long it will take to learn the trick. For the method of locations, the answer seems to be "not very long." The same is true for other tricks. For example, consider the many tricks we all use every day when asked such questions as "How do you spell *receive?*" or "How many days does July have?" or "What is the order of the planets from the sun?" In answering the first question, you solemnly recite: "*I* before *E* except after *C*"; in answering the second, you dutifully recite: "Thirty days hath September . . ."; in response to the third, you recite the sentence "Men Very Easily Make All Jobs Serve Useful Needs Promptly" (for Mercury, Venus, Earth, Mars, Asteroids, Jupiter, and so on). In all cases, the **mnemonic**—the memory trick—involves your having learned a rather trivial, if not downright meaningless, phrase, which you then use to "read off" your answer.

Probably the simplest and best-studied mnemonic to have found its way into the psychological laboratory is the following rhyme:

One is a bun	Six is sticks
Two is a shoe	Seven is a heaven
Three is a tree	Eight is a gate
Four is a door	Nine is a line
Five is a hive	Ten is a hen

Generally, the one-bun rhyme is used when the material to be remembered consists of ten or fewer items. For example, the subject may be asked to recall in order the following set of items:

1. ashtray	6. matchbook
2. firewood	7. glass
3. picture	8. lamp
4. cigarette	9. shoe
5. table	10. phonograph

Before the words to be recalled are selected, the person is asked to learn the one-bun rhyme. Then he or she is instructed as follows: "When I tell you a word [one of the ten above], your job is to form a bizarre association with the first word of the rhyme and the word you have just heard. All you have to do is to remember the rhyme and then form an association." As an example of what happens when a subject is asked to do this, I have often found that the 10-phonograph set works out as a hen bending over a record player, using its beak as a needle.

This technique does help people recall a list of ten words. In one early experiment on this topic, Bugelski (1968) found that subjects who had first learned the one-bun rhyme and then were asked to learn six lists of ten words each were able to remember 63% of the words presented. Subjects who were just asked to learn the six lists were able to recall only 22% of the words. In a more elaborate experiment using not only a variation of the one-bun technique but the method of locations as well, Bower and Reitman (1972) found that their subjects were able to recall 85% of 100 words presented. Although recall 1 week later was better for the method of locations than for the one-bun rhyme, the point remains that memory tricks are quite helpful in enabling people to recall more than they would on the basis of "brute" rote recall.

The unexpectedly poor recall produced by witnesses and patients is balanced a bit by findings such as these: people recall a great deal of material quite accurately if they go about it with just a little help from their friends. Such mnemonic friends are not so far removed from our ordinary ways of doing things (as in the "Thirty Days Hath September" technique) and suggest that when we think about it, we can be quite good in recalling individual items that may not always be meaningfully related. The crucial difference between the professional rememberer and the patient is a simple one and comes down to the difference between recall as a reflected and an unreflected act. To go at remembering by using a technique is to do it reflectedly; to go at remembering in a therapist's office is a much more unreflected act. For this reason, the act of the master rememberer is much less affected by the characteristics of the situation than is true for either the patient or the witness. This is as it should be: the professional mnemonist is interested only in remembering; the patient and the witness are interested in trying to reconstruct their past in a personally meaningful and coherent way.

The mnemonist is much freer of his or her ordinary context and even of his or her past. To recall a series of unconnected items by the numbers is a technical act independent of time, place, or person. Anybody can do what the mnemonist does if he or she knows the trick. For the witness, as for the patient, recall is always a unique retelling of a set of very personal experiences located in a very personal past. No one else can do it in exactly the same way I do it. Personal recall is embedded in a set of past experiences as well as within a present situation: it is of, by, and for me.

Another difference between the unreflected act of personal recall and the more reflected act of the professional rememberer (laboratory subject or mnemonist) has to do with the type of material recalled. Generally, mnemonic tricks are used (and needed) to the degree that the material does not form a unified whole—that is, to the degree that it consists of a set of unrelated words or events. Personal recall almost always involves an implicit "story line" originating in the ongoing flow of a life. Such facts as the number of days in the months or the sequence of planets from the sun have no natural story line. To recall these items, I must invent a "story" or a scene, thereby tying the items to one another by a reflected plot. Personal remembering unfolds, more or less, on its own; technical recall is the outcome of planful activity.

C. The politics of mnemonic techniques

One psychologist, Steiner Kvale, sees far more sinister motives in the attempt of psychologists to understand recall by studying how mnemonists or laboratory subjects go about recalling a series of unconnected items. Kvale argues that this approach is simply an unwitting outcome of the fact that most experimental psychologists are members of a capitalistic, technological society and are unfamiliar with a more organic approach to recall suggested by Marxian theory. Although such a statement may raise nationalistic tempers, Kvale argues that we in America (and in much of Europe) follow an "assembly line" model of memory. Kvale phrases the argument as follows:

> The psychological research on memory has often "preformed" the experimental subjects' remembering activity in correspondence with the workers' behavior at the assembly lines of industry, by techniques such as 1) *fragmentation,* 2) *indoctrination,* 3) *time pressure,* and 4) *quantification.* . . . (1) [fragmentation occurs when] the learning and remembering required of the subjects are usually mechanical responses to isolated fragments: lists of nonsense syllables and words; (2) [indoctrination is shown by] experimental instructions that demand

that the subjects learn mechanically by rote; (3) [time pressure is shown by requiring that] learning and remembering take place under the [time constraints] of a memory drum, making any search for meaning difficult; and (4) [quantification appears when] the products of the subjects' remembering activity are quantified and combined into anonymous group averages.... However, while the fragmented work at the assembly line results in a final integrated product, the nature of the final result of the mechanical memorizing is more vague [1976a, p. 5].[3]

In his analysis of these methods, Kvale lays most, if not all, of the blame at the feet of a capitalistic society.

This critique is a bit polemic and perhaps even a bit too political. The answer is surely not as simple as Kvale suggests. Capitalism and laboratory psychology grow out of the same basic human urge: to subjugate the material world and put it at the disposal of the human being. Both go about doing this by dividing the world into manageable pieces and then letting an "expert" work on each piece. Capitalism is not the parent of a word-by-word approach to recall any more than a fragmented approach to recall produces capitalism. Both are children of a more general analytic way of looking at the world. To be sure, the experimental psychologist—no matter how pure he or she claims to be—is a member of his or her society, and there is never a simple one-to-one relationship between any two parts of that society. The experimental laboratory is part of the economic system, but both the laboratory and the economic system are aspects of an individual's particular philosophical, social, and political history. Both interact within the individual scientist's world.

D. Mnemonics as a theory of remembering

One final, and boringly nonpolitical, aspect of the use of mnemonic techniques concerns the trouble human beings have in recalling individual items in the first place. Miller, Galanter, and Pribram (1960) long ago noted that the major problem in recall had to do with getting the correct items to occur in the proper place, hardly ever with knowing them. It isn't that we don't know the words or events we have been asked to recall; rather, the bottleneck is in our inability to "retrieve" them during the act of recall itself.

In talking about recall as **retrieval,** a natural analogue suggests itself: a library. Surely we all have had the experience of going to a library as children and wondering how we would ever be able to find a book in all those shelves. Without knowing how to use the card catalogue, we didn't know where to look. To find books in a library, even a small neighborhood one, we first need to know how the library is organized and how to use its organization. Here, the card catalogue is equivalent to the mnemonist's trick: it is the plan by which we retrieve books from storage.

It is also possible to look at remembering on the model of a less extensive device, such as a filing system. McKellar (1968, p. 136) gives a very clear description of this approach:

As new information comes in ... it is stored into appropriate categories: these categories themselves have been built up out of past experience. This analogy with a filing system may be taken a stage further: in remembering, as in many office filing systems, information may be lost but later found. Moreover, as additional information comes in to be stored, the filing system itself is altered and refined: it becomes necessary to reorganize the file headings, to subdivide categories, and to reclassify.[4]

The idea of a file heading or, more generally, of a mnemonic category is important. There is a very old finding in experimental psychology that most people can recall only **seven, plus or minus two,** pieces of information. For example, most people can remember a series of 7 ± 2 numbers or words if these are presented to them only once, but not a longer series. The strange fact is that it does not matter what the items in the series—the "chunks" (as Miller, 1956b, called them)—consist of: it is just as easy to recall seven words of 12 letters each as to recall seven single letters. For optimum recall—here we come back to the mnemonist—the trick is to get each "chunk" to contain as much information as possible. In a filing-system approach to memory, each category (file heading) can be considered a

[3]From "Dialectics and Research on Remembering," by S. Kvale. Paper presented at the Fifth Life-Span Developmental Psychology Conference, Morgantown, West Virginia, May 1976. This and all other quotations from this source are reprinted by permission of the author.

[4]From *Experience and Behavior*, by P. McKellar. Copyright 1968 by Penguin Books, Ltd. This and all other quotations from this source are reprinted by permission.

very rich chunk of information in the total memory system. Given this system, the act of recall consists of two parts: getting hold of the appropriate category and then "emptying" its contents. With this as a basic model, it seems clear that retrieval of both the category and its contents is crucial in determining whether we will recall a particular item.

Whether we consider the library or a filing system our best guess about how human recall works, what is important for both is their organization, not their content. The only problem in looking at remembering in terms of a filing system or a library is that remembering gets information out of storage much faster. Even though we may occasionally take a few seconds or even a minute or two to remember something, our usual experience is of virtually instantaneous recall. What needs to be added to our filing system is a procedure that will work quickly and efficiently. Fortunately, such a device is already quite well known to us through the courtesy of IBM. No wonder psychologists have recently become so enthusiastic in talking about recall in terms of a "computer model." Here, surely, is a rapid-fire, no-mistakes, perfectly organized filing system.

V. THE COMPUTER REMEMBERS

But what exactly is a computer? In Chapter 5 four components that make up computers were described: an encoding device, a central processor, a memory bank, and a decoding device. In talking about thinking, psychologists were most interested in the central processor; in talking about recall, psychologists have been most interested in the memory bank.

A. Storage systems

Many computers have not one but two, and sometimes even three, components that can be said to mimic human memory. The most obvious pair of these separates memory into **short-term** and **long-term storage**. A third division is **sensory**, or perceptual, **storage**, which deals with the way the computer—human or machine—gets its information. There are theoretical reasons to suspect that getting one's information by seeing it is different from getting it by hearing it or by smelling it, for instance.

Given these three components, the total process involved in having a computer remember (that is, retrieve information) goes as shown in Figure 8-1. In this diagram, information flows from left to right. The first storage area involves a sensory-storage system from which the two subsequent memory systems get their information. In sensory storage, either the information is attended to, or it leaves the sensory system. If it decays or is interfered with by a new piece of information, the study ends; if it is attended to, the information then goes to short-term storage.

Short-term storage, as the name implies, deals with material for a very short time—usually a few seconds, as in looking up a telephone number and forgetting it once the number is dialed. If the material placed in short-term storage is not rehearsed, it too decays and disappears. By rehearsing a telephone number, so the theory assumes, we prevent it from decaying. As experience teaches, however, the number of things that can be rehearsed at one time is small. For this reason short-term storage contains a constantly shifting set of a small number of items (in humans, 7 ± 2). Information is rehearsed until the rememberer either lets go of it or codes it for transfer to long-term memory.

Long-term storage, which is what is usually meant by "memory," is thought to be virtually unlimited: the computer, after all, can always add another component to hold any overflow. It is possible to get directly at material in short-term storage (mostly because it is kept current by continuing rehearsal); access to long-term storage is much slower. Here the problem is retrieval—getting the item out—and remembering occurs to the degree that appropriate cues are available for a given item. Long-term storage is similar to a filing system (such as described for the mnemonist), and items are always coded for later retrieval under different category headings. Category headings and their related content can be of the type agreed on by almost everyone—"The Months of the Year"—or quite idiosyncratic—"The Most Unforgettable Character I've Ever Met."

B. Forgetting in the various storage systems

In a model such as this, forgetting can occur in different ways. Forgetting in short-term storage can occur when a subsequent piece of information prevents us from rehearsing the present piece of information, causing it to decay. Long-term storage can fail either because the information never gets from short- to long-term storage or because there are not

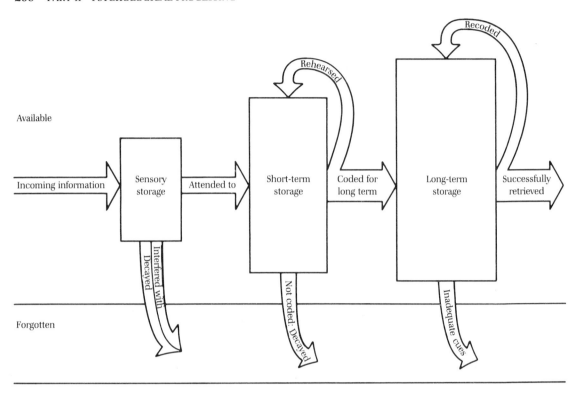

Figure 8-1. The computer remembers.

enough cues to locate an item. Sometimes we get the right category, but retrieving one item interferes with retrieving another.

A final consequence of this way of looking at long-term storage concerns items that we use over and over again, such as our home address or division tables. Theoretically, such items can be multiply indexed so that a great many cues lead to their retrieval. Using a filing system as our analogy, such a situation is similar to cross-indexing a letter or an income-tax return so that you can always find it when you need it.

1. Sensory storage.   The first part of a total computer memory system is sensory storage. The idea of how it works is very simple: you have to notice something before you can remember it. Although the idea is simple, it is quite difficult to demonstrate experimentally. In one of the earliest experiments (Auerbach & Coriell, 1961), a series of 16 letters arranged in two rows of eight each were presented on a screen for 1/20 sec. Then the screen went blank for a varying period of time, up to 1/2 sec. (In some trials it did not go blank at all, so that the period was zero.) At the end of this so-called retention period, a signal appeared over the previous location of one of the 16 letters, and the subject was asked what the letter was.

Results were quite clear in showing that subjects were best able to recall the correct letter when there was no delay period and that recall reached its low point at 1/5 sec and got better from then on up to 1/2 sec. The 1/5 sec, however, should not be considered a fixed value, as other work indicated that recall could last a good bit longer, especially if the display was darker or the background was duller.

One other important aspect of these early experiments concerns what happens when the experimenter changes the signal used to ask the subject to recall one rather than another letter. In one condition, the signal was a simple line that appeared above where the letter had been. In a second condition, the letter to be recalled was circled. Under this second condition, subjects were unable to recall the letter even after as short a period as 1/10 sec, and for this reason the circle was said to have "erased" the trace.

The type of event presumed to go on in visual sensory storage can be experienced directly. One way to do this is to move your finger or a pencil back and forth across your field of vision. You should be able to see the finger or pencil at more than a single place. A similar experience can be had using a lighted cigarette in a darkened room; here you should be able to see continuous waves even when the cigarette tip is no longer moving. In both cases, as well as in many other more controlled laboratory experiments, we tend to be able to see events no longer physically present. This finding suggests a visual storage system that allows us to "read out" an event after it is gone for 2/10 to 3/10 sec. Although we do not ordinarily notice these perceptual/memory effects, we can experience them if we are told what to look for and if we adopt a special way of looking for them.

2. Short-term storage.   The most ordinary and best example of short-term memory, and through it of short-term storage, is given by how we recall a telephone number. After the operator tells us what the number is, we somehow manage to hold onto it while we dial. Personally, I find this a very difficult task and am often forced to repeat the number over and over to myself. Usually, I feel under a great deal of tension as I repeat the number, and I sigh a great sigh of relief when the call goes through. Unfortunately, if I have dialed a wrong number, I usually find I no longer remember the number and have to call Directory Assistance again, hoping this time to get a different operator.

This example, as ordinary as it is, tells us a good bit about short-term storage. For one, forgetting can be rapid, and our short-term capacities are limited; for another, one way to prevent such forgetting is to rehearse and re-rehearse the material. The very small storage capacity of short-term memory has been an acknowledged personal and experimental fact for a long time. In the laboratory, early results indicated that adults can recall only about 7 $\pm$ 2 items. Although what an item is may change from experiment to experiment (it can be a word, a num-

ber, a sentence, or something else), what is important is not the item itself but that there is a definite limit to immediate memory.

More recent, and in some senses more surprising, data supporting the idea of a limited short-term storage area were presented by Peterson and Peterson (1959), who found that college-student subjects could not give 100% recall (or anything near it) for a sequence of three letters, such as BQR, when asked to do this after 3, 6, 9, 12, 15, or 18 sec. To fill the interval between the time subjects saw the three letters and the time they were asked for recall, Peterson and Peterson asked them to count backward by threes. For example, if the subject was shown the sequence BQR and then the number 582, he or she then had to say "579, 576, . . ." until told to stop. Then the subject was to tell the experimenter the three letters just seen. As it turns out, counting backward by threes is a fairly difficult and compelling job. After 3 sec of counting backward, only 60% of subjects were able to produce correct recalls. By 18 sec, the value had dropped to 10%.

In a similar experiment, Murdock (1961) tested students' ability to recall three types of material— three-letter sequences, common words, and sets of three unrelated words—again asking them to count backward until asked for recall. Results for the three-letter sequences were quite similar to those reported by the Petersons. For single words, however, there was little or no loss over the entire 18-sec recall interval. For sets of three unrelated words, results were comparable to those for the three-letter sequences.

Murdock's results suggest that subjects recall *any* three unrelated units in just about the same way. Even if from one point of view three unrelated letters and three unrelated words seem to be different kinds of units, they were dealt with in the same way under the conditions of the experiment. This result suggests that the span of short-term memory is determined by the number of "chunks" of information rather than by the number of elements that make up a given item (or chunk).

One further type of experiment that has been used to explore short-term storage concerns confusions that occur in recalling words or letters. Some of the earliest experiments were done by Conrad (1964). In the first of his experiments, subjects heard a series of letters recorded on tape against a background of noise. These letters were presented at the rate of one every 5 sec, and subjects were asked to write down the letters they thought they heard. The most significant result was that letters that sound alike when spoken, such as *B, V,* and *D,* were frequently confused with one another, whereas letters that only look alike, such as *B* and *R,* were rarely or never confused.

In a second experiment, subjects were presented with sequences of letters. This time, however, letters were shown to them visually, and they were asked to recall them immediately. Subjects still tended to confuse letters on the basis of sound *(B* and *V)* rather than on the basis of written similarity *(B* and *R).* Evidently hearing errors occur for visually presented materials, just as for those presented auditorily.

What all this means is that people "talk to themselves" during an experiment in which they are asked to recall something, even if the material to be remembered was visually presented. Such "inner speaking" is, of course, a very well known part of short-term recall: don't we all repeat that phone number over and over, and haven't there been times when you've just heard something that you know you need to remember and waved people away until you've written it down? All this "inner talk"— more properly called **rehearsal**—seems designed to help us hold onto an item in short-term storage, mostly because our short-term storage system seems to have a very limited capacity. To prevent new items from replacing old items, the rememberer rehearses the old item, which prevents it from getting lost (being forgotten).

In the most ambitious attempt to study how subjects rehearse items that later appear in recall, Rundus (1971) asked subjects to say aloud whatever word or words they were "thinking of or rehearsing" as they went about trying to remember a list of 24 words they had seen. Such rehearsals were tape-recorded and later compared with the number of words recalled. For the recall part of the experiment, subjects were asked to write out the items they remembered.

Perhaps the most important part of this experiment concerns one particular type of word list in which the 24 items were divided into two equal subsets. In one set of 12 items, 6 of the words were members of one category, such as "types of furniture," while the other 6 were members of a second category, such as "fruit." The remaining 12 words were unrelated. When Rundus looked at his re-

hearsal data in conjunction with his recall data, he found that subjects not only rehearsed the item they had just seen ("orange, orange"), they also rehearsed other items from the same category: "orange, orange, pear, apple, ..." Some of the items easily formed categories while others did not, and subjects rehearsed category items more frequently than noncategory items; this fact probably helps explain why such items were better recalled.

3. Long-term storage. One model of organization that is quite helpful in thinking about long-term storage is that of a library. Here "books" (the items to be retrieved later) are filed by topic. When a particular book is wanted, the borrower can get it in one of three ways: by knowing the author, by knowing the title, or by knowing the topic. This third procedure seems a reasonable first guess as to how long-term storage is organized and how we retrieve items from it. Such a starting point also receives support from experimental facts about human recall.

First there is **clustering** by category, a phenomenon first described by Bousfield in 1953. If a subject is presented with a list of words drawn from several categories but listed in random order, the subject will tend to recall them largely according to category, even if he or she is not instructed to.

How might this occur? Let us assume that when the subject is shown a list of words in random order, such as *peach, Bob, East, Jim, apple, West, . . . ,* he or she is likely to say and then rehearse each item as it appears: "Now I see the word *apple . . . apple, apple.*" During the course of this rehearsal (as Rundus' results showed), the subject is likely to say "Apple—let's see, there was another fruit— yeah, peach: apple, peach; apple, peach." In this way items get put into their respective categories even if presented in random order.

Once all categories are decided on—fruits, directions, names—all the subject has to do to recall is to expand the category. In this way recall can be described as a complicated coding/storing/retrieving/decoding procedure, in which the specific nature of the recall output tells us something about the subject's categories and category system.

The order in which items are recalled is important, but if we ask subjects to say their recalls aloud, we can also look at how long they take to produce successive items. Pollio, Richards, and Lucas (1969) found that subjects tended to produce items in recall bursts such as occur in Figure 8-2. The first burst of responses—the first four "blips" on the record—all come from the same category. Where there was a slightly longer time between words, the subject shifted to a different category. This same pattern holds for the entire record of five clusters—sequences of very fast responses appear at intervals.

This pattern suggests that items from the same category occur together in recall and are produced extremely rapidly. We may say intuitively that such a process may reflect the subject thinking "Let's see, I've already recalled all the sports and furniture items; now let's try the fruits"; "Let's see, I've already recalled sports, furniture, and fruits; how about men's names," and so on.

Although the category-clustering procedure tells us something about how a long-term storage system might be organized, other techniques, such as the one suggested by Lindsay and Norman (1972), can also be used to probe such storage. In this technique, Lindsay and Norman were interested in relating retrieval to other types of complex problem-solving activity. Their fictional example begins with the following question:

What were you doing on Monday afternoon in the third week of September two years ago?

Don't give up right away. Take some time to think about it and see if you can come up with the answer. Try writing down your thoughts as you attempt to recover this information. Better still, ask a friend to think out loud as he tries to answer the query.

The type of response people typically produce when asked this kind of question goes something like this:

1. Come on. How should I know? (Experimenter: Just try it, anyhow.)
2. OK. Let's see: two years ago . . .
3. I would be in high school in Pittsburgh . . .
4. That would be my senior year.
5. Third week in September—that's just after summer—that would be the fall term . . .
6. Let me see. I think I had chemistry lab on Mondays.
7. I don't know. I was probably in the chemistry lab . . .

8. Wait a minute—that would be the second week of school. I remember he started off with the atomic table—a big, fancy chart. I thought he was crazy, trying to make us memorize that thing.
9. You know, I think I can remember sitting . . . [Lindsay & Norman, 1972, p. 379].[5]

Here, then, is a new twist on human memory: No longer does a person have to retrieve a particular event. Instead, his or her answer can be constructed out of information already available. From this point of view, remembering is not so much a matter of retrieving one or another event as it is an inferential problem-solving activity. To be sure, the "constructed" memory is built of prior knowledge; however, there would seem to be no specific memory to retrieve. In this way, remembering and problem solving make contact with each other, and both can now be seen as part of the more general ability of the human being to think.

C. Computers and memory: An evaluation

The work on computers has taken an interesting turn. Memory is no longer seen as a unique and isolated human process; rather, it is placed among a large number of cognitive activities all of which can be described in terms of information and information processing. No longer is it necessary to keep "remembering" and "thinking" in separate theoretical compartments: they are now understood to concern similar processes. To be sure, there are differences in emphasis between remembering and thinking, but similarities can now also be emphasized. Largely because such integration seems possible in the near future, many psychologists have joined what can only be called the "computer revolution" and see in it a new direction for the psychology of the future.

Because of the significance of the computer approach for contemporary psychology, it is crucial to

[5]From *Human Information Processing*, by P. H. Lindsay and D. A. Norman. Copyright 1972 by Academic Press, Inc. Reprinted by permission.

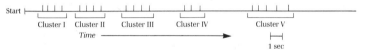

Figure 8-2. Schematic drawing of a typical record, revealing time properties for the free recall of categorized word lists. *(From "Temporal Properties of Category Recall," by H. R. Pollio, S. Richards, and R. Lucas. In H. R. Pollio,* The Psychology of Symbolic Activity, *page 253. © 1974 by Addison-Wesley, Reading, Massachusetts. Reprinted by permission.)*

look carefully at both its successes and its short-comings, particularly as they relate to remembering. The analysis of memory inspired by the computer is an elegant and precise one. Distinctions are made that have an intuitive first-person appeal as well as a possible realization within the technology of a third-person computer. Experiments have been designed and carried out in a way that is at once rigorous and theoretically orderly. The results of these experiments have been described precisely in mathematical terms and seem as applicable to the world of the computer engineer as to the world of the college student. Memory is no longer an isolated process but is placed in relation to other cognitive processes, such as problem solving, so as to suggest an active role for the person/computer in bringing about an organization that is useful not only for storage but for retrieval as well. All in all, the computer revolution is a neat package.

But perhaps the package is too neat. Perhaps the distinctions made, such as those between short-term and long-term storage, do not grow out of our experiences as remembering human beings, but are imposed on them by trying to describe people in terms of the computer. Maybe it is not so much that people are primarily problem solvers when they go after their past as that computers work by finding answers to clearly formulated questions about events already in storage. Perhaps the emphasis on certain kinds of organization and organizing processes does not have to do with things human, but with computers and the organization of computer storage. And perhaps the rigor and neatness of computer analysis is purchased only at the price of distorting a less well defined and apparently more disorderly process that occurs when a human being searches after the meaning of a past event in his or her life.

In fact, what may be described as disorderly from the perspective of the computer is not *dis*order but *different* order. The computer requires a certain logical sequencing if it is to do its job. Human remembering reveals the order of human Being-in-the world with all its spatial/temporal/cognitive/emotional/social/linguistic complexity. The "order" in memory, as in all human activities, is the order of what is involved in being a person. Even if this order is not that of a rational sequence, it is the order of human living and experiencing.

1. Nouns versus gerunds. A different way to evaluate the computer revolution in regard to remembering is to ask whether the analogy between computer storage and retrieval and human recall is a good one. Unfortunately, the computer analogy seems to produce a great many nouns rather than gerunds. For example, *memory* (a noun) is divided into nouns such as short- and long-term *storage*, while *information* is said to pass from one (storage) *system* to another. To remember is to engage a *rehearsal process* for short-term storage or a *retrieval process* for long-term storage. And what is it that is stored and later retrieved? *Images* (or "chunks") of information in short-term storage, and *mental structures*, such as *categories*, *hierarchies*, and so on, in long-term storage. To remember is to retrieve *something* from *some place.*

For the computer, memory is reducible to getting back a relatively fixed and changeless something: an image, a structure, or, more generally, a **memory trace.** The idea that there is a something to be got back can be related, in part, to a bit of uncritical language use. From the point of view of a witness recalling an event in court, there are only questions and answers. Even if helped by appropriate questioning, first-person experience hardly ever seems to contain an inner storehouse or library of events that get "read out" in response to a question. From a third-person point of view, however, it seems that when a person remembers, what he or she says must have been stored away, like a pair of shoes on a shelf somewhere. Given the flow of the story as heard (not as produced), it is not unreasonable to describe it as "playing a memory tape." Unfortunately, there is no tape or any tape recorder on which to play it. All there is is a person trying to relate to a personal event that has passed.

2. Neisser's analysis. Cognitive psychologists have not been unmindful of the problem of "lifeless storage." For example, Neisser, in his very influential early book *Cognitive Psychology* (1967), talked about problems involved in what he calls the **reappearance hypothesis.** He cites approvingly James' ideas on the matter: "A permanently existing idea . . . which makes its appearance before the footlights of consciousness at periodic intervals, is as mythical an entity as the Jack of Spades" (Neisser, p. 282). Continuing in this vein, Neisser notes:

This assumption is so ingrained in our thinking that we rarely notice how poorly it fits experience. If Reappearance were really the governing principle of mental life, repetition of earlier acts or thoughts should be the natural thing, and variation the exception. In fact, the opposite is true. Precise repetition of any movement, any spoken sentence, or any sequence of thought is extremely difficult to achieve. When repetition does occur, as in dramatic acting or nonsense-syllable learning or a compulsive sequence of actions, we ascribe it either to long, highly motivated practice or to neurotic defensiveness [p. 282].[6]

Given his aversion to a simple reappearance hypothesis, Neisser then notes that recall does, however, need to work on something that has changed in the person as a consequence of past experience. Neisser suggests the analogy of a paleontologist trying to reconstruct a prehistoric animal from a few bone chips. The "bone chips" are meant to describe what does get stored; the act of the paleontologist is meant to describe how we "construct a memory" from a few stored and somewhat chaotic fragments.

But what can the nature of these "bone chips" be? According to Neisser, they must not be considered static, lifeless entities. Rather, they can only be described as traces of prior attempts at constructing our past. Given this analogy, the whole process works as follows:

> The present proposal is, therefore, that we store traces of earlier cognitive acts.... The traces are not simply "revived" or "reactivated" in recall; instead, the stored fragments are used as information to support a new construction. It is as if the bone fragments used by the paleontologist did not appear in the model he builds at all—as indeed they need not, if it is to represent a fully fleshed-out, skin-covered dinosaur. The bones can be thought of, somewhat loosely, as remnants of the structure which created and supported the original dinosaur, and thus as sources of information about how to reconstruct it [pp. 285–286].

Although this proposal does not entirely get rid of the idea of a static memory trace, it gives it some life, so that in remembering we continually remake our understanding of the past and are not totally

trapped by unchanging traces. After all, if we "made" Dinosaur I (Memory I), we can also make a slightly different "model" for Dinosaur II.

Neisser's "traces" are much more alive than many other proposals dealing with this same problem. The idea, so well expressed in Neisser's model, that what we remember is our past rememberings seems to have been considered seriously by only a few cognitive psychologists. Neisser's analysis is quite different from the many theories that talk of much more static events that get stored, transferred, and/or retrieved.

The noun-ness of computer psychology yields a harvest of pieces. If these pieces were as dynamic as Neisser's "bones," it might be all right. Unfortunately, most of these concepts are dry bones, and, with apologies to Ezekiel, them bones ain't ever going to rise, mostly because they are products of definition rather than of experience. Take the most famous of these bones—the "chunk" of information. When psychologists such as George Miller (1956a, 1956b) first used this term, it was quite clear that they were talking about a scientific fiction useful in helping organize many facts about human memory. Unfortunately, Miller's "chunk" too soon lost its quotation marks and improperly came to be considered the "real thing."

In the study of short-term memory a chunk of information can now consist of anything: letters, words, numbers, sentences, pictures, or whatever. Only under an extended categorizing of material as "part" or "not part" of a chunk did it become possible to talk about a "memory span" of 7 ± 2 "chunks." The fact that "memory span" was a statistical product (a kind of memory threshold) was lost sight of: not only did "chunks" become real, so did a constant-size short-term memory. In both cases, events derived from a large number of observations were lumped together and, once given the same name, came to be treated as identical. Once this happened, these bones could never live again, mostly because they never came from living experience in the first place.

3. Time and memory. Neisser's reconstruction theory of memory has other implications. The most important concerns the problem of time and memory. If what I remember now depends, in part, on how I remembered it last time, what I remember

[6]From *Cognitive Psychology*, by U. Neisser. Copyright 1967 by Appleton-Century-Crofts, a division of Prentice-Hall, Inc. This and all other quotations from this source are reprinted by permission.

must be from a little to a lot different every time I remember. Remembering can only be described as an ongoing event that is never independent of my particular situation now. Remembering is never done "out of time" or "out of place," and so where I am, when I am, and what I have already remembered about a particular topic must all affect how and what I remember. Remembering, like all living behavior, is a relation between me and my situation in which I try to make some sense out of that situation. In remembering, my task is to connect a present first-person situation to a past first-person situation that I alone have had. To remember is a personal act that can only grow out of a very personal history.

A major consequence of this approach is that as our understanding of an event changes, so will our remembering of it. In this regard, Kvale (1976a) notes:

> With respect to changes in the world of the remembering subject, the Munich Treaty of 1938 provides an example of how the understanding of a historical event depends on the temporal and social context, and how the memory of the event can be changed when seen within a new context. This Treaty that lay Czechoslovakia open to Hitler was originally celebrated as a victory for peace by the Western Allies. But at the outbreak of World War II, it came to be regarded as a political blunder. In the post-war years, the Treaty was also interpreted as a tactical postponement of the Western Allies in order to gain time for rearmament. In the Soviet Union the Pact has been viewed as a deliberate attempt by the Western Allies to open Eastern Europe to Hitler. Such a necessary social and temporal perspectivity in the interpretation of the past must be distinguished from a total relativity of interpretations as well as from dogmatic, political manipulation and falsification of the past described by Orwell in *1984* [p. 9].

What might be expected is that the Munich Treaty would originally have been recalled within the context of a discussion having to do with peacekeeping techniques. Next, it might have come up (that is, have been remembered) in the context of an argument against appeasement; still later it would be recalled as an example of how to delay politically while continuing to build militarily. For the Russian rememberer, however, no such changes in meaning or memory would have occurred. He or she would always have recalled (and rerecalled) the Munich Treaty as an example of Western treachery before

and during World War II. How an event is understood and categorized at Time 1 and then at Time 2 helps to predict how it will (or will not) be recalled at Times 1 and 2.

If some of this discussion seems overly critical of the computer approach to memory, that is not quite what I mean. If one thing is clear from the cognitive point of view, it must be that categorizing, thinking, problem solving, and remembering are not separate activities. Rather, each process must involve aspects of the others, so that at the time of recall how we see our present task as well as how an event is categorized or thought about will determine whether we remember it in the present context. A total person remembers, and each rememberer brings a great many skills and intentions to bear in any particular act of remembering.

To remember is to make contact in some way with what we remembered or experienced before. Only if we grant some life and flux to these prior rememberings will we begin to have some reasonable idea of how human beings continually reevaluate their past. Only if we give some life and flux to all of "computer memory" will it be possible to talk about a computer that remembers rather than one that can only fetch "Neisser's bones." And only if we do this will it be reasonable to talk about the recall of a human being in terms of the recall of a computer.

It seems good to end on a note of conciliation. Earlier it seemed that any attempt to explore recall experimentally was doomed to failure and that all that was left the poor experimental psychologist was pity: no subjects, no laboratory, no elegant mathematics, no computer, no data, no nothing. Experimental inquiry is possible and desirable if we constantly keep in mind that we are interested in human beings, not pretty models of human beings. Sometimes, in the experimentalist's zeal for precision and control, the phenomenon of interest gets defined away or at least distorted, so that studies of remembering have little to do with how a human being recalls. Although it is difficult to do experiments that respect both the person and the phenomenon, such experiments can be done. Fortunately, just such a series of experiments on remembering has been done. These experiments were begun in the early 1900s under the direction of Sir Frederic Bartlett, and it is to this work that we now turn.

VI. REMEMBERING AS A HUMAN ACT: BARTLETT'S STUDIES

Bartlett first published his book *Remembering* in 1932. The title itself announced the break that Bartlett was trying to make from earlier work, especially since the major earlier book having to do with this topic was published by Hermann Ebbinghaus under the title *On Memory* (1885). For Ebbinghaus, the problem was *memory*—a noun—whereas for Bartlett the problem was *remembering*—a gerund. To study memory scientifically, Ebbinghaus decided that he needed to purify his experiment, so that very little if any of the subject's humanness was left. To do this, he studied the recall of nonsense syllables—that is, material that has little or no immediate meaning to a person. Although it is impossible to stop human beings from developing meaning for almost anything, the job is awfully difficult if you do not allow them much time. For this reason, investigators in this tradition present nonsense syllables to subjects at quite fast rates, sometimes as fast as 1 per sec and never slower than 1 every 12 sec or so.

To Bartlett, such procedures ruled out the most important part of the experiment: the remembering human being. To study remembering his way, Bartlett invented or borrowed different techniques. In all his procedures, however, Bartlett tried to use interesting (or at least meaningful) material and to give his subjects full scope in doing what they (not he) wanted to do with the material. He also felt no great compunction to follow the same procedure with every subject. He would sometimes question his subjects to find out whether they could describe what they were doing in any clearer way than he could. Similarly, it was not unlike Bartlett to stop former subjects on the street—two, five, or even ten years after they had been subjects in his experiments—and, after the initial hellos, ask them whether they remembered anything at all about what had gone on in his experiment many years before.

A. Cultural influences on remembering

The most widely known of Bartlett's somewhat unorthodox procedures is the method of repeated reproductions. In one variation on this method, subjects were asked to read a North American folktale called "The War of the Ghosts." A short time later, they were asked to write out whatever they remembered of the story. The original story went as follows (Bartlett, 1932, p. 65).

THE WAR OF THE GHOSTS

One night two young men from Egulac went down to the river to hunt seals, and while they were there it became foggy and calm. Then they heard war-cries, and they thought: "Maybe this is a war-party." They escaped to the shore, and hid behind a log. Now canoes came up, and they heard the noise of paddles, and saw one canoe coming up to them. There were five men in the canoe, and they said:

"What do you think? We wish to take you along. We are going up the river to make war on the people."

One of the young men said: "I have no arrows."

"Arrows are in the canoe," they said.

"I will not go along. I might be killed. My relatives do not know where I have gone. But you," he said, turning to the other, "may go with them."

So one of the young men went, but the other returned home.

And the warriors went on up the river to a town on the other side of Kalama. The people came down to the water, and they began to fight, and many were killed. But presently the young man heard one of the warriors say: "Quick, let us go home: that Indian has been hit." Now he thought: "Oh, they are ghosts." He did not feel sick, but they said he had been shot.

So the canoes went back to Egulac, and the young man went ashore to his house, and made a fire. And he told everybody and said: "Behold I accompanied the ghosts, and we went to fight. Many of our fellows were killed, and many of those who attacked us were killed. They said I was hit, and I did not feel sick."

He told it all, and then he became quiet. When the sun rose he fell down. Something black came out of his mouth. His face became contorted. The people jumped up and cried.

He was dead.[7]

As Bartlett points out, he chose to work with this story and others of its type for four major reasons: it deals with a culture different from our own; some of the incidents would have to appear disconnected to an English subject, and Bartlett wanted to see how subjects would deal with such discontinuity; the dramatic nature of the story seemed likely to arouse strong emotional reactions; and the supernatural

[7]From *Remembering*, by F. C. Bartlett. Copyright 1932 by Cambridge University Press. This and all other quotations from this source are reprinted by permission.

events involved in the story might produce interesting effects in remembering.

What happened when these stories were read and then recalled? Here is the first reproduction of the story by Subject P, after a 15-minute interval.

THE WAR OF THE GHOSTS

Two youths were standing by a river about to start seal-catching, when a boat appeared with five men in it. They were all armed for war.

The youths were at first frightened, but they were asked by the men to come and help them fight some enemies on the other bank. One youth said he could not come as his relations would be anxious about him; the other said he would go, and entered the boat.

In the evening he returned to his hut, and told his friends that he had been in a battle. A great many had been slain, and he had been wounded by an arrow; he had not felt any pain, he said. They told him that he must have been fighting in a battle of ghosts. Then he remembered that it had been quiet and he became very excited.

In the morning, however, he became ill, and his friends gathered round; he fell down and his face became very pale. Then he writhed and shrieked and his friends were filled with terror. At last he became calm. Something hard and black came out of his mouth, and he lay contorted and dead [Bartlett, 1932, p. 72].

Aside from an obvious shortening and loss of detail, other modifications are quite evident. Most of these have to do with making the story more sensible, often by dropping "peculiar" ideas and phrases: the young warrior is now wounded "by an arrow"; he "became ill" and "writhed and shrieked," thereby filling his friends "with terror." These phrases never appeared in the original story; rather, they represent Person P's attempts to make the story fit a more Western frame of reference. The phrases "writhed and shrieked" and "his friends were filled with terror" seem to indicate that P was trying to capture the supernatural parts of the story, particularly in its eerie and emotional aspects. Emotional elements are not only remembered (such as the death scene); they are often elaborated and dealt with in detail. Finally, the strangest part of the story—the battle itself—is dropped out entirely and the spooky parts do not appear, even 15 minutes after the story was first read.

Person P produced many other recalls. Each of these showed progressive changes that served to drop out more and more of the supernatural parts.

After two months, the warrior no longer fought alongside ghosts; instead, "The neighbors said he must have been at war *with* the ghosts." People fight against, not with, ghosts, and this detail has been "tamed" to do away with the spookiness of the original story. The final retelling of the story by this subject, two and a half years later, went as follows:

Some warriors went to wage war against the ghosts. They fought all day and one of their number was wounded.

They returned home in the evening, bearing their sick comrade. As the day drew to a close, he became rapidly worse and the villagers came round him. At sunset he sighed; something black came out of his mouth. He was dead [Bartlett, 1932, p. 75].

Now the warriors are fighting the ghosts. The story has a John Wayne aura to it, as the good guys "bear their sick comrade" home, who just happens to die at sunset rather than at sunrise. The story has metamorphosed from a Native American folktale to an American movie: after two years everything now fits a Western frame of reference. Only one dramatic bit of the original story remains—something black still comes from the dying warrior's mouth.

Changes such as these are found not only in successive recalls written by the same person. In another experiment, Bartlett showed one subject in a group of subjects the first picture (marked A) in Figure 8-3 and asked him to draw it. The original figure is a stylized Egyptian owl. Each of ten subjects, in turn, was asked to draw a picture of the previous picture shown to him. Under this procedure, the subjects produced a series of drawings, each further removed from the original. As can be seen, the Egyptian owl becomes a quite civilized Western pussycat after only ten persons. The crucial turn seems to have been taken by Person 3, where the wavy lines at the right of the picture become a tail; from then on, successive drawings go their own irresistible way to Reproduction 10.

Thus, the course of group recall strongly resembles the course of individual recall. This is as it should be, for it is the person—emotions, attitudes, language, cultural frame of reference, and so on—who decides what will and what will not be remembered. The use of a group procedure only allows us to show that many of the same effects occur whether remembering is done by a single subject over and over or by a group of people. In both cases, quite

Figure 8-3. Elaboration of a figure drawn by ten persons in succession. *(From* Remembering, *by F. C. Bartlett. Copyright 1932 by Cambridge University Press. Reprinted by permission of the publisher.)*

clearly, many of the changes introduced in successive recalls have their origin not only or even primarily in the material but in the social frame of reference of the remembering subject. English college students can no more permit warriors to fight with ghosts than they can permit Egyptian birds not to change into pussycats.

B. Bartlett's theory of remembering

The theory of remembering that comes out of all these experiments has perhaps been Bartlett's most important contribution to a psychology of remembering. The major assumption in this theory is that remembering can only be described as an active process; it is never appropriate to talk of remembering as the retrieval of "innumerable lifeless and fragmentary traces." For Bartlett, to remember is to reconstruct or even to construct a description of some past aspect of experience. Each reconstruction is built out of the person's very personal and changing relationships to a continuously changing mass of past reactions. Remembering is scarcely ever exact, for as I change, so must the what, as well as the how, of what I recall.

For Bartlett, the past leaves some trace, but it is neither a static nor a lifeless trace. Rather, the schema, as Bartlett more technically calls the rememberer's "mass of past reactions," is alive—alive with a sensitivity to new situations, new interests, and new interpretations. And it is precisely this sensitivity that allows us to turn continuously around on what it is we have experienced and to separate out of the mass that is our experience those elements that are needed in a particular situation.

Remembering has to do not only with making contact with our past but also with weaving our past into the present. For this reason, our interests and even the very questions we and others put to our past determine what we will remember and how we will remember it. Recalling, like all human action, is an act of a person, and to strip it of its human foibles and qualities is to strip it of its significance in and to our lives. We could do no better than close with a quotation from Bartlett:

> I have written a book preoccupied with problems of remembering and its individual and social determination. But I have never regarded memory as . . . a reaction narrowed and ringed round, containing all its peculiarities and all their explanations within itself. I have regarded it rather as one achievement in the line of the ceaseless struggle to master and enjoy a world full of variety and rapid change. Memory, and all the life of images and words which goes with it, is one with . . . constructive imagination and constructive thought wherein at length we find the most complete release from the narrowness of present time and place (1932, p. 314).

VII. SUMMARY

Each situation in which remembering occurs creates its own unique set of demands, and these demands strongly affect not only how, but also what, we finally remember. Remembering, like every other human act, always occurs in some present situation. This is true whether we are concerned with "uninvited" recall such as that described by Proust or Van Den Berg or with more ordinary remembering such as might occur in a classroom or laboratory.

In uninvited recall the event remembered is so strongly experienced as to capture the person totally. The person often suspends his or her ongoing activities so as to enter the world evoked. Higher senses, such as sight and hearing, do not seem to evoke the past as strongly as taste or smell, largely because what we see often becomes dissociated from uniquely meaningful prior experience.

In a second type of remembering, we consider a segment of our past from a somewhat detached and logical third-person point of view. Although this is a more common form of remembering, it is not always as accurate as we might expect, largely because we often try to fill in gaps to produce a logical and orderly recall.

One good example of such remembering occurs when a witness gives testimony in court. It seems that honest people with no reason to lie often make obvious errors in testimony. One reason is that we do not attend to events that do not interest us, and what might be important to our present testimony might not have been important to us when we experienced it. A second reason is that even with the best of motives, witnesses try to produce the most logically complete description they can (what has been called "logification"), and this attempt often yields an orderly but inaccurate recollection.

Another reason for inaccurate testimony concerns differences in the person between the time an event occurred and the time of the trial. Still other errors occur when an attorney attempts to lead our testimony astray simply by changing a word or two in his or her questions—for example, in substituting *smashed* for *contacted* in asking us to describe an automobile accident. What is important to keep in mind about remembering in the courtroom (as elsewhere) is that to recall something represents an attempt in the present to speak with the past and that the living link between then and now is a living, remembering person.

Freud pioneered research into small errors of speech and writing ("Freudian slips") on the assumption that such errors revealed the operation of unconscious processes. Freud assumed that the meaning of a slip was unrecognized because it was "pushed" or "held" from reflected experience by strong counterforces called repression. Repression, which became Freud's major principle of forgetting and memory, was seen to occur when we forgot something we did not want to remember or do. Repression was also seen to have more serious consequences, particularly as it made its influence felt in pathological symptoms. Freud believed he had to understand the repressed event before he could help the patient overcome the symptoms. The patient, like the witness, sometimes filled in details from his or her past so as to make a memory sensible. With the patient, the personal meaning of his or her past was at issue, not the truth or falsity of the event remembered as some outside observer might have described it.

Mnemonics, or methods for improving memory, have been used for centuries. The Greek poet Simonides is credited with the method of loci, in which a series of imaginary locations is used to "place" pieces of information to be remembered. In general, the use of memory tricks seems to be necessary to the degree that the information to be recalled is a series of unrelated words or events. Meaningful personal memories tend simply to "unfold," compared with the more forced and mechanical process of remembering unrelated information.

The crucial difference between the professional rememberer and the witness or patient is a difference between recall as a technical and as an unpremeditated act. For this reason, the act of the master rememberer is much less affected by the situation than is true for either patient or witness. The mnemonist is interested only in remembering; patient and witness are trying to reconstruct the past in a personally meaningful and coherent way. Technical recall can only be the outcome of planful activity.

The use of mnemonics in recall, with its emphasis on rules and planful activity, has led to the idea that computers might provide a good analogy for describing human recall. The computer has three basic memory systems: sensory storage, short-term storage, and long-term storage. Sensory storage lasts only a fraction of a second. Short-term storage is wider in scope but still is limited to 7 ± 2 items held for a few minutes only. Long-term storage is much larger in capacity, although adequate indexing and recall are not as direct as for short-term storage. Within long-term storage, information is often highly organized, suggesting the model of a library as appropriate for either human or machine retrieval.

The problem with using the computer as a model of human remembering can be seen most clearly in cases in which the cognitive psychologist has forgotten the *as if* quality of the model. When this happens, the semanticist's quotation marks tend to get lost; for example, "chunks" of information become *chunks* of information, and what was an analogy takes on a quality of thingness. The process of remembering then becomes the retrieval of a "real" thing (a memory trace) from some "real" place (memory storage). Under these conditions, the model loses sight of remembering as a unique and per-

sonal process that must be different from the simple retrieval of a static piece of information. In remembering, the person's task is always to connect a present first-person situation to a past first-person situation, never to retrieve lifeless memory traces.

In contrast to this somewhat naive use of the computer model, Neisser has argued that remembering can better be described as an act of reconstructing rather than one of retrieving. From his point of view, the act of recall is best compared to the work of a paleontologist who reconstructs a long-dead dinosaur from a handful of bones. Memory traces are analogous to bones, while reconstruction is the process by which past events are re-created. Generally speaking, each successive remembering of an event comes progressively to be based more on prior reconstructions than on direct experience with the "memory trace" itself.

Neisser's view is an attempt to bridge the gap between computer models of memory and earlier work by Bartlett, who tried to take the topic of remembering out of the laboratory and return it to the extralaboratory world in which it usually occurred. Bartlett's studies, involving both linguistic and pictorial elements, revealed that changes in the recall of unfamiliar events often followed personal or cultural lines, suggesting that in recall the person seeks to eliminate or change unfamiliar elements in order to produce a more sensible and reasonable version. Each reconstruction is built out of the person's unique relationship to a continuously changing schema of past reactions. Remembering is hardly ever exact, for as I change, so must the what, as well as the how, of what I recall. Like all human action, remembering is a personal act, and to strip it of its human foibles and qualities is to strip it of its significance in and for our lives.

VIII. GLOSSARY OF IMPORTANT CONCEPTS

"Chunk". A term used in computer analyses of memory to denote a meaningful unit of information.

Clustering. A phenomenon of recall in which randomly presented words are remembered according to category.

Freudian slips. Slips of the tongue or pen, used as evidence by Freud for the existence of unconscious processes.

Leading question. A type of question used by attorneys to direct the flow of recall.

Logification. A recall process that acts to produce the best and most logically complete description of an event. Logification sometimes acts against remembering events accurately.

Memory trace. A relatively fixed and changeless image or structure thought to be stored in a person's memory and reactivated during recall.

Method of locations. A memory "trick" attributed to Simonides and Cicero whereby one can recall ideas or objects by assigning each of them a fixed and unique location in an imaginary space.

Mnemonics. Memory "tricks," such as the methods used in "professional remembering" situations.

Mnemonist. A professional rememberer.

Personal recall. Recollection differentiated from mnemonic recall by the unique and personal character of the recollection, which originates in the ongoing flow of life.

Reappearance hypothesis. The belief that memory consists of discrete permanent traces that can be recalled exactly, much as a tape replays the same information.

Reconstruction. A process of recall by which the person creates an impression out of a few remembered details. Used by Neisser in an attempt to coordinate schema and computer theories of recall.

Rehearsal. Talking to oneself in order to hold onto an item in short-term memory storage.

Remembering. An act of the present designed to recapture the past through either a first-person reentry into the past or a third-person "looking back" at some event experienced in that past.

Repression. A psychological process described by Freud, designed to hold back events in the unconscious so that they do not become conscious.

Retrieval. A process by which information is obtained from a storage system. It is a major principle in the computer theory of remembering.

Schema. Bartlett's term for a person's "mass of past reactions," which he believes to be alive with a sensitivity to new situations and new interpretations.

Seven, plus or minus two. The memory threshold; the "size" of short-term memory in "chunks."

Short-term, long-term, and **sensory memory storage.** Aspects of a cognitive (or computer-based) approach to remembering. Short-term memory stores information easily for a brief time. Long-term memory stores information for a long time, but retrieval may be slow. Incoming information is held in sensory storage until it decays or is attended to.

IX. SUGGESTED READINGS

Major sources

Bartlett, F. C. *Remembering*. Cambridge: Cambridge University Press, 1932.

Freud, S. *The psychopathology of everyday life*. In S. Freud, *The basic writings of Sigmund Freud*. New York: Random House, 1938. (Originally published, 1905.)

Neisser, U. *Cognitive psychology*. New York: Appleton-Century-Crofts, 1967. Chapters 1, 8–11.

Van Den Berg, J. H. *The changing nature of man*. New York: Dell, 1961. Chapter 1.

Secondary source

Pollio, H. R. *The psychology of symbolic activity*. Reading, Mass.: Addison-Wesley, 1974. Chapters 4, 11.

On Becoming:
The Human Life Cycle

9

Prologue:
A Question of Time

Some birthdays seem more important than they ought to be. Although it does not quite make sense, society manages to make a big deal out of being 10, 13, 16, 18, 21, 30, 40, 50, and 65. Ten seems important because, as my son put it, "that's when you're not one number anymore"; 13 because that's when you're a teenager; 16 because that's when you're sweet and can drive; 18 because that's when you're really an adult; 30 because that's when you can't be trusted anymore and when you're only five years from Geritol; 40 because that's when you get to do one more stupid thing before you enter middle age forever; 50 because that's when you're half a century old; and 65 because that's when you have to slow down, retire, and wait. There is no simple way to organize this set of socially important ages: some have to do with the numbers game (10, 50), others with legal matters (18, 21), while still others seem to mark the end of one phase in a life and the beginning of another (13, 65).

In passing from one phase of a life to another, some societies have special rites. For example, in our own society the retiring employee (age 65) has this occasion noted with a check and a gold watch; the 13-year-old Jewish child gets a public celebration and a fountain pen. In some other societies, the rites are a bit more elaborate: Among the Ndembu of northern Zambia, manhood is noted by a ceremony taking 4 months. On the last day of childhood (at roughly 12 years of age), the young males of the tribe are fed a final meal by their mothers. Following this, they are publicly circumcised in the "place of dying." Then they are forced to remain as novices in a camp of male elders until they can prove that they are capable of "being reborn" as men. When the appropriate tests of manhood are passed, the young men return to their tribal units and are given warrior's clothing. They are then required to perform a war dance as the final achievement of their newly attained manhood (Turner, 1967).

Not all the significant changes in a life, however, are clearly marked. For this reason we often commemorate personally significant events with anniversaries or other public observances. In the case of marriage, not only do we celebrate the yearly date

of the wedding, we also single out as of special significance 10, 25, and 50 years of marriage. These events are often noted by parties and even by public mention in the newspaper. Clearly defined units also mark our progress through various educational institutions. So, for example, we divide our learning time into elementary school, junior high school, high school, college, and for the particularly masochistic, graduate school. Each phase has its own subdivisions, some simply marked by a number— third grade—and others by a change in status, such as lower classman to upper classman. Similarly, finishing college (and later graduate school) is marked by a formal change in status: Jane Doe, B.A., M.A., Ph.D.

Professional careers are similarly marked out. In this case, however, success is correlated with age and experience. Although some college professors are "old" (45 +), a number of extraordinary people have been promoted to full professor at age 22 or so. In the military, enlisted personnel have their time marked out from private to sergeant, while officers have their time marked out from lieutenant to general. Not every member of the military reaches the highest ranks; even so, everyone does have some expectation to advance to a higher rank after some time. Academic and military ranks are not always directly related to chronological age. An outstanding achievement in research or in battle usually speeds up a promotion; a crowded field slows one down. In either case, progress is marked by formal changes in status and rank.

I. BENCHMARKS AS MEASURES OF TIME AND PROGRESS

Sometimes changes in status are not signaled quite so formally, nor are the end results so sure. For a patient in a tuberculosis hospital, there is only one goal: to be released as healthy. Perhaps the best way to get some feel for a patient's view of his own hospital timetable is to listen to one such patient. The patient we have in mind is sitting outside an X-ray room in a TB hospital, talking to the man next to him:

"You know, I was supposed to get this X-ray five days ago, but somebody slipped up. You have to keep after these people or else they forget all about you. When there is a delay in your X-ray once, it's passed along to the next time, and so on. It means you get out of this goddam place that much later. Every day an X-ray is delayed is another day of your life" [Roth, 1963, p. xv].

As far as this patient is concerned (who is in no sense atypical), being in a hospital is considered the same as "doing time" in prison; in both cases the person wants to know when it will end. Because there are no precise markings, patients try to deal with this uncertainty by structuring their time in the hospital in terms of a series of what Roth (1963) has called **benchmarks.** Some of these are formal, such as a change in the patient's health category as determined by physical examination; others are informal, such as getting one's first X ray or one's first pass to the exercise room. By means of both kinds of benchmarks, the course of a patient's stay in the hospital is carefully monitored by the patient as well as by the hospital staff. Even though these benchmarks are not nearly as well delineated as those of the military or educational establishment, they are there.

In all three cases—academia, the military, and the hospital—benchmarks serve not only to mark out the person's progress toward a goal but also to segment time into more manageable units. If the present is difficult or uncertain, one way to make it more manageable is to develop a set of norms that will enable you to evaluate progress toward a different (and, you hope, better) time.

II. OPEN AND CLOSED SYSTEMS OF TIME

Whole societies, as well as individuals within such societies, also testify to the powerful presence of time in human life. In the short range, such concerns are shown by the organization of an ordinary day, week, season, or year; in the longer range, they deal with the unique history of a people. Although every society recognizes time in one way or another, ideas about ordinary or historical time are remarkably different in different cultures. One way to describe these differences is in terms of what have come to be called **open** and **closed systems of time** (Wax, as cited in Roth, 1963).

In societies that have a closed system of time, accurate measures of time are rarely kept. Thus, Paw-

nee Indians keep little track of personal age or calendar time. Life is seen as a series of repetitions: day and night, one season to another and return, misfortune and blessing, poverty and wealth, and so on. There is no need to plan the future, for, as Roth (1963) notes, good fortune is not thought to be the result of planning and labor.

Among the Nuer of north central Africa, almost every aspect of life is determined not by how it relates to the clock but by how it relates to their cattle. In this society, a man says "I'll be home at milking" or "I'll go to the other village when the calves come home," not "I'll be home at 4 o'clock" or "I'll go to the other village in June." Although the Nuer do recognize day and night and two seasons (drought and raining), they orient themselves on the basis of daily routines relating to cattle rather than to the sun, moon, or seasons (Evans-Pritchard, 1940).

Although Westerners such as the anthropologist Evans-Pritchard may talk about "**Nuer time,**" Nuer language has no single word or expression equivalent to *time* in our language. For this reason, the Nuer cannot use *time* as the subject of a sentence, and they find meaningless such expressions as "saving (wasting) time," "real time," "the passing of time," or "being on time." As Evans-Pritchard (1940, p. 103) notes:

> I do not think that they ever experience the same feeling of fighting against time or of moving to coordinate activities with an abstract passage of time, because their points of reference are mainly the activities themselves, which are usually of a leisurely character. Events follow a logical order, but they are not controlled by an abstract system, there being no autonomous frame of reference to which activities have to conform with precision. Nuer are fortunate.[1]

Although it is difficult to say which came first—the Nuer's concept of time or their lack of concern about it—it is clear that a closed-system conception of time produces a quite different attitude toward time than an open-system conception such as we have in our everyday world. As Evans-Pritchard put it, Nuer are fortunate.

But how did we get unfortunate, and why, in contrast to the Nuer, do we worry about "being on time," "saving (or wasting) time," "losing (gaining)

[1]From *The Nuer,* by E. E. Evans-Pritchard. Copyright 1940 by Clarendon Press, imprint of Oxford University Press. Reprinted by permission.

time," and so on? We seem forever to be on time, ahead of time, or behind time, and, more than most others, we seem to be mad about timing things, whether they be eggs, foot races, or orgasms. In truth, some of us seem to live under the **tyranny of the clock.**

To a large extent, we regulate our lives by an abstract system we do not understand, at least not in the same precise sense as the physicist or astronomer does. Nevertheless, we do seem to be very well oriented with respect to time, especially in regard to its working units: hours, half hours, minutes, seconds, tenths of seconds, hundredths, thousandths, and so on. When asked to draw how we order the course of things, we usually represent time as a line running from left to right. History for us always seems to move in a reasonably straightforward sequence of cause and effect, with one problem (society, era) following another to no determinate goal.

It is this last idea, that human history has no definite goal or end point, that gives the feeling that time must be open-ended. Whether it scares us or not, and whether we like it or not, we seldom ask where time began or where it will end. Time is always uncomfortably open, even if some Western religions do suggest a clear stopping point for human history, such as the coming of the Kingdom of God. Even in these cases, God is forever ("He who always was and always will be"), and the same seems to be true for time.

III. IMAGES OF TIME

Because time is so continuously open, we and our ancestors in the Western world have done a lot of thinking about it. Even if we disregard the highly ordered and precise definitions of physical science, it is clear that our literature, our mythology, and even our everyday language are filled with references and allusions to time. The Greeks, for example, had a god named Cronus, who was their symbol for time. And what was this disreputable fellow's claim to fame? Eating his children as they were born until one, Zeus, was strong enough to kill Cronus and take the world and the heavens for himself and his offspring.

Western societies have produced other interesting images of time. One is the contrast between Father Time and Baby New Year. If Cronus cut an

unpleasant figure in the ancient world, Father Time's scythe is just as unfriendly. Since many people fear time, it is not surprising to find that one young woman, when asked for her specific image of time, described it "as a great monster that is always chasing me ... [it's] dark brown, a prehistoric type, somewhat like a buffalo" (McKellar, 1968, p. 158).

When most people are questioned about their images of time, they give rather conventional responses: watches, clocks, hourglasses, and calendars. A few, however, give somewhat more dramatic images:

> "Historical personages dying in sequence; a corridor through which one walks backwards so that the past is before and the future ahead; movement of a long ribbon; a mental picture of sun, moon, and stars; a winged chariot hurrying; the week being imaged as a track with each day divided from its neighbor by a small hurdle" [McKellar, 1968, p. 173].

Among larger cultural images, one of the most frequent is a river or stream. We often talk about the "flow of events" or use some other such figure of speech. In ancient Greece, Heraclitus talked about our experience of time as a river that could never be the same the second time we put our foot in it as the first. For him, as for many of the Greeks, life was constantly in flux, and a river of change was their way of talking about it. The sands of time flow from one part of an hourglass to the other and provide a similar image of continuity-in-change.

History is also said to have a "flow." Here again the idea of continuity-in-change seems to be what the historian is trying to talk about. Depending on where historians sit, they see the river of a single culture (for example, Turkish history) or the rivers of many cultures (for example, the history of Western civilization). Some accounts even lay out these historical streams side by side so that there is one column for the United States, one for England, one for Russia, and so on. Even if these historical rivers join, coalesce, or break apart, historical time is presented as a river or some other straight-line model of change-in-continuity.

The image of a river as expressing our understanding of time has much to recommend it, at least as far as the Western industrialized world is concerned: it changes, it can be measured, it comes from someplace unknown, it flows in the same direction, only a limited section can be seen at one time, and, finally, it is ongoing and continuous. If we look carefully at this list of qualities, and if we go back to the chapter on thinking and creating (Chapter 5), we must be struck by the fact that human consciousness is also often described in terms of living water—compare James' stream of consciousness—as well as by many of this same list of properties. Is all this simply a coincidence, or is there some deeper significance to the fact that the stream of our consciousness merges at points with the river of time?

IV. TIME AND THE CHILD

One thing that is sure in all this discussion of time is that time, as we come to know and live with it, is a culture-bound phenomenon. Not all cultures see time as a river or a line, nor, even more important, as having a clear-cut beginning or end. To look at our (unreflected) experiences in (and of) time independent of the clock, it may help to begin by describing how the infant's lived time changes into the child's sense of time, which, in turn, changes into the adult's concept of time—scientific, historical, and otherwise.

A. Using time words

One way of looking at the development of the child's understanding of time is to trace his or her use of time words. According to standards used in intelligence tests, the "average" child is supposed to know the difference between morning and night by age 5. In addition, he or she is expected to know the days of the week and what today's day and date are at about this same age. By the time our mythical average child is 6 or so, he or she will know the names of all 12 months.

One of the most extensive studies dealing with the young child's ability to speak of time was a doctoral dissertation by Richard Cromer in 1968. Cromer kept a detailed and exhaustive record of what a child named Sarah said from the time she began to speak until she was almost 6. Cromer's work provides natural observations of a speaking child rather than the results of questioning Sarah in the laboratory or even at home.

Sarah began to use time-related words in the interval between 3 years 10 months and 4 years 2 months. At just about her fourth birthday, not only

did Sarah know *yesterday* from *today* and *sometime* from *never*, she also showed good use of such phrases as *a few minutes* and *so long*.

Another way of looking at the child's ability to "talk time" concerns a clear use of grammatical tense. From a careful examination of Sarah's conversations, Cromer found a strong increase in her command of tense at around 4 years of age (from 4.0 to 4.6). It was at this point, for example, that Sarah began to use different time references in the same utterance: "I *will* show you what I *got* for Christmas" (age 4.6). Even more significant are what Cromer called **time reversals**—that is, sentences in which time references were not kept in the same order in which they were experienced. For example, in the Christmas sentence quoted above, Sarah mentions what she is going to do (future) before mentioning what happened a while ago (past).

All in all, the child's sense of time (as reflected in speaking) takes a good-sized jump in the fourth year. Even though tense is not always used correctly, the child can now talk about imagined and real events. Sarah can even combine tenses in the same statement. Taking these findings in combination with those having to do with changes in vocabulary led to the conclusion that, for Sarah, time came into its own around age 4–5.

B. The clock

But what of the clock: when and how do children learn to tell time? Here a set of early studies by Springer (1951, 1952) is quite interesting. In the first of these studies, children ranging in age from 4 to 6 were asked to draw a clock. Results showed that about 41% of the 4-year-olds did not know what clocks looked like, while only 11% did not know at age 5. In a second study, children were asked "Why does a clock have two hands?" For the answer "One is for minutes, one is for hours," the values were 0%, 8%, and 10% for children aged 4, 5, and 6, respectively. Taking into account other answers that were almost as good (for example, "One for hours, one for 2:30, 4:15" or "You need two hands to tell time"), the values were 9%, 31%, and 58%, respectively. Other answers that occurred more than 14% of the time for the 4-year-olds were "One to go one place, one to go another place," "To pass the numbers by," and "It has to, because it's a clock." Probably the most unusual answers were "God thought it would be a good idea" and "Because it's like a girl."

C. The calendar

Children do not know how to deal with the calendar early in life. Although there has been no single large-scale analysis of the child's use and knowledge of the calendar, there have been some fairly well documented anecdotes. Werner (1948) reports that many children believe that calendars "make" time and that if you rip off a calendar sheet—oops, there goes Wednesday (or October, depending on the calendar and the date). Katz and Katz (1928) believe that, for children, calendars are not just things adults use; rather, they are significant in their own right: "Sunday is the day when the calendar is red" or "A weekday is when the number is black." Similarly, a boy as old as 6 years 8 months has been observed to say after tearing off June 30th "Look, no more June bugs" (Scupin & Scupin, 1931).

Although calendars do not mark out the various seasons, it is clear that children know the names of the seasons fairly early, at about age 4 or 5. Knowing the names of the seasons, however, does not necessarily mean that the child understands their ordered relations to one another. As one set of early investigators put it: "The seasons to children seem much less a work of time than a description of concrete things that enter directly into their experiences. Winter really means snow . . . spring, flowers. On a very warm day in March a child may say: 'It's summer . . . it's so hot today' " (Oakden & Sturt, 1922, p. 315).

For the child, even the child of 5, 6, or 7, time is not the continuous system adults understand it to be. It is much more personal, much more individual, much more discontinuous. Events are organized into personal meanings ("Snow equals winter," "June bugs go on July 1"), and events from different units of time need not be seen in an ordered relation to one another. There is no "universal" time for the child, only his or her own personal time organized in his or her own personal way.

D. Personal and abstract time

One of the best illustrations of the difference between a "personal" and an "abstract" sense of time is given in the following observations. Sturt, in 1925, asked children ages 4 through 10 two questions: what time is it for your mother at home now, and what time is it in another nearby city? (Since the children questioned were in Cambridge, the other city was London.) At age 4, 50% of the children answered the first question correctly, while only 14% answered the second correctly. Even by age 10, when all children answered Question 1 correctly, 14% were still unable to get Question 2 right. At age 7, the values for correct responses were 84% and 54%, respectively.

One of the more interesting aspects of these results is that although children may be able to deal with time in a general sort of way so far as their family or town is concerned, they may still be unable to extend the same courtesy to distant towns and distant scenes. If time varies so much between Cambridge and London, it seems reasonable to wonder how children deal with larger hunks of time, such as get talked about in history or geology. Here again work by Oakden and Sturt (1922) provides an answer. In their studies, children were asked to place historical figures in order. For example, a child might be given the following names and dates and asked to place them in a chronologically correct sequence: Attila lived in 438, Philip of Spain in 1585, Nero in 50, and so on. Only 67% of 10-year-olds were able to produce a correct sequence. Not until age 13 were better than 90% of those tested able to do this task correctly.

Even more interesting than correct responses were mistakes: younger children often arranged figures in the order in which they had first heard of them. As one child explained, "I put Robin Hood first because I heard of him in infant school [kindergarten through second grade]. I put King Alfred next because I didn't hear of him until the first form [fourth grade]." Other children produced equally individual responses: one child knew for sure that his "grandmother was a friend of Robin Hood."

On the basis of Sturt's work it seems reasonable to conclude that a genuinely historical concept of time does not emerge in children until about age 11. This finding would seem of some importance for the way history ought to be taught in elementary school. If we are a bit surprised that the child is not able to deal with the idea of history until about age 11, we surely must wonder what a child understands of history in the first through fourth grades. It must be quite difficult for children in these grades to understand a unit on ancient Egypt or even one on Jerusalem at Christmastime. The child's time is clearly not the historian's time, and one can only wonder what sense a young child can make of geological time. In this latter regard, Jersild (1954, p. 469) describes an incident reported by one of his colleagues:

> In a fifth-grade class the children were discussing the Appalachian Mountains, and the teacher took this opportunity to question them on what they had retained from previous discussions of the age of the earth. The question, "How old do you think those mountains are?" stumped the group, until a hardy youngster answered, "I think those mountains came there at about the same time as the Pilgrim Fathers."

For small and not-so-small children, the idea of time is not easy to grasp. Observation reveals two critical ages at which the child comes to handle time and concepts of time. The first of these occurs at between 4 and 5, the second at between 11 and 13. During the first of these stages, the child begins to use time words and grammatical tenses. In addition, there is a beginning orientation toward the clock even though the child will not learn how to tell time for two or three years. The achievements of this first stage include a preliminary ability to deal with time in a way that is at once general, yet personal. The child is able to do things in and about time, but it is always a personal time—a time near at hand. The idea of time as a system is still well beyond the 4- or 5-year-old child.

The child's ability to extend time from the personal to the abstract occurs at around age 11. Only at this age does the child understand that seasonal change is cyclic, that years form a continuous series, and that different locales have one and the same time. Time, as a fact in the child's life, has clearly moved from a personal and narrowly defined event to one of more general significance. Everyone is now seen and understood to live within the same system of temporal reference.

E. Piaget's analysis

Although the child's developing concept of time has been described in terms of two stages, only in Piaget's work does the idea of a developmental stage reach its best and most complete description. As in all his work, Piaget began by observing how infants and children performed in tasks concerning time. His early observations showed that one critical early point occurred between 3 and 4 months of age: only at this age did the infant begin to make

even a brief search for an object that had been hidden. Before 3 or 4 months, infants never seemed to look for an object if it was not in plain view. By about 8 to 12 months, Piaget found, infants would spend a long time looking for a rattle that was not in their crib or for some other favored but now absent object. They had attained object constancy— they knew that an object persisted when it was out of sight.

In addition to results having to do with absent objects, infants also can handle time in terms of their dealings with important people. Piaget observed that 5- to 8-month-old children not only recognized their mother but were able to keep track of where she was in the room even if they had not been looking directly at her. If mother comes into a room and the infant is playing, he or she will note her entrance and then go back to playing. A few moments later, the infant may look to where mother was seated, indicating that he or she "remembers" where mother was and where she is still expected to be. On the basis of such results Piaget described the first period of development as one in which the infant comes to have a "practical ability" in dealing with events that extend in time. This first stage begins at about 3 months of age and continues to about 8 or 9 months.

According to Piaget, the next major period extends from 9 to 18 months and concerns the infant's growing mastery of a series of events extending in time. So, for example, Piaget (1954) reports that his son Laurent, at 11 months 22 days, did the following:

> Observation 54:
> Laurent . . . is seated between two cushions, A and B. I [Piaget] hide the watch alternately under each; Laurent constantly searches for the object where it has just disappeared—that is, sometimes under A, and sometimes under B, without remaining attached to a privileged position [p. 67].[2]

This behavior is in marked contrast to what Laurent did in this same situation when he was only 2 months younger (age 9 months 17 days):

> Observation 44:
> Laurent is placed on a sofa between a coverlet A on the

[2] From *The Construction of Reality in the Child*, by J. Piaget. Copyright 1954 by Basic Books, Inc. This and all other quotations from this source are reprinted by permission.

right and a wool garment B on the left. I place my watch under A; he gently raises the coverlet, perceives part of the object, uncovers it, and grasps it. The same thing happens a second and a third time . . . I then place the watch under B; Laurent watches this maneuver attentively, but at the moment the watch has disappeared under garment B, he turns back toward coverlet A and searches for the object under that screen. I again place the watch under B; he again searches for it under A [p. 53].

Only 2 months earlier, then, Laurent was unable to follow what had happened to an object although he had seen it being placed under location B. What Laurent did not seem to be able to understand at this earlier age was that the same object could be put in a different location a second time. At 11 months of age he is quite able to handle this problem: a second time is now just a second time.

The final achievement of this second phase in the child's ability to deal with time shows that objects are now understood to endure over time and that you do not have to see what happened to know what to do. Consider the following description of Piaget's then almost 20-month-old daughter, Jacqueline:

Observation 64:
Jacqueline watches me as I put a coin in my hand, then put my hand under a coverlet. I withdraw my hand closed; Jacqueline opens it, and then finding no coin, she searches under the coverlet till she finds the object [p. 79].

Although it is impossible to describe in detail all the relevant research dealing with the child's understanding of time, Table 9-1 gives some idea of how time comes to the child and the child comes to time.

What is the overall impression produced by these findings? They suggest that the infant and then the child comes to have an ever-widening ability to do things in and with time. At first, the infant behaves as if he or she were out of time—as if there were only the present. During this period, things and events are experienced as having little or no duration, and the infant seems to live from one event to the next. Slowly, the horizon of time spreads out, so that the 9-month-old child comes to live in a situation in which objects endure and can even be transformed: Mamma is recognized, anticipated, and remembered.

The horizon spreads further as the child comes to search for lost objects and to look in places where an object has been or where it is likely to be. By 2 or 3 years of age, speaking and language extend the child's experience of and in time; by 4, the child is secure in his or her initial world of time.

TABLE 9-1. The Child's Mastery of Time (Based on data summarized from many sources by Orme, 1969, pp. 48–55)

Age	Achievements in time
0–3 months	No real evidence or sense of ordering of events in time.
3–5 months	Searches for absent objects but not for long.
6–8 months	Will look for mother where she was last seen.
8–12 months	Searches for absent object for a reasonable period of time; is unable to look in two places for an object previously found in one place.
11–18 months	Able to follow sequential placements if seen; searches for absent objects.
19–24 months	Searches for absent objects quite persistently; able to understand and deal with sequential placements even when not seen.
24–28 months	Begins use of time words, tense, and order words.
4–8 years	Increase in time vocabulary; tells time by clock, later by calendar; is able to talk of time in an order different from the one in which events occurred; time not yet an abstraction or system, still a system of personal meanings.
8–10 years	Good use of time and time concepts in regard to immediate surroundings, tells time well; is able to see relation of time to space, especially in regard to speed, "faster and slower."
11 years on	Sense of historical and calendar time; beginning of scientific understanding of time as system; understands relations of time to space; can estimate duration of a conversation, time before holidays, and so on; large times and large distances are understood, such as speed of light and its relation to time.

The temporal world of the 4-year-old is personal and idiosyncratic, and the child must next learn not only what his or her time world is like but also that of the society in which he or she lives. In Western society, the child must and does learn to use the clock, the calendar, and the historical era. When this occurs, the horizon is no longer personal; it also extends to the social context. The child can now measure out the grains of time used by his or her society; not only does time come before and after me, it also belongs to my family, my school, and my neighborhood.

The use and idea of time continue to evolve, so that by age 8 or 10 the child is able to deal not only with "slow" and "fast" but with that abstract relation of time and space known as speed. The car goes so-and-so many miles per hour, and I know (or can figure out) that 20 mph is slower than 55 mph. Although the relation of time and space is there and larger numbers mean faster travel, the speed of sound, light years, and other such measurements are still beyond my grasp.

As adolescence approaches, birthdays come to mean more than just parties and visits from friends and relatives: they suggest that I have a personal history. By the same token, my family also has a history stretching beyond my father, mother, and grandparents. My country and even the world have their histories, and even though I do not experience them directly, they exist as a past horizon in my life. Similarly, the adolescent understands the idea of an infinite future stretching away from him or her as well as the existence of an abstract system of time he or she can never reach. The adolescent is located in the situation of time as much as in the situation of space.

With the advent of Time (the formal system), I am likely to become absorbed into some of my own and society's madness about it. No longer is personal time limitless; only Time, the abstract concept, is without end. With this comes the realization of my own death, not only as an abstract possibility but as a distinctly personal event. Similarly, Time becomes a precious commodity. Personal time comes increasingly under the control of Time, and my life is measured out without much help or control by me. Thus, the adolescent's newly acquired knowledge of Time is not a simple blessing. Increasingly more often, personal time becomes less important than clock time. In just this sense does Cronus eat his children and the Grim Reaper come to claim his due.

The one fact that often gets lost in our relations with Time is that each of us has participated in creating the concept of Time within which we live. If we compare this concept with the visual horizon of space, it becomes clear (for both space and time) that a horizon exists *for me* only if I am there to experience it. Although I can no more complete my **temporal horizon** than my spatial horizon, it is important to realize that both depend on me for their existence: no me, no horizon. This means that Time is irrelevant unless I choose or allow it to be relevant. I need not be a slave to the clock, my past, or the future: as a thinking, choosing human being, I can choose when to respond to Time and when not to respond. Here as elsewhere, I can choose to enslave myself to my own creation, or I can recognize it for what it is and live accordingly. Time is neither a Grim Reaper nor a sullen God: it is an aspect of human life that can either support my plans or stand in their way, and it is I who choose which it will do.

V. DISORIENTATION IN TIME

Much of the human world is organized on the basis of time: what day it is, what time we should meet for drinks, what year it is, and so on. Although we are sometimes free not to keep an appointment or not to worry about what time it is, time is one of the major backgrounds against which human events appear, disappear, and reappear. Even if we do not give ourselves over totally to the tyranny of the clock, we, as adults, do order much of our personal lives on the basis of time.

Sometimes, however, when we are confused and lose our way, we come to have a great deal of difficulty in regard to time. No longer is it possible for us to make an appointment that we then have the option of keeping or not keeping. In our confused state, we seem totally unable to deal with the ordered aspects of our human world. In fact, one of the first things a person being tested for admission to a psychiatric hospital is often asked is to tell the examiner the day, the date, the hour, or the year. If the person is unable to answer one or more of these questions correctly—that is, shows **disorientation in time**—the interviewer is likely to recommend admission to the hospital.

Being unable to tell someone the day, date, or year seems a trivial failing. As a matter of fact, many patients have much more profound disorientations in and about time. To appreciate what these are like, we can do no better than to examine the relation of personal disorder to disorientation in time in clearly defined styles of abnormal behavior, such as occur in severe **depression** or **mania**. Although these terms have fairly specific meanings in psychiatric settings, their everyday meanings provide a good idea of the disorders. We can get some understanding of what these disorders involve if we multiply by a good bit our own experiences with depression and excitement.

A. Depression

The clinical picture of a severely depressed person is usually presented as underactivity and a dejected mood. In its mildest form, depression shades into the normal state of discouragement. In more severe cases, underactivity shows itself in slowness of movement and speech. Patients often sit in one place with folded hands and are unable to summon the energy to perform even the simplest of tasks. If questioned, they speak slowly, in a low tone, and with great economy of words. They prefer not to speak at all. Ideas do not come to mind, and problem solving seems almost impossible. As one patient described it, "At these times my brain feels paralyzed; I have not the strength or ambition to do anything . . . I have the impulse to act, but it seems as if something shuts down and prohibits action."

The dejected mood may take the form of unrelieved sadness. The patient cannot be cheered; everything looks horrible. If he or she does talk about troubles, a picture of utter hopelessness is presented. The patient often believes he or she has committed unforgivable sins and is responsible for all the misery in the world. The patient is full of self-accusations, and the one theme that comes up over and over is the patient's wickedness and the expectation that dire punishments must surely come. There is so much self-blame and so much hopelessness that the possibility of suicide must always be considered (paraphrased from White, 1964, pp. 315–316).

B. Mania

The manic, in contrast, shows an incredible excess of excited activity. Outstanding among these is talking, which never seems to stop. The rapid flow of words is full of puns and word play. In short units, such talk seems perfectly coherent, although change from topic to topic takes place constantly. Patients are also quite distractible. Whatever they see or hear may divert their attention completely and may cause them to make personal remarks that often take visitors by surprise: "My, how gray your hair is" or "Your pants really need to be pressed."

There is constant restlessness. Patients are always busy, never tired. They sleep little at night and begin the day long before sunrise. If there are not enough ways to use up their energy, they may burst into shouts and song, smash furniture, or do sitting-up exercises.

The prevailing mood is joyous elation. Patients are full of confidence and are quite willing to take their projects to the White House, to Wall Street, to Hollywood, or wherever else they believe the projects will most rapidly reach their undeniable conclusions. This mood easily reaches an unpleasant arrogance, especially toward those in authority. If the patient's thoughts take a sexual turn, he or she will show a lack of restraint. All impulses come to immediate expression in words and acts. Any kind of restraint is extremely uncomfortable because of the pressure to activity (paraphrased from White, 1964, p. 520).

C. Experiences of time in depression and mania

How is time experienced by the depressed or manic individual? Here are the words of a severely depressed patient:

> "The hands of the clock move blankly, the clock ticks emptily . . . they are the lost hours of the years when I could not work." . . . "The world is all of a piece and cannot go forward or backward; this is my great anxiety. I have lost time. . . ."
>
> On looking back, on recovery, the patient said: "It seems to me that January and February passed just like a blank, all of a piece, at a standstill; I couldn't believe time really went on. As I kept working and working and nothing came of it, I had the feeling that everything was going backwards and I would never be done" [Jaspers, 1968, p. 84].[3]

Time, for this patient, existed only in the past; the

[3]From *General Psychopathology*, by K. Jaspers. Translated by J. Hoenig and M. W. Hamilton. Copyright 1968 by the University of Chicago Press. Reprinted by permission.

present was still, never seeming to move forward toward the future. The patient behaved (and talked about his experiences) as if he did not want time to go on—as if, for him, time stood still and the future was totally closed down.

But not only the future is at issue. There seem to be similar disorders in regard to the past and the present. As the psychiatrist Straus (1963) noted, the clinically depressed patient experiences the past and the present in a way that can be summed up best by the patient who said "There is no beginning and no end to things." What this means is that things that happened this morning are forgotten, while events of yesterday are as remote as those of years ago. Tomorrow does not exist, and the patient is unable to mark out time in units of any kind. The clock, our instrument of time, is distorted, and it is not uncommon for the hands of the clock to move backward or for its face to have eyes that figure strongly in the patient's hallucinations. For the severely depressed, the basic structure of time has broken down, and one can find no place for oneself within the void of this formless structure.

But why does this come about: why is the depressive lost in an unaccented situation having none of the familiar landmarks known to us all? Straus argues that the central aspect in severe depression is that the person no longer experiences any possibility of personal change, no longer has any "possibility of becoming." Under this loss of personal becoming, the depressed person is at a standstill. Any projection into the now-empty future is impossible, for I, as patient, am unable to give any definition or direction to my future.

We might therefore expect the depressed patient to be thrown back on the past; yet here too there is no refuge, for it was in the past that the person lost his or her way. Although how and why the person got lost varies, the past always seems to pronounce a terrible judgment for things done (or not done). The depressive patient is trapped: if bad things were done or good things left undone, then some punishment awaits in the future. The past—done or undone—is an area of failure that can be set right only by terrible punishment. As one patient saw it: "I will be condemned to live, covered with vermin, in a cage with wild beasts, with rats in the sewer until I die. The whole world knows of my crimes and knows that punishment awaits me" (Minkowski, 1970, p. 180).

Thus, the future is closed on the basis of the past. If the future is unbearable because ruin will surely occur, the past is unbearable because it is the source of failure. As I have no future, I have no past. My present is overwhelming. I move as if clothed in wet sand, and the sand closes in, destroying familiar landmarks that might have helped me determine where I had been or where I might go. Without past and future—without being able to come from someplace or get to someplace—I exist in an unyielding and lifeless situation. For the depressive, the past "is experienced as unpardonable guilt, the future as inevitable catastrophe and the present as irreparable ruin" (Straus, 1947, p. 255).

Severe depression sometimes alternates with excited mania. If the depressive barely moves, the manic moves all too frequently. If there is one word to capture how the manic behaves, it must be the word *NOW*. The manic wants to do everything now: to talk, to run, to jump, to defecate, to scream, to do, to *do*, TO DO!

Like the depressive (and perhaps for many of the same reasons), the manic seems to have lost contact with the past and the future: time seems to have shrunk so that all that exists is the present (Fraisse, 1963, p. 184). Although being able to live fully in the present is often a good and healthy way to be, the manic lives in a present that has been torn out of the usual fabric of time. It is an "instantaneous present" that has no location in the "before" and no projections into the "after." What the manic patient lacks is an "unfolding" in time (Minkowski, 1970), a sensible location in the flow of things.

The world of the manic, like that of the depressive that it sometimes becomes, is a shrunken world—a world of the instantaneous present. Although a person in the manic state may appear more in contact with the world than a depressed person, both have lost their way. In neither case is there a reasonable ordering of and for the person in time. The sense of order (and even of security) that an integrated experience in time provides is missing: time and the person have collapsed.

If there is one thing to be learned from this destruction of a sense of time, it is that time is a human response to the world. As such, it is sensitive to all the problems, disorientations, and successes of the person. If we are whole and well functioning, our sense of time forms a sensible horizon that

stretches ahead of and behind us. Under these conditions, we have a past and a future that seem to be
given all at once. As T. S. Eliot wrote:

> Time present and time past
> Are both perhaps present in time future
> And time future contained in time past.
> ....
> Time past and time future
> What might have been and what has been
> Point to one end, which is always present.[4]

Under the conditions of normal life we always
seem to deal with all of time at one and the same
time—that is, as horizon in which past, present,
and future are always present. When we reflect or
think seriously about time, we divide it into fixed
units that can be used by everyone. We call these
units seconds, hours, milliseconds, days, or whatever, and we know that each of us in our particular
social world will come to the same evaluation of
time when we use these units. Consequently, each
person comes to orient himself or herself to the
world in approximately the same way. For this reason we are also able to agree on how fast some
event happened, how long it took, as well as to plan
for a determinate future and describe a common
past. The **domestication of time** for public use, both
social and scientific, represents a great advance that
the disoriented among us cannot always share in.

The collapse of a temporal world so common in
disordered lives can occur at both reflected and unreflected levels. Not only does the patient do things
that take no account of time, he or she also is unable to deal with time as an ordered and ordering
system. Being out of time, unfortunately, is not only
symptomatic of a more general disorder, it also contributes to further collapse. Losing one's horizon of
time, at either a reflected or an unreflected level,
only increases personal disorder further. To lose
our way in time is to lose one of the basic structures of human life: where there is no present, past,
or future, can there be anything at all?

VI. PERCEPTION OF TIME IN ADULTS

Clocks notwithstanding, it is quite clear that time
does not divide itself neatly into equal units even
for the most sane among us. "My, how time flies

---

[4]From "Burnt Norton" in *Four Quartets*, by T. S. Eliot.
Copyright 1943 by Harcourt Brace Jovanovich. Reprinted
by permission of Harcourt Brace Jovanovich, Inc. and Faber & Faber, Ltd.

when you're having a good time!" is something we
often say, and it is quite true. What we are doing
and how we are or are not enjoying ourselves determine how long we feel we have spent in doing this
or that particular activity. A few years ago there was
an unkind maxim suggesting that if you wanted to
have a longer life, all you had to do was to stand in
line for something you wanted to do but never do
it. Waiting in line for a movie is surely one way to
drag out our experience of time.

Although time may seem to go slowly during boring experiences (such as riding 14 hours in a car between Atlanta and Miami), there is the paradoxical
experience that in looking back on such experiences a week or a year later, the amount of time
spent in traveling does not seem long at all. If it did,
we would probably never subject ourselves to the
trip again. Time during the trip also does not flow
at the same rate; somehow the beginning and the
end of a trip (say, the first and last 2 hours of our
14-hour drive) go the fastest, whereas the middle
goes more slowly.

If, however, we have an exciting experience, such
as seeing an engaging hour-and-a-half play or movie, the time "seems to fly by." Yet rapidly passing
experiences have a way of becoming longer when
we describe them to someone else or think about
them again by ourselves. At this later time we are
able to recall so many details and so many exciting
parts that we feel sure the play or movie must have
lasted longer than it did according to our clock. The
enjoyable event, which was so very brief in the experiencing, seems, from a later point of view, to
have lasted so very long. In contrast, the dull,
dragged-out event seems short in retrospect—surely peculiar things to happen to so orderly an aspect
of our world as Time.

A. Laboratory work on the perception of time

Because such experiences (and many others) are
common in everyday life, it is not surprising that research psychologists have tried to examine in the
laboratory how people estimate time. The general
method is to ask people to estimate the length of an
interval that is either empty or filled with one or another activity. One of the earliest studies of this type
was done by Axel (1924), who asked subjects to estimate the amount of time they had spent in doing
five tasks: (1) estimating an unfilled interval, (2) tapping with a pencil on a sheet of paper, (3) crossing

out various designs, (4) solving an analogy, and (5) completing a series of figures. Results were clear in showing that subjects overestimated empty-time and tapping tasks by about 2 sec (the time seemed longer, "went more slowly"). The amount of clock time by which they underestimated the remaining three tasks varied from about 5 sec for crossing out designs to about 9 sec for completing a series of figures. (For example, a 30-sec figure-series task was estimated to have taken only 21 sec.)

Fortunately, Axel asked his subjects how they came to their estimates. What he found, to take the most extreme case, was that subjects filled empty time by counting numbers or by making rhythmic body movements. Since Axel's subjects were unable to use a similar strategy for the more complicated analogy and figure-series tasks, they reported that they used the "amount of mental effort involved," or, more simply, they guessed. For the crossing-out task, 81% of the subjects reported counting the number done and then assuming a constant value (say, 1 sec for each item). Using this approach, the interval was estimated in terms of how much work was done.

From this and similar studies, Fraisse (1963) concluded that time was over- or underestimated on the basis of how the subject figured it: if the subject figured it on the basis of a repetitive and rapid event (body movements, number of taps), time appeared long. If the subject estimated it using a non-regular event, such as solving a difficult series of figures, time appeared short. This interpretation suggests that "marking time," by whatever regular means this might be done, leads to an overestimate of time (judging 20 sec as 30), whereas working at a unified task (which cannot easily be "marked out") leads to an underestimate of time (judging 30 sec as 20). Anything that serves to organize a task into a single meaningful unit for the person reduces our judgment of how long it took. Perhaps, for this reason, a long automobile trip seems long because we mark it out in terms of the most regular of units—minutes, miles, and hours—whereas an interesting movie or play seems short because all aspects of such an event come to form a single, unified whole for the person experiencing them.

B. Experiences of time during uncontrollable events

Whether we are bored or excited by something we do is only one of a number of factors affecting how long a particular experience appears in retrospect. One of the more interesting observations has to do with accidents. Although there are only a few scattered reports, one general consensus is that everything moves quite slowly during a severe accident, particularly if you cannot do anything except wait until it is over. As one observer put it, "I had the impression that the car turned over in slow motion" (McKellar, 1968, p. 159). In this situation, our usual experience is that once the car gets out of control, we become spectators to an event over which we no longer are able to exercise any control.

Other results also support the idea that spectators at an event, even if involved in the outcome, experience a "lengthening" of time. In 1916, for example, Myers asked a number of spectators at a basketball game to estimate the time from the beginning of the game until a serious accident occurred. According to the clock, the accident took place 6 min 15 sec after the opening tipoff; 80% of the spectators overestimated the interval. The average judgment was 10 min 7 sec, or about 3.9 minutes longer than it was according to the clock. Fraisse (1963) reports that in a series of studies dealing with estimates of how long a movie sequence was, subjects overestimated the interval on the order of 100%. For example, for one film running 2 min 47 sec, subjects' estimates averaged 5 min 54 sec; for a second film running 3 min 14 sec, the estimate was 7 minutes. Such estimates suggest that when you are a spectator, time goes by very slowly.

There are, however, a few observations dealing with accidental situations in which people can do something about their fate—that is, they are participants, not spectators—and here results show that time is under- rather than overestimated. Fraisse (1963) describes two such incidents. The first was a mine accident in Courriers, France, in 1906; in the second, three brothers were buried under the rubble of an earthquake in Italy. All the miners, on emerging from 3 weeks in the mine shaft, spontaneously volunteered that they were glad to have been rescued after "only 4 or 5 days." Similarly, all three brothers were quite happy to have been trapped for "only 4 or 5 days"; they had been trying to dig out for 18 days.

Thus, it is not the occurrence of an accident that is crucial in determining how long you will estimate an experience to have lasted; rather, it is whether you could only wait for it to run its course or were able to do something about it. Whenever you are a spectator rather than a participant, time "goes slowly." Only when you can do something in an emotionally demanding or dangerous situation is time experienced as going by more rapidly. It is not the situation of an accident that is critical; rather, it is our field of possible moves in dealing with that situation. The greater our possible (and actual) actions, the "faster" time goes; the more restricted our possibilities, the "slower" time goes.

C. Experiences of time in altered states of consciousness

A different set of observations concerns the nature of our experiences in and of time in what can best be called **altered states of consciousness** (Tart, 1969). These include (among others) states produced by alcohol, drugs, sleep, hypnosis, Zen meditation, and mystical experiences. Most investigators (such as Ludwig, 1969) have found that one of the major defining properties of altered states of consciousness is a "distorted time sense": clock time is sometimes experienced as speeded up, sometimes as slowed down, sometimes as reversed, and sometimes even as irrelevant. Occasionally, the same experience may exhibit two, three, or even all four of these possibilities.

Consider an analysis of Zen meditation offered by Deikman (1963). In his attempt to understand this process, Deikman taught four colleagues to perform a Zen concentration exercise for 12 sessions. At the end of this period, most subjects reported striking changes. Some of these had to do with the object concentrated on (a blue vase), others with experiences of pleasure evoked by the object, still others with experiences of time. Although not all people experienced similar changes in their perception of time, most did report surprise at how much or how little clock time had passed. "This sense of time having passed quickly occurred despite . . . occasional . . . feelings during meditation that the session had been going on for a very long time" (Deikman, 1963, p. 334). Perhaps the most accurate statement that can be made is that time varied: the whole episode seemed to be both shorter and longer than subjects expected (or wanted) it to be.

A second, somewhat special situation in which changes in a person's experience of time are reported concerns the use of marijuana. In an anonymous article written for Charles Tart's book *Altered States of Consciousness*, the writer noted that under the

influence of marijuana events seemed to take up more clock time than he or she had expected. For example, this person reported that Bach's First Brandenburg Concerto appeared to last over an hour; the record takes 25 minutes of clock time to play. Neither the music nor the fantasies that accompanied it seemed to move at a faster pace; they were experienced as moving at their own proper rate. The overwhelming impression was that clock time had slowed down while "internal experience continued at its ordinary rate. There was no impression of speed or rapidity, only that the time available to the user was magnified" (Anonymous, 1969, p. 339).

People who habitually use marijuana often report that they are supersensitive to events going on around them—whether these events concern ideas, an awareness of one's own body, or more perceptual phenomena such as the vividness of a particular color. The general consensus seems to be that the person is more attuned to his or her experiences in the present than to the implications of present events for either past or future actions.

Similar to meditation, marijuana seems to induce experiences that are quite present-centered. Taken together, these observations suggest that any state in which the person is directed to the here-and-now of his or her situation is likely to induce a change in his or her ordinary perception of clock time. This conclusion applies equally to other altered states of consciousness, including those experienced under hypnosis, while dreaming, and so on. Each of these conditions seems to produce a strong orientation to the present, with this orientation serving to break our usual relationship to past and future and, through them, to our usual measure of Time: the clock.

A somewhat more common example of being totally immersed in an ongoing activity is artistic or scientific creation. Although the role of dreaming and extraordinary imagery in creative thinking was described in Chapter 5, no attempt was made to describe the person's experience of time during the creative episode. Many creative thinkers and artists experience what Doyle (1976) has called a period of "centration," which she has described as follows:

Actions and thoughts interact directly with the problem . . . without being distracted or narrowed by other concerns. . . .

These are wonderful times; they have been described as moments of full spontaneity and freedom. But freedom and spontaneity do not come from an absence of structure or direction to the flow of thought . . . but from such total concentration on a task . . . that all resources are directed toward it. The person is freed of self-consciousness . . . and can respond fully and freely . . . to whatever he is centered on. . . .

During the period of total centration . . . there is a center toward which all activity flows, and . . . that center is . . . those ideas-in-flesh developing in relation to that initial intuition which started the creative episode. . . . This is the magnet that attracts and patterns all those resources which become available.

These periods are recalled as periods of incredible joy, even ecstasy. Thought and action [become] as smooth and flowing as a dance, and ideas seem to emerge out of nowhere. The work seems to create itself, because the creator's picture of himself as working does not obstruct the flow between himself and his work [pp. 15–17].

What is important about the period of centration is that it removes the person from the world of everyday experience and places him or her squarely within the world of an ongoing problem. During this period, many thinkers later report, they were "out of time," and they were surprised to find just afterward that so much clock time had passed. What is clear here, as elsewhere, is that being totally immersed in a present-centered situation alters our ordinary relationship to clock time. This conclusion should not be surprising, for whenever a person "enters" an altered state of consciousness, he or she (by definition) has left the world of everyday reality. This means that the ordinary supports and roles of that world are abandoned as the person gives himself or herself over to a different style of being in and dealing with the world.

The person in the midst of one of the various states described above is not "out of time"; he or she is simply in time in a different way. Whereas realistic, third-person demands for order and regularity make linear, equal-unit time a valuable part of our everyday world, highly centered first-person experiences make a more personal description of time a necessity. When ongoing, present-centered events are the focus of our experience, clock time is often irrelevant. Where present, ongoing activities are primarily a means to some past memory or future event, clock time can provide a useful measure of our experience. That personal and clock time can sometimes be out of synchrony should come as no surprise: after all, it is the person who defines what is or is not a relevant standard of measurement, and

this is no less true for time than for any other significant aspect of human living.

D. Age and the perception of time

One of the more peculiar aspects of our everyday ability to estimate time is that time seems to move more slowly for children than for adults. Even at age 20 or 25 we can all sense that the four years it took us to get through high school plus the first two years of college went by much more quickly than the first six years of elementary school. As long ago as 1890, James noted that the same duration of time (say, the six years of our two different schoolings) seemed much shorter when we were older than when we were younger. The speed with which time passes continues to accelerate, so that our parents do not exaggerate their experiences when they tell us that "it seems like only yesterday you were a little child."

Many explanations have been proposed to account for this phenomenon. The French psychologist Pierre Janet (1877) thought it was a ratio effect: 6 years out of 12 is a larger proportion than 6 out of 20; hence the first 6 ought to seem longer than the second. William James explained it in terms of vividness and habit: In youth, events are vivid and exciting; hence everything has more detail as the person lingers over each event. In old age, few events strike us as noteworthy. For this reason there is nothing to linger over; we know it all, and it is all of a piece. Finally, Lecomte du Nouy (1936), drawing on the fact that physical wounds heal much more rapidly in infancy and childhood than in old age, suggested that we need larger "quantities" of time when older to do the same work; hence six years for the faster-living child amounts to more time, biologically and psychologically, than six years for the slower-living adult.

These are all interesting speculations, yet Fraisse (1963, p. 248), in evaluating these hypotheses, asks:

> But what connection do these facts have with the appreciation of time? It is quite possible that in old age, decreased biological activity makes us register fewer changes and, by the same token, days and hours seem to be shorter by contrast than before. In our opinion, however, these are only basic tendencies which are corrected, all through adult life, by our social habits. Although old people all agree that time passes more quickly than it used to, it is nonetheless true that there is hardly any change in their objective time judgments. Psychological time is doubtless conditioned by biologi-

cal time, but one cannot be equated with the other, for the psychological processes are more complex, since they involve all the functions: contrast, automatic corrections, habit, etc. [p. 248].[5]

Here, as elsewhere, the facts reveal a complex human event. It is the total human being who experiences and estimates time, no more or less than any other phenomenon. And here, as in all other aspects of a life, it is difficult to disentangle the various threads that enter into the human experience of time. Rather, **time**, the quantity estimated, and **Time**, the abstract system, both emerge from our experiences in, of, and with lived time. The construction of human time is not to be found in physics or philosophy; instead we must look to that aspect of our experience in which we always live—the present. Only in this way can we even begin to have a chance at describing how it is that human beings come to some understanding of time.

VII. THE PSYCHOLOGICAL PRESENT AND THE CONSTRUCTION OF TIME

The present is one of those aspects of human life everyone recognizes as a universal human experience. However, no one seems able to describe it very successfully. Perhaps this explains why we have so many names for it: James (1893) gave it two names—the *specious present* (after an earlier philosopher named Clay) and the *sensible present* (after James himself); Piéron (1923) called it the *mental present*; Koffka (1935) the *actually present*; and Fraisse (1963), most recently, called it the **psychological present** or *perceived present*. No matter how we name it, there is a "present" to our experience, and we do well to let William James help us understand it.

A. James' analysis

As James so correctly noted, we cannot grasp the present when we turn our attention to it. Just as resting places in the stream of our conscious life (ideas) are more easily noted than changes (transitions), so too are the ends of an interval of time more noticeable than the "passage of time" itself. We are able to mark a transition from one moment to the next only because we perceive a change. For

[5]From *The Psychology of Time*, by P. Fraisse. Copyright 1963 by Harper & Row, Publishers, Inc. Reprinted by permission.

this reason, the psychological present cannot be a fixed bit of clock time; instead it is better thought of as an interval just long enough for a meaningful part of the task in progress to occur.

Although James gave his psychological present an upper boundary of a few minutes, it is probably better to leave it more open than that. What seems more important is that the "psychological present" not be fixed as a unit of so-and-so many seconds or minutes; rather, its size must be allowed to vary with the task and our interest in it. Although it may be scientifically uncomfortable to deal with a unit that changes from task to task as well as from person to person, it seems we must do so. Even if the psychological present never turns out to be of constant size, it is significant and real for the person living it.

The interval James described is empty of content. Yet the truth is that the present teems with activity and that many times the end of one "present" is defined by changing the object of our interest. During the time that you speak and I try to understand, there is a single present for both of us. If I listen only halfheartedly or if you "do go on," the unit changes. To be sure, during our talk I am usually not aware of any interval, although I could be should you ask "How long was I talking?" or "Did I talk too long?" We usually pay attention to what we are doing, not to time; "what we are doing" appears as a figure against the quiet background of time—a background that is silent until we are asked to turn round on it and summon it for inspection.

As in all acts of reflecting, we can talk to someone else about a particular moment only after that moment has passed. The present we talk about is not the present we talk in. It was present until we started to talk about it, but it is now (as we talk) a "recent past." For this reason, James (1890) called the present "the specious or apparent present" because it could never be present at the same time it was being talked or thought about. James proposed that we consider the present we live in an unreflected, uncatchable aspect of our experience.

All our actions take place in the present, and it does not seem wrong to say that we live in the psychological present and that it is the past and the future we must worry about. After all, past and future can be experienced only in the present. The idea of time, then, must grow in two directions from the present, and our task must be to describe exactly which events in the present help extend it to times past and times future.

There seem to be only two sets of alternatives: remembering for the past and anticipating, planning, or problem solving for the future. Although we can talk and even think of time as a line running from past to future through present, the truth seems to be that past and future are only past and future for us in the present. The idea of Time (note the capital *T*) has somehow or other to be derived from the unreflected present.

The process of coming to Time involves several phases. First there are the interconnected psychological processes of remembering and anticipating. Remembering seems not only to help us order and be ordered by our experiences, it also helps us note that the present "time" was preceded by a preceding "time," which was preceded by an earlier one, and so on. Anticipating and its more formal counterpart, planning, extend our projects ahead of us. Whenever a project comes to some conclusion, we must surely realize that when we first planned it, the "present of its being finished" was not yet upon us. Planning builds the future out of both the present and the past. Only if we are able to remember an hour from now that an hour ago we planned to do what we are now doing is it possible for us to plan again, secure in the possibility that the future will become the present and then the past.

B. Time, the abstract system

Remembering gives us a past; planning, a future—but where do we get the idea of Time, the abstract system? There can be only one answer: from reflecting on our experiences in time and then trying to formulate some general understanding for them. Abstract thinking allows us (in the present) to hover over *the present, the recently present,* and *the soon-to-be-present* and to order these times one after the other. Perhaps the best way to think of the whole business is in terms of a picture such as Figure 9-1. The total area falling under the boxes provided by abstract thinking gives us some idea of the ordering of our lives in time as well as some feeling for the ground against which this ordering occurs.

So far we have described a very limited bit of Time: the recently present, the "presently" present, and the soon-to-be-present. To come to some more conclusive picture, we need to consider a larger segment. One of the most obvious ways to do this would be to drop the three boxes labeled 1, 2, and 3 in Figure 9-1 and subsume them under a larger unit, perhaps something called "personal time." "Personal time" includes those past and future projections of our actions that form a unit for us. Among the more important of these is the continuing nature of our own unique stream of consciousness: the "where" we have come from and the "where" we are trying to get to.

Because it seems so reasonable to tie all the threads of personal time together in a single image—that of a line or a river—we tend to extend our ideas beyond the boundaries of our own unique bit of personal time. When we do, we come to imagine the possibility of a Time that we are un-

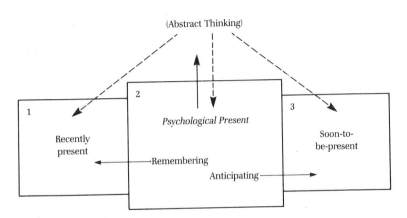

Figure 9-1. Steps in the development of an abstract concept of Time.

able to experience directly: a Time that came before us and a Time that will come after us. Since we are much better at looking backward than ahead, we tend to systematize our backward glances into reminiscences and then more carefully into history. The line can then be extended to a time when there were no people, and here we have geology, paleontology, and so on. Similarly, we are able to project a sense of the forward direction: first in the sense of personal planning, then of social planning, and finally of a study of the future. Religions have long been concerned about the "end of days"; scientific theory has likewise come to be concerned with the future and what will happen to our earth and solar system.

Thus, from a small interval of the directly experienced present, human beings build up a concept of infinite Time. But the job is not yet done: we are not content to develop the idea of Time and let it go at that. What is yet to be done is to subdue Time for our purposes, to make it "work" for us. This was done by developing a usable system of measuring and ordering Time. We divide Time into equal units (seconds) that can be added (60 seconds make a minute), divided (1/1000 of a second is a millisecond), and so on. In this way we produce something direct experience could never have provided with any degree of certainty—an equal unit of Time that is now available to meet our needs and our purposes.

Because clock time meets so many needs so well, we require our children to learn how to deal with it and to adjust their lives to it. This learning does not occur immediately, for in order for any measure of Time to make sense, the child first must have had the experience of living in time. Not until the child is 11, 12, or even 13 does Time, the abstract system, emerge.

For the adolescent or the adult, the achievement is so complete that we tend to lose sight of the fact that Time was constructed out of experiences that preceded our understanding of Time as a system. Only occasionally does this fact of construction return to us, and then only because personal time is out of phase with clock time. When this happens, we are often so "brainwashed" as to imagine that the clock's minutes and hours are somehow more real than our minutes and hours. We should not be surprised that equal clock units sometimes go slowly and sometimes rapidly; rather, we should be surprised that the clock is so indifferent to our lives.

The world we have carved out of time is not always helpful to us, for sometimes we let the mechanism run away with us. When this happens, we no longer adjust the clock to our lives, but only adjust our lives to it. About all that can be said then is what Humpty-Dumpty said to Alice about using words: "The question is which is to be master— that's all." In regard to time, the question is "Which is to be master: me or my clock?"

VIII. SUMMARY

Time is both a system of reference and an ongoing human experience. To miss this fact is to give too much importance to the clock and the calendar and too little importance to our own first-person experiences in and of time. Although it is too arrogant to say that we create time, what is true is that we are always free to create our own unique way of measuring it—if indeed we choose to measure it at all. It is absolutely necessary for human beings to concern themselves with time, but reflected, linear Time is not the only choice we could have made.

Different cultures deal with time in one of two ways: as an open system or as a closed system. In an open-system approach, time is thought to be continuous, irreversible, and capable of being measured in equal units (seconds, hours, years). Such an approach leads to an image of time as a river or a stream. There is much to recommend this image, for it suggests that Time can be measured, that it comes from (and gets to) someplace unknown, and that only a limited section of it can be seen at any one time.

A closed-system approach to Time does not allow accurate measures, nor does it encourage planning. In societies following a closed system, there is no drive to plan because success is not seen to be the result of planning or work. Time is not considered a precious commodity and is most often dealt with in terms of the significant events in that society; for example, in Nuer society time is established around the routines of raising cattle.

Within an open system such as ours, different ages take on a special significance: entering our teens, becoming 40, retiring at 65, and so on. As we move from childhood through retirement, we tend to divide our lives into units relating to years of service or training or into experiences such as apply to academic or military organizations. Progress within these latter two systems is marked by formal changes in status and rank. These changes—whether formally organized or not—are called "benchmarks" and are used not only to indicate personal progress but to suggest that an orderly approach to change is not only possible but desirable.

Because any human reaction to time is culture-specific, it is necessary to approach the developmental pattern by which children come to understand Time within a particular culture. In Western culture, the infant's lived time changes into the child's usable sense of time, which, in turn, changes into the adult's reflected concept of Time—scientific, cultural, and otherwise. As revealed in many studies, the child's sense of time first comes into its own at age 4 or 5, and it is only then that children learn to use clocks and calendars effectively. For children of this age, however, units of time do not so much mark time as they describe aspects of experience: winter means snow; spring, flowers; summer, heat; and fall, leaves.

Until age 7, time is not the continuous system of reference adults understand it to be; it is experienced as personal and discontinuous. Sturt's work indicates that a genuinely historical concept of Time does not emerge in children until about age 11. By 12 the child has a good idea of time appropriate to most situations. The temporal horizon ceases to be merely personal and now extends to social and historical contexts as well. No longer is personal time limitless; only Time, the abstract concept, is without end.

Disorientation in time—the inability to relate one's personal experience to a more general experience of time—is often symptomatic of personal disintegration. In such cases time is experienced as collapsing. For the severely depressed patient, time becomes blank: past and future are remote and inaccessible; the present, detached and empty. Time no longer produces a sensible structure within which the person is able to order or orient his or her life. The depressed person no longer experiences any possibility of change: the future is closed on the basis of the past, while the present remains insufferable, unyielding, and lifeless.

The manic, like the depressive, has lost reference to a meaningful past and a meaningful future and comes to live in a present that can only be described as instantaneous. Time no longer evolves from past to future but is an overwhelmingly "present" present, demanding constant activity. For both the depressive and the manic, the usual ordering system of Time has collapsed, as have other aspects of the person's life.

Although we order time in terms of units by which we then evaluate duration, the experience of time for each of us is always personal. Measured time, although composed of equal units, may be experienced either as rapidly moving or as dragging along slowly. What we are doing, how involved we are in the activity, how much we are enjoying ourselves all influence our perceptions of a particular event in time. There is a paradox here: events which we enjoy greatly and which pass quickly seem much longer when we describe them in retrospect; conversely, seemingly long, dull, dragged-out events are later remembered as being shorter than we originally experienced them to be. In accidents and other such emergencies, time passes more quickly when we can do something to escape than when we must merely wait for the situation to improve.

Time is also experienced as having varying rates in altered states of consciousness, such as those brought on by creative centration, meditation, drugs, or hypnosis. In all these experiences, the person's primary focus is on the present. Although events do move sensibly within that present, the person seems to lose his or her ordinary relationship to clock time. This is as it should be: to be in an altered state of consciousness means, by definition, to relate to the world in terms other than those ordinarily experienced and used.

Time seems to pass much slower for the child than for the adult. Janet attributed this difference to the proportion of one's life involved: a year is a larger proportion of a child's life than an adult's. Lecomte du Nouy believed that the same clock time is biologically and psychologically longer for children.

The best-developed description of how we come to Time was offered by William James, who based his analysis on the fact that any experience I might have in the present is impossible to grasp if I turn my attention specifically to it. Rather, human beings can only mark the transition from one moment to the next when they perceive a change. The psychological present, as James called it, is not a set unit containing so-and-so many minutes: its size varies with the task and my interest in it. The psychological present is never present to reflection; our ideas about it can only be derived from unreflected experiences in some prior present. Remembering the past and anticipating the future are psychological processes by which we are able to extend time present to times past and times future.

In addition to remembering and planning, there is also the process of abstract thinking. This process allows us simultaneously to hover over the present, the recently present, and the soon-to-be-present. When we do this, we have begun to construct an abstract (and somewhat linear) approach to time that ultimately will lead us to the more abstract understanding of Time as an open system. What must always be remembered, however, is that we know and experience time long before we are able to measure it. In this way it is possible to see the measurement of time for what it is: a human construction designed to help order human life. If we forget this, the clock is likely to get the upper hand, and all we can do then is to bow obediently before the tyranny of measured Time.

IX. GLOSSARY OF IMPORTANT CONCEPTS

Altered states of consciousness. States that differ from those usually experienced in the world of everyday reality. Included are states such as those induced by creative work, meditation, drugs, sleep, alcohol, and hypnosis.

Benchmarks. In this chapter, units of time by which individuals monitor progress within some social system. Although these events concern time, their primary importance is their subjective content—for example, how long until the TB patient will leave the hospital.

Closed system of time. A system in which accurate measures of time are rarely kept. Time is seen as a series of repetitions: day and night, change in the seasons, birth and death, and so on. Cultures using such systems often have little or no concept of cause and effect.

Depression. A psychological condition of unremitting sadness. A severely depressed person experiences time as standing still. Straus explained this experience as a loss of any possibility for becoming and a loss of meaning for one's past.

Disorientation in time. A frequent aspect of various pathological conditions (see **Depression** and **Mania**).

Domestication of time. Organizing the flow of events in time for societal purposes.

Mania. A psychological condition of extreme excitement and agitation. Time is experienced as a series of instantaneous presents ripped from a sensible unfolding of events in time.

Nuer time. A closed system of time used by the Nuer tribe of north central Africa. For this group, time is dealt with (when it is) in terms of the daily and seasonal routines appropriate to their herds of cattle.

Object constancy. As identified by Piaget, the idea that objects endure in time; acquired sometime in the first year of life.

Open system of time. A system in which Time is seen as a linear progression without a specific beginning or end. For such systems, Time is often described as a stream or river.

Psychological present. The time it takes for a meaningful segment of a task in progress to occur; the point from which one remembers and anticipates. It is sometimes also called specious present, sensible present, mental present, actually present, or perceived present.

Ratio effect. Janet's explanation that time seems to pass more quickly as we get older because each year is a smaller proportion of our total age.

Temporal horizon. The sense of having a personal past and a personal future that results from an individual's experiences in (and of) time.

Time. (1) Spelled with a lower-case *t*—one's experience of personal time; the quantity estimated. (2) Spelled with a capital *T*—the abstract system of time; clock time.

Time reversals. References to experiences that are not kept in order of occurrence. The ability to talk of experiences this way is first established at 4–5 years of age.

Tyranny of the clock. A Western attitude toward clock time in which it is seen as more important than lived (or personal) time.

X. SUGGESTED READINGS

Major sources

Fraisse, P. *The psychology of time.* New York: Harper & Row, 1963.

James, W. *The principles of psychology* (2 vols.). New York: Dover, 1950. (Originally published, 1890.) Chapters 9, 15.

Merleau-Ponty, M. *The phenomenology of perception.* London: Routledge and Kegan Paul, 1962. Part 3, Chapter 2.

Secondary sources

McKellar, P. *Experience and behavior.* Harmondsworth, England: Penguin Books, 1968. Chapters 5, 6.

Orme, J. E. *Time, experience, and behavior.* London: Iliffe Books, 1969.

10

Milestones in Contemporary Human Life

In the north central part of the city of Oslo is a large and beautiful park. There you can find the usual assortment of things that go into city parks anywhere: trees, benches, shady walks, children's playgrounds, and so on. What is unusual about Frogner Park is that it also has 250 stone and bronze statues by the Norwegian sculptor Gustav Vigeland. And these are not just your ordinary, decorative outdoor statues designed to make the park a pleasant place to stroll through on a summer afternoon. Instead, these pieces of sculpture were all designed to present Vigeland's unique perspective on that most complicated of topics, the human life cycle. For this reason, a stroll through Frogner Park is just the right place to begin thinking about significant milestones in contemporary human life.

On entering the park, you pass through a large stone-and-iron gate. After a walk of 150 feet or so, you come to the first major group of sculptures: the Bridge of Bronze. On this 180-foot bridge are over 30 groupings of bronze statues depicting various human activities. Once across the bridge, you walk through an open, grassy area of some 200 feet to a second major grouping, called "The Fountain and the Maze." The Maze, a mosaic floor decoration, surrounds a stone-and-bronze fountain containing 20 subgroupings of sculpture, all placed around a 70×70-foot fountain. From the fountain, you pass through another open, grassy area, ending at a granite platform called the "Middle Terrace." From there, your walk leads you to the main sculpture grouping in the park: a 55-foot carved stone monolith surrounded by 12 major groups of statues. There, at the base of the Monolith, by turning around, you can see the ¾ mile or so of sculpture and park you have just walked through from the main entrance.

If this description makes the park seem on a grand scale, it should, for the park *is* on a grand scale. Its gates, statues, fountains, and bridges all deal with nothing less than the complete cycle of human life. Because it is difficult to convey in words what the park and its statues look like, two pages of examples of Vigeland's work are presented. One purpose of this chapter is to provide an overview of

human life from birth to death, and statues were chosen with this goal in mind. They are neither the best nor the worst of Vigeland's work: they are simply meant to provide a vivid set of images to go along with the more wordy prose of the psychologist.

Frogner Park represents one man's attempt to answer the question of what are the significant events in contemporary human life. For Vigeland's answer to be of more than just artistic interest, however, we must expand it into two somewhat more precise questions: (1) what are the significant developmental changes that occur in human life, and (2) at what ages do these events occur?

Before these questions can be pursued, the lesson taught by Chapter 9 must be emphasized once again: Clock time and human time are not equivalent. Each individual lives out his or her relationship to time in a special and unique way. Any attempt to describe the overall course of human development must be understood to represent no one's life exactly and everyone's life to some degree. If we take any single approach—Vigeland's included—as "the normal" course of development, we are in for trouble. What this chapter will do, instead, is to provide a general overview of some of the more significant events in contemporary human life. It is not a recipe for human growth and development.

I. SOME CONTEMPORARY MILESTONES

One way to find out about significant milestones is to ask people what they think are the most important events. Figure 10-1 presents a fairly representative set of answers to this question given by 150 undergraduate psychology students at the University of Tennessee. Because so many of the students complained that they were unable to give an exact time (within one year) for some of the events they thought should be included, these items were marked with an asterisk. There was also some argument, from both the political right and the political left, that certain events (such as sexual intercourse or marriage) were optional and that one could be a perfectly good human being without going through

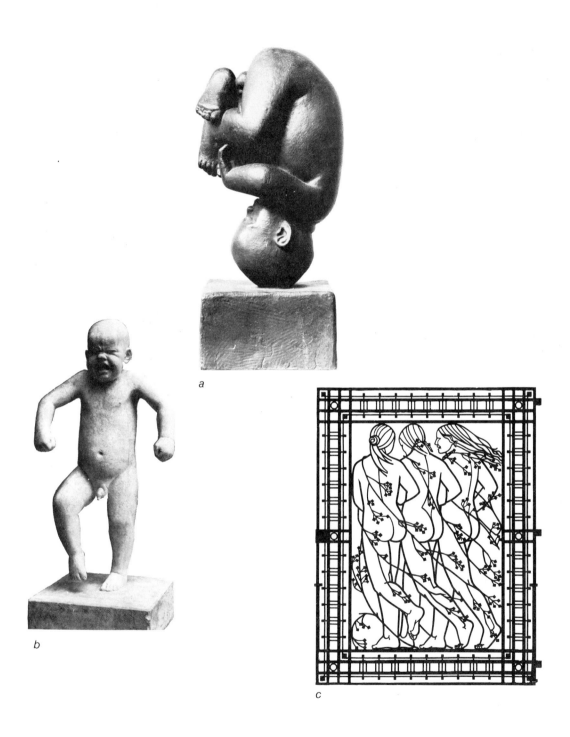

(A) *The Fetus*. The Vigeland Park, Oslo, Norway. (B) *Angry Boy*. The Vigeland Park, Oslo, Norway.
(C) *Three Women*. Wrought iron gate in the Vigeland Park, Oslo, Norway.

(D) *Man Fighting with Lizard.* The Vigeland Park, Oslo, Norway. (E) *Man with Small Child in His Arms.* The Vigeland Park, Oslo, Norway. (F) *Old Man and Woman.* The Vigeland Park, Oslo, Norway. All the above sculptures are by Gustav Vigeland and are reproduced by permission.

this or that particular experience. Events such as these are italicized in Figure 10-1. Finally, the students agreed that it would do little violence to what they were thinking if events were grouped into three categories: body development, intellectual development, and interpersonal, or social, development.

One of the most obvious things about Figure 10-1 is that events in the three major categories cluster around different chronological ages. The majority of body events occur early, many before the teenage years are completed. Many of the more dramatic intellectual milestones take place between ages 4 and 12, and most significant interpersonal events take place after the bodily and intellectual ones have occurred. The starred events—that is, events difficult to place at a precise age—occur relatively later in the human life cycle and seem to relate more to the interpersonal/social aspects of living than to the intellectual or body spheres.

From even this simple study, two conclusions suggest themselves: one, that it is meaningful to mark off human life into "units" of one or another type; and two, that such units are often not very precise. Such results also suggest that if we want to

develop a precise theory of development, it would probably be best to start with body-maturation events. Any attempt to describe the unfolding of human life on the basis of social/interpersonal factors would seem to have to be a good deal more vague to account for all the events that might (or might not) occur. In addition, social/interpersonal events seem to occur at less predictable ages than bodily events.

II. THE CONCEPT OF A DEVELOPMENTAL STAGE

Each of these three categories—the maturing body, the developing intellect, and the person in society—has given rise to a different and far-reaching understanding of what it means to be human. Each of these approaches—one by Sigmund Freud, one by Jean Piaget, and one by Erik H. Erikson—has had to deal with some of the same data that are presented in Figure 10-1, and each of these theorists has used some of the same concepts in coming to his own unique conclusions. The one concept that is general to all three theorists is that of a **developmental stage**. Freud described such stages in terms of psychosexual factors; Piaget, as stages in the de-

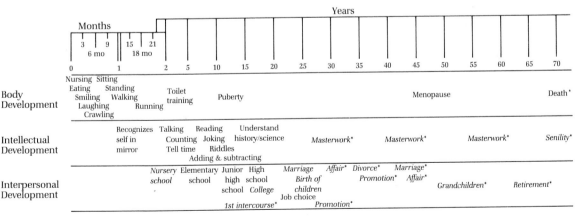

Figure 10-1. Milestones in contemporary human life.

velopment of intelligence; Erikson, in terms of psychosocial factors.

What exactly is a developmental stage, and how should it be understood? One way to think about a developmental stage is from the point of view of a theorist trying to understand, reflectedly, the overall course of a human life. From this point of view, a stage represents one way of grouping together events a particular theorist thinks make a meaningful unit *for him or her*. For example, organizing the milestones of human life into bodily, intellectual, and social groupings is one attempt to categorize some of the more obvious milestones. Categories, however, need not be "real" in any first-person sense of the term—that is, to the person whose life is being categorized. They are theoretical fictions, useful in organizing the mass of information that scientific and everyday observation provides about the developing human being.

There is, however, a deeper sense in which a category—developmental stages included—can be used, and this concerns the first-person point of view of the individual whose life is being considered. For a stage to be personally meaningful (not just theoretically useful), the world of the person in question must be different in one stage than in another. For example, if we divide human life into the stages of infant, child, adolescent, and adult, we must assume that the world of the infant is different in some important first-person way from the worlds of the child, the adolescent, and the adult. Under this condition the idea of a stage ceases to be a useful third-person fiction; instead it represents an attempt to describe a change in the living perspective of the person being talked about.

A. Movement through stages

One of the most important problems in looking at human life in terms of developmental stages is to describe how (and why) we get from one stage to another. The general argument seems to be that we move from one stage to the next for one of two reasons: one, because it is our "nature" to become interested in different things at different times in life; two, because there is some contradiction or, to use a more general term, some crisis in how we do things and how we feel they might be done differently. To take the first of these reasons first: Erikson, following Freud, is insistent on critical periods in human development. For Erikson, as for Freud,

such periods are the biological "givens" of being human, and they occur at certain critical ages in the development of the child and adult.

Each aspect of the adult has a critical time of emergence. This means that the child comes to stand, walk, talk, regulate his or her bowels, and so on only when he or she has reached the **critical period** appropriate for that behavior. For many of the things children come to do on their way toward becoming adults, everything works out quite well: both the child and the world are glad of the child's achievements. Some events, however, do not make the society glad—for example, the infant's tendency to defecate whenever he or she (rather than the parent) wants. Under this condition conflict must arise as society and infant collide over the "when" and the "where" of moving one's bowels. At this point in the infant's life there is some need for a change (no pun intended) if the child is to adapt to his or her world, and here the idea of a crisis as crucial for change comes into play.

Not all crises are as dramatic as that between an infant, his or her bowels, and society; rather, many subtle crises also occur in regard to the child's more general way of dealing intellectually with the world. Consider the following example provided by Piaget (1951). A child of 2 years 7 months saw her sister dressed in a new bathing suit and cap and asked her mother quite seriously: "What's that little baby's name?" Even after the mother explained that it was the child's own sister wearing a new bathing suit, the child still asked (pointing to the child's face): "But what's the name of that?" As soon as her sister again put on her dress, the child noted very seriously, "Why, it's Lucienne again."

Although, depending on mood, we find this example cute or odd, the questioning child did not notice anything wrong with her analysis: different clothes, different children. There will come a time when the child will recognize that it's Lucienne in the bathing suit as well as in the dress: it will be difficult for the child to hold onto the idea of different dress/different child in the face of continued dealings with Lucienne and her changing wardrobe. What must happen is that the child will experience a contradiction and will have to resolve it by coming to some new understanding: people who change clothing are not different people. Intellectual contradiction forces reevaluation, and such reevaluation pushes the child from the stage of seeing something as different every time she encounters it to the stage of knowing that people (and objects) have a permanence to them that is unchanged by changing clothes.

Moving from one stage to another depends both on the developmental level of the child and on his or her ability to experience a contradiction between how he or she is now doing something and how it might be done. In "intellectual" growth, such contradictions involve me with others. Although *crisis* is the word usually applied to issues concerning the social world, Riegel (1975a, 1975b) has suggested that this word has far too many negative implications to describe the situation correctly. For this reason he proposes that we look at "developmental crises" not as uninvited catastrophes but as challenges to development.

B. Developmental stages and cultural history

In all this talk about stages, we seem to have blissfully disregarded time and human history and assumed that what is a stage of development to us in the 20th century must also have been a stage to our ancestors in earlier historical eras. This may not be a valid assumption. Consider the stage of "childhood." It seems reasonable to expect that childhood is (and always was) a "meaningful stage" from the point of view of both the observer and the child (and his or her parents). Despite the obvious nature of childhood to our 20th-century eyes, there are strong historical reasons for assuming that human beings have not always seen childhood as a distinct stage in human life. There are two sources of evidence: one, paintings made of children in the 14th through 17th centuries; and two, analysis of child-rearing practices in these same centuries (Van Den Berg, 1961).

As an example of what went on in painting, look at a picture painted in the 17th century entitled *Boy with a Dog*. The boy in *Boy with a Dog* is nothing like the way we would think of a boy in the 20th century. Quellin's boy is a miniature adult in dress and bearing. Clearly, the child and the adult were not as different from each other then as now. As an antidote to Quellin's 17th-century view, look at the wickedly funny painting by the contemporary Belgian artist René Magritte. Childhood is now seen as a separate stage, even if Magritte does have more to say about the matter than just that. Although some 17th-century artists did represent infants and children in a manner somewhat closer to our own understanding of childhood and infancy, the general social attitude was that there was little distinction between child and adult.

Van Den Berg makes this same point even more emphatically in *The Changing Nature of Man* (1961). As he notes, the philosopher Montaigne advised the Countess of Curson to teach her child philosophical discourse "almost from the moment it was weaned." Montaigne went on to caution her that philosophy was much to be preferred to Boccaccio's *Decameron*—that bawdy 14th-century work we aren't allowed to read until college. John Locke, who was fairly astute in other matters, noted: "If I misobserve not, children like to be treated as rational creatures."

Although Van Den Berg then goes on to list the staggering achievements of preteen writers, philosophers, soldiers, and even kings, perhaps the best example of how little the young child was perceived as different from the adult is an anecdote told of a 6-year-old princess in the 17th century. A seemingly cruel hoax was played on the young princess: she was told by some members of the court that she was pregnant.

> The little one denied it, but the joke was carried further. When she woke up one day, she found a newborn baby in her bed, put there by the ladies-in-waiting when she had been asleep. She was surprised, and said that it was apparently not only the Holy Virgin to whom a thing like that could happen. Everybody was delighted at this remark, and she got lying-in visits, and the queen herself offered to be the child's godmother. Eventually she was asked who might be the father. The little one thought deeply for a moment, and then replied that only the King and the Count of Guiche could be considered, for, said she, "Only those two had kissed me." Nobody considered this joke the least improper; in all probability because in those days there was nothing improper about it. But imagine such a joke being played on a six-year-old child today! Bad effects would be unavoidable [Van Den Berg, 1961, pp. 31–32].

The point of Van Den Berg's story is not to destroy the "innocence" of childhood but to show that human ideas about human life have been quite different at different points in history. The human being is always a part, as well as an originator, of the historical process, and how we look at one or another aspect of culture changes over historical eras. There is another point to Van Den Berg's story:

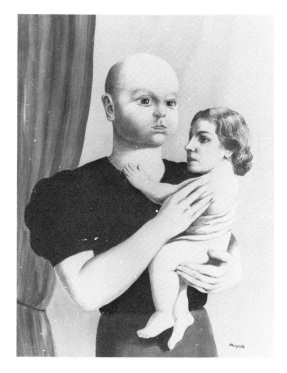

Figure 10-2. Changing images of childhood. Left: Erasmus Quellin, *Boy with a Dog* (*c.* 1634), Koninklijk Museum, Antwerp. Right: René Magritte, *The Spirit of Geometry* (*c.* 1937), The Tate Gallery, London.

to raise the possibility that human beings are different at different times in history. What it means to be human changes from generation to generation, so that a caveman is not a simple historical variant on a Renaissance man, nor is the Renaissance man simply a variation on contemporary man. The human being is not static, and each historical period gives rise to its own unique type of person.

Accordingly, we have to place the whole of human lives within the proper time frame of their own century and their own culture. Although we may find stages helpful in talking about the cycle of human life, we must also recognize that any set of stages is probably most appropriate to a particular time and a particular place. Any description of a human being made at the end of the 19th century may be somewhat less correct today than it was even the short 80 or so years ago when it was written. It is a sad fact of intellectual history that the more accurate a particular description of a society is at one period in history, the sooner it will be in-

correct in the next. The reason is that the more correctly a thinker diagnoses a society's ills, the sooner that society will take pains to remedy them. In our own day, have we not changed dramatically in, for example, our public attitudes toward premarital sex since a short 75 years ago?

Any description of the human life cycle is correct only for the "us" who live here and now. We must never expect any description to pierce, once and for all, the mystery of what it means to be human. We should be satisfied with the idea that even sensitive thinkers of the stature of Freud, Piaget, and Erikson will probably be right only for the time being.

III. THE CHILD AND THE THREE WISE MEN: FREUD, PIAGET, AND ERIKSON

A. Freud

The 20th-century intellectual world belongs in large part to Sigmund Freud. Everywhere we turn—literature, advertising, drama, psychology, sociology, philosophy—Freud is among the most important thinkers of our contemporary world. Yet what is not often kept in mind is that Freud was a clinical practitioner and that many of his most original ideas came from his work as a therapist. Even Freud noted that his own self-analysis was one of the most significant achievements in his life, for not only did it teach him about himself, it also gave him a good deal of insight into the more general nature of human beings.

Freud's role as a therapist should never be overlooked in presenting his approach to human development. The people Freud saw were almost all suffering from difficulties in their current lives. When he examined these difficulties carefully, he found that many of them had roots in the patient's experiences as a child. On the basis of long clinical work, Freud concluded that not only was the child father to the man, but how we functioned (or did not function) as adults depended on how we and our families had dealt with a small number of critical periods Freud came to call **psychosexual stages.**

1. The psychosexual stages.   Although different lists vary, the major psychosexual stages turn out to be six: oral, anal, phallic, latency, puberty, and genital. These stages (and their ordering in time) are charted in Table 10-1. For the moment consider only the first two columns. Of the six stages, five are begun before age 13. For the remaining 55 years or so, Freud saw only one or, at most, two stages for the human being to pass through.

The first two stages are easy enough to understand: they deal with the child's attempts, both successes and failures, at being fed and toilet-trained. Both stages are usually completed before the child is 3 years old. Dividing the **oral stage** into two parts means simply that before an infant gets teeth, his or her primary way of dealing with the world is by taking it in, the model for this behavior obviously being nursing. The eruption of teeth is important because the mouth, which up to this time has been the source of so much pleasure, suddenly gives pain. A breast-fed infant may bite the mother during this stage, possibly bringing the infant into conflict with her for the first time. In addition, babies become very fussy at this age and can be quite difficult for the caregiver.

The **anal stage** is almost self-explanatory: this is the first time society makes a strong and insistent demand on the infant to conform—to do his or her social duty, if you will. Before this time, infants have not had society define any part of their world as consistently bad or unpleasant. By age 1½ or 2 (depending on the attitudes of the society and of the caregiver), children learn that feces (a part of themselves) are bad, dirty, or both. This may come as a bit of a shock, for if children have ever played with their feces before this age, it likely was not at all unpleasant: for the infant, feces are warm and intimate, not bad or dirty. The strength of social evaluation can nowhere better be seen than in the fact that among the earliest words an infant will use are *dirty* and *bad,* and they usually get applied to that stuff "I just made."

The third stage carries three names, **phallic** being the most general one. *Phallic* is, of course, the adjective derived from the word *phallus,* meaning

TABLE 10-1. Freud's Psychosexual Stages

Age	Stage	Significant Individuals Involved	Thought Processes		Psychic Structures		
0–1½	Oral (a) Incorporative (b) Biting	Caregiver	Primary		Id		
1½–2½ +	Anal	Parents		Secondary		Superego	
4–6	Phallic (Oedipal, Electra)	Parents and siblings					Ego
6–12	Latency	Peers, "chums"					
12–17	Puberty	Self, peers					
18 +	Adult (Genital)	Opposite-sex partner, children, social and work peers.					

"penis." Unfortunately, the word *phallic* and one of the other names for this stage—*Oedipal*—are male-oriented terms and exclude females. For this reason a third term, *Electra*, has been given to this stage with specific regard to little girls. Whatever we call it, the third stage deals with the family romance, the original triangle. The terms *Oedipus complex* and *Electra complex* come from Greek mythology. Oedipus was a royal character who unknowingly killed his father and then married his mother; Electra was the child of King Agamemnon who incited her brother Orestes to avenge Agamemnon's murder at the hand of his adulterous wife and her lover.

Each legend revolves around the sexual attachment of the male child to his mother or of the female to her father. Does Freud mean to suggest that these stories are more than just 2000-year-old legends? As a matter of fact, yes. Freud found in these two classical dramas support for the idea that a child's first sexual attachment is always to the parent of the opposite sex. Although this may sound scandalous at first—and Freud suffered greatly for his views when they were first presented in the early part of this century—such a state of affairs does make sense. Whom better to love in all ways than your parents, and from whom would it be better to learn that you cannot have everything you want than from your own father (in the case of a little Oedipus) or from your own mother (in the case of a little Electra)?

The family romance can come to only one resolution: mommy gets to keep daddy or daddy gets to keep mommy, and both give Oedipus or Electra a bit more room to move around in. Although no one ever quite solves the problem of separating love from sex in the context of the family, we all do have to put it aside and get on with the business of discovering what the world is like and of finding someone else (aside from mother and father) to deal with in a sexually loving way.

And get on with the business of life we do, particularly in the next stage. For the child, as well as for the parents, the period from 5 or 6 until 12 is one of the most conflict-free times in life. Behind us are the problems of *giving and getting*, as in the oral stage; behind us are the problems of *holding on and letting go*, as in the anal stage; and behind us too are the problems of family intrigue and conflict. Ahead of us is the **latency stage**—six years in which we experience the world with our peers and in which we become competent in how we move, how we think, and how we are.

Unfortunately, this fine set of days comes to an abrupt end and many of the conflicts that we felt were safely behind us suddenly reappear with the onset of puberty. What a strange and eerie time: everything changes so fast that all the solutions of childhood problems that worked up to this point in life seem undone, and a whole new set of solutions has to be renegotiated between me and my world. For a year or two (sometimes even more) I am overwhelmed by the reemergence of oral, anal, and phallic problems. In addition, I am stumped by questions of "Who am I?," "Whom can I trust?," "How do I relate to my parents?," and "Why is everything that I ever thought I knew useless now?" For the adolescent, according to Freud, all the unresolved and half-resolved conflicts of the preceding years resurface, and the growing person becomes temporarily overwhelmed and lost.

For most of us, adolescence does come to a more successful conclusion than ever seemed possible when we were in the midst of it. This is accomplished, according to Freud, not because we really ever resolve our earlier and continuing conflicts but because we learn to live with the paradoxes of human social life. One reason this learning occurs is that we change some of the things that satisfy us. The process of **sublimation** (as Freud called it) allows us to gain socially acceptable gratification for childish wishes that stay unresolved. For example, the child who never learned to deal with his anger or hostility may, according to Freud, become a football player or surgeon—occupations in which the force to hurt is rigorously controlled and used in a contest of skill or to help others become well.

Although there are a great many other mechanisms serving to transform the will and drive of the infant and child into the purposeful directedness of the adult, the important point is that all the strands (resolved and unresolved, helpful and debilitating) combine to fashion a unique adult. At this point, the person enters the final Freudian stage, that of **genitality.** *Genitality* is a strange word. The dictionary gives us two meanings: one pertaining to generation and the other pertaining to the organs of generation. Since we have read and thought about Freud enough by now, we know that he intended the second meaning.

In one sense this is quite true. For Freud no life

is complete or can be considered even partly successful without having children. Yet might Freud not also mean that I must be productive in my own right, that I must do work that I can come to see as valuable? If so, to be satisfied as an adult in this final stage (and for Freud, this is the best we can hope for) is to be productive in both love and work. There is a curious lack of sensational sex in this last stage. To be sure, the mature person is able to behave sexually with someone else. But this is not enough. Let one of Freud's disciples tell us what Freud thought about the business of maturity:

> Freud was once asked what he thought a normal person should be able to do well. The questioner probably expected a complicated answer. But Freud . . . is reported to have said: "Lieben und arbeiten" [to love and to work]. It pays to ponder on this simple formula; it gets deeper as you think about it. For when Freud said . . . love *and* work, he meant a general work-productiveness which would not preoccupy the individual to the extent that he loses his right or capacity to be a genital and a loving being. Thus we may ponder, but we cannot improve on "the professor's" formula [Erikson, 1963, pp. 264–265].[1]

Freudian psychology has often been accused of being more concerned with sickness than with health. Although it is quite true that Freud was a therapist, it is also clear that we do need to worry about what the quality of adult life might be like if not encroached upon by childish perceptions and bargains. The answer that Freud gives is not one of unbridled lust, but rather one stressing the very human capacities to accept the joys and constraints of a personally and socially productive life: "to love and to work."

2. Primary and secondary process. The remaining two columns in Table 10-1 are "Thought Processes" and "Psychic Structures." Since differences between **primary-process** and **secondary-process thinking** have been handled in Chapter 5, we need only remind ourselves that primary process (the chaotic, non-time-oriented, non-space-oriented way of thinking and dealing with the world) is with the child from the very first and that

[1]Reprinted from *Childhood and Society, Second Edition, Revised*, by Erik H. Erikson, by permission of W.W. Norton & Company, Inc. Copyright © 1950, 1963 by W.W. Norton & Company, Inc. and The Hogarth Press, Ltd. This and all other quotations from this source are reprinted by permission.

only later does more orderly and rational activity develop. From the second or third year of life, all of us are capable of moving back and forth between these two types of thinking. Sometimes, as in dreams or in people under pressure, such shifting results in unclear and disorganized thinking, which is most noticeable when primary process dominates unchecked by secondary control. Sometimes such shifting will result in innovative, or at least original, thinking, when we use primary process in producing novel combinations and then secondary process in checking them out as possible or not. In any case, from earliest years on, we live in the invigorating tension created by shifting from primary to secondary process and back again.

The change from primary to secondary process is not the only, or even the most significant, tension we have to experience as children and adults. Rather, the most significant tensions to be dealt with come from conflicts between the biological aspects of the person (such as can be seen in sexual and aggressive behaviors) and the social aspects of the person (such as can be seen in our conscience, or sense of morality). To dramatize the constant friction between these two aspects of our life, Freud chose to talk about a battle between two entities within the person known as the **id** and the **superego**. *Id* is the name Freud gave to our biological strivings, whereas *superego* represents an early (and continuing) form of human conscience.

Both these fictional structures are "with" the child very early on: the id from birth and the superego from about the time of toilet training, or at just that time when society makes its first real demands on the infant to control himself or herself. Because they come on the scene so early, the id and the superego are really too "immature" to deal well with each other or with the world. For this reason, a third "actor" comes into the picture: the ego. The ego's job is to mediate between its two harsh masters, the id and the superego. It does this by delaying the id from getting everything it wants when it wants it. Such delaying tactics seem to pacify the strict superego of the young child. For life to continue, however, the id must be satisfied at least some of the time. For this reason, the ego constantly mediates between the id, the superego, and the world in order to maximize the probability of getting some goodies for the id.

The ego is best characterized as the "executive

director" of the person. In other contexts we might want to call it the rational part, the personal executive, or something of the sort. The important thing to keep in mind is what Freud was trying to do by inventing these structures: to describe the developmental course of a human being as he or she progresses from a basically illogical and asocial biological entity to a fully functioning, rational/social/biological being. He chose to do this by emphasizing the increasing role of secondary process in human thinking as well as by vividly describing the emergence of the ego. In so doing, Freud also meant to remind us that no matter how much we may want to see ourselves as rational, orderly, and planful adults, we must always remember that chaotic and powerful forces go along with our rationality and our planfulness. There is a tension to human life, and whether we talk about it in terms of a conflict between styles of thinking or among fictional parts of the personal psyche, we must always recognize that to experience tension is to be alive.

B. Piaget

Freud described childhood largely from the recollections of suffering adults seemingly trapped by their bodies and their social traditions. Although we do not know for sure whether Freud directly observed many children other than his own, we do know that he came to describe children and childhood on the basis of how adults talked about their own childhoods rather than on the basis of direct observation of children.

1. Piaget as observer.   With Piaget the story is different. Most of his long and productive scholarly life has been concerned with a sympathetic and almost intuitive attempt to understand the first-person world of the infant and the child. This is no accident, for his early interest was in biology, particularly in the study of animals in their natural environments. With his Ph.D. behind him at age 22 (in 1918), Piaget went off to study psychology, ending up in 1920 at the Binet Laboratory in Paris. The Binet Laboratory was where (for better or worse) the very first IQ tests were developed. As the new Ph.D. in the laboratory, Piaget was assigned the "menial" job of finding out at what age children were able to do various tasks.

At first this did not seem a very interesting job.

Fortunately, Piaget was not an ordinary research worker. He soon became quite fascinated not with the correct answers to a question but with the incorrect ones. As an example of what might happen, consider the following case. An 8- or 9-year-old child was asked to work on the following problem: Suppose you have three girls, Edith, Suzanne, and Lillie, and suppose that Edith has lighter hair than Suzanne and darker hair than Lillie. Which of the three girls has the darkest hair: Edith, Suzanne, or Lillie? One child answered: "You can't tell, because you said that Edith has the lightest hair *and* the darkest hair" (Piaget, 1926, p. 88). Although we may think the child missed the point, it is quite clear why the child had so much trouble: he was simply unable to consider Edith in connection with *both* Suzanne and Lillie and was therefore unable to construct a single order capable of describing the overall relations among the three girls—namely, that Lillie has the lightest hair and Suzanne has the darkest.

In the hands of a lesser observer than Piaget, the child's incorrect answer might have been dutifully recorded and forgotten or simply left as "one of those things kids do." Not so with Piaget; from this and similar observations Piaget concluded that the reason the young child could not order all three girls on a single dimension was that 8- to 9-year-old children are not yet able to hold in mind at the same time two aspects of a situation. The child of this age is only able to see Edith "as lighter" and Edith "as darker" and for this reason is unable to order all three girls by hair color.

In looking at a great many answers given by children to this and other problems, Piaget found that the same wrong answer often was given by many children of the same age but not by many children either younger or older. These observations led Piaget to conclude that the ways children think at different ages are qualitatively different. He also came to conclude that IQ tests could not tell us much about human intelligence other than to put people in rank order. For Piaget, the most important problem of intelligence was to discover the various stages of intellectual growth, not how to order people from "best" to "worst." In setting himself this task, Piaget realized from the start that the infant's thought was not the child's thought and both were not the adult's.

2. The developmental nature of intelligence.
With this change of direction, Piaget stopped trying to describe intelligence in terms of objective tests administered under rigorous third-person conditions. Instead, he tried to enter the first-person world of the developing child so as to describe what it might be like. No more would it be enough to say that Child A, age 10, was able to do so-and-so many tasks that other 7-, 9-, or 11-year-olds could or could not do. Rather, the task now became describing how the world looked to Child A at age 10. The growth of intelligence was not so much a piling up of an ever greater number of facts and skills; instead it consisted in developing new and different ways of looking at and understanding the world and its problems. Children not only are often unable to solve certain problems (Is Suzanne lighter-haired than Lillie?); at a certain age they are also unable to see why a given problem is a problem at all.

Intelligence—the person's ability to deal with the world in a consistent and effective way—develops in stages. For Piaget, each of the major stages of intellectual development is the conclusion of a continuing process of organization and reorganization of what the child knows and can do. In this way, the child carries forward everything he or she has learned in an earlier stage to the presently emerging one. As with Freud, it would be wrong to take the chronological ages offered by Piaget as absolutely correct for each and every child. Instead they are meant to provide very general landmarks for what a child of 2, 6, or 15 might be expected to know. What is absolute is the order of stages: for Piaget it would be impossible for a child to do Stage III thinking without having passed through Stages I and II.

3. Stages in intellectual development. The major stages of intellectual development, according to Piaget, are four in number and occur (roughly) at the following ages: (1) sensorimotor intelligence, birth to 2 years; (2) preoperational intelligence, 2 to 6 years; (3) concrete operational intelligence, 7 to 11 years; and (4) formal operational intelligence, 12 years and onward.

Three of the four stages (excluding the preoperational stage) are named for the intellectual process that has recently become available to the developing person. To understand exactly what this means, consider the very first stage, **sensorimotor intelli-**

gence. To most of us, the newborn infant seems small, fragile, and passive, a helpless lump of stuff quite unable to deal with its world in any reasonable way. Here, Piaget the observer shows how wrong we are. Consider the following exciting bit of behavior by Laurent (one of Piaget's children, whom he observed) in the second day of life: "Laurent again begins to make sucking-movements between meals. . . . His lips open and close as if to receive a real nippleful but without having any object. This behavior subsequently becomes more frequent" (Piaget, 1952, pp. 25–26).[2] Although this does not seem like much—perhaps at best a confirmation of Freud's oral stage—Piaget believes it is significant because it shows that the infant, even as young as 2 days, has a basic tendency to deal with the world. Since this observation occurred shortly after Laurent had eaten, it seems unlikely that he was sucking because he was hungry. Because it was only Day 2 in the life of Laurent, it also seems unlikely that sucking had been "reinforced" by having been fed: learned responses seem to take longer than that to get learned. The conclusion must be that even as young as Day 2, the infant shows a basic directedness (intentionality) toward the world and that this directedness does not have to reduce a bodily need or to be the result of learning. As Freud assumed and Piaget found, the mouth is a crucial body area for the very young infant, and it is not surprising that the infant first deals with the world by means of his or her mouth.

If infants exhibit a tendency to direct themselves toward the world as early as Day 2, it should come as no surprise that much of their early learning concerns their increasing ability to act intentionally—that is, to explore and deal with various aspects of their early world in a meaningful way. Piaget reports the following observation of his child Lucienne at age 3 months 16 days: "As soon as I suspend the dolls [from the bassinet] she immediately shakes them, without smiling, with precise rhythmical movements with quite an interval between shakes" (1952, p. 158). At age 7 months 13 days:

> I present a box behind my [hand] . . . so that he cannot reach [it] without setting the obstacle aside. After trying to take no notice of it, Laurent suddenly hits my

[2] From *The Origins of Intelligence in Children,* by J. Piaget. Copyright © 1952 by International Universities Press, Inc. Reprinted by permission.

obstacle hand as though to remove or lower it. I let him [lower the hand], and he grasps the box. I recommence to bar his passage, but I use as a screen a sufficiently supple cushion to keep the impress of the child's gestures. Laurent tries to reach the box, and, bothered by the obstacle, he at once strikes it, definitely lowering it until the way is clear [1952, pp. 217–218].

There can be no doubt: Laurent continuously seeks mastery over his world. At just past the middle of his first year of life, he, like other infants, shows dogged determination and a good deal of personal order in getting exactly what he wants.

If children seem competent in expressing their intentions during the first year of life, they are surprisingly incompetent in dealing with certain types of problems. Look at the two pictures presented in Figure 10-3. The upper picture shows a 7-month-old infant focusing on a toy elephant placed directly in front of him or her. So far, so good: the infant shows clear bodily orientation toward his or her world. When, however, a barrier is placed between the infant and the toy (in the lower picture), the infant directs himself or herself toward some other aspect of his or her world and does not seem particularly disturbed. "Out of sight, out of mind" seems to be the rule describing how the 6- or 7-month-old infant deals with objects.

This is a curious state of affairs: an infant who is sometimes perfectly capable of behaving in a directed and purposeful way is totally unable to maintain directedness toward an object when that object is removed from the infant's line of sight or touch. Piaget concluded that objects have no permanence for an infant of this age unless they can be seen directly. For the 6- or 7-month-old, objects do not exist independently of the infant looking at them. By 10 months or thereabouts, Piaget found, an infant will continue to look for a hidden object, such as the toy elephant, but will not continue the search for very long. In contrast, the 14–16-month-old will make every attempt to look for and get an object hidden from view.

With the infant's greater ability to understand that objects have a permanence to them, the infant begins to sense that he or she too endures. The discovery of **object permanence** leads to the discovery of Me. If things exist and endure, so too must an I exist (and endure) to deal with these objects. For this reason, the discovery of permanent objects signals the advent of Me, and both come to signal a

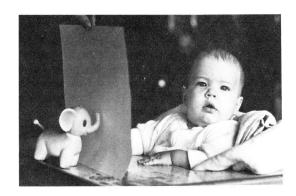

Figure 10-3.   Object permanence. When the toy is hidden by a screen, the infant acts as if it no longer exists. He or she does not yet have the concept of object permanence. *(From* Introduction to Psychology, Sixth Edition, *by E. R. Hilgard, R. C. Atkinson, and R. L. Atkinson. Copyright 1975 by Harcourt Brace Jovanovich, Inc. Reprinted by permission of Monkmeyer Press Photo Service.* Photo by George Zimbel.)

beginning to the concept of personal time (see Chapter 9).

With the early separation of an enduring Me from an enduring Not-Me, the child leaves the world of sensorimotor intelligence and enters into a world in which objects exist even when I am not present. At this time, the infant begins to deal with a world of objects that can be imagined or symbolized. Although Piaget has called this second stage the stage of **preoperational intelligence**, it is perhaps better to think of it as the stage of early symbolic activity. In this stage the young child's focus shifts away from direct bodily (sensorimotor) dealings with the world to dealings with representations of that world known as images, thoughts, or, most important, words. Speaking begins at between 2 and 2½ years, and it comes as no surprise that the period between 2 and 5 or 6 is concerned with the early world of symbols.

The phenomenal growth of the young child's ability to speak has been described in the following terms:

> At the age of two, if he can produce any sentences at all, a child will tend to say things such as: "All gone milk," "Jono car," "Bye-bye Mommy," and so on. By the time he is six, he may be able to say such things as: "The stegosaurus has armor like a knight; but that's impossible because he's prehistoric." The difference between these two utterances involves more than just vocabulary; it involves a difference between the crude beginnings of language and the use of language in a delicate and literate form.
>
> The changes that take a child from vaguely verbal teddy bear to fully productive speaker seem to occur in all normal children at about the same time, and more or less at about the same rate. Although most children and perhaps many adults never reach the level attained by our dinosaur-loving six-year-old, most do come to have command of their language by the time they are four years of age. In the two-year period between two and four, the child comes to adult language estate [Pollio, 1974, p. 442].[3]

If the achievements of the preoperational child are astounding, so too are some of his or her shortcomings. The most notable of these have come to be known as **nonconservation.** As an example of what is meant by this term, consider the case of a 4- or 5-year-old who is shown a round ball of clay and the same amount of clay in a hot-dog shape. Under these conditions the child is likely to report that the hot-dog-shaped object has more clay than the round ball. The child makes this judgment even though he or she has previously seen that the two items contained equal amounts of clay. Another example involves two rows of seven checkers each; the child will say there are more checkers in an

[3]From *The Psychology of Symbolic Activity*, by H. R. Pollio. Copyright 1974 by Addison-Wesley Publishing Company. Reprinted by permission.

evenly spaced row than in a tight circle of the same seven checkers. In both cases, the longer object is judged as "more." The child has seen the adult change the shape of the clay or the pattern of the checkers, but that does not seem to matter. The 4- or 5-year-old is tied to the present situation; the fact that he saw the transformation occur is of little importance. Because the preoperational child deals with the world in terms of states rather than transformations, Piaget believes, children of this age lack the ability to reverse a present situation to that which went before. The 4-year-old cannot see that if he were to reroll the hot dog or rearrange the checkers, they would be the "same" as they were before.

The child of this age shows another curious tendency: he or she usually centers attention on only one aspect of what has just been seen or on what is now being seen. For example, the child may see that the hot dog is longer than the ball and come to the conclusion that it must be "more." The fact that it is thinner is not taken into account: the preoperational child centers his or her attention on only one thing at a time.

The child's ability to "conserve" mass, number, and so on occurs at about the end of the sixth or seventh year. Only then can the child regularly reverse an operation mentally, and only then can he or she **decenter** (that is, simultaneously take account of more than one aspect of a present situation or event). With the mastery of these processes, the child's world becomes more orderly and predictable and less self-centered ("egocentric," to use Piaget's term). Just as achieving preoperational intelligence frees the child from the egocentric idea that "the world is my actions on it," so overcoming preoperational thinking frees the child from the view that "the world is as it now looks to me."

With these achievements, the child enters a much more dynamic and changed world of thinking and doing. The stage of **concrete operations** presents the picture of a child who can conserve mass and number, who can decenter and reverse, and who can deal with his or her world in terms of ideas as well as in terms of actions. The ability of the child to think symbolically is perhaps nowhere better illustrated than in the use of maps. Whereas the 5- or 6-year-old can get from her home to her school by herself, not until 8 or 9 is the child able to draw a map of the route. This is only one aspect of the child's increasing ability to represent his or her experiences from the perspective of a symbolic, third-person point of view.

In addition to being able to draw maps and to do many kinds of conservation experiments successfully, the concrete-operational child shows two other intellectual skills: the ability to classify things in different ways and the ability to take other people's points of view into account. As an example of the child's newly emerging classification skills, consider the set of nine items in Figure 10-4. Any adult, as well as any concrete-operational child, would describe this arrangement as reflecting a type of grouping based on both shape and color.

Although younger children might also organize these nine items in the same way, asking them to explain why they did it that way would probably produce some strange answers. For example, the preoperational child might say "It looks like a choo-choo train." A somewhat older child might describe it in terms of shape or color but never both. Not until the child can say "I've organized them into squares and circles and then into white and black squares" can we feel sure the child can classify according to a rule. If we do not like questioning the child, we can offer him a choice of the two organizations in Figure 10-5. Only if he chooses the first rather than the second (or something similar) will we be likely to feel that he is grouping according to a joint, or double, rule of classification.

The idea of rule is important not only for classifying things but also for playing games with other people. Until concrete operations, the young child has difficulty in playing games, such as baseball, football, or even dodgeball. It is not unusual for the preoperational child to say "Why do I have to be out—couldn't I have another turn?" Although the concrete-operational child may want to ask the same question, an answer such as "That's not the way we play the game" or "It's against the rules" will now satisfy her. After all, if the rule applies to her, it must also apply to everyone, and that is only fair.

With this understanding, I can now shift between your point of view and my point of view and need not feel overwhelmed by what is going on. I now think of myself as a separate person who has the option of going with you, of opposing you, or of being indifferent to you. Thus does the beginning of the social world and its multiple realities come into

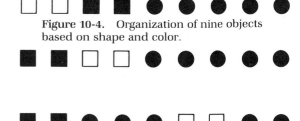

Figure 10-4. Organization of nine objects based on shape and color.

Figure 10-5. Two different organizations of nine objects useful in testing grouping according to a joint rule of classification.

existence. And it all begins with the child's ability to understand rules and change perspectives.

But concrete operations are not the be-all and end-all of the intellectual world of the adult. To be sure, representations and symbolic knowledge now take priority over perception where the two are in conflict. Just as surely, however, we are not yet free from our concrete situation: our thinking is not yet the "soaring eagle" of Chapter 5 and will not be until we move from dealing with the "world of *as is*" to the "world of *as if.*"

Consider the following conversation between an adolescent and himself: "I found myself thinking about that class. Then I began to think why was I thinking about that class and then I began to think about why I was thinking about my thinking about that class." Although this may sound a bit like the discussion of reflected consciousness begun in Chapter 1, it does indicate that in the stage of **formal operations,** from age 12 onward, the emphasis is on the *form* of thinking as well as on events thought about.

A complete record of this (or any other) adolescent's interior monologue would likely show that "thinking about thinking" does not describe all the adolescent can do. There surely would be some attempt on his or her part to organize ideas about thinking in some logical way. With this done, the adolescent might then try to develop hypotheses about some of the gaps in his or her theory of thinking and then test out certain conclusions from the newly developed theory. The ability to provide a systematic ordering to what we know, to develop hypotheses about what we do not know, to test these hypotheses fully, and finally to revise the original system on the basis of these tests not only represents thinking done by adolescents; it is a thumbnail sketch of scientific thinking as well. The achievement of formal-operational intelligence signals the entry of an adolescent into the intellectual world of rational Western society. For Piaget, there could be no lesser achievement as the final stage of human intellectual development.

If the adolescent is so able intellectually, why is he or she so often confused and so likely to do outrageous things? The answer seems to be that until formal-operational thinking is well mastered, it often is used **egocentrically**. Egocentric thinking is most often discussed in reference to the preoperational child. Here children are said to think or speak "egocentrically" because their thinking and speaking take no account of anyone other than themselves. Adolescent thinking, for all its high-powered possibilities, initially lacks grounding in the realities of the day-to-day world. Instead it deals with an adolescent's very private and very idiosyncratic problems. Just as the preoperational child is initially unable to put speaking to use in meaningful interpersonal communication, so too the formal-operational adolescent does not initially think about anything except his or her immediate concerns. Since such thinking is largely about the "as if" rather than the "what is," the adolescent is likely to build airy abstraction on top of airy abstraction and make no attempt to solve the problems of his or her day-to-day life.

At his or her best, the adolescent is able to perform outstanding feats of logical as well as fanciful thinking. Because he or she partakes of both fact and fancy, the adolescent has mastered the lessons of both the preoperational and the concrete-operational child. As one textbook put it:

> The preoperational child is capable of preposterous flights of fancy; the concrete operational child's thinking is limited by his concern for organizing the actual data of his senses. The adolescent in the Period of Formal Operations is like both of those and different from each. He is capable of departures from reality, but those departures are lawful; he is concerned with reality, but reality is only a subset within a much larger set of possibilities [Phillips, 1975, p. 131].[4]

[4]From *The Origins of Intellect: Piaget's Theory*, by J. L. Phillips, Jr. Copyright 1975 by W. H. Freeman and Company. Reprinted by permission.

4. Piaget and Descartes. If there is one criticism to be made of Piaget's analysis of intellectual development, it must be that Piaget follows Descartes (see Chapter 1) too closely: Piaget, like Descartes, thinks that a rational understanding of the world according to Western scientific and logical standards is desirable; more important, he sees such thinking as a natural final stage to human intellectual development. For Piaget the ideal adult must certainly be someone very much like René Descartes (or is it Jean Piaget?). Although Piaget does not initially separate mind and body (the stage of early sensorimotor intelligence is remarkable for its lack of a mind/body split), the final two stages of intelligence firmly come out in favor of mind over matter.

Such a conclusion is not surprising given Piaget's single-minded emphasis on intellectual development independent of what other theorists would call psychosexual or, perhaps more simply, personal development. Although Piaget recognizes that "emotional" aspects of a person may have an influence on the content of thinking—see his insightful discussion of early adolescent thinking—he tends to view such influences as outside the scope of intellectual development. Although the content of what is thought depends on personal facts, the essential nature of thinking runs its own course relatively independent of such content. Descartes' *Cogito*—the rational facility of the adult thinker—may be knocked about by being part of this or that person in this or that crisis, but such factors, according to Piaget, never significantly change our style of actual or potential thinking.

C. Erikson

Both Freud and Piaget have described the human life cycle with insight and brilliance; yet we, as adults, must feel somewhat slighted by their analyses. Both theorists conclude their descriptions at early adolescence, and those of us who are older than 15 cannot help feeling that there must be something important left to do in life. Surely we do not spend the next 50 or so years living out a plan set down in final form during early adolescence and before. If the advertisements say life begins at 40, Freud and Piaget seem to say it stops at 15.

It remained for Erik H. Erikson to try to spell out what might go on in the years between adolescence and death. Not that Erikson disagrees with what

Freud and Piaget have said; he simply is not content to see much of human life worked out so early. Erikson's work is not so much a departure from Freud's or Piaget's theory as an extension built on their earlier and continuing work.

Erikson is a Freudian (he was trained in psychoanalysis by the Freudian school of Vienna) and very much a clinician. Indeed, one of his most important books, *Childhood and Society* (1963), is built around case studies gathered during his long and distinguished career as a child therapist. Unlike Freud, however, Erikson writes about children from a first-hand knowledge of their doings. This is true not only for unhappy children in our own society but for children of other societies (Native American, German, and others). In addition, he has concerned himself with one of the most perplexing of life situations in many societies—adolescence. As a matter of fact, Erikson is probably best known for his sympathetic picture of the adolescent in crisis as well as for his discussion of the healthy resolution of that crisis, resulting in an enduring sense of personal identity and worth.

Erikson, every bit as much as Freud and Piaget, is concerned with each person's unique developmental history. He is also interested in each person's plans and aspirations. In all of this, however, he is careful to take account of the social situation in which we live. Perhaps more than either Freud or Piaget, Erikson shows a sense of place, and it is this emphasis that makes his approach the most inclusive of the three (as well as the least explicit). There is often a trade-off between breadth and precision, and Erikson has always been more concerned with breadth than either Freud or Piaget.

1. Modes and zones.   Erikson is nevertheless quite skillful in using what Freud and, to a lesser extent, Piaget have provided. Take the developmental stages first proposed by Freud. Here Erikson is not content to note that the child becomes strongly interested in different parts of his or her body at different ages, although that certainly is true enough. Instead, Erikson uses these facts as a starting point for his far-reaching distinction between bodily zones and bodily modes and how our experience with modes and zones relates to our early and continuing dealings with the world.

Because the distinction between modes and zones is difficult to grasp, it seems best to begin, as

Erikson does, with the clinical study of a little girl named Ann. At the time of her interview by Erikson, Ann was 4 years old. She was brought to Erikson for several reasons, the most obvious of which was that she was not yet completely toilet-trained: she tended to hold onto her bowel movements until early in the morning, just before her mother was able to get to her.

But this was not the only problem, for, as Erikson noted, "she seems to be losing her usual resilience; in one way she is too babyish, in another . . . too unchildlike" (1963, p. 49). When excited, she tended to "explode" and become silly. Just before being brought to the clinical interview, she had been knocked down by a car, and although she was not hurt seriously, she seemed to have withdrawn further from her parents.

Upon entering Erikson's office, Ann sucked on her thumb and paid very little attention to what was going on. Erikson began not by talking with Ann but by building a simple house of blocks, the most important part of which was a bedroom with a little girl in bed and a woman standing close to her. The door to the nearby bathroom was open, and some distance away was the garage, with a man standing next to his car. The house obviously was set up to suggest the morning routine, in which momma tried to "catch" Ann and daddy got ready to leave for work. What happened next in this drama without words was as follows (1963, pp. 50–51):

> [Ann], increasingly fascinated with this wordless statement of a problem, suddenly goes into action. She relinquishes her thumb to make space for a broad and toothy grin. Her face flushes and she runs over to the toy scene. With a mighty kick she disposes of the woman doll; she bangs the bathroom door shut, and she hurries to the toy shelf to get three shiny cars, which she puts into the garage beside the man. . . .
>
> I am still pondering over the power of her aggressive exuberance when she, in turn, seems suddenly overpowered by an entirely different set of emotions. She bursts into tears and into a desperate whimper, "Where is my mummy?" In panicky haste she takes a handful of pencils from my desk and runs out into the waiting room. Pressing the pencils into her mother's hand, she sits down close to her. The thumb goes back into the mouth, the child's face becomes uncommunicative, and I can see the game is over. . . .
>
> Half an hour later the telephone rings. They have hardly reached home when the little girl asks her mother whether she may see me again that same day. To-

morrow is not early enough. She insists with signs of despair that the mother call me immediately for an appointment the same day so that she may return the pencils. I must assure the child over the phone that I appreciate her intentions but that she is quite welcome to keep the pencils until the next day.

The next day . . . Ann sits beside her mother in the waiting room. In the one hand she holds the pencils, unable to give them to me. In the other she clutches a small object. She shows no inclination to come with me. It suddenly becomes quite noticeable that she has soiled herself. As she is picked up to be taken to the bathroom, the pencils fall to the floor and with them the object from the other hand. It is a tiny dog, one of whose legs has been broken off.

I must add here the information that at this time a neighbor's dog plays a significant role in the child's life. This dog soils too; but he is beaten for it, and the child is not. And the dog, too, has recently been knocked down by a car; but he has lost a leg. Her friend in the animal world, then, is much like herself, only more so; and he is much worse off. Does she expect (or maybe even wish) to be punished likewise?[5]

Here, then, is a young child unable to master the problem of how to give without taking (how to love her father without letting go of her mother). In presenting this problem to her parents and the world, she seems to have fallen back on a very obvious body process, a process that presents her dilemma clearly and dramatically: to hold onto or to let go of her urine and feces. The parts of the body involved in soiling are the anus and urethra, and for this reason Erikson calls these body locations the **zone** through which Ann's conflict is expressed. Associated with the anal-urethral zone is a particular way of dealing with the world, and this is called its mode of operation or, more simply, its **mode**. The major mode associated with the anal-urethral zone is one of alternately holding on and letting go, of withholding and giving, of opening and closing. This zone, in short, is the anatomical model for the "retentive and eliminative modes," which seem to describe a great many behaviors, not only those having to do with bodily elimination.

It is easy to see how the mode of holding on and letting go describes a great many of the things Ann does. Her general orientation to the world is a

closed one: she does not smile or talk much; when she does, it has an "explosive" (letting go) quality to it. She is also emotionally closed, and one of the few ways she deals with the world is by being scared, so that when she does "open up," she must immediately "close up" again.

The kind of problem Erikson is talking about here is what Freud would probably have called a problem in the anal stage of development. But Erikson refuses to talk about it in just this way. The emphasis is not on the child's ability (or lack of ability) to control his or her body; the emphasis is on the interpersonal aspects of "holding on" and "letting go." Erikson does not deny Freud's analysis of the anal stage; rather, what he has tried to do is to show that the child learns a way of dealing with the social world that has implications far beyond the child's body. For this reason, Erikson talks about psycho*social* rather than psycho*sexual* stages of development.

2. Erikson's reinterpretation of Freud's psychosexual stages. Using this strategy, Erikson has devised a psychosocial interpretation for each of Freud's psychosexual stages. Table 10-2 compares Erikson's and Freud's approaches to development from infancy through adolescence.

In separating modes from zones, Erikson has tried to extend Freud's approach in ways that are compatible with the original. Erikson's modes get a bit removed from their bodily zones by the time Freud's Oedipal/Electra stage is reached. Although our list separates males and females and talks (as Erikson sometimes does) about intrusion and inclusion, some of Erikson's psychosocial modes apply to both sexes (for example, "make" equals "go after" in the sense of "being on the make"). Those aspects of the mode/zone list that are specified least clearly begin at the Oedipal/Electra stage and continue from there. Perhaps a mode/zone approach is most valid for the earliest two or three years of life—before the child is able to speak and move easily and well within his or her world. As the child's world expands because of his or her increasing ability to get around and to talk with others, the idea of strict body zones (and their associated modes) becomes less accurate and more diffuse.

The world the 4-, 5-, or 6-year-old lives, moves, and talks in is largely a social world—a world in which the child has to deal not only with his or her

[5]From *Childhood and Society*, 2nd Edition, Revised, by Erik H. Erikson. Reprinted by permission of W. W. Norton & Company, Inc. and Hogarth Press, Ltd. Copyright © 1950, 1963 by W. W. Norton & Company, Inc.

TABLE 10-2. Erikson's and Freud's Summaries of Early Development

Zone	Eriksonian mode	Freudian stage
Mouth	To get; to give in return	Oral
Anus and urethra	To hold on or to let go	Anal
Genitals	Male: to intrude, to assert	Oedipal/Electra; phallic
	Female: to include, to accept	
	Both: to "make" (to go after a person) or to "make like" (to play)	
Unspecified—probably skilled body movements	To make things (complete projects); to move skillfully	Latency
Genitals/total body	To change rapidly; to become	Puberty and beyond

Adapted table of Erikson's Eight Stages of Psychosocial Development, from *Childhood and Society*, 2nd Edition, Revised, by Erik H. Erikson. Reprinted by permission of W. W. Norton & Company, Inc. and Hogarth Press, Ltd. Copyright © 1950, 1963 by W. W. Norton & Company, Inc.

body but with the bodies and actions of a whole range of others, none of whom will ever allow him or her to live in as egocentric a world as the one from which he or she has come. By 5, although we may still be in close contact with our bodies, we also need to be in touch with the larger and more important social worlds around us.

Erikson's separation of modes from zones points up the fundamental role of the human body in directing our lives in many subtle and unreflected ways. If we stay close to the earliest stages—where the idea of zones and modes is most obvious—it is clear that the infant experiences and deals with the world in terms of his or her own, highly specific actions. But these actions also generalize to other aspects of the infant's (and later the adult's) life, and it does not seem wrong to feel that "holding on" and "letting go" have to do not only with how our sphincter muscles work but also with how we deal with our ideas, with our emotions, and even with other people. The infant's body provides a model capable of applying to many aspects of life. Because "the model" comes to us so early on, we are likely to lose sight of its bodily origin and the wide range of its application in adult life. For the infant, to be in the world is a very bodily business and one we find increasingly more difficult to reexperience as we come to live more and more in a world of words and ideas.

Piaget has also emphasized that the infant's earliest way of dealing with the world is through actions rather than concepts. The very idea of space and objects in that space, as well as that of time and objects that endure in time, originates in the infant's actions in and on the world. The infant's self-world

forms the basis of the most abstract and wordy worlds that in due course will come to all infants as they become children and then adults. As always in such matters, the adult easily loses sight of the world of action that preceded the worlds of language and logical thinking.

What Erikson and Piaget suggest is that our bodies provide the original symbols not only for intelligent behavior but for much of social behavior as well. Beneath the wordy surface of adult intellectual and social activity is the original presence of our earliest dealings with the world, and these dealings shape and determine what we now do. The human body is not only the basic experience out of which our later social and intellectual lives emerge; it is also the continuing center around and through which we express patterns that come to define us.

3. Eight ages of the developing person.
Even if Piaget, Freud, and Erikson see eye-to-eye on the significance of early bodily actions for the developing child, Erikson alone has attempted to chart a complete course for the human life cycle. This he has done in the form of a series of eight stages, which he calls the Eight Ages of Man. Table 10-3 summarizes these stages. The first column presents the approximate ages for each stage. The first four or five stages are quite comparable to those described by Freud and Piaget. Stages 6, 7, and 8, however, represent new ideas about the human life cycle and deal with early adulthood, middle adult life, and old age.

The second column describes the primary nature of the social world accompanying a given stage. For the first three stages, the family provides the focus.

For the next two stages, the focus shifts to the neighborhood and one's age peers. For the sixth and seventh stages, the focus is a loved one and the person's newly emerging family. In the final stage, the person shifts to the domain of all human beings. For Erikson, the old have a special way of seeing from the broadest of possible perspectives.

The third column in Table 10-3 presents the heart of Erikson's approach to human development. Here the human life cycle is presented in terms of a series of psychosocial confrontations. For example, the infant struggles in his or her way with the crisis of whether the world is a place that can be trusted. For Erikson a successful resolution of this crisis results in a genuinely good feeling about the world ("hope") that will endure throughout the person's life. To take another example: the old person faces the crisis of whether he or she will feel a sense of wholeness and integrity about life or, more sadly, a sense of despair and futility. Human life sets a series of problems that emerge at different ages, and each of these crises can be either mastered (the outcome being trust, autonomy, and so on through integrity) or left undone (the outcome being mistrust, shame and doubt, and so on through despair).

If left undone—to take the more unfavorable outcome first—a crisis leaves the person with "unfinished business" that will crop up over and over during the course of a life. For example, a person with a basic sense of mistrust would not only experience a lack of confidence in the world in general, he or she could only respond to each remaining psychosocial crisis with a feeling of basic mistrust. It is difficult to see how such a person could ever achieve continuing love and intimacy with someone else.

"Successful" resolution of any crisis leaves the person with a lifelong resource. If we achieve a sense of trust, we are more likely to be able to be confident in our autonomy, to show initiative, to be intimate, and so on. Each resolution permeates all other aspects of our life, and for this reason the earliest crises have the most far-reaching effects. Perhaps that is why Freud the clinician came to emphasize experiences in early life and to treat later experience as of lesser importance. Without a good beginning, it is difficult to deal openly and directly with later crises, and in just this way does the troubled person continue to relive and, unfortunately, to redo the problems and mistakes of the past.

But such change (difficult as it is) can be

TABLE 10-3. Eight Stages of Psychosocial Development

Stages (ages are approximate)	Radius of significant relations	Psychosocial crises	Favorable outcome	Related elements of social order
1. Birth through first year	Mother or mother substitute	Trust vs. mistrust	Drive and hope	Cosmic order; religion
2. Second year	Parents	Antonomy vs. shame and doubt	Self-control and willpower	"Law and order"; social order
3. Third through fifth year	Basic family	Initiative vs. guilt	Direction and purpose	Ideal prototypes heroes
4. Sixth year to onset of puberty	Neighborhood; school	Industry vs. inferiority	Method and competence	Technology
5. Adolescence	Peer groups and out-groups; models of leadership	Identity vs. identity confusion	Devotion and fidelity	Ideological perspectives
6. Early adulthood	Partners in friendship, sex, competition, cooperation	Intimacy and solidarity vs. isolation	Affiliation and love	Patterns of cooperation and competition
7. Young and middle adulthood	Divided labor and shared household	Generativity vs. stagnation	Production and care	Currents of education and tradition
8. Old age	"Mankind" "My kind"	Integrity vs. despair	Renunciation and wisdom	Wisdom

From *Introduction to Psychology*, Sixth Edition, by E. R. Hilgard, R. C. Atkinson, and R. L. Atkinson. © 1975 by Harcourt Brace Jovanovich, Inc. Reprinted by permission of the publisher. Adapted table of Erikson's Eight Stages of Psychosocial Development by E. R. Hilgard, R. C. Atkinson, and R. L. Atkinson, from *Childhood and Society*, by Erik H. Erikson. Used with permission of W. W. Norton & Company, Inc. Copyright 1950, 1963 by W. W. Norton & Company, Inc.

achieved, partly because appropriate resolutions are possible in the face of conflicts left over from the past. The young adult who emerges from adolescence with a secure sense of personal identity is more trusting of his or her world, even if he or she had never resolved the issue of trust before. To be sure, it is less likely for a person who does not have a good sense of trust in himself and others to achieve a secure identity, but it can and does occur. In this way the present can reshape or "undo" the past, and in this way it is possible to see how interconnected the various stages of the human life cycle are.

Because Erikson firmly roots his understanding of human development in the social order, it is not surprising that each of the psychosocial crises not only gives rise to a personally favorable outcome but also relates to concerns of the society in which it occurs. The last column of Erikson's chart extends developmental stages to social patterns. As a counterpart to trust, in its individual form, we have the social institution of religion, with its belief that the world is in God's trust and that God will not violate that trust. Similarly, law and order emerge easily out of concerns for body regulation so obvious in the crises of autonomy that occur during the second year of life. Similar pairings are made for each of the remaining six stages. The important point is that society builds on and sustains the favorable outcome of each stage in the individual's development. If Erikson begins by setting the child securely in society, he concludes by finding the institutions of that society developing out of the context provided by the changing person.

IV. TIME AND THE CYCLES OF HUMAN LIFE

Whenever we see the major milestones of a human life laid out on paper, as in Figure 10-1, we may be surprised by how much open space there is from year 20 on. For the first 20 or so years, important milestones seem to be happening all the time; after that, much less seems to happen.

If this impression is even partly true to our experience as adults, then the last two-thirds of a life must be quite boring. The truth, however, is that this period is not boring; for proof, there is the observation that time goes much more quickly for older people than for younger ones. Why, then, does the figure have so much open space? The answer is

to be found not in our experience but in our diagram. Such diagrams tend to use the same scale throughout (for example, 1 inch = 1 year). In using this convention, we seem to be saying that time has an equal value everywhere in life: it does not matter whether you are old or young, whether you are doing exciting or boring things, whether you are a participant or a spectator. All the evidence we have from the laboratory and from our living experiences, however, tells us that this is just not so. Clock time is not the same as lived time, and only an abstract point of view would represent the time of a human life as a straight line of equal intervals.

If we know that this way of presenting time in human life is not likely to be true to our experiences, why continue to use it? Mostly because we have no alternative if we want to present many different aspects of a human life all at one glance. Although the line is surely not correct and may introduce distortion, it still is a reasonably good way of ordering the milestones of a life. As with most diagrams, we have to remember that the time line is, after all, *only* a line, not necessarily an accurate presentation of our experiences of (and in) time at the various ages in human life.

As a matter of fact, in Western society there are quite clearly a very desirable time of life and a very undesirable one. Western societies tend to talk about a "prime of life." Although its location in time varies quite a bit, it usually refers to the early and middle adult years—say, between 20 and 40 or 45. We also have a nondesirable period of life called old age, which is so unfavored that we invent words to disguise it: *senior citizen, golden years,* and so on. In our world, we ascend to our prime, live in it for a while, and then descend from it.

There is nothing unusual about a society's selecting one aspect of life as more valuable than another, but it makes for very rough going for the person past his or her prime. For one thing, the definition of what a desirable human being is like is often presented in terms of that society's prime time. Thus, "You look young and trim" is a compliment; "You don't look as young as you used to" and "Your hair is turning gray" are not compliments. In our society, to be in one's prime is to possess and display the major virtues of this society. In America, as in much of Europe, these come down to being sexy, powerful, or both.

If we extend Erikson's approach, it is not unreasonable to feel that there may be many primes and that although some of these may come early (physical grace and beauty), others (knowledge and wisdom) will come later. Although it may be going a bit too far to say that a favorable outcome for each psychosocial stage represents a prime, it does seem proper to propose that no single set of years need be defined as "the prime of life."

The idea that there might be different primes for different achievements shows how strongly the society you happen to be born into decides how you will value the stages of your own life's experiences. The choice made by a society not only reflects its values (we value youth, beauty, and power), it also suggests that there is no universal blueprint for how things "have to" turn out.

If this is true across societies, is it also true across historical eras? Here we can do no better than restate the point made initially by Van Den Berg: Different historical periods produce different kinds of people. The "nature" of what it means to be human is constantly changing. Different ages, as well as different societies, come to define what it means to be human for them. There is no biological blueprint that can be applied directly to different social environments or to different historical eras.

In human development, as in all other aspects of the human world, nothing is ever completely determined: there is always the possibility for something new, something unique. Although it is comforting to know that Erikson can tell us, here and now, what crises we are likely to meet, we should not expect *our* crises and *our* resolutions to be correct for even the next few generations. Everything, even crises and resolutions, moves and changes as we move and change. For this reason, we should not be surprised that the developmental conflicts and solutions of one era will not be the conflicts and solutions of another. In development, as in all other aspects of being human, there are always possibilities. The past can guide us; it never specifies what will be. Only we can do that.

V. SUMMARY

It is almost impossible to think about the nature of human life without dividing it up into units of one or another type. Even so simple a request as asking someone to describe what he or she considers the most important milestones in contempo-

rary life produces some intriguing answers. As a start, some events or accomplishments just naturally seem to fall at certain fairly specific ages. Many of these milestones deal with the developing, functioning body, such as crawling and walking, or with more intellectual skills, such as talking or counting. In addition to events of this type, we also find some for which the "proper" age is less clear. This latter set of milestones includes events having to do with our relationships to other people and more formal social institutions, such as business, education, and marriage.

On the basis of such fairly obvious (and almost intuitive) data, psychological theorists have categorized developmental changes into three major groups: bodily development, intellectual development, and interpersonal development. Each of these categories has given rise to a far-reaching analysis of what it means to be human. For example, Freud placed primary emphasis on biological factors, most especially sexual ones, and for this reason his theory has come to be called a psychosexual theory of development. Piaget stressed cognitive factors, and so his theory is described as a theory of intellectual development. Finally, Erikson stressed social factors, thereby producing a theory of psychosocial development. Although these three theories concern different aspects of development, we should never forget that they all deal with the same event—the developing human being.

Each of these theorists makes use of the concept of a developmental stage. From one point of view, a stage simply represents a grouping of events into a theoretically meaningful unit. This is obviously a third-person description. For a stage to be personally meaningful, however, the developing person's world must be different in each stage. This is a first-person definition. For all stage theories there seem to be two ways to describe how the developing person gets from one stage to the next. One principle assumes that it is in the "nature" of the human being to be interested in different things at different times. A second assumes that the developing person experiences a contradiction, crisis, or challenge in how he or she does things now and how he or she thinks they might be done and that such a crisis brings about movement from one stage to another.

Freud, Piaget, and Erikson maintain that different aspects of the adult person all arose at different critical ages in development. Van Den Berg, however, has argued that people—scholars and clinicians included—must see and understand things differently at different points in history. For this reason Van Den Berg has stressed that developmental theories must be understood within their own proper historical (and cultural) contexts: no theory is forever.

In his clinical work, Freud found that many problems in adult life had roots in the person's experiences as a child. Such data suggested that the way we function as an adult often depends on how we and our families dealt with a small number of critical events in early human life—the so-called psychosexual stages. The first two of these stages—the oral and the anal stages—concern the child's experiences involving feeding and toilet training. The third, or phallic, stage deals with the family romance, involving young Oedipus or young Electra. The latency stage, from about age 6 to age 12, is a period relatively free of strife. At puberty, however, all the unresolved and half-resolved problems of early childhood reemerge, and it is at this time that we must begin to learn how to live with the paradoxes of life on the basis of a process known as sublimation. Freud's final stage, genitality, ends by defining a "healthy" adult as one who is productive in both love and work.

For Freud, the most significant tensions we have to deal with concern conflicts between biological (id) and social (superego) aspects of the person. The ego (or executive "part" of the person) mediates between these two warring partners. Freud described the development of a human being as involving changes that take the person from an illogical and asocial biological entity to a fully functioning, rational/social/biological being.

Piaget, the second of our three wise men, outlines the development of intelligence in terms of four stages:

1. *Sensorimotor intelligence* (birth to age 2). The infant at first has no sense of object permanence and throughout this stage deals with his or her world egocentrically—that is, only in terms of his or her own perceptions and desires.

2. *Preoperational intelligence* (2–6). The child has a sense of object permanence. In addition, he or she has a beginning concept of personal time (discovery of an enduring Me) and a beginning use of symbols (speaking begins at about 2 or 2½). As yet, the child has little or no sense of conservation of mass or number.

3. *Concrete-operational intelligence* (7–11). The child can conserve mass and number, reverse an operation mentally, decenter, and use rules to classify things as well as to play games. The child is able to take another person's point of view and thus begins his or her understanding of the social world and its multiple realities. At this time thinking is still limited to organizing the data of relatively immediate experience.

4. *Formal-operational intelligence* (12–15 and on). The person is able to deal with the world in terms of "as if" as well as in terms of "as is." He or she is able to perform feats of logical as well as fanciful thinking. At this stage the person has come of age intellectually and is sometimes able to deal with the world as either a philosopher or a scientist might.

The third major developmental theorist to consider is Erik Erikson. Like Freud, Erikson based many of his most important insights on experiences as a therapist. His primary theoretical advance over other theories concerns his interest in the years between adolescence and death. This work should be seen not as a departure from, but as an extension of, both Freud's and Piaget's work.

Erikson is best known for his concern with the adolescent in crisis. He uses the fact of an infant's interest in different parts of his or her body at different ages as a starting point for a distinction between zones (body locations) and modes (ways of dealing with the world, initially specific to a zone). The separation of modes from zones is only one aspect of his attempt to describe the more general relation of person to society. For Erikson (as for Piaget and Freud) the body always provides the original symbols for social as well as intelligent behavior. In this Erikson makes good use of body metaphors such as "holding on" or "letting go" as appropriate for describing later personal and social behavior.

Erikson carried his analysis of personal development well beyond the adolescent years, charting a course for human life in the form of eight stages. These stages include the following specific contrasts:

1. Trust vs. mistrust (birth to 1 year).
2. Autonomy vs. shame and doubt (2 years)
3. Initiative vs. guilt (3 to 5 years)
4. Industry vs. inferiority (6 to 12 years)

5. Identity vs. identity confusion (adolescence)
6. Intimacy vs. isolation (early adulthood)
7. Generativity vs. stagnation (middle adulthood)
8. Integrity vs. despair (old age)

Successful resolution of any stage—for example, the development of trust rather than mistrust—leaves the person with a lifelong resource. If an early crisis has an unfavorable outcome, it is difficult to deal openly and directly with later crises; there always seems to be too much unfinished business. The troubled person continues to relive and redo the mistakes of the past, although Erikson does believe there is always an "open area" for change.

As a final word, it is important to think about each of these theories in light of Van Den Berg's analysis. The society one is born into strongly affects how one feels about the course of one's life's experiences. Different historical ages, as well as different societies, define what it means to be human for them. The developmental conflicts and solutions within a society move and change as societies move and change. There are always possibilities—the past only guides us, it never totally defines or determines us.

VI. GLOSSARY OF IMPORTANT CONCEPTS

Anal stage. In Freud's theory, the stage at which a child's dominant source of pleasure is derived from the anal region (about 1½–2½ years of age).

Concrete operations. In Piaget's theory, the stage from 7 to 11 years of age, in which the child is first able to conserve, reverse, and decenter—that is, to understand some of the concrete workings of the world.

Critical period. A stage in development in which new behavior or understanding emerges as a result of a subtle (or obvious) crisis.

Decenter. In Piaget's theory, to take into account more than one aspect of a situation simultaneously.

Developmental stage. From a third-person point of view, a theorist's way of grouping together developmental events in an attempt to understand, intellectually, the overall course of human life. From a first-person point of view, an individual's experience of change in the way he or she goes about dealing with the world.

Ego. In Freud's theory, the rational aspect of a person that is constantly mediating between the id and superego to provide satisfaction for both.

Egocentric thinking. The process in which a person can see the world only in terms of his or her actions on it, not how the world is perceived and acted on by others.

Electra complex. In Freud's theory, a girl's feelings of hostility and rivalry toward her mother as well as her specific sexual feelings for her father.

Formal operations. In Piaget's theory, the stage from 12 years onward, in which the person is able to think logically, hypothetically, propositionally, and combinatorially—that is, like a scientist or philosopher.

Genitality. The stage pertaining to the organs of generation or reproduction; Freud's name for the adult stage.

Id. In Freud's theory, the theoretical entity within a person that represents his or her biological strivings.

Intelligence. A person's ability to deal with his or her world in a consistent and effective way.

Latency stage. The stage at which children are psychodynamically quiet, about ages 6–11. During this period the child becomes competent in dealing with his or her world.

Mode. In Erikson's theory, the method of operation for dealing with the world that is associated with a particular zone (body location).

Nonconservation. As observed by Piaget, the inability of the preoperational child to understand that changing the shape of an object, such as a piece of clay, does not change its quantity.

Object permanence. The idea that objects endure even if I am not there to see them; object constancy (see glossary, Chapter 9). Up to about 6–8 months an infant exhibits little or no object permanence. Object permanence also leads to the experience of "me" as an enduring entity.

Oedipus complex. In Freud's theory, a boy's feelings of hostility and rivalry toward his father, as well as his specifically sexual feelings for his mother.

Oral stage. In Freud's theory, the period when the infant's primary source of pleasure and gratification is the mouth, which also provides his or her way of dealing with the world; the first year.

Phallic stage. In Freud's theory, the period when the child's dominant source of pleasure is the genital region; age 3–5.

Preoperational intelligence. In Piaget's theory, the stage from age 2 to age 6 or so, of early symbolic activity, in which the child deals with representatives of his or her world, such as images, thoughts, and words.

Primary-process thinking. A chaotic way of thinking and dealing with the world, not ordered in time and space. According to Freud, it occurs in young children and during dreams in adults.

Psychosexual stages. Freud's ordering of development, focusing on how wishes, mainly sexual, are expressed and managed in different ways at different ages.

Secondary-process thinking. An orderly and rational way of thinking and dealing with the world; originates later in life than primary process.

Sensorimotor intelligence. In Piaget's theory of intellectual development, the stage from birth to about age 2. In this way of dealing with the world, the infant says, in effect, "The world is my actions on it."

Sublimation. In Freud's theory, the conversion of id energy (libidinal drives) into socially acceptable channels.

Superego. In Freud's theory, the theoretical entity within a person that is an early and continuing form of human conscience.

Zone. In Erikson's theory, a bodily location toward which a person is oriented during a particular developmental stage, such as the mouth or the anus.

VII. SUGGESTED READINGS

Major sources

Erikson, E. H. *Childhood and society.* New York: Norton, 1963. Parts 1–3.

Freud, S. *A general introduction to psychoanalysis.* New York: Simon & Schuster, 1935.

Piaget, J. *The construction of reality in the child* (M. Cook, trans.). New York: Basic Books, 1954.

Van Den Berg, J. H. *The changing nature of man.* New York: Dell, 1961.

Secondary sources

Ginsburg, H., & Opper, S. (Eds.). *Piaget's theory of intellectual development: An introduction* (2nd ed.). Englewood Cliffs, N. J.: Prentice-Hall, 1969.

Hall, C. S., & Lindzey, G. *Theories of personality* (2nd ed.). New York: Wiley, 1970. Chapters 2, 13, 14.

11

Growing and Becoming Unique: Identity, Self, and Ego

At age 20, where are you and what do you know? One of the things you undoubtedly know is that you will not stay 20 forever: you must decide on some kind of future for yourself. If you are not in college, you have to make a decision either to go to college or to begin learning a trade that will last you a good part of the rest of your life. Either way, 20 is a time for wondering "What should I become?"; "What should I do for the next few years?"

If you are romantically involved with someone, it is also a time for deciding. There is no getting away from it: do you want to set up house or not? For a male, society isn't much help: on the one hand, it holds out the option of being a swinging single and tasting life (as the beer commercial says); on the other, it extols the virtues of being a father and a respectable citizen (as the bank commercial says). For a woman, there is also a double message: swinging single or devoted mom. If you choose the second alternative, you may still feel caught—motherhood or a career. Whichever way you turn, and whether you are female or male, there are a great many things still to be resolved.

Although you may be disappointed that you haven't closed the issue of "Who am I?" by age 20, don't be too upset: this issue will recur throughout the course of your life. As an example of what could happen, consider a woman in our society at age 30 or 35. If she is unmarried, she finds herself with a few decisions to make: Should she have a child even if not married? Should she continue the strenuous pursuit of a career even if it means coming into increasingly greater conflict with peers and family? Should she deal directly with her own needs to be loved even if it means violating certain religious and social expectations? And so on. If she is married, she also finds herself having to decide a few things: Should she have children or continue her career? Should she go back to school (or work) when the kids are 3, 5, or 10 years of age? Should she attempt to coordinate these interests? And so on.

I. IDENTITY, YOUTH, AND SOCIETY

If you begin to feel sorry for yourself or for our hypothetical 30–35-year-old woman, there is one consoling thought: the indecision and conflict you are experiencing now is surely less than it was when you entered the teen years. Could any period of life be as difficult as the one between age 12 and 16? The problem then was not "What shall I become?" but "Who am I?" Although you may not have the whole answer right now, you no longer worry about it so much. Worries about your identity now seem more under control and more related to the more manageable problems of learning an occupation and picking a partner.

But why should the years between 12 and 16 have been so difficult? The "cause" of it all had to be the body: There I was, a perfectly happy and competent 12- or 13-year-old, when suddenly my body changed in ways I couldn't understand. There were the unmistakable signs of growing sexuality: body hair, a general change in size and build, specific changes in my sexual organs. I grew taller; my favorite clothes no longer fit. I began to experience strange and inexplicable urges within my body. Looking at my friends, I found that some were even larger and more changed than I; others were smaller and less changed.

Then at age 14 or 15 I began to think differently. Suddenly I had the capacity to deal with all kinds of ideas and concepts in a more abstract way. And think about things I did—at first egocentrically, then idealistically, and finally realistically.

At about 15 or 16, I began to feel that while I was changing, there was also something stable about me. What I experienced was a growing sense of sameness in the meaning I had for myself and others—a stable yet changing core to which I referred everything that had to do with me. Although I did not know it then, this "core" is what Erikson (1968) called a sense of ego identity. What I did know then was that my identity was not an automatic gift of being so-and-so many years old. Rather, it was the outcome of an active struggle to find a place for me in regard to myself, my society, and my history.

A. Adolescence, preadolescence, and youth

The problems involved in coming to a secure sense of personal identity occur over a wide range of years. Some of them, such as a rapidly changing body, occur early in the teenage years; others, such as the decision to go to college, occur much later. The period of adolescence, in Western society, usually extends from about 12 to about 17 years of age. It is flanked by an early period called preadolescence (ages 10–12) and a later period called youth (18–22+).

Preadolescence, like all age-graded schemes of describing people, ought not to be thought of as beginning sharply at 10 and ending sharply at 12. Individual variation is great, and this two-year period merely represents the most typical span in contemporary society. At this time, boys and girls often form groups or clubs composed of other children of the same age and sex. Often, boys show a vigorous interest in sports and a vigorous avoidance of girls. Girls often show a strong interest in group activities as well as a strong avoidance of boys. Preadolescence seems best described as a "growing away" from childhood and family and a "growing toward" one's peers. As such, it enables the growing person to move away from his or her family and toward an adult sexual and emotional life, usually in conjunction with someone of the opposite sex outside the immediate family.

If preadolescence is well described as a breaking with childhood, adolescence (12–17) is probably better described as a growing toward adulthood. This decision is seen most strongly in some fairly characteristic behaviors of adolescents. Among these are a more selective but stronger attraction to, and dependence on, one's peers; a growing and highly variable relationship to adolescents of the opposite sex; an increase in the time spent in thinking about oneself and other fascinating topics; and a genuine commitment to be excellent at something, whether it be drinking more beer than anyone else or becoming a concert pianist.

Although particular stresses and strains may break out at different points in the teenage years for different people, they usually occur in the earlier rather than the later teens. The years between 15 and 18 or 19 are relatively good and exciting ones for many people. At this point, growth away from the family and toward adult status is well underway. The major new situations that late adolescents find themselves enmeshed in concern, first, sex and love and, second, deciding on an occupation.

The stage following adolescence is often called "youth." In the United States, it includes the years between 18 and 22 or 24. In many European countries, the range is much larger, and it is common to

find individuals as old as 25 or 30 still being included in this category. Although in the United States there is now a strong tendency for 18–22-year-olds to be quietly in college, there was a time during the late 1960s and early 1970s when American youth was a much more powerful and significant political force. Many of the demonstrations that took place in protest of the Vietnam war, for example, involved American youth to an unprecedented degree. The strength of this involvement surprised many American political observers.

American higher education, which should have known better, was also surprised by the strength of political power shown by students in the late 1960s. During this period it was not uncommon for university life to be disrupted and even stopped as professors and students met outside the classroom to discuss the moral and political issues of the day. Folk-song rallies and discussions of future political and personal action took place on the lawns of many of the major American universities and colleges. Book learning was suspended as American youth and its teachers sought their values.

Such happenings were going on in Europe as well. Major reforms in the university system were initiated and completed in countries such as France, Germany, England, and Sweden—reforms that could only be described as the "democratization" of the university. Students were no longer to be treated as children, nor were professors expected to be unreachable, grand, parental. Instead, the university was to be a society of people governed with the consent and advice of everyone concerned. It was during this time that a European student leader wrote:

> A spectre is haunting Europe—the spectre of student revolt. All the powers of old Europe have entered into a holy alliance to exorcise this spectre. Pope and Central Committee, Kissinger and de Gaulle, French Communists and German police-spies.
>
> But now it has become world-wide; Berkeley, Berlin, Tokyo, Madrid, Warsaw—the student rebellion is spreading like wildfire, and authorities everywhere are frantically asking themselves what has hit them [Cohn-Bendit, 1968, p. 23].

The fact that college students, and youth more generally, could bring about such reforms should have surprised no one. At many points in history a few political leaders have always understood how effectively and how totally youth is able to respond when touched by a particular insight or by a particular viewpoint. The reasons are not hard to find. Personally and intellectually, the late adolescent is likely to be "high-minded" and given over to great and enduring ideas and ideals. Adolescence and youth are times when formal-operational thinking can be used skillfully, and what better topics to use it on than humankind and the nature of the social order? Economically, youth is usually not hampered by worrying about a family or by having job obligations. Of all social institutions, colleges and universities can be the most open to innovation and change. Finally, young people tend toward direct action, and open public response meets such very well indeed.

All of this suggests that youth has the possibility of exercising great political and social power. It would be a mistake, however, to suggest that such power is necessarily asserted for politically and socially just goals. The vigor and power of youth is neither intrinsically good nor intrinsically bad; it simply is. For the duly elected individuals responsible for a college, a city, and even a country, there is only one way to deal with the power of youth: to treat it as a partner, proportionate in responsibility and power to other aspects of the institution. To treat youth permissively or autocratically is to grant it less than equal status.

Erik Erikson, in talking to a reporter from *Newsweek* magazine, discussed the issues of youth and authority in the following terms:

I would say, first, that authoritativeness and permissiveness are two sides of ... the same frame of mind. The permissive as well as the authoritarian adult makes decisions for the young without considering what reasonability and responsibility they may be ready for themselves. The ability to confer delegated authority [Erikson's alternative] would require that one learn to sense that readiness and become ready, deep down, to share that responsibility. Only thus can one gauge how far the young of today can learn to participate in decisions—if with some tumult on their part, and some anxiety on ours. But it would also require the will to exert whatever authority cannot be delegated in areas where experience counts. Such authority, if true, the young can respect once they are permitted to exert the responsibility which is prepared in their development and fostered by history [Erikson, 1970, p. 86].[1]

[1]From "The Quest for Identity," by E. H. Erikson. In *Newsweek*, December 21, 1970, pp. 84–89. Copyright 1970 by Newsweek, Inc. All Rights Reserved. Reprinted by permission.

B. Social aspects of the adolescent identity crisis

The search for identity always takes place within a particular historical era and a particular social situation. In talking specifically about American culture in the 20th century, Erikson notes that

adolescence is least stormy in that segment of youth which is gifted and well trained in the pursuit of expanding technological trends, and thus able to identify with new roles of competency and invention.... Where this is not given, the adolescent mind becomes a more explicitly ideological one, by which we mean one searching for some inspiring unification of tradition or anticipated techniques, ideas, and ideals. And, indeed, it is the ideological potential of a society which speaks most clearly to the adolescent who is so eager ... to be inspired by worthwhile "ways of life." ... Should a young person feel that the environment tries to deprive him too radically of all the forms of expression which permit him to develop and integrate the next step, he may resist with the wild strength encountered in animals who are suddenly forced to defend their lives. For, indeed, in the social jungle of human existence there is no feeling of being alive without a sense of identity [1968, p. 129].

Even the adolescent comfortable with technology still experiences some of the **adolescent storm** Erikson talks about, and we may well wonder whether this always has to happen. A bit of anthropology will tell us how the teenage years unfold in societies other than those of Western Europe and America. One early book on this topic, *Coming of Age in Samoa* (1928/1950), contains field reports of Margaret Mead's observations made during her stay in the 1920s on some islands in the South Pacific. Mead noted that many of the sudden changes in expectations we place on our adolescents are absent in Samoan society. For example, we expect our young children (and this was more true when Mead wrote than now) to be relatively sexless. In Samoa, young children not only witness the birth of siblings and other infants, they also are allowed to engage in sexual explorations with one another as early as they choose. In adolescence casual sexual behavior is permitted and sometimes even encouraged. Mead noted that the early-teenage girl spent a good deal of time in "clandestine" sexual adventures that were really not so clandestine at all. Many a young Samoan girl postponed marriage to enjoy a carefree and uninhibited sexual adolescence.

1. Social discontinuities here and elsewhere. Adolescents in Western cultures differ from Samoan adolescents not only in terms of sexual behavior. Ruth Benedict (1954), a close friend of Margaret Mead, noted two other areas in which teenagers in our society experience strongly changed expectations between late childhood and early adolescence. The so-called **social discontinuities** are (1) being responsible or irresponsible, (2) being dominant or submissive, and (3) being sexual or asexual. In our society, the child is expected to behave on the "don't" side of each category: young children are not expected to be responsible, they are expected to be submissive, and they are expected to be asexual.

Other cultures have different expectations. As Mead noted, the Samoan child is expected to be sexual all through life. The only difference in Samoa between the sexual behavior of children and adolescents is in what behaviors are thought appropriate: masturbation for the child, heterosexual experimentation and diversity for the adolescent.

In societies other than our own, the same is also true in regard to dominance and responsibility. It is not unusual to hear a Crow Indian father brag about the difficulty he has with his son simply because any such "difficulty" is taken to indicate that the son "will grow up to be a man worthy of the name." Mead notes that Samoan girls as young as 6 or 7 are expected to take care of their younger brothers and sisters. Not surprisingly, the 6- or 7-year-old is taken care of by her 9- or 10-year-old sister. Young male children are also asked to behave responsibly, and 6- and 7-year-old boys do some of the fishing for the family. Here, as in all other areas, tasks are age-graded: the young boy fishes off the reefs, as going out in the fishing boats is more dangerous. The idea of "play for children" and "work for adults" is unknown: children and adults both work and play.

These cross-cultural findings indicate that not all societies emphasize adolescence nearly as much as we do. Instead of discontinuities in social expectations, some societies emphasize **cultural continuities** among the child, the adolescent, and the adult. All members of the society, regardless of age, are allowed and even expected to be sexual, dominant, and responsible (provided the tasks are age-appropriate). The idea of separate stages such as child/adolescent/adult/old-aged is much less sharply drawn in these societies than in our own. Although age-defined stages do exist, they are less important than in contemporary Western societies.

Ruth Benedict (1954) was quite explicit in pointing out the problems brought about by our way of doing things. If a society is discontinuously age-graded (as ours is), people have to cope not only with how well they are doing right now but also with how well they are doing relative to some social norm. For example, if a 10-year-old girl starts dating, her family is very much up in arms: "She's too young." Similarly, if an 18-year-old is not dating, her parents will worry: "Why isn't she dating?"

Some societies tolerate continuing sexual contact between boys and girls as early as 10; others deny such contact until as late as a formal marriage at 18 or older. The latter situation would seem to be the more disturbing of the two. There is a sharp and painful discontinuity between what the young man or woman has been trained to do and be and what he or she is expected to become all at once. No wonder the story is told that Victorian mothers advised their Victorian daughters "to close their eyes, grit their teeth, and think of the Queen" during sexual intercourse with their Victorian husbands. Despite the jarring discontinuity of marriage during this era, there was probably some comfort in the fact that every other young woman also experienced these same feelings of discomfort. In one sense the discontinuity was an expected part of being "well brought up."

2. A psychosocial moratorium. In more contemporary society, discontinuities not only occur, they are part and parcel of implicit and very subtle social contradictions. The young male child is trained to be submissive and at the same time is expected "to be a man" when he grows up. The young female child is expected to be submissive but, when she grows up, to master the harder job of being assertive in Situations 1, 2, and 3 and submissive in ten other situations. Not only are there discontinuities between child and adult life, there also are inconsistencies about what is the "right" thing to do after the person has moved to a new status. Benedict (1954) and Mead (1961) have emphasized that our social institutions do not furnish adequate or consistent support for the growing person as he or she changes status. The adolescent is not only supposed to be "grown up," he or she is also expected to behave with restraint and concern in most situations.

Perhaps that is why Mead and Erikson have both talked, with approval, about the more European idea of allowing an adolescent a period of experimentation—what Erikson called a psychosocial **moratorium**. During this period the growing adolescent is allowed to try out things without necessarily being expected to succeed. As Mead put it, the moratorium is "an *as if* period in which heights of aspirations and depths of despair can both be experienced without final economic, social, or personal psychological consequences" (1961, p. 46). Erikson himself went through such a period when, after finishing high school, he hitchhiked across Europe without any obvious goal and without any specific direction. Such a trip was a perfectly acceptable way for a sensitive young man to find himself.

3. Is adolescent storm inevitable?   Adolescence is often described as if it must be a period of great personal upheaval and disorientation. Yet it is clear that not everyone experiences that much storm and stress. Some individuals even report that adolescence was a particularly happy and gratifying period in their lives and that there was no sharp break between any of the stages usually assumed to describe the developing person. Indeed, one strong advocate of this "frictionless" (or continuity) view noted that the adult must have

> evolved by imperceptible degrees [from] the pubescent girl or boy of thirteen or fourteen years; and therefore by degrees still very gradual, though somewhat more noticeable, total growth is achieved, till we have at last the matured human adult.... The quality of the organism is a constant, which shows itself from the beginning to the end of individual life.... The widespread myth that every child ... comes forth (at puberty) as a different personality is doubtless a survival in folklore of the ceremonial rebirth, which constituted the formal initiation of our savage ancestors into manhood and womanhood [Hollingsworth, 1928, pp. 16–17].[2]

By this reckoning, the storms of adolescence do not have to happen to everyone, nor is everyone overwhelmed. Indeed, one eight-year survey (Offer, 1969; Offer & Offer, 1975) found that of 73 middle-class adolescent males interviewed from age 14

[2]From *The Psychology of the Adolescent*, by L. S. Hollingsworth. Copyright 1928 by Appleton-Century. Reprinted by permission.

through age 22, only 21% showed the pattern of adolescent turmoil often assumed to describe the usual adolescent experience; 23% were described as experiencing a continuing process of growth from earliest years on, 35% were characterized as experiencing a pattern of successful development that was episodic rather than continuous, and 21% could not be placed into any of the other categories.

What is important about this work is that it self-consciously chose to examine the lives of "normal" rather than "abnormal" adolescents. Although *normal* is a tricky word that means both more and less than it ought to, the young men studied by Offer and associates were picked so as to be representative of middle-income, mid-American youth who displayed no overt symptoms of personal difficulty according to their own, their parents', their teachers', or even the investigating psychiatrist's report.

Should we be surprised that only 21% of these students expressed an **identity crisis** of the extent required by many developmental theories? Writing a few years earlier, Bandura (1964) took sharp issue with the idea of adolescence as invariably stormy. He saw the idea of adolescent turmoil as a social myth having little or no basis in fact. By his estimate, only 10% or so of adolescents experienced storms, and those reactions could be tied rather directly to clear factors in the child's life history. Far from being a regular stage in human development, Bandura argued, adolescent disorientation was the result of a unique personal history and of a special set of social expectations. Bandura suggested that 90% of all adolescents were probably better described as "responsible, well-adjusted, and respectful of parents."

If adolescent turmoil is only a myth, we still need to understand the origin and prestige of the myth. Bandura offers five reasons the myth of turmoil is so popular: (1) We tend to overinterpret superficial signs of nonconformity. One reason teenagers seem more "faddish" than 8–10-year-olds is that they, not their parents, are now selecting their clothing, recreation, wall posters, and so on. (2) Mass media, such as radio, TV, and newspapers, tend to pay more attention to the deviant than to the typical individual. (3) We overgeneralize, from clinical work done on adolescents in trouble. (4) We overemphasize dramatic biological changes rather than more continuously cumulative social development. (5)

There is a tendency toward self-fulfilling prophecy; that is, we expect "pathology," and we get it.

II. FROM CHILD TO ADULT: SOME DEVELOPMENTAL PATTERNS IN IDENTITY

Bandura's analysis strongly suggests that the storm and stress described as capturing what it means to be an adolescent is an overglib generalization covering at most only a quarter of the total teenage population. Although Bandura and Hollingsworth are right in emphasizing that not *all* adolescents experience an adolescent storm, this does not mean no difficulties are involved in making the change from child to adult. Instead, we ought to recognize that there are many roads from childhood to adult life.

A. Research on "normal" adolescents
As a partial guide to these routes, Offer and Offer (1969, 1975) proposed three styles of development during adolescence. In one of these, growth is **continuous** and ongoing—quite similar to what might be predicted from Hollingsworth's and Bandura's suggestions. A second, much more episodelike pattern consists of series of starts and stops. Adolescents showing this second (**surgent**) pattern can usually be distinguished from those in the continuous-growth group by a less fortunate life situation: for these adolescents, Offer and Offer found that parental divorce or death was more frequent than for teenagers in the continuous group. Adolescents in the surgent group were nevertheless able to keep an overall sense of balance, particularly in regard to their general life goals and expectations.

A third pattern described by Offer and Offer comes closest to what both psychological theory and educated common sense have long held to be *the* pattern of adolescent experience. In this, the **tumultuous** pattern, recurrent self-doubts and strong conflicts with parents are clearly in evidence. The 15 young men interviewed by Offer and Offer in this group described their adolescent years as a period of discordance; 7 were judged to have clinically definable symptoms, such as depression or overtly delinquent behavior.

Although Offer and Offer's results are clear, interpretation of them is not. For example, because only 15 male adolescents out of 79 reported experiencing great turmoil, is it reasonable to conclude that teenagers today are having an easier time than during the period written about by Freud, Piaget, or Erikson? Or should we worry that our young men are growing up into very predictable and unidimensional adults and therefore no longer require a moratorium because there are no longer any significant choices open to them? Then again, should we focus on the fact that only 21% developed according to the tumultuous route, or should we emphasize that only 23% grew according to a continuous route? Finally, should we pay particular attention to the 35% of the young men in this study who experienced the so-called surgent, or episodic, pattern?

These questions all need answering if the significance of Offer and Offer's results is to emerge for us in the here-and-now of contemporary society. One response that seems possible in connection with these results is that the psychological literature may overemphasize the emotional crises that occur in some adolescent lives. Such crises are indeed profoundly disturbing to the people experiencing them, but they do not characterize everyone's life. There is always something heroic about the not-quite-adult's struggle against society and himself or herself that evokes a romantic response in us.

The case of the continuous-growth group—less than a quarter of the sample—is also hard to understand in any simple way. To be sure, there are some children who grow into adults on a productive and continuous path beginning in early life, and many of these children do grow to be productive and innovative adults. But an opposite interpretation of continuous growth is also possible: some children seem to grow up as carbon copies of their parents and tend to see life not as a series of choices and challenges but as a pleasant enough obligation to pass through as effortlessly and securely as possible. These children grow up to be boring and unidimensional adults. By itself, the continuous pattern does not mean a person must be a bore or a social innovator. Continuous growth simply describes one way in which some children make the passage from child to adult life.

Neither the tumultuous nor the continuous growth pattern would seem to be an obvious blessing or curse in its own right. Tumult may signal potential greatness or potential madness; continuity may signal resolute purpose or resolute boredom. There is no simple way to read the significance of these patterns independent of the person whose life is being lived. Both patterns describe ongoing human lives, and continuity and turmoil both have to be accepted as different paths of growth.

Even if we grant that these extremes do not exhaust the various ways adolescents experience their world, they do provide a clue to what is at issue: continuity and turmoil. This combination would seem best realized in the third and major group described by Offer and Offer: that of episodic, or surgent, growth. Although it is difficult to capture exactly what might be experienced by members of this group, the best description seems to be that they experience personal continuity in a discontinuous way. The major adjective used to describe this group, *surgent*, means "tending to move forward in a series of episodes." Although these young men did things in a seemingly discontinuous way, they never lost unreflected sight of where they were going. Their adolescent years seemed to be a highly skillful balancing act held together by a concern for where they had come from and a concern for where they might get to. Because balancing is a difficult skill, they could bring off this trick only at somewhat separated points in their lives. When they did get their acts together, they surged forward to a new place—a place, however, that they had known they would get to all along, even though it was slightly uncomfortable when they got there.

B. Identity during the college years

Because the idea of continuity in the face of change is at the heart of Erikson's (1963) analysis of identity, or what it is an adolescent is seeking, it is not surprising that his approach to adolescent development has also given rise to a typology of developmental options. Here the major work was done by James Marcia (1966, 1968) of the University of Buffalo, who questioned a group of students on such issues as choice of occupation, religious identity, and political ideology. Two of the questions asked by Marcia and his collaborators were as follows: (1) "How willing do you think you'd be to give up going into [your chosen occupation] if something better came along?" (2) "Have you ever had any doubts about your religious beliefs?" Characteristic of the answers given were those by the following four students:

Student A
Answer 1: Well, I might, but I doubt it. I can't see what "something better" would be for me.

Answer 2: Yeah, I even started wondering whether or not there was a God. I've pretty much resolved that now, though. The way it seems to me . . .
Student B
Answer 1: I guess if I knew for sure, I could answer that better. It would have to be something in the same general area—something related.
Answer 2: Yes, I guess I'm going through that now. I just don't see how there can be a God and yet so much evil in the world or . . .
Student C
Answer 1: Not very willing. It's what I've always wanted to do. The folks are happy with it, and so am I.
Answer 2: No, not really, our family is pretty much in agreement on these things.
Student D
Answer 1: Oh, sure. If something better came along, I'd change just like that.
Answer 2: Oh, I don't know. I guess so. Everyone goes through some sort of stage like that. But it really doesn't bother me much. I figure one's about as good as the other!

Each of these students represents one of four patterns that Marcia thought described where many (if not all) college students were with respect to the development of a secure personal identity—four **categories of identity.** Student A would be considered as having achieved a sense of personal identity—that is, as having experienced a period of indecision that gave rise to certain commitments concerning the direction of his present and future life-style.

Student B seems much less sure of his commitments and his direction. There is still something open and questioning about his approach to both occupation and religion. He sounds most like the vaguely naive and strongly idealistic youth described by much that has been written about adolescent development. According to Marcia, Student B is in the midst of a moratorium, or rest period.

Student C, in contrast to B and in agreement with A, has made some quite firm religious and occupational choices. Unlike A and B, however, he seems to have closed down his options without any prolonged period of questioning. He has committed himself to values that were given to him by parents, society, or both, and he has probably not gone through any strong period of evaluation and reevaluation. Student C seems to have foreclosed his options and is committed, on an unquestioning basis, to the values of his ancestors.

Student D is quite diffuse in his handling of both questions. He clearly has no real commitment to any vocation or to his religious beliefs. As he puts it, "I figure one's about as good as the other." The youth who talks about the world this way may or may not have experienced a crisis. As it now stands, however, he is apathetic, uninvolved, and uncommitted.

Do the four types of personal identity defined by Marcia have anything to do with young adults' behavior apart from interviews? To show that such differences make a difference in how our four students would behave, Marcia (1966, 1967) ran a set of experiments in which 84 male college students were first classified into the four groups on the basis of how they answered Marcia's questions. These four groups corresponded to the four students described and were called the Identity Achieved group, the Moratorium group, the Foreclosure group, and the Identity Diffusion group. Of the 84 students, 18 could be classified as Identity Achieved, 22 as Moratorium, 23 as Foreclosure, and 21 as Diffusion. Each student was asked to perform three tasks: to learn a difficult concept; to talk about feelings of self-worth and self-confidence; and to answer questions concerning attitudes about authority.

Results were quite clear in showing that Identity Achieved students were more successful than any other group at the concept-learning task. In addition, they tended not to give up when a problem was difficult and to endorse less-authoritarian values than any other group. In general, Foreclosure students endorsed more statements in support of authoritarian values than any other group. Finally, subjects in the Diffusion group were not very different from subjects in the remaining three groups except that they scored lower on the concept-learning task than the Identity Achieved group and lower on the authoritarian-values questionnaire (less authoritarian) than the Foreclosure group. (Differences among all four groups on the self-worth questionnaire were insignificant.)

How do these findings, and their associated categories of personal growth, relate to the more naturalistically derived categories proposed by Offer and Offer? In making this comparison, we have to remember that Offer and Offer's students were the same age as Marcia's, only at the end of their fourth year of being interviewed. Despite this difference,

the studies are in agreement in describing the experiences of "identity diffusion" students—that is, those young men who were involved in crises of personal identity. The major conclusion here seems to be that such students act and think in a relatively diffuse and uncommitted way. In addition, some small part of this group is definitely directed away from other people.

The major cross-experiment problem comes in comparing "Foreclosure" students with any of Offer and Offer's groups. At first glance Foreclosure students would seem most similar to Offer's continuous-growth group. Yet this equation does not ring true, especially since students in Marcia's Foreclosure group never did come to any very distinctive sense of personal identity. Students in the continuous-growth group, although not experiencing much adolescent conflict, did nonetheless achieve a unique and individual personal identity.

Does this mean the continuous-growth group is similar to the Identity Achieved group? Again the answer is no, primarily because students in the Identity Achieved group did experience a period of crisis before coming to a sense of personal identity. In truth, the Identity Achieved group seems more like the surgent-growth group in that both had direction, both struggled a bit, and both came through it all right. Offer and Offer's continuous-growth group seems to have no direct counterpart in Marcia's scheme of things, just as Marcia's Foreclosure group has no direct counterpart in Offer and Offer's scheme of things. Both descriptions, however, do seem to express a unique style of dealing with the adolescent years that does not fit comfortably within any of the other descriptions—suggesting that there are many ways of describing patterns of adolescent growth and that one should not be surprised when different systems fail to agree. The problem may not be in the adolescent's behavior, only in our categories.

C. Intimacy, sex, and love
All this discussion about personal crisis and commitment to a social ideology seems a bit removed from two topics often taken to be at the very center of adolescent experience—love and sex (or is it sex and love?). Up to now, adolescent growth has been described in a sexless and loveless way. Yet who among us does not remember the excitement of early passion or the disorienting effects of early in-

fatuation? Any attempt to talk about the adolescent experience that does not deal with the issues of sex and love must surely be one-sided and prissily incomplete.

Although the adolescent may sometimes talk about sex with his or her own group as early as 11 or 12, the issue doesn't come out of the closet until about 14 or 15, sometimes even as late as 16 or 17. One reason, no doubt, is the social taboo against talking about sex. More significant, however, is the adolescent's fear of being overwhelmed by the strength of his or her attachment to another person. Although such attachment may at first be quite satisfying, it may also be quite frightening, especially if it involves giving up one's so recently won freedom and individuality.

Adolescents may experience a strong distinction between lust and idealized love, even though they seldom talk about it in precisely these words. Indeed, as Muuss (1975) has noted, it is not uncommon to find that an adolescent boy (or girl) will direct lust toward one girl (boy) and idealized love toward another. "Putting someone on a pedestal" is one way to talk about idealized love.

Since many of the social, personal, and economic attitudes in our society serve to separate love and sex, one of the major tasks faced by an adolescent is to grow from a strictly sexual orientation toward people of the opposite sex to one in which love and sex can be invested in the same person. Unfortunately, investing a single other person with so much that is so valuable is frightening, and this possibility is sometimes beyond the late adolescent as well as the young adult. Perhaps that is why Erikson sees the major crisis of the postadolescent years as the issue of intimacy: to whom should I give myself, and will such giving be reciprocated?

Fortunately, most of us do not stay scared, and we do give ourselves over in loving someone else. But what exactly is the nature of this love, and how have we been prepared for it? One of the most insightful discussions of this complex issue within the context of the developing human being has been offered by Erikson, who notes that each stage preceding the crisis of **intimacy vs. isolation** must make its own unique contribution to how we resolve that crisis. Trust, autonomy, initiative, industry, and identity all prepare the youth and then the young adult for entering into an intimate relationship. So, too, do the negative poles of each stage:

mistrust, shame, guilt, inferiority, and identity confusion.

Because the development of identity precedes intimacy as a psychosocial situation, the nature of the identity attained must strongly affect the type of intimacy possible. Past the age of the family triangle, the earliest experiences most of us have of cross-sex intimacy occur during middle or late adolescence. Erikson is quite clear in pointing out that teenage intimacy, as it may occur in "going steady," is not so much a matter of love as it is one of self-definition: "I lose myself in you so as to find me." The adolescent requires all kinds of relationships through which to define himself or herself, and giving oneself over to another person is often not so much a question of intimacy as of defining the boundaries of me.

Being in love is no simple matter for anyone, especially the adolescent. Because the adolescent is still in the process of answering the question "Who am I?," it is impossible for him or her to use the pronoun *we* with much conviction, especially if *we* implies a new union in which the *I* has to be partly given up. Although in a lasting and satisfactory relationship, the *I* returns to take its proper place alongside the *we*, the early stages of being in love involve a going beyond oneself in the strongest and most dramatic of terms. The adolescent, unfortunately, is least likely to be able to juggle *I* and *we* in a skillful way, and about 75% of adolescent marriages end in divorce.

The relationship between *I* and *we* is one that is not easily handled by contemporary society. If we pay too much attention to *we*, the *I* suffers; if we attend to the *I* alone, the *we* suffers. As adults we have to live with the continuing problem that *I* and *we* are both inclusive and exclusive: inclusive because *we* is larger than *I*; exclusive because in order to stay an *I*, I sometimes have to exclude you.

For the adolescent, the solution seems to require that the young person has to be an *I* before he or she can become part of an enduring *we*. If the person brings no solid *I* to a relationship, the *we* is fragile and easily disrupted. To love is to take a chance on giving yourself over to someone else in the hope that he or she will respect the significance of your mutual and precious gifts. This event is so important that you cannot leave it to reason or intellect alone; instead it must be a commitment of the total person if a loving *we* is to last.

That love endures is what love is about. Although it is difficult to describe the exact course loving takes, Kinget (1975) has suggested that it makes sense to divide love into three phases. The first phase is called "falling in love," the second "being in love," and the third "being fulfilled in love." Each of these phases creates its own tempo and its own set of concerns, from the point of view of an observer as well as from the point of view of each of the people involved.

What could be more exciting than falling in love? Although no two people ever experience falling in love in exactly the same way, Kinget notes that the phrase "falling in love" is a good one, and one that appears in many languages. The fall is never without excitement. It can be graceful or awkward, slow or fast, but it always involves a fall: a precipitous change in your way of looking at yourself, someone else, and, indeed, the whole of your world. Kinget talks of love in this phase as "addictive": you can never have enough of the look, the talk, the touch of the person you have just fallen in love with.

Unfortunately, addiction fades. When it does, "It was great fun / but it was just one of those things." If, however, loving endures, the tempo slows a bit, and a second phase, that of being in love, is reached. "Being in love" is perhaps the most pleasant time in anybody's life. It is in this phase that warmth spreads from the very center of one person to another and provides the experiences out of which enduring relationships are made. Yet such experiences are not always pleasant, for sometimes during this phase quarrels occur as each person comes to recognize some of the limitations of the other. Such quarrels not only reveal the other person, they also reveal the *me*; and how you and I work these problems out (or do not work them out) can have a beneficial or damaging effect on both of us.

Kinget talks of this second period as a "joyful apprenticeship," and, again, the phrase seems apt. Both members of a pair in love have to learn a lot about each other as well as about themselves. What used to be called the courtship or the engagement period often served this purpose. The more recent arrangement known as living together can serve much the same purpose. The major difference would seem to be sexual activity—and if the preceding generation of parents are honest, they will tell you that not much has changed. A more significant difference between courting and living together

concerns the day-to-day experiences made possible by the latter arrangement. Although couples 50 and even 25 years ago saw a good deal of each other during the courting period, they hardly ever worried together about the day-to-day work required initially by living together and later by staying together.

The final phase of a love relationship involves an enduring fulfillment in which two persons share a large portion of themselves and their lives with each other. Kinget suggests that the relationship changes from one of "face to face" to one of "side by side," so that a couple who endure as a couple come to live and work together as two individuals rather than only as a single unit. Members of a couple come to know each other, and if they are not undone by the knowledge of limitations brought on by such familiarity, the magic formula becomes "To know, yet to love."

These, then, are three phases of love described by Kinget. In the early adult years, it is unlikely that many people will experience much beyond infatuation and perhaps the beginning moments of "being in love." For the adolescent, as for the young adult, the task of identity—who am I—is much more significant than almost any other. For this reason, love also concerns this topic, as love becomes one more way in which I try to discover myself. The more mature forms of loving, and the intimacy that results from sharing oneself with someone else, are tasks left for future years. Indeed, the task of the decade from 20 to 30 is to define the nature of loving and bring it to a significant and human conclusion.

The decade that begins with being 20 leaves the person with a reasonable hold on himself or herself. During the next ten years this will change as the person enters into new and intimate relationships. In Western society one of the most important of these relationships is marriage. Within this relationship, the human life cycle takes a new turn for the growing person: no longer is he or she simply a participant in his or her parents' family; rather, he or she is the start of a new family. The decade between 20 and 30 represents an end to the "time between families" and marks the beginning of a new cycle in human life: that of *my* family. How it turns out no longer depends only or even primarily on my parents; it now depends on you and me and what we do.

III. THE ME, THE NOT-ME, AND WILLIAM JAMES

For most people, the adolescent years serve to resolve the issue of identity. By the time we are 20 or 25, we have a good idea of what we can do, how we look to others, what kind of career we would like to follow, and so on. Each of us, ideally, has also begun to explore intimate relationships in the hope of finding someone with whom to share a portion of the rest of our life.

A. Word problems in discussing "self"

Although most of us decide on an identity fairly early in life, the poor psychologist has never been able to decide exactly what it is each of us has accomplished in coming to a "sense of personal identity." One reason must surely be that the psychologist has too many words and concepts to deal with. In the course of this book, for example, the following terms have been used as synonyms for *identity* in one or another sense of the term: *I, me, person, mind, cogito, body, self, ego, consciousness, stream of consciousness, subject, individual, self-concept.* This excess of words suggests that something important needs to be talked about but no one can decide exactly how to do it. To help us talk about whatever "it" is, it seems best to select one of these words and then use it to represent the lot. But which one? Here let us be guided by William James (1893) and use his word, *self,* to deal with the various issues raised by each of the other words.

One reason for starting with James is that he had a knack for bringing order to a messy field, and "self" is a messy field. Consider the opening paragraph of his chapter on self written in 1893:

> Whatever I may be thinking of, I am always at the same time more or less aware of myself, of my personal existence. At the same time it is I who am aware, so that the total self of me [is] partly known and partly knower, partly object and partly subject.... For shortness we may call one the Me and the other, I [p. 176].

In this single paragraph, James poses many of the problems that need to be handled in discussing this topic of self. At the very beginning he points out that a silent I is involved in everything I think. We may extend this notion from thinking to doing and paraphrase James' first sentence: "Whatever I may be doing, be it thinking, moving, seeing, learning, perceiving, or something else, I am always at the same time more or less aware of myself." Another way of saying this is that I am always a part of the ground out of which one or another figure in my life emerges, whether this figure is an object or some action I am now doing.

Because our own personal "ground" is so usual and so close to us, it is extremely hard to recognize. Changing ground into figure is never easy, even in looking at simple drawings, and it is very difficult to bring the personal self to the foreground. The self is like the air we breathe: it takes the rather special (and unpleasant) condition of suffocation for us to recognize that the usually available air is no longer around. Perhaps it is for a similar reason that the psychiatrist or psychotherapist has been more involved in dealing with the idea of self than people in other areas of psychology have. After all, the theoretical or experimental psychologist scarcely, if ever, deals with people who are "falling apart"—people whose certainty about self has been undermined. Perhaps it takes the rather special situation of personal dissolution for us, either as people or as psychologists, to come face to face with the quiet presence of self in everyday life.

B. The I and the Me

The second part of James' paragraph draws a distinction between the words *I* and *Me.* In terms of grammar, *I* is the subject of a sentence, whereas *Me* is the object of a sentence. In a phrase such as "Me, a name I call myself" we can begin to see some of the complicated issues involved. In order for an I to name some aspect of its experiences as Me, it must already have had some experience with a "myself." This is not meant to be a bit of word play; instead, it is meant to suggest that the I, or I-who-knows, is different from the Me, or I-as-known.

This distinction does not exhaust all the things that can be experienced in connection with the words *I* and *me.* I, for one, find a striking difference in the familiarity (or personal warmth) I experience in talking with and about these two words. I find *I* a much less intimate pronoun than *me.* Somehow I always feel that the *Me* is more Me than any I could ever be. This suggests that my *Me* was around long before my *I* ever was—that is, that "I was known" long before "I knew." The full rich I of adult life seems to grow out of the more diffuse (and earlier) experience of being known by someone else. The world was probably divided up into a Me and a

Not-Me long before any grammatical I ever came on the scene.

All this fancy wordsmanship seems to leave us with two separate entities, an I and a Me. If we take the Me (the self as known) as our major category, we can never know who it is that knows the Me. If we take the I as primary (the self as knower), we face the opposite problem of trying to determine what exactly it is the I knows when it says "I know myself." For *either* an I or a Me to make sense, there have to be *both* an I and a Me. It was James who first pointed out that there could not be *only* an I or a Me: both had to be seen as aspects of the same process or event. What James had in mind was the stream of personal experience or, as he more usually called it, the stream of consciousness. For James the stream of consciousness was never a physical or even a psychological phenomenon. Instead, he presented it as an irreducible first-person fact of human experience. As such, it is a perfectly good place to begin any psychological approach to self.

Although James went back and forth between talking about the stream of consciousness as having to do mainly with thinking and other "mental" activities (see Chapter 5 for an example of this specific use) and as having to do with other, more general aspects of human existence, many other psychologists and philosophers have insisted that psychology must include the study of human conscious experience. Foremost among these have been people such as Merleau-Ponty (see Chapter 1), Buber (Chapter 2), Goldstein (Chapter 3), Werner (Chapter 4), Köhler (Chapter 5), Edie (Chapter 6), Giorgi (Chapter 7), Van Den Berg (Chapter 8), and Minkowski (Chapter 9), to list only a few who found their way onto the pages of this book. Although each of these thinkers has given a somewhat individual interpretation to the idea of consciousness, all have agreed on the distinction between reflected and unreflected consciousness as well as on the idea that consciousness is an ongoing event, never a static "thing."

It is not surprising, given this agreement, to see that the self-as-knower refers to unreflected aspects of self and that the self-as-known refers to reflected aspects of self. Thus, I and Me are not two different phenomena: they simply represent two relationships a person can have with his or her own unique stream of conscious experience. If we fail to make this distinction, we can end up by seeing *I* and *Me*

as two totally different theoretical events—a situation quite contrary to what James meant to suggest.

C. *Self and* Dasein

Any attempt to describe "self" as an ongoing event runs into the problem that the word *self* (like the word *consciousness*) is a noun. As such, it seems to suggest a static object quite at odds with James' (and many other) descriptions. For this reason, we need to think and talk in terms of some image that recognizes the ongoing nature of the event usually called "self" and recognizes that the image is only an imitation of our experience, never the experience. One way out of this dilemma is to try never to use the word *self* or any of its synonyms. Barrett (1958) has suggested that the philosopher Martin Heidegger tried to talk about human existence without using any of the ordinary words such as *self, person, ego,* or *consciousness.* In place of these words Heidegger chose to use the relatively simple German word *Dasein,* which is probably best translated as "being there" or "existence." Although Heidegger wants to include these meanings, *Dasein* is much more complex. It is hard to define what Heidegger means exactly; *Dasein* may also be described as "a clearing within a forest" or as "the place where Being reveals itself" (Harries, 1967) or, finally, as a "field or region of concern" (Barrett, 1958).

In talking about the idea of *Dasein* as a field, Barrett describes the case of a young child who has just learned to respond to his own name. When called, the child comes promptly enough; if asked to point out who it was that was called, he is much less certain. Sometimes he may point to himself and sometimes even to his mother or father. When asked the question some months or years later, the child will unhesitatingly point to himself. Before he reaches that stage, however, the child

> has heard his name as describing a field or region of Being with which he is concerned, and to which he responds, whether the call is to come to food, to mother, or whatever. And the child is right. His name is not the name of an existence that takes place within the envelope of his skin: that is merely the abstract social convention that has imposed itself not only on his parents but on the history of philosophy. The basic meaning the child's name has for him does not disappear as he grows older: it only becomes covered over by the more abstract social convention. He secretly hears his own

name called whenever he hears any region of Being named with which he is vitally involved [Barrett, 1958, p. 195].[3]

Heidegger sometimes thinks of the person as a gap and sometimes as a special region of Being. As a gap, the person is defined by being absent; as a field, the person is defined by spreading over everything he or she is vitally involved with. Once before (in Chapter 3) we encountered the poet Mark Strand's idea that a person could be thought of as something missing in a field. As he put it, "In a field / I am the absence of field," and this poetic image seems to capture at least one part of Heidegger's attempt to talk about self without using any of the ordinary words.

Unfortunately, the idea of a gap or a field still seems a bit too static to capture my experience. Often I find myself wanting to give this gap movement and life. For this reason I always try to think of Heidegger's *Dasein* as an amebalike opening in Being. Here I am thinking about the constantly shifting form that defines what the textbook will freeze as the ameba's shape. I prefer to think of the ameba as I see it, alive and flowing, under the microscope. With this in mind, it is possible to think of *Dasein* as a continuously moving and changing form within the larger ground of a continuously moving and varying world—in short, the Jamesian self.

This description is also close to what Merleau-Ponty described as the **living body**. A long and detailed analysis of this topic (see Chapter 3) convinced Merleau-Ponty that the human body is described best not in terms of biology but in terms of personal intentions. For him, the living body is the way each of us relates to and is related to the world. The human body expresses and reveals us in everything we do. It is not an object that does things because some intelligence "tells" it to, nor is it pure intelligence that makes an "I" out of lifeless flesh. Rather, the body is me; and I, as body, am always alive and always in the world.

The living body is neither spirit nor flesh in the usual sense of these terms. It is better to think of the living body as the most basic aspect of what we

usually call the person. As such, it is that region of the world which I call *me* and through which I deal with my living human world. My body is never just another object in the world; it is always that unique part of the world from which I do whatever it is I do, whether it be eating, thinking, walking, talking, or any of the hundreds of other ways I am able to relate (and be related) to the world.

D. Self and selves

When Lyndon Johnson was asked to describe himself, he did so in the following terms: "I am a free man, an American, a U.S. Senator, a Democrat, a liberal, a conservative, a Texan, a rancher and not as young as I used to be nor as old as I expect to be" (Gergen, 1971, p. 19). This list does not seem extraordinary: each of us could probably also list some characteristics we thought could describe us to others (and to ourselves).

A list like the one created by LBJ is a reflected attempt to describe the most familiar of all things: oneself. Because it is a description, the particular facts chosen to present one's concept of oneself to someone else must vary in at least four ways: how central they are to us, how clear they are to us, to whom we are describing ourselves, and for what purpose.

We all know that some parts of our self-concept are more important to us than others. As William James noted some 90 years ago:

> I, who for the time have staked my all on being a psychologist, am mortified if others know much more psychology than I. But I am contented to wallow in the grossest ignorance of Greek. My deficiencies there give me no sense of personal humiliation. Had I "pretensions" to be a linguist, it would have been just the reverse. So we have the paradox of a man shamed to death because he is only the second pugilist in the world . . . that he is able to beat the whole population of the globe minus one is nothing; he has "pitted" himself to beat that one; and as long as he doesn't do that nothing else counts [1890/1950, p. 310].

Not all the adjectives used by a person in describing himself or herself are equally clear to the person using them. For example, in LBJ's self-description, "a Texan" is a much clearer and more easily defined characteristic than "a liberal." A more significant way a descriptive term may be unclear to the person using it concerns the user's degree of familiarity with that term. For example, describing

[3]Excerpted from *Irrational Man: A Study in Existential Philosophy*, by William Barrett. Copyright © 1958 by William Barrett. This and all other quotations from this source are reprinted by permission of Doubleday & Company, Inc.

oneself as an adult is much less clear to an early adolescent than it is to a 30–35-year-old (Combs, Richards, & Richards, 1976).

Over and above these problems are the reasons a particular person has for describing himself or herself. It is quite one thing to attempt an "honest" private definition and quite another to define oneself for a prospective employer. Each situation selects its own adjectives, and even if the person is not trying to lie, there will probably be little overlap in the two lists. Describing oneself is never done out of context or without some reasons, and the contexts and the reasons profoundly determine what will or will not appear in one's description.

It is impossible for anyone to describe himself or herself in only one or two adjectives; we are much more complicated than that. LBJ's list, which (depending on how you count them) contains nine or ten characteristics, does not seem unreasonably long; we all could produce a list equally long, if not longer. What these everyday facts suggest is that "the self" can never be described as a single, unified entity. Rather, we seem to have many "subselves," and these are defined by the groups each of us feels are important to us.

E. The looking-glass self

When we think about the matter in this way, it is quite clear that we are not only our own creation. Rather, our ideas about ourselves must be strongly determined by how other people deal with us— both in what they do to and with us and in how they think of us. At the beginning of this century, the sociologist Herbert Cooley described this state of affairs as leading to a **"looking-glass self"**; that is, each of us comes to an evaluation of self in the mirror provided by the actions of other important people in our life. A later sociologist, G. H. Mead, extended this idea to suggest that we come to respond to ourselves in terms of how others respond to us, and hence each of us comes to develop many different "selves." Each self mirrors the responses made to us by a different social group, such as our playmates, our family, or our teachers. Each of us develops a "family-self," a "peer-self," a "school-self," and so on.

But exactly where and how does this happen? One of the major settings in which the child comes to some realization of herself as others see her is in play and its more formal counterpart, games. Who

has not seen a young child, after being scolded for leaving her toys around, scold herself the next day even though her parents are nowhere in sight? And who has not seen the same young child compliment herself for a job well done? These very ordinary behaviors suggest that the young child practices the reactions other people have toward her and on this basis comes to learn two very important things: one, that she is "third-person" to all other people; and two, that there are proper (expected) things to do in certain situations.

A more complicated example of how social selves might develop can be seen by watching a mother feeding her baby. The mother's facial expression of "opening wide" as the spoon approaches the baby's mouth shows she is taking the role of the child. To learn how to be fed, the child must imitate what the mother does. In this imitation, the child takes the role of the mother (as she takes the role of the child). The mother acts as if she were being fed, and the child, acting like the mother acting as if she were being fed, is fed. The whole business involves mother and child taking the role of each other and, for a time, becoming the other.

The child's ability to take the perspective of a great many others—mothers, fathers, friends, and so on—reaches its most developed form not in imitative play but in that highly structured situation known as a game. In order to play a rule-governed game such as baseball (or even marbles), the child has to learn to anticipate the responses of other people playing the game with him. To do this, the child has to "put himself in their place." What the child learns in learning how to play a particular game is not only the rules of the game but how to take another person's point of view. In learning how to do this, the child comes to define himself as others do. If different situations call out different ways of dealing with the world, it is possible to see how the young child develops a "baseball-self," a "family-self," a "school-self," and so on.

Mead's analysis of self is a strongly reflected one. The definition one has of oneself comes from seeing and thinking about oneself as others do. This means that Mead's social self (really, selves) is part of the Jamesian *Me* rather than the Jamesian *I*. For Mead the person's selves are always "objects of consciousness," not personal consciousness itself. Yet there is no reason to restrict Mead's analysis to reflected selves. We may also learn what is expected of us, and do it, in the absence of ever reflecting on it. We all sit more properly when we are our "good girl" selves than when we are our "slumber party" selves. The reactions others have toward us not only appear in the various self-concepts we have of ourselves; they also appear in the style and manner in which we, as living people, participate in various settings. Far from applying only to the reflected self, Mead's analysis is also quite relevant to the unreflected domain as well.

On either a reflected or unreflected level, we seem to have many different selves. Although it is possible to argue that each of us can have as many social selves as there are people who know us, it seems more reasonable to put these "selves" (and the people who define them) into personally meaningful groups. We often show a "different self" to different groups. Sometimes these selves are in conflict, as when the psychologist, as his teacher self, flunks a student even though he, as his clinical self, understands the student's personal problems. Sometimes there is a perfectly harmonious split, "as where one is teacher to his children, but stern to the soldiers or prisoners under his command" (James, 1890/1950, p. 254). The reason such a split can be harmonious is that there are clear social expectations of what is proper behavior for a "father" and a "general," and these expectations are specific to specific situations. Splits are difficult only to the degree that there is no consistent social expectation of the proper behavior for a particular person in a particular situation.

If there are "so many" different social selves, how do we ever resolve conflicts among them? Here James suggests that each person picks out "his strongest and deepest" self and places his "self-contentment" on the fortunes of this "self." A person's selves are not equally important; some are more central than others. It is the person's own evaluation of which are the "important" and the "unimportant" selves that protects him from humiliation and helps him decide on the proper grounds for personal satisfaction.

So far, so good: James has divided the self into selves and, along with Mead, has studied the social nature of many of these selves, and he finally has described the conditions under which conflict will or will not arise. Yet there is still a problem: we as people never experience only a collection of selves;

we often seem to experience a certain unity of self, and this "self of selves" still needs to be described. What is missing, of course, is the other part of the I/Me relationship. In fact, it is the experience of an I that comes closest to satisfying what might be meant by the idea of a "self of selves." Somehow or other there seems to be some unchanging core to each of us, and it is this core that seems to capture best what we mean by *self* or *I*.

In talking about this issue, Combs, Richards, and Richards (1976) present Figure 11-1, which represents a single person's phenomenal field at a single moment. The outer ring, marked C, is meant to show that the phenomenal field includes all the personally relevant aspects of the world, whether these relate directly to the self or not. The second ring, marked B, includes everything about the person that is of some importance to the person, whether or not it is important in this situation. Rings B and C are always defined for a specific situa-

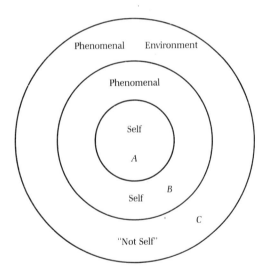

Figure 11-1. A simple diagram of the personal field at a given moment. *(Figure 7.1, page 160, in* Perceptual Psychology: A Humanistic Approach to the Study of Persons, *by Arthur W. Combs, Anne Cohen Richards, and Fred Richards. Copyright 1949 by Harper & Row, Publishers, Inc. Copyright © 1959 by Arthur W. Combs and Donald Snygg. Copyright © 1976 by Harper & Row, Publishers, Inc. Reprinted by permission of the publishers.)*

ation and represent the total "pool" of reflected and unreflected "selves" that are of relevance in the situation.

The center circle, labeled A, seems best defined as including the most stable, important, and characteristic aspects of the person—in short, the essence of "me." This core defines the person in all situations and at all times, and the loss of this center can only be regarded by the person as equal to personal destruction. Even though much of the phenomenal field varies from situation to situation and from time to time, there is a continuity to the field, and it is this continuity we call "self."

IV. THE DEVELOPMENT OF SELF

To summarize, there are several aspects to what we might mean by the word *self*. These fall into three categories: (1) A bodily aspect defined not in terms of physiology but in terms of the unique pattern of intentions expressed by the nature and style of our actions. (2) A social aspect defined in terms of differentially significant selves growing out of a wide variety of interpersonal experiences and situations. (3) An intellectual or reflected aspect defined in terms of our own private and public reflections on ourselves at various points in life. Any approach to the idea of self must include a discussion of at least the following three "sets of selves": a bodily, or intending self; a social, or interpersonal, self; and a reflected, or thought-about, self.

With these categories in mind, we can describe the way each of the various aspects of self develops. In going about this, let us take whatever help we can get from wherever we can get it: let us look both at experimental and observational facts and at Freud's, Erikson's, and Piaget's theories of development. In the end, let us hope the facts will yield a picture of the developing self that is consistent with our experiences as people as well as with the major theories describing how the self develops.

A. Facts on the bodily (intending) self

Since almost all the facts relevant to the task of understanding the **intending self** have been presented in Chapter 3, all that needs to be done now is to point out a few of the more important ones, especially those that seem to have a clear age range at which they first occur.

1. Recognizing oneself in the mirror.   The data are quite clear in showing that infants recognize others in the mirror before they recognize themselves. When infants do behave in regard to their own reflected images, they usually behave socially—that is, as if the image were another infant. Following this early period, they often respond emotionally to their image—by either laughing or crying. Not until about age 2 do children come to recognize themselves as separate and bounded entities: as objects. Up to this point, they seem to be without boundaries, and although they can recognize others, they do not seem to recognize that unique location in the world that they will later call Me or I. In the beginning, the first-person world of the infant is best described as a formless void in which events happen and in which there are no secure personal boundaries.

2. Phantom limbs.   For amputations occurring before age 4, only 23% of patients report phantoms. For amputations occurring after age 8, 100% report phantoms. Research by Simmel shows that if a limb that is not usable is amputated, no phantom results. Simmel also found that individuals suffering from leprosy, in which there is a gradual loss of use sometimes taking ten years or more, never experience phantoms.

3. Skilled actions.   Data from a fairly diverse set of moving people—athletes, artistic performers, more ordinary adults doing skilled typing and so on—suggest that for the skilled person there is no division between thinking and doing the performance itself. A description of the athlete's first-person world provides the best examples of the simultaneity between body and will, action and intent, movement and meaning. Not only do these usually separate events form a unity, so do the person and his or her situation. Such unity has been described in terms of the pattern of forces in the athlete's self-world; within the constraints of a game, the skilled athlete often "abandons" himself or herself to the process so that person and situation form a single dynamic system.

The fact that training allows us to "get outside" (or transcend) ourselves suggests that the self-less state of the infant is different from the self-less state of the adult. The infant has no "self" to come back to, whereas the adult does experience a personally unique sense of self-continuity after the skilled activity has run its course. To relinquish self in some activity is not the same as having no self at all. Although it may be an extraordinary experience to give up one's self (as in athletes), it does not signal the end of a personal core. Indeed, such experiences are exhilarating and may make the rest of our existence all the more full and meaningful.

B. Facts on the interpersonal (social) self

The facts suggest that the first glimmerings of bodily self occur at about age 2. Is there anything comparable for the social, or interpersonal, self? The most important single fact seems to be that speaking occurs at about this age. With the advent of speaking, the child automatically comes into greater and more enduring contact with his or her social world.

1. Use of personal names and pronouns.

More relevant to the case of self, however, is the question of how and when children come to use those words in their language that refer to themselves as well as to others. What is the developmental course of children's use of proper names (including their own) and of their equivalents, the pronouns? The overwhelming bulk of evidence suggests that important proper nouns are learned well in advance of personal pronouns, such as *I* or *you*. Children begin to use pronouns considerably after they have used a wide variety of nouns, adjectives, and verbs. The earliest words (nouns) are produced, on the average, at about 60 weeks of age. In addition, most children recognize their own names at about 35 weeks of age and use them by 80 weeks. In contrast, they use the personal pronoun *I* correctly only at about 100 weeks of age and not very regularly until about 130 weeks.

Many studies have also found that the young child does not interchange *I* and *you* in an ongoing conversation until well over age 2½. This observation would seem quite relevant to our concern with the development of social selves. To use the words *I* and *you* correctly, the "I" must be able to switch roles with the "you." It is a peculiar fact of language that when you speak, you are *I* and I am *you*, but that when I speak, you are *you* and I am *I*. The ability to use *I* and *you* correctly must signal a better-

than-beginning knowledge of intersubjectivity. It would seem to signal the development of secure but fluid personal boundaries—boundaries that enable me to stay *me* when I speak or to become *you* when you speak. Probably because this is such a difficult bit of learning to accomplish, we often hear children as old as 3 or 4 years refer to themselves as Jonathan or Michele, rather than as I or me.

To use pronouns well relates directly to G. H. Mead's ideas about how the social self develops. According to Mead, to define oneself always involves taking the point of view of someone else. Changing from *I* to *you* and perhaps then to *he* or *she* shows that I can deal with the ongoing flux of social interactions from more than a single point of view. It also shows that I am sometimes able to see myself as an object (a *he, she,* or *it*) for someone else.

2. Social play.

Mead, however, did not focus on the child's use of pronouns; he was more interested in the role of play (and later of games) in providing the young child with experiences appropriate to the task of defining a Me. Because of Mead's theoretical position, it is important to look for the development of an interpersonal self in the child's manner of playing with someone else. Nursery-school children often engage in what is called **parallel play**, in which two or more children play at individual games while sitting or standing next to each other.

Parten (1932) made some early observations on children's play. Although she divided play activities into six categories, it seems more useful to reduce them to the two categories of "self-play" and "play involving others." Even by age 4½, play involving others accounted for only 35% of the cases Parten observed. The comparable value for **solitary play** at this age was 24%. As a point of contrast, at age 2½, self-play accounted for 41% of the cases, play with others for only 13%. It seems that not until about age 6 does play involving others come to be the major way in which children play. Unfortunately, playing alone (or with others) ceases to be a very reasonable measure of social interaction when the child enters school, because play is no longer self-determined but is now firmly in somebody else's hands: the teacher's.

Perhaps the only possible follow-up to these results concerns the child's playing rule-governed games with other children. According to Piaget, children show evidence of being able to follow the rules of a game (marbles) concerning other players at about 5 or 6 years. Only at 7 or 8, however, does the child play the game in a consistent and rule-oriented way that clearly takes others into account. The child still cannot tell you in any clear way what the rules are; this ability will come only much later, at about 11 or 12. For our purposes, the child is first able to behave appropriately with others in a game at between 6 and 7 years and does not become proficient until a few years later.

C. Facts on the reflected self

Whenever we ask who it is that worries most about the question "Who am I?," the answer always seems to be "The adolescent." To talk about the reflected self automatically demands that we consider the world of the adolescent as a critical point. But the adolescent is not alone in having to deal with this question: people older and younger than this age also deal with it from time to time. A slightly different but related question is "At what age is the child first able to answer the question 'who am I'?" The answer seems to be 5 or 6. If we ask a slightly more specific question, such as "Are you a boy or a girl?," the child as young as 3 or 4 can answer it.

These values represent a lower limit to when the child is able to talk in one way or another about who or what he or she is. They do not, however, represent the age at which such questions assume prime importance on their own. If anything, the young child (3–5) considers questions about himself or herself as "funny things adults like to know," not as points of compelling personal interest. Self-generated interest in questions of this sort begins in early adolescence and continues throughout adult life.

Perhaps one reason children do not spontaneously ask questions of the "Who am I?" type early in life is that they are not yet comfortable enough with speaking to extend it to speaking about oneself. Children younger than 12, however, do seem to reflect on what it means to be a person, and these reflections are perhaps best captured in young children's drawings of the human body. Work on figure drawing (see Chapter 3) shows clearly that children like to draw pictures of human beings and that such drawings can be used as measures of "intelli-

gence" only from about age 4 to about age 9. By 9, almost everybody gets everything right; at age 4 each drawing is almost unique to the particular child.

These data suggest that although self-reflection can be prompted by adult questions at age 3 or 4, it does not emerge on its own even in figure drawings until somewhere between 4 and 9. Self-reflection in the form of asking questions about oneself does not begin until about 11 or 12. By this time, the child has long since observed all his or her body parts, and so the reflections of a 12-year-old usually have to do with social rather than bodily matters. Together, the data on figure drawing, on children's answers to questions, and on children's spontaneous introspection suggest that the growing child is first able to reflect about himself or herself somewhere between 3 and 9 years of age. A second major peak is reached at 12 or 13. In addition, the tendency to think about oneself, who one is, what one is like, what one is likely to do, and so on seems to continue, at irregular intervals, throughout life.

One further set of reflected self-concerns is those that go by the names of **self-esteem**, self-regard, self-identity, and so on. All such concepts represent specific functions or concerns of a person that are thought about and decided upon throughout life. Self-reflection is an ongoing process, and when we talk about a "reflected self," we must be careful to remember that any reflected self is always in a continual state of redefinition. If there is one topic that interests us, and one that we come back to over and over again, it must be the topic of Me as understood by I.

D. A summary and some theory

All these facts have been brought together to look at the developing self as it grows out of dealings with the world. The conclusion from this somewhat selective review of the evidence is that we can single out at least three distinct phases in the development of self as of greatest importance.

First, results involving children's dealing with their own reflections in the mirror suggest 2 (or just before) as a critical age. Simmel's work on phantom limbs implicates a period between 4 and 8 as critical. Work on pronouns suggests 2 as a critical time for the development of a "social self." Research on children at play suggests that it is only at about 5 or

6 that the child comes to play well and regularly with others; only at 7 or 8 can more formal games (such as marbles or dodgeball) be played cooperatively, and not until 12 can children describe the rules of a game to someone else. Finally, the child's ability to reflect on himself or herself seems to arise somewhere between 3 and 9 years, and it is not until 11 or 12 that the child raises such questions spontaneously.

Considering all these findings together suggests that the development of self occurs in three critical phases, at about 2, 6, and 12 years of age. Although not all aspects of self are equally visible at each age, such values provide a reasonable set of benchmarks. It is also worth noting that these ages are almost identical to Piaget's stages of intellectual development. In addition, they are quite compatible with both Freud's and Erikson's approaches to human development.

In talking about specific ages in the growth of self, such as 2, 6, and 12, such values should never be taken as absolute and fixed. Rather, these ages can best be thought of as mnemonic devices; each age provides a rough idea of when important things might be happening in the growing child's or ado-

lescent's life. It is never the exact year that matters; what does matter is the order in which each aspect of self appears as well as its interrelationship to all the other aspects of self that have emerged or are yet to emerge.

All these facts are combined in Figure 11-2, which presents the major milestones in the development of various aspects of self. This figure tries to take into account all the ideas and conclusions suggested by what we know of human development.

One feature of Figure 11-2 is that it shows the ever more differentiated nature of the developing self. The earliest aspects of self clearly concern intentional action by the infant on his or her world. It is through the body that the child relates and is related to the world, and for this reason the term *body self* is used in Figure 11-2 to describe the pattern of these unreflected relationships. Here, as elsewhere, *body* does not mean the fleshy body known to biology; rather, it means the embodiment of an individual's intentional relationships in the world.

The second aspect of self to be differentiated once there is a functioning/intending body is the social (or interpersonal) self. This aspect of self can

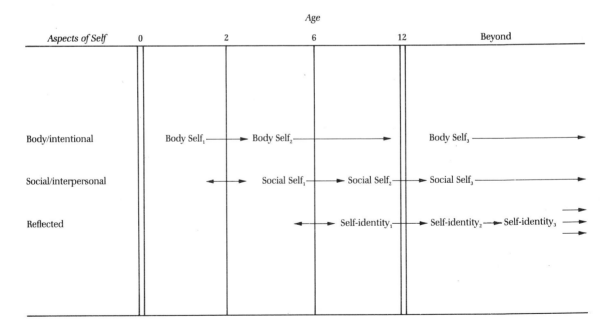

Figure 11-2. Developmental milestones in the bodily, social, and reflected aspects of Self.

begin to emerge only when the person has established a flexible but viable form for himself or herself. Even though the "body" and "social" selves have been described as different aspects of self, they are not separate and unrelated parts. Rather, at this point in life, as at all others, the person is a unity, and how well a young child can do things surely determines the nature of his or her unreflected social self. *Self* always suggests a patterned whole—a Gestalt—of everything the person is and can do; it is never simply a collection of separate functions and pieces. Every developmental change brings about a new and different organization of the person. Although Figure 11-2 might suggest that body self$_2$ is a simple continuation of body self$_1$, this is not at all the way the person experiences his or her development. It may be reasonable to study separately the development of various aspects of self, but such study is meaningful only when the developing aspect is seen as a part of a growing child. All aspects of the developing self are interdependent; individual study of them makes sense only if the total pattern is firmly held in mind.

The third major aspect of this emerging pattern concerns children's developing ability to distance themselves from themselves. As Piaget has shown, at about age 6 (and even a year or two before), the child is able to think about many topics, including body and social self. At first, the child is limited to concrete aspects of self. Most of the things a young child says about himself or herself are concrete: "My name is Jon; I live on Sheffield Drive; I'm 7 years old; I have blond hair." Only later will such reflections include "who I am" (my identity), "what I'd like to be" (my ideal self), and so on.

The self-reflection of the 6-year-old changes the personal Gestalt once more. The relatively simple changes that occur at this point bring about a new and relatively stable personal organization that will last until puberty. At that time, formal-operational thinking will force a dramatic and far-reaching reorganization. Because the organization attained during this earlier period is quite stable, the years between 6 and 12 may be among the most satisfying in a child's life. Perhaps it was for this reason that Freud termed a roughly comparable span of years the developing child's period of latency.

As presented in Figure 11-2, the developmental pattern is reasonably clear from birth to age 12. Aspects of the person arrive on the scene in their appropriate sequence. Each aspect serves to shape further the pattern that is now the person. The changes that occur in the person at puberty, however, are probably more far-reaching than at any other single time. Not only is there a rapid change in body size, weight, and so on, but new modes of behavior become possible. The body, which up to now provided a secure foundation for my ability to deal with the world, suddenly becomes different. New bodily fluids appear in both the female and male adolescent, and even though I can still walk, talk, stand, and so on, my body is no longer the well-known friend it has been up to now.

If the adolescent experiences discomfort with his or her bodily self, he or she is likely to experience a good deal of discomfort in social expectations as well. There is a sharp discontinuity in our expectations of what is right and proper for children and adults to do, and the adolescent sits precariously balanced in the borderland between child and adult. The secure, unreflected social world of the child comes increasingly to be replaced by a confused and confusing world of conflicting and rapidly changing expectations. Under the joint onslaught of changing body and changing social world, it is no wonder that the child turns to reflect on the one question that needs answering: "Who am I?"

Unfortunately, the smoothly functioning and totally reliable process of thinking that up to this time has guided the child has recently also become a bit less reliable. As Piaget and many others have shown, the reflected world of the child suddenly breaks out of the world of "as is" to become the world of "as if." But the world of "as if" is unruly and at first controls the adolescent rather than vice versa. With experience, the possibilities of "as if" are tamed and finally come under the control of the growing person.

There will be many future evaluations of self, and each of these will change the person. Because much of our postadolescent life is lived in a world of planning and symbols, many of these progressive changes will begin as reflections about one's self and one's life. Each resolution will disorganize the person for a time, yet each will also serve to re-form the person into a new and sensitively balanced pattern.

The development of self is thus a lifelong process. Although it is possible to tie each of the three major aspects of development to one or another specific point in time, the important thing about such development is that it is continuous and interrelated. Some aspects emerge before others and come to provide the background on which a new and different aspect will depend. For example, body and social selves interrelate, and both are changed as a result: If the infant never learned to move intentionally, it would be very unlikely that he or she could deal with other people except as a "getter." Having control of our intentions (via bodily movements) would seem to be a precondition for intentional movement toward other people. Similarly, once the infant becomes a toddler and enters bodily into the social world, new movement skills are needed and even taught.

The self always emerges not only out of the developing aspects of the person but also out of the interaction between these aspects and the world. For this reason, different situations may affect the time of arrival of each new stage, though most likely not the order. Here, as elsewhere, there is a reasonableness to the order in which the person develops, and it is only out of such order that an infant comes to move ever more precisely from body to society and from society to the varying worlds of theoretical possibility and beyond. It is this order that defines the development of self.

V. SELF: EAST AND WEST

All this talk about self seems far removed from the Zen Master Archer who felt that one could be expected to hit a bull's-eye only to the degree that one was a "selfless" self (see Chapter 7). What the Zen Master meant was that during the act of shooting at a target, there must be no separation among any of the "parts." To hit a target, the archer, bow, and bull's-eye must all form a single unity. When this occurs, the archer is effortlessly involved with his target, not with himself.

According to the more Western views offered by James, Piaget, Erikson, and Freud, every act has at least two reference points: the actor (self) and the action done. For James, the self is always a quiet participant in everything we do. Each of us experiences a bit of self in every act, reflected or unreflected.

How different this is from the Eastern view of self as "no-self," most especially that presented by Zen

Buddhism. In trying to convey the difference between East and West, the eminent Japanese interpreter of Zen theory D. T. Suzuki (1960) presented two poems, both concerned with the issue of what it means to say that a human being understands something. One of these poems is by the Japanese poet Bashō, the second by Alfred, Lord Tennyson. Bashō's poem goes as follows:

> When I look carefully
> I see the nazuna blooming
> By the hedge!

Bashō's poem is a haiku, a verse form of Japanese origin in which the poet describes his experiences with a single aspect of the world as simply and concretely as possible: in this case, his experiences of a nazuna flower.

Tennyson's more complicated poem goes as follows:

> Flower in the crannied wall,
> I pluck you out of the crannies;
> Hold you here, root and all, in my hand,
> Little flower—but if I could understand
> What you are, root and all, and all in all,
> I should know what God and man is.

Suzuki (1960) points out that these two poets are obviously dealing with the same situation, their reactions to a flower. Just as obviously, they deal with it in quite different ways. For one, Tennyson plucks the flower, while Bashō simply looks at it, as he says, "carefully." In this difference the poets reveal a basic difference between East and West: whereas East is able to leave things alone and try to grasp the meaning of things in their entirety, West analyzes and, by its analysis, destroys what it is trying to understand. Suzuki also points out that Tennyson is filled with the desire to understand ("what God and man is"); Bashō is content simply to experience, without any explicit reflection on this experience.

There is also a difference in style. Bashō accepts the limits of a 17-syllable form (the haiku) and expresses his relationship to the world quite simply. Tennyson uses an intricate and complicated rhyming scheme involving over 50 syllables and, as Suzuki says, "transforms the word into flesh and makes the flesh too voluptuous."

But what of self in all of this? Tennyson, like

Westerners in general, treats the flower as an object separate from himself. For Tennyson, to understand any object fully is to understand the world, and it is always a separated self that does the understanding of a separated world. For Tennyson (as for Descartes and the rest of us) there is a break between subject and object; we in the Western world always seem to sit at an uncomfortable distance from a world we can look at but never feel integrated within.

Contrast Bashō's view. There, the self experiences the world directly. For Bashō there is no split between "me" and "it." What could be more natural and effortless—one part of the world flowing in and through another? There is no division of person from world: the human being is not encapsulated in his or her mental cocoon; world and person form an indivisible unity. Note also that Bashō presents a very ordinary experience as it occurs in everyday life. He does not "study" a plucked and dead flower; he is involved with his flower in a very ordinary, everyday sort of way. The Zen view of self presents it not as an abstract thing but as a seamless garment in which world and person are united.

In presenting Suzuki's view of Zen to the Western world, the American philosopher William Barrett described it as follows:

> [The] passion for ... living facts accounts for that quality in the Zen masters which must seem most amazing to the Westerner; their supreme matter-of-factness. "What is the truth?" asks the disciple. "Your everyday mind," replies the Master; and he goes on to amplify: "When I am hungry, I eat; when tired, I sleep." The disciple is puzzled, and asks whether this is not what everybody else does too. No, the Master replies; most people are never wholly in what they are doing; when eating, they may be absent-mindedly preoccupied with a thousand different fantasies; when sleeping, they are not sleeping. The supreme mark of the thoroughly integrated man is to be without a divided mind. This matter-of-fact spirit of Zen is expressed in another paradoxical statement: "Before you have studied Zen, mountains are mountains and rivers are rivers; while you are studying it, mountains are no longer mountains and rivers no longer rivers; but once you have had Enlightenment, mountains are once again mountains and rivers are rivers" [Barrett, 1956, p. xvi].[4]

[4]Excerpted from "Introduction" in *Zen Buddhism: Selected Writings of D. T. Suzuki*, edited by William Barrett. Copyright © 1956 by Rider & Co. Reprinted by permission of Rider & Co. and Doubleday & Company, Inc.

The last part of this passage expresses an important truth about Zen truth: it is not something that *just* comes to you. As the German philosopher struggling to learn archery found, it takes time and training. Once there, however, you are no longer separate from the world, and mountains and rivers are free to be mountains and rivers once again.

This point draws us back again to the idea of the living body. In the beginning there is no body. The infant experiences every action as individual and unique. With time and further experience, the body "comes together," and the infant comes to be in unreflected and continuous contact with his or her world. The growth of reflection serves to define subject and object, first somewhat tentatively, then somewhat more forcefully. The early culmination of thinking ends at about age 12. At this time reflection turns back on itself, and the major object of interest turns out to be the person. The adolescent works hard at defining himself or herself, and only when this issue is resolved is he or she able to reenter a world of concerns larger than self. Most of us, unfortunately, continue all our lives in the split between subject and object, and only occasionally in music, in athletics, or perhaps even in thinking do we come back into comfortable and continuous contact with what Heidegger called Being. The Zen Master—whether in archery, painting, or flower arranging—is regularly able to reenter Being for a timeless bit of time. Even the Zen Master must return to a state of dividedness, in which person and world relate but are not in seamless contact.

The goal of total immersion in Being, where "self disappears," is a state that only few are able to enter. Many Zen Masters are never able to enter and live in this condition. Although the "selfless self" of Zen is possible for all of us, only a few get there and then only after much training and much discipline.

Should we in the Western world feel cheated that we usually end up with a Jamesian rather than a Zen self? The answer must be no, for here we must remember that the idea (and the reality) of a selfless self grows out of a particular culture, and it is not our culture that it grows out of. Any attempt to transplant this ideal to Western soil must surely alter the nature of Zen no less than the nature of Western society. For us, as for much of the East, the Zen self seems better thought of as a possibility than as something to be rigorously sought. To take the Zen self as the "proper self" for Westerners is to ask for too big a change in our style of living. After all, it took over 2000 years for the appropriate conditions to develop in the East. Only a hopelessly Western person would expect to duplicate these conditions within a single lifetime. As the Zen Master said, attaining a selfless self, even in the East, is so difficult that it is like "a mosquito trying to bite an iron ball." How much more so for the Western person!

VI. SUMMARY

Human beings have always struggled with the question "Who am I?" If at certain times this question does not seem to come up, this is only a respite, not a reprieve. Although we all have to deal with this question, adolescence seems to be a more fertile time for the question than any other. One obvious reason for this concern is the changes that occur in the body at puberty. An equally important reason is the sometimes confusing messages given by parents and society, such as "You can't do that; you're not an adult yet." Finally, significant intellectual changes (formal-operational thinking) also occur at this age to complicate the adolescent's self-world even further.

The adolescent period in technological societies has within it strong forces for change as well as an implicit imperative to break with the (childish) past. Adolescence is not like that in all cultures. Margaret Mead's study of Samoan society shows that the transition between childhood and adult life can be relatively smooth, uncomplicated, and continuous. For example, there are fewer taboos concerning responsibility or sexuality all through the life of a Samoan, and Samoan children (and adults) deal with both responsibility and sexuality in a more continuous way throughout life than we do.

Why does adolescence stand out in Western society as a particularly difficult period for many people? Perhaps, as Benedict noted, because we place more emphasis on discontinuities in development rather than on its continuities. As one example, adolescents in Western societies are expected to be in control and to practice restraint in most situations; during childhood, control was not expected or was vested in someone else. Because of the dramatic changes required by society, some psychologists have proposed that adolescents be granted a period of experimentation known as a moratorium during

which time the adolescent is encouraged to work things through on his or her own.

Not everyone experiences the "storms of adolescence" to the same degree. To describe adolescent development in more general terms, Offer and Offer proposed three styles of development. In the "continuous" style, growth was smooth and steady, with no cataclysmic events or volcanic eruptions. In the "surgent" style, the person experienced a series of stops and starts, often brought about by a major event, such as divorce or death of a parent. The third style, termed "tumultuous," was characterized by recurring self-doubts and strong conflicts with parents. These styles of development, though different, are all similar in one respect—they each reflect the person's attempt (sometimes, struggle) to make the transition from early to later life and thereby to move from total dependence on one's family of origin to a more integrated balance of reliance on family, close friends, loved ones, and self. Order and change are the polarities that must be reconciled, and such reconciliation must be consistent with the individual's ever-changing understanding of himself or herself during adolescence.

A different analysis of adolescent growth patterns, by Marcia, is based on Erikson's psychosocial theory of development. On the basis of both interviews and experimental results, Marcia described four styles of dealing with identity conflict among college students:

1. *Identity Achieved.* The person has made lasting commitments after going through a period of questioning.
2. *Moratorium.* The person is still in a period of openness and questioning.
3. *Foreclosure.* The person has made lasting commitments without experiencing much questioning or doubt.
4. *Diffusion.* The person has made no commitments nor asked any questions; such a person is still drifting and undefined.

Although these two analyses of adolescent "styles" agree in some respects, each emphasizes a different aspect of the situation. For Offer and Offer, the lack of "real conflict" for most adolescents is emphasized; for Marcia, the issue of whether questioning occurred seems most significant. In either case, the important point seems to be that there are many routes to a sense of identity, and this is as we might expect, given the open-ended nature of human growth and change.

The question of sex and love is a fundamental one in coming to an understanding of the adolescent and later the adult. The adolescent has a strong desire for attachment; at the same time, there are also demands for interperson separateness. The degree to which one has resolved the issue of identity is often the degree to which one is prepared for a meaningfully intimate relationship. Trust, autonomy, industry, and identity (as well as their opposites) all prepare (or retard) the young adult for intimacy ahead. It is crucial that the developing individual be an "I" before he or she can participate in creating a "we."

Love opens its participants to a number of new experiences. "Falling in love," "being in love," and "being fulfilled in love" are stages describing various aspects of this experience, and it is the task of the 20- to 30-year-old to define the challenge of love and to meet it personally. If a stable relationship results, the person is likely to find himself or herself beginning a new family. The emergence of this new context often marks the final break with the person's earlier dependence on his or her family of origin.

Out of the struggle with body, parents, teachers, and friends (and with the issue of intimacy) emerges a fairly autonomous person with a strong sense of what can best be called "self." William James described the self from two perspectives: the "I" (as knower) and the "Me" (as known by others). In addition, *Dasein* (Heidegger) and *living body* (Merleau-Ponty) have been used as terms to describe one's experience of self. In all cases, we must remember that even though *self* and its synonyms are nouns, the self is neither a thing nor unchanging. Rather, these words are meant to capture an experience we all have, throughout the course of a life, of a reassuring sense of sameness in the face of continuing change.

For purposes of discussion it seems reasonable to talk about three "sets of selves": a bodily, or intending, self; a social, or interpersonal, self; and a reflected, or thought-about, self. Pivotal ages in the development of these "sets of selves" are 2, 6, and 12, for it is at these ages that human beings begin to take the step that will lead them from bodily being in the world to an evaluation of self based on reflection. Although such reflections will continue, the

adolescent years represent the first major attempt to apply "formal operational" thinking (Piaget) to the problems of a personal self.

A final distinction to be made in any discussion of self must concern differences in this concept between West and East. Western approaches often separate "self" into two parts, the actor (self) and the action done, and this split leaves us sitting at an uncomfortable distance from our world. The Eastern approach is different in that the Zen person leaves the world undisturbed. Here the person attempts to grasp the meaning of a situation (self included) in a single, unified way, never in a fragmentary or a selfish sense. Through sensitive observation he or she loses himself or herself and thereby seeks to gain a far deeper understanding of both self and world.

We in the West cannot duplicate the cultural conditions that enabled the doctrine of Zen to develop. We can, however, acknowledge its value and hear its goal: to lose oneself to find deeper meaning in human living. Eastern wisdom points the way to this rich tradition. Before we in the Western world can lose ourselves in the world, however, we must find ourselves, and this goal first begins to be approached during the adolescent years.

VII. GLOSSARY OF IMPORTANT CONCEPTS

Adolescence. The period between ages 12 and 17 when new and often discontinuous societal demands must be coped with; "growing toward adulthood."

Adolescent storm. A period of upheaval and disorientation; rarely does the experience live up to the scale required by the romantic tradition of Western thought.

Categories of identity. Four patterns found by Marcia in young adults. (1) Identity Achieved—the person has made some important commitments after a period of questioning. (2) Moratorium—the person is in a period of openness and questioning. (3) Foreclosure—commitments have been made but without real questioning. (4) Diffusion—no commitments, no questioning: such a person might be either a "playboy" or a "loner."

Continuous, surgent, tumultuous. Three adolescent growth-pattern types suggested by Offer and Offer to encompass the majority of adolescent experiences involved in growing up.

Cultural continuities. Uniformities in what is expected of persons as children and as adults. Expectations are usually age-appropriate—for example, younger children are given the easier task of fishing off the rocks rather than from boats.

Dasein. A concept Heidegger used to present his understanding of personal Being. As such, it leads to a description of the person as constantly alive and flowing within the larger ground of a continuously moving and varying world.

I. That aspect of self which knows, distinguished from the **Me** by William James.

Identity. An individual's style and beliefs, especially as they relate to his or her meaning to other people. A reassuring sense of personal continuity in change.

Identity crisis. An event recurrent throughout life when a person reflects on such questions as "Who am I?" and "What shall I do from now on?" A major focus in adolescence.

Intending self. Merleau-Ponty's way of describing the person not just in a biological way but as the pattern of intentions involved in how one finds oneself related to the world as well as how one chooses to relate to that world.

Intimacy vs. isolation. The critical task of early adulthood, described by Erikson, during which individuals seek to establish sexual and loving relationships; conflicts may arise if such relationships are not established, sometimes resulting in withdrawal and isolation.

Living body. The way each of us relates to and is related to our world; that region of the world which I call "me" and through which I deal with my living human world (see **intending self**).

Looking-glass self. An evaluation of oneself in the mirror provided by actions of important people in our lives (a concept developed initially by the sociologists Cooley and Mead).

Me. That aspect of self which is known, distinguished from the I by William James.

Moratorium. An adolescent period of freedom of experimentation without repercussions, described by Erikson. A more European idea than American; "approved" by M. Mead and Erikson.

Parallel play. A form of children's play characterized by playing alongside others with no direct interaction.

Preadolescence. Age 10–12—a period of "growing away from" the family and "growing toward" one's peers.

Self-esteem. The amount and quality of the regard that a person has toward himself or herself.

Social discontinuities. Changes in expectations placed on persons as adults from what was expected of them as children. For example, children are expected to be submissive; adults are expected to be more dominant.

Solitary play. An early form of play characterized by interactions with inanimate objects, such as toys, rather than with other people.

Youth. Age 18–22 or so—a time when educational, career, and marital goals become central; also a period of direct action often guided by abstract ideals.

VIII. SUGGESTED READINGS

Major sources

Combs, A. W., Richards, A. C., & Richards, F. *Perceptual psychology: A humanistic approach to the study of persons.* New York: Harper & Row, 1976.

Erikson, E. H. *Identity: Youth and crisis.* New York: Norton, 1968. Parts 1–5.

James, W. *The principles of psychology* (2 vols.). New York: Dover, 1950. (Originally published, 1890.) Book 1, Chapter 10.

Suzuki, D. T. Zen. In D. T. Suzuki, E. Fromm, & R. Martino (Eds.), *Zen Buddhism and psychoanalysis.* New York: Harper, 1960.

Secondary sources

Barrett, W. *Irrational man: A study in existential philosophy.* Garden City, N.Y.: Doubleday, 1958. Chapters on Heidegger and Buber.

Gergen, K. J. *The concept of self.* New York: Holt, Rinehart & Winston, 1971.

Muuss, R. E. *Theories of adolescence* (3rd ed.). New York: Random House, 1975.

12

Making and Doing:
The Adult Years

So you're 45 now. Where have you been, what do you know, and what do you have yet to do?

I. WHAT IT MEANS TO BE IN MIDLIFE

One thing you know is that being 45 is not as bad as you thought it would be. When you were younger, everyone told you that at 45 you would feel old and tired. Although you sometimes do feel old and tired, it is not much different from being tired at 35, 30, or even 25. Sometimes you still feel surprisingly spry.

Forty-five, however, does seem a turning point of sorts. If 20 marked your entry into adult life, then the period between 40 and 50 marks the beginning of a time to think about what you have achieved and what you might still do or leave undone. At 45 you are also likely to begin noticing certain signs of aging: some of your friends are disabled—or, worse, have died. Even some of your friends' children may have died. If you are a man, there is also always the possibility of a heart attack, an ulcer, and only Marcus Welby knows what else. If you are a woman and you have not yet gone through menopause, you are likely to worry about when it will occur and what it will mean for you.

In addition to these biological signs of aging, there are other, social signals. If you have had a family, your children are growing up. Some may already have left home; others may be on the verge of going. Whether or not you have had a family, you notice that people have begun to call you "ma'am" or "sir" more of the time than you find comfortable. Being 45 clearly demands a second look at what is important to you, what you care about.

Despite this occasionally unsettling state of affairs, which is sometimes called the **midlife crisis**, you also have a sense of fulfillment and accomplishment, particularly if you have had a successful life. In talking to successful 40–50-year-olds, Neugarten (1968) reports conversations like the following:

> "You feel you have lived long enough to have learned a few things that nobody can learn earlier. That's the reward . . . and also the excitement. I now see things in books, in people, in music that I couldn't see when I

was younger. . . . It's a form of ripening that I attribute largely to my present age" [p. 97].[1]

A vice-president of a large publishing company said:

> "When I think back over the errors I made when I was 28 or 30 or 35, I am amazed at the young men today who think they can take over their companies at 28. They can't possibly have the maturity required. . . . True maturity doesn't come until around 45. . . . And while some of the young men are excellently educated, we middle-aged men are no longer learning from a book. We've learned from past experience" [p. 97].

Even though as a 40–50-year-old you are more aware of time and aging, you do not have any real desire to "go back." As one person put it,

> "There is a difference between wanting to feel young and wanting to be young. Of course it would be pleasant to maintain the vigour and appearance of youth; but I would not trade those things for the authority or the autonomy I feel—no, nor the ease of interpersonal relationships nor the self-confidence that comes from experience" [p. 97].

At 45, as at all other stages in human life, there are both pluses and minuses. Most of the disadvantages have to do with a decrease in bodily health and an occasionally ominous sense of time, while many of the more positive aspects concern a feeling of competence in dealing with others and with the changing situations in life. The middle years are neither a fearful introduction to biological decline and death nor years of unmixed power; rather, there is a little of this and a little of that in being 45. These years, in short, are no different from any other age in human living in terms of providing the person with both problems and possibilities. Although the same word, *adult*, is applied to everyone from the twenties on, we should not think that people are static and unchanging once they become adults. Change and possibility are as much a part of this phase in life as was true for the adolescent and (before that) the child.

[1]From *Middle Age and Aging*, by B. L. Neugarten (Ed.). Copyright 1968 by the University of Chicago Press. This and all other quotations from this source are reprinted by permission.

A. Disadvantages in being 45

Some of the most unsettling events to deal with in midlife have to do with changes in one's body. Two of the most frequently studied of these are heart attacks in men and menopause in women. Although both of these events are more dramatic than others occurring at the same time, a careful examination of what we know about how both are experienced should provide insight into how other, less dramatic types of bodily decline are dealt with in midlife.

1. Heart attack. How do men react to a heart attack and the subsequent period of hospital bed rest? Rosen and Bibring (1968) present some relevant information. They observed 50 male patients in the hospital immediately after a serious heart attack. Of these patients, 7 were under age 40, 6 were between 40 and 49, 22 were between 50 and 59, and 15 were over 60. On the basis of numerous ratings and interviews, Rosen and Bibring described each man in terms of how depressed he was, how anxious, and how cooperative in regard to staying in bed and following doctor's orders.

Results showed clearly that men under 40 or over 60 were generally cheerful, while men between 40 and 50 tended to be depressed much of the time. Although about 50% of the men in all groups were understandably anxious and tense, about 65% of the men in the 40–59-year-old group showed regular signs of being extremely upset. Men in this group were also the least cooperative in following a regimen of bed rest, while men over 60 were most cooperative.

Such results are quite understandable. The man who is over 60 has already come to terms with the fact that he can no longer pursue the goals of young men. The man under 40 is still full of confidence in being young and vigorous. It is the man between 40 and 60 who is in the midst of a struggle to come to terms with reduced capacities. This struggle involves a conflict between the active role of a young man and the more passive-dependent role of an old one. Having a heart attack serves only to emphasize once more the normal problems of being 50.

Even if the 50-year-old had already begun to give up some activities, he often still has doubts about what the future will hold. After a heart attack, he can no longer deny that his style of living will have

to change. The immediate demands of the doctor or nurse that he be passive only serve to represent concretely the social situation which advancing age will come increasingly to put on him but which he is not yet ready to accept. For this reason his being-in-time is disturbed, for not only is he depressed about his present, he is also anxious about his future. The very act of defying doctor's orders betrays a loss of personal relationship to the future.

2. Menopause. Although having a heart attack accentuates the problems associated with aging in men, not all men have heart attacks. All men, however, do make the transition to midlife, even if not marked by so dramatic an event as a heart attack. For women the story is different: here there is a clear and definite physical event marking the passage from "young" to "middle-aged": **menopause.** The major symptoms are well known and start with the obvious fact that the woman no longer menstruates, although, as one woman put it, "This change is gradual and damnably unpredictable." The woman in menopause also experiences a certain lack of body tonus, most noticeably in the skin and breasts. There sometimes are more negative symptoms, including dizziness, insomnia, tingling sensations, and so-called hot flashes. About three out of four women experience one or more of these symptoms.

Although menopause is a biological given for women, their experience of it is not. Survey data (Neugarten, Wood, Kraines, & Loomis, 1963) indicate that 10–15% of women have physical and/or emotional problems serious enough for them to seek medical or psychological help. The most frequent psychological complaint is depression coupled with feelings of personal worthlessness. Social factors leading to depression are somewhat predictable, and Williams (1977) has related them to the social and personal possibilities the woman feels are still available to her once she can no longer have children. If a woman sees youthful beauty and motherhood as the only possible roles for her, she is more likely to become depressed than if other options are available. The more a woman experiences herself as a valuable person in addition to her role as mother and wife, the more likely she is to handle menopause with little difficulty.

One interesting aspect of women's reaction to menopause is that it is more fearful for younger women (age 21–44) than for women in it or past it. In one questionnaire study (Neugarten et al., 1963), women aged 45–65 more often agreed with the following statements than women aged 21–44: "Women generally feel better after menopause," "A woman gets more confidence in herself after menopause," "Going through menopause doesn't really change a woman in any way," and "Women who have trouble during menopause are those who are expecting it."[2]

Perhaps the best way to understand what menopause is like for the woman going through it is to listen to comments made by some of the women Neugarten et al. interviewed: "Yes, the change of life is an unpleasant time. No one enjoys hot flashes, the headaches, or the nervous tension. Sometimes it's even a little frightening. But I've gone through changes before, and I can weather another one. Besides, it is only a temporary condition." Another woman joked, "It's not the pause that refreshes." A third woman noted:

> My experience has been that I've been healthier and in much better spirits since the change of life. I've been relieved of a lot of aches and pains.
> Since I have had my menopause, I have felt like a teenager again. I can remember my mother saying that after her menopause she really got her vigor, and I can say the same thing about myself. I'm just never tired now [Neugarten et al., pp. 149–150].

B. Possibilities in being 45

All this talk about the disadvantages of being 45 misses the fact that being older can also provide a good deal of freedom. Much of this freedom comes about because society recognizes that people gain more competence in dealing with their world as they get older. By *competence*, we simply mean that the person comes to feel that he or she is able to speak the snappy dialogue of the novelist and actually does; that he or she makes the right decisions in most situations; that he or she is the person other people ask questions of, whether such questions deal with fixing a motor or making a cake. In short, feeling competent is knowing that you are good at what you do and needing no one else's opinion to confirm it. To be competent is to know and feel that

[2]From "Women's Attitudes Toward the Menopause," by B. L. Neugarten, V. Wood, R. J. Kraines, and B. Loomis. In *Vita Humana*, 1963, 6, 140–151. Copyright 1963 by S. Karger AG. Reprinted by permission.

the world is at least as much affected by you as you are by it.

Robert W. White (1959), who has been quite influential in making us recognize the nature and importance of competence in human life, often stressed that a feeling of competence does not just happen to a person at 45; rather, the growth of competence is a developmental process having roots at least as far back as the first time an infant tried to feed himself or herself or a child tried to have his or her own way with parents. Like any developmental process, it depends very strongly on the way important people dealt with the person in the past. Here we need only think back to the Crow Indian father who bragged about what a difficult child his son was. This father knew that his son's sense of being able to affect his world was an important one for him to keep, and the father did nothing to rob the growing boy of his sense of competence in dealing with his world.

Each human being starts out, as White (1959) put it, with "a restless urge to find out about the environment and to test the effects of action on it." The environment can either facilitate or interfere with this urge, and although it is a robust urge, it does take a bit of time to overcome an environment that is not easily impressed. The person may also contribute to his or her sense of personal competence by learning how to do a number of things competently. For this reason, it may take until 40 or even 50 for the person to acknowledge, in an honestly felt way: "I know what I am doing."

Because Western society is so complex, it may take a good many years to become competent at one's job, and a person may not become competent at more than one or at most a few tasks. For this reason, a mature person's sense of competence cannot possibly be the simple summation of his or her separate competencies; rather, it must come from an evaluation of how important the things we do well are to us. William James noted that we base our self-esteem on a small number of tasks that we have set ourselves to do. How well we do these specific tasks determines our overall sense of competence in dealing with all aspects of our life. The person is a totality, and a few strong areas of competence provide the person with a favorable self-evaluation.

The urge toward competence is, by itself, neither good nor bad. The strong child who develops a sense of physical competence can as easily become a bully as an athlete (or may become both). The socially sensitive child can just as easily become a flirt as a genuinely loving human being. There is no necessity for a personal sense of competence to produce a moral person. As White (1972) sadly notes, "The great villains of history have often been uncommonly competent." Competence is no guarantee of goodness, and the person at midlife knows this as well as anyone.

Taking into account both the pluses and the minuses of being 45 suggests that the middle years are neither all bad nor all good. This period is just as open and filled with possibility as any of the preceding years. To recognize this fact, we need only shift the field of concern from more narrowly defined bodily issues to more broadly defined, and far-ranging, social ones. When this occurs, the shift from youth to adult life and then to midlife has been made. Personal restriction occurs only to the degree that we accept the bodily self as the one measure of our value and significance and come to deal with our social and intellectual worlds in rigid and unvarying ways.

II. MAJOR ISSUES IN GOING FROM YOUTH TO MIDLIFE

Erikson's analysis of the human life cycle led him to conclude, along with Freud, that what is important in adult life is *Lieben,* the ability to love, and *Arbeiten,* the ability to work. As Erikson could not improve on his teacher's formula, neither can we: generativity (or productivity) in adult life relates not only to jobs but to people, and the possibilities of relating in a meaningful and productive way to other people and to one's work would seem to be the major issues that need handling as we make the passage from youth to middle age.

A. Lieben: *Productivity in intimate relationships*

Although it is true that love between two adults spiced by mutual and exciting sex is among the great joys of being human, it is not the only kind of love possible. To be sure, it grabs the headlines, the songs, the poems, the plays, and the novels. Yet there are other kinds of love, and these should be talked about especially insofar as they occur for the first time or in their most powerful form between 25 and 55.

The ancient Greeks identified three types of love that are still meaningful to us today: eros, philia, and agape. Eros (the one we are most familiar with) comes from the name of a cherubic little god called Eros by the Greeks and, later, Cupid by the Romans. Eros is that type of love which gives its name to the word *erotic.* Philia is a quieter love: it is perhaps best described as loving friendship or, more simply, as friendship. Agape is the most difficult of the three to define, simply because it occurs so infrequently and is often so extraordinary as to defy definition. Historically it meant God's love for human beings; in our time, it refers to a person's love for humankind in its entirety.

1. Agape. In trying to describe her understanding of agape, Kinget (1975) presents the following story of an incident during World War II that is reported by Gordon (1962).

> The day's work had ended; the tools were being counted. When the detail was about to be dismissed, the Japanese guard declared that a shovel was missing. He insisted someone had stolen it to sell to the Thais. He strode up and down in front of the men, ranting and denouncing them for their wickedness, their stupidity, and most unforgivable of all, their ingratitude to the Emperor.
>
> Screaming in broken English, he demanded that the guilty one step forward to take his punishment. No one moved. The guard's rage reached new heights of violence.
>
> "All die! All die!" he shrieked.
>
> To show that he meant what he said, he pulled back the bolt, put the rifle to his shoulder, and looked down the sights, ready to fire at the first man he saw at the end of them.
>
> At that moment, the Argyll [a Scotsman] stepped forward, stood stiffly to attention and said calmly, "I did it."
>
> The guard unleashed all his whipped-up hatred; he kicked the hapless prisoner and beat him with his fists. Still the Argyll stood rigidly at attention. The blood was streaming down his face, but he made no sound. His silence goaded the guard to an excess of rage. He seized his rifle by the barrel and lifted it high over his head. With a final howl he brought the butt down on the skull of the Argyll, who sank limply to the ground and did not move. Although it was perfectly evident that he was dead, the guard continued to beat him and stopped only when exhausted.

The men of the work detail picked up their comrade's body, shouldered their tools, and marched back to camp. When the tools were counted again, at the guardhouse, no shovel was missing [Gordon, 1962, pp. 104–105].[3]

There are a great many adjectives we might apply to the Scotsman, such as *heroic, noble,* and *self-sacrificing.* Because we are sophisticated 20th-century people, we might also want to use such adjectives as *naive, foolish,* and even *masochistic.* However, the Scotsman was neither naive, foolish, nor masochistic; he was, instead, one of those rare individuals who offered by his death a significance to his and our lives. Unfortunately, we tend to have an unhealthy skepticism about such acts, often interpreting them as pathological. "Such behavior couldn't be healthy because it's so rare" seems to be the way we state our case.

Here the psychologist is as much to blame as anyone else. With our penchant for averages, groups, and normality, we seem to have created the idea that any behavior that is rare is somehow suspect, if not totally inappropriate. There is something about a psychologist that likes a category. Events, some as dramatic as and some less dramatic than the one involving the Scotsman, do occur, and there is no reason to deny their meaning. For psychology to be a truthful or at least an unbiased discipline, agape needs to be recognized as a valid category of what it might be like to be human.

2. Philia.   Friendship is another aspect of what it means to be human that seems, for the contemporary mind, to have a certain darker interpretation to it. The biblical pair David and Jonathan would seem to represent the best in friends. Not only did Jonathan protect David when Jonathan's father, Saul, tried to kill him; he even went against his father's command by helping David escape. As a clear and dramatic gesture of friendship, Jonathan exchanged armor with David to symbolize that an enduring bond existed between them.

David and Jonathan represent a particularly vivid example of friendship, and it is easy for us to wonder whether there was some hidden erotic aspect to their relationship. Although it is true that friendship in antiquity did allow and sometimes even suggest an erotic element (as in the case of Socrates and Alcibiades or of Alexander and Hephaestion; Kinget, 1975), we tend to find eros in place of philia because simple friendship is difficult for us to understand. One reason may be that friends often place undesirable and (to our way of looking at it) illegitimate demands on our privacy of action; another may be that we are suspicious of gift horses; another may be that friends do not play a large part in our lives. Whatever the reasons, we often view friends in terms of "what's in it for me," thereby making the idea of philia a bit suspect to the modern person.

3. Other types of love: Maternal, infant, and paternal.   Even though much has been written about maternal love from literary and artistic points of view, some of the more psychologically revealing studies of mother love were done on rhesus monkeys by Harry Harlow. Although not everything Harlow observed is directly relevant to the human case, the parallels are intriguing enough to be included in any discussion of this theme.

On the basis of careful observation, Harlow noted that **maternal love** in the monkey shows a complete cycle for each infant. In the beginning, the mother initiates all contact; only later is what she does modified by what the baby does. All monkey mothers seem to go through three phases of mother love: (1) care and comfort, (2) ambivalence, and (3) relative separation (Harlow, Harlow, & Hansen, 1963).

For monkeys, the sequence is care, protect, and then reject. Although some monkey mothers reject their young by pushing them away or biting them, chimpanzee mothers observed in natural environments use a much more benign strategy. According to Jane Goodall (1967), who spent many years observing chimps in the wild, chimp mothers do not pinch or hit their offspring. Rather, they distract them by playing with them or by tickling them whenever they try to renew contact. In either the natural or the laboratory setting, punishment or play is designed to break the maternal tie. Talking more, perhaps, to the human than the monkey mother, Harlow notes: "Maternal rejection during this period is truly one of the forms of mother love; a mother who loves her infant will emancipate him" (Harlow, 1971, p. 14).

[3]From *Through the Valley of the Kwai,* by E. Gordon. Copyright 1962 by Harper & Row, Publishers, Inc. Reprinted by permission.

A second type of love observed by Harlow is the infant monkey's love for the mother. One major difference between infant and maternal love is that while a monkey mother's love is directed only toward her offspring, **infant love** is more indiscriminate. Indeed, Harlow has shown that all that is required in the way of an object for the infant to love is that it be soft and cuddly. In some of Harlow's experiments an object about the size of a monkey mother, covered with terrycloth, did very well indeed even if the infant was fed by some other device.

Infant love, like maternal love, passes through a series of stages, the last of which results in a relatively independent young monkey. Because there is a close correspondence between what mother and infant do, the mother's tendency to push the infant away (at about 5 months) coincides with the infant's tendency to explore its environment. As a matter of fact, the 5-month-old infant monkey spends a good deal of time away from the mother, and the infant's and mother's affectional systems are in harmony so as to produce an independent young animal.

A third type of love defined by Harlow has been called **paternal love.** Although this type of love has not been studied nearly as well as maternal and infant love, it has its own unique properties. In the developmental course of things, paternal love is generally the stage after maternal love and the one before heterosexual love. The major aspect of this affectional system is that an adult male monkey will take care of almost any infant monkey, whether or not the infant is his offspring. This type of love is, thus, much less fixed in its target than the other varieties described by Harlow. Mostly it takes the form of a secondary protection system for the infant.

These data, interesting as they are, do not tell the whole story for human beings. What they suggest is that in addition to heterosexual love (even among monkeys) there are strong affectional ties that automatically occur between mother and child and between father and child and that these bonds develop from both the adult's and the infant's side of the relationship. If we add these types of love to those of philia and agape, it is reasonable to propose that at least five varieties of love are possible for the developing human being. This number is reassuringly large in showing the diversity and developmental progression of this most important aspect of interpersonal behavior.

B. Experiences in being a parent

Harlow's work, for all its relevance to human beings, is still about monkeys. As such, it does not help much in describing the experiences involved in any of the various kinds of human loving. We all know or have read novelists', poets', or playwrights' first-person accounts of romantic love. Similarly, we have all heard learned psychologists and pediatricians talk of the infant's (first-person) love for his or her mother and father. In addition, theologians and priests have talked about the experiences of agape and philia. What we have not heard, however, is the first-person voice of a parent talking about his or her experiences as a loving parent. Without this perspective, the story of familial love is incomplete.

1. Pregnancy. To find out how parents experience themselves and their children in a loving way, it seems best to begin at the beginning: with pregnancy. Although there are a great many jokes about 6-month pregnancies, most couples do take the decision to have a baby seriously. There are a great many reasons for having a baby; some are easily recognized, others are not. For both mother and father, pregnancy will provide obvious and public proof of their femaleness and maleness. During the deciding time, mother and father are also likely to experience a reidentification with their own parents and, through them, a reawakening of personal continuity with the past (and future). In addition, having a child will assure the parents, at least initially, that they have done the right thing; that is, they have done what is socially expected of them as a married couple.

There will be some negative experiences as well. For one, there is no "going back" when you are going to have a baby. Perhaps more than the marriage vows themselves, having a child means you are *really* married and *really* grown up. Husband and wife must now realize that they have to try to make the marriage work. If there is ambivalence or fear, assurances that they will work to make the marriage work are not easily and comfortably given. After all, the child will need care for a very long time. Then, too, there is the peculiar prejudice (fear) that being a good parent means that neither partner can be as openly erotic and sexual as before the baby was born. Coupled with this is the woman's fear that her husband will not love her if her figure is ruined. Finally, she may even fear being hurt during delivery.

One might think that the decision to have a second or third baby is not as difficult as the first one; yet here too there are problems. Although most of the problems associated with a first pregnancy (fear of childbirth, commitment to partner, lessened erotic satisfaction, and so on) are no longer very important, there are other problems. The situation is perhaps best illustrated by a dream a woman had in the beginning of her third pregnancy. In this dream the woman "was swimming in a pool with three children. One was drowning; she hastened to save him. Meanwhile, the others were drowning. When she hurried to them, the first one was drowning. The dream continued: one child was attacked by a bull. While saving him, the bull attacked the other ones. When she came to their rescue, the first was attacked again" (Jessner, Weigert, & Foy, 1970, p. 215).[4]

Despite these somewhat unpleasant possibilities, people do commit to each other and to an as yet unborn child, and somehow or other we all do get born. The course of a woman's experiences in pregnancy seems best described in terms of three 3-month periods, called "trimesters." The first trimester focuses the woman on her body: her breasts swell, she has a great appetite (or aversion) for certain foods (the "pickles and cashew-nut phenomenon"), and she may experience nausea throughout the day or during part of the day ("morning sickness"). Not surprisingly, this collection of changes often brings about a certain aloneness and distance from others, including the husband. It can also focus the newly pregnant woman on her own personal history as well as on her special connection to the generations of her family.

The second trimester is filled with early movings of the fetus and the experience of a "living otherness within me." Sometimes fetal movements are experienced as a "moving, fluttering butterfly" or as "gentle stroking from a soft glove"; sometimes they are experienced as a stranger within who "placidly

leeches food from my body without even an invitation."

The emphasis on the body so strongly experienced in the first 3 months continues, especially as the body comes to lose its familiar shape. This outward sign of coming motherhood has both a calming and a disturbing aspect. On the bad side, women worry about losing their husbands to some slender, slinky, sexy lady in a black dress. On the good side, many pregnant women come to exude a personal warmth and glow that, on occasion, seem to radiate waves of tenderness toward the whole world.

The actuality of a moving fetus forces the pregnant woman to redefine herself. No longer can she be a tomboy or a little girl. She will soon be an "adult," a "mother," and this is both comforting and frightening. The person figuring most importantly in the woman's personal musings at this point is her mother. Pregnant women are often flooded with memories during this time; some women idealize their mothers, others repudiate them. Either way, the woman's mother becomes crucial.

The third trimester begins with a flurry of activity and ends in waiting. The activity deals, of course, with preparing a place for the baby and with planning what has to be done so as to get to the hospital on time. In general, the third trimester (especially the eighth and ninth months) is a heavy and boring time. The body, which to this point had been seen as altered, now comes to be experienced as distorted, as a burdensome weight.

In addition to the discomfort and the waiting, many women experience an eerie dread of producing a monster or a deformed child. Such concerns, which alternate with happy projections about the child, strike the pregnant woman as odd, yet they persist. During the last trimester, women also experience a fear that they will die in childbirth. Sometimes expectant mothers experience fantasies of death and rebirth, and there is an occasional confusion between the mother and the infant in these fears.

During the last trimester, everything focuses on the expected date of birth. Everything the mother- and father-to-be do during the last month orients around "the date." No longer is pregnancy regarded as an interesting or frightening event; all that is now wanted is an end to it and to the anxieties that have

---

[4]From "The Development of Parental Attitudes During Pregnancy," by L. Jessner, E. Weigert, and J. L. Foy. In E. J. Anthony and T. Benedek (Eds.), *Parenthood: Its Psychology and Psychopathology.* Copyright 1970 by Little, Brown and Company, Inc. This and all other quotations from this source are reprinted by permission.

to do with becoming a mother or father. Observations of pregnant mothers (Jessner et al., 1970) show that all the women studied experienced morbid preoccupations and anxieties during the last week or weeks of pregnancy. This finding suggests that such fears are natural reactions, almost always unfounded.

These observations on the total course of pregnancy can be summarized as follows: During the first trimester, there is a preoccupation with one's body, one's individuality, and one's relationship to time and significant others, such as the woman's mother. The second trimester focuses the pregnant woman on the (now moving) fetus and (again) on her relationships to it and to her own mother. The fetus can be seen as an "enemy within," as a fulfillment of being a woman, as an intruder in her marriage, and as a personal link with time, generation, and history. The third trimester focuses on discomfort and possible damage to the woman and her infant. In addition, the third trimester focuses on the woman's experience of time. During this period, time is experienced as "dragging on" as everything and everyone focuses on the predicted delivery date and beyond. The present is boring; the future is where the woman now lives.

2. The "pregnant" father. With all this talk about pregnant women, what about the "pregnant" father? Most expectant fathers feel the same way: "Yeah, what about me, the father!" All attention seems directed toward the pregnant mother, and many fathers may well feel "I don't get anything. I seem to be totally unimportant." The father's role seems limited to giving out cigars after the baby is born. (Giving out cigars is a good symbol: smoking cigars signifies being an adult, and the cigar is our old friend the phallic symbol.) Despite this one ceremonial act, most young fathers experience themselves, and are experienced by others, as slightly comical and awkward figures.

A father, however, is important to the wife both when she is pregnant and once she has given birth. How men become fathers and learn the ropes of fatherhood seems to depend a good deal on their first-person understanding of what it means to be a father. On the basis of a series of interviews, McCorkel (cited in Jessner et al., 1970) described three styles 29 young fathers adopted: (1) a romantic style, (2) a family style, and (3) a career-oriented style.

Husbands in the romantic group had a somewhat casual approach to being a parent. Pregnancy brought about a general feeling of awe in these young men. In addition, they were a bit scared at the idea of having a wife *and* a child. Men in the career-oriented group felt that prospective fatherhood was a burden. One young man noted to his wife, "This is our last chance to be human beings. After this we're going to be parents." Men in the family-oriented group accepted new responsibilities easily and felt very good about the idea of becoming a father. Pregnancy was considered a gift, and they tended to grow closer to their wives.

Career-oriented husbands often denied changes they experienced. They felt they and their family would continue to go on just as before. Family-oriented husbands, in contrast, experienced a deep and continuing change in who they were and how they acted. Romantically oriented husbands experienced becoming a father as a period of personal growth. Pregnancy was seen as a reminder that they were soon to be adults and were no longer carefree adolescents. This change was sometimes accompanied by marital problems and/or conflict with relatives. "One of them remarked how he did a lot of thinking about having children, who grow up to have children, whose children had children, and so on to infinity" (Jessner et al., 1970, p. 233).

3. Parental love. Once the baby is born, two life cycles have to be taken into account—the parents' and the child's. The milestones of the growing child are well known (see Chapter 10); what are the experiences of the parents (the "other" from the child's point of view) during these same years? Although we know a great deal about the effects parents have on children, we know very little about the effects children have on parents. The crucial milestones from the infant's point of view seem to come during Year 1 (nursing stage), Year 2 (stage of independence), Year 4 (family romance), Years 6–12 (latency), and Years 13 + (adolescence). Year 18 or so also seems important because that is when many young people leave home for military service, a job, or college.

The first of these stages for the parents is a period of having to deal with the exciting and frightening reality of a fragile new life. The first baby seems so fragile and so much in need of wise parental care. An example is the seemingly innocent business of holding the baby. The nurse told me, just before we took my oldest child home from the hospital, to "be careful. The spinal column isn't yet strong enough to support the infant's head. So when you pick him up or hold him, make sure you always have your hand under his head to support it." Such advice terrifies the new parent. "What happens if I don't hold the neck properly? Could I kill my baby? What happens if I hold him too tight? Will his neck be deformed?" The first five or ten times I picked the newborn up, there was (to my way of looking at things) the imminent possibility of disaster.

If such a simple task as holding the baby is so scary, what do parents experience when they have to do something more complicated with the newborn, such as feeding him? Breast feeding is one of the most touching, frightening, and challenging experiences a new mother has. Even though women are told about the benefits of breast feeding, most women in Western society choose not to. Fewer than 50% of mothers nurse their children more than 1 month, and fewer than 30% nurse as long as 3 months, according to surveys in the United States, England, New Zealand, France, Guatemala, and just about any other country in which such surveys have been taken (Newton & Newton, 1967).

Generally, mothers offer the following reasons for not breast feeding (Newsom & Newsom, 1962): (1) Nursing formulas are cheap, easy to prepare, and readily available. In contrast, new mothers often find breast feeding bothersome, time-consuming, and difficult. (2) Many mothers report being embarrassed by publicly exposing their breasts to feed the infant. Despite the sexual revolution, certain kinds of modesty are still with us. (3) Some mothers are ill at ease with the newborn and would prefer to have as little to do with him or her as possible. (4) Finally, there is the chance of some slight pain and the somewhat greater probability of initial insufficiency of milk. As most pediatricians confirm, however, the act of nursing increases the flow of milk to the needed level within a few feedings.

Despite these real, potential, and imagined problems, the nursing situation provides some of the most profound experiences for both mother and child. Women who breast-feed successfully

often talk about the extraordinarily tender feelings they have for their baby during feeding and afterward. Many women report that when they nurse, they reestablish a physical tie to the newborn.

Although nursing babies supposedly do very little, careful observation reveals that this is just not so. First, babies look at the mother during feeding, and just putting a crying baby near the breast will often quiet him or her. By 12 weeks, not only does the infant look at the mother and assume a restful and comfortable position in her arms, he or she will also, ever so gently, touch the mother.

Nursing also produces strong physical reactions in the mother. First, there is the obvious and continual stimulation of the breast by the newborn. Second, the uterus contracts during nursing. Both these effects are associated not only with nursing but with adult sexual activity. Perhaps the most complete attempt to tie nursing to sexual excitement was made by Newton and Newton (1967), who wrote that

the survival of the human race, long before the concept of "duty" evolved, depended upon the satisfactions gained from the two voluntary acts of reproduction— coitus and breast feeding. These had to be sufficiently pleasurable to ensure their frequent occurrence.

The physiologic responses in coitus and lactation are closely allied. Uterine contractions occur both during suckling and during sexual excitement. Nipple erection occurs during both. Milk ejection has been observed to occur during sexual excitement in women. Moreover, the degree of ejection appears to be related to the degree of sexual response.

Extensive breast stimulation occurs during breast feeding. Breast stimulation alone can induce orgasm in some women. . . . Masters and Johnson found that nursing women had a higher level of sexual interest than non-nursing post-partum women. Nursing mothers not only reported sexual stimulation from suckling but also, as a group, were interested in as rapid a return to active intercourse with their husbands as possible [p. 1180].[5]

Does this mean that nursing is meaningful to the mother only because of its similarity to sexual excitement? The answer clearly is no, especially if we distinguish properly between "sexual" and "sen-

[5]From "Medical progress: Psychologic aspects of lactation," by N. Newton and M. Newton. In *New England Journal of Medicine*, 1967, *277*, 1179–1188. Copyright 1967 by the New England Journal of Medicine. Reprinted by permission.

sual." Nursing involves a sensual relationship between unequals—between a caregiver and a care receiver. Sexual intercourse involves a sensual relationship between (ideally) equal adults. Although tenderness, love, and care, as well as sensual arousal, may be aspects of both situations, maternal concern is not the same as female sexuality. Psychology always seems to have an unfortunate tendency to reduce one emotion (maternal tenderness) to another (sexuality) and, in so doing, to miss essential differences between the two. Nursing is a sensual experience, but just as surely, it is a different sensual experience from lovemaking.

Many of the feelings, actions, and reactions of nursing can also be experienced if the infant is fed by bottle. The tenderness, the communication, the developing and deepening mutuality, and the fondling and body contact are still there. The one thing that is missing is the very direct and immediate reaction of the "nursing body," and it is this unreflected reaction that differentiates nursing from bottle feeding. Without the direct and deep bodily involvement of nursing, more reflected aspects of mothering, such as "duty," can be aroused and satisfied. As any woman who has both breast-fed and bottle-fed will report, there are clear differences between the two. This does not mean that breast feeding will save the baby or the mother from all the calamities of existence; all it means is that, like birth itself, breast feeding is a unique experience reserved for those who choose to do it.

Feeding a baby and watching him or her grow can occupy much of the parents' first year. But profound changes occur in the baby so that by Year 1 the baby's territory has increased mightily, mostly because baby can now walk and soon will be able to talk. Because of these developing skills, the infant becomes more of an individual and moves out from the safe shelter of parents' arms and laps to the less safe confines of house and yard. How do the parents experience these changes?

First, there is a sigh of relief that baby can now get around and is so able to make his or her needs known. The relief soon fades, however, as baby gets into everything. This situation occurs so regularly (and is so exasperating) that it has been given a special name: the "terrible twos." What is so terrible about this early period is that baby is no longer a baby, and mamma and papa begin to experience the real pangs of a first separation from their child.

Thus begins the child's drive to become a unique and competent individual.

In describing parents' experiences during this period, Mahler, Pine, and Bergman (1970) note that part of the problem is that the baby changes and develops much faster than the parents do and that such changes upset any personal equilibrium mother and father and baby have developed to that point. For example, if the parents did have some fears about handling so "precious" a bit of stuff as baby, it is unsettling to find that once again they do not know what to do with their new-found walking and talking machine. The major problem for the mother during this period is separation and individuation; that is, can she change from a symbiotic relationship with her child to one in which the child is allowed increasingly greater scope? What is important is whether she perceives the change as a loss or as a step forward.

Although most mothers experience the force of this change at about 24 months, the process began much earlier (at about 6 months) and will come to a final resolution only much later (at about 36 months). The earliest examples of baby's independence occur between 5 and 7 months, when baby ceases to allow himself or herself to be completely enveloped by mamma. The more "adult" forms of individualization occur around 2 years of age and continue until both parents are able to deal with their child as a child rather than as a baby. In our society it is during the period between 20 and 36 months of age that the father becomes increasingly important, for it is at this time that father/child play begins to become a regular event. This playing often begins as roughhouse and tumbling, or precisely those types of play that will help develop the well-defined and skillful movement of the child.

4. "Erotic" love in the family. Even though it may be hard for us as parents to let go of our children, we all do. Because the child is always developing and changing, the next phase in parent growth must relate to the child's growing interest in sex and in the situation of the family romance.

The family romance is a test not only of the parents' relationship to the child but also of their relationship to each other. The difficulty involved here usually surfaces at around age 3 or 4 in the father's complaint that the mother "is babying her boy" as well as in the mother's complaint that father is "rejecting his boy." Mothers of little girls often complain that father "is spoiling his little princess," while fathers complain that mother "doesn't like her little rival." In either case, the test is as much between parents as it is between parent and child.

During this period, the child is often treated "with an inconsistent mixture of teasing acceptance and angry repudiations; at times admired and at times laughed at" (Anthony, 1970a, p. 276).[6] And it is this continuing variation that drives the family crazy. Fortunately, these issues usually resolve themselves quickly (within a year or so), and both parents sense with relief that their child has settled down (or grown up) and that he or she will be much easier to handle than before. With the passing of this situation many parents feel (correctly) that they have come through a rather trying time and have done a good job.

5. School and part-time parenthood. By the time the family romance is over, the child has begun to go to school and enter into the nicest of childhood stages, latency. From the parents' point of view, this may be a particularly sensitive time, for it marks the beginning of "part-time parenthood" (Kestenberg, 1970). The period around the child's fifth and sixth birthdays represents a further development of the conflict between dependence and independence begun by the 2½-year-old. The most notable series of events activating this conflict has to do with starting school. To be sure, some children do go to nursery school and kindergarten; by age 6, however, almost every child is in school. As a matter of fact, almost all societies see the 6-year-old as ready to take on individual activities away from his or her parents.

This transition can be difficult, although in principle it is no different from each of the transitions the parent (and child) endures. In changing from one phase of living to the next, the child forces the parent to change, and this causes difficulty. Sometimes the child even seems to reject the parent during periods of transition. Consequently, parents

often feel neglected and on this basis come to estrange themselves from the child. Before parents can develop their identities as parents, they must give up the "Johnny they know to become acquainted with a new Johnny. But once the strange child loses his strangeness and becomes familiar again, the discontinuity of the relationship is bridged over and the period of alienation passed" (Kestenberg, 1970, p. 291).[7]

One context in which Johnny is extremely strange to his parents is that of the classroom. Here, a stranger, the teacher, tests him and judges his performance so that all can see how good (or how poor) a job the parents have done. Many parents see the teacher as representing the cruel, hard world that determines whether they "pass" or "fail." In many important ways the teacher, an outsider, validates or refutes the good job parents have (or haven't) done with their child.

Exactly how to relate to a child's teacher is a difficult situation for many parents. Even though the teacher may be only the parents' age (or even younger), he or she is regarded as an authority. Parents may reexperience their own attitudes toward teachers—attitudes that developed when they were children. In addition, the teacher is among the first officials of society the parent, as parent, runs into; hence, the teacher can help the parent grow both by helping him or her "let the child go" and by reminding the parent of social and personal morality and redefining it in accord with contemporary values. The teacher's influence is not only important to the child; it can be important to the growth of the parent as well.

One final consequence of the child's going to school is that it provides a bit of free time for the parents. In a multichild family the change is likely to be small until the last child goes to school; in a single-child family the effect is likely to be quite profound. When the day is emptied of children, mothers (and, still to a lesser extent, fathers) feel the need for a reorganization of how and where they spend their time. The increasingly common result is that a young mother goes back to school, enters

[6]From "The Reactions of Parents to the Oedipal Child," by E. J. Anthony. In E. J. Anthony and T. Benedek (Eds.), *Parenthood: Its Psychology and Psychopathology.* Copyright 1970 by Little, Brown and Company, Inc. This and all other quotations from this source are reprinted by permission.

[7]From "The Effect on Parents of the Child's Transition Into and Out of Latency," by J. S. Kestenberg. In E. J. Anthony and T. Benedek (Eds.), *Parenthood: Its Psychology and Psychopathology.* Copyright 1970 by Little, Brown and Company, Inc. This and all other quotations from this source are reprinted by permission.

into charitable or religious work, or resumes a previously interrupted career.

Under these conditions, papa must also change. With a change in how mother spends her day, father may be expected to take more responsibility for the day-to-day chores. He may take on an increasingly important role in being with the children or in guiding them through social/educational groups, such as Scouts. At this time fathers also begin to teach their children how to play ball, swim, do work, or whatever. In these ways the tremendous intellectual and physical vitality of the latency-age child spurs both the father and the mother into new activities and new roles. To keep up with their child, they too must grow and experience new feelings unknown until now.

6. Puberty and parents. Unfortunately, the calm of latency comes to an end with puberty. If puberty and adolescence upset the child, they also stress and upset the family. Initially, when the child is 10, 11, or even 12, parents may try to deny changes they see. Perhaps the most difficult aspect of these changes is that they hint of the child's impending adult sexuality—the change first from a "sexless" child into a sexy adolescent and later into a sexual adult. In the early phases of adolescence, both mother and father may deny the evidence of womanhood or manhood in their children. Soon, however, they will come to see themselves in their growing child.

If each previous change has brought about its own bit of disorganization, a subsequent calm always seemed to follow the turmoil. The resolution of the teenage years, however, involves a final separation of child from parent, and even where adolescence is at its most calm, parents sense the undercurrent of separation.

Perhaps the hardest part of the adolescent years for parents is that they are often in the beginning or the midst of their own midlife crises, which can only be exaggerated by having teenagers in the house. Even if the male or female adolescent is a model of decorum and propriety, the physical, sexual, and intellectual changes in the child must give both parents a good deal to contend with. Since one part of being 45 has to do with real or imagined decreases in physical and intellectual vigor, the adolescent can only serve as a constant reminder of one's own decline.

Generally speaking, parents deal with the fact of their own decline and of their teenage child's ascent in one of two ways: by identifying with or by competing with their child. Competition is seen when a father asks his teenage son to race him or to play tennis "just to see if the kid can beat me." Similarly, mothers often compare their daughters' figures with their own. Sometimes such comparisons develop into an envy of the child that shows up in a continuing comparison of the parent's worldliness and skill against the child's awkwardness and stupidity. Envy may also occur because of differences between the opportunities that were available to the parent and those that are available to the child. It is not infrequent to hear parents charge their children with not appreciating the advantages they have. "Why, when I was your age . . ." is the way the story usually begins.

But it is not all negative: some parents actively identify with their adolescent child. Who has not heard a mother brag about her daughter's brains and beauty or a father about his son's good looks and manliness? Unfortunately, in some of these cases identification is designed to cover the parents' fears about not being what they used to be. Sometimes parents respond to their adolescent children's problems and concerns in terms of their own unresolved conflicts in such areas as personal identity, productivity in work, and aging.

Nowhere is the father and mother's uncertainty better displayed than in the sexual domain. There can be no doubt about it: the adolescent's oversexiness and physical beauty can serve to turn on the whole family. What the mother and the father do with this upsurge depends on who they are: no one would ever deny the existence of a strong sexual tone in a house of teenagers. Under this upsurge in sexual awareness parents may act out and "unfaithfulness may enter the marriage for the first time. . . . The sexuality of the adolescent [may serve] as a stimulus for the sexuality of the parent" (Anthony, 1970b, p. 317).

7. The changing nature of being a parent. Despite these problems, parents (and children) do manage to get through each of the stages. The important point is that all is not always quiet on the home front. Parents are not immovable and unchangeable objects that help or hinder the growth of their offspring; rather, both children and parents grow and change in response to each other. Although this seems obvious once said, many theorists have had great difficulty in taking the changing patterns of adult life into account. A "parent" is no more a fixed entity than an "adult" is; both parents and adults are in constant change, and one focus for such change must be the "significant others" the adult loves. To be a good parent for one phase of a child's life is not enough; like our children, all of us have to change and grow if we are to deal with the changing pattern that is our child's life.

The experience of growing up with one's children—a second run through the psychosocial stages of childhood—co-occurs with changes in many of the more significant aspects of being human. First, there is the body. The years between 25 and 55 see an initial increase in one's bodily possibilities to an inevitable decline in which we sometimes make unflattering comparisons with our own children. If a person's body was the initial repository for a new life, by midlife it can become the uncertain repository of a competent but declining human being.

Another aspect concerns other people, especially those we love. We experience the continuing dialectic of growing toward and then away from each other so that in the end our children end up as loved strangers pursuing their own destiny in their own way. For us as parents there is little we can do but stand aside and help it happen.

During this span of years we are also forced to develop a new relationship to time and history. In the beginning this relationship was experienced as a continuity of my family in me; later it will be experienced as an acceptance of my only life as part and parcel of a single and unique moment in history. In this the mid-years of life make common union with the stream of human living that went before and will continue after my life. Changing relationships to time, body, and others serve to define the currents of midlife as they have done before and will continue to do until the current runs no more.

C. Arbeiten: *Productivity in work*

Change and growth are key concepts in understanding our relationships to work as well as our loving relationships. Erikson described the more general nature of the opportunities and problems set by the middle years in terms of a psychosocial crisis between generativity and stagnation (see

Chapter 10). Erikson extended the notion of generativity from parenthood to include loving and working. **Generativity in loving** consists in an ability to deal in an ever-fresh way with the changing natures of the people we love—our children, our colleagues, our students, or, more narrowly, our lovers.

In the realm of work, generativity, or **creativity,** means dealing in a continuously innovative and fresh way with one's job and what is done at that job. To talk about growth and change in one's job, it is first necessary to locate the idea of work within the values and concerns of our society. To set this analysis within its appropriate historical context, it will also be necessary to consider the meaning of work in past and present times. Only in this way will it be possible to understand the meaning of work then and now.

1. The historical meaning of work. For most of the ancients—Hebrews, Greeks, Romans, and their contemporaries—work was something to be avoided; indeed, in Hebrew the word for "work" and the word for "slave" have the same root. *Labor* comes from the Latin word meaning "trouble," while the French word for "work", *travail,* is derived from a Latin word naming a three-pronged instrument of torture used by the Roman legions (Braude, 1975, p. 5). In addition, all the Western world knows that Adam's punishment for eating the apple was work. Up to the time of the Protestant Reformation, work was viewed as a necessary, if unpleasant, aspect of human life.

With the rise of Protestantism, however, work took a turn for the better with "salvation through work," a reasonable motto describing this change in attitude. Hard work was no longer something to be avoided. Success in heaven was equated with success on earth, and work became the crucial testing ground whereby a person might learn whether or not God held him or her in high enough esteem to allow entry into the Kingdom of Heaven. To the Protestant view, work was an essential part of life, for, as everyone knows, "the devil easily finds work for idle hands."

The contemporary meaning of work for the Western world must, therefore, take account of two contradictory traditions: one that sees human work as a reflection of "God's work" and one that sees it as partly equivalent to slavery, travail, and woe. Our ambivalence in this regard can be seen in such sayings as "I have to go to work" (we never "have to" go to play) as well as in our tendency to decrease the work week as much as possible. In addition, we often separate work from the things we like to do (playing) or from things that are intrinsically important (praying).

Although it is possible to discuss our ambivalence toward work from lofty economic, historical, or sociological perspectives, it seems better to ask working people how they (not the sociologist, historian, or psychologist) feel about their jobs to find out what work means in contemporary society. One of the earliest studies done on this topic was completed in 1947 by Friedman and Havighurst (1954), who asked five groups of workers to describe the meaning work held for them in their everyday lives. Friedman and Havighurst coded the answers using a seven-category system. Table 12-1 presents the percentage of respondents estimated to have given answers appropriate to each category. The first thing that strikes us in this table is that for none of the five occupations was the highest value given in response to Category 1: no occupation, from the least to the most skilled, was thought of exclusively as a means of making money (although money was seen as important in all five occupations). What is also obvious is that 28% of the unskilled or semi-skilled workers did see work as meaningful primarily in terms of providing money, whereas fewer than 10% of skilled craftsmen, salespersons, or physicians saw this as its primary meaning.

Category 2, Routine, represents such answers as "Work gives me something to do" or "It's a way of passing time." Although all groups see routine as one possible meaning for work, it was a major meaning only for the least skilled group, where 28% saw it as *the* major meaning. If we combine this value with the 28% of unskilled workers responding in Category 1 (that is, that the only meaning of work is to earn money), we see that 56% of these workers view work as of no real significance in its own right. For no other group does this combined value reach 40%; for physicians it does not even reach 20%.

Perhaps the relative meaninglessness of work in American society can be understood more dramatically if we note that of 85 million or so adults working in America, about 38 million are blue-collar workers (Braude, 1975, p. 45). This means that about 22 million Americans, or 58% of these workers, essentially find that their work has little meaning other than "it fills time" and/or "it pays the bills." If we take the percentage of workers in each of the remaining categories (37% of coalminers, 25% of skilled craftsmen, 21% of salespeople, and 15% of physicians), the total number of people sharing this attitude goes to 34 million. This means that just about 4 of every 10 working people find little in their job that is intrinsically interesting, meaningful, or satisfying.

Categories 3 and 4—self-respect and association with others—represent answers of the following sorts: "Work is a way of achieving recognition or re-

TABLE 12-1. Comparison of Five Occupational Groups on the Meanings of Work
(Relative Percentages Assuming Each Group to Have Given One Response per Person)

Meaning	Steelworkers (Unskilled and semiskilled)	Coalminers	Skilled Craftsmen 20–64	Skilled Craftsmen Over 65	Salespeople	Physicians
1. No meaning other than money	28%	18%	10%	11%	0%	0%
2. Routine	28	19	–	15	21	15
3. a. Self-respect	....		30	....	12	7
3. b. Prestige, respect of others	16(3a, b)	18(3a, b)	15	24(3a, b)	11	13
4. Association	15	19	18	20	20	19
5. a, b, c. Purposeful activity, self-expression, new experience	13	11	28	30	26	15
5. d. Service to others	–	16	–	–	10	32
No. of people responding	128	153	242	208	74	39

Derived from *The Meaning of Work and Retirement*, by E. A. Friedman and R. J. Havighurst. Copyright 1954 by the University of Chicago Press. Reprinted by permission.

spect from others"; "Work is a place where I meet friends"; "Work is a place where I get to know what I'm supposed to do." Although each of these answers reveals a social and interpersonal meaning to work, none of them comes anywhere near the ideal of work as a meaningful activity that is valuable in its own right and one that enables the person to do new things or to grow in some way.

The only categories suggesting such possibilities are Categories 5a–d, and here values range from 11 to 32%. If we do the appropriate multiplications for the entire work force of 85 million or so people, we can estimate that only about 10 million Americans find their work a source of meaningful life experiences. This is in contrast to the 34 million or so who find work without much significant social or personal meaning. Meaninglessness has it 3 to 1 over meaningfulness—and this seems a reasonable commentary on the meaning of work in contemporary America. Parenthetically, we should note that the values given in Table 12-1 were derived from surveys done in about 1950, and there is no one around who feels that working conditions have now become more stimulating. To the contrary, most discussions of work in America see it as becoming more, rather than less, meaningless.

2. Work as a social problem. The implication of this exercise in arithmetic must be that work has (or will) become a problem in contemporary society, perhaps not as dramatic as drugs or alcohol, but a problem nonetheless. The most important part of this problem seems to be that for about 40% of the total working population, work is a meaningless activity, simply done to earn a salary or to fill time. While there may be many reasons this situation has come about, Braude (1975) summarized a good deal of thinking about this topic when he wrote:

> The specialization that was spawned by the Industrial Revolution, with the consequent growth of technology, led not only to the progressive estrangement of the worker from his work but also the loss of a sense of and a concern for beauty in material culture. The potter at his wheel and the lacemaker and the carriage-builder could take pride in what they made, could see that it was aesthetically as well as functionally pleasing, because they could follow their work from concept to completion. They were, so to say, re-enacting the very

mystery of Creation, partners with God in the beautification and refreshment of His world. But the division of a task into its component parts has prevented the worker from seeing beyond the immediate because he is geared to the pressure to produce in the here and now. Because he is not permitted to see beyond the demands of the moment, he has no idea, except perhaps in the most abstract sense, of what the finished material ought to be, or of his part in bringing the "creation" of this material to fruition. And if he cannot see what his labor will eventually bring forth, why then should he take pride in what he does? Why care whether it is beautiful or not, whether the item even operates or not? The worker is no longer a partner with God, for the Protestant Ethic, the intellectual tradition that shaped so much of Europe and North America, has been shorn of its religious significance and God has been dethroned. Specialization and secularization arose from the same set of ideas [p. 180].[8]

Now, these are strong words, and strong words they must be. Work, which occupies half of what one does each waking day as an adult, is in danger of becoming meaningless. How can we reverse the trend of becoming further isolated from our work and our productivity? The answer must be that each one of us has to remember that we always have the possibility of changing the nature and quality of what we do, and this includes our work as well as our play. Although it may be difficult to think of ways to change the nature of work in our society, we must be aware that it can be done and that it need not involve revolutionary violence. After all, those who are strong enough and organized enough to overthrow the present machine, as would occur in a revolution, would probably also be strong enough and orderly enough to impose their own machine (see Chapter 2).

As an alternative, then, it seems that workers and bosses must get together for their own collective good, or else it is likely that workers will gum up the works by slowdowns or by outright acts of destruction. No one likes to feel superfluous or exploited. One young worker expressed the matter clearly when he said: "I don't even feel necessary .... Every day I come out of [the factory], I feel ripped off.... A good day's work is being tired but not exhausted" (Braude, 1975, p. 181).

[8]From *Work and Workers*, by L. Braude. Copyright 1975 by L. Braude. This and all other quotations from this source are reprinted by permission.

All this suggests that workers and bosses have to reestablish the meaning of work. One way to do so would be to enable a worker to see the importance of his or her particular job in the production of a complete product. An example is the Volvo company in Sweden. In 1973 Volvo changed from an assembly-line process to a work-team approach in which individuals who made relatively large components of the car were able to see how their work fit into the completed product. Although "work teams" are not the final answer, they do indicate a sensitivity to this issue. It seems a shame that we have come so far in separating work from its meaning that we now have to concern ourselves with turning things around. This time, let's recognize that *human beings* work and that work must be revalued if it is to be a meaningful human activity rather than one that simply fills time.

3. Work and personal identity. Work is important not only because it allows us to earn a living but because there is an intimate relation between how we feel about what we do for a living and how we feel about and define ourselves. In this regard, the sociologist Everett Hughes wrote: "A man's work is one of the more important parts of his social identity, of his self; indeed, of his fate in the one life he has to live, for there is something almost as irrevocable about choice of occupation as there is about choice of mate" (1958, p. 43).

In this remark Hughes recognizes that the major choices of adult life come down to the two major issues of intimate relationships and occupational role. If people are asked to describe themselves—for example, by answering the question "Who am I?"—almost all of us respond with words such as *male* or *female; father, mother,* or *grandmother; college professor, mail carrier, electrician,* or *teacher.* In fact most research using the "Who am I?" technique has found that about 50% of all responses include social evaluations, such as one's position in the family, as well as one's occupation (Gordon, 1968). Occupation, gender, and family strongly serve to define a person. They do this by setting the person within a specific social context, and occupation is one of the more crucial ways in which a person places himself or herself within the larger setting of social reality.

We do not establish or define our identity

through work all at once. Rather, it takes up the better part of our adult lives, and our work identity comes to us slowly over the course of years. As one example of how a person comes to his or her work identity, consider a college professor. Basing his work on an analysis of adult growth patterns and problems by Levinson and his associates at Yale (Levinson, 1978; Levinson, Darrow, Klein, Levinson, & McKee, 1974), Hodgkinson (1974) proposed that two crucial aspects involved in making a deep commitment to one's career (college professors included) concern the issues of what Levinson has called the **Dream** and the **Mentor.** The occupational Dream of the person in the middle to late twenties is usually linked to a particular job—for a worker on the assembly line, becoming a foreman; for a person new to business, becoming a manager. The Dream for most young faculty members

> may include becoming a famous scholar in one's field, writing successful books (both financially and intellectually), advising political figures at the local, state, or federal level, being an officer in one's learned society, gaining leadership positions on committees, moving into administration, . . . getting tenure, getting large research grants, and being beloved by generations of students (the Mr. Chips syndrome) [Hodgkinson, 1974, p. 266].[9]

The Dream at this and other ages is supported by the encouragement of an older and wiser colleague called the Mentor. The Mentor is not a parental figure; rather, he or she is a person selected by the young professional as a model and guide. Although Mentors show young professionals around and may even take them under their wing, what is important, as Levinson put it, is not the "teaching or the sponsoring" but the "blessing" by the Mentor of the junior person's activities. It seems we ought to have Mentors throughout our work lives, but few of us have more than two or three Mentors, and some may have none.

Using the joint ideas of the Dream and the Mentor, Hodgkinson, following Levinson, describes the development of a full-fledged work identity for a

[9]From "Adult Development: Implications for Faculty and Administrators," by H. L. Hodgkinson. In *Educational Record,* 1974, *55,* 263–274. Copyright 1974 by the American Council on Education. This and all other quotations from this source are reprinted by permission.

college professor in terms of the following age scheme:

Stage I	Mentor for a Dream	Ages 22–29
Stage II	Age 30—Transition	Ages 29–31
Stage III	Settling Down	Ages 31–35
Stage IV	Shedding the Mentor	Ages 35–39
Stage V	Midlife Discomfort	Ages 39–43
Stage VI	Reestablishing Commitments	Ages 44–50
Stage VII	Toughing It Out to Retirement, or the Happy Few	Ages 50–62 +

Perhaps the most revealing phase is the period from Stage IV through Stage VI—that is, after the Dream has (or has not) been attained and the person has (or has not) become his or her own person. At about age 35, the person may begin to feel that he or she is competent and no longer needs the Mentor. This, then, is the time when the person may start his or her own business, become a foreman, or get tenure at a college or university. The key word here is autonomy—I know what I'm doing, and I do it well.

Stage V, Midlife Discomfort, may come about because each of us has to deal with the gap between the Dream and the reality made possible by the Dream. Oddly enough, accomplishing the Dream can sometimes be worse than not accomplishing it. If the Dream is attained, we discover it is not all we dreamed it to be, and we are stuck at age 40 with no new occupational Dream to aim toward. This discomfort can bring about a period of reconstructing our relationship not only to our career but to our intimate life as well. Although there is very little in the way of secure research data relevant to this point, Hodgkinson does note that the period between 43 and 50 can be one of the best in life. As he puts it,

> New goals can be established that will be meaningful in terms of work and one's entire life as a person. New sources of marital happiness can be discovered . . . and the individual can become more fulfilled in more ways than at any stage in the past. However, it is important to notice that this can be accomplished most effectively by those who have dealt satisfactorily with the midcareer crisis.
>
> The crisis, then, is a vital stimulus for growth. This is a time when individuals often expand their horizons and begin to take up other sorts of activities that hold

special meaning unrelated to their jobs. Because physically one is still relatively strong, the sky is virtually the limit regarding what one wishes to do to find fulfillment. In addition, new activities often bring new friendship patterns and a more varied social life [1974, p. 271].

In this description, we find that the joint themes of *Lieben* and *Arbeiten* rejoin. It seems clear that the person must grow, both personally and professionally, into a new stance toward the self, others, job, and society and that such growth is strongly prompted by problems that reach their most acute form at about age 40. Only if this conflict is understood as an opportunity for change can the person make the satisfying transition from striving young professor (shop steward, business person, lawyer, physician, mechanic) to helpful and productive Mentor for the next generation. Only in this way can we come to a new definition of ourselves as "teacher" as well as "doer," and this is as true for the shop steward or master mechanic as for the lawyer, doctor, or college professor.

D. Age and creative work

The natural history of a person's work identity seems to fall easily into a series of phases. Even a superficial examination of the seven stages described by Levinson and Hodgkinson suggests that we are not likely to be equally innovative in all stages: one of these stages is likely to be more open and productive than most others. If we had to pick, it seems that the years between 35 and 45 or 50 ought to be the ones in which we are maximally creative. During this time not only do we have the technical competence necessary for innovative work, we also have the personal confidence required to push innovative ideas.

Although there is no obvious and completely clear way to evaluate the relation of age to creative ability, an extensive series of studies by Lehman (1953) has been directed toward answering one very basic question: at what age is a person most likely to do his or her most outstanding work? In answering this question, Lehman tried to determine the ages at which outstanding contributions in different fields (art, science, philosophy, and so on) were made. Characteristic of many graphs Lehman has compiled are the two presented in Figure 12-1. For each of the seven fields included—chemistry, mathematics, astronomy, physics, poetry, short-story writing, and invention—the peak of outstanding

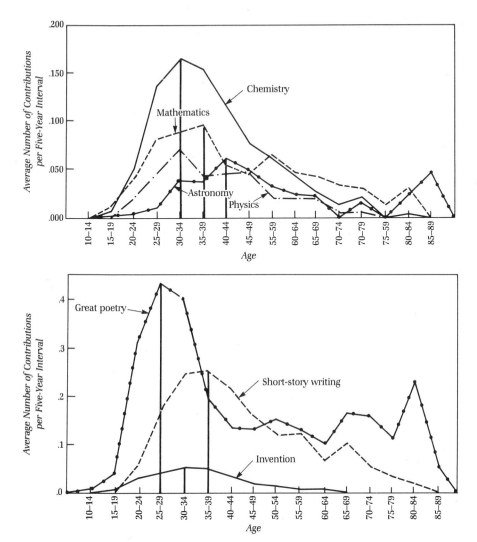

Figure 12-1. Age trends in productivity in various areas of science and literature. *(From Harvey C. Lehman, Age and Achievement, Figs. 7 and 80, pp. 11 and 119. Copyright 1953 by the American Philosophical Society and published by Princeton University Press. Reprinted by permission of Princeton University Press.)*

achievement fell in the 20-year period between 25 and 45. A closer look at both figures also reveals that five of these seven fields peak within the decade from 30 to 40. Although there are funny bumps in some of the curves (poetry, astronomy), most *great* works do seem to be done at around age 35.

A different way to measure productivity over the life span was reported by Dennis (1966), who stud-

ied the total output of 738 persons who lived to be at least 80. Dennis undertook his study to examine creative productivity across a set of achievements, rather than for one "outstanding" achievement as Lehman had done. Dennis consulted reference books in three areas: science and invention; the arts; and general scholarship, such as social criticism, philosophy, and history. In contrast to much of the work reported earlier, he was interested in how productive people were at each age, rather than at what age a single outstanding contribution was made. Dennis' data, while still concerned with extraordinary people, would seem to tell us more about general changes in work productivity. For this reason, such data are probably more relevant for people like you and me.

Figure 12-2 presents the mean percentage of total works done in each decade for the three major areas of scholarship, science and invention, and art. Individuals in the three areas do not reach or maintain their maximum productivity during the same decade. For example, the Scholars group shows a steady and continuing rise in productivity that does not diminish even in the seventies. The Artists group shows a more dramatic rise, an earlier peak, and a more rapid decline than either of the other two groups. In the six subgroups of scientists and inventors studied by Dennis, productivity was at its peak in midlife (40–50) and decreased thereafter.

Although Dennis' results show some of the same properties as Lehman's, there are notable differences. These are particularly obvious for the Scholars group. In the Scientists and Artists groups, Dennis' results show that maximum productivity neither rises nor declines as sharply as might be expected from Lehman's data. Although there may be many reasons for these differences, the major one seems to be that Lehman was concerned with "out-

standing" contributions, rather than with the total course of productivity over a lifetime. In addition, Dennis not only examined contributions by the most eminent people in a given field; he also included work produced by "lesser" individuals who met his criterion of having lived to age 80.

Despite these differences, Lehman and Dennis did find maximally productive decades for both ordinary and extraordinary work. Dennis was most concerned with differences among fields, and here he argued that the three fields discussed—art, scholarship, and science—require different styles of work. For example, in some fields it is proper to have collaborators; in others the individual only works alone. Similarly, in some fields it is necessary and proper to collect and store information for later use; in other fields such procedures are minimal or unnecessary. Finally, in some fields a person receives credit for modifying, applying, or restating previous views; in other areas each contribution must be a new work. For each of these three possibilities, the first alternative describes the work situation of the scholar, while the second describes the situation of the artist. Scientists present an intermediate situation.

Despite differences among fields, Lehman's evidence suggests that outstanding contributions are likely to occur fairly soon after the person enters a given field. Only at this point is the person unlikely to be "fixed" in his or her way of looking at a partic-

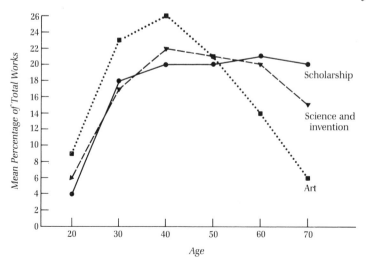

Figure 12-2. The total course of productivity over the life span for scholars, scientists and inventors, and artists. (Data from Dennis, 1966.)

ular problem. Even if a person makes a discovery that will later be regarded as outstanding, there is no guarantee that it will be appreciated immediately. Initially, only a small group of specialists may be able to appreciate the discovery, and only later will the discovery spread to other parts of the field. Only once a discovery has been accepted within the limits of a given field will it be possible for its influence to spread to other fields, and then and only then is the discoverer likely to be considered outstanding by other creative thinkers. This process takes time, and it is not surprising that many of the pictures finding their way into history books show middle-aged or even old men and women. Portraits are made only once the person is famous, not when the discovery occurred.

The number of years a person has been in a profession enters into the creativity picture in still another way, particularly in scientific and academic careers: many scientists and scholars, after a few productive years, come to head a laboratory or a school. This means that in the middle or later years they administer, rather than create as they did before. To be sure, some scientists encourage younger colleagues to be creative or are themselves encour-

aged by younger colleagues, but the more usual course of events is for the creative worker to redirect his or her energies toward administration during the mid-years and beyond.

Obviously, talented people who enter fields in which early achievement is not possible will come to a position of eminence only in later life. Some professions have a long apprenticeship before the person can be recognized as outstanding. Figure 12-3 shows the peak age for each of four fields in which great maturity would seem to be required before a person reached his or her maximum level of achievement. Each of these fields—business, the Supreme Court, the House of Representatives, and the Catholic Church—not only requires a long apprenticeship, it also requires a degree of social and political skill. If early middle age is a time of great creativity and innovation in science, arts, and general scholarship, late middle age and after is a time of maximum leadership and political power.

These data agree with the conclusions of an earlier discussion concerning the "prime of life" (Chapter 10). Even if original and creative thinking characterizes early midlife, there is still more to come if the person is able to pursue it and so chooses. If

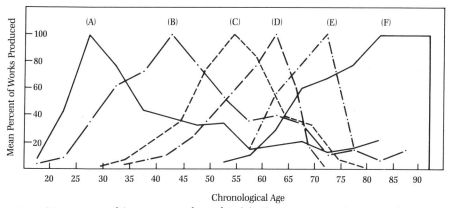

Figure 12-3. Age versus achievement and productivity in maturity and old age. (A) 480 superior secular poems by 93 poets. (B) 459 superior novels, essays, and other prose selections by 149 authors. (C) Age data for recipients of 426 "earned" annual incomes of $100,000 or more during the years 1934 to 1938 inclusive. (Data for movie people omitted.) (D) Justices of the Supreme Court. (E) Speakers of the United States House of Representatives from 1900 to 1940—similar age data were obtained for the prime ministers of England for the years 1834 to 1945. (F) Age data for the last 26 deceased popes of the Roman Catholic Church—a similar curve was found for 99 presidents of religious organizations of the U.S.A. elected to office prior to the year 1900. (*After Harvey C. Lehman,* Age and Achievement, *combination of Figs. 1-67, pp. 5-97. Copyright 1953 by the American Philosophical Society and published by Princeton University Press. Reprinted by permission of Princeton University Press.)*

youth is a time of vigor, beauty, and strength, and old age a time of leadership and wisdom, then midlife is that period in which the person tends to make his or her most distinctive and most innovative contribution. Such innovation need not be restricted to the work of the scientist, inventor, or scholar; it can refer to the little innovations each of us makes in the large and small of our work and social worlds. The decade between 35 and 45 seems to be a time when most human beings are ripe to change some aspect of themselves or of their world. Whether they (we) choose to do so depends primarily on their skills and themselves. No one can make anyone else change things or be responsive to innovation: only the individual can do it, should he or she dare.

E. A small problem: Age, stage, and human choice

With all this talk about stages of occupational development, creative productivity, and intimate relationships, we may well wonder how all these "stages" are related to the issue of human freedom. Once before, in Chapter 10, we discussed the more general problem of what exactly we mean by a "stage of development." The issue is not only first-person versus third-person point of view but also why people move from one stage to the next. In much of this discussion one disturbing issue about stages has been left untouched: how can we say a person has any freedom of choice if it is inevitable that we all pass through a series of predetermined stages? Where, exactly, is the experience (and the anxiety) of human choice in all this?

Put just this way, the idea of a developmental stage seems so fixed and so impervious to human choice. A stage, after all, *is* a stage, and there is little we can do about it except enter and possibly pass through it. Even if we view each stage as a comfort (that is, if we remind ourselves that we all suffer adolescent and midlife crises, and everyone gets through them), that does not lessen our fear that how it will all turn out is already settled. The most we end up with is a choice (reflected or unreflected) between two alternatives: identity diffusion *or* identity achieved, generativity *or* stagnation, and so on. To exercise "free choice" surely means more than to choose one or another preordained alternative.

The answer to this concern involves three main points: (1) stages are not independent of social or historical context (Van Den Berg's argument), (2) choice is always choice from the specific point of view of some specific someone (first-person-perspective argument), and (3) choice is always choice within limits (situation argument). Although all these considerations have been raised before, it is important to see what implications they have for the issues of age, stage, and human choice.

All three considerations seem to point to the same conclusion: the timetable a particular society in a particular historical era chooses to emphasize is important in that it sets a task for each of us that we can only respond to in terms of what we choose to do in *this* situation, in *this* crisis, in *this* society, in *this* era. Developmental stages are thus not independent of person, time, or context, and to treat them as if they were is to miss the experience of crisis (or challenge) they set for the living individual. Although someone (perhaps the developmental psychologist) may *think* he or she knows what the eventual resolution will be, and although most of us do resolve an issue in predictable ways, we must never miss the drama and the uncertainty of the first-person perspective of the particular life in question. We must also not miss the possibility that some one of us might just come to a different resolution than everyone else and thereby force the rest of us (if we are brave enough) to a reevaluation not only of our personal resolutions but of our stage theories as well. In just this way might the personal and theoretical situations of contemporary developmental psychology change and become less, rather than more, restrictive.

Stages do not set down an automatic and inviolate grand plan for human development; they are better thought of as providing a series of situations that limit, but do not coerce, human change and growth. In the end, the developing human being decides in which direction he or she will go.

III. THE FULLY FUNCTIONING ADULT: MASLOW'S IDEAS ON SELF-ACTUALIZATION

Much of the research dealing with creativity in midlife and elsewhere has to do with famous individuals. It seems reasonable to wonder whether more ordinary people have a chance to be creative as well. Do I have to be a superperson to live a full and productive life in the years preceding and following 45? A different, perhaps more manageable way of asking this question would be to examine what the characteristics are of a "fully functioning" adult, whether or not the adult happened to be famous.

No one has approached this topic more carefully (or more often) than Abraham H. Maslow, who saw the major issue in adult life as **self-actualization.** For Maslow, self-actualization means the full use of one's human potential in a unique and individual way. No two self-actualizing persons need have the same traits, skills, or ways of Being-in-the-world. The emphasis is clearly on each individual's unique mode of being human: for some it may take the form of being an ideal teacher or parent, for others it may be expressed athletically, while for still others it may be expressed in poetry, painting, or invention.

Maslow is trying to describe what it means to be a "healthy" human being. He came to focus on the healthy rather than on the neurotic or deprived adult because of some of his own personal experiences—most especially with two colleagues, Ruth Benedict and Max Wertheimer. Maslow was struck by the "humanness" of his two friends and because of them decided to study the nature of exemplary, or, as he called them, self-actualizing, people. At first, Maslow reflected on his dealings with self-actualizing people in a highly impressionistic and personal way. He soon became convinced that for psychology to come to any understanding of human beings at all, it was necessary to study those who best exemplified what it might mean to be human. All his life, Maslow was critical of personality theories developed on the basis of observing only poorly functioning or neurotic people. Instead, he argued, why not study healthy people to understand what human potential might be like in its most highly developed state?

Maslow searched for individuals who seemed to be self-actualizing in their everyday lives. Because no other work had ever been done on this topic, Maslow started by using whatever procedures he could to study the people available—informal observations, interviews, reading of dramas and biographies, and so on. In his earliest work Maslow began by looking for self-actualizing college students. As it turned out, these were almost impossible to find. After screening a large number of undergraduate students, Maslow was able to find only one college student who met his standards and only about 20 who might be able to meet these standards in the future. For this reason, Maslow decided that "self-actualization of the sort I had found in my older subjects perhaps was not possible in our society for young developing people" (1970, p. 150).[10]

Because self-actualizing individuals are so difficult to come by, Maslow based his descriptions of the self-actualizing person on an analysis of the following 60 actual, partial, and possible cases. *Actual cases:* Seven fairly sure and two highly probable contemporaries (interviewed); two fairly sure historical figures (Lincoln in his last years and Thomas Jefferson); seven highly probable public and historical figures (Albert Einstein, Eleanor Roosevelt, Jane Addams, William James, Albert Schweitzer, Aldous Huxley, and Baruch Spinoza). *Partial cases:* Five contemporaries who fairly certainly fell short somewhat but who nonetheless could be used for study. *Potential or possible cases* and *cases suggested or studied by others:* G. W. Carver, Eugene V. Debs, Thomas Eakins, Fritz Kreisler, Goethe, Pablo Casals, Martin Buber, Danilo Dolci, Arthur E. Morgan, John Keats, David Hilbert, Arthur Waley, D. T. Suzuki, Adlai Stevenson, Sholom Aleichem, Robert Browning, Ralph Waldo Emerson, Frederick Douglass, Joseph Schumpeter, Robert Benchley, Ida Tarbell, Harriet Tubman, George Washington, Karl Muenzinger, Franz Josef Haydn, Camille Pissarro, Edward Bibring, George William Russell, Pierre Renoir, Henry Wadsworth Longfellow, Peter Kropotkin, John Altgeld, Thomas More, Edward Bellamy, Benjamin Franklin, John Muir, Walt Whitman.

Because data resulting from this kind of impressionistic analysis tend to be somewhat imprecise, Maslow described the self-actualized person in terms of a series of personal characteristics. His final set of 15 can be summarized as follows:

1. Self-actualizing people tend to have a more adequate perception of what is enduring; they are able to detect the spurious, the fake, and the dishonest in interpersonal relationships and are attuned to what is significant in all spheres of living. They prefer to deal with unpleasant reality rather than retreat into pleasant fantasy.

[10]From *Motivation and Personality, Second Edition,* by A. H. Maslow. Copyright 1970 by Harper & Row Publishers, Inc. This and all other quotations from this source are reprinted by permission.

2. Such people have a high degree of acceptance of themselves, of others, and of human nature. They are not ashamed of being what they are, nor are they shocked to find shortcomings in themselves or in others.

3. Self-actualizing individuals display spontaneity in their thinking, emotions, and behavior to a greater extent than most people.

4. Such individuals are problem-centered, usually focusing on problems rather than on themselves. They are not overly self-conscious; they are not problems to themselves, and therefore they are able to devote their attention to a task, duty, or mission that seems peculiarly appropriate for them.

5. The self-actualizing person enjoys privacy. He or she enjoys solitude, even seeking it on occasion, and uses such periods for intense concentration on subjects of interest.

6. Such people are highly autonomous. They seem to be themselves in the face of rejection or unpopularity; they pursue their interests and maintain integrity even when it hurts to do so.

7. Self-actualizing people have a continued freshness of appreciation. Such people show a capacity to "appreciate again and again, freshly and naively, the basic goods of life . . . a sunset, . . . a flower, . . . a baby, . . . a person" (1970, p. 163). They avoid grouping experiences into categories; rather, they see the unique in commonplace experiences.

8. Such people often have "mystical experiences," in which their personal boundaries are experienced as evaporating and in which they become a part of all humankind and even of nature.

9. Self-actualizing people experience feelings of belonging to humanity as a whole. For this reason they not only are concerned with the lot of members of their immediate family but also concern themselves with the situation of people from different cultures.

10. Such people maintain close relationships with only a few friends or loved ones. Even though self-actualizing people are not necessarily popular, they establish close, loving relationships with at least one or two other people.

11. They tend to have democratic character structures and to associate with people not on the basis of race, status, or religion but as individual human beings.

12. Self-actualizing people have a highly developed sense of ethics. Though their notions of right and wrong are not totally conventional, they usually do what they do with its ethical meaning in mind.

13. Such individuals have a special sense of humor in which common human foibles, pretensions, and foolishness are the subject of laughter, rather than sadism, obscenity, or rebellion against authority.

14. Self-actualizing people are creative and inventive in at least a few areas and only infrequently are followers of usual ways of doing things.

15. Self-actualizing people detach themselves somewhat from brainwashing by their cultures, thereby permitting themselves to adopt a critical attitude toward cultural inconsistencies within their society.

Now, this is quite a list. We all certainly would like to meet such a person or (if we have enough good feelings about ourselves) would like to become one. At first the idea may seem overwhelming, but it need not be if we keep in mind that self-actualizing people get irritable, angry, and jealous just like the rest of us. They can be temperamental, vain, and ruthless; and, like us, they can be downright stupid and nasty some of the time—all of which led Maslow to note:

> What this [research] has taught me I think all of us had better learn. There are no perfect human beings! Persons can be found who are good, very good indeed, in fact, great. There do in fact exist creators, seers, sages, saints, shakers, and movers. This can certainly give us hope for the future of the species even if they are uncommon and do not come by the dozen. And yet these very same people can at times be boring, irritating, petulant, selfish, angry, or depressed. To avoid disillusionment with human nature, we must first give up our illusions about it [1970, p. 176].

Despite this last statement, Maslow does have illusions about being human and has tried to place before the psychologist his idea of what it means to be a "human" being more forcefully than anyone else.

A. The hierarchy of human needs

Maslow's analysis of self-actualization is part of a much more ambitious attempt to define what he called human needs and to describe their role in directing what human beings do. According to Maslow, we are all directed by a set of inborn needs that can be arranged in the form of a hierarchy, with the more primitive ones at the bottom and the more complex and human ones at the top, as in Figure 12-4. Maslow presented his ideas about human needs in the form of a hierarchy because he assumed that higher needs become important only when lower needs have been at least partly satisfied. The logic here seems to be that a person worrying about food, safety, belongingness, or esteem cannot be concerned about realizing his or her potential.

Although it makes some sense to describe what human beings need in the form of a hierarchy, the lower four levels of the hierarchy seem very different from the highest level, that of self-actualization. In his more recent work Maslow (1970) has come to describe **physiological, safety, belongingness and love,** and **esteem** as "deficiency" needs and self-actualization as a "being" or "growth" need. There are three major differences between deficiency and growth needs: (1) A person tries to get rid of deficiency needs and to enjoy the pleasure of a growth need. (2) Deficiency needs tend to set off tensions, so that the person does what is necessary to restore a lower state of arousal. Growth needs usually involve an increase in arousal or tension. (3) Deficiency needs tend to produce episodic behaviors (eating three times a day, going to the bathroom in the morning), whereas growth needs tend to be continuous. Thus, meeting a deficiency need leads to a sense of relief and rest; meeting a growth need leads to a feeling of fulfillment and change.

In addition to self-actualization, Maslow described two other types of growth needs: **cognitive** and **esthetic.** Most simply described, cognitive needs include the need to know, to understand, and to explore; esthetic needs include symmetry, order, and beauty. Maslow, strongly committed to a

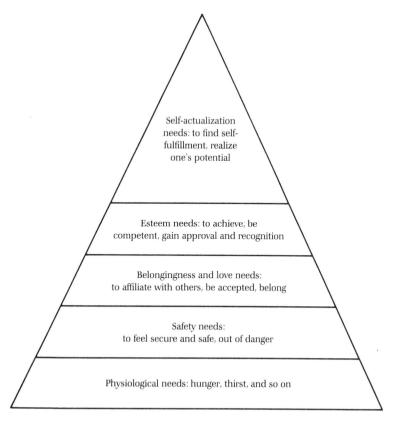

Self-actualization needs: to find self-fulfillment, realize one's potential

Esteem needs: to achieve; be competent, gain approval and recognition

Belongingness and love needs: to affiliate with others, be accepted, belong

Safety needs: to feel secure and safe, out of danger

Physiological needs: hunger, thirst, and so on

Figure 12-4. Maslow's hierarchy of human needs. *(From* Introduction to Psychology, Sixth Edition, *by Ernest R. Hilgard, Richard C. Atkinson, and Rita L. Atkinson, © 1975 by Harcourt Brace Jovanovich, Inc. Reprinted by permission of the publisher.)*

hierarchal organization of needs, considers cognitive needs "lower" (and hence more demanding of action) than esthetic needs, so that esthetic needs come to the fore only after cognitive needs have been taken care of.

The idea of personal self-actualization is thus seen as one part in the larger tendency of human beings to grow and change. Although these tendencies are natural, most of us never experience them fully, and it seems reasonable to wonder what one has to do to be self-actualizing. As Maslow put it, "Do we grit our teeth and squeeze?" No, we don't grit our teeth and squeeze; rather, there are actions we can take to help us on the road to self-actualizing. These include—

1. Experiencing life as a child does, with full absorption and concentration; trying something new rather than sticking to safe ways.

2. Listening to our own feelings in evaluating experiences rather than to the voice of tradition, authority, or the majority.

3. Being honest and avoiding game playing.

4. Being prepared to be unpopular if our views do not agree with most people's.

5. Assuming responsibility.

6. Working hard at whatever we do.

7. Trying to identify problems and having the courage to modify them or give them up.

Although this is not a sure-fire recipe for "health," it does represent some good advice on how to go about actualizing our life and our style of being.

This, then, is the house that Maslow built. How satisfactory is it to us as individuals, and how well does it describe what it means to be human? On the positive side there is Maslow's strong emphasis on change and growth as an essential aspect of being human. This part of his approach is quite in tune with the idea that human beings are not static entities but are constantly changing. Maslow's ideas, however, are not about change alone; rather, they are meant to serve as an (optimistic) guide to what it means to be human and what we have to do to get there.

One reason Maslow can be optimistic about human beings is that he does not consider aggressiveness or sexuality necessarily bad and in need of suppression. Rather, Maslow recognizes the whole human being as his territory and does not condemn any one aspect as "bad" or "problematic."

Maslow's emphasis on seeing each "need" in terms of its relationship to other needs within the person allows him to call his approach to human behavior **dynamic holism**—*dynamic* because it deals with the constantly changing flux that is human living, *holism* because it deals with the complete person. In this regard the theory is reminiscent of Kurt Goldstein's (see Chapter 3).

Despite these generally positive aspects, there are also problems. For one, Maslow tends to an uncritical use of words and facts. Take the idea of self-actualization itself: although it may make us feel good, is any one of us sure that we could definitely pick out a self-actualizing person if we were to come upon one? Indeed, everyone might not agree that Maslow's conclusions, provocative as they are in providing a model for healthy human functioning, apply to the list of people whose case histories he looked at in the first place. It seems to me that Abraham Lincoln and Eleanor Roosevelt, despite their tremendous compassion for the lives of others, were not very actualizing in their own personal lives.

Probably the most troublesome part of Maslow's theory concerns his concept of a need hierarchy. Although Maslow often noted that we should not try to develop a list of basic drives because "such a listing implies an isolatedness of each of these drives from each of the others" (1970, p. 25), he has in fact developed such a list. He does allow that security needs may be less important than belongingness needs for some people, but this concession does not go far enough toward seeing "needs" as part of a total living person.

Perhaps the most useful distinction drawn by Maslow in this regard is the distinction between deficiency and growth needs. If we interpret these categories more generally than Maslow, it seems reasonable to think of deficiency needs as those tending to preserve a person's present state and growth needs as those serving to promote change in the person. People who function primarily in terms of meeting deficiency needs will usually try to maintain their present situation; people who function in terms of growth needs are constantly alert to possible changes in their style of living. Under this interpretation, human beings do things to conserve as well as to change, with the relative importance of change and conservation defining each person's unique mode of Being-in-the-world.

B. Self-actualization and midlife

It is at this point that self-actualization theory makes contact with the experience of being 45. According to almost everyone who has written about it, the situation to be explored in midlife involves a contrast between the opposing tendencies of stagnation and generativity, conservation and change— that is, between growth and deficiency needs. In being 45, the problem is often whether the person will continue to go on as he or she has been or will come to a newer and more open approach to the world and his or her life.

Although such conflict may peak during these years, similar crises and challenges have occurred throughout all the preceding years and will continue to occur during all the succeeding ones. The contrast between stagnation and change seems woven into the very fabric of what it means to be human. No one escapes it, and we all have to come to terms with whether we will remain as we are or whether we will be open to opportunities and problems that come up throughout the course of living. These problems and our answers to them come to define the nature of our life, most especially in the mid-years, for it is only here that we have finally become our own person. Self-actualizers are rarely found among the young because it takes a bit of living to know what might be possible in the way of being fully human.

IV. SUMMARY

The age of 45 appears to be a turning point in adult life that brings about both a sense of accomplishment and one of disappointment. Many negative aspects of the "middle years" have to do with one's perception of declining physical strength and health, while many advantages are associated with the increasing degree of mastery and competence an adult brings to her or his present dealings with the world.

Two of the most frequently studied physiological events during this period are heart attacks in men and menopause in women. For men, the crucial issue is to accept the fact of reduced capacities. Although a similar issue is involved for women, further issues may arise to the degree that a woman's sense of her value as a person is linked to her identity as an attractive female, a mother, or both.

Men and women alike suffer from the social defi- nition of no longer "being young," although women in early stages of midlife are likely to experience this evaluation more strongly because a man in our society is still considered to be in his prime from 35 to 50, whereas women of this age are often no longer encouraged to consider themselves attractive or even significant.

In general, the major concerns of this period, as is true for much of adult human life, are the crucial issues of loving and working. Erikson maintains that the central challenge of the middle adult years is the issue of generativity versus stagnation, especially as it occurs in the areas of love and work.

Lieben, or loving, was described by the Greeks as consisting of three types: eros (sexual love), philia (loving friendship), and agape (love for mankind, altruism). Other types of love, however, can also be defined. Maternal love, for example, enables an infant to survive his or her delicate early period although it entails later rejection. Infant love (the child's love for the mother) is of comparable strength to maternal love but much less tied to a particular person. Paternal love (as studied by Harlow in monkeys) seems best defined as a secondary protection system for the infant as much as a specific type of affectional relationship.

Though the effects that parents have on their children's development is a common topic in psychology, little notice has been given to the effects children have in bringing about changes in their parents' lives. Indeed, in humans, the effect children have on their parents can be seen to occur as early as the decision to become pregnant. This decision involves a great deal more in the way of a commitment between partners than the marriage vows and, for this reason, is a significant one for both father and mother as well as for the unborn infant.

A woman's experience of pregnancy seems best discussed in terms of three 3-month periods called trimesters. The first trimester focuses the mother on her changing body and sometimes brings about an interperson distance from her husband as well as from the rest of her world. The second trimester brings an awareness of the fetus as a separate life within and often serves to renew attachments by the mother to her own family of origin, particularly to her mother. The final trimester is taken up with preparations for the infant's birth and may be experienced as a "heavy" and difficult time.

The expectant father, though biologically unaffected by pregnancy, is definitely affected by the social process surrounding it. Expectant fathers behave in such a way as to fit into one of three categories: romantic (the father takes a casual approach to paternity, punctuated with a bit of awe concerning the whole business); familial (he accepts familial responsibilities easily and well); and career-oriented (he denies that any changes will occur and is unsure what having a baby might mean for him). Each father thus deals in his own way with the situation of pregnancy.

The first stage experienced by parents once the child is born is characterized by the prospect of caring for a new and fragile life. Feeding represents an early significant milestone, and despite advantages of breast feeding, such as increased intimacy between mother and child, not all women nurse their babies. A second early milestone that becomes noteworthy to the developing parents involves the child's drive to become an individual—a drive that is both a relief because of the child's increasing competence and a vexation because of the parents' inability to control and protect the child as easily as before.

At around age 4, the child enters into the "stage" of the family romance. This stage is as much a test of parent/parent as parent/child relationships. Some parents resent growing "competition" with a child of the same sex; some overidentify with the child. Regardless of how this situation is dealt with by a particular family, the child starts school at the close of this period, thereby changing parenting from a full- to a part-time job. Here, parents must decide how to deal with the child's teacher—usually the first evaluating authority figure they encounter in their capacity as parents.

With puberty a more openly sexual tone is introduced into family life. At this time, the conflicts of the adolescent may coincide with the midlife crises of the parents. Parents can respond either by identifying with the child or by competing with him or her, with competition producing envy, and identification, overcontrol. In either case, it is important to remember that parents, like children, are changing and that adolescence and midlife problems often greatly complicate each other.

Arbeiten, or working, involves the same set of problems present in the evolution of loving—being stagnant versus being innovative. Although work sometimes was seen by the ancients as something to be avoided, it became valuable in the Protestant ethic. This joint historical evolution is reflected in contemporary attitudes toward work as something desirable *and* as something to be avoided. An unfortunately high percentage of workers, particularly those in low-status and low-skill positions, see work merely as a way of earning money or passing time. Such meaninglessness may result from an extreme division of labor in which pride in workmanship is sacrificed for increased efficiency. Work is important to the adult because much of adults' self-identity is derived from what they do for a living.

We come to our adult work identity only through a relatively long developmental process. This process involves different stages in which the person grows from (and through) an apprentice relationship with his or her Mentor. At about age 40 the worker often seeks to become his or her "own person" and thereby to give up the Mentor/Apprentice relationship. Crisis is likely at this age if the occupational "Dream" (for example, to be a master carpenter or to own one's own business) is or is not reached; in either case, the adult has begun to realize that he or she is no longer "growing up" but is now "growing old."

One important aspect of the developmental process involved in work concerns that period in which a person is likely to be most creative. In the careers of special people defined as creative or innovative by their society, maximum productivity is usually achieved a reasonably short time after entering the field. Many of the exceptions are explained by requirements imposed by various fields; for example, it takes longer to become a judge than a plant foreman.

The idea of stages in the development of a work identity (as in the more general development of a person) may suggest that the individuals involved are never exercising free choice but are only following a preordained blueprint. However, choice always operates within limiting situations, and choice is always choice for the person whose life is at issue—never for some third-person observer, not even a developmental psychologist. And even though everyone up to the present has resolved a given developmental crisis in a particular way, someone might resolve the crisis in some new and unexpected way, which would necessitate a change in everyone's perspective from then on. Stages limit our choices; they need not coerce them.

Full functioning in midlife can be defined (according to Maslow) by the self-actualizing adult. Since self-actualization entails both experience and preparation, people before midlife are not likely to deal with their world in a self-actualized way. According to Maslow, self-actualization is the full use of one's human potential in a unique, individual way. As such, it provides one definition of what it might mean to be a healthy adult human being.

In his more general theory of human development, Maslow divides human needs into two basic types: deficiency (for example, food, acceptance, self-preservation) and growth (self-actualization, cognitive, esthetic). Growth needs can emerge only when deficiency needs are met. The distinction between deficiency needs (which attempt to preserve the present self) and growth needs (which support the person in his or her attempts to change) relate Maslow's views to those proposed by Erikson, who noted that stagnation and change represent the most important challenge of what it means to be a human being at midlife. In this, Maslow and Erikson agree; the human being must always choose between remaining what he or she is or becoming what he or she might become. Only the latter set of concerns will set the person on a road that might lead to a self-actualized style of dealing with the world and with one's place in it.

V. GLOSSARY OF IMPORTANT CONCEPTS

Agape. The Greek term for God's love for man, which has been applied to humans in the sense of a profound love for one's fellow human beings.

Arbeiten. To work productively; one of Freud's and Erikson's concepts describing significant midlife activities in Western society.

Belongingness and love needs. The needs to affiliate with others, to be accepted, and to belong. A class of needs at the intermediate levels of Maslow's hierarchy of needs.

Cognitive needs. The need to know, to understand, and to explore. A class of needs near the top of Maslow's need hierarchy, although lower than esthetic needs.

Competence. A person's experience indicating that he or she controls events as well as being controlled by them. Described as a master motive by White.

Creativity. The capacity to deal in a continuously innovative and fresh way with one's job or with other aspects of life, such as loving.

The "Dream." The final state a young professional aspires to attain. By midlife, the Dream is often changed to accord with one's achievements rather than with one's early wishes.

Dynamic holism. Maslow's approach to personality, in which he views needs in relation to other needs within the total person, all needs being in constant flux.

Eros. Erotic love, in which sexuality plays a significant role in the relationship. The Greek term for sexual and romantic love.

Esteem needs. The needs to achieve, to be competent, and to gain approval and recognition. A class of needs at the upper levels of Maslow's hierarchy of needs.

Esthetic needs. The needs for symmetry, order, and beauty. A class of needs proposed by Maslow near the top of his hierarchy of needs.

Generativity. The term by which Erikson characterizes the middle-adulthood stage of development when this is marked by creativity, productivity, and a concern for the next generation.

Generativity in loving. Dealing in an ever-fresh way with the changing nature and problems of the people we love.

Infant love. An infant's love for the parents, which begins as a symbiotic union with the mother, then progresses into a specific attachment to mother or father, and finally allows for an attachment to siblings and other relatives.

Lieben. To love. One of the two major areas of concern during midlife as described by Freud and Erikson.

Love. Eros is that type of love which gives its name to the word *erotic.* Philia is a quieter love—friendship. Agape is a person's love for mankind in its entirety.

Love, within the monkey family. Maternal—the mother monkey's love for her child. Infant—the love shown by the infant for the parent. Paternal—the stage in development after maternal love and the one before heterosexual love. These stages first observed and described by Harlow.

Menopause. The natural cessation of menstruation in middle age, often accompanied by such symptoms as dizziness, insomnia, tingling sensations, and "hot flashes." The severity of these symptoms is related to the woman's perception of what is important to her self-definition.

Mentor. An older colleague who guides the person during an early stage of his or her career. Generally "outgrown" by age 40.

Midlife crisis. Turmoil precipitated by the review and reevaluation of one's past, typically occurring in the early to middle forties.

Philia. A Greek term best translated as "(loving) friendship." Exemplified by the biblical pair David and Jonathan.

Physiological needs. Hunger, thirst, and so on—the lowest level of Maslow's need hierarchy.

Safety needs. The need to feel secure and safe, out of danger. A class of needs at the lower level of Maslow's hierarchy of needs.

Self-actualization. A person's fundamental tendency to be all that he or she can possibly be. A tendency toward maximum realization of human potential stressed by Maslow in his analysis of what it means to be a fully functioning human being.

VI. SUGGESTED READINGS

Major sources

Anthony, E. J., & Benedek, T. (Eds.). *Parenthood: Its psychology and psychopathology.* Boston: Little, Brown, 1970.

Lehman, H. C. *Age and achievement.* Princeton, N.J.: Princeton University Press, 1953.

Levinson, D. J. *The seasons of a man's life.* New York: Knopf, 1978.

Maslow, A. H. *Motivation and personality* (2nd ed.). New York: Harper & Row, 1970.

Neugarten, B. L. (Ed.). *Middle age and aging.* Chicago: University of Chicago Press, 1968.

Secondary sources

Braude, L. *Work and workers: A sociological analysis.* New York: Praeger, 1975.

Kinget, G. M. *On being human.* New York: Harcourt Brace Jovanovich, 1975. Part 3.

Sheehy, G. *Passages.* New York: Dutton, 1976.

White, R. W. *The enterprise of living.* New York: Holt, Rinehart & Winston, 1972.

13

Making It Bad: Disorder and Woe in Human Living

You might think life would be easy for a healthy person of normal intelligence born in North America in the present century. Not always; many Americans find themselves with sufficiently strong problems in living to require the services of a psychologist, psychiatrist, or social worker. From 1923 until 1975, between a quarter-million and a half-million people a year were resident patients in state and county hospitals in the United States. This does not include people being treated by private therapists or those seen at outpatient clinics, day hospitals, or related mental-health facilities. One author (Coleman, 1976) has estimated that in 1975 there were 80 million people in the United States suffering from some sort of severe personal woe—about 38% of the population.

Now these are only numbers, abstract entities, adding up the miseries of four of every ten Americans. For some idea of what a few of these 80 million people experience in their day-to-day lives, we need to take a careful and sympathetic look at a small number of quite specific case studies. Only in this way will it be possible to find the living person behind the numbers. A word of caution: When we read about disordered lives, we see ourselves in the person whose life and troubles are being described. As a result, we often experience the "Medical Student's Disease," in which we are sure we have the symptoms of each and every problem we read about. Be forewarned: after reading this chapter, you may feel a little crazy yourself.

I. THE CASE OF JOHN KNIGHT

John Knight was an extremely successful 30-year-old industrial chemist who came for therapy because of a bleeding ulcer. This was not his first attack; an earlier one had taken place during his master's-level examinations when he was 25. Although he did well on the exams (he always did), Knight was forced to go to the hospital. There he became friends with an older internist who took a fatherly interest in him. Although the first attack was not severe, a second one, at age 30, was, and after this attack Knight was told his ulcer would never clear

up until he cleared up the mess his personal life was in.

John had spent his early years in a Midwestern town of 30,000. His father and mother had both come from Europe and had settled initially as immigrants in the Jewish ghetto in Manhattan. Since Knight's uncle (his father's older brother) owned a profitable business in the Midwest, John's family moved there when his father was unable to find work in New York.

Although Knight's father didn't like working under his older brother's control, they did well together in business. By a stroke of luck, a speculative property investment made by the brothers yielded a high profit. In later years both brothers, in telling of this venture, always attributed its success to their superior skill and intelligence in the world of business. John, however, described his attitude about their skill in the following story he later told to his therapist:

> Once, two cockroaches lived together in a compost heap. They became the closest of friends and shared their lives and secrets. One day the farmer began shifting the manure pile and he pitched the home of the two roaches far away. One roach landed on an even richer pile, but the other fell into a clay ditch where he could barely find enough to eat. He withered away almost to the vanishing point.
> One day the starving roach wandered away from his ditch and encountered his friend who looked fat, sleek and prosperous. "Hello," said the scrawny one. "Go away," said the other, "I don't know you." The starving roach reminded his friend of their former life together in the farmer's yard. He received a grudging acknowledgement. Said the starving one, "Please tell me the secret of your success." Said the other roach, somewhat grandly: "It's all a matter of brains and personality" [Knight, 1950, pp. 29–30].

Knight was the third of eight children. He had a brother five years his senior, a sister two years older, and five younger sisters. The youngest died in infancy; all the others grew to adulthood.

Knight was quite successful in school. Because of his intellectual abilities and achievements, young Knight was popular with peers, and except for one anti-Semitic incident (in Grade 6, when he fought a local bully), schooling went extremely well. This pattern continued during college, where he made good grades and ultimately gained admission into a prestigious graduate program in chemistry.

Knight's desire to become a chemist derived from personal and academic experience in high school. While at high school, he won the chemistry prize. In addition, the father of one of his very good friends encouraged him to pursue a career in chemistry. When Knight proposed that he become a chemist, his father said that he had never heard of a Jewish chemist, adding that "I'll pay for it, but I don't like it."

John's earliest dating included young women in his home town. The one he remembers best was a slightly older non-Jewish girl whom he followed around in his sophomore year until she finally accepted him. Most of their dates consisted of playing tennis together, including one final game after which the girl's father chased young Knight off, saying "I don't want any Jews hanging around here." In describing this incident, the adult John Knight reported that he had had a strong desire to strangle the father. Instead, he had walked off quietly.

One of the major events that sent John Knight to seek psychiatric treatment occurred just after his 30th birthday—the severe attack of bleeding ulcers already described. Even though he went to the hospital following this attack, Knight refused to enter psychotherapy although he was warned that he might die if he didn't straighten out the "emotional side" of his life. The final event forcing him into therapy occurred just after Knight had been told by an old friend that she was remarrying and would no longer be able to see him. Margaret, however, was not just an old friend; she had also been John's high school teacher. The intimate aspect of their relationship had begun a few years before his 30th birthday and just a few years after Margaret's husband had died. Knight, who always visited Margaret when he came to New York, soon found himself in an intermittent liaison that both parties knew could never end in a more permanent arrangement.

After Margaret told him of her plans to remarry and dropped him off at the airport, he suddenly became "breathless, unable to walk and gripped by a wild tide of fear." He later wrote of this incident:

> This episode had been genuinely terrifying. One must experience it to realize its absolute horror. The fear appears to strike from nowhere; it has a deathly quality about it; it seems to obstruct one's ability to breathe. The breathlessness and sensation of suffocation became so severe that I felt at first that I must be having a heart attack [1950, p. 20].

This attack of anxiety finally persuaded John to seek help. The unfolding of his treatment is clearly described in his book, *The Story of My Psychoanalysis* (1950).

The case of John Knight offers us a first glimpse at the power and significance of personal disorder in a seemingly well-run and successful life. Although there is much to be learned from this case, it is perhaps enough to talk about the terrible divisions that pervade John Knight's style of living. Even from this brief description it is clear that some of the issues giving him trouble concern his being Jewish, his relationship to women, his tendency to equate intellectual ability with physical well-being, his fear and distrust of men, and an ulcerous estrangement from his body. Although we have not talked about it in this excerpt, Knight was also confused about what was important to him in his job: was it doing new and daring research or being rewarded by large sums of money?

In John Knight we have a person who is unclear about many of the major themes in adult life. His intimate life was one in which he could experience men only as people to be feared (like his father) and could experience women as people to be loved only if they somehow were like his mother. He was confused in terms of religious origins and background as well as in terms of job. By age 30, John Knight had become a man divided and at war with himself and his body. Without productivity in love or work and estranged from both past and body, is it surprising that this seemingly successful and smoothly functioning man should come to express these conflicts in the form of a festering decay at the very center of his physical body?

A. Psychophysiological problems in living

John Knight is only one of a great many people whose disordered lives reveal themselves in dramatic bodily terms. Such **psychophysiologic disorders** can involve any and all bodily parts and systems. To get some idea how widespread psychosomatic reactions can be, consider the following partial list:

1. Skin disorders—for example, neurodermatitis, hives, excessive sweating.
2. Musculoskeletal disorders—for example, arthritis, backache, cramps.
3. Respiratory disorders—for example, asthma, hay fever, sinusitis.
4. Cardiovascular disorders—for example, hypertension, migraine, angina.
5. Hemic and lymphatic disorders—for example, hemorrhaging.
6. Gastrointestinal disorders—for example, ulcers, constipation, heartburn.
7. Genitourinary disorders—for example, certain menstrual disturbances, problems with urinary function.
8. Endocrine disorders—for example, obesity, certain types of hyperthyroidism.
9. Nervous-system disorders—for example, loss of strength.
10. Disorders of special sense organs—for example, vertigo.

To see in some detail how psychosomatic disorders occur, let us look at two specific classes of disordered bodily reactions: one concerning the most external of organs, the skin, and a second concerning structures deeper within the body, such as those involved in hypertension.

1. Psychophysiological skin reactions. Everyone already knows that changes in the skin relate quite directly to emotional events. All of us have turned red with anger or white with fright or have blushed when embarrassed. Similarly, we all know that personal traits can be described in terms that are no more than skin-deep: for example, a "thin-skinned" person is one who is easily upset. A person who "gets under your skin" is annoying, while someone "itching for a fight" is to be avoided. All these ordinary phrases suggest that the skin provides a richly symbolic language by which an individual can express important events in his or her life. This is as it should be if we remember that the human body is not only or even primarily a physical "thing," but the living contour at which personal intentions and the social world come into contact (see Chapter 3).

The phenomenon of **religious stigmatization** also points to this conclusion. In cases of this type, the person displays certain skin reactions (such as bleeding) that directly recall the crucifixion of Christ. A well-documented, recent case of religious stigmatization concerned a woman named Therese Neumann of Konnersreuth, Germany (Hyneck, 1932). Ms. Neumann, who died in 1962, was annually observed during Easter week not only by thousands of pilgrims but also by a select group of physicians and psychiatrists. They reported that Ms. Neumann developed wounds on her face, head, and feet in exactly the same bodily locations as Christ had at crucifixion. There was no question about it: even the doubting physicians saw it and, though not believing it a "miracle," could not dispute the fact that the wounds were there and that they occurred on Good Friday.

Most skin disorders do not involve stigmatization; rather, they usually involve more ordinary reactions, such as rashes and hives. No part of the body is immune. Although the meaning of such events is usually not nearly so obvious as for Ms. Neumann, what is clear is that they do express a meaning for and about the person having them. Perhaps the most important thing to keep in mind about skin reactions is that they are visible not only to the person concerned but to other people as well. For this reason the interpersonal significance of such reactions has to be taken into account.

Skin disorders tend to bring about strong reactions in other people because they may disfigure the person involved. In trying to understand a given skin reaction it is always important to determine for whom the reaction is intended. It seems obvious that more people are going to notice a rash if it is in a very easily noticed place (such as the face or the hands) than if it is in a less easily seen place (such as between the toes or on the genitals). Location would seem to have a lot to do with who is to get the message: me, the world, or only someone who knows me intimately. After all, you do not have to be a psychologist to know that a rash under the wedding ring might have something to do with what's going on in a person's marriage. Then too, it might mean something different if it is on the outside rather than on the inside of the finger.

Skin disorders are clearly related to who the person is and what is important to him or her. This is a theme that will come up over and over again and one that has been described in detail before (see Chapters 1 and 3). In these earlier discussions, the human body was described as reflecting the person in his or her dealings with the world. In psychosomatic disorders, bodily dysfunction can be seen as reflecting difficult or problematic aspects of living. The person is *always* his or her body, whether life is going well or poorly.

2. Cardiovascular reactions.   All body systems have their own unique possibilities for symbolic expression. From the gastrointestinal system we have such expressions as "I had no stomach for that," "I've had a bellyful," "She's gutsy." The respiratory system gives us "That was a great weight on his chest," "I need to catch my breath," "I was so excited I could hardly breathe." To come to the topic of the present section, we often use expressions that refer to cardiovascular reactions: "I was heartbroken," "She's got lots of heart," "People are good-hearted (or bad-hearted), hot-blooded (or cold-blooded)," and "I left my heart in San Francisco."

Anatomically, the cardiovascular system includes the heart and blood vessels. Although there are a great many pathological cardiovascular reactions having to do with how a person feels, the major ones are rapid heart rate (tachycardia), chest pains (angina), high blood pressure, heart attack, and stroke.

For our purposes, hypertension, or high blood pressure, presents a very interesting symptom. What is most interesting about it is that there are no obvious signs that a person does or does not have it. Although we may be aware of a rapidly beating heart or of a fast pulse, there is no obvious way to know we have high blood pressure. A diagnosis can be made only with a blood-pressure gauge.

Not everybody is equally likely to develop hypertension. For example, hypertension is more common in women than in men and more common in Blacks than in Caucasians. It has been measured to occur in about 6% of the population (Rimm & Somerville, 1977, p. 204). Although this is the official figure, it seems far too low. For example, in one survey of three middle-class neighborhoods in Los Angeles, about one-third of the people tested had high blood pressure. Only about 50% of these people, however, were aware of this fact.

Although stroke, headache, and other cardiovascular accidents may result from chronic hypertension, perhaps its most significant consequence is a coronary, or heart attack. Physical factors are involved in heart attacks, but so are personal ones. To cite just one study: When Rahe and Lind (1971) looked at what they called life-stress factors in the history of 39 people who had suffered fatal heart attacks, they found a marked upswing in the experience of stress in the 6-month period before death. This was true whether or not the patients had a previous history of heart attacks. In a related study, Thiel, Parker, and Bruce (1973) found significant differences between 50 patients, aged 40–60, who had their first heart attack and 50 non-heart-attack patients. In this study, there was a strong relation between personal stress and heart attack.

Although heart attacks are easy to measure, personal stress is not. T. H. Holmes and his colleagues at the University of Washington, however, have developed a procedure capable of evaluating such stress in a numerically useful way (Holmes & Rahe, 1967). The impacts of various life events are given fixed values (as in Table 13-1), and a person's present total life-stress score is found by adding up the units. Among many other findings, Holmes and associates have discovered that if a person's present life-style produces a total score of 300 or more in any given year, he or she is likely to develop a major illness within the next two years.

B. Voodoo death

One of the most intense and dramatic relations between a person's experience of stress and severe psychophysiological responses concerns the strange case of **voodoo.** Although **voodoo death** seems like something only Hollywood could invent, a very complete study of this topic by Cannon (1942) shows that people who believe in voodoo indeed die when put under a voodoo curse. From a wide variety of field studies in places as diverse as Africa, New Zealand, South America, and Haiti, Cannon concluded that voodoo death was a genuine phenomenon not due to disease or poisons in any usual sense of these terms. He also found that such deaths seemed to follow a regular and predictable course in persons affected.

Among the factors Cannon described as of particular importance were (1) strong bodily reactions brought about by the person's belief in a voodoo curse, (2) a strong belief among the person's tribal group supporting his or her personal belief that voodoo curses kill, and (3) social isolation of the

TABLE 13-1. Measuring Life Stress

Events	Scale of impact
Death of spouse	100
Divorce	73
Marital separation	65
Jail term	63
Death of close family member	63
Personal injury or illness	53
Marriage	50
Fired at work	47
Marital reconciliation	45
Retirement	45
Change in health of family member	44
Pregnancy	40
Sex difficulties	39
Gain of new family member	39
Business readjustment	39
Change in financial state	38
Death of close friend	37
Change to different line of work	36
Change in number of arguments with spouse	35
Mortgage over $10,000	31
Foreclosure of mortgage or loan	30
Change in responsibilities at work	29
Son or daughter leaving home	29
Trouble with in-laws	29
Outstanding personal achievement	28
Wife begins or stops work	26
Begin or end school	26
Change in living conditions	25
Revision of personal habits	24
Trouble with boss	23
Change in work hours or conditions	20
Change in residence	20
Change in schools	20
Change in recreation	19
Change in church activities	19
Change in social activities	18
Mortgage or loan less than $10,000	17
Change in sleeping habits	16
Change in number of family get-togethers	15
Change in eating habits	15
Vacation	13
Christmas	12
Minor violations of the law	11

From "The Social Readjustment Rating Scale," by T. H. Holmes and R. H. Rahe. In *Journal of Psychosomatic Research*, 1967, *11*, 213–218. Copyright 1967 by Pergamon Press, Ltd. Reprinted by permission.

person by other members of the tribe, sometimes followed by public prayer for the victim's death. If we look at these factors with an open (that is, neither an evil nor a modern) eye, we see that they all concern the victim's personal and social belief in the significance of being put under a killing voodoo curse. That such victims faint and experience over-whelming fear would seem a natural consequence of such beliefs. Under these conditions, is it any wonder that once the victim's personal and social world collapses, his or her physical boundaries should suffer a similar catastrophic fate?

Voodoo death is neither a surprising nor a curious oddity if we keep in mind that the human body is not only or even primarily a physical structure. Rather, it is *the person*, and events and ideas having to do with the person can only be experienced by and through the body. When the boundaries of personal existence are in doubt, it is reasonable to expect a catastrophic bodily reaction. For the primitive, the outcome is ritual death; for the more sophisticated, psychophysiological disorder.

II. THE CASE OF PETER OBERMAN

After 2 months in the army, Peter Oberman cracked up. He was overcome with anxiety and found himself in need of professional help. At the time of his discharge he entered therapy, where he described a style of living that was incredibly cramped and debilitating for a man in his early twenties.

Peter's troubles had started when he was 11. It was then that he lost "faith in both of his parents" (White & Watt, 1973, p. 217). Before that, Peter was well taken care of by his mother. To tell the truth, he was too well taken care of, for his mother was a fearful woman who felt the world was full of dangers—sickness, accidents, injury, kidnappers, and so on. Although Peter had not always been restricted by his mother, in his 11th year he and a friend became interested in electricity and how it might work in radios. His mother, afraid of electricity, tried to dissuade him from continuing his interest, and Peter consequently came to feel that she was totally absurd.

Peter's father, who had been a traveling man, changed jobs when Peter was 11 and was now in town more often. While home he interfered with Peter's affairs and ran the house in a dictatorial way. He was unfeeling for both Peter and his mother, and should the boy ever come home even a minute late, he was severely scolded. The worst thing for Peter happened when his father started an affair. When Peter screamed at him and called his father's girlfriend a "bitch," the father did not hit him but stalked away, seemingly in guilt and anger.

Through all of this, only one figure continued to be solid to Peter: a grandfather who lived upstairs. The grandfather, who had recently become a widower, greatly enjoyed the boy's friendship, and the two had long discussions. Unfortunately, the grandfather spoke of philosophy and history in ways young Peter couldn't always understand. But the boy spent time with his grandfather, for, after all, who else was there to turn to? As a consequence of their conversations, Peter came to the idea that if he could but understand the order of the physical world, he would find himself in a world more to his liking.

Even though his grandfather's ideas were not always meaningful to Peter, he began to worry that his grandfather might die: he was old, older than Peter's grandmother and hadn't she died? Peter soon began to have horrible thoughts that seemed to "push themselves into his head." He thought of the house catching fire and was afraid it might be struck by lightning or knocked over by a tornado. He thought of various ways in which something bad might happen to his grandfather, and he began to do "magical" things to prevent these events. If the thought crossed his mind that his house might burn, he felt compelled to touch something to avoid the danger. If he had such a thought while stepping on a crack, he had to step on the crack again to cancel the thought.

Soon he needed to do lots of extra touchings for good luck; sometimes he would spend almost an hour going through a complete ritual. When people noticed his peculiar behavior, he developed a technique for getting rid of all the unlucky thoughts by himself at night. If he pointed four times (a lucky number) to the southwest (a lucky direction), he could take care of things. Unfortunately, he never felt satisfied: often he had to point $4 \times 4 \times 4 \times 4$ times, and this sometimes took over half an hour. Although he tried to invent short cuts, such as stamping his foot to stand for groups of numbers, in the end no time was saved. If he could not complete the ritual, he was upset and unhappy.

It may seem peculiar that Peter developed bad thoughts about his grandfather. The idea is less peculiar if we look at the world from Peter's 11-year-old point of view. For Peter, his grandfather represented a source of affection and security. But it could only be a false security, for he was old and would soon die. Even though Peter needed love

very badly, spending so much time with an old man and listening to him talk endlessly must have been difficult. Even though he could not stand the idea of his grandfather's death, there were times when a part of him might secretly have wanted it.

When Peter was 12, his grandfather died. His relatives all attributed his death to distress over the father's love affair, and this was a further proof that the father could destroy Peter's happiness. Peter's grief was uncontrollable, and he tried to preserve his grandfather's apartment just as it had been. When this turned out to be impossible, he photographed it from every angle and kept the negatives locked up in his room.

Unfortunately, his feeling of helplessness was so overwhelming that he needed further reassurance. He soon developed the idea of a universal determinism, which he felt grew out of his grandfather's discussion of science and history. Finally, he began to draw up a life plan listing his liabilities and assets, taking hours to get every detail just right. At 14 he tried to read Einstein, believing that if he could understand Einstein's theories, he could understand everything.

That Peter should become interested in science and philosophy at between 12 and 14 years of age is not surprising: many young adolescents go the same route. Yet one of his therapists said of the whole business:

> In Peter's case curiosity was a secondary motive; he was using philosophy to compensate himself for a feeling of weakness, to make himself feel masterful and omnipotent. His preoccupation ... was more than a natural unfolding of real powers; it was a desperate measure designed to avert anxiety. As a result he overdid it and spent fruitless hours struggling to work out an unchallengeable system of truth. It is this excess, this rigidity, that distinguished his overdriven striving from a straightforward expression of healthy impulses [White & Watt, 1973, p. 220].[1]

It should not be surprising to find that Peter did well in school. For the most part his grand philosophical scheme helped him through high school and through the early parts of college. When college got to be tough, he found comfort in his system. Unfortunately, his first course in philosophy chal-

[1]From *The Abnormal Personality*, by R. W. White and N. F. Watt. Copyright 1973 by John Wiley & Sons, Inc. This and all other quotations from this source are reprinted by permission.

lenged the system he had worked out for himself, and he spent so much time in trying to rework it that he neglected his regular studies. Any little failure in school brought on daydreams of power and achievement. One day he messed up a recitation in elementary German, and for hours on end he daydreamed about a future invitation from a German university to give a series of lectures in German.

All this took its final toll after 2 months in army training camp, when Peter cracked up and was released from the service. When out of the service, he sought help for his problem, and he is now, many years later, in a successful career.

A. The world of the obsessive

The case of Peter Oberman gives us good entry into the world of an obsessive. This world, according to White and Watt (1973, p. 220), who first described the case, has four major aspects.

1. The obsessive ideas that run through the person's head belong to the person thinking them. Although the person may be unable to explain the meaning of his repetitive ideas, he does know that the ideas are his. Nevertheless, such ideas "feel like foreign bodies" and come uninvited from unknown regions of the person.

2. The areas of conflict experienced by the person are handled by not thinking about them. For example, Peter found himself worrying about the philosophical problem of determinism rather than about the issue of a totally disordered emotional life.

3. Obsessive thoughts often concern aggression or destructive actions—for example, Peter's worry that his grandfather might die, that his home might burn, and so on.

4. Obsessive people often show extreme interest in order and cleanliness; they seem stingy and stubborn.

Adding these characteristics together produces a mode of Being-in-the world that is often called the **obsessive** style. One way to describe this style is in terms of control: the obsessive person experiences anything less than perfect control as unbearably upsetting. To get as close to perfect control as possible, the obsessive thinks everything through before he or she does it so as to get it right. White and Watt (1973) describe an obsessive style of being in the following terms:

"It is a mode of activity in which the individual exerts a more or less continuous pressure on himself, while at the same time living and working under the strain of that pressure." But the demands are not experienced as one's own; rather, they seem to arise from a job to be done, an expectation to be met, a duty to be performed—some inherent requirement outside the self. There is little room for zest and enthusiasm in a life thus structured [p. 216].

All these aspects of **obsession** can occur in most of us: who has not had a sentence run endlessly through her head, who has not wondered whether the door and windows were shut when he left for a trip, and who has not thought endlessly about some event that would soon happen? In an obsessional neurotic (to use the technical term) such as Peter Oberman, such thoughts occur in exaggerated form. Often they are combined with ritualized acts called **compulsions** (such as not stepping on a crack), and this whole mode of incredibly ordered thinking and doing comes to define an obsessive-compulsive style of being in which there is no joy and there is no room for free, spontaneous activity.

But what does it mean to be such a person, and how is the world experienced? The simplest description would seem to be that the world is experienced as an extremely frightening place that has to be controlled and mastered. For the person living out an obsessive-compulsive style, the way to control things is to think about them, for to reflect is to conquer. But reflecting has an unfortunate side effect: not only does it conquer the fearfulness of the world, it also puts distance between the person and that part of the world being thought about.

The person who obsesses about every little thing gets increasingly out of contact with his or her world. Everything is turned into an "idea," and people, things, and situations are no longer responded to as they occur. Instead, they are responded to in terms of the person's continuing ruminations about them. The world is not a place to be alive in or one to be dealt with unreflectingly. What the obsessive loses is the possibility for spontaneous, unreflected dealings with the world. The world is tame because it is at a distance. If the person is compulsive, the world is also controlled by repetitive actions that provide a predictable, even if sterile, way of dealing with things. The obsessive-compulsive person sits frozen (or meaninglessly active) in a world he or she no longer inhabits. To reflect may conquer the world by reducing it to mental objects; unfortunately, it also robs the world of living possibility.

The obsessive person no longer has the freely functioning, unreflected body of the nonobsessive. Instead, the body is experienced as an object, and the self as subject is unattainable. The unreflected world no longer speaks freely to the obsessive, and if it did, the obsessive would not allow himself to hear it. The bodily self as subject is "smothered by obsession," and the person no longer experiences a living body, only a thought-about and distant object.

Time is also experienced differently by the obsessive-compulsive person. Like the living body, which is turned into a thing, time becomes a static object. Time and the body form an unholy and unhappy alliance: because the living body is now a static body-object, the obsessive worries about its eventual deterioration. Time, instead of being both a condition for hope and a condition for fear, comes to have only the second meaning. To stop time in order to control its consequences of aging and deteriorating is to close the future and make the past unredeemable and oppressive. The present does not move, and the obsessive person loses contact not only with self and body but with time as well. Is it any wonder that he or she tries to make the future predictable?

In a first summing-up of the obsessive style of Being-in-the-world, Keen (1970) notes:

> It is well to recall that the obsessive experience of time and of the world are unreflected choices made at an earlier time. The choice was to avoid anxiety; the result is paradoxically to experience it more painfully in its neurotic form. Like death, pain, ambiguity, and a thousand other kinds of human finitude, anxiety can be escaped only at the cost of one's being-in-the world and of the perversion of one's being-for-oneself [p. 162].[2]

One final observation to be made in regard to the world of the obsessive is that all of us obsess from time to time. The philosopher with her problem, the lawyer with his case, and the physician with her diagnosis are all obsessing. The major difference between what is being done by these people and by an obsessive such as Peter Oberman is that their thoughts represent a choice of how and to what they will devote their energy. The obsessive has no choice: he or she must think over and over again about a world and a self that is too dangerous to be

trusted. To reflect is to put distance between the world and me and in so doing to subdue it.

Such a state of affairs is no different from what is involved in all acts of thinking, in which a person, by reflecting, fixes the boundaries of events that are in motion and have no solid boundary. To think about an event is to experience the act of thinking about that event; it is never to have unreflected contact with the event itself. The obsessive and the scholar share more than their continuing involvement with thinking; what they share is an attempt to render the boundaries of unreflected experience ever more precisely. In so doing they hope to change and control what it is they feel needs changing and controlling.

B. Additional categories for describing problems in human living

Being obsessive is only one of many ways an everyday human action can be diverted (or even distorted) from its ordinary use. Traditionally, the American Psychiatric Association listed seven categories of diminished human living that together were termed **neuroses.** Although this specific set of categories (as well as the word *neurosis* itself) is no longer the only one used in psychiatric settings, a careful examination of the conditions described by these categories should shed some light on the nature and range of normal and more disordered styles of dealing with the world.

For each of the following conditions, it is important to keep in mind that no individual ever goes around as lost, as anxious, or even as unhappy as these descriptions might suggest. Rather, the following list describes how some people live in and experience the world at their worst moments—not at every moment of their lives.

1. *Anxiety neurosis.* Diffuse but severe anxiety not referable to a particular situation or threat.
2. *Phobias.* Various irrational fears people may have from which they cannot free themselves.
3. *Hysteria.* This category consists of two subtypes: (a) a conversion type, with symptoms of physical illness, such as paralysis or loss of hearing, without underlying physical pathology, and (b) a dissociative type, which includes such reactions as amnesia and multiple personality.
4. *Hypochondriasis.* Preoccupation with one's bodily functioning and various presumed diseases.

[2] From *Three Faces of Being: Toward an Existential Clinical Psychology,* by E. Keen. Copyright © 1970 by Irvington Publishers, Inc. Reprinted by permission.

5. *Neurasthenia*. Chronic fatigue, weakness, and lack of enthusiasm.
6. *Depression*. Abnormally prolonged dejection associated with personal conflict, interpersonal loss, or environmental setback.

In addition, there is the seventh major category already described, that of the obsessive-compulsive.

These categories seem to fall into three main groups: one concerning distortions in a person's bodily being; a second, in his or her emotions or moods; and a third, in his or her ability to think. The first category includes hypochondriasis (4), neurasthenia (5), and hysteria (3a). The second category includes anxiety neurosis (1), phobias (2), and depression (6). Under disorders of reflected activity would fall the conditions of disassociation (3b) and obsessive-compulsive neurosis (7).

Looking at these categories in this way reminds us how close neurotic patterns can be to more ordinary functioning. The person described by one or another of these categories seems to relate to his or her world in an exaggerated way; that is, he or she seems strangely out of touch with certain aspects of bodily, emotional, and/or reflective being. Although each of us may be out of touch with one or another of these from time to time, the neurotic person does the job more consistently and more thoroughly. It is as if he had split himself off from one or another aspect of being on a continuing basis. When this happens, the part that has been split off comes to dominate the person in a compelling and demanding way, and the person often experiences a loss of the very joy of living itself.

Part of this "loss" comes about because the person feels inadequate in dealing with his or her everyday world. There is the ever-present danger of losing oneself in a world that cannot be trusted. Because the person's general view of things is that they are bad, he or she tends to be oversensitive to even the simplest of criticisms and circumstances of everyday life. All of us get upset when something goes wrong; the neurotic person is sometimes overwhelmed. Even success may be an occasion for anxiety: "If I'm promoted to a new position, everyone will see how inadequate and dumb I really am." Again, this is an exaggeration of the "normal" concern we all experience in assuming a new task or job.

Part of the person's inability to deal with day-to-day activities has to do with the fact that changes, even small ones, require the person to change. To change means to accept risks, and this is the one thing the neurotic person cannot and will not do. The person clings desperately to whatever has worked in the past and arrives at a defensive position requiring constant vigilance. Is it any wonder that a person whose style of being is that of defense loses his or her capacity to experience joy or the possibility to change?

One further consequence of a neurotic style is that such individuals often have a terrible time with interpersonal relationships. To be comfortable with another person requires trust, mutuality, and openness—precisely the things a neurotic person cannot or will not give. Depending on the specific pattern, the person may be so preoccupied with himself or herself as to neglect your being, or else he or she may experience such a lack of being for himself or herself that he or she has nothing to give to you.

All this is to be contrasted with more healthy Being-in-the-world, in which the world is experienced as a home, not as a dirty, closed hotel room in some unknown country. To be sure, when I think about myself and my fate, I sometimes do fall short in my own eyes. But never for any extended period of time do I feel that I am totally incompetent and unworthy. Rather, I come to achieve a more balanced picture of myself and of my dealings with others. In this the person having problems in living is unable to follow: he is a child, lost in a world he can look at but never feel comfortable in; he is lost in a dark forest, afraid of the night, knowing that he has never been, nor is he likely to be, happy or good.

To show how such themes work themselves out in individual lives, consider the following two case studies. One of these concerns a person diagnosed as neurasthenic-depressive; the second, a person diagnosed as showing a conversion reaction. To get some feel for what the first person might experience and be like, consider the following conversation between patient and therapist (Coleman, 1976, pp. 252–253).

P: I used to talk rather fluently, but now I'm more nervous than I've ever been, my tongue seems to catch on my teeth so that I don't speak plainly. Everything seems such an effort ... even the simplest things ...
T: Even the simplest things ...
P: Ah, hm, I mean, the phone is there and I'm lonesome and yet I don't even phone ... I don't even talk to my

neighbors much any more even though I know that I should be with people and I like people, but I've gotten so that . . . [long pause] . . . that . . . [sigh] . . . I feel too bad to even talk or do anything [voice breaks into tears].

I've tried so many things to get well, but it's just awful . . . I mean . . . sometimes I can just barely live . . . I mean just listen to the radio or read, or eat . . . I mean just like being in a daze or something . . . I don't know . . . I just feel so horribly tired and sick.

Two months ago I felt better than I had been. I mean I was able . . . well, I went to several shows and I actually even went to a dance. Often I would begin to get tired, and I was very frightened that I would break down, but I would go on . . . I mean like some people would go to a battle or to a battlefront [proud tone of voice]. But . . . now . . . well I am just so tired and run-down that I can't even go to a show . . . if I do go . . . I have to leave in the middle because I am not strong enough . . . I mean I don't have enough strength to sit through it.

T: Two months ago you felt better?

P: Well, yes . . . you see, my husband's brother came to visit us . . . and he would talk to me and he had such a way of diverting me and he was very interesting, and you'd be amazed, within a few minutes or a few hours I'd be just different . . . and he took me to several shows and to the dance. I felt so much better and I had a really good time. So I can see it ain't sleeping or eating. I mean . . . I need someone who'd give me something different to think about . . . someone who'd show you affection . . . But my husband . . . well, I just can't understand how he can treat a woman who is ill . . . and trying her best . . . well, [tears] . . . I have just sort of withdrawn . . .[3]

The picture is one of hopelessness; things are just too much, the world is heavy, unresponsive, and taxing—in short, "the diary of a mad housewife." The world is not only a difficult and boring place; it is a thwarting place. Although this person may feel that she is putting up a "noble battle," the battle can only be lost once and for all. Any person attempting to deal with the world in this way is acutely aware of his or her bodily symptoms and will go to great lengths to tell anyone about them who will listen.

In a case such as this, bodily fatigue serves as a focus for problems, and the person is often quite anxious about the body's seeming lack of function.

[3]From *Abnormal Psychology and Modern Life*, (5th ed.), by James C. Coleman. Copyright © 1976 by Scott, Foresman and Company. This and all other quotations from this source are reprinted by permission.

In a conversion reaction, the picture is quite different. Here the person's body ceases to function and he or she is remarkably casual about the whole business. Conversion reactions are not difficult to understand. After all, our language does contain such clichés as "I was so scared I couldn't move" or "I was paralyzed with fear."

The following case presents a particularly good example of symbolic paralysis.

Fred K. is a fifty-year-old married man who developed a marked contracture of his left hand, and a partial paralysis of his arm. He held his arm bent in front of him, as if it were in a sling, and his fingers were curled inward toward the palm of his hand. He was unable to raise his arm above the level of his shoulder, and he could move his fingers only slightly.

The symptoms came on suddenly and before he was referred for psychological treatment, the patient had undergone medical and neurological examinations. Various diagnoses were made, including vertebral dislocation, with the recommendation of surgery on the spine. Other medical treatments were tried; but the patient did not respond, and the symptoms remained unaltered. . . .

[The patient] was a well-to-do executive, . . . married to an attractive and considerably younger wife, and while he seemed anxious to be cured of his disorder, nevertheless showed remarkable casualness about it. In fact, one sensed that the patient took a certain pride in it. He displayed his hand and arm with some satisfaction, demonstrating the lack of feeling by touching a lit cigarette to the back of his hand to show he felt no pain. The attitude of the patient toward his symptom, combined with the lack of positive neurological findings, pointed to the possibility of a conversion reaction. Psychotherapy was recommended and at the end of several treatment hours, the symptom was removed. While it returned a few days later, the psychological nature of the disorder had been proved, and psychotherapy was continued.

It was clear to the therapist that the patient had been using his neurotic symptoms to solve his problems. His young and attractive wife was fond of nightclubs, while the patient merely wanted to come home at night, have dinner, read his paper, and go to bed. The difference in age and interests resulted in serious conflict. Finally, the wife began to go out without her husband. It was at this point that the symptoms appeared.

The paralysis served a number of purposes. It gave the patient a good excuse for staying home at night. After all, who would expect a man with a paralyzed arm to go to nightclubs? It also forced the patient's wife to spend more time with him in the evenings. Moreover, the paralysis brought the patient the sympathy and attention of friends and relatives. Previously, being a rather colorless and uninteresting person, he had been overshadowed by his attractive and vivacious wife. Now he was the center of things. Finally, because the patient was jealous of his wife, and suspected her fidelity, he used his symptom as an excuse to come home from his office at any hour of the day. Sometimes he would return home, complaining about his arm, an hour after leaving in the morning.

Interestingly enough, the eventual cure of this case was not brought about through the efforts of a psychotherapist, but rather by a policeman! The patient's suspicions about his wife had not been unfounded, and one day he awoke to find that his wife had run off with a police officer. Days later, when he was convinced that his wife would never return to him, his symptom disappeared spontaneously. It had served its purpose; without his wife and the problems of living with her, [he] no longer needed it [Kisker, 1972, pp. 266–267].[4]

One other characteristic of how a person showing a conversion reaction presents himself to the world concerns his style of speaking. Generally, the person talks in flowery and exaggerated terms. Events and people are described in terms of the impact they make on people, and such individuals often speak in a rush, thereby conveying a sense of urgency and excitement.

As one patient said to her therapist about some problems she was having in communicating:

> It scared me pea green ... I find myself thinking absolutely rigid, stiff as a board ... let me cogitate. I'm afraid I'm projecting ... that gibbering about myself is an imposition, silly. This business of being terribly conscious of your talking. Torturing myself with name calling ... I was terrified, it horrified me ... thinking in non sequiturs, such a queer situation anyway. I can't feel differences, messy gray area where you can't jell [Sarason, 1976, pp. 228–229].

Everything the patient says, does, or does not do is geared to calling attention to himself. It is as if the ordinary body were not quite imposing enough to express messages skillfully or compellingly. For this reason, the person tries to call attention to himself in such a way that someone must and will notice and take care of him. Once the person makes a dramatic impact, either through language or through paralysis, the problem seems momentarily

solved, and the person can feel comfortable with his symptom even if not with his situation.

This benign neglect, or unconcern about one's symptom, is quite different from the neurasthenic person's attitude. The neurasthenic calls attention to himself not by means of a focused disability but by means of a style of being that is punctuated by withdrawal and complaint. Again the person's body is experienced as ineffective and without expression; here, however, personal struggle can only go on to inevitable defeat. Although the hysteric can function in some areas of life, the neurasthenic has given up and cannot (or will not) do anything.

The problem in both cases comes down to dealing with the body as a not too well-functioning object. Turning the body into such an object seems designed to save the person from having to be a subject—that is, having to be a person and to face all the indecision and conflict of choosing a specific way in the world. To be a subject is too frightening, and all that is left for the person is to live in the light of others. Keen (1970) calls this "being-only-for-others," and such a description fits both the neurasthenic and hysterical person's constant attempt to get others to pay attention to them. Such a style of being, in which the body is experienced as an object, is in marked contrast to the more usual style characteristic of functioning adults. As Keen notes:

> By examining the pathological experience of the body [we are able] to specify what is a healthy experience of the body, for which we used the phrase, "lived body" in contrast to "used body." To "live" one's body is to "be one's body." It is a core of self-experience rather than extraneous to it: it expresses who and how we are rather than being a kind of limit that condemns us to be what we are [Keen, 1970, pp. 205–206].

The idea of the body as object is not limited to these cases alone. The obsessive, Peter Oberman, also turned his body into an object. In his case, the body became an object for him, not for someone else. In all these cases, the body is no longer the living body of a fully functioning human being. Instead it is the object-body of a person lost in a world he or she no longer feels competent to inhabit as a person. For such individuals the world of spontaneous, joyful action is shut down, and all that remains is the misery of a precarious object-like existence. Is it any wonder the neurotic person suffers?

[4]From *The Disorganized Personality*, (2nd ed.), by G. W. Kisker. Copyright 1972 by McGraw-Hill, Inc. This and all other quotations from this source are reprinted by permission of McGraw-Hill Book Company.

III. THE CASE OF JOAN SMITH

Sometimes the anguish a person experiences is best told in the person's own words. In the case of Joan Smith, originally reported by Hayward and Taylor in 1956, Joan described her experiences in a very direct and first-person way. For this reason it is best to let her speak and let us listen as she makes her way through therapy.

As background, we need only know the following few facts: At the beginning of therapy Joan was 26. Her illness first appeared early in 1947, when she was 17. In the ensuing two years, she lived in four private hospitals and was subject to intensive psychotherapy, accompanied by 34 electric-shock and 60 insulin-shock treatments. Fifty comas occurred. She showed "little, if any improvement" and was finally referred to a state hospital, where she appeared to be hopelessly insane.

At the start of Dr. Hayward's treatment, Joan was cold, withdrawn, seclusive, and suspicious (his words). Visual and auditory hallucinations were regular occurrences. She did not enter into any hospital activities, and frequently it was difficult to get any response from her. If asked whether she needed treatment, she would become sullen or argue that she wanted to be left alone. She made three attempts at suicide, one by slashing herself with broken glass and two by taking overdoses of sedatives. At times she fought so violently that she was placed on a closed ward.

In spite of this discouraging picture, Joan responded well to a course of intensive psychotherapy by Dr. Hayward. In 6 months she was declared free of "committable psychosis," and 2 months later she was moved successfully to an open ward. She is now married and has been free of hospital restrictions since the fall of 1949.

The following selections were taken from material written by Joan during the course of her 6-month therapy with Dr. Hayward. They are presented roughly in the order in which they occurred; the numbers give the location of each session in the sequence of sessions. The first selection discusses Joan's feeling at the very beginning of therapy.

I

At the start, I didn't listen to what you said most of the time but I watched like a hawk for your expression and the sound of your voice. After the interview, I would add all this up to see if it seemed to show love.

The words were nothing compared to the feelings you showed. I sensed that you felt confident I could be helped and that there was hope for the future.

It's like talking to a frightened horse or dog. They may not know your words but the calm and strength and confidence that you convey helps them to feel safe again. . . .

II

I had to tell you things by doing them instead of talking . . . I was sure you would turn things against me and use what I said to hurt me. Also, no one ever paid attention to what I asked for, but they usually did react if I did something. I wanted terribly for you to help me, but I had to be sure I could trust you.

We schizophrenics say and do a lot of stuff that is unimportant, and then we mix important things in with all this to see if the doctor cares enough to see them and feel them. . . .

III

Patients kick and scream and fight when they aren't sure the doctor can see them. It's a most terrifying feeling to realize that the doctor can't see the real you, that he can't understand what you feel . . . I would start to feel that I was invisible or maybe not there at all.

IV

I hated you when you first came in. So many other doctors had tried things with me and got discouraged that I had thought that now at last I would be left alone, in peace. But you just wouldn't go away so I wanted to kill you.

I couldn't trust love, that's why I kept planning ways to make you mad. You were too blank unless you were mad. That was more real and warm and genuine. When my parents loved me, they never saw the real me. They could only love me by destroying the real me. . . .

V

Hate has to come first. The patient hates the doctor for opening the wound again and hates herself for allowing herself to be touched again. She really wants to be dead and hidden in a place where nothing can touch her. . . .

The patient is terribly afraid of her own problems [and] . . . feels guilty in allowing the doctor to get mixed up in them. The patient is convinced the doctor will be smashed too. It's not fair for the doctor to ask permission to come in. The doctor must fight his way in; then the patient doesn't have to feel guilty. The patient can feel that she has done her best to protect the doctor; she can even feel it is O.K. to destroy the doctor. The doctor must say by his manner, "I'm coming in no matter what you feel."

VI

Hating is like shitting. If you shit, it shows you are alive but, if the doctor can't accept your shit, it means he doesn't want you to be alive. It makes him like a mother who can't accept her child's mess.

X

Meeting you made me feel like a traveler who's been lost in a land where no one speaks her language.... Then, suddenly, she meets a stranger who can speak English. Even if the stranger doesn't know the way to go, it feels so much better to be able to share the problem with someone, to have him understand how badly you feel.

Being crazy is like one of those nightmares where you try to call for help and no sound comes out. Or if you can call, no one hears or understands....

XI

I felt like a moving picture projected on the wall. I only existed because you wanted me to and I could only be what you wanted to see. I only felt real because of the reactions I could produce in you. If I had scratched you and you didn't feel it, then I'd be really dead.

XII

I had to have control. I had to know you could control me. It was the only way I felt safe because I couldn't control myself. I went wild when you seemed doubtful about this. That's why I slashed my wrists. I thought you didn't care about my fear or my anger or you didn't feel you could handle me, so I had to kill myself before I could harm you.

I needed terribly to feel safe as a little girl so that I could rebel and still wouldn't need to punish myself. I could play at being grown up without having to be in complete self-control.

My interviews were the only place where I felt safe to be myself—to let out all my feelings and see what they were really like without fear that you would get upset and leave me. I needed you to be a great rock that I could push and push, and still you would never roll away and leave me. It was safe for me to be bitchy with you. With everyone else I was trying to change myself to please them.

XIV

You should have made it clear that I would have to feel and think like a baby; that I would have to start in infancy and live my life all over again.... For most peo-

ple nothing that happened before the age of six seems important. For the schizophrenic, nothing that happened after the age of six seems important.

XV

Everyone should be able to look back in their memory and be sure he had a mother who loved him, all of him; even his piss and shit; not for what he could do. Otherwise he feels he has no right to exist.

No matter what happens to this person in life, no matter how much he gets hurt, he can always look back to this and feel that he is lovable. He can love himself and he cannot be broken. If he can't fall back on this, he can be broken.

XVI

If you could have given me a bath it would have helped me to accept my body sooner. You could have been mummy and there would have been no danger and guilt about liking my body. You could have shown that you liked my body; then I could have liked it.

I kept asking you to beat me because I was sure you could never like my bottom but, if you could beat it, at least you would be accepting it in a sort of way. Then I could accept it and make it part of me.

XX

The first time I cried, you made a terrible mistake; you wiped away my tears with a handkerchief. You had no idea how I wanted to feel those tears roll down my face. At least I had some feelings that were on the outside. If only you could have licked my tears with your tongue. I would have been completely happy. Then you would have shared my feelings.

XXII

Patients dribble and smear their food or smear their B.M. in an effort to test it out. They want to get to know what is going in and coming out of them. They want to know what it feels like on the outside. Then they can feel safe when it's inside.

I used to beg to go outdoors because I needed to be warmed by the sun. It's terrible to feel empty and cold inside. Rainy weather is very hard because it forces patients to look inside themselves for warmth, but they can't find any. It helped me a lot to lie on the beach because then I could feel that mother was holding me and giving me warmth and life.

XXIV

When I was catatonic I tried to be dead and gray and motionless. I thought mother would like that. She would carry me around like a doll.

I felt as though I were in a bottle. I could feel that everything was outside and couldn't touch me.

I had to die to keep from dying. I know that sounds crazy but one time somebody hurt my feelings very much and I wanted to jump in front of a subway. Instead I went a little catatonic so I wouldn't feel anything. (I guess you had to die emotionally or your feelings would have killed you.) I guess I'd rather kill myself than harm somebody else.

XXV

I had to be able to tease you sexually so that I could be sure that I really was attractive, but before I could do this I had to be sure that nothing bad would come of it.

If you had actually screwed me it would have wrecked everything. It would have convinced me that you were only interested in pleasure with my animal body and that you didn't really care about the part that was a person. It would have meant that you were using me like a woman when I really wasn't one and needed a lot of help to grow into one. The real me would have been up on the ceiling watching you do things with my body. You would have . . . let the real me die. When you feed a girl, you make her feel that both her body and her self are wanted. This helps her get joined together. When you screw her she can feel that her body is separate and dead. People can screw dead bodies, but they never feed them.

XXVI

It was terribly hard for me to stop being a schizophrenic. I knew I didn't want to be a Smith because then I was nothing but old Professor Smith's granddaughter. I couldn't feel as though I were your child, and I wasn't sure of myself. The only thing I was sure of was being a "catatonic, paranoid schizophrenic." I had seen that written on my chart. That at least had substance and gave me an identity and personality.

I walked back to see the hospital recently, and for a moment I could lose myself in the feeling of the past. In there I could be left alone. The world was going by outside, but I had a whole world inside me. Nobody could get at it and disturb it. For a moment I felt a tremendous longing to be back. . . . But then I realized that I can have love and fun in the real world and I started to hate the hospital. I hated the four walls and the feeling of being locked in. I hated the memory of never being really satisfied by my fantasies [Hayward & Taylor, 1956, pp. 212–238].[5]

[5]From "A Schizophrenic Patient Describes the Action of Intensive Psychotherapy," by M. L. Hayward and J. E. Taylor. In *Psychiatry Quarterly*, 1956, *30*, 211–248. Copyright 1956 by *Psychiatric Quarterly*. Reprinted by permission.

A number of things strike us on reading this material. First there is Joan's sheer horror of being crazy and, at the same time, her sheer horror of not being crazy. In the very last selection, she tells us how hard it was to stop "being a schizophrenic" and how hard it was to step back into the everyday world most of us live in. One reason this was so difficult is hinted at in these selections: Joan never felt very sure that she was a real person. One theme that runs through a great many of the selections is that Joan has no sense of being an effective self (person). She knows that she has a real self, but she is not sure that anyone else can get in touch with it. She is in a bottle where "everything was outside and couldn't touch me."

The major themes that come up in these selections have to do with some very unusual perceptions and some very crazy ways of experiencing them. To begin with, there is a preoccupation with hate, feces, and dying. These three themes always seem to be confused. A second set of themes concerns the idea of being understood despite the fact that Joan does everything to avoid helping you understand her. A third set of themes concerns the need to be a fully loved infant who can grow up and thereby undo her first run-through. Finally there is Joan's peculiar relationship to her body.

A. The "disembodied self"

According to R. D. Laing (1965), the place to begin an understanding of Joan's experience is with her disembodied self. For Joan, as for many schizophrenics, Laing sets up the situation as follows:

$$\text{self} \longleftrightarrow \text{(body/other)}$$

Under this arrangement, the experience of "self" is separated not only from the experience of others but from the person's experience of her body. As a point of contrast, Laing suggests that the more ordinary state of affairs can be described as follows:

$$\text{(self/body)} \longleftrightarrow \text{other}$$

Here "self" is always experienced as in contact with "body." Joan's "real" self could get into contact with the world of others by first getting into contact with her body. Her body was not "part of her-self," and for this reason she was shut out from any and all relationships in and to her world.

Although we may all at times step outside our bodies (for example, when we are in a situation in which we can do nothing, as might occur in surgery), the schizophrenic person has this as her usual mode of Being-in-the-world. Although being disembodied may provide moments of relief, it can only lead to "unreal" perceptions and futile actions. Under this condition, I (as body) am never in contact with my world. Since I can perceive and act only in unreal and futile ways, I must come to a very idiosyncratic style of existence. Laing has called the experience of this continuingly distorted style of existence the "false" self in order to distinguish it from the "real" self. In contrast to the real self, the false self is dead and unmoving, and as Joan said, "When I was catatonic, I tried to be dead. . . . I had to die to keep from dying."

Becoming disembodied represents an attempt to escape a world full of horrors. Unfortunately, by escaping from intimate and spontaneous contact with the world, entering "a bottle" where "everything was outside and couldn't touch me," the person is likely to stay outside of meaningful experiencing and acting. Laing says that under these conditions the self

> becomes a vacuum. Everything is there, outside; nothing is here, inside. The constant dread . . . of being overwhelmed, is [increased rather than decreased] by the need to keep the world at bay. Yet the self may at the same time long more than anything for participation in the world. . . . Its greatest longing is felt as its greatest weakness and giving into this weakness is its greatest dread . . . in participation [with the world] the individual fears that his vacuum will be obliterated, that he will be engulfed or otherwise lose his identity [1965, p. 80].[6]

The personal situation set up by the schizophrenic splits him or her in two parts: a disembodied "real" self and a "separated" body experienced as part of the outside world. This split disrupts the ordinary difficulty we all have in understanding our body as both subject (I) and object (me, mine) and leads to confusion between such ordinary relations as *here/there* or *inside/outside*. Dealing with each of these relations requires a continuing shift between *I* and *me*, a shift the schizophrenic person can no

---

[6]From *The Divided Self*, by R. D. Laing. Copyright 1965 by Tavistock Publications, Ltd. Reprinted by permission of Associated Book Publishers, Ltd.

longer accomplish. For this reason there is a continual running together, or merging, of the schizophrenic and his or her world—between "here" and "there," between "inside" and "outside"—until finally the person can only flow endlessly through and around events that are meaningless and personally disordering.

How does all this come about? Here Joan gives us a clue: "For most people nothing that happened before the age of six seems important. For the schizophrenic, nothing that happened after the age of six seems important." What Joan suggests is that we must look to very early experiences. As we saw in Chapters 3 and 9, the idea of Me-as-body takes hold early on, and it does not seem far-fetched to suggest that the very earliest of our experiences give us a sense of worth and a beginning sense of unity. "Everyone should . . . be sure he had a mother who loved him, all of him. . . . Otherwise, he feels he has no right to exist. . . . If he can't fall back on this, he can be broken."

In Joan's dealing with her therapist we feel as if we were watching the regrowth of an infant and then a child. Her therapy process gives us some hints about the terrible confusion Joan had in dealing with hating and loving and dying. People have to love all of a person—"even his piss and shit"—and hating "is like shitting." Thus, to hate is to "shit on someone," and only if you can be loved when you are messy and hateful do you have a right to be alive and to grow.

The course of therapy involved remeshing Joan's experience of her body with herself, as well as redeveloping firm yet permeable boundaries that allowed someone else to see her live emotionally. "The first time I cried, . . . you had no idea how I wanted to feel those tears roll down my face. At least I had some feelings . . . on the outside." But emotion is not all that Joan had to learn about and express in a bodily way. She had to learn the distinction between "outside" and "inside"; she had to learn about sexuality and, perhaps more important, about what it means to be alive. It was no easy job, for "it was hard . . . to stop being a schizophrenic." Fortunately, Joan Smith made the journey.

B. Other patterns of psychotic Being-in-the-world

Joan's psychiatric pattern was diagnosed, as she herself noted, as "catatonic paranoid schizophrenia." That seems an awfully long title, but the truth is that "pure" cases of one or another type of psychosis are rare in practice, even if "pure" forms are easy to describe on paper. Most psychiatric categories distinguish between two large categories of psychotic reaction: one that comprises all the various types of schizophrenia (catatonic-paranoid included) and one that comprises the so-called mood, or affective, disorders.

1. Mood disorders and schizophrenia. The major types of mood disorders can be described easily: first, there is depression, second, there is mania, and third, there is the alternation between these two states known as **manic-depressive** psychosis. The category system for **schizophrenia** is more complex, and one author (Coleman, 1976) described the following types of schizophrenic reactions.

1. *Acute.* This condition is characterized by a sudden onset of symptoms, often involving confusion, emotional turmoil, delusions, excitement, dreamlike dissociation, depression, and fear. The person seems to undergo a total breakdown, with the result that experience becomes fragmented and disorganized.

2. *Paranoid.* Here the person is dominated by illogical and changeable delusions, frequently accompanied by hallucinations. He or she tends to have poor judgment and behaves in an unpredictable and sometimes dangerous way. In long-term cases, there can be reasonably good dealings with other people.

3. *Catatonic.* This condition is often characterized by periods of withdrawal and excitement, although in some cases one or the other state predominates. In withdrawal, there is a sudden loss of movement as well as a tendency to remain motionless for hours or even days. Sometimes the picture changes abruptly and the person suddenly becomes excited. In this state the person may talk or shout, pace rapidly, and do a wide variety of uninhibited, impulsive, and frenzied acts.

4. *Hebephrenic.* Usually occurs at an earlier age than most other types of schizophrenia. The hebephrenic person is severely disorganized and shows inappropriate laughter and silliness, peculiar mannerisms, and bizarre, obscene actions.

5. *Simple.* In this condition, the person shows a continuous downhill loss of clear thinking, feeling, and doing, beginning early in life and gradually getting worse until the person becomes inaccessible, isolated, colorless, and remote. Because disorganization is usually less severe than in other types of schizophrenia, the person is not always hospitalized.

6. *Latent.* Characterized by various long-standing symptoms but lacking full-blown schizophrenic history or behavior.

7. *Chronic undifferentiated.* In this state, the person is not clearly classifiable into any one of the other categories although he or she definitely shows schizophrenic types of thinking, feeling, and doing [paraphrased from Coleman, 1976, p. 308].

2. Paranoia. In addition to manic-depressive and schizophrenic reactions, a third category of psychosis is **paranoia.** Here the person develops an intricate and well-worked-out system of delusions. Such false ideas often center on a single topic, are well systematized, and do not keep the person from dealing with the world on a day-to-day basis. The person rarely, if ever, hallucinates and is seldom out of contact with the world of everyday reality. In terms of Laing's approach, a *single* aspect of the self-system splits off, becomes systematized, and no longer remains in direct and spontaneous contact with either the bodily-self, others, or the world.

Freud once said that paranoia was perhaps the most perfect form of psychosis. Not only does it tie up in a neat package many of the problems that threaten to overwhelm a person, it does so without destroying the person's ability to deal with his or her ordinary world. As a matter of fact, such people often deal quite easily and well with their world. They are also not without a sense of humor even though such humor may be but another expression of what is problematic in their life.

Keen (1970) presents the following bizarre but quite witty parody of Edgar Allan Poe's poem *Annabel Lee.* It was written by a young paranoid writer who called his version of the poem *Cannibalee.*

It was many and many a day ago,
    In a city you all can see,
That a maiden lived whom you might know
    By the name of Cannibalee;
And this maiden she lived with no other thought
    Than a passionate fondness for me.

I was a lad and she was a lass;
    I hoped that her tastes were free.
But she loved with a love that was more than a love,

My yearning Cannibalee;
With a love that could take me roasted, or fried,
    Or raw, as the case might be.

And that is the reason that long ago,
    In a city you all can see,
I had to turn the tables and eat
    My ardent Cannibalee—
Not really because I was fond of her,
    But to check her fondness for me.

But the stars never rise but I think of the size
    Of my pot-potted Cannibalee.
And the moon never stares but it brings me nightmares
    Of my spare-rib Cannibalee
And all the night tide she is restless inside
Is my still indigestible dinner belle bride,
    In her pallid tomb, all rent free
In her carnivorous sepulchre—me.
        [Searles, 1965, pp. 484–485; also cited in Keen, 1970][7]

If you know the poem from which this parody
was derived, you can see how cleverly done it is; if
not, you can still sense the difference between this
person's ability to use language, rhythm, and sound
and the more disordered way in which we expect
people diagnosed as "psychotic" to speak and
write. The paranoid is much more in tune with
things than people having any of the other psychotic life-styles considered. If the conversation never
gets around to his or her specific delusional system,
it is very difficult to see the person as crazy.

Yet he or she is crazy: once the critical topic or
topics surface, the whole story comes tumbling out
in all its bizarre, logically illogical form. Consider
the case of Walter P., described by Kisker (1972):

> Walter P. was a twenty-three-year-old single man
> when he was admitted to a psychiatric hospital. When
> he was twenty, his family and friends began to notice a
> change in his behavior. He became increasingly talka-
> tive and developed an idea that he was destined to
> make the world over. His preoccupation with this proj-
> ect became so great that he quit his job, neglected his
> health and personal appearance, and refused to speak
> to members of his family. He became more and more
> withdrawn and spent his entire time making entries in
> a series of notebooks in which he outlined, in the most
> minute detail, his plans for a utopian community. The
> first notebook bears the title The Pictopisist Movement,
> and starts with the following paragraph: "An Interna-
> tional Society, the members of which stand for the cre-

ating of a Modern Utopia, in which that strata of people
with the proper Intellect, Perspective, Nature, and Phy-
sique, will form a society where all are Happy, Content-
ed, and Peaceful, just as their Creator meant them to.
We will segregate ourselves from the general society of
the world until such time when those who are outside
our New Movement shall look upon Life in general as
we do."

> The notebooks contain detailed entries on various lo-
> cations in different parts of the world where the utopi-
> an community might be located. The patient decided fi-
> nally that the ideal location would be the Galapagos
> Islands, off the coast of South America. He planned to
> build a schooner to transport his "disciples" and their
> supplies down the Ohio and Mississippi Rivers to the
> Gulf of Mexico, and then to the Islands. The notebooks
> contain not only detailed drawings of the schooner and
> long lists of supplies but hundreds of notes on new re-
> ligious, economic, and social systems. Public buildings
> are sketched, and several pages are devoted to specifi-
> cations for a communal bakery. Every detail was care-
> fully entered, from the cost of elaborate baking equip-
> ment to the cost of a dozen muffin cups [pp. 341–342].

So Walter P. created a world in which he hoped
to live. It obviously would be a far less threatening
one than the world in which he now lived—and
one he could control. It would also shield him from
feeling powerless in the present and thus would allow him to bear the indignities of the present. Once
encapsulated, Walter was safe and in charge.

Walter P. constructed a world in which he was
the hero, the conqueror, the supreme king. For this
reason, Walter's delusion would be called a delusion of grandeur, or, more simply, a delusion of
greatness. Not all delusions are of this type. In
many cases the person feels persecuted by demons
or enemy agents. Such a delusion, for obvious reasons, is called a delusion of persecution or conspiracy. You might think that the person who suffers
from persecutory delusions is in worse shape than
the person who suffers from delusions of greatness.
Therapists, however, find it much more difficult to
work with a person suffering a delusion of greatness.

Delusions of persecution and of greatness are not
the only symptoms shown by the paranoid. One investigator (Lorr, 1964) asked therapists to describe
and then rank-order paranoid symptoms from least
to most severe. Their ranking was as follows: hostile
attitude, verbal expression of hostility, feelings of re-
sentment, blaming others, suspicion of others, delusions of persecution, delusions of conspiracy, ideas

[7]From Three Faces of Being: Toward an Existential Clinical Psychology, by E. Keen. Copyright © 1970 by Irvington
Publishers, Inc. Reprinted by permission.

of reference, ideas of control by people, ideas of control by forces, ideas of grandeur, ideas of divine mission. Why should therapists who deal with paranoid patients find delusions of greatness among the most difficult aspects of paranoia to work with? One reason seems to be that there is much greater "distance from reality" in delusions of greatness than in delusions of persecution. If you are great, you are in charge and there is no reason to change. If you are scared, as in delusions of persecution, then you are probably still in there trying. Under this analysis, the Savior is in worse shape than the Sinner, although neither is making it very well.

The paranoid, like the obsessive, again shows an ordinary human ability gone wrong: in these two cases, the ability to reflect. If an obsessive like Peter Oberman wants to deny the world of unreflected thinking and doing, a paranoid like Walter P. goes one step further: he develops a systematic reconstruction from which he can safely look out on a threatening world. From this orderly capsule, the living world is held at a distance, and each and every Walter P. can go on with his everyday life because he has a secret that is more important to him than anything else ever could be.

Some paranoids do manage to get along quite well in handling the events of an ordinary day, week, month, or year. If no one questions the delusion—or, just as important, no one accepts it—everything goes well. If this is so, are we right in seeing the paranoid as so very different from you and me? After all, he or she has only constructed a world that gives comfort; in no way need it harm others. Isn't our judgment that the person is "a paranoid" simply a political decision—aren't we saying "My reality is more real than yours"? Isn't the paranoid's delusion an attempt to solve the very human concerns we all have?

The answer, of course, is yes: the paranoid simply describes, with more quietly angry strokes, the problems all of us have in trying to order our world. The difference, however, is that he is crazy, not just because I say so but because the whole texture of his or her life tells us so. It is easy to romanticize madness and equate it with creativity or prophecy, but at some very basic level it is nothing other than misery for the person experiencing the world in this way. Speaking specifically for the paranoid (and perhaps for other disordered styles of Being-in-the-world as well), the psychiatrist Harold Searles noted:

The paranoid patient is not sufficiently in tune with his fellow-man; not sufficiently able to integrate the ever-flowing nature of life with change and growth, fulfillment and loss, birth and death; not sufficiently matured in his thought-processes to distinguish the more significant from the less significant incidents and threads in his life; and not sufficiently loving and trusting to experience love as the ingredient which gives human existence cohesiveness and meaning; to be able to feel the wholeness, the genuine "master plan" which the healthy individual comes to see in his life [1965, p. 469].

IV. THE CASE OF FERDINAND W. DEMARA, JR., THE GREAT IMPOSTOR

One of the boldest impostors of recent times was Ferdinand Waldo Demara, Jr. As an adolescent, he ran away from his family, and after unsuccessful attempts first to become a Trappist monk and then to teach school, he joined the army. Soon thereafter he went AWOL, joined the navy, and was assigned to duty on a destroyer during World War II. Here, by a ruse, he got hold of some navy stationery, with which he managed to obtain the college transcript of an officer who was on leave. He then doctored this transcript by substituting his own name and adding some courses; when photostated, it looked so impressive that he used it to apply for a commission. While waiting for his commission to come through, he amused himself by obtaining other records, including the full credentials of a doctor who had received a Ph.D. in psychology from Harvard. Informed during a visit to Norfolk that he could expect his commission as soon as a routine security check was completed, he realized that such a check would surely expose him. Under cover of darkness, he left his navy clothes on the end of the pier with a note that "this was the only way out."

Now that Demara was "dead"—drowned off Norfolk—he became Dr. French. He obtained an appointment as professor of psychology in a small Canadian college and taught courses in general, industrial, and abnormal psychology. Eventually, however, he had a disagreement with his supervisor and reluctantly left.

During this period he became friends with a physician by the name of Joseph Cyr and learned about the practice of medicine from him during the cold winter months when neither man had much to occupy his time. Interested in the possibility of getting a license to practice in the United States, the trusting doctor had given Demara a complete packet including his baptism and confirmation certifications, school records, and license to practice medicine in Canada.

Using these credentials and without Dr. Cyr's knowledge, Demara obtained a commission for himself as a lieutenant in the Royal Canadian Navy. His first assignment was to take sick call each morning at the base. To help solve his problem of not knowing what to do, he went to his superior officer and told him that he had been asked to work up a rule-of-thumb guide for people in lumber camps, most of whom did not have physicians readily available. The officer, delighted with the project, prepared a manual covering the most serious medical situations. Demara used this manual to help him in his early-morning rounds. He also studied medical books and picked up considerable additional knowledge.

Assigned to duty on the aircraft carrier *Magnificent*, Demara was criticized by a senior medical officer for his lack of training in medicine and surgery, especially for his deficiency in diagnosing certain medical problems. Learning of the report, Demara took characteristic action. He commandeered several compartments in the lower area of the ship, posted them with quarantine signs, and sent there for observation the patients whose maladies he was having trouble diagnosing—in the meantime giving them penicillin. The chief medical officer knew nothing of his plan, and reports of Demara's performance, based only on cases that Demara reviewed with his superior officer, became more favorable.

Perhaps the climax of Demara's incredible career came during the Korean War, when he was assigned as ship's doctor to the Canadian destroyer *Cayuga*. As the *Cayuga* proceeded to the combat zone, Demara studied medical books and hoped his skill would never be put to test. Fate decreed otherwise. One afternoon the destroyer spotted a small Korean junk littered with wounded men who had been caught in an ambush. "Dr. Cyr" was summoned and knew that there was no escape for him.

Nineteen suffering men were lifted from the junk. Three were so gravely wounded that only emergency surgery could save them. Demara had read books on surgery but had never seen an operation performed.

The self-taught "M.D." cleaned and sutured the 16 less seriously wounded men while gathering his

courage for the great ordeal. Then he took over the captain's cabin as an emergency operating room. Working hour after hour with a slow, unskilled hand, Demara performed the demanding operations while the ship's officers and dozens of enlisted men helped and watched.

When his ship was sent to Japan for refitting, an eager young press officer seized on "Dr. Cyr's" exploits and wrote them up in full. His story was released to the civilian press, and the "miracle doctor" became world-famous. This publicity proved to be Demara's temporary undoing, for it led to queries from the real Dr. Joseph Cyr whether the physician mentioned was a relative, and when Dr. Cyr saw the newspaper picture, he was shocked to find it was his old friend Demara.

Dropped from the Canadian navy without fanfare, Demara went through a difficult period. Wherever he went, he was soon recognized, and he lost job after job. He managed to work for a year at a state school for retarded children and did so well that he received a promotion and a transfer to the state hospital for the criminally insane. Here he found that the patients seemed to like him and that he was able to communicate with them. Unfortunately, he started to drink heavily and eventually had to resign.

One morning after a prolonged drinking bout, he woke up in a different city and realized his drinking was getting out of hand. He joined the local chapter of Alcoholics Anonymous as Ben W. Jones, whose credentials he had acquired along the way. With the help of sympathetic friends in Alcoholics Anonymous and a few fraudulent references obtained by his usual methods, he was hired as a guard in a state penitentiary. Here he did a good job, instituting a number of badly needed reforms in the maximum-security block. Again he found himself able to communicate with the men and soon was promoted to assistant warden of maximum security. Ironically, one of his reform measures was to ask the townspeople to contribute old magazines, and before long one of the prisoners read the issue of *Life* magazine that contained his picture and case history.

Trying to get away lest he wind up as a prisoner in the same penitentiary, Demara was jailed in a nearby state and given considerable publicity but eventually released. Some time later he telephoned a friend of his, Dr. Crichton, from whose report most of this material was derived, to say "I'm on the biggest caper of them all. Oh, I wish I could tell you" (Coleman, 1976, pp. 376–377).

What can we say of Ferdinand W. Demara, Jr.? It is easy to find the Great Ferdinand a rogue and a scoundrel, but a charming and capable one nonetheless. There is something in us that responds to his exploits and makes us want to forget that all his credentials were forged and that his style of living was a lie. Yet we do respond, and it is a characteristic reaction to people like Ferdinand, who technically can be categorized as a **psychopathic** personality.

Why are some psychopaths so fascinating to us? The answer must be that psychopaths like Demara seem to live out what the rest of us only fantasize. And what is the nature of our fantasy? Not to be subject to the ordinary rules of social convention. Under one interpretation this "freedom from social restraint" can be seen to suggest an immature child or adolescent. Under a second interpretation, and this is the more important point, a psychopathic style of living shows that the limitations we accept in our own personal actions are not fixed aspects of the world but unreflected choices we have made about our functioning in a given society. If we are not careful in our thinking, a charming psychopath such as Demara may appear the model of a "free man"—a man who transcends the ordinary and flies in the face of social convention.

By his style of living the psychopath escapes the continuing tension we all experience when our wishes conflict with those of the social world. When and if we respond to the Demaras of this world, we often are responding to the stupid and senseless restrictions we feel in regard to social norms and laws. What we do not take into account is that social laws and norms have a justifiable as well as an unjustifiable aspect. Many laws and norms are just and justifiable, and the fact that many are not should not lead us to exalt the fraud. Instead, it ought to make us insist that our laws and our conventions be based on reasonable human grounds rather than on power or caprice.

A different face of the psychopath is not seen in the charming and bright Demara; instead, it is more clearly seen in the criminal behavior of many antisocial individuals. Consider the following case of a man named Charles:

When Charles was four years old he was "arrested" for vandalism and taken to the police station. A few hours later when his parents retrieved him, he came home and broke several windows in the house. His parents, believing he was just "bored," brought him an erector set to keep him occupied. During his school years, he was persistently in trouble with school and law officials and, although he was of superior intelligence, did barely passing work.

When he was 14, he ran away with a 15-year-old girl in a stolen car. When they were caught and returned home two months later, Charles promised that he would "turn over a new leaf" and make something of his life. He returned to school but did not put out much effort at studies. He left school at age 16 and went to California, using money he had acquired by selling some of his mother's jewelry. After several months, most of which were spent in jail, he returned home. He got a job at a service station and bought an automobile on credit. His carefree attitudes about business—he was casually giving away merchandise and on one busy day did not bother to charge for gasoline— soon resulted in his being fired.

He was a master at obtaining jobs, since he appeared as a bright young man with a wealth of new ideas. However, he was just as adept at losing them (either because of his unreliability or the liberties he took with the cash register). In three months he changed jobs fourteen times. Charles soon became bored with the world of work and left home again after selling the mortgaged car for a fraction of its original value.

Several months later Charles came home again. He and his new wife (a former prostitute, eight years his senior) had hitchhiked a thousand miles and appeared at the parents' home drunk and disheveled during a reception for a prominent politician.

Charles and his wife moved in much to the dismay of his father (whose patience was beginning to run out). Charles drank heavily and smoked dope daily. After several weeks, he took up residence with an elderly lady in town who was quite flattered by Charles' interest and affection. (Charles' wife stayed at his parents' home eating, drinking heavily and watching television.)

After a few weeks Charles became tired of "family life," borrowed $2,000 from the elderly lady under the pretense of opening up a market, and left town alone. He was last heard of several months later in a city 600 miles away, when his father received a note demanding payment for a large loan made to Charles on which he had allegedly been a co-signer [Butcher, 1971, pp. 50–51].[8]

This, then, is the other face of the psychopath and the one that is hard for us even to begin to understand. The whole life-style seems beyond belief.

[8]From *Abnormal Psychology*, by J. N. Butcher. Copyright 1971 by Wadsworth, Inc. Reprinted by permission of the publisher, Brooks/Cole Publishing Company, Monterey, California.

There are several ways to describe the "psychopathic style"; Table 13-2 shows how Kleinmuntz summarized his understanding of it. Both Charles and Demara show a great many of the characteristics described in Table 13-2. The only difference between them would seem to be whether the face wore a smile or a scowl.

Keen (1970), in discussing the psychopath, notes that when a therapist comes in contact with a psychopath, the therapist is likely to feel he has stepped into an alien culture. Everything the therapist, as a person, takes to be reliable and "true" of his world is questioned by the doings and sayings of the person confronting him. The psychopathic person seems to negate our typical ways of dealing with the world and seems to suffer no guilt or anxiety about it. The psychopathic person seems frighteningly in touch with the social realities he or she casually ignores. It is an unsettling experience to step into such a world.

But what is this world like, and how is it experienced by the person we describe as psychopathic? As should be obvious, it is radically different from ours in a great many ways. Take the important categories of time, body, self, other, and world. To start with time: As many therapists have stressed, the psychopathic person lives almost exclusively in a present unrelated to his or her past and having few projections into the future. As one set of authors put it, for the psychopath "the moment is a segment of time detached from all others" (McCord & McCord, 1964, p. 16). Under this style of rootedness in time, is it any wonder that the psychopathic person is "impulsive and immature" or that he or she

TABLE 13-2. Characteristics and Typical Behavior of the Antisocial Personality

Characteristic	Typical behavior
Inability to form loyal relationships	Treats persons as if they were objects; might marry but then deserts family.
Inability to feel guilt	Feels no pangs of remorse, although he can express sorrow and other emotions.
Inability to learn from experience, special attention, or punishment	Commits repeated crimes, and neither rewards nor severe deprivations seem to deter him.
Tendency to seek thrills and excitement	Behaves bizarrely and sometimes grotesquely as a rule rather than as an exception.
Impulsiveness	Cannot defer immediate pleasures, cannot tolerate long-term commitments.
Aggressiveness	Reacts to frustration with destructive fury.
Superficial charm and intelligence	Often becomes a confidence man because of "winning" personality and astuteness.
Unreliability and irresponsibility	Unpredictably responsible during some periods but completely irresponsible during others.
Pathological lying	Plays many roles—doctor, lawyer, soldier—all according to whim.
Does antisocial acts on a whim	Impulsively steals and destroys "just for the hell of it."
Egocentric	Lives off others because of a wish to be believed, served, and supported.
Poorness of emotion	Incapable of true anger or genuine grief.
Lack of self-insight	Can analyze the motivations underlying the behavior of others—and often does—but has no appreciation of the impact he has on others.
Casual but excessive sexual behavior	Has a casual attitude toward sex; sexual contacts, like most of his behavior, are outlandish and erratic.
Has a "need to fail"	Has no apparent life plan, except perhaps the need to make a failure of himself.

From *Essentials of Abnormal Psychology*, (2nd ed.), by B. Kleinmuntz. Copyright © 1980 by Benjamin Kleinmuntz. Reprinted by permission of Harper & Row, Publishers, Inc.

seems unable to learn from the past for the future? If time is instantaneous, there is no reason to learn, to plan, or to obey anything other than the momentary whim that captures one's fancy. Since the psychopath experiences little or no future, he or she cannot "fear" what will happen in a nonexistent future and for this reason experiences little or no anxiety.

Perhaps the most outstanding trait of the psychopathic person is his or her tendency to "use" other people—that is, to treat them as objects at his or her disposal. Other people are not dealt with as if they were in any way like me or as if they might be hurt if I used them. There is only one point of view for this type of person—Mine!—and this accounts for the trait of egocentricity and the seemingly childish way the person pursues his or her activities. If there are no "real" others, then there is only a single center to the world, and that center is forever, and only, me.

Since the personal, subjective point of view is so significant, the Me must be grandiose and almost without bounds. The psychopathic person thus comes to "trudge on through life without giving credit to the world for existing" (Keen, 1970, p. 313). If the self is grand, it is not the same grand self the paranoid builds: rather, it is a self that is large simply because the world is small and unimportant. The psychopathic person never becomes someone else's object (as everyone else is his) and for this reason exists in a strange, superpowerful relationship to a world that can sometimes make the rest of us small and insignificant.

Thus, the ordinary categories of our world do not exist, reflectedly or unreflectedly, for the psychopath. Although we may assign a value judgment of "bad" or even "wicked" to his behavior, these are our judgments, not his. More than any other style of living, the psychopathic person's shows us that all our worlds are constructed and not God-given. The psychopath forcibly reminds us that it is difficult (and demanding) to accept the constraints of being human—that is, of being mortal, of being responsible, of being afraid. He also forces us to guarantee a world for him to live in, while he seemingly has free scope within a timeless, free world. The only problem in the psychopathic resolution is that it is a lie, for it denies that we are all embedded, whether we like it or not, within a social and physical world that is both our creation and our limit. Without

other people, we are not; the psychopath cannot and will not understand this.

V. SOME GENERAL ISSUES IN PROBLEMS IN LIVING

The neurotic, the psychotic, the psychopath, and the person suffering from psychosomatic disorder only emphasize what it is we all find difficult to deal with in our lives. Time, body, the nature of reality, death, anxiety, social constraints, and personal meaning are among the most significant issues in every human life. A person such as Peter Oberman experiences a world in which the very human facility of thinking runs away with and from him. A person such as John Knight finds that he is locked in mortal combat with his body in much the same way that Ferdinand Demara is at odds with his society. Joan Smith, for a time, was "disembodied" and thus was cut off from meaningful contact with her world.

In each of these cases, the unity of the person was destroyed by his or her being in a distorted relationship to significant aspects of self and world. Under these conditions we may take the word *disorganized* quite seriously: each of these people was disorganized to such an extent that the total person who was or could be Joan Smith, Ferdinand Demara, Peter Oberman, or John Knight could be considered as in pieces, as less than a well-integrated, fully functioning human being. Being in many pieces (*fragmented* seems a good word) in regard to self, others, and/or one's social world leads to an experience of the world as chaotic and dangerous, a place in which existence is always at issue and nonbeing never far from hand.

Under these conditions two "symptoms" accompany almost all the various life-styles discussed. One of these is anxiety, and the second concerns the issue of nonbeing—that is, of dying and its more active form, suicide. These two themes occur in every human life, and here as elsewhere, they appear more sharply and better defined in people who are not making it in the world.

A. The problem of anxiety
The poet W. H. Auden called the present era the Age of Anxiety. Although anxiety is an important contemporary problem, many psychologists have been more concerned with measuring anxiety and

determining its effects from a third-person point of view than with describing our experiences of the world when we are anxious.

1. A phenomenological analysis.

To correct this imbalance and describe what the world is like when we live it anxiously, let us begin with a highly specific and detailed description of what one person—a young man named Roger—experienced when he was anxious. Roger was about to take a final exam in college.

When I think about the exam I really feel sick . . . I know I'm not prepared . . . but I keep hoping that I can sort of snow my way through it. He [the professor] said we would get to choose two of three essay questions. I've heard about his questions . . . they sort of cover the whole course. Maybe I'll be able to mention a few of the right names and places. He can't expect us to put down everything in two hours . . . I keep trying to remember some of the things he said in class, but my mind keeps wandering.

God, my folks—What will they think if I don't pass and can't graduate? Will they have a fit! Boy! I can see their faces. Worse yet, I can hear their voices: "And with all the money we spent on your education." Mom's going to be hurt. She'll let me know I let her down. She'll be a martyr: "Well, Roger, didn't you realize how this reflects on us? Didn't you know how much we worked and saved so you could get an education? . . . You were probably too busy with other things. I don't know what I'm going to tell your aunt and uncle. They were planning to come to the graduation, you know."

Hell! What about me? What'll I do if I don't graduate? How about the plans I made? I had a good job lined up with that company. They really sounded like they wanted me, like I was going to be somebody . . . And what about the car? I had it all planned out. I was going to pay seventy a month and still have enough left for fun. I've got to pass. Oh hell! What about Anne [girlfriend]? She's counting on my graduating. We had plans. What will she think? She knows I'm no brain, but . . . hell, I won't be anybody. I've got to find some way to remember those names. If I can just get him to think that I really know the material, but don't have time to put it all down. If I can just . . . if . . . too goddam many ifs.

Poor dad. He'll really be hurt. All the plans we made . . . I was going to be somebody. What did he say? "People will respect you. People respect a college graduate. You'll be something more than a storekeeper." What am I going to do? God, I can't think. You know, I might just luck out. I've done it before.

He could ask just the right questions. What could he ask? Boy, I feel like I want to vomit. Do you think others

are as scared as I am? They probably know it all or don't give a damn. I'll bet you most of them have parents who can set them up whether they have college degrees or not. God, it means so much to me. I've got to pass. I've just got to.

Dammit, what are those names? What could he ask? I can't think. I can't . . . Maybe if I had a beer I'd be able to relax a little. Is there anybody around who wants to get a beer? God, I don't want to go alone. Who wants to go to the show? What the hell am I thinking about? I've got to study . . . I can't go. What's going to happen to me? . . . *The whole damn world is coming apart* [Fischer, 1970, pp. 121–122].[9]

This is not an extraordinary record; we all have experienced something of this sort, even if not with the same content or intensity. Several themes are involved in Roger's experience of being anxious. First, there is a focus on his body: "I really feel sick . . . I feel like I want to vomit." Second, there is a focus on time past and time future. Past—" 'And with all the money we spent on your education.' " Future—"How about the plans I made? I had a good job lined up with that company."

Third, there is a focus on Roger's Being-for-others. Included in this category are parents ("Mom's going to be hurt. . . . I let her down"), teachers ("He can't expect us to put down everything in two hours"), relatives (" 'Your aunt and uncle . . . were planning to come to the graduation' "), girlfriend ("What about Anne? She's counting on my graduating"), and peers ("Do you think others are as scared as I am?"). Finally, there is the exaggerated concern that "the whole damn world [is coming] apart" and the wonder "What's going to happen to me?"

Although Roger's experience of being anxious would seem directly related to having to take an exam, a more sensitive reading suggests that doing well on the test is part of the larger issue of what is important to Roger as a person. This particular exam was experienced as a hurdle that much depended on. As Fischer (1970) notes in regard to Roger's experience of being anxious,

The meaning of [Roger's anxiety] reveals itself to be a complex network of relationships (to parents, to girlfriend, to peers, etc.), projects (graduation, securing

[9]From *Theories of Anxiety*, by W. F. Fischer. Copyright © 1970 by William F. Fischer. This and all other quotations from this source are reprinted by permission of Harper & Row, Publishers, Inc.

the job, paying for the car), and identities (being somebody). The meaning of his possible performance on the exam ... points not only toward an anticipated future, but also it illuminates a past ... in which plans ... were made and promises enacted. There is a continuity, an unfolding ... at stake here. ... The ... meaning of the ... exam is that of a hurdle or milestone. If passed, a door is open to a world of "being somebody," a world that has already been envisioned and experienced. If it proves to be insurmountable, this lived-and-planned-for-world vanishes into meaningless oblivion; the past goes nowhere; the future is being nobody [1970, p. 123].

Anxiety is thus experienced about an event that is important for Roger's sense of being worthwhile, of being up to snuff, of validating his past, and of producing happy extensions into the future. For Roger a good part of his world is at issue: to do well is to have or to be somebody; to do poorly is to lose a great deal and maybe even to be nobody. Anxiety signals a world in which Roger stands at the edge of nothingness.

In this situation Roger is alone. The experience of anxiety yields a shrunken world, a world reduced to the point of including only one's body in a limited and objectlike sense. When I am anxious, I can do nothing but listen to the humming of my heart and sense the nonmoving of my body. The world is small and I am alone, in constant fear of nonbeing.

Roger also experiences continuous fluctuations in what he thinks about. At one moment he is worried about the past, in the next, the future; at one moment he thinks about his parents, in the next, his professor and then his girlfriend. He also worries about what he should be doing: I ought to study, I ought to get a beer, I want to go to the movies. Under the experience of anxiety, Roger's world is so fragile that it does not support any single project from start to finish.

Although Roger's anxiety seems to have a specific focus—the test—it is clear that parts of his whole life are also at issue. Perhaps that is why anxiety, even when it has a focus, is experienced as diffuse and vague. Most severe experiences of anxiety seem to involve feelings of uncertainty and helplessness in the face of personal danger. Many writers, such as Kurt Goldstein, Rollo May, and Sigmund Freud, have distinguished between **fear** and **anxiety** according to whether there is a specified focus: Fear (and its more severe counterpart, **phobia**) is always

brought about by some specific thing or event. Anxiety, though equally terrifying, is without a specific anchor.

Severe anxiety changes the whole texture of personal experience, so that when I live my world anxiously, I can lose my sense of self and my ordinary integration in time. Severe anxiety breaks down the difference between the Me and the Not-Me and threatens the Me with a sense of nonbeing. Under this condition, I not only fear for life itself; I am also afraid of becoming nothing, of lapsing into nonbeing.

2. Defensive and facilitative ways of dealing with anxiety.   All this talk about anxiety suggests that it is an overwhelmingly powerful and an overwhelmingly useless experience in human life. Some people, however, are able to use their anxiety constructively. We have two possibilities in regard to anxiety: to defend ourselves against it or to recognize it as one aspect of our attempt to grow and change. On the defensive side of the ledger, Freud described techniques called **defense mechanisms** that all of us use at one time or another in coming to grips with our anxieties. Perhaps the simplest one is to keep thoughts and ideas that make us anxious out of awareness. Freud called this process "repression," for he believed that we prevent such thoughts from being conscious by forcing, or repressing, them into the unconscious.

It is not necessary to give defense mechanisms a Freudian interpretation; instead, they can be described as strategies a person might use in defending against a threat of personal nonbeing. Although the number of defense mechanisms varies across different attempts to list them, Ruch and Zimbardo (1971) present a list of 15 that covers the major ones clearly and well (see Table 13-3).

The constructive use of anxiety can be described as a person's moving *through* anxiety-creating experiences rather than *around* them. Viewed in this way, human growth can be seen to depend on our tendency to take risks and to confront and move through experiences that require us to deal with the world as new, different, and frightening. The freedom a healthy person experiences often concerns his or her considering new possibilities in meeting and overcoming threats to his or her present style of being. A person can become self-actualized (to use Goldstein's and Maslow's word) only to

TABLE 13-3. Summary Chart of Ego Defense Mechanisms

Compensation	Covering up weakness by emphasizing desirable trait or making up for frustration in one area by overgratification in another
Denial of reality	Protecting self from unpleasant reality by refusal to perceive it
Displacement	Discharging pent-up feelings, usually of hostility, on objects less dangerous than those which initially aroused the emotion
Emotional insulation	Withdrawing into passivity to protect self from being hurt
Fantasy	Gratifying frustrated desires in imaginary achievements ("daydreaming" is a common form)
Identification	Increasing feelings of worth by identifying self with person or institution of illustrious standing
Introjection	Incorporating external values and standards into ego structure so individual is not at the mercy of them as external threats
Isolation	Cutting off emotional charge from hurtful situations or separating incompatible attitudes by logic-tight compartments (holding conflicting attitudes which are never thought of simultaneously or in relation to each other); also called *compartmentalization*
Projection	Placing blame for one's difficulties upon others, or attributing one's own unethical desires to others
Rationalization	Attempting to prove that one's behavior is "rational" and justifiable and thus worthy of the approval of self and others
Reaction formation	Preventing dangerous desires from being expressed by exaggerating opposing attitudes and types of behavior and using them as "barriers"
Regression	Retreating to earlier developmental level involving less mature responses and usually a lower level of aspiration
Repression	Preventing painful or dangerous thoughts from entering consciousness
Sublimation	Gratifying or working off frustrated desires in substitutive activities socially accepted by one's culture
Undoing	Atoning for, and thus counteracting, immoral desires or acts

From *Psychology and Life*, by Floyd L. Ruch and Philip G. Zimbardo. Copyright © 1971, 1967 by Scott, Foresman and Company. Reprinted by permission.

the degree that he or she can bear the anxiety of continuing growth. Kierkegaard put it best when he wrote: "To venture causes anxiety, but not to venture is to lose oneself" (cited in May, 1950, p. 234).

Anxiety is not always to be viewed as something undesirable or something extraordinary. To be human is to experience anxiety, and this experience becomes a barrier to healthy functioning only if the person gives in to the experience and is overwhelmed by it. In severe anxiety, the person is lost, and the project that up to that time was his or her life comes to be futile and without direction. Under this condition, the person experiences what Goldstein (see Chapter 3) called a catastrophic collapse, and the rest of his or her life may become nothing more than an attempt to avoid ever having to face the experience of nonbeing again. For this reason such individuals turn away from choosing and toward avoiding. Under this strategy, all living becomes defensive, for there is no room for change.

One is always defending oneself against the possibility of a new catastrophic collapse.

3. Anxiety and dread. If the experience of anxiety is related to experiences of nonbeing, then we must all eventually face this possibility in the form of **death**. None of us can escape, and each of us must live with the dread such knowledge creates throughout our lives. Perhaps it was for this reason that the philosopher Martin Heidegger believed that one of the most important categories of human existence was anxiety, or, as he called it, dread (*Angst* in German). Heidegger saw dread as significant in human life precisely because he saw human living as uncertain and ever open. The same situation that gives rise to change and growth can give rise to the possibility of collapse as well as to the experience of dread.

Human beings, once adult, come to realize that they will die. A crucial difference, however, occurs when I change from thinking and talking about death in general terms, such as "People die," to thinking and talking about death in personal terms, such as "I will die." To say "I will die" changes the whole game: Death ceases to be only an abstract and distant idea. Most of us cringe when we make Death *my* death. Heidegger tells us that only because I take my death seriously does authentic living become possible. William Barrett (1958), speaking more directly than Heidegger, describes the situation as follows:

> Touched by this interior angel of death, I cease to be the impersonal and social one among many . . . and I am free to become myself. Though terrifying, the taking of death into ourselves is also liberating: It frees us from the petty cares that threaten to engulf our daily life and thereby opens us to the essential projects by which we can make our lives personally and significantly our own [p. 201].

The nature of what it means to be human has anxiety built into it from the start. From both philosophical and psychological points of view, living anxiously is always a reaction to the possibility of nonbeing, and the best we can do is to face this possibility head on. To do this gives living a certain boundary and in so doing may free us from the "petty cares" that come up in our daily lives.

For the person who is not making it, anxiety is not something to live through but something to run away from. Even though we all do run from time to time, such a person pursues a style of existence that is always concerned with running from his or her experiences of anxiety. If the person is unsuccessful in avoiding some of these experiences (as many neurotics are) or is unable to tie them to fairly specific bodily patterns (as in psychosomatic reactions), he or she is likely to fall into that extraordinary style of living known as schizophrenia. Even the seemingly nonanxious psychopath takes anxiety into account—by denying that anyone or anything could be sufficiently important so that to lose it would be catastrophic. The person not making it comes to define, in a negative way, what each of us must face and work through. To live in an uncertain world of human projects is always to risk anxiety; it is both our blessing and our curse.

B. The question of suicide

Philosophers such as Martin Heidegger and Maurice Merleau-Ponty seem to say that life can be lived at full intensity only to the degree that the possibility of one's own, very personal death is taken into account. Illustrating this point, Merleau-Ponty (1962, p. 84) cited an experience reported by a pilot during a raid in World War II: "It is as if my life were given to me every second, as if my life became every moment more keenly felt. I live. I am alive. I am still alive. I am always alive. I am now nothing but a source of life." Similarly, Rollo May cited the following bit of folk knowledge used by men fishing the North Sea.

> The fishermen bringing in their herring from the North Sea were faced with the problem of the fish becoming sluggish in their tanks and thus losing some of their market value for freshness. Then one fisherman conceived the idea of placing a couple of catfish in the herring tanks. Because of the threat of death in the presence of these catfish, the herring not only did not grow sluggish but became even more active and flourishing [1977, p. 14].

To live fully and authentically is to be fully aware of dying, not as some abstract possibility but as a very real possibility for me.

None of the postwar existential philosophers took this point of view more seriously or more dramatically than Albert Camus. Camus felt that the only question worth considering in a world that could only be described as absurd was that of suicide: the possibility of my own death brought about by me. Only if we accept the possibility of suicide seriously is there any future at all. For Camus, the most basic of human decisions is always "Am I to die voluntarily or to hope in spite of everything?"

1. A failed attempt.   To gain some feel for the experience that characterizes an attempt at suicide, we can do no better that let the English poet and essayist Al Alvarez describe his own "failed attempt at suicide." The entire account is too long to be quoted in full, but some excerpts will give a flavor for Alverez's present understanding of the attempt.

> I built up to the act carefully and for a long time. . . . It was the one constant focus of my life, making everything else irrelevant, a diversion. . . .
> I see now that I had been incubating this death far longer than I recognized at the time. When I was a child, both my parents had half-heartedly put their heads in the gas-oven. Or so they claimed. . . .
> Maybe that is why, when I grew up and things went

particularly badly, I used to say to myself, over and over, "I wish I were dead." ...

Then one day I understood what I was saying. I was walking along the edge of Hampstead Heath after some standard domestic squabble, and suddenly I heard the phrase as though for the first time. I stood still to attend to the words. I repeated them slowly, listening. And realized that I meant it. ...

My life felt so cluttered and obstructed that I could hardly breathe. I inhabited a closed, concentrated world, airless and without exits. I doubt if any of this was noticeable socially ... I simply was tenser, more nervous than usual. ... But underneath I was going a bit mad. I had entered the closed world of suicide and my life was being lived for me by forces I couldn't control. ...

I remember that Christmas standing at the front door, joking with the guests as they left. "Happy Christmas," we call to each other. I closed the door and turned back to my wife.

After that, I remember nothing at all until I woke up in the hospital and saw my wife's face swimming vaguely towards me through a yellowish fog. She was crying. But that was three days later, three days of oblivion, a hole in my head. ...

As I reconstruct it I went upstairs to the bathroom and swallowed forty-five sleeping pills. I had been collecting the things for months obsessively, like Green Stamps. This was an almost legitimate activity since I rarely got more than two consecutive hours of sleep a night. But I had always made sure of having more than I needed. Weeks before ... I stopped taking the things and began hoarding them in preparation for the time I knew was coming. When it finally arrived, a box was waiting stuffed with pills in all colors, like M&M's. I gobbled the lot. ...

A week later, I returned to finish the university term. When I was packing, I found a large, bright yellow, torpedo-shaped pill. I stared at the thing, turning it over and over on my palm, wondering how I'd missed it on the night. It looked lethal. I had survived forty-five pills. Would forty-six have done it? I flushed the thing down the lavatory. ...

The truth is, in some way I had died. The over-intensity, the tiresome excess of sensitivity and self-consciousness, of arrogance and idealism, which came in adolescence and stayed on and on beyond their due time, had not survived the coma. It was as though I had finally, and sadly late in the day, lost my innocence. ...

Somehow, I felt, death had let me down; I had expected more of it. I had looked for something overwhelming, an experience which would clarify all my confusions. ... But all I had got was oblivion. To all intents and purposes, I had died: my face had been blue, my pulse erratic, my breathing ineffectual; the doctors

had given me up. I went to the edge and most of the way over; then gradually, unwillingly and despite everything, I inched my way back. And now I knew nothing at all about it. I felt cheated.

Months later, I began to understand that I had my answer, after all. The despair that led me to try to kill myself had been pure and unadulterated, like the final, unanswerable despair a child feels, with no before or after. And, childishly, I had expected death not merely to end it but also to explain it. ...

Once I had accepted that there weren't ever going to be any answers, even in death, I found to my surprise that I didn't much care whether I was happy or unhappy; "problems" and "the problem of problems" no longer existed. And that in itself is already the beginning of happiness [Alvarez, 1974, pp. 291–306].[10]

A number of themes can be picked out of Alvarez's description quite easily. For one, it is clear that Alvarez didn't just decide one day to kill himself. Quite the contrary, "I had been incubating this death far longer than I recognized. ... It was the one constant focus of my life. ... I had been collecting the [pills] for months." The only thing that was sudden was the realization that he could do it.

A second theme concerns the world as experienced before the attempt. It was a closed and suffocating world that contained only himself. Although this experience may have been noticed by others, Alvarez feels that socially he was only "tense [and] a bit more nervous than usual."

A third theme in this narrative is that the suicide attempt occurred during a holiday, Christmas, and during a vacation from work. The immediate event was a fight with his wife, but the fight had been part of a larger series of frequent fights. The "cause," however, was Alvarez's adolescent fantasy that death had all the answers.

As Alvarez was to find in the days and years after, death had "let him down"; there was no answer that would satisfy the adolescent *and* the adult, and so in the end he had to turn to living and give up the idea that there would ever be answers. Death and rebirth are possible only for the living.

Two further themes also deserve comment: one has to do with Alvarez's experience of time, the other with his experience of what was still possible

[10]From *The Savage God: A Study of Suicide*, by A. Alvarez. Copyright © 1974 by Random House, Inc., and Weidenfeld Publishers, Limited. This and all other quotations from this source are reprinted by permission.

for him to do. Time had "no before or after." Alvarez had lost his foothold in the past, and extension into the future could be considered only with difficulty. He was, in a word, stuck: stuck in a "closed, concentrated world" without possibility. Without hope and possibility the person is not alive, and the act of suicide is an inevitable and almost logical conclusion.

2. "Testimony" from other suicides. The description provided by Alvarez agrees with conclusions based on studies by more dispassionate observers. Although many "factors" have been listed (interpersonal crisis, failure and self-devaluation, anxiety and personal confusion, loss of meaning and hope, and others), the one sure thing about suicide is that it can only be seen "as an expression of the most catastrophic shock caused by the realization that existence is meaningless and impossible" (Goldstein, 1939, p. 446). In this it answers Camus' question: to die voluntarily is to have lost all hope that life is or will become meaningful.

Alvarez's description also agrees with the clinical observation that to attempt suicide is not necessarily to die. As of 1970, there were about 25,000 suicides a year in the United States, out of 225,000 attempts. Statistics also show that more women than men attempt suicide but that men complete the act between 4 and 10 times more often. One reason this occurs is that men usually use violent means of committing suicide, such as shooting, while women use less violent means, such as taking an overdose of sleeping pills. In cases of "failed suicide," perhaps Alvarez is right in feeling that something nonetheless dies, something that was holding the person back from living: in his case, a simplistic, romanticized view of himself and his world.

Although Alvarez did not leave a suicide note, about one-third of suicides do. About half of such notes contain what can only be called positive emotion: "Please forgive me. . . . I'll always love you. . . . All I ever had was you" (Tuckman, Kleiner, & Lavell, 1959). Only 6% of the notes are completely hostile in tone: "I hate you and all of your family . . . . I hope you never have peace of mind" (Tuckman et al., 1959). Neutral matter-of-fact statements occur ("I, Mary Smith, being of sound mind . . . make my last will as follows . . .") in about 25%, while about 18% contain a mixture of all three types of statements. The final communication of a person committing

suicide seems to shed no more light on the issue of suicide than any of the other approaches considered thus far.

Also in agreement with Alvarez, most suicides share the idea that death ought to provide an experience "capable of clarifying all of life's confusions." The research literature, derived from an analysis of suicide notes, agrees with Alvarez's conclusion that death by suicide is a cheat: it never provides a magic answer. After reading 220 suicide notes, Cohen and Fiedler (1974) feel that the romantic concept of suicide as a "window into the great mysteries of living and dying" is wrong. What they found were a great many references to the ordinary, daily events of human life. On this basis they concluded that the suicide note seems best considered a letter "tailored to the needs of both the suicide and his survivors as these are perceived by the person committing suicide at the time the act was undertaken" (p. 94).

Should we be disappointed that no mysteries are unraveled and that the last communication made by most suicides (among those who leave such a communication) contains so many references to the ordinary? Why is it that the experience of suicide is not nearly so grand as all of us might imagine it to be? The answer seems to be that there is a great difference between a disoriented person committing (or trying to commit) suicide and a somewhat thoughtful and perplexed person thinking about the meaning such an act might have. In one case the person is in disorder and disarray: all that is possible is nonbeing; there is nothing else. In the other case we have a person actively involved in trying to find meaning in his or her life. Here suicide is considered only in terms of its implications for living, never in terms of its implications for nonbeing. Is it any wonder that such a person chooses life? To wonder about the meaning of one's existence is already an affirmation (not a negation) of that existence, even though human existence is often brutal and senseless. After all, even Camus, who saw the problem most clearly, could do no better than affirm life, with all of its absurdity.

C. The politics of diagnosis
A psychiatric diagnosis, especially one concerned with determining whether a person is or is not sane, is not the statement of an objective fact, but a decision based on moral as well as professional

grounds. To say that someone is mad is to say that he or she is out of step with the world. In some cases, this conclusion is a fairly straightforward one: the person is not functioning well, either in dealing with friends and relatives or in dealing with his or her job.

Even when a person seems to be totally mad, R. D. Laing (1967) has suggested that the psychotic state may be an attempt at self-healing. The person has to retreat to rebuild herself if she is ever to have a chance at living a more satisfying life. As support for this point of view, Laing describes the case of one of his friends, Mary Barnes, who for a time resided in a treatment center in London called Kingsley Hall. Mary first came there, as she said, "to have a breakdown, to go back before I was born and come up again." To do this, she worked at an ordinary job during the day and literally went mad at Kingsley Hall at night:

> Life soon became quite fantastic. Every night at Kingsley Hall I tore off my clothes, feeling I had to be naked. I lay on the floor with my shits and water, smeared the walls with feces. Was wild and noisy about the house or sitting in a heap on the kitchen floor. Half-aware that I was going mad, there was the terror that I might not know what I was doing away, outside of Kingsley Hall.
>
> The tempo was increasing. Down, down, oh God, would I never break [Schatzman, 1971, pp. 256–257].[11]

According to Mary's report (as well as the report of others working at Kingsley Hall), she did get better: "Eventually, I 'came up'—was 'reborn'. I wanted new clothes, nothing black, the color I used to wear . . . I was coming out of the web, working free. Coming to know I was a separate, distinct person" [p. 263].

A description such as this makes exciting reading. Although it is undoubtedly true that some schizophrenic episodes can be described as attempts at personal reintegration, most episodes simply represent madness and woe for the person whose life is at issue. There is some truth to the view that a person has to be "undone" to remake herself, but most schizophrenics do not, unfortunately, seem to be Mary Barnes.

There is, however, a more general point to Laing's

view: schizophrenics, paranoids, and the whole long list of psychiatric categories are people, not categories. To be crazy is to live a different existence, and it is a question of contemporary moral judgment whether this different existence is to be encouraged or rejected. Laing obviously feels that schizophrenia is a journey to rebirth, and the job of the psychiatrist is to let it happen and to be there when the person needs him or her.

There are further implications to seeing the schizophrenic person as a person rather than as a schizophrenic, and no one has been more resourceful in trying to make these points than the psychiatrist Thomas Szasz. In a series of articles and books over the last 15 years and more, Szasz has repeatedly pointed out that being schizophrenic does not make you a nonperson. The person diagnosed as schizophrenic is still a member of society and, as such, has legal rights. For this reason, Szasz believes that neither the psychiatrist nor the judge should have any power to commit people to a hospital if they are not obviously dangerous to themselves or society. Too often a schizophrenic person is put away for the convenience of his or her family, not necessarily for his or her own therapeutic good.

Szasz also notes that a person who has committed a punishable crime and who is judged insane can be put away and never brought to trial. From one perspective, this is a kind act: the person didn't know what he was doing. From a different point of view, the person is being denied a fair trial and the possibility of a fixed repayment for the crime. A sane person committing a crime and found guilty is required to serve a sentence, and that is the end of it; the debt is cancelled. A psychotic, in contrast, may languish in a psychiatric hospital without a trial and without any chance to make restitution for the crime. Under this circumstance, the sentence is without end. Except in the most severe cases (in which the person does not seem to know at all what is going on), Szasz believes that trial and restitution ought to be asked of the insane as well as of the sane person. To be insane should not mean you lose your civil rights or responsibilities.

There is one further point to make in talking about schizophrenics as people-with-problems rather than as psychiatric "patients." Considering them "patients" is likely to mislead us into thinking of madness as a disease like pneumonia or tuberculosis. Under this guise, problems in living should be treatable, as other illnesses are, by bed rest and

---

[11]From "Madness and Morals," by M. Schatzman. In R. Boyers and R. Orroll (Eds.), *R. D. Laing and Anti-Psychiatry.* Copyright © 1971 by Skidmore College. Reprinted by permission.

pills; unfortunately, they are not. One reason psychiatrists tend to talk about severe problems in living as a "disease," Szasz thinks, is that this view shields them from their own lack of skill in dealing with madness. It also shields them from the more difficult problem of seeing madness as an example of "moral conflict in human relations."

In one early summary of his position, Szasz (1960) wrote:

> The myth of mental illness encourages us to believe that social intercourse would be harmonious, satisfying, and the secure basis of a "good life" were it not for the disrupting influences of mental illness. The potentiality for universal human happiness, in this form at least, seems to be but another example of the I-wish-it-were-true type of fantasy. This goal could be achieved if we had the courage and integrity to forego waging battles on false fronts, finding solutions for substitute problems—for instance, fighting the battle of stomach acid and chronic fatigue instead of facing up to a marital conflict.
>
> Our adversaries are not demons, witches, fate, or mental illness. We have no enemy whom we can fight, exorcise, or dispel by "cure." What we do have are problems in living. My argument is that mental illness is a myth, whose function it is to disguise and thus render more palatable the bitter pill of moral conflicts in human relations [p. 118].

Most psychiatrists, however, disagree with Laing's (and to a lesser extent with Szasz's) attitudes toward psychiatric diagnosis and treatment. The people they see on a day-to-day basis need help and seem not so much on a journey as lost and abandoned. Patients in a mental hospital are there not because they went on a trip to some mystic region that will enable them to be reborn but because they are disembodied and scared. It is the job of the psychiatrist and the hospital to help the psychotic person in whatever way possible given the person, the era, and the society. Although patients certainly should not be deprived of their rights, they should not be allowed to run around mad, either.

Thus, the decision to call someone mad (or sane) is not an easy one given by the unthinking use of a simple formula that is once and forever valid. Instead, it is always a social act done responsibly, we can only hope, by people who have made it their life's work to deal openly and reasonably with matters of human sanity. The decision is not arbitrary or mechanical; rather, it is the act of a specially trained person operating both within and above a particular social and historical context. In this, the definitions of *sane* and *insane* are no less products of human invention than the definition of *time* or *society*. Only if we recognize this can we see the schizophrenic person for what he or she is: a person and a schizophrenic. To lose sight of either is to render a decision that ignores its context—an act as irresponsible as it is immoral.

VI. SUMMARY

When looking at the various categories of "mental illness" described by psychologists, it is important to realize that these categories do not exist in the same sense that physical or chemical entities exist. Rather, personal problems can be defined only in terms of a dialectical relation between self and body, self and others, and self and society, with society usually defined by some specific psychologist or psychiatrist. As Szasz (1960) noted, there are no demons, witches, or even mental illnesses—only people with problems in living. Mental illness, understood in this way, concerns people whose mode of Being-in-the-world is defined by others as abnormal. Sometimes these modes are not seen as disordered or abnormal from the first-person perspective of the individual in question. There is a sociopolitical aspect to the definition of mental illness, and this fact must never be lost sight of.

The intimate relationship between self, body, and social world is illustrated quite well by psychosomatic disorders (as in the case of John Knight). These disorders include skin, musculoskeletal, cardiovascular, gastrointestinal, and other types of problems. The common quality shared by these various conditions is the unreflected expression of personal style (problems included) in dramatic bodily terms. In psychosomatic dysfunction, the stresses and strains of living are expressed for the person by and through the physical body.

Psychosomatic disorders take many forms. In the present chapter, two types—those involving the skin and the cardiovascular system—received particular consideration. The skin reacts quite dramatically and obviously to emotional states (as in blushing) and for this reason can serve to symbolize personal or even religious concerns quite directly. Cardiovascular reactions can also express a personal meaning, usually a response to stress. It follows that severe enough problems in living can kill the person by producing the cardiovascular reaction of heart attack or stroke. To measure the effects of perceived stress on health, Holmes and his coworkers developed a life-stress scale by asking people to assign numerical values to stressful life events. Research conducted by this group has supported a correlation between perceived stress and physical illness.

A different and less familiar context in which the role of personal stress can be seen concerns voodoo death. Although such occurrences seem quite impossible to Western eyes, careful field research has shown that a voodoo curse can kill if the victim (and his or her society) believes it can. A person under a curse is isolated from his or her social context, and personal surrender to the curse is not only possible but likely. Without social support, the person is open to a number of damaging psychosomatic reactions; the ensuing physical death only mirrors the sociopsychological death exacted by the curse in the first place.

Another class of personal disorder is illustrated by the case of Peter Oberman. Peter's obsession exemplifies the unreflected (and extreme) need for control characteristic of obsessive thinking. Although such action may tie up personal anxiety, it also has the consequence of tying up the person in his or her attempt to deal with the world in a spontaneous and open way. Obsessions are often accompanied by compulsive, ritualized behaviors, which are another way to control a world experienced as frightening. In both cases, the person splits himself or herself from the world by trading in a living, spontaneous existence for one in which reflection controls the world by isolating the person from it.

A so-called obsessional neurosis is only one of several categories of disordered behavior described by psychologists. These, more generally, can be described in terms of three different classes of problems: (1) distortions of one's relationship to the body, (2) problems with one's emotions, and (3) problems involving reflected activity. The person categorized as neurotic often exaggerates or distorts one of these ordinarily helpful aspects of living so that it becomes perverted and therefore out of contact with the world of everyday reality. Open and trusting relationships become impossible.

Schizophrenia is a third large category of personal woe; here the case of Joan Smith presents the relevant information. R. D. Laing, in his discussion of this case, has suggested that the person described

as schizophrenic has separated body from self and self from society. Since to act in (and on) the world requires a more integrated style of existence, Joan Smith would be described as a person who created a barrier between herself and the world by denying her body as a valid expression of herself. Joan's need to relive her early life can be interpreted as her attempt to unify self and body via the symbolic reexperiencing of a second childhood.

Although many types of psychoses have been distinguished, most can be accommodated in a single system involving only a few categories. Pure types of schizophrenia are rare; most cases involve a combination of types. One major category of psychotic behavior concerns mood disorders and includes the manic, the depressive, and the manic-depressive conditions. In addition to manic-depressive and schizophrenic reaction, a third category of psychosis is paranoia. Freud is said to have termed paranoia "the most perfect form of psychosis" largely because it allows the person to deal with his or her problems by means of a complex system of delusions without incapacitating him or her in other areas of living. Delusional styles are generally either ones of grandeur or of persecution; the former is more difficult for the clinician to work with than the latter. In general, it seems best to describe paranoid disorders as the person's attempt to construct an ordered world in which he or she can feel at ease.

The case of Ferdinand W. Demara, Jr., presents the idiosyncratic and often antisocial pursuits of a psychopathic personality. The psychopath ignores conventional rules and, if we are uncritical, can seem to transcend the (over) controlled life-style each of us experiences at times. Psychopathy, however, is not an answer to the constraints of social organization; rather, it represents an abuse of other people's rights. When the world of the psychopath is explored more carefully, we find it consists only of an instantaneous present with no sensible unfolding in time. Within this world, other people lose their rights, so that in the end the psychopath denies the existence of the world except insofar as it benefits himself or herself.

One common denominator that seems to apply across all areas of "not making it" is the issue of personal fragmentation. Such fragmentation lends itself to disorientation in one's dealing with the social and personal world and often co-occurs with severe anxiety. In this, anxiety may be understood as an expression of the fearful possibility of total personal disintegration—that is, the possibility of personal nonbeing.

Anxiety can be dealt with in two ways: the person can accept and try to deal with the anxiety or can try to defend himself or herself against the experience. In this second strategy, the person will use procedures called defense mechanisms to reduce the anxiety produced by the threat of nonbeing. Although anxiety is often considered something to be avoided, dealing with anxiety in a productive way can lead to growth, especially if the person is not overwhelmed by the experience and allows himself or herself to work through the issue involved.

The threat of nonbeing can also be discussed in terms of *Angst*, or existential dread, brought about by knowing that eventually I will die. We all have to deal with a sense of purposelessness or helplessness from time to time, but the person contemplating suicide experiences hopelessness to a much greater degree. Although suicide is a complicated topic, its meaning for some people can perhaps be read in statistics. For example, in 1970, statistics indicated that only one out of nine suicide attempts was successful. Four to ten times as many men as women succeeded in the attempt. In general, it seems that suicide is not necessarily an attempt to find an answer to the meaninglessness of one's life—an answer it cannot provide—but a personal reaction to the frustrations of everyday living. An examination of suicide notes often confirms this conclusion.

Although some theorists (such as Laing) have attempted to describe psychiatric disorders as an attempt by the person to build a more satisfying style of living, most individuals judged as falling within one or another psychiatric category are ineffective in dealing with themselves and their worlds. Still, diagnosis is not an objectifiable fact and is always the result of someone's personal evaluation of the individual under consideration. While some diagnoses may have sociopolitical motivations, most simply suggest that a given life-style is unsatisfactory for the person whose problem is being diagnosed.

In this more general context, Szasz has argued that a person judged "mentally ill" need (and should) not automatically become a nonperson, nor should the person be deprived of legal rights accorded others. In this regard, the use of the medical model is misleading, as it implies an ability to cure objectifiable biological diseases and disguises the fact that personal disorder is as much a social as an individual process. Only if we keep these larger issues in mind will we be able to remember that the person labeled "mentally ill" is still a person—not simply an example of one or another diagnostic category.

VII. GLOSSARY OF IMPORTANT CONCEPTS

Anxiety. An unpleasant and often unspecified emotional experience that has no definite focus or specific anchor.

Compulsion. An irresistible impulse or ritualized act usually done repetitively.

Death. In existential theory, a state of nonbeing. A condition for existential anxiety, known as *Angst*.

Defense mechanisms. As described by Freud, ways of avoiding and/or coping with anxiety. These include such processes as repression and projection.

Disembodied self. The term used by R. D. Laing to describe a schizophrenic mode of Being-in-the-world in which the "self" is experienced as separated from other people as well as from the person's own body.

Fear. An unpleasant emotional experience tied to a particular event, object, or situation, which is perceived as threatening.

Manic-depressive. A category of psychotic behavior in which a person's actions alternate between depression and mania.

Neurosis. A class of psychological problems in living in which the person is often unable to deal with aspects of his or her day-to-day world. Not as severe a class of reactions as psychosis. Some of the major categories are:

  Anxiety. Diffuse but often severe anxiety not referable to a particular situation or threat.

  Phobic. A fear which the person may realize is irrational but from which he or she cannot free himself or herself.

  Hysterical. Consists of two subtypes: (1) a conversion type with symptoms of physical illness, such as paralysis or loss of hearing, without underlying physical pathology and (2) a dissociative type, which includes such reactions as amnesia and multiple personality.

  Hypochondriacal. Preoccupation with one's bodily functioning and various presumed diseases.

  Neurasthenic. Chronic fatigue, weakness, and/or lack of enthusiasm.

Depressive. Abnormally prolonged dejection associated with personal conflict, interpersonal loss, or environmental setback.

Obsession. A persistent preoccupation with an idea or feeling. Often used to control a world otherwise experienced as disordered and frightening.

Obsessive. A style of being in which the person experiences the world as a frightening place that must be controlled and mastered in any way possible, often by continuous reflection.

Paranoia. A type of psychotic Being-in-the-world in which the person develops a highly systematized pattern of delusions. Such delusions do not get in the way of dealing with day-to-day events unless the delusional system becomes an issue of discussion or concern.

Phobia. An irrational, morbid fear usually centered on a particular object or event.

Psychopathic. A style of being in which the person relates to the world in an antisocial way, seemingly not subject to conventional rules of society.

Psychophysiologic disorder. A bodily reaction that often reveals (or is symbolic of) an emotional event in a disordered life.

Psychotic Being-in-the-world. A (psychiatric) category for the most debilitating ways people come to deal with problems in living. Generally described as consisting of three subtypes: schizophrenia, mood disorders, and paranoia.

Religious stigmatization. A bodily reaction in which the person displays certain skin reactions (such as bleeding) that recall the crucifixion of Christ.

Schizophrenia. A class of psychiatric disorders marked by loss of contact with the world of everyday reality, personal disintegration, and (often) hallucinations. Some major categories are these:

Acute. Characterized by a sudden onset of symptoms, involving turmoil and confusion; a total breakdown of personal functioning.

Paranoid. The person is dominated by nonrational and changeable delusions, frequently accompanied by hallucination.

Catatonic. Characterized by periods of withdrawal and excitement; one or the other state may predominate.

Hebephrenic. A severely disorganized state, sometimes involving inappropriate laughter, peculiar mannerisms, and/or bizarre actions.

Simple. The person shows a continuous downhill loss of clear thinking, feeling, and doing, beginning early in life and gradually getting worse until the person can be described as inaccessible to others.

Latent. Characterized by various long-standing symptoms but lacking full-blown schizophrenic history or behavior.

Chronic undifferentiated. The person is not clearly classifiable into any one of the other categories although he or she definitely shows irrational and personally disturbing types of thinking, feeling, and doing.

Voodoo. A body of superstitious beliefs and practices including sorcery and magical rites.

Voodoo death. Death brought about by a voodoo curse. The direct "cause" is the victim's and a society's belief in the power of voodoo ritual.

VIII. SUGGESTED READINGS

Major sources

Fischer, W. F. *Theories of anxiety.* New York: Harper & Row, 1970.

Keen, E. *Three faces of being: Toward an existential clinical psychology.* New York: Appleton-Century-Crofts, 1970.

Laing, R. D. *The divided self.* Harmondsworth, England: Penguin Books, 1965.

Secondary sources

Coleman, J. C. *Abnormal psychology and modern life* (5th ed.). Glenview, Ill.: Scott, Foresman, 1976.

Kisker, G. W. *The disorganized personality* (2nd ed.). New York: McGraw-Hill, 1972.

14

Making It Better: The Nature and Possibilities of Psychotherapy

Almost everyone who has ever sought psychotherapy has begun with a great many questions and worries. Each of us seems to start out by asking "What am I doing here?," and when the answer comes back "You need it, friend, you need it," we generally change to more practical questions, such as "I wonder what it will be like to be in therapy?," "I wonder how other people will feel about me when they find out?," and, perhaps most important, "Will I be a different person when I finish?"

The prospect of psychotherapy can be unsettling, especially if you think it will remake you into a completely new person. The purpose of **psychotherapy** is not to remake you or turn you into something you were not; instead, it is to help you change in ways that were not possible for you when you weren't making it. Psychotherapy never forces anyone to do anything he or she doesn't want to do. It is not a magical process: you have to want to change, and you have to help it along.

But what happens when you go for psychotherapy? What does the therapist do, what do you do, and how does what happens happen? To get some feeling for what goes on in psychotherapy, ask yourself what you would do if someone asked you to help her work out some problem she was having. First, you would probably want to talk with the person to get some idea of the problem. Once you thought you understood the problem a bit, you would probably want to find out what kind of person you were dealing with: what were her skills and liabilities, how did she approach doing certain things, and how might she do them differently? Finally you would get down to the business of trying to help the person work out her problem.

This state of affairs is similar to what happens in psychotherapy. To begin with, there is an **initial interview**. During this interview, the therapist and patient try to get their bearings; they try to find out what the problem is and what the person coming for help might want and might be able to do about it. The person then is sometimes given a battery of psychological tests to find out something about the person's strengths and weaknesses as well as to give a quick initial perspective into how the person deals with and experiences his or her world. Once the tests provide what insights they can, the therapist and person come together to begin the process of therapy itself. Depending on the type of therapist, he or she may (or may not) explicitly share impressions derived from the test material.

Psychotherapy can be talked about as if it consisted of three parts: an initial interview, a psychological evaluation, and therapy itself. Although not all the various types of therapy use exactly this sequence, all do have to make an initial contact, and all do make a preliminary evaluation before moving on to the more demanding and time-consuming activity of helping the person come to some better way of dealing with his or her life. Obviously, not all the parts are equally important, nor do they all take the same amount of time. The initial interview and psychological evaluation together usually take only a few days; therapy takes a good deal longer, sometimes weeks, sometimes months, and sometimes even years.

I. THE INITIAL INTERVIEW

What is the first interview like? That depends on who the therapist is. For example, some therapists get started right away and assume that if you are there, you have already made the decision to get help for yourself. Other therapists are more cautious and try to find out whether you know how long and how expensive treatment is likely to be. Still other therapists do not interview you at first; instead the first session is devoted to record taking and concerns such things as your age, your marital status, and your occupation. Sometimes the initial interview is done by a psychiatric social worker rather than by the person who will later become your therapist.

Regardless of the therapist, the first session is designed to allow each person to find out what the other is like. In addition to providing some small hint about what is likely to happen in therapy, the initial interview is also a time when patient and therapist begin to build a relationship. Sometimes if the initial session does not seem to be working, either the patient or the therapist may decide not to go ahead. Psychotherapy is a long and personal relationship, and it just will not work if there is no mutuality between participants. Although patient and therapist do not have to be totally committed to each other, there does have to be a strong enough bond for therapy to continue.

In the first session most therapists do a lot of listening and only a bit of questioning. In the more classic style of psychotherapy, the therapist sees his or her job as attempting to form "a working clinical . . . diagnosis" (Colby, 1951) and to teach the patient what psychotherapy will be like in subsequent sessions. How this happens can be seen in the following excerpts from an initial psychotherapy session (Colby, 1951). The patient is a 26-year-old businessman named Tom who was referred to the therapist because of severe anxiety and a persistent fear of ulcers. (The patient is not John Knight.)

Therapist: Well, where shall we start?
Tom: [Smiling but uneasy] I'm not sure. Perhaps I should go back a little when I got these stomach things. They came on about six months ago. I was working hard and had a lot on my mind. I began to notice sort of a clutching sensation in the pit of my stomach, like something had suddenly clamped tight. I went to the doctor and he advised X-rays to look for an ulcer. The X-rays . . .
Therapist: You said you were under a lot of pressure when this began. Anything else besides your job? [pp. 72–73].[1]

Tom then tells the therapist that some of his "pressure" was coming from a continuing disagreement he and his wife have over how often to have sex. He seems to want it every day; she, two or three times a month. When they argue over this matter, his stomach tightens and he becomes quite anxious. As Tom talks, the therapist notes that he fidgets and, in the therapist's words, looks "angry and bitter." In thinking about this session, the therapist notes some things he wants to remember for future reference: (1) the wife is an important part of Tom's problem, (2) Tom seems to want sexual activity very frequently, and (3) Tom's stomach is the most affected body part.

Following the opening discussion, the therapist turns to a bit of history. Specifically, he asks Tom to describe how he met his wife. This particular thera-

[1] From *A Primer for Psychotherapists*, by K. M. Colby. Copyright 1951 by Ronald Press Company, a division of John Wiley & Sons, Inc. This and all other quotations from this source are reprinted by permission.

pist happens to be a psychoanalyst, and, in general, psychoanalysts do not record a systematic history but consider each item as it comes up and, if it appears significant, explore it briefly.

In describing how he met his wife, Tom reports an interesting fact. Before he was married, Tom was a heavy drinker although only after working hours. Each night he would go out and get drunk. In the beginning, Tom told his girlfriend, later his wife, that he didn't want to get married. One night he passed out and, on coming to, found himself in jail, charged with disorderly conduct. This scared him so badly that he decided to settle down to a more stable life. The next day he proposed marriage.

Therapist: And was the sexual problem present from the first?
Tom: Oh, yes. Even before we were married we tried intercourse and I knew she had trouble enjoying it. But I thought she would get over it as time went by [p. 74].

Thus, it is quite clear that Tom married with full knowledge of his wife's attitude toward sex. He seems to have married in the hope that leading a stable life would help overcome other problems, problems that till then were handled by getting drunk.

Although there are a great many types of therapists, the opening session just described is fairly typical. The patient has made contact with the therapist and has shared some of his history and his concerns with him. To be sure, there are still uncertainty and conflict and maybe even a little fear about what will happen next. At the same time, there is the pleasant surprise that therapy won't be terrible, and for the first time there may be a glimmering of hope: "My problems can be worked through. It won't be easy, but at least I'm doing something and I do have some confidence in my therapist. I hope it keeps up."

But what of the therapist: what does he or she experience in dealing with the patient? One therapist described her concerns as follows (Fitts, 1965, p. 59):

Who am I to be entering into this person's life in such an intimate and, what will probably be, painful way? Will this make a difference in his life, the difference he is wanting? Will I be able to feel and think enough with him? What am I bringing to this experience that will be helpful, and what may not be helpful? How can we use my weaknesses, as well as my strengths, in a therapeutic way?

Questions such as these come to me in one form or another as I meet the new client. Why these questions about myself instead of concentrating on the person sitting in the other chair? Are these self-doubts? It is because I am beginning a new relationship, a relationship which is the agent of the therapeutic process that the person has come seeking. In order for the process to be a creative change, therapeutic, it has to be a living part of reality. I must be real in this relationship. In it I am myself and I act in the service of the client. During the hour in which we are together my total resources are his to use in his therapy. I need, therefore, to have my own feelings and thoughts as material for him, when it is appropriate, as well as to focus on his feelings and thoughts. I look forward to working together with this person in a unique relationship that is designed for his benefit. I know I cannot make him well. My job is to give what I can and to know that he is what he can become. So, the questions are part of my preparation for a new yet familiar experience. And I am glad for the opportunity to meet another person in such a special way.[2]

Like the patient, this therapist experiences uncertainty and doubt, and she is glad for the opportunity to provide hope for another human being.

II. PSYCHOLOGICAL EVALUATION

After the initial interview, many therapists ask the person to take a battery of psychological tests; this step is the **psychological evaluation.** Such tests fall into two major groups. In one set the scoring depends heavily on statistical analysis of how the person does compared with a great many people who have taken the test; in the second it depends more on an individual reading of some fairly unstructured and even ambiguous materials. Tests of the first type, in which an individual's performance is compared with a statistically derived average value, are called **psychometric tests;** those of the second type are called **projective tests.** This division is really too sharply drawn, for projective tests can be evaluated statistically and psychometric tests can be used projectively. As a first step, however, such a grouping will help organize the vast number of tests that psychologists use.

[2]From *The Experience of Psychotherapy,* by W. H. Fitts. Copyright 1965 by Van Nostrand Reinhold Company. This and all other quotations from this source are reprinted by permission of the author.

A. *Psychometric tests*

1. IQ tests. The granddaddy of all psychometric tests is the intelligence test. Although everyone seems to take a good shot at the limitations of intelligence tests (and there are many), such tests have been constructed with care and do make sense if used with care.

The first intelligence tests were constructed by Alfred Binet in Paris and imported to the United States by several psychologists. The most extensive work on the English-language version of the test was done by Lewis Terman of Stanford University, and the earliest such test was therefore called the Stanford-Binet test.

The abbreviation *IQ* stands for *intelligence quotient* and tells a good deal about the way the idea of intelligence was first dealt with. The idea of an intelligence quotient was originally suggested by William Stern, who defined it as mental age (MA) divided by chronological age (CA) times 100 (the MA/CA fraction is multiplied by 100 to get rid of decimals). Thus IQ was defined as:

$$IQ = MA/CA \times 100$$

Chronological age is easy to define: it is simply the person's age in years or months. **Mental age,** however, is not quite so easy. Most work came to define MA in terms of the ability of a group of similar-aged children to solve a problem. For example, if 50% of 2½-year-old children can repeat two digits correctly after hearing the examiner say them, a child completing this task will have an MA of 30 months (2½ years) on this task. Similarly, if 50% of all 7-year-old children can solve the analogy "Brother is a boy; sister is a _____," a child passing this item would get credit for an MA of 84 months on this task.

Since all tests are age-graded, a child's MA is defined in terms of how many items from each age level he or she passes. Suppose a child 4 years 2 months old (CA = 50 months) passed all six of the age-3 items, five of six age-3½ items, three of the six age-4 items, two of the six age-4½ items, two of the six age-5 items, and two of the six age-5½ items. Since the child passed all the age-3 items, he or she would get credit for an MA of 36 months. If we add 1 month for each of the remaining items (5 + 3 + 2 + 2 + 2), we get 14 more months of credit. Adding this to the 36 months of credit earned for the age-3 items produces a total MA of 50 months (4 years 2 months). Since the child's CA was 50 months, the total IQ value is given in the following fraction:

$$IQ = MA/CA \times 100 = 50/50 \times 100 = 100$$

An IQ of 100 means the child can do a great many activities that other children of his or her age do. If the IQ measure does what it is supposed to, most children will get scores of about 100, a somewhat smaller number will get scores of 90 or 110, a still smaller number will get scores of 80 or 120, and so on. When Terman and Merrill gave the Stanford-Binet test to almost 3000 children aged 2–18, they found that the scores produced the curve shown in Figure 14-1. As expected, the majority of children fell in the interval from 85 to 114. (The percentage of cases falling between 85 and 94 was 18%; 24% of cases fell between 95 and 104; 20% fell between 105 and 114. All in all, 62% of the cases fell between 85 and 114.)

A second look at Figure 14-1 will show why a curve such as this one is called a bell-shaped curve. One of the nice things about a bell-shaped curve is that we know a great deal about its statistical properties. In general, bell-shaped curves describe most

situations in which we look at some event or trait that varies around an average value. Because results for the Stanford-Binet test have been found to take this form, Stanford-Binet IQ scores can be interpreted in terms of the statistical definitions shown in Table 14-1.

TABLE 14-1. Interpretation of Intelligence Quotients on the Stanford-Binet

IQ	Verbal Description	Percentage in each group
Above 139	Very superior	1
120–139	Superior	11
110–119	High average	18
90–109	Average	46
80–89	Low average	15
70–79	Borderline	6
Below 70	Mentally retarded	3
		100%

From *Introduction to Psychology*, (6th ed.), by Ernest R. Hilgard, Richard C. Atkinson, and Rita L. Atkinson. © 1975 by Harcourt Brace Jovanovich, Inc. Reprinted by permission of the publisher.

The Stanford-Binet test has a number of disadvantages, even from a statistical point of view. For one, the test has an age ceiling: it probably should not be used for people older than 14 or 15. More important, however, is the fact that passing or failing one kind of item (for example, a verbal one) is scored the same as passing or failing a different kind of item (for example, a mathematical one). Thus, a test of this kind can only provide an overall score. Even though it is possible to look at how well a child did on the vocabulary part of the test compared with the logical reasoning or remembering tasks, the Binet is not set up to measure separate intellectual abilities. Finally, more meaningful use can be made of the fact that IQ test scores distribute themselves in the form of a bell-shaped curve than was done with the original test.

Although revisions of the Stanford-Binet since 1960 have taken this last fact into account, it was David Wechsler who developed the first statistically rigorous intelligence tests for use with adults. In addition to the Wechsler Adult Intelligence Scale (WAIS), Wechsler developed, along similar lines, the Wechsler Intelligence Scale for Children (WISC) and its revision (WISC-R). Even though Wechsler used many items similar to Binet's, he grouped his test

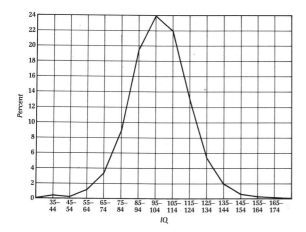

Figure 14-1. Distribution of IQ scores for 2904 children tested by Terman and Merrill. (*From* Measuring Intelligence, *by L. M. Terman and M. A. Merrill. Copyright 1937 by Houghton Mifflin Company. Reprinted by permission.*)

items into two large subareas: Verbal and Performance. Table 14-2 summarizes the 11 tests making up the WAIS (and the WISC), classifying them as primarily verbal- or performance-oriented.

With a test such as the WAIS it is easy to find more than just a total IQ score. What is particularly helpful is that it is possible to look at a person's pattern of intellectual strengths and abilities and from this to draw conclusions not only or even primarily about the person's "intelligence" but about what the person is like as he or she approaches intellectual tasks. Using an analysis of the subtest profile produced by a particular person, the tester is often able to describe a person, not just a score.

2. An example of psychometric evaluation.
But how is this to be done? Consider the WAIS profile in Figure 14-2. This profile was produced by an 18-year-old named Charles who was sent by his school counselor because he wanted to become an

electrical engineer but had taken a commercial course in high school and had failed bookkeeping.

While taking the WAIS, Charles maintained a steady interest in all the tasks although he said the testing made him nervous. He spoke in a high, strained voice, rushed through timed tests, and was constantly dissatisfied with how he was doing. He recognized that his drive for perfection was a bit disabling.

On the WAIS he achieved ratings of "Superior" intellectual ability on the Verbal, Performance, and Full-Scale scores. Although his scores on all subtests were at least average, there was some variation. His score on Information was a bit low, considering all his other scores. His high score on the Similarities subtest showed exceptional ability in dealing with abstract concepts. His general comprehension was also superior, as was his performance on arithmetic reasoning. In solving some of the arithmetical problems he appeared tense but nonetheless performed rapidly.

TABLE 14-2. Composition of the Wechsler Adult Intelligence Scale and Some Examples

Test	Description
VERBAL SCALE	
Information	Questions tap general range of information—for example, "How many weeks in a year?"
Comprehension	Tests practical information and ability to evaluate past experience—for example, "How would you find your way out if lost in a forest?"
Arithmetic	Verbal problems testing arithmetic reasoning.
Similarities	Asks in what way certain objects or concepts (such as *egg* and *seed*) are similar; measures abstract thinking.
Digit Span	Series of digits presented auditorily (for example, 7-5-6-3-8) are repeated in a forward or backward direction. Tests attention and rote memory.
Vocabulary	Tests word knowledge.
PERFORMANCE SCALE	
Digit Symbol	A timed coding task in which numbers must be associated with marks of various shapes; tests speed of learning and writing.
Picture Completion	The missing part of an incompletely drawn picture must be discovered and named; tests visual alertness and visual memory.
Block Design	Pictured designs must be copied with blocks; tests ability to perceive and analyze patterns.
Picture Arrangement	A series of comic-strip-type pictures must be arranged in the right sequence to tell a story; tests understanding of social situations.
Object Assembly	Puzzle pieces must be assembled to form a complete object, such as a human profile or elephant; tests ability to deal with part/whole relationships.

From *Introduction to Psychology*, (6th ed.), by Ernest R. Hilgard, Richard C. Atkinson, and Rita L. Atkinson. © 1975 by Harcourt Brace Jovanovich, Inc. Reprinted by permission of the publisher.

Table of Scaled Score Equivalents — Raw Score

Scaled Score	Information	Comprehension	Arithmetic	Similarities	Digit span	Vocabulary	Digit symbol	Picture completion	Block design	Picture arrangement	Object assembly	Scaled Score
19	29	27–28		26	17	78–80	87–90					19
18	28	26		25		76–77	83–86	21		36	44	18
17	27	25	18	24		74–75	79–82		48	35	43	17
16	26	24	17	23	16	71–73	76–78	20	47	34	42	16
15	25	23	16	22	15	67–70	72–75		46	33	41	15
14	23–24	22	15	21	14	63–66	69–71	19	44–45	32	40	14
13	21–22	21	14	19–20		59–62	66–68	18	42–43	30–31	38–39	13
12	19–20	20	13	17–18	13	54–58	62–65	17	39–41	28–29	36–37	12
11	17–19	19	12	15–16	12	47–53	58–61	15–16	35–38	26–27	34–35	11
10	15–16	17–18	11	13–14	11	40–46	52–57	14	31–34	23–25	31–33	10
9	13–14	15–16	10	11–12	10	32–39	47–51	12–13	28–30	20–22	28–30	9
8	11–12	14	9	9–10		26–31	41–46	10–11	25–27	18–19	25–27	8
7	9–10	12–13	7–8	7–8	9	22–25	35–40	8–9	21–24	15–17	22–24	7
6	7–8	10–11	6	5–6	8	18–21	29–34	6–7	17–20	12–14	19–21	6
5	5–6	8–9	5	4		14–17	23–28	5	13–16	9–11	15–18	5
4	4	6–7	4	3	7	11–13	18–22	4	10–12	8	11–14	4
3	3	5	3	2		10	15–17	3	6–9	7	8–10	3
2	2	4	2	1	6	9	13–14	2	3–5	6	5–7	2
1	1	3	1		4–5	8	12	1	2	5	3–4	1
0	0	0–2	0	0	0–3	0–7	0–11	0	0–1	0–4	0–2	0

Summary

TEST	Scaled score
Information	10
Comprehension	13
Arithmetic	13
Similarities	16
Digit span	11
Vocabulary	12
Verbal score	
Digit symbol	13
Picture completion	12
Block design	16
Picture arrangement	16
Object assembly	13
Performance score	
Total score	

VERBAL SCORE _75_ IQ _121_

PERFORMANCE SCORE _70_ IQ _126_

FULL SCALE SCORE _145_ IQ _127_

Figure 14–2. Profile for Wechsler Adult Intelligence Scale (WAIS). Test scores for an 18-year-old male. The table on the right shows these test scores combined to give a verbal, performance, and full-scale score. *(Wechsler Adult Intelligence Scale (WAIS) from* The Measurement and Appraisal of Adult Intelligence, *Fourth Edition, by D. Wechsler. Copyright © 1958. Reprinted by permission of Oxford University Press, Inc.)*

His highest scores, however, were on the Performance part of the WAIS, most particularly on the Picture Arrangement and Block Design subtests. On the former he was quick to recognize and understand the situation and to interpret what was going on. On the Block Design he completed the tasks rapidly although he did fumble occasionally because of his eagerness.

Overall, Charles' performance on the Wechsler test placed him in the Superior category of intellectual functioning in both Verbal and Performance areas. His handling of the various tests was hampered a bit by some self-doubt, but he was well able to maintain a responsive and flexible style of dealing with the test (paraphrased from Wechsler, 1958, pp. 233–234).

On the basis of these test results and the examiner's generally positive attitude toward Charles, he was counseled to return to school. He was also encouraged to take an academic course and to try to become an engineer, as he had planned.

The case of Charles is not unusual. Most skilled examiners are more interested in Charles as a person than in Charles as a test score. The IQ number is really much less important than how Charles went about doing the various subtests. Although an IQ is given, a skilled examiner (as well as a skilled reader of an IQ-test score) is always interested in the person producing the score. As Fischer (1978) points out in her review of intelligence testing, even Binet warned that "scores on psychological tests should not be taken more seriously than school achievement, that the child's way of reasoning should be observed and that the statistical techniques should not be more sophisticated than . . . the phenomenon being measured" (p. 206).

3. The MMPI. Despite Binet's approach, many people are interested in the statistical definition of such terms as *intelligence* or even *personality*. Although a statistical approach to evaluating human beings may have begun with IQ tests, probably the best-known statistically defined test is used not in intelligence testing but in personality assessment.

This test is the Minnesota Multiphasic Personality Inventory (MMPI).

The one characteristic that sets the MMPI off from almost any other test is the totally statistical way it was developed. The authors of this test selected items by statistical methods from a larger original pool of items. These items are questions about how people feel about certain things, how they act in certain situations, what "symptoms" they have, and so on. All 566 items were administered to groups of people who had unequivocally been judged as falling into diagnostic categories such as schizophrenic, psychopathic, or hysterical (see Chapter 13). Another group of men and women, matched on age and social class to these patients, also answered the same questions. Only those items producing a clear difference between "patient" and "normal" groups were kept for use in the final scale. For example, a test item that tended to get a positive response from hysterical patients but not from matched "normal" respondents would be included as an item on the Hysteria scale of the MMPI.

The MMPI has 14 scales, nine of which deal with obvious clinical categories (Table 14-3 lists all 14). Of the remaining scales, one, the Masculinity-Femininity scale, is used to distinguish between so-called male and female interests; the four others seek to determine whether the person is evading the test (?), lying (L), being careless, faking sick, or responding randomly (F), or being extremely defensive (K). In short, these four scales are designed to find out whether the person is answering the test honestly.

To see exactly how the MMPI works in two cases, look at Figure 14-3. The top figure shows the scores of a group of psychotic patients compared with a nonhospitalized group of people; the bottom figure contrasts delinquent and nondelinquent individuals. The differences are clear and substantial. As should also be obvious, the "psychotic" and "delinquent" profiles differ, as they should.

In the MMPI we have the ultimate in a psychometrically developed personality test. It seems reasonable, however, to wonder whether the MMPI is totally devoid of human subjectivity; that is, is it totally a product of statistical manipulations? Although every item was scrupulously checked to see how well it divided hysterical or depressed or psy-

TABLE 14-3. The Scales of the MMPI

Scale	Interpretation
TESTING SCALES:	
Question (?)	A high score indicates evasiveness.
Lie (L)	Persons trying to present themselves in a favorable light (as, for example, good, wholesome, honest) obtain high L-scale elevations.
Faking (F)	High scores suggest carelessness, confusion, or "faking bad."
Correction (K)	An elevation on the K scale suggests a defensive test-taking attitude. Exceedingly low scores may indicate a lack of ability to deny symptomatology.
CLINICAL SCALES:	
Hypochondriasis (Hs)	High scorers have been described as cynical, defeatist, and crabbed.
Depression (D)	High scorers usually are shy, despondent, and distressed.
Hysteria (Hy)	High scorers tend to complain of multiple symptoms.
Psychopathic Deviate (Pd)	Adjectives used to describe some high scorers are adventurous, courageous, and generous.
Masculinity-Femininity (Mf)	Among males, high scorers have been described as esthetic and sensitive. High-scoring women have been described as rebellious, unrealistic, and indecisive.
Paranoia (Pa)	High scorers on this scale were characterized as shrewd, guarded, and worrisome.
Psychasthenia (Pt)	Fearful, rigid, anxious, and worrisome are some of the adjectives used to describe high Pt scorers.
Schizophrenia (Sc)	Adjectives such as withdrawn and unusual describe high Sc scorers.
Hypomania (Ma)	High scorers are called sociable, energetic, and impulsive.
Social Introversion (Si)	High scorers: modest, shy, and self-effacing. Low scorers: social, colorful, and ambitious.

From *Personality Measurement: An Introduction*, by B. Kleinmuntz. Copyright 1967 by The Dorsey Press. Reprinted by permission of the author.

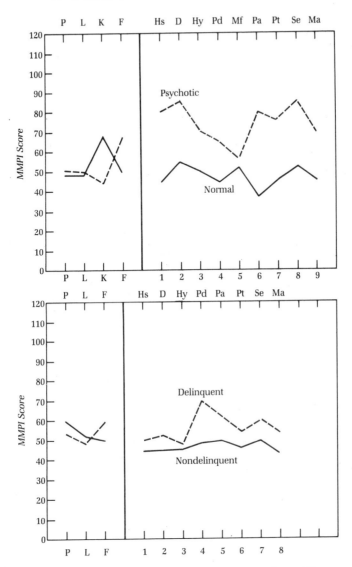

Figure 14-3. MMPI profiles for psychotic and normal groups and for delinquent and nondelinquent groups. *(Top: From* Contributions toward Medical Psychology, *Volume 2, by A. Weider. Copyright 1953 by The Ronald Press Company. Reprinted by permission of the author. Bottom: From* Analyzing and Predicting Juvenile Delinquency with the MMPI, *by S. R. Hathaway and E. D. Monachesi. Copyright 1953 by the University of Minnesota Press. Reprinted by permission.)*

chopathic patients from normals, it seems clear that before the final set of test items was selected, somebody's prestatistical knowledge about what types of people would fall into the various categories had to be used to write items in the first place. The statistical analysis of items only served as a check on the pretest intuitions of a person familiar with the world of the neurotic and psychotic. Behind the

statistical magic used to develop the MMPI are the intuitions of sensitive and perceptive clinicians who knew what madness and woe were long before they wrote test items about them. Objective assessment was the final step, not the inspiration, for the MMPI.

Even though subjectivity has sneaked in for the test *maker*, what about the test *taker?* Is he or she nothing more than a pebble to be cast into an appropriate container? According to many proponents of MMPI-type tests, the answer is yes; a person has to be categorized before he or she can be worked with, and whether we like it or not, that's the way things are with the MMPI.

B. Person-oriented testing

Must we conclude that a person-oriented psychologist will hardly ever use such tests as the MMPI, the Stanford-Binet, or the WISC because they dehumanize the person into a statistically defined object? In her attempt to seek a more positive (and useful) stance toward the use of psychological testing, Constance Fischer of Duquesne University has advised us to restore the person to the testing situation and to get rid of the idea that the person being tested is nothing but an object being measured.

Fischer's approach to psychological testing involves several stages. Let us suppose that she has been asked by a school to find out "what a child's IQ is." Before she does anything else, she is likely to try to find out what events led to the referral. Unfortunately, a teacher will often tell her something like "This student didn't do as well as I expected on his social-studies achievement test, and I thought maybe I had overestimated his intelligence." Even though this seems a reasonable statement, the teacher isn't talking about a child but about some entity (a student) who did not fit a category (his predicted social-studies achievement level) because he did not have as much of something (intelligence) as the teacher expected.

Because Fischer is interested in children and not in IQ or achievement, she is likely to ask what the teacher experiences in dealing with the child. Here the teacher might say "The real problem is I don't know whether to encourage him to try harder or to tell him that he's doing a good job." At this point Fischer is likely to ask the teacher to give some specific examples of when the student met or exceeded her expectations and when he did not.

In one particular case, the teacher was able to tell Fischer that Danny Sanders did quite well in group projects, in homework assignments he could check with his mother, and in classroom discussions. But he didn't seem to do at all well when left alone. Specifically, he didn't do well in writing a book report by himself, nor did he do well on standardized tests. Given this understanding, Fischer (1978, p. 218) went on to note:

The teacher and I agreed that the referral . . . should be revised to explore with Daniel Sanders the meaning of working by himself; develop ways in which he could be encouraged to extend his active participation in groups to his independent work. Note that IQ as such is no longer an issue. Even had Daniel been working below grade expectancy across the board, I would try to put his performance into a specific context to expand whatever already is working for him into other contexts.[3]

For Fischer, the psychologist giving a test is not a technician but a consultant, and the act of testing is designed to uncover a style of living, not to place a person into a pigeonhole. To be sure, it is helpful to know how so-and-so many other people of comparable ages do on this test, but just as surely, the job of the psychologist is to see through the number to the child's everyday world. The test situation is just one more situation a child experiences, and this situation is neither more nor less revealing of the child's style of being than any other.

Fischer thinks of the testing session not as an evaluation but as the beginning of a helping relationship. From even her brief discussion with the teacher, Fischer tried to get some feel for Danny Sanders. As a matter of fact, if the psychologist works in this way, an IQ test may not be needed. In the case of Danny Sanders, for example, Fischer met with him and his teacher. At this meeting Danny helped identify those times he felt comfortable, even when working by himself. With this information, and without an IQ test, Danny and his teacher were able to agree on a plan of action aimed at making him feel more competent when working alone.

Another important part of this approach in using tests is that Fischer always tries to explore with the person how what he or she is doing and experiencing in the present (test) situation is like what he or she does and experiences in other situations. So, for example, a high school student named Link referred to her because of "delinquency problems" had been asked to copy some designs from a test called the Bender-Gestalt Test onto a piece of paper. As Fischer (1978, p. 219) reports:

[3]Excerpted from "Personality and Assessment," by Constance T. Fischer, in *Existential-Phenomenological Alternatives for Psychology*, edited by Ronald S. Valle and Mark King. Copyright © 1978 by Oxford University Press, Inc. Sections of recommendations to the parents and to the school teachers have been deleted. This and all other quotations from this source are reprinted by permission.

Link and I had been trying to understand how Link gets into trouble even when he had intended to stay clean. We both witnessed the first design's completion in the middle of the page. Already I realized that although Link was intending to do a good job, he was going to run out of room. Sure enough, at design seven Link looked up at me, puzzled that there was no space left for it. I just looked at him noncommittally, and Link smashed the pencil point on the sheet, angrily shouting that I had tricked him. "Yes," I said, "the same way Mr. Wilkens 'tricked you' into missing your appointment Tuesday."

In this way Link and Dr. Fischer experienced together how it is that he gets into trouble so often. The test situation served as a model of Link's day-to-day world. For this reason, Link's smashing his pencil is the same as his having thrown a hammer through a shop window. The testing session has made contact with the world, and both Link and Fischer now have something they have experienced together to talk about rather than simply talking about events that only one of them has experienced.

For Constance Fischer, as for any skilled user of psychological tests, the testing session does not consist of an observer and an object to be observed and categorized. The purpose of using test materials, even relatively objective ones such as the WAIS or the MMPI, is to let a second person in on how the person being tested does things. The psychologist's job is to consult *with* the person, not to catalogue him or her like a dead butterfly. The testing situation just happens to be the medium by which both psychologist and client are able to make contact with the client's experienced and lived self-world.

C. Projective tests

Not all tests are as statistical or as structured as the Stanford-Binet, the WAIS, the WISC, or the MMPI. Part of the original appeal of these tests was that they had objective answers that could be easily scored and that the score could be used to describe a large group of people as well as one person's relative standing in that group. Binet was originally interested in selecting retarded children for special attention, and in this his test succeeded quite well. It has only been our later worship of the IQ score that has made us forget that an IQ value is only a number and is not the same thing as a person's

"intelligence"—that is, how well and effectively a person deals with the changing situations of his or her life.

Because it is often helpful *not* to have a correct answer, psychologists and psychiatrists very early in the present century tried to develop tests that give a person room for individual ways of dealing with the test situation. Such tests are relatively unstructured and ask the person to tell what he or she sees in a test item rather than to give a single "correct" answer.

1. The Rorschach Inkblot Test. The most famous (and notorious and misunderstood) of the projective tests is the Rorschach Inkblot Test. This test consists of a series of ten cards similar to Figure 14-4. The cards are shown one at a time to the person being tested, and a complete record is taken of what the person reports seeing in the inkblot, as well as other information, such as how long it took the person to give a response and where on the card the person says he or she saw something. After this first part of the test, there is an inquiry period

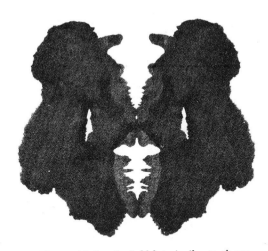

Figure 14-4. An inkblot similar to those used in the Rorschach Inkblot Test. It is deliberately made ambiguous in order to be open to a wide variety of interpretations. *(From* Abnormal Psychology: A Social/Community Approach, *by H. Goldenberg. Copyright © 1977 by Wadsworth, Inc. Reprinted by permission of the publisher, Brooks/Cole Publishing Company, Monterey, California.)*

designed to help the examiner see as the person taking the test has seen. Detailed records are also kept on gestures, comments, mannerisms, and so on.

In scoring, the examiner is careful to note the location on the card where the person "saw" an object as well as what the object was. The examiner notes whether the person used the whole card or a large or small detail. The examiner also notes whether the person was affected by color (five of the cards have color), whether he or she was responsive to shading, how good the form of the object was (that is, could the examiner see it easily), and whether the object was seen as moving or stationary.

Unfortunately, most of us tend to be taken in by content (does the person see a butterfly, a knife, or a wound) and to neglect how the person went about constructing his or her percept. The Rorschach test is not only designed to tell the sensitive examiner the "what" of the person's interpretation; more important, it also tells the "how." The Rorschach examiner does not only administer and score tests; rather, he or she uses them to learn something about how one particular person comes to see what it is he or she sees. Like an IQ test, the Rorschach provides a record of shared experience, experience the psychologist may then use as a basis on which to begin the process of seeing the world as the client does.

As should be obvious, a Rorschach card only partly determines what a person reports he or she sees. In a very important sense, the person *projects* his or her unique style of perceiving onto the card, and for this reason the Rorschach test is called a projective test. Although the idea behind this test originally came from the Freudian concept of projection as a defense, projective tests are better thought of as occasions for projecting one's style of perceiving rather than projecting sexual or antisocial impulses. Some psychologists have suggested that *expressive test* would be a better and more descriptive term.

2. The Thematic Apperception Test. Whether we call it a projective or an expressive test, such a test is designed to give clues to how a particular person experiences and reports about his or her world. If the Rorschach test tells us about perceiving, the Thematic Apperception Test (TAT) helps us

and the client come to some understanding of what a person experiences as the major themes in his or her life. Such themes are not always explicitly recognized by the person, and one helpful aspect of the TAT is that it encourages the person to clarify exactly what these themes might be.

Figure 14-5 gives one example of the type of card used in the TAT. Generally speaking, the examiner presents the person being tested with 20 cards, 19 of which have pictures and one of which is blank. The person being tested is asked to tell a story about each card. For teaching purposes, Kleinmuntz (1974) presents the following story told by a 12-year-old boy in response to a card like the one shown in Figure 14-5.

For purposes of later interpretation, the boy's answer is presented in a line-by-line format:

Line 1: "This boy was supposed to be practicing his violin, but he really doesn't feel like it."
Line 2: "If his mother catches him goofing off from practicing, he is going to get into a lot of trouble."
Line 3: "She does a lot of yelling and screaming about these types of things, and the boy has learned not to excite her."
Line 4: "She really doesn't care whether he learns to play the thing or not, and as long as she doesn't catch him goofing off, she's satisfied."

Figure 14-5. A TAT card similar to the one that elicited the story reproduced in the text. (*From* Essentials of Abnormal Psychology, *(2nd ed.), by B. Kleinmuntz. Copyright © 1980 by Harper & Row, Publishers, Inc. Reprinted by permission. Courtesy of The Dorsey Press.)*

Line 5: "Right now the boy is trying to figure out how to fool his mother, and he thinks maybe he'll tape-record his practice sessions and then in the future play back the tape recordings while he sneaks out the window and plays with his friends."

Line 6: "Wait till he tells his friends about the tape recordings and the way he fooled his mother. They'll find out again how smart he really is."[4]

Even though the card looks innocent enough, the boy tells us (and himself) a good deal about how the world looks to him. Kleinmuntz summarizes and interprets the boy's protocol in the following way. In his commentary, Kleinmuntz is sensitive to story themes that are common to most people (Line 1) as well as to those that are unique to this particular child.

Line 1: The opening comment shows that the boy perceives the violin accurately (most but not all subjects do), that he has been instructed to practice his lessons, and that he does not enjoy playing the instrument.

Line 2: Here the boy suggests that his behavior may make mother unhappy, and she may punish him.

Line 3: There is some cynicism expressed in this remark, and the boy indicates that his mother is to be placated.

Line 4: The boy's mother is presented as uninterested in his progress with the violin and will not reprove him so long as he doesn't confront her. This remark may reveal his opinion of her attitudes toward violin lessons. It also seems to be a facet of their relationship worth exploring.

Line 5: This boy's plan reflects ingenuity and suggests he is willing to take risks.

Line 6: The final sentence indicates his concern about the opinions of others and his fear of being stigmatized as ignorant and slow. It also suggests that he has planned similar deceptions [paraphrased from Kleinmuntz, 1974, p. 79].

The TAT, unlike the Rorschach, is a very content-oriented test. Although the pictures lend themselves to a great many interpretations, they are not nearly so free-form as the Rorschach materials. Although they may tell us and the person being tested what is important to the person, they seem much less

able to provide information on how the person experiences his or her world. For this reason, a combination of the TAT and Rorschach is usually employed whenever projective techniques are used.

3. The Bender-Gestalt Test. One final test that is frequently used in clinical testing is the Bender-Gestalt Test. As the name *Gestalt* implies, this test is concerned with how a person perceives and deals with organized wholes. The test, developed by Laureta Bender in 1938, consists of nine different patterns. Each pattern is presented on a single card, and the person is asked to copy the design. Some psychologists also ask the person to reconstruct all nine patterns from memory after the cards have been removed.

Although, strictly speaking, the Bender is not a projective test, it has been found useful in identifying people who have difficulty in dealing with organized patterns. Sometimes such difficulty suggests certain fairly well known problems in living. An example was described in this chapter in connection with the high school student named Link. In other cases, such difficulty is taken to suggest brain damage. It is believed that brain-damaged individuals have difficulty in dealing with organized designs of any and all kinds, and psychologists who deal with people having known brain damage often find that they have great difficulty in drawing the patterns correctly. Even though there is little statistical "proof" for the Bender test, it is a helpful test in day-to-day clinical practice.

Because there are so many different tests that can be used in clinical work, it seems appropriate to summarize the major ones before we describe how they can be used to help direct the course of psychotherapy. Table 14-4 presents a summary of the major tests currently in use in clinical practice.

D. What the psychologist and the client get from testing

Psychologists have been very industrious in developing tests—too industrious, some might say. The problem is not that there are too many tests, just that sometimes the psychologist and the public forget two things about tests: (1) that they are behavior and therefore cannot give a totally objective and situation-free assessment of the person and (2) that the "object" being tested is not an object but a

---

[4]From *Essentials of Abnormal Psychology,* (2nd ed.), by B. Kleinmuntz. Copyright © 1980 by Harper & Row, Publishers, Inc. This and all other quotations from this source are reprinted by permission.

TABLE 14-4. Some Psychological Tests Commonly Used by Clinical Psychologists

Test	Description
Minnesota Multiphasic Personality Inventory (MMPI)	A 566-item true/false test, administered individually or by group. Suitable for adults and adolescents. Responses are scored on ten diagnostic scales.
Rorschach Inkblot Test	Ten standard inkblots presented one by one, to which the person responds with what he or she "sees" the blots to look like or suggest. Responses are scored for form, color, and movement and other determinants, as well as content. Applicable to all ages.
Thematic Apperception Test (TAT)	A series of pictures presenting scenes of varying content presented one at a time, to which the examinee makes up stories. Various scoring systems available, although clinical interpretation is usually impressionistic. Suitable for adults and adolescents. Children's version, Children's Apperception Test, depicts animal figures.
Draw-A-Person (D-A-P)	Examinee is asked to draw a picture of a person and then of a person of the sex opposite the first drawing. Suitable for all ages. Interpretation is primarily intuitive; can be used as intelligence test up to about 7 years of age. Individually or group administered.
Wechsler Adult Intelligence Scale (WAIS)	Verbal (such as vocabulary and comprehension) and performance (such as block design, object assembly) subtests that measure various abilities that together make up individual's intelligence level. Norms are provided for ages from 16 to over 60. Individually administered.
Wechsler Intelligence Scale for Children—Revised (WISC-R)	Similar to WAIS, but with items suitable for children. Norms available for ages 5–15.
Stanford-Binet	Individual test, with norms from age 2 to adult, arranged by mental-age levels. Most suitable for children.
Bender-Gestalt	Person is required to copy nine designs as they are presented one by one. Several scoring systems available for children and adults. Individually administered. Used to detect certain types of brain damage. Also used as a projective test.

From *Abnormal Psychology, A Social/Community Approach,* by H. Goldenberg. Copyright © 1977 by Wadsworth, Inc. Reprinted by permission of the publisher, Brooks/Cole Publishing Company, Monterey, California.

person. If these two ideas are kept in mind, there is little danger that we will try to read our test results as a fortune-teller reads tea leaves or as a mechanic reads a wheel-balancing device. Tests show what people do, and it is our job to communicate what we have seen to our client and to grant that he or she will be a responsible collaborator in trying to come to some understanding of what these results mean for him or her.

If this is how we are to use tests, how are we to communicate our findings to the people involved? Here, as before, Constance Fischer provides a good example in the form of two letters: one written to a child she tested and the other to his parents (Fischer, 1978, pp. 225–230). These letters, a bit longer than usual (even for Fischer), give a sense of what might be learned from psychological testing. (By way of introduction, it should be noted that the child tested gave his own pseudonym, "Robbie March," for this report as well as his permission to publish it. It is an actual letter, unchanged in substance except for names and other identifying information.)

Dear Mr. and Mrs. March:

The following is a review of the observations, understandings, and suggestions we arrived at together last Thursday. . . . Since there are also a couple of afterthoughts, please telephone me not only with any corrections of fact or additions but also for clarification or possible disagreement. . . . The report is written primarily in third-person form to facilitate reading by the school staff.

The Referral and Assessment Situation

By the time Robbie completed fourth grade this past Spring with grades of D and F, his parents decided that patience with the school system and with Robbie was not succeeding. They enrolled Robbie in a local parochial school for the coming Fall with hopes that he would benefit from its concern with the individual child, together with its tradition of consistent discipline. They were pleased by their visit to the school, especially by what they heard of its use of small-group instruction. I imagine that they also may hope that a Catholic setting might minimize prejudices against a Black student. . . .

Mrs. March's overview of the background was essentially the same picture I came to through examination of Robbie's report cards and school papers and through my visit in the Marches' home. Robbie's kindergarten records describe a regular youngster getting along fine. His first-grade report card describes a likable boy who meets academic expectations but who is overly "talkative" for the classroom setting. The second-grade report indicates that the talkativeness and activity level probably are frustrating to the teacher and are interfering with school achievement. Robbie's third-grade class had a series of substitute teachers, who assigned him grades of B and C. During that year the school reported that Robbie's Otis IQ was 90 (from which teachers would not expect higher achievement than C's and B's). During the past year (fourth grade), Robbie's teacher had described him as "quarrelsome" and a "nuisance" to other students. . . . She regarded him as not being serious about school, [and] . . . she seems to have provided little if any positive response to Robbie's efforts. Her comments on his papers are of the sort: "This is not as bad as before."

My meeting with Robbie took place on 8-7-75 in his home from 10:30 to about 3:15. Mrs. March intercepted me at a nearby crossing and guided me to their house. We entered through the recreation room, where my first view of Robbie was at his full set of drums, enthusiastically and loudly producing what seemed to me as high-quality music. Turning off the amplifier, he looked me over and grinned broadly during a comfortable introduction. That image of an alert, energetic but relaxed, smiling youngster has remained with me as representative of Robbie. He led the way upstairs to the kitchen, where Mr. March met us. (Both parents had taken the day off from work to be available during the assessment.) My first impression of the Marches held up through our five hours together: straightforward, perceptive, unpretentious parents, with high aspirations for their son, eager to help him but also able to confront his limits and difficulties. Physically, all three are slim and evenly featured; all three were dressed neatly in slacks and shirts.

My representative image of Mrs. March is of her . . . preparing our lunch: flowing but efficient movement, quietly and quickly carrying out her earlier plan for a light . . . lunch. . . . Her husband was the quieter of them. He sat back . . . eyes following attentively/alertly, but his features otherwise composed for observation rather than interruption. When he did speak or otherwise take initiative it was done gently but firmly. . . . The parents deferred equally to one another . . . giving me the impression of a long-married couple that has come to terms with differences.

With other families I have always asked to be left alone with the child . . . later bringing the parents back into a discussion of what I observed. In this case, finding no disruptive tension among the participants, and finding that all four of us were able to observe Robbie's test performance, I wound up working with the family for almost all our time. Our discussions centered on Robbie's [work on] . . . the Bender-Gestalt, the Wechsler Intelligence Scale for Children, a drawing, Thematic Apperception Test stories, and responses to selected Rorschach cards. . . .

Robbie as Seen through the Test Materials

Before beginning the Bender, I asked Robbie to tell me what his folks had said about my coming. He sat tall but loosely, with glances at his parents being the only indication of wariness. He hesitated for a moment as though not sure of how to start, and then grinned with what struck me as a self-conscious and somewhat playful "I forgot." As we gave hints, Robbie seemed both to be relieved and to take pleasure in our knowing that he knew more than he appeared to. Eventually he announced that I was a "psychologist to help understand school." Again he hesitated to elaborate, looked for affirmation from us that his guess would be correct, and then launched into an account of school, confidently sending his mother out to bring in documents from time to time. I found myself appreciating his open enjoyment of our attention and his confidence that his parents would not let him down. But it also seemed that he genuinely looked to them rather than to himself for direction. . . .

When I asked Robbie to copy the Bender-Gestalt, he started right away and then had to erase part of the first design. Similarly, he scattered the designs on his paper, without regard for the total number that would have to go on the page. Midway, I interrupted to identify this continuing pattern. Robbie agreed that *starting without planning* is what leads to messy papers. . . . We explored the possibility that he could *stop and think before beginning*. For example, he could have counted the dots beforehand instead of midway as he had done. I suggested that he also could have used an additional sheet of paper, and Robbie mentioned that he could have made each figure smaller. Then he enthusiastically volunteered to start over. This time he numbered the figures, arranged them sequentially, corrected an error from the original sheet, and pronounced that the second sheet was much better (as it indeed was, although both were adequate for a 10-year-old).

Nevertheless, the same pattern of getting started first and *then* reflecting showed up through all of our activities. On the WISC, Robbie tossed out associations first, sometimes stopping there, sometimes (as when I just waited without writing down his answer) working his way to the most appropriate answer. For example (question 1): "What do we celebrate on the Fourth of July?" "Fireworks. Parades. It's independence of America."

A second theme is that of *looking to adults*. Instead of relying on himself, Robbie habitually looked to one of us for guidance once he had jumped in. Examples: "Do I color in the dots?"; "Did I do that one [acceptably]?" "Should I start over?" This turning to us was matter-of-fact and not self-conscious or helpless. But even as he took advantage of our responses, Robbie did not look for principles or an overview as such, but instead worked his way cumulatively to success. During the Bender and the WISC, the three Marches and I pursued the notion of Robbie placing himself "in charge," "being the quarterback," "being the captain" (as of a hockey team or in the navy). We were trying to help him to try out taking responsibility for making overall plans and for deciding when *his* criteria had been met; but in part Robbie confused these features with "choosing whatever I want."

The third theme is perhaps a variation of the first two. As Robbie made up stories to the TAT pictures, we adults noted independently (and later discussed) that his characters *did not have long-range goals or plans; they rarely took initiative, instead reacting to events or waiting for resolutions to happen.* But on the blank card (where Robbie had to make up a picture as well as a story), he launched enthusiastically into a Flash Gordon adventure. He laughingly agreed to my suggestion that the character be called Robbie Gordon, and consistently used that name throughout. Later, when I asked what his three wishes (for anything at all) would be, he named a two-way radio, a Kenmore truck, and finally, after hesitating, said he would like to be a hero. The latter would be like "saving a spaceship from blowing up" or "stopping two trains from hitting each other." I added "hitting a home run that wins a tournament," and Robbie agreed, happily instructing me to "write that down too." At this point I tried to open a middle ground between Robbie's TAT stories and his fantastic heroes. I asked if he could think of less dramatic ways of "being important." Here Robbie came up with "stopping the innocent from going to jail," "stopping the

ocean from flooding a city," and "being an executive" (which turned out to mean being a research scientist concerned with ecology, inventing a phonograph record that doesn't wear out, or developing new ways of transporting things from country to country). It seems to me that at present Robbie does not conceive of himself as able to work his way through the everyday to his own important contributions.

Robbie's TAT scores also contained several references to *false blame that eventually is cleared up by authorities*—parents, police, and "Robbie Gordon." Examples: lying about the main character, others assuming the boy was a killer, "calling him a name." This fourth theme is related to the next concern for his relative isolation; the Marches had enrolled Robbie in Cub Scouts and this summer he went on an overnight camp and played on a Little League baseball team ... right into an all-star tournament. ... He did not speak of special friends. His other prized possessions were related to his parents: a newspaper clipping of the three Marches waiting for Pirate autographs, his autograph book filled with a range of sports figures contacted through his father or through the family's waiting together at sporting events, and crafts projects he has brought home to his mother. When I asked directly if he had any buddies, he mentioned two youngsters "up the hill" with whom he does sometimes play. I do know that Robbie is sensitive to criticism from peers, but otherwise I can only report this character of his social relations.

Concluding Remarks

From the above sorts of observation, it seems to me that Robbie's "lack of motivation," poor grades, and low achievement scores can be understood in terms of (1) his confidence in his parents' respect for him and in a world in which authorities see to it that things eventually will be taken care of; (2) fourth-grade (and in September, fifth-grade) work requires initiative, planning, and relatively independent follow-through, which are contrary to Robbie's current style; (3) standardized tests do not allow Robbie to check with adults or to correct himself after he leaps in; also, although Robbie works quickly, on my tests he seemed oblivious to being timed; and (4) at that critical fourth-grade stage, Robbie's adults apparently failed to evoke the school-related hero in him or to show him how to get from "jumping in" to being a "captain" with his school assignments.

On the WISC, where the individual administration allowed Robbie to work his way through initial approximations to the correct answer, his IQ (conservatively scored) was 122, placing him within the upper 10 percent of his age peers. Performance levels on the various subtests were remarkably consistent—an indication of the reliability of the IQ score. Moreover, Robbie worked steadily at these tests for more than four hours with only a few detours (to tell me about or show me his various other successes). Robbie clearly is not deficient in "intellectual ability" or in "motivation."

Although I probed for possible psychological ... conflicts and the like, I found none. No doubt, as the Marches and Robbie's teachers began to work more systematically to help him toward "captaining" his way to achieved importance, then whatever interpersonal family struggles exist for Robbie would come into focus. I suspect these would be related somehow to Robbie's being the sole nonadult in a working family. . . .

Dear Robbie:

When I scored those tests you took, I found out that you know enough and are smart enough to be making B's and A's in the fifth grade. Of course at first you'll have to work very hard to catch up with your new class. Your Mom and Dad will help you every night with homework and practicing for tests. Maybe you can even make a big "progress chart" together to keep track of what you practice and how well you're doing. Where would be the best place in which to keep it? —on your bedroom door, in the kitchen, or where? Anyway, if you practice hard in school and at home, I think you'll learn a lot—enough to be a research scientist. . . .

I think that your Mom and Dad and your teachers will be trying to help you to plan ahead, stop and think before you get started, like you did on the second sheet of paper with those designs you copied. That means you have to know how you want something to come out before you start, like Robbie Gordon planned his attack on the enemy ship, or like a hockey captain plans his team's strategy. That's the best way to be "cool"—to know who you are and who you want to be, and what you want to do. To help you to be cool that way (to think for yourself) your parents and teachers sometimes will ask you to figure out what *you* think before you ask for help.

I think you're going to have a good year, Robbie. And I think your new teachers and classmates will like you, especially if you work hard and help other people. I know that I liked you very much.

Sincerely,

Constance T. Fischer, Ph.D.

In this report we see all the desirable outcomes of a psychological testing session: (1) It represents a first step in helping the person change. (2) It respects the person (and his parents) as having something to contribute. (3) It seeks their advice. (4) It uses the testing session as one in which the person does things that relate to the rest of his life. (5) It treats the person as a person, not as a number. Although an IQ score is mentioned, its importance is played down relative to Robbie's style of being. This is as it should be. (6) It also offers concrete, itemized suggestions to both the parents and the teachers (these are not reprinted here).

III. PSYCHOTHERAPY AND WHAT HAPPENS THERE

With the initial interview and psychological testing out of the way, the day-to-day work of psychotherapy begins. The first task on the part of the person seeking help would seem to be to open up, to tell someone else what it is that bothers him or her. Such events take place fairly early in the course of therapy. Sometimes people do not realize that they are opening up, sometimes they do so only after they have committed themselves to staying in therapy, and sometimes they do so, on their own, right at the outset.

The initial interview of Tom, who was having problems with his wife and his drinking, has already been presented. In more of his early interviews we can see how Tom opened up to his therapist. The second interview, for which Tom arrived early, went as follows:

Tom: I like this idea of talking over my problems. During the time I was telling you about when I drank so much, I sometimes thought to myself, "You're all screwed up, you should see a psychiatrist." But I guess I didn't have the courage.
Therapist: Now that you can look back on it, why do you think you did drink so much during that period?
Tom: You've got me there. One thing it does is relax my stomach ...
Therapist: [Interrupting] You mean your stomach spasmed all that time?
Tom: Off and on. I guess it's come and gone for years. Nowadays it's the worst it's ever been. In those days I didn't know why it was acting up. Didn't even know my wife then. H'mph [surprised]. That's odd, never thought of it until just now. I had stomach trouble six or seven years ago when I was going to school. That's when my drinking began ...
Therapist: Your parents kept close watch over you?
Tom: [Vehemently] And how! When I was seventeen they still treated me like a child. I couldn't go out at night unless I told them where I was going, who I'd be with, etc. My mother especially, my father didn't care too much ...

Following some discussion about Tom's love life, the therapist directed the conversation back to Tom's drinking.

Therapist: So one thing in drinking was feeling independent?

Tom: And the comradeship. It was fun. We'd have big bull sessions and talk for hours.

Therapist: What do you connect your stomach troubles with at that time?

Tom: Another thing that relaxed me at times were daydreams. One especially about meeting a woman somewhere and getting together with her.

At this point, Tom avoids the question about what he thinks might have been causing his stomach trouble. Although the therapist noted this change in topic, he said nothing but noted to himself that Tom "avoids the question as if he hadn't heard it. Why this reluctance? His anxiety related to being with other men? His mind jumped to having an affair with a woman. His heterosexuality exaggerated as a defense?" (Colby, 1951, pp. 75–76).

The third interview continued the discussion of Tom's drinking problems, his stomach cramps, and their possible relation to anxiety. Tom also gave a brief review of his midadolescent sexual behavior. At that time in his life, he and a girl his age engaged in mutual masturbation three to four times a day. Since they were afraid of pregnancy, their joint sexual activities went no further.

At the end of the third hour of therapy, Tom told the therapist that he had not started drinking until 18 or 19. The therapist came away from this session with the idea that Tom's early hypersexuality was not concerned only with sex but may also have served, as the therapist put it, some "purpose similar to his later heavy drinking."

The fourth interview contained one of the major themes Tom's therapy was to have to confront. The specific discussion began with Tom's lighting a cigarette. The therapist noted that Tom looked a bit more uneasy than in the first three interviews. Tom began this discussion with a question:

Tom: Tell me, what did you think of the Kinsey report?

Therapist: Or of more interest, what did you think of it?

Tom: It was a comfort in one way. Especially the figures on masturbation. And the part about homosexuality. I never realized how many men had such an experience. I must admit I've worried whether I've had any homosexual trends. [Voice shaky.]

Therapist: [Matter-of-factly] Why?

Tom: I've read about men who become homosexual when there are no women around—like in a prison. I've thought that, since my wife wants so little sex, maybe it would drive me in that direction. I knew a guy once who was homosexual. He was a classmate in college, brilliant guy. He was very open about it. We used to talk about it a lot. He claimed homosexuals were a persecuted minority and someone should go to work on this prejudice. That's something I have fights over with my father. He's a real reactionary. Why, he even thinks that labor leaders should be shot [Colby, 1951, p. 80].

Here Tom has "opened up" to a source of great concern: his fear about being homosexual. The therapist does not pursue the issue now because it is still too early in therapy and because Tom is still too frightened of therapy, the therapist, and the topic. It will be dealt with subsequently.

A. The issue of trust

These three sessions present an example of the ways a patient opens up. One of the major issues involved at this point in therapy is trust. Sometimes the patient does not seem to recognize trust as an issue, and the therapist has to help him or her come to this realization. As an example of how this might happen, consider the following excerpt from the 14th interview of a 24-year-old man named Bob.

Therapist: You seem to be having some trouble talking about your relationship with your girl.

Bob: Yes, I am. But I don't know why. I guess I don't know the right words to express it. I mean, it's hard to put your feelings about a relationship into words. They're just feelings, you know . . . I mean words can't really express them well.

Therapist: Yes, I know it's hard at times, but you've been pretty successful in the past when it came to describing your feelings. I wonder if there's something special about this particular relationship that makes it hard for you to talk about it?

Bob: Well, it's a special relationship, of course. It's different from any relationship that I've ever had, so maybe that's why it's hard for me to describe my feelings clearly. I don't know . . . it . . . it's not that the feelings are so vague, or anything. Oh, I don't know. Maybe it's just a bad day for me.

Therapist: A bad day?

Bob: I'm just all confused, and I'm having trouble concentrating. Oh, hell. I'm just disgusted with myself.

Therapist: Disgusted with yourself?

Bob: Yes. I know that I should be able to tell you about

this relationship, but for some reason, I can't. I don't know why. It's stupid.

Therapist: What do you think might happen if you did tell me?

Bob: I don't know. Why do you ask?

Therapist: Well, I just got the impression that you might be afraid to tell me for some reason, and I was wondering what that fear might be about.

Bob: [Silence, 30 seconds.] Well . . . yes. In a way, I guess I am a little frightened to tell you, but I'm really not sure why. There's sort of something inside me that's holding back . . . it's like . . . well, it's just a feeling I have that I'd better not tell you. I can't explain it.

Therapist: Tell me, these feelings you have about your girl, are they painful or upsetting to you?

Bob: Yes, they are.

Therapist: Then perhaps one of the reasons you don't want to tell me is that you're afraid that I wouldn't understand.

Bob: No, I know you'd understand. You always have in the past. I don't know what it is . . . it . . . it's not like I don't trust you or anything . . . but . . . oh, I don't know. Really, I don't.

Therapist: Well, maybe it's that you don't trust me. I know that you've been hurt many times when you did put your trust in someone. It must be very hard for you to trust most people, so I can understand that you might find it hard to trust me, too.

Bob: But I do trust you . . . at least I think I do. You know, I'm not even sure anymore what it means to trust someone.

Therapist: Well, maybe we can talk about that, since it seems to be an important area for you. What does trusting someone mean for you?

Bob: What does trusting someone mean? I wish you hadn't asked me that. I really don't know. It's been so long since I've trusted anyone . . . I can't even remember . . . well, I guess I trusted my mother [laughs]. What a joke. But I learned. I learned fast. It was a hard lesson, but I learned. You wouldn't believe the things she did to embarrass me. Every time I'd tell her something—anything that meant something to me, I'd have it thrown right back in my face. But I learned. After a while, I'd never tell her anything. [Laughs.] It was ridiculous. She once had the gall to ask me why I never confided in her anymore. Can you believe it? That's what I call sick! Really sick! I guess that was the last time I ever trusted anybody. I mean, if you can't even trust your own mother, who can you trust?

Therapist: Sounds like she really ruined your faith in humanity.

Bob: She sure did. Boy, I remember one time—I'll never forget it—I . . . I was . . . well, I used to have this problem with wetting my bed. I don't know why, but I

had that problem for a long time. Do you know what she did? She waited until all her friends were at the house playing cards, and when I came in with a friend of mine and asked if he could sleep over at our house, she said, "Maybe your friend wouldn't be so anxious to sleep over if he knew that you still wet your bed." I was so ashamed . . . they all looked at me . . . all those women . . . and my friend . . . he just looked at me like I was a freak or something. I couldn't stand it. I ran upstairs and locked myself in my room, and I cried for hours. How could she do that to me? How could she? My own mother. Some friend! The next day it was all over school. My "friend" had told everyone. Some friend! My mother and my friend. I didn't ever want to come out of my room again. I was so ashamed. I wanted to run away—to go somewhere they'd never find me. They all kept teasing me about it. . . . Later, when she came up and tried to come into my room, I wouldn't unlock the door. She said, "I did it for your own good, to help you stop." Can you believe it? For my own good! I'll never forgive her, never. She never could understand what she did to me. She kept saying how she'd done it out of love—to try and help me. Christ! If that was out of love, it's a good thing she didn't hate me. Well, that was the last time she ever shamed me. I never told her anything about me. That's when she started this "you don't confide in me anymore" stuff. What a laugh.

Therapist: It was a horrible experience. You must've been furious for a long time afterward.

Bob: You wouldn't believe how angry I've been. Like I said before, I'll never forgive her for that. I guess that's why I find it so hard to believe that it's OK to trust anyone. I guess that's why I was having trouble before telling you about what's been happening with my girl, too. Well, to tell you the truth, things haven't been going very well at all [Duke & Frankel, 1971, pp. 26–28].[5]

This interview takes a few interesting turns. Although the interview starts out as if it were going to concern Bob's relationship to his girlfriend, it ends up by focusing on the problem of trust. Although Bob may have been dimly aware of not trusting someone well enough to tell that person his problems, it is clear that he did not know the extent of his lack of trust, nor did he know how it had come about in the first place. The therapeutic work concerning his inability to trust was carried on for a

[5]From *Inside Psychotherapy*, by M. P. Duke and A. S. Frankel. Copyright 1971 by Markham Press. Reprinted by permission of the author.

few more interviews and facilitated a discussion of many other topics as well.

B. Other issues in therapy

Trust is only one of the issues that have to be dealt with in therapy. Fitts (1965) describes four other issues that often come up in the lengthy middle phases of therapy.

The first of these issues is **learning to feel.** Often people come in for therapy who cannot experience their emotions, mostly negative ones, such as anger. With the discovery that neither I nor my therapist is destroyed by anger, the person comes to express not only negative feelings but positive ones, such as affection and love. To feel is to be alive, and many of us have to relearn how to live in the world emotionally, whether this emotion be anger or love.

The second issue is learning to get rid of personal "garbage." Here one of Fitts' patients remarked:

> Another comparison that I've thought of is that of a faulty garbage disposal system. I feel that while most of the people I know have a well-adjusted and smooth-running mechanism for disposing of the inevitable emotional and mental garbage that all people must encounter, mine is broken. Instead of disposing of wastes in an orderly manner, mine has dumped garbage into the cabinet under the sink. It is very difficult to keep others from noticing the foul stench that surrounds it, and it has become full of all sorts of putrefying materials. There has been a time that I longed so much to be able to get rid of it, but didn't know how, so I've kept covering it and hiding it, making myself very sick of having to see some of it push out into view, and I'm having to open doors to the filthy place, and little by little, with my hands, remove the stuff and try to destroy it. Sometimes I'm so overwhelmed by the nausea of the task that I would almost willingly shut the door on the writhing maggots inside, cover up the place and try to pretend that it wasn't there [Fitts, 1965, p. 67].

Although the language is a bit dramatic, this person is learning to get rid of the (bad) feeling that she is not worthwhile. To be sure, she never does this completely, but she does come to experience herself in a considerably better light.

A third issue is learning not to feel ashamed about needing help. Somehow or other, to seek help seems unadult, and we all feel a bit ashamed about it. One of Fitts' clients reported:

> I feel a little guilty about being in therapy. Guilty!—hmm—No, that's not quite it either. No, it's more like shame. That's it. I feel a little ashamed to be in psychotherapy. I think I must be feeling that I'm weak or something to have to have any of this kind of help, and yet the funny thing is, it was weakness that kept me from seeking therapy for so long. It took more strength to do this than most anything I ever did. Maybe I'm not so weak as I've been feeling, now that I can sort this out. But I've sure been feeling that way [1965, p. 80].

The final issue is learning to see the therapist as simply another person rather than exaggerating his or her importance or his or her similarity to someone else in one's life. Technically, the tendency to see one's therapist as some other important figure in your life, such as father, teacher, or mother, is called **transference.** Transference means only that one acts toward the therapist in the present situation as if he or she were someone else who was significant in the past.

Although transference may be a hard idea to grasp, some therapists, including Freud, saw it as an essential aspect of therapy. A person was said to have been helped to the degree that he or she stopped transferring inappropriate reactions derived from past experiences onto people in the present life situation. Colby (1951) lists five perceptions a person may inappropriately transfer to his or her therapist: the therapist is seen as the giver of all affection, as an all-knowing and powerful authority, as an ideal human being, as a rival to be competed with, or as a precocious child. Although one or more of these transferences may occur in "pure" form, the more usual case presents some combination of two or more of these reactions.

As an example of the third type—seeing the therapist as an ideal human being—consider the following bit of therapeutic dialogue. At the time this conversation takes place, the person is telling the therapist what wonderful things she has heard about him from her friends. The therapist begins:

> *Therapist:* And no one had anything bad to say?
> *Patient:* No. Or maybe I wouldn't let them. To me you are perfect.
> *T:* But nobody could be so perfect as the person you describe.
> *P:* I admit you must have faults, but I haven't found any. Even if you do, your understanding makes up for them. You're the only one who really understands me.
> *T:* And it's this not being understood that angers you about your husband?

P: Yes. He's terrible. What I want is a man who understands that people have feelings and are not just machines. In fact I've thought it would be nice to be married to you. You are the only one who has ever been interested in me.

T: But I'm paid to be interested in people, it's my job.

P: I know. Still, I think you would make a fine husband.

T: If I were your husband, who would be your psychiatrist?

P: I wouldn't need one.

T: Why not?

P: Then I'd be alright. I wouldn't have to go through all this talking and questioning.

T: Maybe in one sense that's what making me your husband means. I couldn't be objective about you, it would take away my powers as a therapist.

P: That comes close to something I once thought—if we were together you'd be on my level, not over me, and you couldn't pry into my life as you do now. Maybe I'd be telling you instead of you telling me.

T: Like your husband now?

P: You mean that I want to snare you like I snared him. You may be right [Colby, 1951, pp. 117–118].

This excerpt is more than a good example of transference; it also shows how one kind of therapist (a psychoanalyst) works in helping make reflected what previously were unreflected aspects of the person. When the patient began, it was not clear where the discussion would end. She did not expect it to end by suggesting that her uncritical admiration of the therapist concealed somewhat unfriendly motives. What started as admiration ended as a snare, and this patient once again tried to act out with the therapist her relationship to her husband. This time, however, the person was not her husband, although here as elsewhere her admiration was meant to disarm rather than to admire.

One other point concerns the therapist's actions. Whereas during the early phases of therapy a therapist might help the patient skirt threatening issues, during the middle phases such issues are dealt with directly. The therapist is certainly not "nice and polite" in dealing with this patient. Instead, she is openly confronted with an interpretation of her behavior, and the therapist tries to function as an objective reflection on what was said and done.

When, and if, a therapist is accurate in his or her reflections, the patient is forced to face the issue just experienced as one that describes her style of living outside therapy as well. This process of dealing with unreflected styles of doing things, called

working through, constitutes a major part of what the patient has to do in therapy. Working through, that mysterious process at the heart of so much of psychotherapy, also goes on outside of therapy. A good interpretation, one that provides the patient with a vivid experience, can be thought and re-thought about many times in the course of a day. As a matter of fact, most working through takes place in the living world outside the safe walls of the therapist's office.

C. Some positive feelings toward the middle phases of therapy

Therapy is not only a disturbing business, it can also be a gratifying one. Although therapy produces pain, uncertainty, and shame, it also may produce positive feelings about oneself. Fitts describes some of these good feelings in the following ways.

1. Many patients, after initial uncertainty, come to use therapy as a safe haven in which they can talk openly about things that concern them deeply. This is not surprising when we consider that therapy deals with one of the most interesting topics in the world: me.

2. Another reaction to therapy is that it provides the person with hope and an opportunity to grow. Coupled with such growth is a feeling of pride in one's accomplishment, when in fact that is justified.

3. Perhaps most important, therapy may restore a sense of joy and excitement that is so curiously absent in neurotic patients. This does not mean new problems will not come up; all it means is that sometimes I now feel that I can face and solve problems without help from my therapist, and this frees me to be more open and joyful in my relations to other people and events.

D. The final phase: Termination

The process of ending the therapeutic relationship is called **termination.** There are many reasons for ending therapy. The best one is that the person comes to feel that he or she can handle his or her life and the therapist agrees. Although it would be nice to say that all patients end on this grand note, most do not. Most psychotherapy concludes when a limited change in the person has occurred and either the therapist or the patient (or, better, both) decides little more is to be accomplished.

Part of the difficulty therapists have in dealing with the issue of when to end therapy concerns the fact that there are no obvious criteria for when a patient is "better." Although it is easy to describe such things as freedom from symptoms and ability to love, to work, to choose, and so on, the decision to end therapy is always an individual one for each person. Sometimes, in the middle phases of therapy, the therapist has a pretty good idea of what might be a reasonable goal for this person. Such predictions "cannot compare in accuracy with those of an astronomer, but they easily rival most of those made by the weatherman" (Colby, 1951, p. 135).

Sometimes a prediction cannot be evaluated because the person moves away from the area and therefore cannot continue therapy. Although such people may try to find a new therapist, many find that they are now better able to deal with the issues that brought them into therapy in the first place. One woman wrote to her former therapist:

I have not yet been able to receive any therapy but I think that my difficulties have been slowly working themselves out. Of course, I would probably have progressed a lot faster if I had been given some professional help. As it is, I am more or less working blindly, but still I do feel as if I am going in the right direction. My relations with my family have improved a great deal from what they were two years ago. Also I have realized that my former hostile attitude toward other people was all wrong, and lately I have been trying to mix with other people, instead of avoiding them. For the first time I have discovered that delightful sensation of expressing my own real feelings and reactions (not without some trepidation) and along with this I have accepted the responsibility of my own self [Fitts, 1965, p. 137].

Not all cases of involuntary ending work out so well. One man wrote:

I won't lie and say that I have thought of you often. To be honest, I have thought as little as possible about it—I don't think that I have made much advance on my problems, other than financial ones. I haven't sought out any therapist here because I have been satisfied up until now to let things ride. The question still remains as to what I am to do with my life . . . I am evading the problems that I have, in favor of more pleasant pursuits . . . I wonder if I am sufficiently disturbed right now to really benefit from any therapy. I'm not sure what the necessary motivation is for therapy but I'm too happy evading my problems. Even so I realize that I'm living in a fool's paradise, albeit enjoying it immensely. Strange how I start therapizing with you in a personal letter [Fitts, p. 137].

This last letter gives the feeling that the final story has yet to be written for and by this person.

A situation that might appear paradoxical occurs when the therapist thinks the patient should end therapy and the patient does not. Most often, in such cases, the person is not sure of himself or herself, and the therapist has to be tactful but firm. One way a therapist can manage this situation is to introduce the topic of ending therapy a few months before the therapist feels it is a good time to end and then let the patient consult with the therapist first on a reduced schedule and finally not at all. In ending a therapeutic relationship, people are not thrust out; rather, they come to realize that although they weren't doing too well when they came in, they aren't doing so poorly anymore. Once this occurs, it is not so much a matter of "cutting the ties" as it is one of "flying on one's own." And that, after all, is the purpose of therapy.

IV. TYPES OF PSYCHOTHERAPY

Several case studies have come our way in the course of this book. Some of these go as far back (in the book) as Chapter 3, where a few of Goldstein's brain-damaged patients were described, most especially one named Schneider. Unfortunately, little could be done for those individuals: keep them comfortable, in a hospital, and keep their day and life orderly. Chapter 5 had a brief excerpt from the case of a man named John Knight, whose more complete history was told in Chapter 13. Chapter 6 described the use of poetic language in helping a woman named Audrey come to a different way of dealing with both her harsh and human sides. Chapter 7 described the use of learning techniques (both operant and classical conditioning) to help people overcome phobias and rapid heart rate.

A wide variety of problems, people, and therapies have appeared in this book. Some of these concerned clearly psychotic individuals (Joan Smith and Mary Barnes in Chapter 13) as well as some unnamed manic and depressive souls suffering distortions in time (Chapter 9). Sometimes the cases described individuals suffering neurotic reactions (Peter Oberman, Fred K., John Knight in Chapter 13; the belltower case in Chapter 8). Some cases concerned psychopathic life-styles (F. W. Demara, Jr., in Chapter 13), and some concerned people in need of simple academic counseling (Roger in Chapter 13; Robbie March in Chapter 14). Sometimes the patients were adults, sometimes children, sometimes men, and sometimes women. Sometimes therapists talked to their patients; sometimes they subjected them to electric shock or gave them M&Ms; sometimes they just left them alone. Sometimes the goal was to have patients experience something new, sometimes to help them gain insight into their conditions, and sometimes to change rather directly what they were doing.

Given all these various problems, goals, people, and therapies, is it possible to say anything general about how therapists go about helping people make it better? Yes: all we need is to find some fairly general themes capable of capturing the similarities and differences among the various types of therapy. Here Ernest Keen (1977) has suggested that the easiest way to compare the major types of therapy is by looking at therapeutic goals and at the roles adopted by patient and therapist.

A. Therapeutic goals: Behavioral or experiential?

There seem to be two major types of goals in psychotherapy; one of these deals with changes in what the person does (his or her behavior), while the second includes the larger category of changes in what the person experiences. As we noted in the very first chapter, there are two ways to think about human experience: as something I reflect on intellectually after I've done it or as equivalent to my total Being-in-the-world. In this latter case, experience is both reflected and unreflected and includes "doing" (behavior) as a special subcategory.

B. Who's in charge?

A second major way to describe psychotherapy is according to who is in charge. In many varieties of therapy, the therapist assumes major control. Such control is based on the idea that the therapist is a professional who knows how to help you if you will only let him. Some therapists take a strong biomedical point of view; others, a much more psychological point of view. In either case, personal problems in living are seen as "caused" either by disordered biology or by disordered personal history, and all that has to be done to help the person "get better" is to discover the cause and help him or her get rid of it.

The particular technique used to "get rid of the cause" allows us to talk about a biological or psy-

chological point of emphasis. For example, **psychosurgery, chemotherapy** (the use of drugs in treatment), and shock therapy all deal directly with the person as a biological entity; these are all examples of **biological therapies.** In psychoanalysis, by contrast, the therapist tries to help you uncover the historical basis of your present disordered situation. In both cases , the therapist is in charge, and you are clearly dealt with as a patient.

A second way therapists and patients can deal with each other is, as Carl Rogers put it, with "shared responsibilities." Here the therapist considers the patient a collaborator in the therapeutic process. Although a therapist can sometimes be "faceless" in those types of psychotherapy in which he or she takes the physician role, the therapist in a "shared responsibilities" situation cannot. Not all therapists reveal themselves to the same degree; Jourard (1974) has gone so far as to suggest that therapy cannot progress very far until both therapist and patient disclose private aspects of their lives to each other. Only in this way can an appropriate degree of openness and trust occur between the two.

C. Major categories of psychotherapy

Using the two categories of "who's in charge" and "type of change" as major organizing principles, we can develop a system that will order many types of psychotherapeutic procedures. Table 14-5 contains some 15 or so procedures and approaches organized on the basis of just this scheme. Included among these are some procedures that still need to be defined.

Almost all the therapies in Table 14-5 are self-evident (such as yoga) or have been described in greater or lesser detail at some point in the book. The only remaining instances that may not be clear are assertiveness training, some of the more directive forms of family and marriage counseling, and finally, Rogerian, or client-centered, therapy. In **assertiveness training** the person is explicitly taught a series of techniques designed to make him more assertive: "When someone does something you don't like, tell her directly you don't like it." Because it is easier to say than use a rule such as this, the person is given practice in using the various rules. In the directive counseling situation, clients are told what will happen if they continue their line of behavior and are helped to role-play their way into a

TABLE 14-5. Major Types of Individualized Psychotherapeutic Procedures

Type of Change Desired	Power, Control, and Responsibility in the Therapy Situation		
	1. Therapist in Control		2. Shared Between Therapist & Patient
	A. Medical	B. Psychological	
BEHAVIOR	Electroshock Psychosurgery Chemotherapy 1. Major Tranquilizers 2. Minor Tranquilizers 3. Antidepressants Biofeedback	Operant Conditioning Systematic Desensitization Aversion Therapy (Alcohol)	Assertiveness Training Marital Counseling Academic Counseling
EXPERIENCE	Drug Therapy (LSD)	Psycho-analysis and other classical interpretive therapies (Jungian, Adlerian, etc.) Hypnosis, yoga—other body therapies	Client-centered (Rogerian) Gestalt Existential Phenomenological

Adapted from "Existential-Phenomenological Therapy," by E. Keen. In D. C. Rimm and J. W. Somerville, *Abnormal Psychology.* Copyright 1977 by Academic Press, Inc. Reprinted by permission.

new style of dealing with each other and with their children, schools, and so on.

Client-centered therapy of the type developed by Carl Rogers would seem to have special merit because of the crucial role Rogers and his particular brand of therapy have had in promoting an existential-phenomenological perspective in psychology. Although client-centered therapy has gone through many changes since Rogers first described it in 1940, some basic principles have not changed. A careful reading of the following four principles will provide a taste of how Rogers conducts therapy.

1. This approach to therapy relies on the individual's drive toward growth, health, and adjustment. Therapy frees the client for normal growth and development.

2. This approach places greater stress upon the feeling aspects of the situation than upon the intellectual aspects.

3. This approach places greater importance on the immediate situation than upon the individual's past.

4. This approach lays stress upon the therapeutic relationship itself as a growth experience—a personal relationship which is a growth-promoting psychological climate [Rogers, 1970, p. viii].[6]

[6]From C. R. Rogers (Foreword) in J. T. Hart and T. M. Tomlinson (Eds.), *New Directions in Client-Centered Therapy.* Copyright 1970 by Houghton Mifflin Company. Reprinted by permission.

In order to carry out this program—particularly the last point—Rogers has emphasized that three conditions must be present for change to occur. These concepts tell us not only about Rogers the therapist but also about Carl Rogers the person. These three essential attitudes have been described as follows:

1. Unconditional positive regard—a value of the client as a person.

2. Empathetic understanding—an ability to understand the client's experience, based on the therapist's answer to the question "What would I be experiencing if I were saying what the client is saying?"

3. Genuineness—an attempt to be honest with the client, including a consistency between what the therapist says verbally and nonverbally [paraphrased from Harren, 1977].

Eugene Gendlin, one of Rogers' students, has described the therapeutic encounter in the following, very human way, showing how empathy, unconditional positive regard, and genuineness all enter into this situation:

[Empathy is] pointing sensitively to [the patient's] felt meaning to help him focus on it and carry it further. . . . Unconditional positive regard really means appreciating the client as a person regardless of not liking what he is up against in himself (responding to him in his always positive struggle against whatever he is trapped in). It includes our expressions of dismay and even anger, but always in the context of both of us knowing we are seeking to meet each other warmly and honestly as people, exactly at the point at which we each are and feel [Gendlin, 1970, p. 549].[7]

Although it is easy to draw a table such as 14-5 and put the various therapies into their "proper" places, not all therapists fall quite so easily into place. As a matter of fact, most therapists use a variety of techniques and approaches. Even though a given therapist might call himself or herself a psychoanalyst, a behavior therapist, or a medical psychiatrist, he or she would likely use whatever technique was felt to be most helpful for the patient. Tables have a way of drawing lines between people a bit more sharply than is true for the people they describe. This is no less true for therapists and therapeutic procedures than for anything else.

D. Therapy groups

Human living always takes place in the presence of other people, whether a person deals with other people in a satisfying and productive way or whether he or she has little or no success in dealing with other people. Whether we like it or not, we are always in a social situation, and many of our satisfactions and our frustrations must have their origins in the social world.

Group psychotherapy uses this human fact as its basic reason for being. Because group procedures resemble everyday living more closely than individual psychotherapy procedures seem to, such procedures should have a number of advantages. Goldenberg mentions six considerations as of special importance:

1. The person in a group learns that he or she is not the only one in the world with a certain problem.
2. Because people share personally meaningful material, the person learns that it is easier to share problems and feelings than he or she had thought.
3. A process of modeling goes on in which group members have an opportunity to observe how other (more skillful) people deal with one another.
4. The person learns that it is all right to show strong emotions in public and that other people

will not necessarily be hurt or upset by the person's behaving emotionally toward and with them.
5. The person has an opportunity to help someone else. This is likely to raise the person's sense of self-worth.
6. There is a general increase in the person's sensitivity to others and to himself or herself. Since a major difficulty experienced by many people is their insensitivity to how they affect others, the group provides a good situation for many people to experience how to get along with others [paraphrased from Goldenberg, 1977, p. 231].

Group therapy did not start out by being very different from individual psychotherapy. It became popular during and just after World War II, when highly skilled psychotherapists were scarce. At that time, group therapy was seen as a more economical way of doing therapy: a single therapist could see a larger number of people at the same time. The original groups were run according to the training of the therapist. So, for example, if the therapist had been trained to give interpretations (as in psychoanalysis), the therapist (as group leader) interpreted for the group what the person said and did. Similarly, if the therapist was trained to be supportive every time the client talked about emotions, that strategy was applied to the group setting.

As time went by and therapists became skilled in the therapeutic possibilities of a group setting, they came to realize that people were changed by their participation in a functioning group and that the group had its own rules and dynamics. Group process came to be seen as a model for certain types of interpersonal experiences, experiences that could not occur in one-on-one therapy. Such experiences involved learning how to deal with groups of people who were not necessarily sympathetic, supportive, or even friendly. The group also served as a somewhat sheltered tryout situation for doing things with other people that the person was not yet ready to do outside the group.

Therapists continued to encourage or to interpret what went on; at the same time, the group often took on a much more open and leaderless style. In a well-functioning group, many of the participants came increasingly to model the leader's actions. In long-term groups, the therapist often found that group members became progressively more able to deal with problems that were bothering themselves and other group members. Groups would end

[7]From "A Short Summary and Some Long Predictions," by E. T. Gendlin. In J. T. Hart and T. M. Tomlinson (Eds.), *New Directions in Client-Centered Therapy.* Copyright 1970 by Houghton Mifflin Company. Reprinted by permission.

when all members of the group felt more competent in dealing with personal problems and situations.

There was, however, one group movement that did not begin as a simple extension of more conventional one-on-one therapies. **Psychodrama** was created around 1910 by the Austrian psychiatrist Jacob Moreno. In psychodrama, one of the people in a group is asked to act out some past or present interpersonal situation that is troubling him. The drama is performed on a stage, and other group members not only serve as an audience but also act out various other parts. Sometimes these parts concern other people—a wife, a boss, or a doctor. At other times they represent a part of the person—his lust, his anger. Sometimes the therapist/director stops the ongoing action to ask the person to take someone else's role. In this way, the person can experience the impact he has on someone else. The purpose of psychodrama is to provide a situation within which the person (and the audience) reexperiences a personally difficult situation and in so doing comes to be able to handle it better next time. Obviously it was also designed to help the person avoid getting into such situations in the future.

E. Encounter and growth groups

Around 1970 a new type of group procedure was developed. The purpose of this group was not to deal with people who weren't making it but to deal with people who wanted to make it better. The vast majority of these new groups were set up to enable people to deal with each other in new, different, and, ideally, more open ways. For this reason, such groups came to be called **growth** or **encounter groups.**

Such groups differ from therapy groups in a number of ways. For one, the leader is much less in charge and much more a participant. Second, the participants have not usually come for "therapy"; rather, they are there to learn to experience others and themselves more fully. A third difference concerns technique: growth groups focus exclusively on the here-and-now of group experience rather than on family life or on things that go on outside the group. Finally, growth groups lay great stress on a direct confrontation of one's here-and-now feelings rather than on the feelings one has had in the past or expects to have in the future.

As should be obvious, growth, or encounter, groups expect a great deal from their participants. The emotional intensity of the group is quite dramatic and the stakes in terms of personal growth quite high. An example of the type of personal involvement generated in such groups is the following excerpt describing interaction in a group that ran continuously for 84 hours. The business currently under group consideration involved asking one member of the group to "affirm" his deformed leg as a part of himself. The narrator is another (male) member of the group (Kleinmuntz, 1974, p. 470):

> The game that affected me most was when Nickolas was asked to affirm his deformed leg as a part of him even if unsightly because of the paralysis. He was asked to sit in the center of the room without his shoe and sock and let us all see it. His deep resentment was about to preclude him from continuing when, almost as one, the group went to him to give their love and encouragement. At this point I sat behind him and when somebody first touched his foot, he fell back almost in agony into my arms. He was encouraged to speak words of acceptance to his leg as they finally bared it and laid their hands on it and caressed it. After a while I laid his head in the lap of one of the women and continued to stroke his shoulder as others in the group used physical touch to affirm their support of him and their loving acceptance. I had never expressed love in a physical way to a man before this day, I myself, in a certain sense also "crippled" by my phobia against physical contact, was freed to experience its rightness and genuine human warmth. My "homo hang-up" disappeared as a result of this experience. It was the involvement of the entire group that made it possible for me to act and feel as I did.

As should be obvious, growth groups demand that their participants express frank and honest opinions about one another and that they remove the social masks they often wear in their lives outside the group. Since this is a difficult and unsettling task, it seems reasonable to wonder whether growth groups might be dangerous to some participants. Most people who have gone through an intense group experience require no follow-up data: they know that they have been changed in ways that are personally significant and beneficial to them. Unfortunately, some of the follow-up work done by Yalom and Lieberman and their colleagues (Yalom, 1971; Yalom & Lieberman, 1971; Lieberman, Yalom, & Miles, 1973) has found that not all group members profit from this experience. In fact, many authors have talked about encounter-group "casualties"—people who are so unsettled by their experiences in such groups as to require psychological attention.

One follow-up study of 16 such "casualties" found that 3 of these individuals became psychotic, 1 committed suicide, and the remaining 12 were more depressed and disordered after their group experience than before, as long as 8 months after the group ended. Perhaps the most poignant casualty uncovered by the Lieberman research group concerned the suicide of a college student after the second meeting of his group. Although this student did have a long history of personal difficulty, his suicide note "vividly illustrates the extreme difficulty a vulnerable person can have in an encounter group" (Coleman, 1976, p. 707):

> "I felt great pain that I could not stop any other way. It would have been helpful if there had been anyone to understand and care about my pain, but there wasn't. People did not believe me when I told them about my problems or pain or else [said] that it was just self pity; or if there had been someone to share my feelings with, but all they said was that I was hiding myself, not showing my true feelings, talking to myself. They kept saying this no matter how hard I tried to reach them. This is what I mean when I say they do not understand or care about my pain; they just discredited it or ignored it and I was left alone with it. I ask that anyone who asks about me see this, it is my only last request" [p. 19].[8]

A further study attempting to evaluate the effectiveness of growth groups (Lieberman, Yalom, & Miles, 1973) found that of all the participants in ten groups, over 60% stayed in the group until it ended. Almost all these people considered the experience worthwhile, although their feeling of how important the group was to them 6 months after it ended was much less than it had been immediately after the group ended. Ratings made by group leaders, as might be expected, were much more favorable concerning the beneficial effects of having been in a group, both for themselves and for other group members. Perhaps the most critical outcome was that approximately one-third of participants either dropped out of the group before it finished or re-

ported that they were less able to deal with their world after the group than before.

Overall, this research suggests that although many people benefit from an intense group experience, a large enough number get hurt. Probably the best remedy would be to screen applicants before permitting them to enter the group. The most important thing to keep in mind is that growth or encounter groups are not without risk. As in other forms of trying to make it better, such risks should not be overlooked, for we are dealing here (as elsewhere) with that most precious of human commodities: the meaningfulness and continuity of individual human existence.

F. The medical model and the behavioral model

Each of the various techniques to help make it better has behind it a different philosophy of what it means to be a human being. At one end of the spectrum, a person coming to seek therapy is considered a patient suffering from a disease and, therefore, very different from the therapist, who is presumably "well." At the other extreme, a person coming for help is seen not as a patient but as someone who has somehow or other learned to go about his or her life in ways that are personally unproductive and/or dangerous.

There are several ways to describe the difference between these two approaches; perhaps the most obvious one concerns the idea of a symptom. In the patient/therapist approach—the so-called **medical model**—a given behavior, such as compulsive eating or compulsive sexual behavior, is always seen as a symptom of some "underlying" cause or problem. In the more medical sense of this approach, the therapist might look for something like a chemical imbalance in the blood. In its more psychological sense, the therapist would help the patient try to discover what events make him anxious and would then try to help the patient deal with the underlying problem in more reasonable and constructive ways.

The **behavioral model** (or "learning model") takes issue with the idea that disordered behavior is always a symptom of a disordered physical body or of a disordered psyche. In this approach to therapy, ongoing behavior is what is important, not some theoretical conception of what it might reveal about a person's underlying bodily or psychological func-

---

[8]From "A Study of Encounter Group Casualties," by I. D. Yalom and M. A. Lieberman. In *Archives of General Psychiatry*, 1971, *25*, 16–30. Copyright 1971 by the American Medical Association. Reprinted by permission.

tioning. The medical model, so the argument goes, places far too little emphasis on the person's present situation and far too much on his or her history. History is important only to the degree to which the present situation is responded to as similar to those the person has gone through in the past.

Milton and Wahler (1969) have summarized, in the form of Figure 14-6, some of the issues involved in behavioral- and medical-model approaches to disordered behavior. They describe the approach of the medical model in the following terms:

> As a result of certain historical experiences (e.g., a demanding and critical mother during early childhood) an individual may develop disturbances in his mental apparatus (e.g., an inadequate self-concept); and the mental apparatus then becomes the present-day cause of adult deviant behavior (e.g., consumption of excessive amounts of alcohol to the point of being unable to keep a job). For this reason the long-range, developmental, or historical antecedents are outside of the person although they were within his social environment at one time [p. 6].

The behavioral, or psychosocial, model, which derives most of its support from the learning laboratory, considers disordered behavior similar to any other type of behavior. As such, disordered behavior is learned and can only be maintained by reinforcing events in the present environment. In alcoholism, for example, the present environment must be reinforcing the behavior in some way; let us say the person drinks to avoid the anxiety evoked by his present life situation. If the environment/person re-

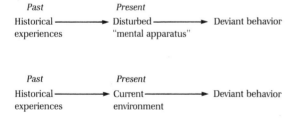

Figure 14-6. Two models of causation of deviant behavior. Top: The medical model. Bottom: The behavioral model. *(From* Behavior Disorders: Perspectives and Trends, *Second Edition, by E.O. Milton and R. G. Wahler (Eds.). Copyright © 1965, 1969 by J. B. Lippincott Company. Reprinted by permission of Harper & Row, Publishers, Inc.)*

lationship is sufficiently strong, it may be necessary to get rid of cues that evoke the behavior (for example, feeling anxious) before the behavior will extinguish.

Obviously such differences in theoretical approach must have some effect on the kind of therapy a medical-model or a behavioral-model therapist would use in a given case. For example, consider the problem of anxiety. Suppose a person went to a therapist because she often "felt nervous." A medical-model therapist, if biological, might prescribe tranquilizers and then gradually decrease the dosage until the person could tolerate anxiety without medication. A more usual procedure, however, would be to prescribe tranquilizers only if absolutely necessary and try at the same time to get the person out of the "reasons" for her anxieties. Here the major tools used by the therapist include suggestion, dream interpretation, and transference, as well as insight achieved after a long and detailed analysis of the patient's life history. In this kind of therapy, the therapist does little talking and hardly ever evaluates the morality of what the patient says or does. Therapy is usually done in an office, far removed from the current life situation of the patient. The case of John Knight is a good example of this type of therapy.

By contrast, the behavior therapist would not make a detailed inquiry into the person's past history. Instead, he or she would focus on events in the person's current situation that evoke anxiety. Once these were identified, some therapists would try to extinguish the anxiety responses evoked. Other therapists might try systematically to desensitize the person (see Chapter 7 for an example of Wolpe's approach) so that the cues evoking anxiety would no longer be effective. If the patient did not seem to know what to do in a particular situation (that is, "had no relevant and/or appropriate behavior"), some therapist might even train her to respond in certain socially and personally useful ways.

Although there are many differences between medical and behavior therapists, there are also many similarities. Both approaches involve a power relationship between therapist and patient. In trying to help a patient come to insight, a therapist may interpret, advise, and even express genuine liking for the patient. There is, however, no doubt who's in charge or whose judgment "really matters." In behavioral therapies, it is the therapist who trains and reinforces the patient and is always in charge of the situation. To be sure, the therapist/patient relationship is important for both insight and learning therapies, and the therapist is assumed to have the right answer in both.

A second and more important similarity between the behavioral and medical models concerns the therapist's philosophy of what makes human beings tick. Although the two types of therapy differ in how they understand disordered behavior, both do see it as describable in terms of scientific laws. For the psychologically oriented medical-model therapist, underlying "internal" factors are most important; for the learning therapist, the stimulus world is most important. In both cases, what the patient does is "caused," and the person is thought of as an object acting in accordance with scientific laws. Neither approach renders unto the person a full measure of self-as-subject.

Both approaches, however, do make some concessions to the person's subjective life. The insight therapist tries to provide the person with a new perspective on his or her style of living. In so doing, the therapist has sneaked in the idea of a personal world as important to how one lives one's life. Then, too, patient insight is never solely an intellectual experience, and the degree to which insight involves the total person determines how changed a person's point of view will be. Behavioral therapies also are sensitive to some of these same issues.

Behavior therapists criticize the medical model on many grounds; perhaps the most important has to do with their analysis of "where" the problem is in a particular case. Therapists who operate from a behavioral point of view always stress the rootedness of a person in his or her *current* situation. In addition, behavior therapists usually talk about the patient's problem in terms of relationships *between* people rather than in terms of a disease *within* the person seeking help. This emphasis on the current interperson situation suggests that behavior therapists are trying to understand disordered behavior as an ongoing problem in living rather than as a symptom of a disease to be handled medically.

G. The existential model

Both medical insight and behavioral therapies seem to be moving toward the view that disordered living depends on how the person coming for help perceives and understands his or her current interpersonal situation. In so doing, they still are a long way from providing more equal roles for patient and therapist. In addition, neither model has made any systematic attempt to recognize personal experience as of crucial importance to the therapeutic process.

This is not to say that either kind of therapist sees a person's past history or current way of dealing with situations as unimportant. As one existential therapist put it:

> In no sense does [existential therapy] make the insights of behaviorism and psychoanalysis irrelevant to the understanding of people. Principles of conditioning are essential to understanding the [emotional] overtones of an action observed or performed. Understanding character structure is helpful in judging what a particular behavior means to the individual. But the existential approach to human psychology does not seek the conditioned habits or characterological peculiarities as explanations of the troubled person's troubles. They are only guides to understanding his experience of himself and the world. The abnormality, the problem that is attacked, is in the person's experience rather than in his behavior or his character structure [Keen, 1970, p. 4].

In therapy, as in other aspects of psychology, what is at issue is neither movement nor psychic style alone. What is important is the person's experience of his or her world. This includes both what the person does and the style in which he or she does it. If in "experience" we include both its reflected and unreflected aspects, it seems clear that the person defines which aspects of his or her past and present situation are relevant and meaningful right now. Situation and response are always situation and response for some person, and whether what the person does is disordered or not, it is always an expression of that person's style of existence.

The existential therapist, while recognizing the importance of both behavior and past history, operates on the basis of assumptions about people that differ quite markedly from those of behavior or insight therapies. Keen (1977) has reduced these to four major points.

First, the person is an active agent in changing his or her life. The goal of therapy is to help liberate the person from as many restrictive and disruptive prior choices as possible. Therapy, thus, becomes a cooperative venture between individuals of equal responsibility, where the patient has to take as much responsibility for change as the therapist.

Second, the critical area of change must be the person's experience. So, for example, it does no good to unravel an "Oedipus complex" or to teach the person to get rid of smoking if the person's experience of the world in regard to loved ones or smoking is unchanged. Helping the person free himself or herself from restrictions means enabling the person to experience and interpret his or her world in new and different ways.

Third, the meanings a person gives to certain events, problems, or situations are (unreflected or reflected) choices, and there are always alternative possibilties to choose from. In this regard, Keen (1977) notes that both possibilities and limits are crucial.

> One cannot transcend limits imposed by the existential situation, such as the eventual . . . death of oneself and others, the inevitability of disappointments, pain, and physical illness, and of anxiety in the face of an always uncertain future. But one need not be condemned to depression over loss of loved ones, conditioned or imagined transgressions of the past. There are always alternative meanings of both past and future, and we actively choose what they shall mean to us [p. 551].[9]

Fourth, the therapist and the person coming for help are in a demanding relationship where the outcome of an entire life is at stake. The person is asked to evaluate a style of existence, and in so doing the therapist must be willing to take as many chances in rethinking his or her life as the patient does. Coming for help is not as simple as repairing a poorly functioning watch; the person coming for help must be challenged in his or her total style of experiencing the world.

Does this mean that every therapist is or ought to be an existential therapist? No. What it does mean is that there is a general tendency among therapists of all theoretical positions to treat human beings less as patients and more as people. People who make it their life's work to deal with other people experiencing problems in living are much less interested in a particular theoretical point of view than

in helping the person who sits before them. A good therapist's experience is usually more important than his or her theory. Therapists hide behind theory and routinized technique only to the degree that they are frightened by the new problem and the new person now confronting them. In this, existential therapy is no less of a risk for the therapist than for the patient.

V. HOW GOOD IS PSYCHOTHERAPY: ARE PEOPLE HELPED?

The question whether psychotherapy works ought to be very easy to decide; we have all the statistical and experimental expertise for the job. What seems to be required is to select a group of people before they enter therapy and find out how well (or poorly) their lives are going at that time. After psychotherapy, we again find out how well they are doing. In statistical terms, this group of people would be called the experimental group. We also need a control group—that is, a group of people who are similar to those in the experimental group but who do not go through psychotherapy. To make the experiment completely above suspicion, people in the control group must be evaluated at the same time as people in the experimental group—that is, just before the experimental group's therapy and just after it. To assure objectivity, we have to make sure we never know which group a person is in when we do the evaluations.

Unfortunately, the question whether psychotherapy "works" cannot be handled this easily; there are a great many problems in doing the experiment just described. One problem is that there are always at least three persons involved in deciding whether psychotherapy has been helpful: the patient, the therapist, and one or more outside evaluators (us). Each of these three has his or her own first-person world and his or her own first-person reasons for being interested in the usefulness of therapy in the first place. Each also probably has a different idea of what "success" means.

Let's take the outside observer first. Perhaps the most often cited study relevant to this issue was presented by Eysenck in 1952. In this study, Eysenck reported that 44% of the patients seen by psychoanalytic therapists could be considered "cured," while 64% of patients seen by other, more eclectic therapists could be considered "cured."

[9]From "Existential-Phenomenological Therapy," by E. Keen. In D. C. Rimm and J. W. Somerville, *Abnormal Psychology.* Copyright 1977 by Academic Press, Inc. Reprinted by permission.

More to the point, Eysenck reported that 72% of patients not treated by any sort of psychotherapy could also be considered "cured."

Now, these are astounding results against psychotherapy in general and psychoanalysis in particular. They suggest that more people "get better" when left alone than when treated by any type of psychotherapy. Such results seem to undermine the whole idea of psychotherapy.

Despite Eysenck's results, the whole of psychotherapy has not come tumbling down, and it is reasonable to wonder why. Probably the major reason these data have had so little effect concerns the ways Eysenck chose to define someone as "cured." For psychoanalytic and other therapeutic procedures, judgments of "cured" were made by the therapists. For psychoanalysis, a "cure" was counted by the therapist only if the person was dramatically improved in his or her style of dealing with the world. A lesser, but still strong, demand for good personal functioning was also made by other therapists before they would claim their patient had been "cured."

A careful examination of the 72% figure produced by the no-therapy group indicates that this figure was derived from two studies using an entirely different definition of "cured." One of these studies was a survey of 500 patients receiving disability checks for neurotic problems from an insurance company (Denker, 1946); the second (Landis, 1937) concerned patients released from a mental hospital who had received no therapy and who had originally been diagnosed as "neurotic." In the first study, patients were under the care of general practitioners, and a two-year follow-up showed that 72% had resumed work and felt no need to seek psychiatric help. In the second study, simply being released from the hospital was taken as evidence of "cure." In neither case was the definition of "cure" nearly so demanding as that used by the therapists.

Thus Eysenck, the "unbiased" observer, seems neither so unbiased nor, perhaps, such a good observer. If we leave the 72% figure alone (as we should), it seems possible to reinterpret his data to suggest that between one-half and two-thirds of people seeking psychotherapeutic help are in fact much improved by their experience. One out of two or two out of three is not a bad average unless we *want* to interpret it as bad. More recent figures cited by White and Watt (1973, p. 279) suggest a 70% help-

ing rate, using the more stringent criterion of therapist judgment.

But why take the therapist's word for it, Eysenck would argue? After all, therapists do have a vested interest in showing that their particular brand of therapy works. It seems clear that a behavior therapist evaluating the outcome of behavior therapy would have a quite different slant on things than a behavior therapist evaluating psychoanalytic therapy. Much contemporary research (by Eysenck and by other behaviorally oriented researchers) has the air of a contest about it: "My therapy is better than yours." As a matter of fact, behavior therapists report "success" rates of 70–90% in almost all their published reports and far lower figures for any other kinds of therapies dealing with the same problem.

In evaluating these results, Kleinmuntz (1974) has summarized the situation in the following terms:

> Whenever carefully controlled studies of behavior therapy are available and unfortunately they are not as frequent as one might expect in an area dominated by research-oriented psychologists, favorable outcomes have been reported only in cases where specific and easily identifiable problems—phobias, obsessive rituals, tics, stuttering, and other isolated symptoms—were the main source of difficulty. Ultimately, perhaps, it may turn out that for these seemingly single symptom cases, behavior therapy is the method of choice and that for other and more complex problems behavior therapy is inappropriate. In the meantime, however, it is essential that many more controlled studies be conducted [p. 499].

The argument presented here in reference to behavior therapy applies to other types of psychotherapy as well. Psychoanalysts, for example, have maintained a smug silence about the efficacy of their treatment procedures. Their argument seems to be that anyone who argues against the effectiveness of psychoanalytic therapy is simply protecting himself or herself from the insights of psychoanalytic theory: to oppose psychoanalysis is to be defensive about your own problems. No wonder psychoanalysts tolerated Eysenck's awarding them such a low rate of cure: after all, they knew that they were right and that poor Eysenck was only being defensive.

A third way to assess the effectiveness of therapy would be to ask the patient's evaluation. Here success (cure) might be defined in terms of what patients say about changes in their lives as a consequence of having been in therapy. In criticizing this criterion, as early as 1948, Hathaway described what he called the "hello-goodbye effect." When a person first comes for therapy (hello), he or she has a vested interest in appearing as disordered as possible so as to get "help." When therapy terminates (goodbye), after the expenditure of a good deal of time, energy, and money, the person now has a vested interest in appearing as healthy and well-functioning as possible. Even though this is an overstatement of the problem, it seems quite clear that a patient's report can no more be taken at face value than a therapist's or an outside observer's.

What, then, is the public (not to mention the psychologist) to do with experimental results of this type? Here the best summary of a great deal of work is that psychotherapy of almost any kind does have beneficial effects for some people. At a practical level this means that a person seeking help ought to consider carefully the person to whom he or she plans to go for help. The experience of the therapist and his or her ability to deal with you in a way that is helpful to you are both of crucial importance in predicting whether you will get anything out of therapy. The therapist is more important than his or her technique. Therapy always involves a relationship between two (or more) persons, and what could be more reasonable than to expect that the more skillful the helping person, the better the outcome? In matters of human relationships, method would always seem to be less important than the person using the method.

VI. SUMMARY

Psychotherapy is a process involving two persons interacting and working together toward the goal of "making it better" for one of them. Traditionally, therapy can be described as involving three basic stages: an initial interview, a psychological evaluation, and the process of therapy itself. The initial interview consists of helping the person define a problem and of then enabling him or her to establish a relationship with the therapist. After the initial interview, the person is sometimes asked to undergo psychological testing. The battery of tests will often include such statistically constructed measures as the WAIS or the MMPI. Since such tests provide a profile for the client that allows a statistical comparison between him or her and the "aver-

age person," it is easy to lose sight of the unique individual taking the test. For individualized testing the examiner is much more concerned with understanding the client's style of being than with classifying him or her according to a statistically derived diagnosis.

Sometimes projective tests, such as the Rorschach or the TAT, are also used. Although this type of test is designed to allow the unique style of the client to emerge, it does not guarantee that the individual will be better understood. To ensure that diagnostic evaluations do not block an understanding of the person, two things must be kept in mind about tests: (1) they are situations in which people behave, and, as such, they cannot give a totally objective and situation-free assessment, and (2) the "object" being tested is not an object but a person.

After testing, therapy continues, ideally with additional understanding of the client by the therapist. For therapy to progress, however, the client must be willing to share much of his or her life history and present experience. Development of such openness is a very gradual process. Basic to the progress of therapy is the issue of trust: the client must trust the therapist, and any reluctance on the client's part must be dealt with by both the therapist and the client.

As therapy continues, personal feelings will usually be explored as the person comes to release much of the destructive "garbage" he or she carries around. The person must also come to experience the therapist as another human being and stop transferring characteristics to the therapist from significant others in the past. If therapy is successful, a point of termination will occur at which both client and therapist agree that the person is now able to handle his or her own life without professional support or advice.

The many approaches to therapy can be differentiated according to what the goals of therapy are and who is responsible for change. The therapist may have a psychological approach, be in total control, and focus directly on behavior, as in reinforcement or operant therapy. Or the approach may be a more psychoanalytic one in which the therapist is still in control, although now he or she will focus on patient experiences rather than on behavior. At the other end of the spectrum, responsibility for change may be shared equally between client and therapist. Here the focus may be either on behavior, as in assertiveness training, or on experience, as in client-centered or more existential therapies.

Because social relationships are so important in human living, group therapy would seem to be an ideal situation for treatment. According to Goldenberg, group therapy has two basic advantages: (1) by sharing feelings and difficulties in a group, participants learn that they are not the only ones who experience particular problems, and (2) they learn in a group that it is easier to share concerns than they had believed. Within the situation of a group, participants become more sensitive to others and to themselves and learn to express feelings more freely and easily. The group gives the person an opportunity to model the behavior of other group members as well as to feel better about himself or herself through helping others.

Most group approaches to therapy were originally developed as economical forms of traditional therapy and only later evolved into unique treatment approaches. Psychodrama, however, was developed in its own right by Moreno and differs greatly from traditional approaches. Here, participants act out their concerns with and for other group members, each person exploring alternative ways of understanding a given problem.

Not all groups are specifically set up to be therapeutic; some are designed to help participants "make it even better." In these groups, usually called "growth" or "encounter" groups, the leader is a participant and, along with other participants, engages in intensive interactions ranging from confrontation to support. In this intensive situation, some individuals experience adverse effects. For this reason, participants should be carefully screened before being admitted into an encounter group.

Two dominant models of therapy (and of conceptualizing human problems) are the medical and the behavioral models. In the medical model, the reason a person comes to therapy is seen as a symptom of some underlying problem(s) related to the past. Personal insight is the means by which the therapist helps a patient change his or her "character structure." In the behavioral model, the therapist focuses the person on present behavior and on reinforcing events in the present situation that maintain that behavior. Both approaches, however, involve power relationships between therapist and client, and both describe problems in living in terms of cause and effect. Neither allows the person a full measure of self-as-subject.

For the existential therapist, however, the client's behavior and history are important only in helping the therapist understand how the client experiences the world and thereby enable the client to come to some evaluation of his or her present situation.

In general, there are four basic assumptions in existential therapy: (1) The client has an active role in producing change in his or her life and shares responsibility for change equally with the therapist. (2) The area of focus is the person's experience of the world, and changing behavior alone is superfluous if the experience of the world remains unchanged. (3) The meaning an individual applies to a situation is not fixed, for he or she actively chooses (reflectedly or unreflectedly) such meaning. (4) The therapy is a process of rethinking one's mode of experiencing the world, one's very style of existence, and is therefore very demanding for both client and therapist. In these assumptions, existential therapy recognizes the role of choice and personal experience in helping to "make it better." As such, it makes contact with the person as an ongoing event, not simply a "diseased entity" in need of curing.

VII. GLOSSARY OF IMPORTANT CONCEPTS

Assertiveness training. A type of training (therapy) in which people are taught a series of techniques to make them more assertive in presenting their own points of view.

Behavioral model. The assumption that ongoing behavior is best described in relation to the contemporary environment, with no reference to inner dynamics.

Biological therapies. Therapies based on a biological approach to the person—for example, shock therapy, psychosurgery, and chemotherapy.

Chemotherapy. Treatment of behavior disorders by means of drugs. Used with both "neurotic" and "psychotic" problems in living.

Chronological age. Time elapsed between date of birth and the present. Used as part of the original formula defining IQ.

Client-centered therapy. A form of therapy developed by Carl Rogers, characterized by unconditional acceptance of the patient by the therapist, a high degree of permissiveness (nondirectiveness), and reflection of client feelings by the therapist.

Encounter (growth) group. A type of interpersonal situation that focuses the individual on here-and-now experiences rather than on events outside the group. The leader is more a participant than a therapist.

Existential model. The assumption that a person's experience, both reflected and unreflected, is important and that the person chooses which aspects of his or her past or present situation are relevant and meaningful. For this type of therapy, there is a fairly equal relationship between therapist and patient.

"Garbage." Feelings of inferiority or worthlessness that patients must get rid of before they can accept themselves as worthwhile persons and move on to a successful therapy experience.

Group psychotherapy. A type of group setting in which people learn about themselves through interaction with one another. The group has a leader who not only encourages interactions but may even offer interpretations of what goes on.

Initial interview. The first step in therapy, in which introductions are made, relationships founded, and ground rules established. The goal of this initial contact is to allow each person to find out what the other is like.

Learning to feel. An aspect of psychotherapy in which the patient is asked to learn to live the world emotionally.

Medical model. An assumption in many therapies that behavior is a symptom of a disordered psychic or biological structure. Therapy attempts to discover the roots of a person's symptoms and does not focus directly on the behavior itself.

Mental age. A concept used by Binet, defined by a person's ability to solve a number of problems compared with the performance of a group of people the same age.

Person-oriented testing. An approach to testing that takes a person's environment into account and tries to experience the person's particular way of being in that environment. Treats testing not just as evaluation but as an initial therapeutic contact.

Projective tests. A class of tests in which a person is asked to describe what he or she "sees" in some fairly ambiguous materials. These tests are designed to allow the person to project his or her style of perceiving onto the materials described.

Psychoanalysis. A style of psychotherapy, originated by Freud, in which the therapist helps the patient gain insight into his or her present problems by working through the meaning of the patient's life history and by interpreting the symbolic content of dreams, symptoms, and slips of the tongue.

Psychodrama. A group-therapy situation in which a member or a group of members act out past or present interpersonal situations that are troubling them.

Psychological evaluation. A formal procedure in which psychological tests are used to determine a person's strengths and weaknesses as well as to give a quick overview of how the person experiences his or her world.

Psychometric test. A test such as the Wechsler tests of intelligence in which an individual's performance is compared with a statistically derived average value.

Psychosurgery. Surgical techniques that involve severing connections between certain areas of the cerebral cortex and other parts of the central nervous system in order to change the patient's behavior.

Psychotherapy. A situation involving two persons trying to make it better for one of them; designed to help the person change in ways that were not possible when he or she was not making it.

Shock therapy. The induction of coma or convulsion by the use of drugs or electricity as a means of treating severe problems in living, such as psychotic depression.

Termination. In therapy, the process of ending the present therapeutic relationship.

Transference. The tendency in a patient undergoing psychotherapy to express toward the therapist attitudes and feelings held toward parents and/or significant others. Working through these transferred attitudes and feelings is an important part of psychoanalytic therapy.

Working through. The patient's efforts to deal with his or her previously unreflected style of doing things that has led to problems in the past.

VIII. SUGGESTED READINGS

Major sources

Colby, K. M. *A primer for psychotherapists.* New York: Ronald Press, 1951.

Fischer, C. T. Personality and Assessment. In R. S. Valle and M. King, *Existential-phenomenological alternatives for psychology.* New York: Oxford, 1978, pp. 203–231.

Fitts, W. H. *The experience of psychotherapy.* New York: Van Nostrand Reinhold, 1965.

Secondary sources

Goldenberg, H. *Abnormal psychology: A social/community approach.* Monterey, Calif.: Brooks/Cole, 1977. Chapters 4–9.

Keen, E. Existential-phenomenological therapy. In D. C. Rimm & J. W. Somerville (Eds.), *Abnormal psychology.* New York: Academic Press, 1977.

Kleinmuntz, B. *Essentials of abnormal psychology.* New York: Harper & Row, 1974. Part 6.

15

Aging, Being Old, and Dying

"So, old man, you're 72. What's it like, and what do you know now that you're 72 that you didn't before?"

"Right off, I can tell I'm going to like talking to you because you had the good sense to call me 'old.' Most people shy away from that word. They call old people 'senior citizens' or something cute like that, as if *old* were a dirty word. As for me, I don't mind being called old. I've earned it and I'm glad to be here.

"You know, my life spans most of the 20th century, and I'll tell you, a lot has happened since 1900. Take transportation, for example, which I happen to be interested in. I have ridden behind Old Dobbin in a buggy. I have used public transportation in the form of the Toonerville Trolley, and I have obeyed the law that prohibited shooting jackrabbits from the rear platform of a horse car. More recently, on television I watched men walking on the moon."

"What changes do you personally find most interesting in how transportation has changed over the years?"

"Well, in later preteens and early teens my regular means of transportation was a bicycle, and it was a better bicycle, I can tell you, than most of those sold today. I never did own a motorcycle, but I had friends who did and who disobeyed the law requiring them to disassemble it and hide the pieces behind the nearest bush at the approach of a horse.

"My family's first car was a 1914 Studebaker, which I learned to drive at 16. We took, among others, a trip over the Coast Range to Santa Cruz. There was a spare wheel, another spare tire and tube, an additional tube, and a tube-repair kit. This wasn't enough! We had two ordinary punctures and three blowouts on the 70-mile trip.

"Our second car was an Oakland, also used. Its demise occurred when in trying to turn around on a narrow dirt road, I backed it over a low cliff into a dry, rocky creek bed about 12 feet below. The brakes were peculiar; they held well going forward but hardly at all going backward. The car backed over the cliff, hit its rear on a large rock, and tilted over backward. No one was hurt seriously. As soon as the passengers crawled out, Grandfather crawled

back to get the picnic basket, and although he wasn't seriously upset about the accident, he was greatly perturbed when he found that acid from the battery had ruined lunch."

"How about some other differences in the way you lived then and how we live now?"

"Take the case of housing. I remember complaints in 1920 that houses were not as well built as they were around the turn of the century. In 1940 the houses were said to be not as well built as those of 1920. In 1960 the houses were said to be not as well built as those of 1940. And I have no doubt that in 1980 the houses will be said to be not as well built as those of 1960.

"My childhood was spent in a turn-of-the-century house which my grandfather built at a cost of a little over $200. It was a three-bedroom house on a 50-foot lot in a California city with about 35,000 inhabitants at the 1910 census. The foundation consisted of redwood two-by-fours laid on the ground. The walls were one-by-ten boards standing vertically, with one-by-two battens on the outside over the cracks. Canvas was pasted to these walls on the inside and covered with paper. A six-inch iron well pipe connected to a pump just outside the kitchen door, and there was an outhouse. But my family was high-class. There was real tissue in the outhouse, not last year's Sears Roebuck catalogue!

"Improvements came over the years. First, city water and connection to the city sewer. Then a nickel-plated copper bathtub replaced the 30-inch round iron tub in which my earliest baths were taken. Then gas lights replaced kerosene lamps, and later, electric lights replaced the gas lights. This house survived the 1906, 1923, and later earthquakes, and so far as I know it still stands. Eventually I inherited it and sold it for about 20 times its original cost."

"I didn't know you were from California. Some Easterners, Woody Allen included, find the West Coast a contemporary Sodom and Gomorrah. What do you remember of California in the early days, and do you think we're all going to hell, California in the lead?"

"My earliest certain memory of California has to do with the 1906 earthquake, and it consists of one visual image. My mother had grabbed me and rushed out the front door. The people from the house across the street had done likewise. The remembered image is of the man of that family standing on the sidewalk in a red flannel union suit.

"As to whether we're all going to hell, I can tell you there are a lot of problems now that didn't exist 70 years ago. For example, we hear a lot about overpopulation, the depletion of natural resources, and the pollution of the environment. The increase in population from 10,000 B.C. or thereabouts to the present has been described as roughly exponential. One author calculates that at some time during the 21st century the human race will occupy all the land surface of the earth with standing room only, and shortly thereafter they will all die by being squeezed to death. I am not worried at this prospect. When expansion is no longer possible, expansion will slow down and stop. The process, however, will be painful. Despite all material progress, social progress is incredibly slow. Each step hereafter will probably be deferred until it is forced on us by a major disaster.

"Evidences of resistance to social change are all about us. One of them is the continued existence of counties. Counties are a relic of the horse-and-buggy age. We have counties because every citizen has a right to his day in court: at the county courthouse. This includes the right to get from his home to the courthouse in one day in a horse and buggy. We have had pretty good automobiles for about half a century. The day when the whole population of America could climb into automobiles and ride off in all directions was reached a quarter-century ago. But there is as yet no whisper of a movement to consolidate the counties into larger units based on the realities of the auto age."

"Since there have been such great changes in your lifetime, how well do you feel you've adapted to them?"

"There have been a great many changes in my lifetime, but I have no recollection of 'adapting' to them. I just missed seeing the coming of the streetcars, and I *have* seen the going of most of them. Crime has been said to be on the increase in every year I can remember. But I have not seen figures corrected for both population increase and changes in how many people there are at each age. We hear a lot about the national debt, but no one prints a long-term graph with corrections for both the value

of the dollar and the gross national product. Much is said about auto accidents, but what *is* the number of accidents per million miles driven or per passenger-mile?"

"So what's next; are we moving toward a better or a worse society?"

"Here's a speculation. Anthropologists recognize three major forms of human society: barbarism, under which the people merely gather vegetable food wherever it can be found and obtain animal food by hunting; nomadism, under which they live mainly on their flocks, moving from pasture to pasture without permanent homes; and civilization. Classical civilization is based on agriculture and animal husbandry: most of the people grow plant foods and tend herds. A few, however, congregate in cities, develop crafts, and trade their handiwork for food grown by others.

"During the last 500 years the basis has been laid for a type of society as different from agrarian civilization as the latter is from nomadism and barbarism. With the Renaissance, the growth of science, the industrial revolution, and the further growth of science and technology, the economic bases of society have changed radically. Food is now grown by only a small proportion of the population. Work has become increasingly specialized. Transportation and communication have so improved that most of the population is mobile, without permanent homes that continue from generation to generation. The first result has been the breakdown of the patriarchal family, which, with related nearby families, formed something akin to clans, and the growth of the small, mobile, democratic nuclear family. Since the nuclear family is not tied closely to a neighborhood, social control by neighborhood standards and gossip has lost its effectiveness, and religious sanctions no longer have their former power in controlling morals.

"But social change lags far behind technological and economic change. The upheavals that have taken place in the 20th century are the beginnings of social adjustments necessary to the transition from agrarian civilization to industrialism. This process must continue for a long time before we have a new social organization, new moral codes, and new philosophies of life appropriate to the new economic and technological structures. The new social stability will not be reached in my lifetime nor in yours. Much trial and error will be required. But I am confident that a new stability will be reached eventually."

"What about today's youth? How do you feel about them?"

"I am amused at the consternation of some of my friends over the behavior of modern youth. I remember reading of an archeologist who dug up a Sumerian clay tablet that might just possibly have been the oldest written record so far discovered. The inscription was by a father who was complaining about the younger generation for loose morals and failing to respect and obey its elders. I remember the complaints of my own elders when I was in college. Those complaints were the same as those of the Sumerian father and the same as those of my contemporaries today. My generation in the 1920s was called 'flaming youth.' But the flames died down, and now we are the representatives of the establishment."

The conversation you have just read is one that actually took place, although some of the names have been changed. The occasion for this conversation was the last class taught by my colleague—let's call him Ted Edwards—at the University of Tennessee. Edwards invited everyone (faculty included) to hear his recollections and comments on a career that spanned, as he put it, almost all of the 20th century. I have taken some liberties with the text, mostly by adding things he has said to me on other occasions. Overall, the comments are much as he made them, and I have tried not to change his style.

What does this document mean for those of us who are not yet 72 and who are still wondering what we will be like when we retire? First, to me, it suggests that old age does not have to be a time of unpleasantness or despair. It suggests that retirement has as many possibilities and limitations as any other milestone in contemporary human society.

I also find that there is a lot I can learn from the reminiscences of a person a few years my senior and that Erikson's notions of old age as a time of wisdom seem well founded. Curiously, I find very little mention of death and dying, and I think that we who are younger may perpetuate the myth that old people are more preoccupied with these topics than we are. I also find a strong optimism in Ted Edwards, both for himself and for humankind, even though the 20th century has at times been the most bloody and inhuman in recorded history.

Mostly, however, I find myself surprised by the notes of optimism and good feeling that come my way through these recollections. I wonder: aren't old people supposed to be without hope, disregarded, and tossed aside, and isn't this a unique document?

I. ATTITUDES TOWARD AGING AND RETIREMENT

To answer this question on the basis of something other than opinion, we need to go back about 25 years, when a group of researchers at the University of California began to study some of the human problems associated with aging and retirement in an industrial society such as ours (Reichard, Livson, & Peterson, 1962). As part of this research, 87 men aged 55–84 were interviewed for 10–16 hours each concerning their attitudes, experiences, feelings, and beliefs about who they were and what was important to them. All were White males. About half the group (42 men) had already retired.

On the basis of a comprehensive interview with each man (an interview consisting of a battery of psychological tests as well as questions concerning retirement, income, work, health, social and family activities, political attitudes, self-evaluations, and so on), Reichard et al. tried to describe satisfying and unsatisfying ways of dealing with old age and retirement. To do this, they tried to select a group of men who were "making it" and then contrast them with another group who were not. As it turned out, the initial pool of 87 men contained 47 who could be categorized into one of these two extreme groups, and when examined more closely, they could be further subdivided into five groups. Of these groups, three contained men who were dealing with old age and retirement in personally satisfying ways; the remaining two contained men who were not dealing with these issues in ways that satisfied them or anyone else.

The largest group of men who were doing well consisted of 14 individuals. To give some feel for what these men were like, let's allow the members of this group to speak for themselves.

When asked about his attitude toward aging, one man in this group said:

> People ought to take their age for granted. They're not young any more. I don't know why people are so sensitive. Everybody passes through these stages. If people

call me an old goat, I just laugh and say, "Well, I am an old goat!" I think a lot of it is the way old people dress themselves—wear clothes that don't fit—that's what makes them old. If you keep yourself up, shaved, dressed right, you never grow old, I think. It's how you feel—in a person's feeling—in your makeup. If a person thinks he's old and done for, by golly he's going to be done for; that's all there is to it [Reichard et al., p. 127].[1]

When asked which period of his life was most satisfying, another man noted:

Well, I suppose when I was small, everything was a bowl of cherries then. Things happen as you go along—different things—different kinds of happiness. I know when I met my wife, I was very happy then. When I married her, I was happy. When we got our girl, I was happy. We was very happy when we moved into the home we have now. No, I really can't choose [p. 128].

When asked how he approached living and dying, a third man said: "I try to work like I was going to live forever, and I try to live like this was my last day" (p. 128).

For obvious reasons, this group of men was called the **mature** group; each man seemed to be integrated quite well and to have himself pretty much under control. By way of summarizing the style of these men, Reichard et al. offered the following third-person account:

Relatively free of [personal] conflict, they were able to accept themselves realistically and to find genuine satisfaction in activities and personal relationships. Feeling their lives had been rewarding, they were able to grow old without regret for the past or loss in the present. They took old age for granted and made the best of it [p. 170].

A second group who were experiencing little or no difficulty in aging consisted of six men whom the authors described as **rocking-chair** men. Men in this group liked the idea of retiring from the world of work and of having an old age in which they could "take it easy." Although they did report some disadvantages in being old, such as being unable to eat certain foods and having less money, they felt "more truly themselves" when not pushed by competition as they had been during their years of work.

When asked about his attitude toward life, one of these men answered: "I'm not dissatisfied with the way I've lived my life. Of course, my success hasn't been great compared to some people that I know of, but it takes care of my tastes and my habits and those of my wife" (p. 135). A second noted: "I haven't accomplished a great deal that's of any benefit to the world, but, on the whole, I've been pretty satisfied with my life" (p. 135).

As can be seen, these men were not nearly so active as men in the "mature" group. In fact, they seem a bit passive and quite willing to have others take control of their lives. Some of these men reported that although they had spent money freely when younger, they now left financial matters pretty much up to their wives. The attitude of one man toward responsibility was well summed up in his answer to the question "What was the happiest period in your life?" "I think a person's boyhood is the happiest time in his life. There are other happy periods, but the responsibilities sort of take away happiness from it" (p. 132).

A third group of men who were handling old age in a personally acceptable way consisted of seven men who made up the so-called **armored** group. This group had a defensive style of dealing with aging. Reichard et al. defined men in the "armored" group in the following terms: "[This] group consisted of persons who maintained a highly developed but smoothly functioning system of defenses against anxiety. Unable to face passivity or helplessness in old age, they warded off their dread of physical decline by keeping active. Their strong defenses protected them from their fear of growing old" (p. 171). One striking difference between "armored" men and men in the other two groups was their tendency to dislike being interviewed as well as their tendency to cut off discussion on any topic they chose not to talk about. Often they would end such discussion by saying such things as "I don't get the drift of that" or "That's enough of that." All seven of these men had not looked forward to retirement and seemed most happy as long as they could keep busy. When asked about full retirement (that is, not doing any part-time work), one 83-year-old man noted: "That would be terrible . . . that's what keeps you alive; that's what keeps you young" (p. 139).

The major difference between men in the "armored" and "mature" groups concerned insight

[1]From *Aging and Personality*, by S. Reichard, F. Livson, and P. G. Peterson. Copyright 1962 by The Institute of Industrial Relations. This and all other quotations from this source are reprinted by permission.

into themselves and their society. When asked "What kind of person are you?," one "armored" man said "That's a crazy question; I really don't know." When asked about changes in his marriage over the course of a lifetime, one replied "We're still married." When asked what kind of person he likes for a friend, another member of this group gave the following no-nonsense reply: "I like people who are straightforward and such as that. You can have faith in them. I don't like people who are cranks. Just ordinary people, I guess that would fill it" (p. 140).

In addition to these three groups of men who seemed to be handling aging well, two further groups were identified who were not handling it quite so well: the **angry** men and the **self-haters**.

> Among those who were poorly adjusted to aging, the largest group of individuals we called the "angry men." Bitter over having failed to achieve their goals earlier in life, they blamed others for their disappointments and were unable to reconcile themselves to growing old. A second group of men also looked back on their past lives with a sense of disappointment and failure, but unlike the angry men they turned their resentment inward, blaming themselves for their misfortunes. These men tended to be depressed as they approached old age. Growing old underscored their feelings of inadequacy and worthlessness. We called this group the "self-haters" [p. 171].

The 16 men in the "angry man" group were not only personally angry, they looked for anger in the actions of other people as well. For them, the world now (as before) was a jungle where people were out to get you if you didn't get them first. The practical implication was that it was not good to retire because other people wouldn't want to take care of an old man who didn't have much money and who couldn't do very much by himself.

Men in the "angry" group had a generally pessimistic and even cynical attitude toward the world. For this reason, they tended to look at everything—themselves and their lives included—in terms of either/or: either it's good or it's bad. Old age for them was the beginning of the end, and although they did not talk much about dying, they did expect to die in a short while if and when they "really" retired.

The final group uncovered by this study was the "self-haters." These four men felt that they had been failures and that life, now as before, was essentially meaningless to them. Three of the four were quite depressed and openly admitted that it would be pleasant to die. All four talked about death as a wished-for release from a miserable existence.

Men in the "self-hate" group considered their lives a series of wasted possibilities. Their general fear and desperation in the face of old age was best summed up by one man who noted: "I don't like the idea of being put to one side and discarded. Your mental faculties slow down; you can't help it. You're more or less ready for the bargain table" (p. 160).

II. THE TASK OF BEING OLD

These interviews have a rather sobering quality. In thinking about these men and their ways of dealing with old age, it is important to remember that of the total group of 87 men, 27 were judged to be making it, 20 were judged not to be making it, and 40 fell somewhere in between. Although it would be hard for one of the 20 older men not making it to take consolation from these figures, we should not lose sight of the fact that 30% of the men were, in their own way, very much like Ted Edwards.

Erikson (1963) has described the choice in old age as involving **integrity vs. despair,** and the extremes reported by Reichard et al. seem to support this point of view. The word *integrity* is a good one in this context, for it has two definitions: one has to do with being honorable, the other with being whole or complete. To "have integrity" requires the person to sense a wholeness to his or her life and to feel that such wholeness guarantees a meaningful relationship to the larger concerns of being human. Erikson says that "an individual life is the accidental coincidence of but one life cycle with but one segment of history; and . . . for [each person] all human integrity stands or falls with the one style of integrity of which he partakes" (p. 268].

What of integrity in the sense of being honorable or of good character? As applied to aging, this concept of integrity suggests that the person does not seriously wish to undo what he or she has done and does not envy the youth and power of the next generation. The integrated old person tries not to whine about his or her fate, nor does he or she experience total isolation, anger, or depression.

Unfortunately, as both Reichard's interviews and Erikson's theory have it, not everyone comes to an experience of this sort in old age. Some of us fall victim to time and pressure and experience our "one and only life" as worthless and out of synchrony with history and our contemporary world. Under such conditions, the individual falls into despair, asking either for more time to start again or for an end to time because there is no way to begin. Under such conditions all there can be is an embittered old age and personal descent to a meaningless end.

Thus the central task of old age is to find a connection between myself and my world as I now am rather than as I used to be. The task is difficult not only because I know intellectually that death is in waiting but because loved ones have died and my world is diminished because of my now-diminished capabilities. At the same time, I have the possibility of feeling satisfaction over what I have done and how I have lived, and this sense of satisfaction provides me with a link to time and human society.

Although ultimately I choose my own style and meaning in old age, certain events give me courage, others stand in my way, while still others are open for individual interpretation. Among these events that provide support and joy are recollections of my past, my involvement with family members, and finally the knowledge that I have lived well and have something to share with others. On the more negative side are such taxing but ordinary events as the death of my spouse, friends, or children, my increased tendency to be sick, and the intellectual notion that I am sometimes useless to those I hold dear. This latter idea can be very strongly affected by my society's attitude toward old age, so that sometimes I may experience the coming of age as "nothing but a parody of my life and a bad one at that" (de Beauvoir, 1972, p. 802).[2]

Old age, however, is no different from any other stage in life in that there are here both possibilities and drawbacks. One does not become old suddenly, as one suddenly begins to walk or talk or suddenly has a first child. Although there may be the public milestone of retirement, many people consider themselves old and feeble well before this time, while others never come to consider themselves old or feeble. In the end, each person chooses when (and whether) he will define himself as old and whether he will take the title of "old" as his own.

III. BIOLOGICAL ASPECTS OF AGING

Perhaps the most universally accepted way to define old age has been in terms of biological considerations. It will come as no surprise that a great many biological changes occur as a person ages. One physiologist, seeking the security of numbers, calculated the "functional efficiency" of 19 physical capacities in the "average" 75-year-old compared with the "average" 30-year-old. Table 15-1 presents his results. If we look at the highest and lowest percentages in this table—80% and above and 55% and below—we can see that although central-nervous-system structures are somewhat diminished (brain weight, number of nerve fibers), neither the flow of blood to the brain nor the rate of nerve conduction

TABLE 15-1. Functional Capacity of an Average 75-year-old Man Compared with 100% Functional Capacity of a 30-year-old Man

Physical Characteristic	Comparative Percentage
Nerve conduction velocity	90
Body weight for males	88
Basal metabolic rate	84
Body water content	82
Blood flow to brain	80
Maximum work rate	70
Cardiac output (at rest)	70
Glomerular filtration rate	69
Number of nerve trunk fibers	63
Brain weight	56
Number of glomeruli in kidney	56
Vital capacity	56
Hand grip	55
Maximum ventilation volume (during exercise)	53
Kidney plasma flow	50
Maximum breathing capacity (voluntary)	43
Maximum oxygen uptake (during exercise)	40
Number of taste buds	36
Speed of return to equilibrium of blood acidity	17

From "The Physiology of Aging," by N. W. Shock. In *Scientific American*, 1962, *206*, 100–110. Copyright © 1962 by Scientific American, Inc. All rights reserved.

[2]This and all other quotations from this source are reprinted by permission of G. P. Putnam's Sons and Andre Deutsch from *The Coming of Age*, by Simone de Beauvoir. Copyright © 1973 by Andre Deutsch and Weidenfeld and Nicolson and G. P. Putnam's Sons.

is much less efficient at age 75 than at age 30. The major decreases (55% and less) seem to involve recovery from exertion or change. Thus, blood acid level is slower to return to equilibrium, and ability to increase oxygen uptake during exercise is less. The central nervous system seems less affected by aging than the ability of various body systems to restore themselves to equilibrium.

Although it is not specifically noted in this table, the digestive and circulatory systems also show marked changes with age. For example, there is a reduction in saliva, gastric juices, and stomach enzymes, with the result that digestion becomes a more skittish business. Aging also affects the heart in a number of ways: heart muscles become stringy and the amount of fatty tissue increases. As Shock noted in Table 15-1, the heart is only 70% as efficient in the 75-year-old as in the 30-year-old. In addition to changes in the heart, arteries have a tendency to harden and become blocked.

There are also musculoskeletal changes. Muscles, if not used, show a decrease in number of fibers, while ligaments tend to harden and contract. There are also biochemical changes in protein molecules such that muscular strength decreases from a little to a lot, depending on the person.

In summarizing these changes, Kaluger and Kaluger (1974, pp. 299–300, following Wolff, 1959) note that the most common physical changes in old age can be described in the following terms: (1) An increase in connective tissue. (2) The disappearance of cellular elements in the central nervous system. (3) The loss of elastic properties in connective tissue. (4) A reduction in the number of normally functioning cells. (5) An increase in fatty tissue. (6) A decrease in the utilization of oxygen. (7) A decrease in the volume of air expired by the lungs. (8) An overall decrease in muscular strength. (9) A decrease in the secretion of hormones, especially by gonads and adrenal glands.[3]

All these decreases sound so final and hopeless: as you get older, it seems there is a sharp and dramatic decrease in most bodily functions, and that's that. Shock (1962), in presenting his findings, however, was careful to note that there are large individual differences in all body functions, even in so clearly decreasing a function as kidney plasma flow

(remember, this was one of those 50%-dropoff systems). Although the general trend of the dots in Figure 15-1 does decline as people get older, one 62-year-old (noted by a circle) is clearly above the average for this group of 70 or so men. Even for this one isolated aspect of the physical body, not everyone declines as rapidly as the average of 50% would suggest, leading to the conclusion that some young men are considerably "worse off" than some much older men. A few older people are still holding their own even as late as 70 or 80 years of age.

A. Disease and aging

Not all changes in the physical body can be attributed to simple "biological aging," whatever that is. Disease also plays a major role. Before describing the nature and role of disease in aging, however, it is important to note that disease never involves only a part of the person; rather, the whole person gets sick. To say that "older people get sick this or that often" or that they are more likely to have "this or that disease" is not to deny that disease is an event affecting the total person. What we mean to say is that aging and disease are interrelated and that it is impossible to decide "how much" of what happens to an old person is due to age or to disease or, for that matter, to any other isolated aspect of the ongoing world of the old person.

Disease in old age, as at all other ages, must always be viewed within the total framework of a person's life as well as in terms of his or her understanding of it. If we adopt this perspective, it becomes easier to figure out why certain sociopersonal factors are so strongly related to a given disease in this or that person at this or that age. Take the seemingly simple issue of acute versus chronic disease. The upper graph in Figure 15-2 shows the number (per 100 persons) of *acute* illnesses, such as are due to infection, injury, influenza, and so on, for males and females for the period July 1969–June 1970. There is a striking decline in the frequency of acute illness for older people compared with younger people. In addition, the decline is slightly sharper for males than for females.

The lower graph in Figure 15-2 shows the frequency of *chronic* diseases in people aged 45 to 75 + . The picture here is quite different: whereas acute diseases decrease up to age 45 (and beyond), chronic diseases increase steadily from age 45 on. In addition to differences between acute and chronic disease, these results also show differences be-

---

[3]From *The Biological, Sociological and Psychological Aspects of Aging*, by K. Wolff. Copyright 1959 by Charles C Thomas, Publisher, Springfield, Illinois. Reprinted by permission.

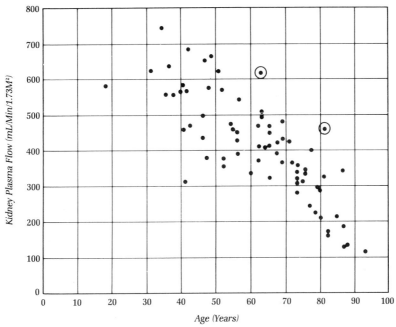

Figure 15-1. Decline in kidney plasma flow with age. Large individual differences in aging show up when, for example, the rate of flow of blood plasma through the kidney is plotted against age for some 70 men. The plasma flow is measured in milliliters per minute per 1.73 square meters of body-surface area. *(From "The Physiology of Aging," by N. W. Shock. In* Scientific American, *1962, 206, 101–107. Copyright © 1962 by Scientific American, Inc. All rights reserved.)*

tween men and women (and boys and girls). For acute diseases, young girls are slightly healthier than young boys, but this pattern changes by mid-childhood, so that females become more susceptible to acute diseases and remain so through old age.

Examining cause-of-death statistics, Timiras (1972) found that young men were more likely to die in accidents than young women and that women in the age range 40–60 were more likely to die from cancer than comparable-age males. Thus, what one dies of, as well as how often one is sick, seems to depend on a great many factors other than simply age and disease.

A different, and perhaps more direct, way to examine the health of older poor people is given in a study reported by Ostfeld in 1966. In this study, physicians examined over 1500 welfare recipients aged 65 and above. On the basis of complete physical examinations, and although only a few of the people considered themselves sick, only about 18% of those examined were judged to be in "good" health. About 33% were judged to be in "poor"

health or "gravely ill." Contrasts between Blacks and Caucasians showed striking differences: whereas 22% of the Black people (both men and women) were judged to be in "good" health, only 16% of the Caucasians were so judged. The "poor and worse" end of the scale included 27% of the Black males and 37% of the White males. Although there is no sure way to know what these data mean, Kimmel (1974) suggests that since life expectancy is lower for Black males in general, Black survivors over age 65 may be more robust than their White counterparts.

B. Personal evaluations of health and sickness

In addition to the physical, social, and economic aspects of health, it is important to examine its "personal side" as well. Physicians usually base their description of a patient's health on how much and what kind of physical pathology is present. A person's evaluation of his or her own health, however, is usually made on the basis of a much more complicated reading of signs. Consider the follow-

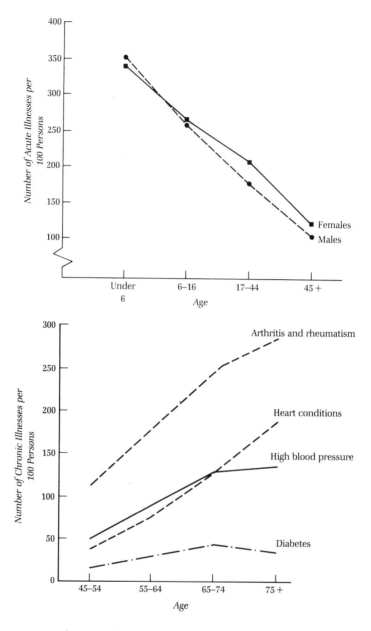

Figure 15-2. Age and sex trends in frequency of acute and chronic illness. Top: Number of acute illnesses per 100 persons, by age and sex, July 1969–June 1970. Bottom: Number of chronic illnesses per 100 persons, by age and sex, July 1969–June 1970. *(From* Adulthood and Aging: An Interdisciplinary Development View, *by D. C. Kimmel. Copyright © 1974 by John Wiley & Sons, Inc. Reprinted by permission.)*

ing three cases described by Shanas, Townsend, Wedderburn, Friis, Milhøj, and Stehouwer (1968, pp. 49–50).

> Mrs. Robinson is 81 years old. She shares a home with two divorced daughters, both in their 50's. She says she often feels as though she is going to fall "flat on my face"; she has difficulty in seeing; she has gall bladder trouble and arthritis. Mrs. Robinson was ill in bed during the last year, and saw the doctor during the last month. Although Mrs. Robinson says that her health is "poor," on the whole she considers her health to be about the same as the health of other people her age.
>
> Mrs. Slayton is . . . an 80-year-old widow. She lives alone. She is hard of hearing, badly crippled by arthritis, and reports that she has difficulty in going out of doors, washing and bathing, dressing, and putting on her shoes. She often feels as though she is about to fall. Mrs. Slayton says that she cannot walk stairs at all and that a neighbour has to help her dress. The housework is done by her daughters, who live about ten minutes' distance. Despite her impairments, Mrs. Slayton says that her health is good for her age. She spent no time in bed during the past year and has not seen the doctor for several months. In fact, Mrs. Slayton says that her health is better than the health of most people her age.
>
> Mrs. Igoe is 82 years old, a widow, and like Mrs. Slayton she lives alone. Mrs. Igoe can get about indoors and out. She reports some difficulty in walking stairs, but otherwise reports no physical impairments. She says that she can and does do heavy household tasks like washing windows and cleaning floors. Mrs. Igoe was ill in bed during the past year, and her daughter who lives nearby came in to take care of her. Mrs. Igoe sees the doctor every month. She considers her health to be poor, but about the same as the health of other people her age.
>
> Mrs. Robinson is a health realist; Mrs. Slayton, a health optimist; and Mrs. Igoe, a health pessimist.[4]

Cases such as these are common, and it becomes an important general problem to determine just how older people view their own health. To answer this question, Shanas and associates (1968) asked 200 people age 65–80 + in the United States, Britain, and Denmark to describe their health using the categories "good," "fair," and "poor." They were also asked how well they could do six tasks: going outdoors alone, walking up and down the stairs, get-

ting around alone in the house, washing and bathing, dressing and putting on shoes, and cutting their toenails. Using these tasks, Shanas et al. could compute an "incapacity score," which served as an estimate of how well the person was able to do things on his or her own.

How do older people at the various ages studied describe their health? A look at Figure 15-3 shows that at least half the people asked this question reported that their health was "good." Two other conclusions can be read from this graph: one, men more often reported "good" health than women, and two, there was an upswing in the perception of good health for people in the oldest group, both males and females. There also were differences among the three countries, not shown in Figure 15-3. More older people (57%) in Great Britain reported being in good health than in either the United States or Denmark (52% for both countries).

1. Male/female and national differences. In an attempt to understand differences found between males and females, Shanas and associates point out that such results make sense if we think about the social attitudes most people hold toward health. In Western society, for example, men are expected to be stronger (and less complaining) than women, even though statistics show women live considerably longer. The only time men do not conform to this expectation occurs in the years immediately following retirement (ages 65–66). Here the men not only produce a smaller percentage of "good" evaluations of themselves than women, they also produce a smaller percentage of "good" evaluations than they will any time in the next eight years (that is, the years 67–74). Evidently the first few years of retirement are understood to suggest that a person "must be in poor health"; this diagnosis is a personal rather than a medical one.

Cross-society differences are also interesting. Although the British aged were, by their own descriptions, more incapacitated than their American or Danish counterparts, they tended to evaluate their state of health more favorably. This tendency seems to go along with the British "stiff upper lip" philosophy: it is "un-British" to complain when the going gets tough. An American, in contrast, seems to regard anything other than perfect health as an impediment to the independent and self-sufficient style demanded by American culture. "Being sick" is a

[4]From *Old People in Three Industrial Societies* by E. Shanas, P. Townsend, D. Wedderburn, H. Friis, P. Milhøj, & J. Stehouwer. Copyright © 1968 by Routledge & Kegan Paul Ltd. Reprinted by permission.

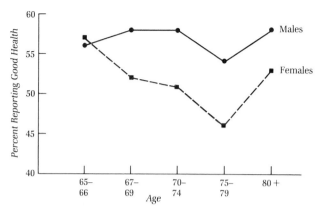

Figure 15–3.   Self-evaluations of good health, by age and sex. *(From* Old People in Three Industrial Societies, *by E. Shanas, P. Townsend, D. Wedderburn, H. Friis, P. Milhøj, and J. Stehouwer. Copyright © 1968 by Routledge & Kegan Paul Ltd. Reprinted by permission.)*

somewhat unacceptable aspect of adult life, and the person's job (not to mention responsibility) is to get well as soon as possible. Unfortunately, "getting well" does not occur quite so quickly among the aged; hence they judge their health "fair" rather than "good."

Differences between the comfort British and American old people reported experiencing in dealing with lessened capabilities suggest two attitudes an old person can take toward his or her body: **preoccupation** and **acceptance.** People who define their worth in terms of bodily well-being can only see old age as a time of pain and woe. For other people (who may suffer equal discomfort and pain), personal worth and well-being are defined in terms of other people or in terms of ideas but not in terms of bodily well-being. People in this latter group see a decrease in body functioning as an inevitable aspect of being an old human being. Such people also feel that it is up to the person to control his or her body rather than vice versa. People who are preoccupied with their bodies do not come to this point of view, with the result that each pain and each discomfort is suffered to the maximum.

2. Old-age survivors.   One final aspect of results gathered by Shanas and coworkers that seems worth mentioning is that there is a marked difference between people in their seventies and those 80 or older. Whereas people in their seventies produced the smallest percentage of "good" evaluations of their health, people in their eighties showed a marked upswing, with average values for both men and women higher at this point in life

than at almost any time in the period from 65 through 79. Taken in combination with other studies involving 80 + -year-old people, these results suggest that once you get to be 80, you are part of a special elite and that people who reach this stage usually know and appreciate their special status. As Cumming and Parlegreco (1961) put it, "Very old people often have a surprisingly high level of social competence and seem able to maintain high spirits.... Among the 'eighties' there is less complaining and more chirpiness, and a mood of using the last days of life in tranquility and with a genuine carefree quality" (p. 201).

Data such as these suggest that the very old (80 +) represent a special group: a group of **survivors** who have made it through the craziness and caprice of the world. Perhaps because the younger-old (that is, those between 65 and 75) still involve themselves with issues of work and retiring, they do not yet treasure (or even understand) their special status as survivors. They have not yet made the transition from being angry about decreasing physical abilities to enjoying the present with cheeriness and transcendence of bodily disability. To be old is to accept the world and our fleeting place in it and still enjoy the sun on warm summer days and the continuity of our lives with the lives of those who have gone before and are still to come. To be old is to survive, and in an absurd world this is no small accomplishment.

C. More research on old-age survivors

If there is one clear-cut theme that runs through almost all the research on old age, it is that people who are healthy into early and late old age represent a special group of human beings. Perhaps the most extensive study presenting this point of view was done by Birren and his associates (Birren, Butler, Greenhouse, Sokoloff, & Yarrow, 1963), who studied 47 men aged 65–91. These men, all of whom were volunteers, lived primarily in urban areas and tended to be above average in educational level and retirement income. The majority (41) lived in their own family households; the rest lived with relatives. Right at the beginning we have to realize that this particular group of men could not in any way be considered representative of their age group: in general, they were healthier, were better educated, had more intact family relationships, and had somewhat higher retirement incomes than most.

When all 47 men were given intensive physical examinations, Birren and coworkers found that it was possible to divide them into two subgroups. Group 1 contained 27 men who were found to be in optimal health in every regard; Group 2 contained 20 men who were found to be without clinical symptoms of illness, although further testing did reveal a few mild disease conditions. Being able to divide the men into these two groups was an important finding, for on almost all tests given to members of both groups, Group 1 individuals were scarcely different from much younger men (aged 20–25), whereas Group 2 individuals showed the usual differences in favor of the younger men.

In each of the areas tested, Birren's results were as follows.

1. Medical examinations revealed little difference between Group 1 men and a sample of much younger men in oxygen consumption during exercise or in brain blood flow. Although there were some small changes in the electrical activity of the brain for Group 1 individuals, overall values were well within the normal range for younger men. In contrast, men in Group 2 scored less well on all medical indices than men in Group 1 or men in the control group of 20–25-year-olds.

2. Intelligence tests covering a wide range of topics and issues revealed that men in Groups 1 and 2 did better than the 20–25-year-olds and that on 21 of 23 tests, men in Group 1 did better than men in Group 2. In addition, scores made by men in both Groups 1 and 2 were better than scores usually achieved by older people not specifically selected as healthy.

3. On almost all the personality measures used,

including psychiatric interviews as well as psychometric and projective tests, neither group of men differed from the younger controls, although 9 of the 47 older men did experience depression as an occasional "symptom." Although it is hard to describe the specific psychological way (or ways) in which these men were able to function so well in old age, it does seem possible to suggest that maintaining a sense of personal identity is crucial. In addition, many of these men made effective use of insight and had accurate perceptions of old age.

4. Interviews concerning how the men dealt with ongoing social problems revealed, not surprisingly, that the loss of a significant person was associated with poorer functioning for both groups of older men.

Perhaps the major conclusion to be drawn from this set of studies is that *people* age and that to talk about age independent of people is to miss the extremely interconnected nature of personal biology, intelligence, adaptability, and social functioning. In fact, it does not even seem reasonable to divide a person into these categories, except for statistical purposes. If there is one thing Birren's data suggest, it must be that healthy old people are "healthy" in almost all respects. It is the person who is in "good" or "poor" health, and even though there are health optimists and health pessimists, a general evaluation of personal health is always of the whole person, never of separate pieces.

A follow-up study, done by Birren and associates 11 years after the original study, provides further evidence of the special nature of Group 1 individuals. Although about half the original sample of 47 subjects had died in the intervening period, a closer examination revealed that 14 (of 20) men in Group 2 had died (70%) whereas only 10 (of 27) men in Group 1 had died (37%). Perhaps an even more significant finding was how little these 17 survivors seemed to have changed as they aged from 70 to 81. Almost the only difference was a now-lessened ability to deal with the death of a loved one.

These findings are not alone in suggesting that it is appropriate to consider healthy older people survivors. In a study originally designed to determine changes in a wide variety of skills, attitudes, and abilities, Riegel, Riegel, and Meyer (1967) tested groups of people aged 55–59, 60–64, 65–69, 70–74, and 75 + at two sessions five years apart. Although this experiment produced a great deal of interesting information relevant to aging, the most important result for present purposes concerns the scores of those who survived the five-year period and those who did not. Of the original group of 380 people, 202 were available for retesting five years later. The remaining 178 could not or would not be retested for various reasons; 62 had died, 32 were too ill, and 84 refused to take part.

When Riegel et al. looked at all 32 of the test measures taken for each person, they found 18 significant differences between those individuals who survived and those who died between the two periods of testing. Most of these differences concerned higher IQ scores for survivors than nonsurvivors. In addition, survivors were found to have a greater variety of interests and lower scores on measures of personal rigidity. Here again the conclusion seems inescapable: the healthy older person must be considered someone special not only in terms of medical health but in terms of interests, attitudes, intelligence, and skills.

To strengthen this conclusion a bit more, consider de Beauvoir's (1973) summary of that very special class of older people: centenarians—people who are 100 or more years old. Such people have been interviewed in different countries (the United States, Cuba, Russia, France, and others), and de Beauvoir's summary of such individuals seems to apply equally to all the various groups studied. As she noted with specific regard to French centenarians:

> There were between six and seven hundred in France in 1959 and the majority of these were to be found in Brittany. Most were under a hundred and two, and ... there are many more women than men. These women had had a great variety of jobs. They had been retired for thirty or forty years; and they were then living in the country with their children or grandchildren, or in some cases in institutions or rest-homes. They had lost their husbands twenty to forty years earlier. They had very little money; they were all thin, not one of them weighing more than 133 lbs. They loved their food but ate little. Many of them were strong and well ... there was one who played billiards at over ninety-nine. Some of the women were slightly shaky, they were a little hard of hearing and their sight was dim, but they were neither blind nor deaf. They slept well. They passed their time reading, knitting or taking short walks. Their minds were clear and their memories excellent. They were independent, even-tempered and sometimes gay; they had a lively sense of humor and were very sociable. They were high-handed towards their seventy-year-old children and treated them as young people. Some-

times they complained of the present-day generation, but they were interested in modern times and kept in touch with what was going on. None of them had any pathological history and none suffered from chronic illness. They did not seem to be afraid of death. In the main, they behaved very differently from old people junior to them [pp. 544–545].

IV. THE EVERYDAY WORLD OF THE OLD PERSON

Contrary to the worst fears of those of us who are not yet 65, 70, or 75, the old person does not live in daily fear of his or her existence any more than the younger person. Instead, there are tasks to be done or avoided, persons to be dealt with or ignored, pleasures or pains to be endured or changed, and so on. The old person lives in his or her self-world as we do in ours, and to understand old age we must come to some understanding of the everyday world of the older person. No simple counting up of medical statistics or changes in IQ scores will ever give us what we seek—a view of old age as it is lived by the old person.

But how can we describe the old person's Being-in-the-world from his or her own point of view? Simone de Beauvoir in her book *The Coming of Age* (1973) suggests that like all self-worlds, the everyday world of old people can be described best only in terms of the categories of body, self, time, and the social world of others, and we can do no better than follow her lead.

The issue concerning the body is clear: does it still function well enough for me to get around, or must I be dependent on others? Almost all the data we have suggest that health in old age is not only a question of the physical body but also a question of whether the well-enough-functioning body is still integrated within a meaningful personal and social context. Those who survive to 70 or 80 and beyond are part of an elite group who have learned how to live and to accept the limitations of being old. The key idea in regard to the issue of body seems to be whether I can accept my decreased possibilities and still find some that are personally worth doing for me. The healthy old person comes to accomplish this, and although I, as an old person, may feel (and be) less able than younger people I still come to define myself as in good enough health "for a person of my age." Fortunately, bodily changes that go along with age are gradual, and all of us learn how to compensate for our shortcomings, if these only come upon us slowly enough.

What this suggests is that we come to our understanding of old age not only as a result of dramatic bodily changes but, more important, as a result of how other people in our social world react to us. Retirement is one of those formal events that signal to us that we are no longer young. Similarly, the actions of coworkers and children (whether these be harsh or concerned) signal a change in status for us. Depending on how we have defined ourselves, we can deal with retirement and all that it involves by accepting it, by rejoicing in it, by denying it, by becoming angry with it, or by feeling that we are defeated and done for. The "meaning" of retirement always depends on whose retirement we are talking about and what that retirement means within the context of a single, unique life.

Other people's actions and opinions, as well as the sheer fact of other people, enter the world of an old person in still other ways. Some of these, such as the way an old person gets along with his or her family (including grandchildren), can provide a measure of support and joy. Others, such as the death of a loved one or friend, provide situations that can only be lived unhappily. Although the significance of a human life depends on its interrelatedness with other people, such relationships can be both a blessing and a curse.

Finally, there is the question of time and my relationships to it. There can be no doubt that age changes a person's attitude toward the whole subject. When one is old, the obvious fact is that there is less time left than has been used up—the future shortens as the past grows. One consequence is a tendency to reminisce, to try to put the events of my life and my society into some sort of order. To be sure, the order is personal, but how else could it be? It is, after all, *my* life and *my* history, and the fact that some "objective" historian may write it all down at some later time is of little interest to me.

Because I tend to think about time and history and often am unable to make much sense of them, it is quite reasonable that I should turn to religion. Sometimes this turning will occur for the first time; more likely it will be a re-turning to issues and ideas I have not been concerned with since youth. Although it may be physically difficult for me to go to church often, this does not mean I am uninter-

ested in God, time, and human values. In one sense, I disengage myself from the formal parts of religion only to reengage myself in personal religious problems and issues.

Time, in old age, is not of a single piece; it can be experienced as exciting as well as oppressive. As one writer put it, "Some sigh for yesterday! Some for tomorrow! But you must reach old age before you can understand the meaning—the splendid absolute, unchallengeable, irreplaceable meaning of the word today." Another put it, "Survival is extraordinary. You are no longer attached to anything and yet you are more sensitive to all." Finally, "I should like to think [in old age] of nothing at all except that I exist and that I am here" (all excerpts quoted from de Beauvoir, 1973, p. 448). Such words from old people suggest that all is not lost in old age, and the fact that there is so little time left is as exciting to some as it is upsetting to others.

Body, retirement (work), time, self, and others are the issues out of which human living is fashioned in old age, as in all ages of life. In old age the issue of body comes down to a question of weakness and health, while that of retirement comes down to a question of accepting socially imposed limits. Time is difficult to pin down at any age, although for old people that issue seems to have something to do with personal history and personal reminiscences on that history. Although relationships to oneself and to others are important all through life, in old age the important concerns are being part of an extended family and being able to deal with personal loss.

Since much of the present chapter has been concerned with the first two of these issues—body and retirement—to set things right we ought to explore the remaining three: reminiscing, losing a loved one, and being involved in a multi-aged and/or extended-family situation.

A. Reminiscing and the process of life review

One of the more important supports and conditions of human life is our relationship to time. For the young person this means the present and the future and, to a lesser extent, the past. For those of us who are not young, it means the present and the past and, to a much lesser degree, the future. Both young and old live (as they must) in the present, and what differs between them is their relationship to, and in, time. When a person is young, plans and long-range achievements are most important, and because a year is "longer" when the person is young, future plans are often vague about how much time they will take. In midlife, planning and doing seem more related to clock and calendar Time; in old age, long-range plans are not undertaken, for each year has now become "so much shorter," and we never know how many years we have left.

If planning and the future it implies are differently understood at each age, so too are remembering and the person's relationship to his or her past. For the young, the idea of searching for significance in the past seems all wrong, for it is surely in the future that I will find myself and become what I will become. In midlife, the past and future are of equal length, and I am defined both by what I have been and done and by what I am still likely to do and be. When I am older, the past serves to remind me of what I have done (and not done), and for this reason it becomes even more important for me to deal with it in a personally meaningful way. This does not mean that old people "live in the past," only that their past is more important to them than it was at any other time in their life.

But in what way is the past important, and why should we continue to think and rethink about it when we are old? One reason for **reminiscence** is that we want to own the past as ours—to reexperience those events that stand out as important for us. Some of these events may be painful (still open) situations we have never resolved; others may provide well-balanced and pleasant memories. In either case, they affirm that we have lived, and this handful of recollections helps validate our having lived.

Sometimes the attempt to recover one's past is a denial. De Beauvoir (1973, p. 362) writes:

> It is the future that decides whether the past is living or not. . . . A man whose project is to get on . . . takes off from his past; he defines his former I as the I that he is no longer. . . . Most old people . . . refuse time because they do not wish to decline; they define their former I as that which they still are. . . . Even if they have accepted a new image of themselves—the dear old grandmother, or the retired person, or the elderly writer— each in his heart preserves the conviction of having remained unalterable: when they summon their memories they justify this assertion. They set up a fixed, unchanging essence against the deteriorations of age, and tirelessly they tell stories of this being that they were, this being that lives on inside them.

There is, however, a more positive way of looking at reminiscing—to consider it as an attempt to make whatever sense we can of our life, past and present. Butler (1968, p. 450), in dealing with the issue of life review, notes the following constructive use of reminiscing in the context of Ingmar Bergman's film *Wild Strawberries.*

> Ingmar Bergman's very fine, remarkable Swedish motion picture . . . provides a beautiful example of the constructive aspects of the life review. Envisioning and dreaming of his past and his death, the protagonist-physician realizes the nonaffectionate and withholding qualities of his life; as the feeling of love reenters his life, the doctor changes even as death hovers upon him.

Whether we see the process of life review as constructive or defensive, one thing is clear: what is at issue in reminiscing is the person's relationship to, and in, time. So much seems to be happening now that I could not have planned for: I have retired, old and dear friends are dying, my body works differently, and so on. All these events force me to find some continuity between the past and present phases of my life, especially since many events of my present are not of my making nor to my liking. Kimmel (1974, p. 413) talks about the old person's attempt to "integrate his new [physical and social] me into his or her relatively continuous sense of self"—a good way to describe the role and meaning of reminiscing in old age.[5] The basic question is "How can I change and be so different, yet feel so much the same?" The way the old person answers this question can lead him or her to a sense of despair or to a final and more profound sense of unity.

Reminiscing is very much an act of the present and, as in all acts of remembering (see Chapter 8), what we choose to remember reveals our attitude toward the topic of our reminiscences. In old age the topic is usually me and my life, and if the best moments can only be remembered as happening a long time ago, that tells something about my present. If, however, I reconstruct both a meaningful near and far past, that too tells something of my present life as an old person. The one thing to keep in mind is that reminiscing is not something that

---

[5]From *Adulthood and Aging: An Interdisciplinary Developmental View*, by D. C. Kimmel. Copyright © 1974 by John Wiley & Sons, Inc. This and all other quotations from this source are reprinted by permission.

happens to me; rather, I choose to do it and in so doing unreflectedly tell something of me and my present situation.

If reminiscing must be described as a personal *act* of the present, this fact suggests that I may also choose *not* to do it. To say that "old people reminisce, and it's good (or bad) for them" is to look at reminiscing from a third-person point of view and to miss the fact that not every old person reminisces all or even much of the time. To reminisce is to relate to one's life in a particular way for some particular reason, and like all the acts of a life, it depends very much for its significance on the particular old person we are talking about. There is no hard and fast single meaning for reminiscing any more than for anything else a person does or does not do at any point in his or her life.

B. Bereavement and grief

One of the most difficult problems in being old is that people you know die. Sometimes these people are important—a child, a wife, a husband. Sometimes they are friends, at other times they are "only" acquaintances. Feeling sad or apprehensive at the loss of another person seems reasonable enough in the first two situations, but why should one feel a sense of loss over the death of an acquaintance or, even more distantly, a famous person of one's generation?

The answer to this question in this last case (and one that relates to all the other cases as well) is that the death of any person I have identified with signals a break with my past. Each death closes down an area of life, which can no longer be reopened except in memory. If the person who died was "only" a celebrity I knew from a distance or through the media, then the era he or she defined is past and no more; if the person who died was a friend or even an acquaintance, then what we shared will be no more; and if the one who died was a spouse or a child, then a complete segment of my adult life is gone. And this is true whether my relationship to the person was pleasant or unpleasant. The death of a child is particularly difficult to deal with, for not only is a part of the past shut down, so is a part of the future. All my plans are in vain, for the future—my child—is no more.

The more usual circumstance of death, however, involves a husband or wife, and so most of what we know about loss and grief concerns reports of wid-owed men and women. One of the more extensive attempts to understand the experience of recently widowed people was done by Clayton, Halikes, and Maurice (1971). In this study 109 people aged 20–89 who were widowed within the preceding month were interviewed on a wide variety of topics related to their experiences of bereavement. Figure 15-4 presents the major reactions reported by this group of people. Not surprisingly, these include crying and a depressed mood. Some of the other reactions reported, such as a lack of appetite, weight loss, loss of interest in TV and news, and a feeling that life was hopeless, also seem related to a general feeling of depression. Still other reactions, such as sleep disturbances, anger, psychosomatic reactions, anxiety, and hallucinations, seem to concern the person's way of dealing with loss in his or her present situation.

Even though we may be somewhat surprised to find anger on the list, almost anyone who has ever worked with people following the death of a loved one reports this as a common symptom. In writing about the need to resolve the issue of anger, Paul (1969) notes that such anger often occurs because the bereaved person feels that the person who died has not only taken away his or her presence but also shattered the family situation and, perhaps more important, abandoned the survivor. Unfortunately, it is inappropriate in our culture to speak badly of the dead or to be angry toward them. For this reason, the bereaved person is often angry with other members of the family rather than with the person who died. If this anger is not dealt with, the family situation can be chaotic for a time and will return to normal only as the experience of anger is worked through. It is at this point that Paul, the psychotherapist, notes how important it is for a therapist to "empathize with the family's grief" and to help them work through it to a more manageable family situation.

1. The "phantom spouse." Another possibly surprising reaction to bereavement is hallucinations. Here a rather interesting study done by Rees (1971) in Wales found that among about 300 widowed individuals interviewed on a one-to-one basis, over 50% reported one or more hallucinations of their dead partners. This figure is obviously much larger than the 6 or 7% reported in Figure 15-4 and includes hallucinations in which the dead person

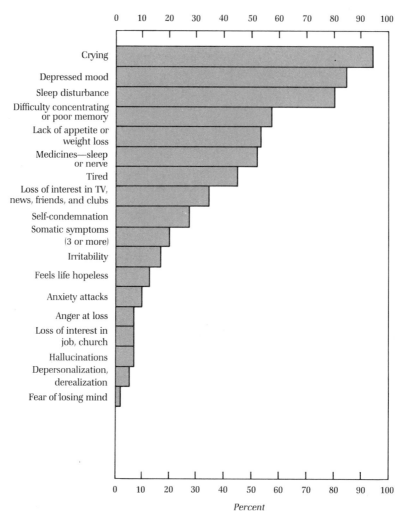

Figure 15-4.   Percentage of randomly selected recently widowed persons reporting various symptoms of bereavement (N = 109). Somatic symptoms include headaches, blurred vision, dyspnea, abdominal pain, constipation, urinary frequency, dysmenorrhea, and other body pains. *(From "The Bereavement of the Widowed," by P. J. Clayton, J. A. Halikes, and W. L. Maurice. In* Diseases of the Nervous System, *1971, 32, 597–604. Copyright 1971 by the Journal of Clinical Psychiatry. Reprinted by permission.)*

was "sensed," "heard," or "seen." It does not include experiences such as fantasies or dreams.

Rees also reports that most of the people interviewed had never told anyone else of these experiences because they were afraid of being ridiculed. When asked whether they were "helped" by their hallucinations, about 70% reported that they were, while 6% reported that they found such experiences unsettling and unpleasant; 24% found the experience neither helpful nor unpleasant.

In summarizing these results, Rees noted:

It seems reasonable to conclude . . . that hallucinations are normal experiences after widowhood, providing psychological help to those experiencing them. Evidence supporting this statement is as follows: hallucinations are common experiences after widowhood; they occur irrespective of sex, race, creed, or domicile; they do not affect overt behavior; they tend to disappear with time; there is no evidence of associated illness or abnormality to suggest they are abnormal features; they are more common in people whose marriages were happy and who became parents; and people are able to integrate the experience and keep it secret [1971, p. 41].[6]

These findings suggest that in strongly bonded couples, the dead husband or wife continues to be present to the widowed partner. Findings such as these have led one investigator, Parkes (1970; 1972), to talk about the "**phantom spouse**" by analogy to the "phantom limb" (see Chapter 3). In support of his feeling that this is more than just an accidental analogy, Parkes notes that a small number of widows report that they experienced great bodily loss after the death of their husbands: "It's as if my inside had been torn out and left a horrible wound there. It's as if half of myself was missing" (1970, p. 448). As in phantom limbs, one explanation may be that the survivor still experiences a wide range of living possibilities in regard to her dead husband, and the fact of death alters the picture only slowly.

The overall pattern of reactions is similar in hallucinations following the loss of a loved one and in the phantom-limb phenomenon (Parkes, 1972). For both, the first stage is a feeling of shock. This stage is followed by a strong tendency to deny that death or amputation has occurred: "It's as if he were still with me." Following these phases of shock and denial there is a period of anxiety and/or grief. In bereavement, such feelings are evoked by almost any event or object associated with the person and often last for about 6 months. By the end of a year or 18 months, the widow (or amputee) finally comes to a period of acceptance.

2. Ghosts. The existence of "phantom husbands" (or wives) may help us make sense of another phenomenon that is both fascinating and puzzling to many people in the Western world—**ghosts.** Anthropological studies are quite clear in showing that if there is one phenomenon typical of preliterate societies, it is the belief in ghosts. Blauner (1968), in reviewing this literature, reports that of 71 tribes studied by anthropologists, all 71 had one or another belief in ghosts. Sometimes the belief concerned a ghost that entered women at childbirth; some-

times it concerned a dead father, chief, or magician; and sometimes it involved the ghosts of warriors or enemies.

The belief in ghosts is not simply a consequence of an unsophisticated, prescientific view of the world; rather, it would seem that ghosts represent "unfinished business" brought about by the death of a person vitally engaged within a small and close-knit tribe. Ghosts give the living a chance to continue a socially and personally important relationship with the person who has died.

This approach may explain why ghosts are sometimes feared. As Blauner put it,

Fear exists because of the belief that the dead man, frustrated in his exclusion from a life in which he was recently involved, wants back in, and, failing this, may attempt to restore his former personal ties by taking others along with him on his journey to the spirit world. . . . It would appear that the dead who were most engaged in the life of society have the strongest motives for restoring their ties, and the most feared ghosts tend to be those whose business has been the least completed. Ghosts of the murdered, the suicide, and others who have met a violent end are especially feared because they have generally died young, with considerable strength and energy remaining. Ghosts of women dying in childbirth and of the unmarried and childless are considered particularly malignant because these souls have been robbed of life's major purpose; at the funeral the unmarried are often given mock marriages to other dead souls. Ghosts of dead husbands or wives are dangerous to their spouses, especially when the latter have remarried [1968, p. 533].[7]

Blauner's analysis suggests that the scarcity of ghosts in contemporary Western society is not so much a matter of our "scientific attitude" (which, to be sure, does make it hard to *talk* about ghosts in public but not to think about them) but a consequence of the fact that we live in a much less close-knit society than preindustrial people do. It matters little to American society if this or that baby, father, or grandmother dies, for the death of one person (or even of one family) is of little consequence to the whole society. When a person significant to the whole social order dies (an event that is quite rare),

[6]From "The Hallucinations of Widowhood," by W. D. Rees. In *British Medical Journal*, 1971, 4, 37–41. Copyright 1971 the British Medical Journal. Reprinted by permission.

[7]From "Death and Social Structure," by R. Blauner. In B. L. Neugarten (Ed.), *Middle Age and Aging.* Excerpted from *Psychiatry, Journal for the Study of Interpersonal Processes*, 1966, 29, 378–394. Copyright 1966 by the William Alanson White Psychiatric Foundation. Reprinted by permission.

it is extremely unsettling to us and takes a number of days or weeks to overcome. The best example in recent years is, of course, the assassination of John F. Kennedy and America's reactions to it.

Ghosts seem very much a social counterpart of "phantom spouses." In both cases, a link continues to exist between those who died and those who live, and in both cases the link is kept alive by "continuing business" concerning the people involved. The more intense and significant the relationship or the unfinished business, the greater and more immediate the phantom (or ghost) to the person still alive. Phantoms and ghosts are spooky phenomena because they are "so real" to the person experiencing them and so impossible for the person not involved. The issue reduces, once again, to the difference between a first- and a third-person point of view, and here, as in many other cases, the difference is enormous.

3. The role of friends and religion in grief and mourning.   Even though each individual takes the loss of a loved one in his or her own unique way, a period of acceptance is decisively entered when (and if) the person comes to involve himself or herself with a new task. As one woman said, "The thing that helped most after my husband died was getting a job" (Parkes, 1972, p. 346). Getting a job, however, is not the only way a period of bereavement is overcome, and perhaps the single most important way in which a person turns from grief and mourning back to the world is through his or her relationships to friends and relatives. Here some work by Lowenthal and Haven (1968) is relevant in showing that older people who had a **confidant** (a friend to whom they could speak openly and freely) were less depressed than those who did not. On the basis of interviewing some 280 old people, Lowenthal and Haven found that 55% of widowed people with a confidant felt satisfied with their situation in old age, compared with 47% satisfied for still-married older people who did not have a confidant. As is to be expected, widowed people not having a confidant were least satisfied (27%), while still-married people having a confidant were most satisfied (65%).

Since Lowenthal and Haven's study was done in an old-age home, it seems reasonable to wonder who the confidants were and who had the confidants. The major confidants for people in this age

group were, not surprisingly, a friend, a child, or a spouse. Brothers, sisters, or other relatives were only infrequently described as confidants. Even though there were far more widows than widowers in this group, more women tended to have confidants than men (69% compared with 57%).

These data suggest that the human being who is strongly involved in a social context is more satisfied with his or her lot than the person not so involved. Using this as a starting point, Lowenthal and Haven wondered whether having a confidant was a generally beneficial state of affairs. Specifically, they suggested (somewhat tentatively, to be sure) that being more socially involved may be one reason women live longer than men, are less likely to commit suicide after the death of a spouse, and have a lower rate of mental illness in old age.

In discussing these speculations and their practical implications, Kimmel (1974) notes that having a confidant is not the be-all and end-all in old age. As he sees it, there are three points to be kept in mind in describing the seemingly beneficial situation of having a confidant:

> First, some persons have maintained adequate levels of functioning with relative isolation over a long period of time; they seem no more prone to mental illness than nonisolates. These isolates may have high morale, but the majority of those who had and lost a confidant are depressed. Second, loss of a confidant may result from a general dislocation (such as moving into a smaller home or into a nursing home) that represents a double loss. Several studies have found an increased rate of death following major relocation, particularly among institutionalized aged; . . . thus, when a confidant is needed most, he may be unavailable. Third, gaining a confidant may help some, but the importance of a stable relationship seems most significant [p. 319].

Formal religion represents another way in which the social world can be of help to an old person. Although this seems a fairly straightforward point, there is some confusion in the research literature over just how religious old people are. First there is the question of what being religious means: does it mean attending formal services, or does it mean having a deeply felt personal conviction? Similarly, we need to know whether religiousness in either (or both) of these senses increases or decreases in importance over the life cycle and whether an increase (or decrease) is necessarily helpful to the person.

An obvious way to go at the problem of religion in old age is to look at church or synagogue attendance for people in various age ranges. The results of many studies reviewed by Moberg (1965) suggest that attendance varies only slightly up to age 60 and decreases somewhat in the years following. The meaning of these results, as Moberg notes, is not entirely clear: an older person is usually not as able to get around as a younger person, and many older people who do not attend church services in person do listen to such services on the radio or television. Among Jewish men, for whom there are few if any "Synagogues of the Air," attendance at services was found to increase in old age (Orbach, 1961).

If attendance does not give a clear picture, do religious beliefs strengthen as the person gets older? Although data on religious beliefs in old people are not extensive, most surveys have found an increased belief in an afterlife. (The values range from 41% for 60–65-year-old Jewish adults to 81% for similarly aged Catholic adults. Comparable figures for people aged 30–50 showed 30% belief for Jewish adults and 70% for Catholic adults.) The aged also seem more conservative in religious beliefs than younger people, although "whether [these] differences are a result of . . . aging or of differing experiences during the years of childhood and youth . . . is unknown" (Moberg, 1965, p. 81).

An increased belief in an afterlife and a feeling of involvement in something larger than oneself both seem to help the bereaved person come to terms with loss. Despite help provided by religion, confidants, and work, the way back from a sense of grief is a long and arduous one that may take as long as two years to accomplish. During this period the person sees himself or herself as diminished and lost and, for this reason, shows a wide range of symptoms indicating that for the person a complete segment of life is forever gone. The way back from a loss of this magnitude is a long and painful one, and even though other people and events may help, in the final analysis we all have to do it alone.

C. On being a grandparent

If the death of a loved one (or even an age peer) closes down certain avenues to the past, then being a grandparent must surely open up certain new ones. One reason grandchildren are so dear is that they grant access to a new future not only for their parents but for their parents' parents. In this,

grandchildren extend older people's history into a future they cannot know and into which they cannot project themselves. As death closes a segment of life, the birth of a grandchild extends new lines into the future.

A person does not have to be a biological grandparent to get a share of the future. Many older people become emotionally involved with people a good many years their junior, and these relationships often become sufficiently important to both partners so that a biological link is unnecessary to cement the relationship. Sometimes the older person will be given the honorific title of *uncle* or *aunt*, and this kinship name is then extended to him or her by the children of the younger person, if there are any.

Perhaps the most important personal benefit to be derived from being involved in a cross-generation network of people (whether it be of friends or relatives) is that it provides the person with an experience of continuity. For this reason it should come as no surprise that when 70 grandmothers and 70 grandfathers were asked what they saw as the most important aspect of being a grandparent, over 30% reported that it provided them with a sense of fulfillment and/or contentment (Neugarten & Weinstein, 1964). Specific statements gleaned from interviews with these individuals included "It's through these children that I see myself going into the future" or "My grandchildren make me feel young again."

Other sources of satisfaction concerned doing things with grandchildren that the grandparents had denied themselves with their own children ("Now I have time to be with them") or being considered a special person by the child. As one grandfather put it, "I take my grandson down to the factory and show him how the business operates . . . . I've also set aside money especially for him. That's something his father can't do yet, although he'll do it for *his* grandchildren."

Among the 140 grandparents interviewed, about 28% felt remote from their grandchildren and were unable to see anything special about this type of relationship. Neugarten and Weinstein summarized their impressions of these people in the following terms:

For both the men and women who fell into this category . . . a certain lack of conviction appeared in their statements, as if the men did not really believe that, once the grandchildren were older, they would indeed become closer to them, and as if the women did not really believe that their busy schedules accounted for their lack of emotional involvement with their grandchildren. Rather, these grandparents imply that the role itself is perceived as being empty of meaningful relationships [p. 203].[8]

Just as being a grandparent has different meanings for different people, so there are different styles of grandparenting. Table 15-2 shows the frequency of the five major styles uncovered by Neugarten and Weinstein among 140 grandmothers and grandfathers. The most common style of being a grandparent was the fairly traditional one of being **formal** and, by that formality, a bit special. For people adopting this style, the grandparent functions as a person who provides special treats for grandchildren but who leaves the day-to-day business of parenting to the child's parents.

A second major style of being a grandparent is **fun-seeking**. In this style the grandparent and the grandchild engage in activities that are fun for both. Although both recognize some generational differences, these are not seen as important to either of them. What is important is that there is mutual enjoyment of the things they do together. In this type of relationship it is not the grandparent who gives and the grandchild who takes; rather, both give and take.

The **parent-surrogate** style of grandparenting is restricted primarily to grandmothers. Often the

grandmother accepts this role as a result of necessity, as when there is no one else to take the place of working parents.

A fourth style of being a grandparent is that of being perceived and responded to as the **reservoir of family wisdom**. Although this role seems an obvious one from many theoretical points of view (such as that suggested by Erikson), it seems rare in contemporary society. For this style of grandparenting, the lines of authority are clear, and it is the grandfather who is in charge. This situation would seem to apply in wealthy and powerful families, with Joseph Kennedy (John F. Kennedy's father) perhaps the best example in our contemporary world.

Finally, there is the **distant** style of being a grandparent, in which little or no contact occurs across the generations. What contact there is usually revolves around formal occasions, such as weddings, births, and holidays. As Neugarten and Weinstein put it, this type of grandparent "is benevolent in stance but essentially distant . . . from the child's life, a somewhat intermittent St. Nicholas" (p. 284).

Although these five styles are quite different, each may be most appropriate at different points in the grandchild's life. For example, many grandparents adopt a "fun-seeking" style when their grandchildren are quite young. As grandchildren grow older, however, some of these same grandparents change style and become "distant" rather than "fun-seeking" grandparents. Although a change of this type may make the grandparent a bit unhappy, it does indicate a sensitivity to the changing nature of the growing grandchild.

In addition to dealing directly with their grandchildren, grandparents can serve other functions. Kalish (1975) notes that young children sometimes

[8]From "The Changing American Grandparent," by B. L. Neugarten and K. K. Weinstein. In *Journal of Marriage and the Family*, 1964, 26, 199–204. Copyright 1964 by the National Council on Family Relations. Reprinted by permission.

TABLE 15-2. Styles of Grandparenting in 70 Grandmothers and 70 Grandfathers

Style	Number of Grandmothers	Number of Grandfathers
The Formal	22	23
The Fun-Seeking	20	17
The Parent Surrogate	10	0
The Reservoir of Family Wisdom	1	4
The Distant Figure	13	20
(Insufficient data)	4	6
Total	70	70

From "The Changing American Grandparent," by B. L. Neugarten and K. K. Weinstein. In *Journal of Marriage and the Family*, 1964, 26, 199–204. Copyright 1964 by the National Council on Family Relations. Reprinted by permission.

learn how to deal with their own parents by watching their parents deal with grandparents. He also points out that grandchildren in their teens or even in their early twenties are sometimes better able to deal with grandparents than with their own parents. One reason is that grandparents often do not live in the same house as the growing young adult, and many of the tensions existing between teenager and parents do not exist between teenager and grandparents. This helpful state of affairs would seem to come about because both the young and the old are usually the less powerful members of the family and as such can form an alliance that is not only mutually satisfying but helpful to both.

Even though some grandchildren and grandparents do develop this type of relationship, many experience tension between the generations, with the older person trying to tell the younger what to do and how to do it and the younger person telling the older not to tell him or her what to do and how to do it. Here, as elsewhere, the style that finally evolves is arrived at by two different human beings, and the choice of alliance or conflict depends on the particular grandparent and the particular grandchild in question.

V. DEATH AND DYING

It is said that when Sir Thomas More (later Saint Thomas) was led to the block during the reign of King Henry VIII to have his head chopped off, he told his executioner two things: one, to make the stroke clean and two, not to worry that anyone would take revenge on him for what he was about to do. Although from our point of view this may seem a hard story to believe, from Sir Thomas' point of view it makes perfectly good sense if we realize that More wanted to make sure his style of dying would reflect his style of living. To die, for Sir Thomas, was the last act a human being did in life, and it was therefore important to die in such a way as to exemplify the values held in life. In his case, these values included not only pity and charity but forgiveness as well.

In the 20th century we find it hard to consider death an act. Rather, our attitude seems to be that death "comes upon us" and that we are powerless to do anything about it. We consider ourselves Death's passive, even if unwilling, victims, and we can make little sense or meaning of the whole business except perhaps that we are afraid of it. With these assumptions, we find it quite reasonable to expect that as we get older, we get more afraid and that dying must be a difficult and frightening business to an old person.

If, however, we look not at our assumptions but at the results of surveys involving respondents of different ages, we find that people do not fear death more when they are old. Rather, the peak of fear occurs much earlier, when death is only a distant possibility. Consider some findings reported by Riley in 1963. The percentages of people agreeing with the statement "Death always comes too soon" were as follows: for people 30 and under, 53%; for people 31–40, 44%; 41–50, 63%; 51–60, 58%; 61 and older, 49%. Thus, people in the 41–50 age range held this attitude more strongly than any other age group—in particular, more than people 61 and older.

In response to the statement "To die is to suffer," results for the same age groups showed little in the way of consistent trends. The one thing that could be said for sure was that no more than 16% of the people interviewed at any age agreed with this statement. Riley (1963) also found that more older people (61 +) had made plans for events surrounding their own death (such as buying a cemetery plot or making a will) than people under 30, and he found a consistently increasing tendency for people to make such plans as they grow older.

Riley's findings suggest that even though older people may think about matters related to death more often than younger people, they tend to be less afraid of dying than people in midlife. In summarizing attitudes toward death among people of various ages, Kalish (1975) said:

> Older people seem to feel that they have lived their lives and have received what they felt they "had coming"; younger people contemplate their own death as coming too soon, as robbing them of their birthright. Many older people have been able to cope with their own eventual death partly because they have had to cope with a variety of other losses: the death of friends and family members, the loss of various functional abilities, youthful appearance, active roles, and important relationships [p. 93].[9]

[9]From *Late Adulthood: Perspectives on Human Development*, by R. A. Kalish. Copyright © 1975 by Wadsworth, Inc. Reprinted by permission of the publisher, Brooks/Cole Publishing Company, Monterey, California.

Many people thus begin to think about their own death during the decade between 40 and 50. It is at this time, perhaps for the first time, that we come to realize that life is "half over" and that we had better begin to think seriously about "how little time we have left." In contrast to this first shock of recognition, the older person has already come to some resolution, and although the issue is still important, most of old age is not given over to a constant concern with death and dying. If anything, old age seems more given over to concerns of the present—either the difficulties of getting around or the satisfactions of still being involved in family, social, or charitable events.

De Beauvoir (1973) also points out that older people do not fear death; many actively welcome it as a relief. Indeed, work done on geriatric wards reveals that terminally ill patients are often quite positive in the way they talk about dying, and many seem to have developed a personal philosophy of death a good many years before (Lieberman, 1968). Thus, the issue of how to come to terms with one's own death is not the most pressing concern when the person is old and sick; to the contrary, old people seem much more concerned with how they will get through this or that sickness than with how they will be able to work out an understanding of what it means to die.

A. Psychological changes before death

Although closeness to death need not trigger an attempt to understand it, Lieberman (1968) did find that certain psychological changes regularly occurred just before a person died. Lieberman first became interested in this topic after he noticed that one nurse in an old-age home had an uncanny knack for predicting which of her patients would soon die. Even though Lieberman never did discover the nurse's trick, he did find differences in performance on psychological tests between people who were to die in less than 3 months and people who were still living one year after testing.

Lieberman used four psychological tests. Two—the Draw-a-Person and the Bender-Gestalt Test—showed significant performance differences between the 8 old people who died within 3 months of testing and the 17 old people who were still living after a year. All subjects in Lieberman's experiments were tested repeatedly on each task.

The records produced by old people in the DI

("death imminent") group are revealing. Figure 15-5 presents an example of one old man's first and last drawings of a human figure and one old woman's first and last drawings of Bender-Gestalt patterns. Consider the Draw-A-Person test first: although the first drawing is not as detailed as we might expect, the final figure is even less detailed. A similar trend appears in the Bender-Gestalt drawings: the final attempt shows greater disorganization and simpler drawings than the first.

A more quantitative way to look at these changes over time is shown in Figure 15-6. Two things are obvious: there are no differences in favor of surviving subjects over death-imminent subjects for the first three testing periods, and there is a marked decrease on both measures for DI subjects at the fourth and fifth testing sessions. These graphs only extend what Figure 15-5 suggests: that there is a dramatic decline in test performance shortly before death. If anything, results for old people in the "death delayed" group (the survivors) improved over the final two or three testing periods.

This study shows clear and obvious changes in an old person's style of dealing with certain psychological tests as he or she nears death. In general, these changes involve a tendency toward smaller, simpler drawings. Lieberman (1968) has interpreted such changes to suggest that old people nearing death experience a sense of personal disorganization. This disorganization is not the reaction to an unknowable event (death) but is better understood as the individual's attempt to deal with disruptions in personal equilibrium. It is not "fear of death" that makes an individual withdraw from the world; it is his or her attempt to deal with the ongoing experience of disorganization and disequilibrium. Thus, "individuals approaching death pull away from those around them not because of a preoccupation with themselves but because they are preoccupied . . . with an attempt to hold themselves together" (Lieberman, 1965, p. 189). For the dying person, death and withdrawal are not the issues; personal integrity and restored balance are.

B. Kübler-Ross' work on stages of dying

Lieberman is not alone in his concern for the last few weeks and months of a dying person's life. In fact, Western society has specified two sets of professional people to be with the dying person: physicians and ministers. For this reason it should come

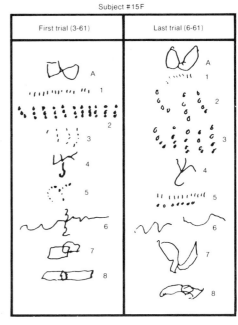

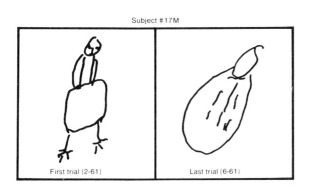

Figure 15-5. Illustration of a decline in complexity in the figure drawings made by an old man in Lieberman's "death imminent" group (left) and of a decline in organization in the Bender-Gestalt figures as drawn by an old woman in the same group (right). *(From "Psychological Correlates of Impending Death: Some Preliminary Observations," by M. A. Lieberman. In Journal of Gerontology, 1965, 20, 181–190. Copyright 1965 by the Gerontological Society. Reprinted by permission.)*

as no surprise that the most important and far-reaching analyses of death and dying were done by the psychiatrist Elisabeth Kübler-Ross (1969). Much of her work was initiated, almost by accident, by a group of theological students seeking her advice on how to research the question of dying. As Kübler-Ross came to discover, the only way to go about this was to talk with dying people and to ask them to be "our teachers."

Although talking to a dying person seemed a relatively straightforward thing to do, Kübler-Ross found that it was quite difficult to accomplish in practice. When she asked physicians to tell her which of their patients were dying, she found to her surprise that there wasn't "one dying patient in the whole 600-bed hospital" she worked in (1969, p. 23).[10] When she probed a bit further, she found

that physicians refused to allow her to interview patients because, they said, the patient was "too weak," "too sick," or "too tired" or "the patient didn't feel like talking."

During this early phase of her work, Kübler-Ross reports, it took about 10 hours of careful and discreet questioning before she could find a single dying patient to talk to. When she did locate a patient, she found that he was quite willing and able to talk to her about his experiences. Talking about death seemed taboo only for the 40- or 50-year-old physician, not for the 60- or 70-year-old patient about to die.

With few exceptions the patients were surprised, amazed, and grateful. Some were plain curious and others expressed their disbelief that "a young, healthy doctor would sit with a dying old woman and really care to know what it is like." In the majority of cases the initial outcome was similar to opening floodgates. It was hard to stop them once the conversation was initiated and the patients responded with great relief to sharing some of their last concerns, expressing their

[10] From *On Death and Dying*, by E. Kübler-Ross. Copyright 1969 by Macmillan Publishing Company, Inc. and Tavistock Publications Ltd. This and all other quotations from this source are reprinted by permission.

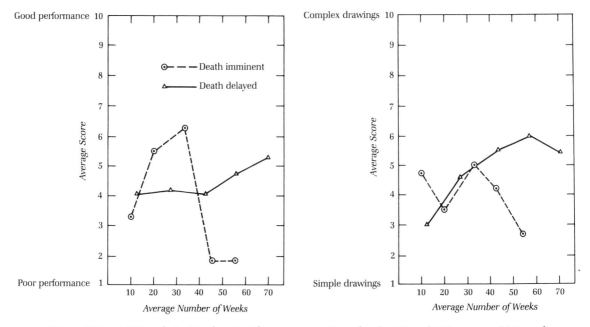

Figure 15-6. (a) Trends in Bender-Gestalt scores over time for the DI and DD groups. (b) Trends in Draw-A-Person complexity scores over time for the DI and DD groups. *(From "Psychological Correlates of Impending Death: Some Preliminary Observations," by M. A. Lieberman. In* Journal of Gerontology, *1965, 20, 181–190. Copyright 1965 by the Gerontological Society. Reprinted by permission.)*

feelings without fear of repercussions [Kübler-Ross, 1970, pp. 157–158].[11]

Over the course of the next decade and more, Kübler-Ross and her associates interviewed over 400 people and came to some conclusions about dying that are relevant not only for the dying person but for the family and the physician. For one, Kübler-Ross is quite convinced that patients know they are terminally ill whether or not they have been told. Sometimes (more often than might be expected) they can even tell you when they will die. The patient, then, knows his or her condition as well as (if not better than) the doctor, and it is pointless to hold out hope for a patient if there is none.

Perhaps the most comforting results to come out of Kübler-Ross' interviews concern her description of six **stages of dying** that many patients go through between their first awareness of a serious illness and death. Figure 15-7 presents the overall course of these stages. The first stage is shock, which shortly merges with the next stage, denial ("It couldn't be true; it couldn't be me"). Denial can last

from a few seconds to a few months, and Kübler-Ross notes that fewer than 1% of all the terminally ill people she interviewed continued to deny their illness until they died.

The third stage is usually anger at having to die: "Why me, why not somebody else?" In a hospital, such anger often takes the form of complaining about things—"My sheets were dirty and wrinkled; don't you care about me?"—or it may take the form of constantly asking for things that cannot be given and then complaining about not getting them. Physicians, but mostly nurses, have a particularly difficult time with the patient during this stage, for they tend to feel that the patient is screaming at them when in fact he or she is screaming at no one in particular.

---

[11]From "The Dying Patient's Point of View," by E. Kübler-Ross. In O. G. Brim, Jr., H. E. Freeman, S. Levine, and N. A. Scotch (Eds.), *The Dying Patient.* Copyright 1970 by the Russell Sage Foundation. Reprinted by permission of Basic Books, Inc. for Russell Sage.

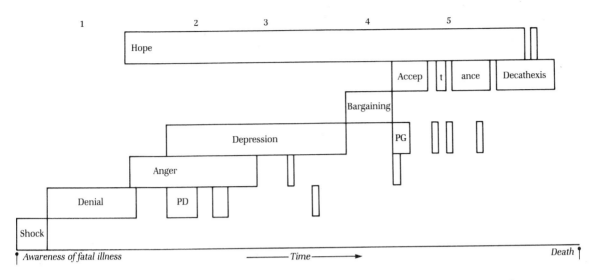

Figure 15-7. Stages of dying in terminal patients. *(From* On Death and Dying, *by E. Kübler-Ross. Copyright 1969 by Macmillan Publishing Company, Inc. and Tavistock Publications Ltd. Reprinted by permission.)*

What the patient wants to scream about can be phrased as "Hey, I'm still alive, don't you forget that. You can hear my voice, I'm not dead yet." The nurse must understand that the patient is not screaming or angry at him or her, and once the nurse comes to this conclusion, the patient is much easier to deal with. Although the patient is still angry, such anger is understandable, and being angry does not make the patient any less vulnerable or any less afraid.

The fourth stage described by Kübler-Ross is called depression. It is at this time that the patient knows he or she is terminally ill and that there is nothing to be done about it. Kübler-Ross notes that there are two types of depression—one that has to do with what the person has already lost (reactive depression) and one that has to do with what the person is about to lose (preparatory depression). In the case of preparatory depression:

> The patient is in the process of losing everything and everybody he loves. If he is allowed to express his sorrow he will find a final acceptance much easier, and he will be grateful to those who can sit with him during this stage of depression without constantly telling him not to be sad. [Kübler-Ross, 1969, p. 87].

The next stage, bargaining, is somewhat harder to understand than any of the preceding four. According to Kimmel (1974, p. 424), it is as if the person, "learning that he cannot get what he wants by demanding it (in anger) now turns to asking nicely and tries to strike a bargain." In bargaining the patient may pray for another year, promising to donate his or her eyes or kidneys to the hospital as payment for this additional time. Unfortunately, the dying person has nothing to give that can buy more life, and bargaining can only, understandably, beget more bargaining.

Kübler-Ross describes the case of a woman who had to have round-the-clock injections to control her pain. The woman wanted to attend her son's wedding. To help her, Kübler-Ross taught her a form of self-hypnosis to relieve the pain so that she could go. The story continues as follows:

> The day preceding the wedding she left the hospital as an elegant lady. Nobody would have believed her real condition. She was "the happiest person in the whole world" and looked radiant. I wondered what her reaction would be when the time was up for which she had bargained.

I will never forget the moment when she returned to the hospital. She looked tired and somewhat exhausted and—before I could say hello—said, "Now don't forget I have another son!" [Kübler-Ross, 1969, p. 83]

The sixth and final stage, which not all people attain, is acceptance. This attitude toward dying occurs only if the person is able to work his or her way through each of the preceding stages, most especially anger and depression. When the stage of acceptance is reached, the patient once again asks to see his or her family, perhaps for the last time. One particularly important aspect of this stage is the tendency of the dying person to want to be with only one other special person. At this time, talk seems superfluous, and all the patient wants is for someone to sit with him or her and, perhaps, to hold his or her hand.

Acceptance is not the same as resignation, which, as Kübler-Ross points out, is more like defeat. Instead, it is perhaps best captured by the attitude that "it's my time now, and it's all right." This is not to say that acceptance is a happy time. It is a time essentially devoid of feeling. The final struggle for survival is over, and the person seems to be taking "a final rest before the long journey," as one of Kübler-Ross' patients put it. It is as if the person feels that he has been able to finish his "business" in an orderly and responsible way.

At the beginning of this section we talked about an element of choice in how one dies. Kübler-Ross' findings show that coming to an acceptance of one's own death is a choice and thus make it clear that dying must be considered the final act of living. In accepting death, a person affirms that he or she accepts the limitations of being human for the last time and thereby reaffirms his or her connectedness to time past and human history.

Not all of us will die in a hospital, nor will all of us experience the pain and suffering of terminal illness. If we are spared this situation, to die is still an act we take upon ourselves. We will usually take this upon ourselves only when the future, our future, is beyond reach—when there is no hope and, therefore, no reason for future projects. In each life there comes a time when we "know we can no longer surpass ourselves and that we can no longer become passionately involved with anything" (de Beauvoir, 1973, p. 447). It is at this time that dying becomes an acceptable possibility. To be human is to transcend and to change, and once these possibilities are too difficult or impossible to accomplish, it is more reasonable to die than to continue in daily struggle and boredom. When this happens, to die is the proper final act of being human.

VI. SUMMARY

Old age, contrary to popular belief, does not have to be a time of unpleasantness and despair. As a conversation with "Ted Edwards" shows, old people do not necessarily preoccupy themselves with death and dying. This time of life (which usually includes retirement) has its own possibilities and limitations, which Erikson has captured in terms of a choice between ego integrity and despair. To experience integrity, an old person must sense a wholeness to his or her life and must not be overwhelmed by despair brought about by the impending end of relationships with other people. Integrated old people are able to accept the limitations of a single lifetime and to find a place for themselves in the more general flow of history and society.

Like younger people, older people construct and live in unique self-worlds. Despite the fears of those of us who are younger, such self-worlds are not preoccupied with a fear for existence; instead, they deal with the particular problems an old person must face in his or her everyday life. Thus, the everyday world of the old person is made up of the very ordinary human experiences of body, time, retirement, and so on, as well as the more specific experiences of bereavement and dying.

The old person experiences time differently than a younger person does, primarily because the older person has a long past and the probability of a shorter future. For this reason, some older people are given to reminiscing in order to reexperience the events of their past lives. Such recollections include both pleasant and painful (still open) situations. Reminiscing is an attempt to affirm the person's relationship to, and in, time. Like all acts of remembering, reminiscing is always an act of the present and, as such, relates to the life in question in a very particular and unique way.

The major changes in one's body in old age involve a diminished ability to recover from exertion or stress. The digestive, circulatory, musculoskeletal, and central nervous systems are also subject to change and deterioration. Disease occurs more often in old age, although it is difficult to specify which particular illnesses in which particular persons are due specifically to aging. Acute diseases (infection, injury, and the like) decline for older people, especially men; chronic diseases increase. Poor people are more likely to be confined to restricted activity in old age than are those better off economically.

In addition to these third-person physical and socioeconomic descriptions of the body in old age, it is necessary to consider the first-person perspective of the individual in question. On the basis of questionnaire results, old people have been divided into health realists, health optimists, and health pessimists. Except for the years immediately following retirement, studies also show that men report they are in better health than women do. Cross-cultural differences also exist; Americans complain more about less-than-optimum health than British people. In general, it is possible to conclude that for those individuals who define personal worth primarily in terms of their bodies, old age is a time of woe. For those who define personal worth in terms of other people or ideas, physical decline is much easier to endure.

Individuals who live to be 80 or beyond tend to appreciate their special status as survivors and to be more tranquil and complain less than people 15 to 20 years their junior. To survive is an accomplishment, and as Birren's and Riegel's studies demonstrate, survivors are a unique group of human beings in terms of interests, attitudes, intelligence, skills, and health. De Beauvoir's study of centenarians in France and other countries only strengthens this conclusion.

Retirement is a particularly important aspect of the first-person world of the old person. One way to determine the (reflected) personal meaning of this situation for old people is to ask them how they perceive the fact of their retirement. An early study by Reichard, Livson, and Peterson found that it was possible to divide older men (women were not included in the study) into five groups on the basis of how they answered questions concerned with old age and retirement. The "mature" group took old age for granted and made the best of it. "Rocking-chair men" liked the idea of retiring, especially as it often served to shift responsibilities to others. Men in the "armored" group refused to accept old age and defended against it vigorously, either by

denying they were old when asked or by continuing to work. "Angry men" tended bitterly to blame others for their failures, while "self-haters" blamed themselves. Only the last two groups contained men having a rough time of it in old age.

Becoming a grandparent concerns some of the more significant themes in old age. For one, becoming a grandparent extends an old person's history into the future; for another, it provides the person with new ways of dealing with important other people, such as children and grandchildren. In this latter regard, Neugarten and Weinstein were able to describe five major styles of grandparenting. Formal grandparents acted as sources of occasional special treats for their grandchildren; otherwise they did not participate in their grandchildren's day-to-day activities. Fun-seeking grandparents were seen to have a give-and-take relationship with their grandchildren, although here again, day-to-day activities were left to the child's parents. Some grandparents (particularly grandmothers) became parent surrogates, especially if parents were widowed or divorced. Here the grandparents of necessity took an active role in the child's day-to-day activities. A fourth (and rare) style of grandparent was called the "reservoir of wisdom." Most decisions involving the extended family were referred to the grandparent(s) for action, his (or her or their) decision being final. Finally, there was the condition of a break between grandparents and their grandchildren, resulting in the fifth, or nonrelational, pattern of grandparenting, known as the distant style.

One of the most important sets of issues to be confronted in old age is that concerning bereavement and dying. Bereavement is especially painful for an old person both because it occurs so frequently and because the death of a person with whom one has identified signals a break with one's own past. By an extension of this line of analysis, the death of a child (or grandchild) signals a break with the future. The usual case of bereavement, however, involves a husband or wife, and here, a study of recently widowed people shows that some or all of the following reactions followed the death of a spouse: crying, depression, lack of appetite, weight loss, loss of interest in TV and news, hopelessness, sleep disturbances, anger, psychosomatic reactions, anxiety, and hallucinations.

Such hallucinations often involve the seen, heard, or felt presence of the deceased, or what has come to be called the "phantom spouse" phenomenon (which most bereaved people are hesitant to report). Ghosts are the social version of this phenomenon, and both cases together suggest that unresolved issues between the dead person and those left behind are the major reason we stay open to the presence and influence of the now-dead person.

From an existential point of view, dying can be described as an act rather than as something that merely comes upon the person. Fear of death, contrary to our naive expectations, seems to peak in the middle years rather than in old age. Lieberman's experiments show that people nearing death experience personal disintegration, and this would seem best understood as an attempt to deal with disruptions in body equilibrium and not usually as an attempt to deal with the "meaning" of human existence.

Kübler-Ross was convinced by interviews with dying people that they know that (and sometimes when) they will die, whether or not they have been told. Between the first awareness of total illness and death, people can be described as going through six stages: shock, denial, anger, depression, bargaining, and (for some) acceptance. This final stage, if reached, means that the person has accepted dying as the final act of living; it is reached only when the person realizes that it is no longer possible for him or her to transcend and change—that is, to continue growing as an individual. When this condition is experienced, the final act of living is to die, and in this act we affirm, for the last time, that we are human and that we have lived.

VII. GLOSSARY OF IMPORTANT CONCEPTS

Acceptance of body. A style in old age of dealing with one's body in which the person accepts diminished body capacities and attempts to deal with this fact. Generally characteristic of people who define their worth in terms of other people or ideas, not in terms of physical activity.

Angry. A personal style described by Reichard, Livson, and Peterson in which the old person feels he or she has failed to achieve goals in life and blames others for disappointments.

Armored. A personal style described by Reichard, Livson, and Peterson in which the old person tends to avoid unpleasant topics and to feel he or she must keep active to avoid thinking about present problems.

Centenarian. A person who is 100 or more years old.

Confidant. A person with whom one shares intimate experiences.

Distant style. A style of grandparenting in which little or no contact occurs across the generations.

Formal style. A style of grandparenting in which the person assumes a traditional role—for example, providing special treats for grandchildren but leaving the day-to-day business of parenting to the child's parents.

Fun-seeking style. A style of grandparenting in which grandparent and grandchild seek out activities that are fun for both.

Ghost. An experience of a person who is dead. More common in nontechnological societies, in which each living person is likely to have a good deal of "unfinished business" with the person who died. A social equivalent of the "phantom spouse" phenomenon.

Health optimist, realist, pessimist. Three styles of dealing with disease in old age. Each style reflects a complex combination of personal and social evaluations of health and aging by the person.

Integrity vs. despair. According to Erikson, the eighth and last critical stage of personality development. With ego integrity, an aged person comes to an acceptance of his or her own life, which then allows him or her to accept death. The developmental alternative, despair, is characterized by failure to accept one's life and, thus, one's death.

Mature. A personal style described by Reichard, Livson, and Peterson in which the old person experiences his or her past life as rewarding, without regret for the past or a sense of loss in the present.

Parent-surrogate style. A style of grandparenting usually restricted to grandmothers in which the person takes over many of the day-to-day activities usually characteristic of the parents. This role is often undertaken out of necessity, as when the parents work.

Phantom spouse. An experience reported by as many as 50% of widowed people in which the spouse was "sensed," "heard," or "seen" (not hallucinated) by the surviving partner.

Preoccupation with body. A style in old age of dealing with one's body in which the person exhibits a continuing and somewhat negative evaluation of reduced body capacities.

Reminiscence. As an activity sometimes engaged in by old people, reminiscing may be either a denial of the present (dwelling in a happier past) or an attempt to integrate one's present life and experiences into the flow of time.

Reservoir of family wisdom. A style of grandparenting that occurs infrequently in contemporary society. In this role the grandparent is the authority in the family and is so recognized by all.

Rocking-chair. A personal style described by Reichard, Livson, and Peterson in which the old person likes the inactivity of retirement and in which he or she is basically satisfied.

Self-hater. A personal style described by Reichard, Livson, and Peterson in which the old person feels that he or she has failed to achieve important goals and turns against himself or herself.

"Stages" of dying. Seven stages characteristic of terminal patients studied by Kübler-Ross. (1) Shock—brief stage after being told of diagnosis. (2) Denial—"It couldn't be true"; may last a few seconds to a few months; for many people, this stage does pass. (3) Hope—may occur concurrently with other stages and lasts until death. (4) Anger—"Why me? Why not somebody else?" (5) Depression—mourning over loss; also, a stage of preparatory grief concerning the impending separation from loved ones. (6) Bargaining—a stage in which the dying person may pray for "just one more year" or "until my kids get through college," for example. (7) Acceptance—a stage not reached by all, in which anger and depression have been worked through and the dying person is able to accept his or her fate and be close to loved ones.

Survivor. A member of a special group of elderly people having good health, good intelligence, and good social functioning.

VIII. SUGGESTED READINGS

Major sources

Kübler-Ross, E. *On death and dying.* New York: Macmillan, 1969.

Neugarten, B. L. (Ed.). *Middle age and aging.* Chicago: University of Chicago Press, 1968.

Reichard, S., Livson, F., & Peterson, P. G. *Aging and personality.* New York: Wiley, 1962.

Secondary sources

de Beauvoir, S. *The coming of age.* New York: Warner Paperback Library, 1973.

Kimmel, D. C. *Adulthood and aging: An interdisciplinary developmental view.* New York: Wiley, 1974.

Newman, B. M., & Newman, P. R. *Development through life: A psychosocial approach.* Homewood, Ill.: Dorsey Press, 1975. Especially Chapters 9–11.

References

Adams, J. A. *Learning and memory: An introduction*. Home-wood, Ill.: Dorsey Press, 1976.

Adamson, R. E., & Taylor, D. W. Functional fixedness as related to elapsed time and to set. *Journal of Experimental Psychology*, 1954, 47, 122–126.

Ajuriaguerra, J. de. Discussion. In S. Wapner & H. Werner (Eds.), *The body percept*. New York: Random House, 1965.

Allport, F. H. *Theories of perception and the concept of structure*. New York: Wiley, 1955.

Alvarez, A. *The savage god: A study of suicide*. Harmondsworth, England: Penguin Books, 1974.

Ames, A., Jr. Visual perception and the rotating trapezoidal window. *Psychological Monographs*, 1951, 65. No. 7. Whole Number 324.

Anonymous. The effects of marijuana on consciousness. In C. T. Tart (Ed.), *Altered states of consciousness*. New York: Wiley, 1969.

Anthony, E. J. The reactions of parents to the oedipal child. In E. J. Anthony & T. Benedek (Eds.), *Parenthood: Its psychology and psychopathology*. Boston: Little, Brown, 1970. (a)

Anthony, E. J. The return of the repressed "Oedipus." In E. J. Anthony & T. Benedek (Eds.), *Parenthood: Its psychology and psychopathology*. Boston: Little, Brown, 1970. (b)

Anthony, E. J., & Benedek, T. (Eds.). *Parenthood: Its psychology and psychopathology*. Boston: Little, Brown, 1970.

Argyle, M. *Social interaction*. New York: Atherton, 1969.

Auden, W. H. An interview with W. H. Auden. *Life*, June 1970.

Auerbach, E., & Coriell, A. S. Short-term memory in vision. *Bell Systems Technology Journal*, 1961, 40, 309–328.

Austin, J. L. *How to do things with words*. London: Oxford University Press, 1962.

Axel, R. Estimation of time. *Archives of Psychology*, 1924, 12, No. 74.

Bales, R. F. Some uniformities of behavior in small social systems. In G. E. Swanson, T. M. Newcomb, & E. L. Hartley (Eds.), *Readings in social psychology* (2nd ed.). New York: Holt, 1952.

Bales, R. F. Task roles and social roles in problem-solving groups. In E. Maccoby, T. M. Newcomb, & E. L. Hartley (Eds.), *Readings in social psychology* (3rd ed.). New York: Holt, 1958.

Bales, R. F., & Strodtbeck, F. L. Phases in group problem solving. *Journal of Abnormal and Social Psychology*, 1951, 46, 485–495.

Bandura, A. The stormy decade: Fact or fiction? *Psychology in the Schools*, 1964, 1, 224–231.

Barnes, H. Introduction. In J.-P. Sartre, *Being and nothingness*. New York: Philosophical Library, 1956.

Barrett, W. (Ed.). *Zen Buddhism: Selected writings of D. T. Suzuki*. Garden City, N.Y.: Doubleday, 1956.

Barrett, W. *Irrational man: A study in existential philosophy*. Garden City, N.Y.: Doubleday, 1958.

Barrett, W. Our contemporary, William James. *Commentary*, January 1975, pp. 55–61.

Bartlett, F. C. *Remembering*. Cambridge: Cambridge University Press, 1932.

Bartlett, F. C. *Thinking*. New York: Basic Books, 1958.

Basso, K. H. 'To give up on words': Silence in western Apache culture. In P. P. Giglioli (Ed.), *Language and social context*. Harmondsworth, England: Penguin Books, 1972.

Bender, L. A visual-motor Gestalt test and its clinical use. *Research Monographs of the American O: thopsychiatric Association*, 1938, No. 3.

Benedict, R. Continuities and discontinuities in cultural conditioning. In C. Kluckhohn & H. A. Murray (Eds.), *Personality in nature, society, and culture* (2nd ed.). New York: Knopf, 1954.

Berger, P. L., & Luckmann, T. *The social construction of reality*. Garden City, N.Y.: Doubleday, 1966.

Beringer, K. Der Mescalinrausch. *Monographien aus dem*

Gesamtgebiete der Neurologie und Psychiatrie, 1927, No. 49.

Berlin, B., & Kay, P. *Basic color terms*. Berkeley and Los Angeles: University of California Press, 1969.

Birren, J. E., Butler, R. N., Greenhouse, S. W., Sokoloff, L., & Yarrow, M. (Eds.). *Human aging: A biological and behavioral study*. National Institute of Mental Health, PHS Publication No. 986. Washington, D.C.: U.S. Government Printing Office, 1963.

Blauner, R. Death and social structure. In B. L. Neugarten (Ed.), *Middle age and aging*. Chicago: University of Chicago Press, 1968. (Excerpted from *Psychiatry*, 1966, *29*, 378–394.)

Bolton, N. *The psychology of thinking*. London: Methuen, 1972.

Borko, H. *Computer applications in the behavioral sciences*. Englewood Cliffs, N.J.: Prentice-Hall, 1962.

Bousfield, W. A. The occurrence of clustering in the recall of randomly arranged associates. *Journal of General Psychology*, 1953, *49*, 229–240.

Bousfield, W. A., & Sedgewick, C. H. W. An analysis of sequences of restricted associative responses. *Journal of General Psychology*, 1944, *30*, 149–165.

Bower, G. H., & Hilgard, E. R. *Theories of learning* (5th ed.). Englewood Cliffs, N.J.: Prentice-Hall, 1980.

Bower, G. H., & Reitman, J. S. Mnemonic elaboration in multilist learning. *Journal of Verbal Learning and Verbal Behavior*, 1972, *11*, 478–485.

Braude, L. *Work and workers: A sociological analysis*. New York: Praeger, 1975.

Brener, J. Heartrate as an avoidance response. *Psychological Record*, 1966, *16*, 329–336.

Broadbent, D. E. *Perception and communication*. New York: Pergamon Press, 1958.

Broughton, P. New peak for newspeak. *Newsweek*, May 6, 1968.

Brown, R. *Social psychology*. New York: Free Press, 1965.

Brown, R., Galanter, E. H., Hess, E. H., & Mandler, G. *New directions in psychology I*. New York: Holt, Rinehart & Winston, 1962.

Brown, R., & Gilman, A. The pronouns of power and solidarity. In T. A. Sebeok (Ed.), *Style in language*. Cambridge, Mass.: MIT Press, 1960.

Brown, R., & Lenneberg, E. H. A study of language and cognition. *Journal of Abnormal and Social Psychology*, 1954, *49*, 454–462.

Brown, R. W., & McNeill, D. The "tip of the tongue" phenomenon. *Journal of Verbal Learning and Verbal Behavior*, 1966, *5*, 325–337.

Bryan, W. L., & Harter, N. Studies in the physiology and psychology of telegraphic language. *Psychological Review*, 1897, *4*, 27–53.

Buber, M. *I and Thou*. New York: Scribner's, 1958.

Bugelski, B. R. Images as mediators in one-trial paired-associate learning: II. Self timing in successive lists. *Journal of Experimental Psychology*, 1968, *77*, 328–334.

Butcher, J. N. *Abnormal psychology*. Belmont, Calif.: Wadsworth, 1971.

Butler, R. N. The life review: An interpretation of reminiscence in the aged. In B. L. Neugarten (Ed.), *Middle age and aging*. Chicago: University of Chicago Press, 1968.

Campbell, D. T. Social attitudes and other acquired behavioral dispositions. In S. Koch (Ed.), *Psychology: A study of a science* (Vol. 6). New York: McGraw-Hill, 1963.

Cannon, W. B. "Voodoo" death. *American Anthropologist*, 1942, *44*, 169–181.

Cartwright, D. C., & Zander, A. (Eds.). *Group dynamics: Research and theory* (3rd ed.). New York: Harper & Row, 1968.

Cherry, E. C. Some experiments on the recognition of speech, with one and with two ears. *Journal of Acoustical Society of America*, 1953, *25*, 975–979.

Clayton, P. J., Halikes, J. A., & Maurice, W. L. The bereavement of the widowed. *Diseases of the Nervous System*, 1971, *32*, 597–604.

Cohen, S. L., & Fiedler, J. E. Content analyses of multiple messages in suicide notes. *Life-Threatening Behavior*, 1974, *4*, 75–95.

Cohn-Bendit, D. Obsolete communism: The left-wing alternative (A. Pomerans, trans.). London: André Deutsch, 1968.

Colaizzi, P. F. *The descriptive methods and the types of subject matter of a phenomenologically based psychology: Exemplified by the phenomenon of learning*. Ann Arbor, Mich.: University Microfilms, 1969.

Colaizzi, P. F. *Reflection and research in psychology: A phenomenological study of learning*. Dubuque, Iowa: Kendall/Hunt, 1973.

Colby, K. M. *A primer for psychotherapists*. New York: Ronald Press, 1951.

Coleman, J. C. *Abnormal psychology and modern life* (5th ed.). Glenview, Ill.: Scott, Foresman, 1976.

Collins, A. M., & Quillian, M. R. Retrieval time from semantic memory. *Journal of Verbal Learning and Verbal Behavior*, 1969, *8*, 240–247.

Combs, A. W., Richards, A. C., & Richards, F. *Perceptual psychology: A humanistic approach to the study of persons*. New York: Harper & Row, 1976.

Conrad, R. Acoustic confusion in immediate memory. *British Journal of Psychology*, 1964, *55*, 75–84.

Cook, M. Anxiety, speech disturbances, and speech rate. *British Journal of Social and Clinical Psychology*, 1969, *8*, 13–21.

Cooley, H. *Human nature and the social order*. New York: Scribner, 1922.

Crichton, R. *The great impostor*. New York: Random House, 1959.

Cromer, R. F. *The development of temporal reference during the acquisition of language*. Unpublished doctoral dissertation, Harvard University, 1968.

Cumming, E., & Henry, W. H. (Eds.). *Growing old: The process of disengagement*. New York: Basic Books, 1961.

Cumming, E., & Parlegreco, M. L. The very old. In E. Cumming & W. H. Henry (Eds.), *Growing old: The process of disengagement*. New York: Basic Books, 1961.

Dashiell, J. F. *Fundamentals of general psychology* (3rd ed.). Boston: Houghton Mifflin, 1949.

de Beauvoir, S. *The coming of age.* New York: Warner Paperback Library, 1973.

DeCecco, J. P. *The psychology of learning and instruction: Educational psychology.* Englewood Cliffs, N.J.: Prentice-Hall, 1968.

Deese, J. Meaning and change in meaning. *American Psychologist,* 1967, *22,* 641–652.

Deikman, A. J. Experimental meditation. *Journal of Nervous and Mental Diseases,* 1963, *136,* 329–343.

Deikman, A. J. Deautomatization and the mystic experience. In C. T. Tart (Ed.), *Altered states of consciousness.* New York: Wiley, 1969.

Dember, W. N. *The psychology of perception.* New York: Holt, Rinehart & Winston, 1961.

Denker, P. G. Results of treatment of psychoneurosis by the general practitioner: A follow-up study of 500 cases. *New York State Journal of Medicine,* 1946, *46,* 2164–2166.

Dennis, W. Creative productivity between the ages of 20 and 80 years. *Journal of Gerontology,* 1966, *21,* 1–8.

Dittman, A. T., & Llewellyn, L. G. Relationship between vocalizations and head nods as listener responses. *Journal of Personality and Social Psychology,* 1968, *9,* 79–84.

Dittman, A. T., & Llewellyn, L. G. Body movement and speech rhythm in social conversation. *Journal of Personality and Social Psychology,* 1969, *11,* 98–106.

Dixon, J. C. Development of self recognition. *Journal of Genetic Psychology,* 1957, *91,* 251–256.

Douglas, M. (Ed.). *Rules and meanings.* Harmondsworth, England: Penguin Books, 1973.

Doyle, C. L. The creative process: A study in paradox. In C. B. Windsor (Ed.), *The creative process.* New York: Bank Street College of Education, 1976.

Duke, M. P., & Frankel, A. S. *Inside psychotherapy.* Chicago: Markham, 1971.

Dulany, D. E., & O'Connell, D. C. Does partial reinforcement dissociate verbal rules and the behavior they might presume to control? *Journal of Verbal Learning and Verbal Behavior,* 1963, *2,* 361–372.

Duncker, K. On problem-solving (L.S. Lees, trans.). *Psychological Monographs,* 1945, *58,* No. 270. (Originally publshed, 1935.)

Ebbinghaus, H. *On memory* (H. Ruger & C. E. Bussenius, trans.). New York: Teachers College, Columbia University, 1913. (Originally published, 1885.)

Edie, J. M. Expression and metaphor. *Philosophy and Phenomenological Research,* 1963, *23,* 538–561.

Edwards, A. E., & Acker, L. E. A demonstration of the long-term retention of a conditioned galvanic skin response. *Psychosomatic Medicine,* 1962, *24,* 459–463.

Einstein, A. A testimonial from Professor Einstein. Appendix II in J. Hadamard, *An essay on the psychology of invention in the mathematical field.* Princeton, N.J.: Princeton University Press, 1949.

Ekman, P. The differential communication of affect by head and body cues. *Journal of Personality and Social Psychology,* 1965, *2,* 726–735.

Eliot, T. S. *Four quartets.* New York: Harcourt, 1943.

Elliott, F. A. *Clinical neurology* (2nd ed.). Philadelphia: Saunders, 1971.

Ellson, D. G., Davis, R. C., Saltzman, I. J., & Burke, C. J. A report on research on detection of deception. (Contract N6onr-180110 with Office of Naval Research.) Bloomington: Department of Psychology, Indiana University, 1952.

Erdelyi, M. H. A new look at the new look: Perceptual defense and vigilance. *Psychological Review,* 1974, *81,* 1–25.

Erdelyi, M. H., & Appelbaum, G. A. Cognitive masking: The disruptive effect of an emotional stimulus upon the perception of contiguous neutral items. *Bulletin of the Psychonomic Society,* 1973, *1,* 59–61.

Erikson, E. H. *Childhood and society* (2nd ed.). New York: Norton, 1963.

Erikson, E. H. *Identity: Youth and crisis.* New York: Norton, 1968.

Erikson, E. H. The quest for identity. *Newsweek,* December 21, 1970, pp. 84–89.

Escher, M. C. *The graphic work of M. C. Escher.* New York: Hawthorn Books, 1960.

Evans-Pritchard, E. E. *The Nuer.* London: Clarendon Press, 1940.

Eysenck, H. J. The effects of psychotherapy: An evaluation. *Journal of Consulting Psychology,* 1952, *16,* 319–338.

Findlay, A. *A hundred years of chemistry* (2nd ed.). London: Duckworth Ltd., 1948.

Fischer, C. T. Personality and assessment. In R. S. Valle & M. King (Eds.), *Existential-phenomenological alternatives for psychology.* New York: Oxford University Press, 1978.

Fischer, W. F. *Theories of anxiety.* New York: Harper & Row, 1970.

Fitts, W. H. *The experience of psychotherapy.* New York: Van Nostrand Reinhold, 1965.

Fowler, R. *Understanding language.* Boston: Routledge and Kegan Paul, 1974.

Fraisse, P. *The psychology of time.* New York: Harper & Row, 1963.

Freud, S. *Introductory lectures on psycho-analysis.* London: George Allen & Unwin, 1922.

Freud, S. *A general introduction to psychoanalysis.* New York: Simon & Schuster, 1935.

Freud, S. *The psychopathology of everyday life.* In S. Freud, *The basic writings of Sigmund Freud.* New York: Random House, 1938. (Originally published, 1905.)

Friedman, E. A., & Havighurst, R. J. *The meaning of work and retirement.* Chicago: University of Chicago Press, 1954.

Galanter, E. H. Contemporary psychophysics. In R. Brown, E. H. Galanter, E. H. Hess, & G. Mandler, *New directions in psychology I.* New York: Holt, Rinehart & Winston, 1962.

Galton, F. *Inquiries into human faculty.* London and New York: Macmillan, 1883.

Gelb, A. Die Farbenkonstanz der Sehlinge. In *Handbuch der normalen und pathologischen Physiologie,* Bethe XII/1. Berlin: Springer, 1927.

Gelb, A., & Goldstein, K. *Psychologische Analysen hirnpathologischer Fälle.* Leipzig: Barth, 1920. (a) Partly translated in W. D. Ellis (Ed.), *Sourcebook of Gestalt psychology.* New York: Harcourt, 1938.

Gelb, A., & Goldstein, K. Zur Psychologie des optischen Wahrnehmungs und Erkennungsvorgangs. In A. Gelb & K. Goldstein (Eds.), *Psychologische Analysen hirnpathologischer Fälle.* Leipzig: Barth, 1920. (b)

Gendlin, E. T. *Experiencing and the creation of meaning.* New York: Free Press, 1962.

Gendlin, E. T. A short summary and some long predictions. In J. T. Hart & T. M. Tomlinson (Eds.), *New directions in client-centered therapy.* Boston: Houghton Mifflin, 1970.

Gergen, K. J. *The concept of self.* New York: Holt, Rinehart & Winston, 1971.

Gibson, J. J. *The perception of the visual world.* Boston: Houghton Mifflin, 1950.

Gibson, J. J. *The senses considered as perceptual systems.* Boston: Houghton Mifflin, 1966.

Ginsburg, H., & Opper, S. (Eds.). *Piaget's theory of intellectual development: An introduction* (2nd ed.). Englewood Cliffs, N.J.: Prentice-Hall, 1969.

Giorgi, A. *Psychology as a human science.* New York: Harper & Row, 1970.

Giorgi, A. Phenomenology and experimental psychology: I. In A. Giorgi, W. F. Fischer, & R. Von Eckartsberg (Eds.), *Duquesne studies in phenomenological psychology* (Vol. 1). Pittsburgh: Duquesne University Press, 1971.

Giorgi, A. An application of phenomenological method in psychology. In A. Giorgi, C. T. Fischer, & E. L. Murray (Eds.), *Duquesne studies in phenomenological psychology* (Vol. 2). Pittsburgh: Duquesne University Press, 1975.

Giorgi, A., Fischer, C. T., & Murray, E. L. (Eds.). *Duquesne studies in phenomenological psychology* (Vol. 2). Pittsburgh: Duquesne University Press, 1975.

Giorgi, A., Fischer, W. F., & Von Eckartsberg, R. (Eds.). *Duquesne studies in phenomenological psychology* (Vol. 1). Pittsburgh: Duquesne University Press, 1971.

Gleason, H. A. *An introduction to descriptive linguistics.* New York: Holt, Rinehart & Winston, 1961.

Glick, I. D., & Kessler, D. R. *Marital and family therapy.* New York: Grune & Stratton, 1974.

Goffman, E. *Interaction ritual.* Garden City, N.Y.: Doubleday, 1967.

Goldenberg, H. *Abnormal psychology: A social/community approach.* Monterey, Calif.: Brooks/Cole, 1977.

Goldiamond, I., & Hawkins, W. I. Vexierversuch: The log relationship between word frequency and recognition obtained in the absence of stimulus words. *Journal of Experimental Psychology,* 1958, *56,* 457–463.

Goldman-Eisler, F. *Psycholinguistics: Experiments in spontaneous speech.* New York: Academic Press, 1968.

Goldstein, K. *The organism.* New York: American Books, 1939.

Goldstein, K. *After-effects of brain injuries in war.* New York: Grune & Stratton, 1942.

Goldstein, K. *Language and language disturbance.* New York: Grune & Stratton, 1948.

Goldstein, K. Health as value. In A. H. Maslow (Ed.), *New knowledge in human values.* New York: Harper, 1959.

Goldstein, K., & Scheerer, M. Abstract and concrete behav-

ior: An experimental study with special tests. *Psychological Monographs,* 1941, *53,* 1–151.

Goodall, J. Mother–offspring relationships in free-ranging chimpanzees. In D. Morris (Ed.), *Primate ethology.* Chicago: Aldine, 1967.

Goodenough, F. L. *The measurement of intelligence by drawings.* Yonkers, N.Y.: World Book Company, 1926.

Goodenough, F. L. Studies in the psychology of children's drawings. *Psychological Bulletin,* 1928, *25,* 272–283.

Goodenough, F. L. *Developmental psychology: An introduction to the study of human behavior.* New York: Appleton-Century, 1934.

Goodenough, F. L., & Harris, D. B. Studies in the psychology of children's drawings. II: 1928–1949. *Psychological Bulletin,* 1950, *47,* 369–433.

Gordon, C. Self-conceptions: Configurations of content. In C. Gordon & K. J. Gergen (Eds.), *The self in social interaction* (Vol. 1). New York: Wiley, 1968.

Gordon, E. *Through the valley of the Kwai.* New York: Harper, 1962.

Gordon, W. J. J. *Synectics: The development of creative capacity.* New York: Harper, 1961.

Groniger, L. D. Mnemonic imagery and forgetting. *Psychonomic Science,* 1971, *23,* 161–163.

Guillaume, P. *L'imitation chez l'enfant.* Paris: Alcan, 1925.

Gusdorf, G. *Speaking* (P. T. Brockelman, trans.). Evanston, Ill.: Northwestern University Press, 1965.

Gustafson, L. A., & Orne, M. T. Effects of perceived role and role success on the detection of deception. *Journal of Applied Psychology,* 1965, *49,* 412–417.

Haber, R. N., & Hershenson, M. *The psychology of visual perception.* New York: Holt, Rinehart & Winston, 1973.

Hadamard, J. *The psychology of invention in the mathematical field.* Princeton, N.J.: Princeton University Press, 1945.

Hadamard, J. *An essay on the psychology of invention in the mathematical field.* Princeton, N.J.: Princeton University Press, 1949.

Hall, C. S., & Lindzey, G. *Theories of personality* (2nd ed.). New York: Wiley, 1970.

Hall, E. T. *The hidden dimension.* Garden City, N.Y.: Doubleday, 1966.

Hanna, T. *Bodies in revolt: A primer in somatic thinking.* New York: Holt, Rinehart & Winston, 1970.

Harlow, H. F. The nature of love. *American Psychologist,* 1958, *13,* 673–685.

Harlow, H. F. Learning set and error factor theory. In S. Koch (Ed.), *Psychology: A study of a science* (Vol. 2). New York: McGraw-Hill, 1959.

Harlow, H. F. *Learning to love.* San Francisco: Albion, 1971.

Harlow, H. F., Harlow, M. K., & Hansen, E. W. The maternal affectional system of rhesus monkeys. In H. L. Rheingold (Ed.), *Maternal behavior in mammals.* New York: Wiley, 1963.

Harren, V. A. The client-centered theory of personality and therapy. In D. C. Rimm & J. W. Somerville (Eds.), *Abnormal psychology.* New York: Academic Press, 1977.

Harries, K. Martin Heidegger: The search for meaning. In G. A. Schrader, Jr. (Ed.), *Existential philosophers:*

Kierkegaard to Merleau-Ponty. New York: McGraw-Hill 1967.

Hartgenbusch, H. G. Gestalt psychology in sport. *Psyche,* 1927, *27,* 41–52.

Hathaway, S. R. Some considerations relative to nondirective counseling as therapy. *Journal of Clinical Psychology,* 1948, *4,* 226–231.

Hathaway, S. R., & Monachesi, E.D. *Analyzing and predicting juvenile delinquency with the MMPI.* Minneapolis: University of Minnesota Press, 1953.

Hayakawa, S. I. *Language in thought and action.* New York: Harcourt Brace, 1949.

Hayward, M. L., & Taylor, J. E. A schizophrenic patient describes the action of intensive psychotherapy. *Psychiatry Quarterly,* 1956, *30,* 211–248.

Herrigel, E. *Zen in the art of archery.* New York: Pantheon, a Division of Random House, Inc., 1964.

Hilgard, E. R., Atkinson, R. C., & Atkinson, R. L. *Introduction to psychology* (6th ed.). New York: Harcourt Brace Jovanovich, 1975.

Hochberg, E. *Perception.* Englewood Cliffs, N.J.: Prentice-Hall, 1964.

Hochberg, J., & Brooks, U. The psychophysics of form: Reversible-perspective drawings of spatial objects. *American Journal of Psychology,* 1960, *73,* 337–354.

Hochberg, J., & McAlister, E. A quantitative approach to figural "goodness." *Journal of Experimental Psychology,* 1953, *46,* 361–364.

Hodgkinson, H. L. Adult development: Implications for faculty and administrators. *Educational Record,* 1974, *55,* 263–274.

Hollander, E. P. *Principles and methods of social psychology.* New York: Oxford University Press, 1971.

Hollingsworth, L. S. *The psychology of the adolescent.* New York: Appleton-Century, 1928.

Holmes, T. H., & Rahe, R. H. The Social Readjustment Rating Scale. *Journal of Psychosomatic Research,* 1967, *11,* 213–218.

Howes, D. H., & Solomon, R. L. A note on McGinnies' "Emotionality and Perceptual Defense." *Psychological Review,* 1950, *57,* 229–234.

Hudson, L. *Human beings.* London: Jonathan Cape, 1975.

Hughes, E. C. *Men and their work.* New York: Free Press, 1958.

Hyneck, R. M. *Konnersreuth: A medical and psychological study of the case of Theresa Neumann* (L. C. Sheppard, trans.). London: Burns, Oates & Washburne, 1932.

Ittelson, W. H. The constancies in perceptual theory. *Psychological Review,* 1951, *58,* 285–294.

Ittelson, W. H. *The Ames demonstrations in perception.* Princeton, N.J.: Princeton University Press, 1952.

Ittelson, W. H. *Visual space perception.* New York: Springer-Verlag, 1960.

James, W. *Psychology.* New York: Holt, 1893.

James, W. *The principles of psychology* (2 vols.). New York: Dover, 1950. (Originally published, 1890.)

Janet, Pierre. *L'évolution de la mémoire et de la notion de temps.* Paris: Chahine, 1928.

Jaspers, K. *General psychopathology* (J. Hoenig & M. W. Hamilton, trans.). Chicago: University of Chicago Press, 1968.

Jenkins, W. O., McFann, H., & Clayton, F. L. A methodological study of extinction following aperiodic and continuous reinforcement. *Journal of Comparative Physiological Psychology,* 1950, *43,* 155–167.

Jersild, A. T. *Child psychology* (4th ed.). Englewood Cliffs, N.J.: Prentice-Hall, 1954.

Jessner, L., Weigert, E., & Foy, J. L. The development of parental attitudes during pregnancy. In E. J. Anthony & T. Benedek (Eds.), *Parenthood: Its psychology and psychopathology.* Boston: Little, Brown, 1970.

Jourard, S. M. An exploratory study of body-accessibility. *British Journal of Social and Clinical Psychology,* 1966, *5,* 221–231.

Jourard, S. *Healthy personality.* New York: Macmillan, 1974.

Joyce, J. *Ulysses.* New York: Random House, 1934.

Kalish, R. A. *Late adulthood: Perspectives on human development.* Monterey, Calif.: Brooks/Cole, 1975.

Kaluger, G., & Kaluger, M. F. *Human development: The span of life.* St. Louis: C. V. Mosby, 1974.

Karwoski, T. F., & Odbert, H. S. Color-music. *Psychological Monographs,* 1938, *50,* 642–643.

Karwoski, T., Odbert, A., & Osgood, C. Studies in synaesthetic thinking II: The role of form in visual responses to music. *Journal of Genetic Psychology,* 1942, *26,* 199–222.

Katz, D., & Katz, R. *Gespräche mit Kindern.* 1928. Cited in H. Werner, *Comparative psychology of mental development.* Chicago: Follett, 1948.

Keen, E. *Three faces of being: Toward an existential clinical psychology.* New York: Appleton-Century-Crofts, 1970.

Keen, E. *A primer in phenomenological psychology.* New York: Holt, Rinehart & Winston, 1975.

Keen, E. Existential-phenomenological therapy. In D. C. Rimm & J. W. Somerville (Eds.), *Abnormal psychology.* New York: Academic Press, 1977.

Kestenberg, J. S. The effect on parents of the child's transition into and out of latency. In E. J. Anthony & T. Benedek (Eds.), *Parenthood: Its psychology and psychopathology.* Boston: Little, Brown, 1970.

Kimble, G. A. *Hilgard and Marquis' conditioning and learning* (2nd ed.). New York: Appleton-Century-Crofts, 1961.

Kimmel, D. C. *Adulthood and aging: An interdisciplinary developmental view.* New York: Wiley, 1974.

Kinget, G. M. *On being human.* New York: Harcourt Brace Jovanovich, 1975.

Kisker, G. W. *The disorganized personality* (2nd ed.). New York: McGraw-Hill, 1972.

Kleinmuntz, B. *Personality measurement: An introduction.* Homewood, Ill.: Dorsey Press, 1967.

Kleinmuntz, B. *Essentials of abnormal psychology.* (2nd ed.). New York: Harper & Row, 1980. (Originally published, 1974.)

Klüver, H. An experimental study of the eidetic type. *Genetic Psychology Monographs,* 1926, *1,* 69–230.

Knapp, M. L. *Nonverbal communication in human interaction.* New York: Holt, Rinehart & Winston, 1972.

Knight, J. *The story of my psychoanalysis.* New York: McGraw-Hill, 1950.

Koestler, A. *The act of creation.* New York: Macmillan, 1964.

Koffka, K. *Principles of Gestalt psychology.* New York: Harcourt, Brace & World, 1935.

Köhler, W. *The mentality of apes.* New York: Harcourt, Brace, 1925.

Köhler, W. *Gestalt psychology.* New York: New American Library, 1947.

Kopfermann, H. Psychologische Untersuchungen über die Wirkung zweidimensionaler Darstellungen korperlicher Gebilde. *Psychologische Forschung,* 1930, *13,* 293–364.

Koppitz, E. M. *Psychological evaluation of children's human figure drawings.* New York: Grune & Stratton, 1968.

Korzybski, A. S. *Science and sanity: An introduction to non-Aristotelian systems and general semantics.* Lancaster: Science Press, 1933.

Kreitler, H., & Kreitler, S. *Cognitive orientation and behavior.* New York: Springer, 1976.

Kübler-Ross, E. *On death and dying.* New York: Macmillan, 1969.

Kübler-Ross, E. The dying patient's point of view. In O. G. Brim, Jr., H. E. Freeman, S. Levine, & N. A. Scotch (Eds.), *The dying patient.* New York: Russell Sage Foundation, 1970.

Kutner, B., Wilkins, C., & Yarrow, P. Verbal attitudes and overt behavior involving race prejudice. *Journal of Abnormal and Social Psychology,* 1952, *47,* 649–652.

Kvale, S. The technological paradigm of psychological research. *Journal of Phenomenological Psychology,* 1973, *3,* 143–159.

Kvale, S. The temporality of memory. *Journal of Phenomenological Psychology,* 1974, *5,* 7–31.

Kvale, S. Dialectics and research on remembering. Paper presented at the fifth Life-Span Developmental Psychology Conference, Morgantown, W.V., May 1976. (a)

Kvale, S. The psychology of learning as ideology and technology. *Behaviorism,* 1976, *4,* 97–116. (b)

Kvale, S., & Grenness, C. E. Skinner and Sartre. *Review of Existential Psychology and Psychiatry,* 1967, *7,* 128–150.

Labov, W. *The social stratification of English in New York City.* Washington, D.C.: Center for Applied Linguistics, 1966.

Laing, R. D. *The divided self.* Harmondsworth, England: Penguin Books, 1965.

Laing, R. D. *The politics of experience.* New York: Pantheon Books, 1967.

Lambert, W. E., & Paivio, A. The influence of noun-adjective order on learning. *Canadian Journal of Psychology,* 1956, *10,* 9–12.

Landis, C. Statistical evaluation of psychotherapeutic methods. In L. E. Hinsie (Ed.), *Concepts and problems of psychotherapy.* New York: Columbia University Press, 1937.

Lantz, D. *Color naming and color recognition: A study in the psychology of language.* Unpublished doctoral dissertation, Harvard University, 1963.

LaPiere, R. T. Attitudes versus actions. *Social Forces,* 1934, *13,* 230–237.

Lawrence, T. E. *The seven pillars of wisdom.* London: Jonathan Cape, 1926.

Lecomte du Nouy. *Le temps et la vie.* Paris: Gallimard, 1936.

Leech, G. *Semantics.* Harmondsworth, England: Penguin Books, 1974.

Lehman, H. C. *Age and achievement.* Princeton, N.J.: Princeton University Press, 1953.

Lemke, E., & Wiersma, W. *Principles of psychological measurement.* Chicago: Rand McNally, 1976.

Lenrow, P. B. The uses of metaphor in facilitating constructive behavior change. *Psychotherapy,* 1966, *3,* 145–148.

Levinger, G., & Schneider, D. J. Test of the "risk is a value" hypothesis. *Journal of Personality and Social Psychology,* 1969, *11,* 165–169.

Levinson, D. J. *The seasons of a man's life.* New York: Knopf, 1978.

Levinson, D. J., Darrow, C. M., Klein, E. B., Levinson, M. H., & McKee, B. The psychosocial development of men in early adulthood and the mid-life transition. In D. F. Ricks, A. Thomas, & M. Roff (Eds.), *Life history research in psychopathology* (Vol. 3). Minneapolis: University of Minnesota Press, 1974.

Lewin, K. *Principles of topological psychology.* New York: McGraw-Hill, 1936.

Liddell, H. S. A laboratory for the study of conditioned motor reflexes. *American Journal of Psychology,* 1926, *37,* 418–419.

Liddell, H. S., James, W. T., & Anderson, O. D. The comparative physiology of the conditioned motor reflex, based on experiments with the pig, dog, sheep, goat, and rabbit. *Comparative Psychology Monographs,* 1934, No. 51.

Lieberman, M. A. Observations on death and dying. *Gerontologist,* 1966, *6,* 70–73.

Lieberman, M. A. Psychological correlates of impending death: Some preliminary observations. *Journal of Gerontology,* 1965, *20,* 181–190.

Lieberman, M. A., Yalom, I. D., & Miles, M. B. *Encounter groups: First facts.* New York: Basic Books, 1973.

Lindsay, P. H., & Norman, D. A. *Human information processing.* New York: Academic Press, 1972.

Loewi, O. Autobiographical sketch. *Perspectives in Biology and Medicine,* 1960, *4,* no. 1.

Loftus, E. F. Leading questions and the eyewitness report. *Cognitive Psychology,* 1975, *7,* 560–572.

Loftus, E. F., & Palmer, J. C. Reconstruction of automobile destruction: An example of the interaction between language and memory. *Journal of Verbal Learning and Verbal Behavior,* 1974, *13,* 585–589.

Loftus, E. F., & Zanni, G. Eyewitness testimony: The influence of the wording of a question. *Bulletin of the Psychonomic Society,* 1975, *5,* 83–99.

Lorr, M. A simplex of paranoid projection. *Journal of Consulting Psychology,* 1964, *28,* 378–380.

Lowenthal, M. F., & Haven, C. Interaction and adaptation:

Intimacy as a critical variable. *American Sociological Review*, 1968, *33*, 20–30.

Luckiesh, M. *Visual illusions: Their causes, characteristics, and application*. New York: Dover, 1965.

Ludwig, A. M. Altered states of consciousness. In C. T. Tart (Ed.), *Altered states of consciousness*. New York: Wiley, 1969.

Luft, J. *Of human interaction*. Palo Alto, Calif.: National Press Books, 1969.

Luft, J. *Group processes: An introduction to group dynamics*. Palo Alto, Calif.: Mayfield, 1970.

Luijpen, W. A. *Existential phenomenology*. Pittsburgh: Duquesne University Press, 1969.

Lyons, J. *Experience: An introduction to a personal psychology*. New York: Harper & Row, 1973.

MacClay, H., & Osgood, C. E. Hesitation phenomena in spontaneous English speech. *Word*, 1959, *15*, 19–44.

Mahl, G. G., & Schulze, G. Psychological research in the extralinguistic area. In T. Sebeok, A. S. Hayes, & M. C. Bateson (Eds.), *Approaches to semiotics*. The Hague: Mouton, 1964.

Mahler, M. S., Pine, F., & Bergman, A. The mother's reaction to her toddler's drive for individuation. In E. J. Anthony & T. Benedek (Eds.), *Parenthood: Its psychology and psychopathology*. Boston: Little, Brown, 1970.

Maier, N. R. F. A gestalt theory of humor. *British Journal of Psychology*, 1932, *23*, 69–74.

Marcia, J. E. Development and validation of ego identity status. *Journal of Personality and Social Psychology*, 1966, *3*, 551–558.

Marcia, J. E. Ego identity status: Relationship to change in self-esteem, "general maladjustment," and authoritarianism. *Journal of Personality*, 1967, *35*, 118–133.

Marcia, J. E. The case history of a construct: Ego identity status. In E. Vinacke (Ed.), *Readings in general psychology*. New York: Van Nostrand Reinhold, 1968.

Marcia, J. E., & Friedman, M. L. Ego identity status in college women. *Journal of Personality*, 1970, *38*, 249–263.

Maslow, A. H. *Motivation and personality* (2nd ed.). New York: Harper & Row, 1970.

Massaro, D. W. *Experimental psychology and information processing*. Chicago: Rand McNally, 1975.

Mawardi, B. H. *Industrial invention: A study in group problem solving*. Unpublished doctoral dissertation, Harvard University, 1959.

May, R. *Meaning of anxiety* (rev. ed.). New York: Norton, 1977. (Originally published, 1950.)

McCord, W., & McCord, J. *The psychopath: An essay on the criminal mind*. New York: Van Nostrand Reinhold, 1964.

McCorkel, R. J., Jr. *Husbands and pregnancy: An exploratory study*. Unpublished master's thesis, University of North Carolina, 1964.

McGinnies, E. Emotionality and perceptual defense. *Psychological Review*, 1949, *56*, 244–251.

McKellar, P. *Imagination and thinking*. New York: Basic Books, 1957.

McKellar, P. *Experience and behavior*. Harmondsworth, England: Penguin Books, 1968.

McKim, R. H. *Experiences in visual thinking*. Monterey, Calif.: Brooks/Cole, 1972.

Mead, G. H. *Mind, self and society*. Chicago: University of Chicago Press, 1934.

Mead, M. *Coming of age in Samoa*. New York: New American Library, 1950. (Originally published, 1928.)

Mead, M. The young adult. In E. Ginzberg (Ed.), *Values and ideals of American youth*. New York: Columbia University Press, 1961.

Mednick, M. T., & Andrews, F. M. Creative thinking and level of intelligence. *Journal of Creative Behavior*, 1967, *1*, 428–431.

Mednick, M. T., Mednick, S. A., & Jung, C. C. Continual association as a function of level of creativity and type of verbal stimulus. *Journal of Abnormal and Social Psychology*, 1964, *69*, 511–515.

Mednick, S. A., Pollio, H. R., & Loftus, E. F. *Learning* (2nd ed.). Englewood Cliffs, N.J.: Prentice-Hall, 1973.

Merleau-Ponty, M. *The phenomenology of perception*. London: Routledge & Kegan Paul, 1962.

Merleau-Ponty, M. *The structure of behavior*. Boston: Beacon Press, 1963.

Miller, G. A. Human memory and the storage of information. *Institute of Radio Engineers Transactions on Information Theory*, 1956, *IT-2*, 129–137. (a)

Miller, G. A. The magical number seven, plus or minus two: Some limits on our capacity for processing information. *Psychological Review*, 1956, *63*, 81–97. (b)

Miller, G. A., Galanter, E., & Pribram, K. H. *Plans and the structure of behavior*. New York: Holt, Rinehart & Winston, 1960.

Miller, N. E., & Banuazizi, A. Instrumental learning by curarized rats of a specific visceral response, intestinal or cardiac. *Journal of Comparative and Physiological Psychology*, 1968, *65*, 1–7.

Miller, N. E., & DiCara, L. Instrumental learning of heart-rate changes in curarized rats: Shaping and specificity to discriminative stimulus. *Journal of Comparative and Physiological Psychology*, 1967, *63*, 12–19.

Mills, L. Psychodynamic factors in hypertension. In J. Nodine & J. Moyer (Eds.), *Psychosomatic medicine*. Philadelphia: Lea & Febiger, 1962.

Milton, E. O., & Wahler, R. G. (Eds.). *Behavior disorders: Perspectives and trends* (2nd ed.). New York: Lippincott, 1969.

Minkowski, E. *Lived time: Phenomenological and psychopathological studies* (N. Metzel, trans.). Evanston, Ill.: Northwestern University Press, 1970.

Moberg, D. O. Religiosity in old age. *Gerontologist*, 1965, *5*, 78–87.

Moray, N. Attention in dichotic listening: Affective cues and the influence of instructions. *Quarterly Journal of Experimental Psychology*, 1959, *11*, 56–60.

Murdock, B. B. The retention of individual items. *Journal of Experimental Psychology*, 1961, *62*, 618–625.

Murphy, B., & Pollio, H. R. The many faces of humor. *Psychological Record*, 1975, *25*, 545–558.

Muuss, R. E. *Theories of adolescence* (3rd ed.). New York: Random House, 1975.

Myers, G. C. Incidental perception. *Journal of Experimental Psychology*, 1916, *1*, 339–350.

Neisser, U. *Cognitive psychology*. New York: Appleton-Century-Crofts, 1967.

Neugarten, B. L. (Ed.). *Middle age and aging*. Chicago: University of Chicago Press, 1968.

Neugarten, B. L., & Moore, J. W. The changing age-status system. In B. L. Neugarten (Ed.), *Middle age and aging*. Chicago: University of Chicago Press, 1968.

Neugarten, B. L., & Weinstein, K. K. The changing American grandparent. *Journal of Marriage and the Family*, 1964, *26*, 199–204.

Neugarten, B. L., Wood, V., Kraines, R. J., & Loomis, B. Women's attitudes toward the menopause. *Vita Humana*, 1963, *6*, 140–151.

Newell, A., Simon, H. A., & Shaw, J. C. Report on a general problem-solving program. In *Proceedings of the International Conference on Information Processing*. Paris: UNESCO, 1960.

Newman, B. M., & Newman, P. R. *Development through life: A psychosocial approach*. Homewood, Ill.: Dorsey Press, 1975.

Newsom, L. J., & Newsom, E. Breast feeding in decline. *British Medical Journal*, 1962, *2*, 1744.

Newton, N., & Newton, M. Medical progress: Psychologic aspects of lactation. *New England Journal of Medicine*, 1967, *277*, 1179–1188.

Nordhøy, F. *Group interaction in decision-making under risk*. Unpublished master's thesis, School of Industrial Management, Massachusetts Institute of Technology, 1962.

Oakden, E. C., & Sturt, M. The development of the knowledge of time in children. *British Journal of Psychology*, 1922, *12*, 309–337.

Offer, D. *The psychological world of the teen-ager*. New York: Basic Books, 1969.

Offer, D., & Offer, J. B. *From teenage to young manhood*. New York: Basic Books, 1975.

O'Neill, N., & O'Neill, G. *Open marriage: A new lifestyle for couples*. New York: Evans, 1972.

Orbach, H. L. Aging and religion: Church attendance in the Detroit metropolitan area. *Geriatrics*, 1961, *16*, 530–540.

Orme, J. E. *Time, experience, and behavior*. London: Iliffe Books, 1969.

Orne, M. T. Demand characteristics and the concept of quasi-controls. In R. Rosenthal & R. L. Rosnow (Eds.), *Artifact in behavioral research*. New York: Academic Press, 1969.

Osborn, M. M., & Ehninger, D. The metaphor in public address. *Speech Monographs*, 1962, *29*, 223–234.

Osgood, C. E. *Method and theory in experimental psychology*. New York: Oxford University Press, 1953.

Ostfeld, A. Frequency and nature of health problems of retired persons. In F. Carp (Ed.), *The retirement process*. PHS Publication No. 1778. Washington, D.C.: U.S. Government Printing Office, 1966.

Paivio, A. Mental imagery in associative learning and memory. *Psychological Review*, 1969, *76*, 241–263.

Paivio, A. *Imagery and verbal processes*. New York: Holt, Rinehart & Winston, 1971.

Parkes, C. M. The first year of bereavement. *Psychiatry*, 1970, *33*, 444–467.

Parkes, C. M. *Bereavement: Studies of grief in adult life*. New York: International Universities Press, 1972.

Parten, M. B. Social participation among pre-school children. *Journal of Abnormal and Social Psychology*, 1932–33, *27*, 243–269.

Paul, N. Psychiatry: Its role in the resolution of grief. In A. H. Kutscher (Ed.), *Death and bereavement*. Springfield, Ill.: Charles C Thomas, 1969.

Pavlov, I. P. *Lectures on conditioned reflexes* (Vol. 1; W. H. Gantt, Ed. and trans.). New York: International Publishers, 1928.

Perky, C. W. An experimental study of imagination. *American Journal of Psychology*, 1910, *21*, 422–452.

Peterson, L. R., & Peterson, M. J. Short-term retention of individual verbal items. *Journal of Experimental Psychology*, 1959, *58*, 193–198.

Phillips, J. L., Jr. *The origins of intellect: Piaget's theory*. San Francisco: W. H. Freeman, 1975.

Piaget, J. *The language and thought of the child* (M. Worden, trans.). New York: Harcourt, Brace, 1926.

Piaget, J. *Play, dreams, and imitation in childhood* (C. Gattegno & F. M. Hodgson, trans.). New York: Norton, 1951.

Piaget, J. *The origins of intelligence in children* (M. Cook, trans.). New York: International Universities Press, 1952.

Piaget, J. *The construction of reality in the child* (M. Cook, trans.). New York: Basic Books, 1954.

Piéron, H. Les problèmes psychophysiologiques de la perception du temps. *Anneé Psychologie*, 1923, *24*, 1–25.

Pollio, H. R. *The psychology of symbolic activity*. Reading, Mass.: Addison-Wesley, 1974.

Pollio, H. R., & Barlow, J. M. A behavioral analysis of figurative language in psychotherapy: One session in a single case study. *Language and Speech*, 1975, *18*, 236–254.

Pollio, H. R., Barlow, J., Fine, H., & Pollio, M. R. *The poetics of growth: Figurative language in psychology, psychotherapy, and education*. Hillsdale, N.J.: Erlbaum, 1977.

Pollio, H. R., Richards, S., & Lucas, R. Temporal properties of category recall. *Journal of Verbal Learning and Verbal Behavior*, 1969, *8*, 529–536.

Polya, G. *How to solve it*. Princeton, N.J.: Princeton University Press, 1945.

Postman, L., Bruner, J. S., & McGinnies, E. Personal values as selective factors in perception. *Journal of Abnormal and Social Psychology*, 1948, *43*, 142–154.

Premack, D. Toward empirical behavior laws: I. Positive reinforcement. *Psychological Review*, 1959, *66*, 219–233.

Prince, M. *Clinical and experimental studies in personality*. Cambridge, Mass.: Sci-Art Publishers, 1929.

Proust, M. *Remembrance of things past.* Vol. 1: *Swann's way.* (C. K. Scott-Moncrieff, trans.). New York: Random House, 1934.

Rahe, R. H., & Lind, E. Psychosocial factors and sudden cardiac death. *Journal of Psychosomatic Research,* 1971, *15,* 19–24.

Rees, W. D. The hallucinations of widowhood. *British Medical Journal,* 1971, *4,* 37–41.

Reichard, S., Livson, F., & Peterson, P. G. *Aging and personality.* New York: Wiley, 1962.

Reynolds, G. S. *A primer of operant conditioning.* Glenview, Ill.: Scott, Foresman, 1968.

Riegel, K. F. Dialectic operations: The final period of cognitive development. *Human Development,* 1973, *16,* 346–370.

Riegel, K. F. Adult life crises: Toward a dialectic theory of development. In N. Datan & L. H. Ginsberg (Eds.), *Life-span developmental psychology: Normative life crises.* New York: Academic Press, 1975. (a)

Riegel, K. F. Toward a dialectical theory of development. *Human Development,* 1975, *18,* 50–64. (b)

Riegel, K. F., Riegel, R. M., & Meyer, G. Sociopsychological factors of aging: A cohort-sequential analysis. *Human Development,* 1967, *10,* 27–56.

Riley, J. W., Jr. Attitudes toward death. Unpublished, 1963. Cited in M. W. Riley, A. Foner, & Associates, *Aging and society.* Vol. 1: *An inventory of research findings.* New York: Russell Sage Foundation, 1968.

Rimm, D. C., & Somerville, J. W. *Abnormal psychology.* New York: Academic Press, 1977.

Rock, I. *An introduction to perception.* New York: Macmillan, 1975.

Rogers, C. R. A theory of therapy, personality, and interpersonal relationships. In S. Koch (Ed.), *Psychology: A study of a science* (Vol. 3). New York: McGraw-Hill, 1959.

Rogers, C. R. *On becoming a person.* Boston: Houghton Mifflin, 1961.

Rogers, C. R. *Freedom to learn: A view of what education might become.* Columbus, Ohio: Merrill, 1969.

Rogers, C. R. Foreword. In J. T. Hart & T. M. Tomlinson (Eds.), *New directions in client-centered therapy.* Boston: Houghton Mifflin, 1970.

Rogers, C. R. In retrospect: Forty-six years. *American Psychologist,* 1974, *29,* 115–123.

Rommetveit, R. *On message structure: A conceptual framework for the study of language and communication.* London: Wiley, 1974.

Rosen, J. L., & Bibring, G. L. Psychological reactions of hospitalized male patients to a heart attack: Age and social-class differences. In B. L. Neugarten (Ed.), *Middle age and aging.* Chicago: University of Chicago Press, 1968.

Roth, J. A. *Timetables.* New York: Bobbs-Merrill, 1963.

Rubin, E. *Visuell wahregenommene Figuren.* Copenhagen: Glydendalske, 1921.

Ruch, F. L., & Zimbardo, P. G. *Psychology and life.* Glenview, Ill.: Scott, Foresman, 1971.

Rundus, D. Analysis of rehearsal processes in free recall. *Journal of Experimental Psychology,* 1971, *89,* 63–77.

Rundus, D., & Atkinson, R. C. Rehearsal processes in free recall: A procedure for direct observation. *Journal of Verbal Learning and Verbal Behavior,* 1970, *9,* 99–105.

Ryle, G. *The concept of mind.* Harmondsworth, England: Penguin Books, 1949.

Samuel, A. L. Some studies in machine learning using the game of checkers. *IBM Journal of Research and Development,* 1961, *3,* 210–229.

Sarason, I. G. *Abnormal psychology: The problem of maladaptive behavior* (2nd ed.). Englewood Cliffs, N.J.: Prentice-Hall, 1976.

Saussure, F. de. *Course in general linguistics* (W. Baskin, trans.). New York: McGraw-Hill, 1959. (Originally published, 1916.)

Schatzman, M. Madness and morals. In R. Boyers & R. Orrell (Eds.), *R. D. Laing and anti-psychiatry.* New York: Harper & Row, 1971.

Scheflen, A. E. The significance of posture in communication systems. *Psychiatry,* 1964, *27,* 316–331.

Schrader, G. A., Jr. (Ed.). *Existential philosophers: Kierkegaard to Merleau-Ponty.* New York: McGraw-Hill, 1967.

Scupin, E., & Scupin, G. I. *Bubis erste Kindheit.* 1907. II. *Bubi im 4.-6. Lebensjahr.* 1910. III. *Lebensbild eines deutschen Schuljungen.* 1931. Cited in H. Werner, *Comparative psychology of mental development.* Chicago: Follett, 1948.

Searle, J. R. *Speech acts: An essay in the philosophy of language.* London: Cambridge University Press, 1969.

Searles, H. R. *Collected papers on schizophrenia and related subjects.* New York: International Universities Press, 1965.

Sebeok, T. *Style in language.* Cambridge, Mass.: MIT Press, 1960.

Segal, S. J., & Fusella, V. Effects of imagery and modes of stimulus onset on signal-to-noise ratio. *British Journal of Psychology,* 1969, *60,* 459–464.

Segal, S. J., & Fusella, V. Influence of imagined pictures and sounds on detection of visual and auditory signals. *Journal of Experimental Psychology,* 1970, *83,* 458–464.

Segal, S. J., & Nathan, S. The perky effect: Incorporation of an external stimulus into an imagery experience under placebo and control conditions. *Perceptual and Motor Skills,* 1964, *18,* 385–395.

Seligman, M. E. P. Fall into helplessness. *Psychology Today,* July 1973, pp. 43–48.

Seligman, M. E. P. Depression and learned helplessness. In R. J. Friedman & M. M. Katz (Eds.), *The psychology of depression: Contemporary theory and research.* Washington, D.C.: Winston-Wiley, 1974.

Seligman, M. E. P., Maier, S., & Geer, J. H. Alleviation of learned helplessness in the dog. *Journal of Abnormal Psychology,* 1968, *73,* 256–262.

Shanas, E., Townsend, P., Wedderburn, D., Friis, H., Milhøj, P., & Stehouwer, J. *Old people in three industrial societies.* London: Routledge and Kegan Paul, 1968.

Shaver, K. G. *An introduction to attribution processes.* Cambridge, Mass.: Winthrop, 1975.

Sheehy, G. *Passages.* New York: Dutton, 1976.

Shock, N. W. The physiology of aging. *Scientific American,* January 1962, *206,* pp. 100–110.

Simmel, M. L. The absence of phantoms for congenitally missing limbs. *American Journal of Psychology,* 1961, *74,* 467–470.

Simmel, M. L. Phantom experiences following amputation in childhood. *Journal of Neurology and Neurological Psychiatry,* 1962, *25,* 69–78.

Simmel, M. L. The body percept in physical medicine and rehabilitation. *Journal of Health and Social Behavior,* 1967, *8,* 60–64.

Simon, H. A., & Newell, A. *Human problem solving.* Englewood Cliffs, N.J.: Prentice-Hall, 1971.

Singer, J. *Daydreaming: An introduction to the experimental study of inner experience.* New York: Random House, 1966.

Skinner, B. F. *The behavior of organisms: An experimental analysis.* New York: Appleton-Century-Crofts, 1938.

Skinner, B. F. *Science and human behavior.* New York: Macmillan, 1953.

Skinner, B. F. *Verbal behavior.* New York: Appleton-Century-Crofts, 1957.

Skinner, B. F. Teaching machines. *Science,* October 1958, *128,* 969–977.

Skinner, B. F. A case history in scientific method. In S. Koch (Ed.), *Psychology: A study of a science* (Vol. 2). New York: McGraw-Hill, 1959.

Skinner, B. F. Pigeons in a pelican. *American Psychologist,* 1960, *15,* 28–37.

Skinner, B. F. Behaviorism at fifty. In T. W. Wann, (Ed.), *Behaviorism and phenomenology.* Chicago: University of Chicago Press, 1964.

Skinner, B. F. *Beyond freedom and dignity.* New York: Knopf, 1971.

Solley, C. M., & Murphy, G. M. *The development of the perceptual world.* New York: Basic Books, 1960.

Solomon, R. L., & Brush, E. S. Experimentally derived conceptions of anxiety and aversion. In M. R. Jones (Ed.), *Nebraska Symposium on Motivation* (Vol. 4). Lincoln: University of Nebraska Press, 1956.

Solomon, R. L., Kamin, L. J., & Wynne, L. C. Traumatic avoidance learning: The outcomes of several extinction procedures with dogs. *Journal of Abnormal and Social Psychology,* 1953, *48,* 291–302.

Solomon, R. L., & Wynne, L. C. Traumatic avoidance learning: Acquisition in normal dogs. *Psychological Monographs,* 1953, *67*(4, Whole No. 354).

Sommer, R. Further studies of small group ecology. *Sociometry,* 1965, *28,* 337–348.

Springer, D. V. Development of concepts related to the clock as shown in young children's drawings. *Journal of Genetic Psychology,* 1951, *79,* 47–54.

Springer, D. V. Development in young children of an understanding of time and the clock. *Journal of Genetic Psychology,* 1952, *80,* 83–96.

Staats, A. W., & Staats, C. K. Attitudes established by classical conditioning. *Journal of Abnormal and Social Psychology,* 1958, *57,* 37–40.

Staats, A. W., & Staats, C. K. Effect of number of trials on the language conditioning of meaning. *Journal of General Psychology,* 1959, *61,* 211–223.

Staats, A. W., & Staats, C. K. *Complex human behavior.* New York: Holt, Rinehart & Winston, 1963.

Staats, C. K., & Staats, A. W. Meaning established by classical conditioning. *Journal of Experimental Psychology,* 1957, *54,* 74–80.

Stern, G. *Meaning and change of meaning.* Bloomington: Indiana University Press, 1954. (Originally published, 1931.)

Stern, W. The psychology of testimony. *Journal of Abnormal and Social Psychology,* 1939, *34,* 3–20.

Stoner, J. A. F. *A comparison of individual and group decisions involving risk.* Unpublished master's thesis, School of Industrial Management, Massachusetts Institute of Technology, 1961.

Strand, M. *Reasons for moving.* New York: Atheneum, 1971.

Straus, E. Disorders of personal time in depressive states. *Southern Medical Journal,* 1947, *40,* 254–259.

Straus, E. *The primary world of senses.* London: Macmillan, 1963.

Straus, E. Chronognosy and chronopathy. In E. Straus (Ed.), *Phenomenology: Pure and applied. The first Lexington conference.* Pittsburgh: Duquesne University Press, 1964.

Sturt, M. *The psychology of time.* London: Kegan Paul, 1925.

Suzuki, D. T. Zen. In D. T. Suzuki, E. Fromm, & R. Martino (Eds.), *Zen Buddhism and psychoanalysis.* New York: Harper, 1960.

Szasz, T. The myth of mental illness. *American Psychologist,* 1960, *15,* 113–118.

Tart, C. T. (Ed.). *Altered states of consciousness.* New York: Wiley, 1969.

Terkel, S. *Working.* New York: Pantheon Books, 1972.

Terman, L. M., & Merrill, M. A. *Measuring intelligence.* Boston: Houghton Mifflin, 1937.

Thiel, H., Parker, D., & Bruce, T. A. Stress factors and the risk of myocardial infarction. *Journal of Psychosomatic Research,* 1973, *17,* 43–57.

Thomas, E. I. Cross-examination and rehabilitation of witnesses. *Defense Law Journal,* 1965, *15,* 247–263.

Thorndike, E. L., & Lorge, I. *The teacher's word book of 30,000 words.* New York: Columbia University Press, 1944.

Timiras, P. S. *Developmental physiology and aging.* New York: Macmillan, 1972.

Tolman, E. C. *Purposive behavior in animals and men.* New York: Appleton-Century-Crofts, 1932.

Tolstoy, L. N. *Anna Karenina* (C. Garnett, trans.). Garden City, N.Y.: Doubleday, 1944.

Treisman, A. M. Monitoring and storage of irrelevant messages in selective attention. *Journal of Verbal Learning and Verbal Behavior,* 1964, *3,* 449–459.

Trudgill, P. *Sociolinguistics: An introduction.* Baltimore: Penguin Books, 1974.

Tuckman, J., Kleiner, R., & Lavell, M. Emotional content of suicide notes. *American Journal of Psychiatry,* 1959, *116,* 59–63.

Turner, V. *Forest of symbols: Aspects of Ndembu ritual.* New York: Cornell University Press, 1967.

Ullmann, S. *The principles of semantics: A linguistic approach to meaning.* New York: Barnes & Noble, 1959.

Valle, R. S., & King, M. *Existential-phenomenological alternatives for psychology.* New York: Oxford University Press, 1978.

Van Den Berg, J. H. *The changing nature of man.* New York: Dell, 1961.

Verplanck, W. S. Unaware of where's awareness. In C. E. Erikson (Ed.), *Behavior and awareness.* Durham, N.C.: Duke University Press, 1962.

von Uexküll, J. A stroll through the worlds of animals and men. In C. H. Schiller (Ed.), *Instinctive behavior.* New York: International Universities Press, 1957.

Vygotsky, L. S. *Thought and Language.* Cambridge, Mass.: MIT Press, 1962.

Wallas, G. *The art of thought.* New York: Harcourt, Brace, 1926.

Wapner, S., & Werner, H. (Eds.). *The body percept.* New York: Random House, 1965.

Watson, J. B., & Rayner, R. Conditional emotional reactions. *Journal of Experimental Psychology,* 1920, 3, 1–14.

Wattenberg, W. W. *The adolescent years* (2nd ed.). New York: Harcourt Brace Jovanovich, 1973.

Wechsler, D. *The measurement and appraisal of adult intelligence* (4th ed.). Baltimore: Williams & Wilkins, 1958.

Weider, A. *Contributions toward medical psychology* (Vol. 2). New York: The Ronald Press Company, 1953.

Weiss, E., & English, O. S. *Psychosomatic medicine.* Philadelphia: Saunders, 1943.

Weiss, P. *The persecution and assassination of Jean-Paul Marat.* New York: Atheneum, 1965.

Werner, H. *Comparative psychology of mental development.* New York: Follett, 1948.

Wertheimer, M. *Productive thinking.* New York: Harper & Row, 1959.

White, R. W. Motivation reconsidered: The concept of competence. *Psychological Review,* 1959, 66, 297–333.

White, R. W. *The abnormal personality* (3rd ed.). New York: Ronald Press, 1964.

White, R. W. *The enterprise of living.* New York: Holt, Rinehart & Winston, 1972.

White, R. W., & Watt, N. F. *The abnormal personality.* New York: Wiley, 1973.

Whorf, B. L. *Language, thought, and reality: Selected papers.* Cambridge, Mass.: MIT Press, 1956.

Whyte, W. F. *The organization man.* New York: Simon & Schuster, 1956.

Williams. J. H. *Psychology of women: Behavior in a biosocial context.* New York: Norton, 1977.

Witkin, H. A., Lewis, A. B., Hertzman, M., Machover, M., Meissner, P. B., & Wapner, S. *Personality through perception: An experimental and clinical study.* New York: Harper, 1954.

Wittgenstein, L. *Philosophical investigations.* Oxford: Basil Blackwell, 1963.

Wolff, K. *The biological, sociological, and psychological aspects of aging.* Springfield, Ill.: Charles C Thomas, 1959.

Wolpe, J. *Psychotherapy by reciprocal inhibition.* Stanford, Calif.: Stanford University Press, 1958.

Wolpe, J. *The practice of behavior therapy* (2nd ed.). Oxford: Pergamon Press, 1973.

Yalom, I. D. Report. *Frontiers of Psychiatry: Roche Report,* 1971, 1(14), 16–30.

Yalom, I. D., & Lieberman, M. A. A study of encounter group casualties. *Archives of General Psychiatry,* 1971, 25, 16–30.

Yarmey, A. D. *The psychology of eyewitness testimony.* New York: Free Press, 1979.

Zimbardo, P. G. The human choice: Individuation, reason and order versus deindividuation, impulse and chaos. In W. J. Arnold & D. Levine (Eds.), *Nebraska symposium on motivation.* Lincoln: University of Nebraska Press, 1969.

Author Index

Subject Index